If Guitars Could Talk

Memories and Stories

By Yuriy Shishkov

"If Guitars Could Talk."

Memories and Stories.

Cover design by author.

Book design by Yuriy Shishkov.

Edited by Autumn Conley.

Printed in the United States of America

First Printing: 2012

ISBN-978-0-615-58637-3

Preface

For many years, I've been asked by my customers and ordinary folks for the full story about the start of my guitar-making career and my life in my homeland, the Soviet Union. This book is about my past, but also about the lives of Soviet people at the time of the Cold War, spanning from 1964 through the end of the USSR history in 1990.

Since 1991, I have had the privilege of working with renowned, large musical instrument companies and for myself, building unique, customized guitars for musicians, celebrities, and collectors. It all started for me in the Soviet Union, where I began making my own instruments using primitive hand tools in our apartment's root cellar, hiding my craft from an oppressive regime that discouraged individual innovation outside of its system. Without knowing the aspects of our Socialistic society, it would be difficult to understand why I had to make guitars in secrecy and why Soviet system considered it a crime.

It is hard for anybody in today's democratic world to picture the injustices and oppression that really happened behind the Iron Curtain. Through the memories and stories on these pages, I will reveal to you in very up-close and personal detail how we grew up, went to school, socialized, and worked in the USSR. I will open your eyes to what it was like to naïvely delight in childhood, only to discover the disappointing and grim reality of the Soviet system in adulthood. You will learn how, even in that society that tried to keep the rest of the world out, rock 'n roll and Western culture found its way in, even though we could not always freely play and listen to the music we liked.

In contrast to modest Soviet social achievements, you will learn why, after twenty-six years of living in the USSR, I—a son of a communist—took a great risk trying to move to the United States.

Chapter 1

Leningrad, Parents, and the Life of Soviet Kids in the 1960's

It was March 17, 1964, in the Russian city of Leningrad. The stubborn sun still hung very low, just above the horizon throughout its short day, but the big piles of snow on the streets were already starting to melt, marking the beginning of spring.

The people were living a typical Soviet day, going to work and then back home, rushing into the crowded city buses and subways. They did their basic grocery shopping and filled the remainder of the day with dinners in the kitchen and late-night Soviet TV. For the most part, life in the USSR at that time was very humble and simple, yet underneath the calm, domestic, everyday routine, it was also complex, intriguing, and harsh for many Russian souls.

Leningrad in 1960's

There was really nothing special on the Soviet calendar for that day in March—no celebrations of national heroes or great achievements of our Motherland. However, for my mother, Ludmila Shishkova, it was a very special day because that was the day I was born, in the "city of Peter" and "home" of the Bolshevik Revolution. That city, while far and distant from me in my life, has and will continue to be a source of inspiration for me.

At the time when I was born, my mother was a student of one of Leningrad's economy colleges and lived with her friend in a small room near the city. Life was tough for her, especially because my father Feodor had much greater priorities in his life than to care for our family and help my mother and me. One day, he simply left.

Only picture of my mom, my dad and me when I was a child.

That same year, my mother graduated college, departed Leningrad, and took me to Gomel to live with my grandmother. Gomel is a smaller and less glorious city than Leningrad. It stands on the beautiful Sozh River in the Belarus Republic, one of the fifteen states of the former Soviet Union.

My relocation to Gomel was the beginning of my big journey in this world, a journey that still continues today.

I heard from my grandmother that my great grandfathers were quite different in origin and blood. One of them was a church keeper, while the other was a "freely" gypsy. Grandmother was always telling me I would be traveling my whole life like a gypsy and I would never find a resting place; I'd be like a wild horse. In the end, her words would prove somewhat prophetic, and this book is something my gypsy grandfather would have been proud of.

Upon our arrival in Gomel, we had to stay in a small one-bedroom apartment with my grandmother and her husband. The Soviet system was failing to provide its citizenry with basic necessities such as roofs above our heads and at that time in that country, living with three to four generations crammed uncomfortably in one small apartment was a harsh reality.

Just over a year old.

My mother Ludmila got a job at the metal fabricating factory, working as an accountant. After work, she vigorously studied the theories and theologies of Marx and Lenin, and she began to really take them to heart. Whether she was driven by a myth of some bright Communist future or just wanted to get involved in the Communist

Party to meet the requirements for a better job, I've always thought she was dedicating too much naively hoping for a utopia that would never really exist.

My grandmother, Lubov (Love), was the sweetest person in the world, kind and friendly with everybody. I cannot recall a time when she ever upset anyone. She worked very hard all her life, first as a train car tender and later at a local hotel. Even after retiring, she went back to work and was adored by everyone who knew her. All my life, she took care of all of her family members, including me. It was my grandmother, in fact, who would ultimately play a fundamental role in my life by purchasing me my first guitar.

Old Mikhail, mom, and my grandma.

Her husband Mikhail worked as a supervisor at one of the city construction companies. I remember him being as loving as my grandmother, but unfortunately, I did not get to live with him for long. Growing up without a father was difficult, just as it is for children today. It was not so much a financial problem for us though. I truly missed my father. At that time, our society had strong family ties, and not many children lived with only one parent. While my grandmother's husband Mikhail was very close to me, I still watched with jealousy when other kids played or walked by with their own fathers. Relying on Mikhail as my guardian, I grew under his care and kind personality, but even that support was not long lasting. In 1968, he passed away. When the red coffin was placed in the middle of our room and everybody began crying around it, I was told, "Mikhail is sleeping and cannot wake up right now," But outside, a rude neighbor lady said, "He's not sleeping. He's dead." My family never told me if it was true or not, even when I started crying. I left with my mom and grandmother, becoming the "head" of our small family at the young age of four years old.

Life of Soviet Children

Like most Soviet children, I had to attend daycare while my family worked. It was an interesting time in history—a time when the Russian government had lavish sympathy and care for children. This was such an endeavor that signs were posted about at parks and children's gathering places reading EVERYTHING BEST—TO CHILDREN. To some degree, it was true, for children were often unaware of the suffering that came with the Soviet reality in their future. Adults, on the other hand, were far too familiar with the difficulties they encountered on a daily basis.

Proper care for future generations, the so-called 'young builders of Communism', was an unavoidable task for the USSR. The country worked hard to keep kids under more government and society control so they'd be less influenced by parents than children in the Western world.

While Communist love for children was overwhelming, the childcare in the country was not free of charge, and parents had to pay for it from their pockets. It was not that expensive, though, and every child had to go because parents had few other options. Even the smallest children, too young for school, were dissuaded from being raised at home, even when grandparents could take care of them all day. Children of all ages were expected to be enrolled in the society daycares.

It was also necessary to have daycare facilities where kids could stay for a whole week and be picked up by parents only on the weekends. This allowed all adults who worked second or third shifts to leave their children there for six days in a row. I just so happened to be one of those children.

At the time when my mother attended night school to study Marxist doctrines and Lenin's teachings, I had to go to one of these daycares, and often for few nights a week. For many kids who were left behind for an overnight stay, this was a real torture, and there was endless crying for home. I, on the contrary, found my overnight stays entertaining and fun. I often had a good time with a couple of other adventurers like me. As soon as the lights were out, all we had to do was quietly slip from our sleeping room to the hallway. Besides observing the night life outside, we had a chance to see for ourselves the first lessons of the Soviet reality. While teaching good things during the day was a standard routine for our teachers, at night we had a chance to see them doing the opposite: drinking, smoking cigarettes, and pilfering food from the daycare to take home to their families. It became clear to us why we at the daycare had to eat poor and meager meals.

Every summer, our daycare headed west to the dacha, similar to a summer camp. Situated on the river and surrounded by mature woods, the dacha was a beautiful home to much of our gorgeous nature. It was a one-month vacation for parents and our teachers. Parents had a chance to forget about the kids for a month, and teachers could relax in the wonderful camp, surrounded by the peaceful outdoors. Some kids hated to be separated from their parents for so long, while others loved it—especially because we had the chance to go to the beach. I always waited anxiously for that time of year, only to be disappointed with the outcome of the expected vacation.

The nature and dacha itself, with its small facilities, were very nice, but it was just a physical amenity we lived amongst. Dacha's rules and regulations in our camp were often quite oppressing, and our daily life was fully under the control of our teachers. We were constantly under the thumbs of their mercy and will. The strict discipline was very different from our daily activities and relaxed living in daycare. Having fun, as we knew it, was a rare opportunity at our dacha.

The most annoying thing at our camp—at least for a majority of the kids—were plays and concerts that we had to put on for our parents. They visited us every weekend, and every time they came, we were forced to put on some kind of performance, ranging from dancing to poetry recitals to singing. The performances themselves were not so bad, but the rehearsals and the practicing was grueling torture for us kids. It occupied most of our time, and I can recall our music teacher, accordion in hands, making us practice for hours and hours. The polkas and hymns had to be executed flawlessly, even by the four- to five-year-old children. The songs were obviously about the Red Army, our brave leaders, or Lenin. While we were practicing all these hymns for the Party, we were dreaming about going to the river or to the forest instead.

My mother and I. 1967

Fortunately, the wilderness isolation was temporary, and the return home was always joyful. We were happy to be reunited with our parents, and the daycare went back to its normal routine in the city.

"No one is too young to be a Proletarian!"

At that time, the function of daycare was not limited to babysitting, and it was not necessarily just a place for kids to play. Prior to going to school by the age of seven, children had to be already politically and morally oriented. In other words, we were expected to be properly brainwashed as early as possible.

Promoting Soviet dogmas and Marxist doctrines to the masses was always an undeniable part of our society. Regardless of many institutions' main purposes or the ages of those who attended them, this kind of brainwashing was a well known responsibility. From the moment, Soviet children could understand spoken words, they were exposed to Bolshevik (same as a Communist or Proletarian) propaganda, and there were absolutely no exceptions—even in the youngest of daycares. No schools were exempt from the philosophy of Communist doctrines.

I remember how heavily the fragile minds and souls of small children were polluted with Communist teachings, slogans, and the history of the Party and its rulers, and it went far beyond the songs they made us sing at the *dacha*. The saturation of the education system by these ideas reached an absurd level. There is an anecdote I recall that exhibits this level of stupidity…

A teacher in a daycare classroom showed the children a picture of a hamster and asked, "Who is in the picture, children?"

No one answered.

Then she said to them, "Well, surely you know him! He can be found in many books. You can see him in movies and often on TV. Come on, children! Everybody knows him!"

One very little girl rose from her chair and said, " I know! This is Vladimir Lenin!"

As bizarre as the story sounds, we were so forcibly focused on what we were being taught that the little girl's answer sadly came as no surprise. Marx, Lenin, and the Communist Party theories and ideals were thrown at us at every corner, so it was in the forefront of our minds from a very young age.

We were told Lenin was our superhero, a genius in every way. Because of this, as a child, I truly believed Lenin was the best at almost everything. I was convinced he could play hockey better than anybody or could paint the coolest pictures of tanks and cars. He was our Soviet god, and it was required that all would worship him as such. The brainwashing worked well on small children who were too young to think for themselves, and our system did not want to miss the opportunity to plant the seeds of Communism in those fragile, impressionable minds.

The purported glory and fame of Communists and their leaders was not limited to the classrooms. It also penetrated literature, movies, theaters, and television. Everything everywhere at every time very purposefully reminded people that every good thing we had was the result of our Bolshevik system. We were told that everything that occurred before 1917 was bad, while everything that came after that was bright and prosperous. In the daycares, children were overwhelmed with these teachings from the moment they could first put a thought together, and there was no escaping the reminders, the pictures of our leaders, Lenin, and Party heroes hanging everywhere we looked.

No Christmas for Soviet Children

Outside of school, for children and adults, all aspects of our lives were required to revolve around the Soviet doctrine. If an idea, a thought, a process, a practice, or any part of life did not fit our dogma, it had to be disregarded, shut down, or tossed aside. Even the holidays known before 1917 were banned or stripped to the bare bone. We only had one neutral, non-political holiday that survived the so-called 'cleaning' of the Tsar era calendar, and that was New Year's Eve. All Christian and religious celebrations were promptly removed from Russian calendars and forbidden—but not forgotten by ordinary people. Around Christian holidays such as Easter or Christmas, in homes and workplaces, the people would quietly offer holiday greetings or even host small celebratory dinners with families and friends.

On Easter, holy bread (pasha) and red painted eggs were stealthily exchanged between people, but we never heard or read in Soviet media about celebrations of these holidays. As a child, on Easter I saw my grandmother making red eggs and cooking pasha, but not many people took the time or the risk to explain to children why they made and exchanged these things at that time of the year. Many feared it would be discovered at work or school and might lead to unwanted complications with the government. I was simply told to eat pasha and Easter eggs and wait until I grew up to understand the meaning behind them or the holidays they represented.

Speaking of religion, Church was officially 'separated' from the State. During the Soviet years, it was under oppression from our Communist regime. Most of the churches were closed or destroyed after the Revolution in 1917, and many monasteries were thereafter converted to prisons, warehouses, museums, or planetariums. The few that did survive lacked funding for restorations and repairs, especially because they were financially dependent on the contributions of their congregations, which declined due to an anti-religious propaganda coming from the government.

Since our Socialist society declared religion as 'opium for the masses', anyone who attended church was considered to be in direct disagreement with that philosophy, and this was especially true when it came to children. Any parent who took their children to church risked getting in severe trouble. Police often patrolled the church entrances, and any youngster who tried to go to church by him/herself would find themselves dragged to the police department, where they would have to wait for their parents to pick them up. Allowing or forcing a child to attend church was considered a 'moral crime' of the family, and reports of this so-called crime were sent to the parents' workplaces and the child's school. While the punishments for these alleged crimes never posed imprisonment, parents who were members of a Communist Party would be faced with losing their membership and often their jobs. For the children, the punishment would entail public humiliation in school, and they faced potential expulsion from the Pioneer or Young Communist (Commsomolets) organizations. For a child, this could represent the beginning of lifelong trouble with the government, ranging from future job opportunities to being monitored by the KGB.

Our Soviet Celebrations

It was irritating for Soviets to keep some churches open, but they knew closing all of them would give the West one more reason to critique their version of freedom and democracy, and the outcry would be far reaching and damaging. So, as an alternative to religious worshiping, the system provided a Proletarian version of honoring our society.

I am dancing at the Daycare's Revolution Day celebration.

Naturally, children were a big part of these manifestations. I can still vividly remember the elaborate daycare celebrations of our Socialist holidays, and there was no lack of them at that time. Big parades honoring our October Revolution and May Day, would be followed by smaller festivities embracing days of Red Army, Boarder Army (KGB), Missile Defense, Air Force, Navy, and birthdays of Lenin and other Communist heroes. We almost always provided plays and concerts for our parents on these days. Kids had to dance with small red flags and flowers, singing songs about the Red Cavalry or Lenin. It would have been near impossible at that time to find anyone who would dare protest or show any dislike toward these kinds of performances. This was how things were: all of this was a part of our lives, and many people truly believed their children would have a better life than they had in the coming bright future.

While these kinds of celebrations were quite lavish in our daycares, the street parades of two major Soviet holidays were colossal by comparison. The most magnificent holiday in our society was obviously the day of the Bolshevik Revolution. It was celebrated in every city and village in the country annually on November 7 and marked the victory of the Bolshevik coup in 1917. Another glorious celebration in the Soviet Union was May Day. It was really two holidays combined into one, and though they both had completely political roots, they were remarkably popular and favored by our entire nation. Regardless of the historical motives behind the holidays, It was a joy for many people to see each other in the streets with happy smiles, dressed in their best attire, sharing happy feelings. As usual, after wild city parades, the people gathered at home for dinner and more than a few drinks before they sometimes danced around old turntables.

These were non-working days for everybody, and participation in these processions was mandatory. Factory workers, students, and employees of government organizations typically gathered by their locations and formed columns. They would then move through the streets to the center of the city. Everyone carried some sort of red banner or flag with slogans and symbols honoring our Communist Party and the celebrated day. Balloons and ribbons flew high in the air, and marching bands played patriotic songs. The atmosphere was truly happy as the processions snaked through the small alleys and streets to create one big river of red flags. The noisy swarm of people then flowed to the center of the city amongst cheering crowds of spectators lined up on the sides of the immaculately decorated streets. From megaphones suspended on streetlights, announcers shouted chants in glory to our society: "Glory to the Communist party of USSR! Forward to the victory of the Communism! Glory to the Soviet people!" to which the people returned hysterical shouts of "Hurray!"

My mom on parade at left with a flag

Much like modern-day parades, every processing column represented a factory or organization, led by a line of its leaders and honored workers carrying the victory flags from the competitions of Socialist labor. These awards were given to the teams or organizations with the delivery of the best products and services. Competition thrived, even under the Socialist regime.

The marching bands trumpeted music from patriotic movies, revolutionary or Socialist hymns. There were also rows of athletic teams performing acrobatics and sports. Trucks were decorated to look like ships or tanks, often as working machinery from the factories where they manufactured their products. Many of the vehicles carried large statues symbolizing the working Proletarian class or Lenin. They followed the processions so slowly that people could climb in to wave their own red flags.

The effort and money spent by the government to make this kind of statement of Soviet superiority and strength was enormous. In Moscow, on November 7, in addition to the civil procession, there was also a big military parade in the Red Square. It was broadcast live on TV, and it was one of my favorite parts of the holiday, absolutely immense and glorious. The pride of military arms and weapons flowed through the Red Square, followed by the honored soldiers marching in front of our government leaders. All this triumphant celebration in Moscow was followed with a tremendous firework display—a very rare treat for us at that time.

This government tradition was established many years earlier, and it was carried by many generations through hard Soviet years and WW2. After the end of the war, our country had to be rebuilt out of the war ruins and decay, so people cherished it. My grandmother and many of her friends were from that very generation. They loved these holidays and celebrated them with so much fun and love that everybody who participated enjoyed it as much as they did.

I am at the October parade in 1969.

As any other Soviet child (or any child, for that matter) I loved these holidays. At that time, my grandmother was working at a hotel in the center of our city, and I was often fortunate to see this magnificent show from the balcony of one of the hotel rooms. When I could not do that, I stayed along the street and waited to see my mom marching within her factory column. I often ran to her while carrying a little red flag and balloons in my hands.

Parade. My mother with her comrades from work.

After the parade, we always got together with friends at our small apartment to enjoy a holiday dinner. The food was always delicious, even though it was nothing extravagant because the meal supplies in the USSR were not as lavish as in the West. Nevertheless, people tried to make holiday miracles in their kitchens, cooking the best they could with what they had. Everyone dressed in their best attire, and gentlemen always wore a tie.

At our place, the table offered the most delicious foods and beverages, and once everybody sat down to eat, the sweet, blended aroma of meals, wine, and cigarettes would fill our apartment. After dinner, music would sound from our turntable, and people got up to dance. Some began singing folk or other popular songs, and everyone joined in for a sing-along . It was a very remarkable time of friendship and honesty, people united by the demands of simple, humble lives, the value of friendship exceeding all other priorities.

I remember that time and that festive atmosphere so well, even though in many ways, I was just an observer because I was a child. Custom and tradition dictated that children were not allowed to be at the table with adults, but no one would kick you out if you dared to join them anyway. We ate the same meal as the adults, but we had more fun playing around the house than sitting in their company. I greatly enjoyed watching them dance and sing as I ran around and blew up balloons. As a child, I was oblivious to the meaning and politics behind the celebrations, and they were always very happy times as far as I was concerned.

New Year's Eves

No matter how elaborately and gloriously the Soviet government celebrated all these working-class holidays, the New Year's celebration was still the favorite amongst the Russian people. It was an all-night party lasting until sunrise, with wild festivities at people's houses and on the streets. In most cities and villages, a Christmas tree was erected in the central square, and the display drew large crowds of people who gathered around it to drink champagne and sing popular songs. In USSR, we had to refer to it as a 'New Year's tree' because the name 'Christmas tree' was banned in 1917 by our government and was never used in public.

We always celebrated the New Year at home, with big crowds of guests, always having a tall decorated Christmas/New Year's tree crowned with a big red star on its top. Right up until the very last day of the old year, people dragged trees of different sizes and shapes to their homes for similar celebrations. There were no special markets or stores that sold holiday trees, so I still don't know where they came from. I do remember that my mother once bought a tree from a person on the street, and she was very happy because it was so beautiful, only to find out that it did not fit in our house. A saw and ax did the job, and it was quickly embellished in sparkly ornaments. As any other child, I loved to be the designated tree decorator, occasionally breaking a couple of ornaments and secretly eating a few candies that were meant to be part of the decorations.

For any Russian child at the time, the New Year's celebration was just as anticipated as our own birthdays. The reason for that was simple: presents. Most Russian children were never spoiled with a lot of toys, but everybody received them on their birthdays and on January 1, New Year's Day. Traditionally, presents were placed under the tree, and children rushed there on the first day of the year to see what Old Man Frost (Russian version of Santa Clause) and the Snow Fairy brought them.

One New Year's, I received my first musical instrument: a xylophone. It was wrapped in a nice box, lying under the tree, waiting for me amongst other smaller gifts. When I opened it, I did not know what it was or how to play with it. It only took a few hours for me to figure it out, and in no time at all, I was beating its wooden planks as hard as I could, drumming up the house. The chaotic notes penetrated the walls of our apartment, notifying the neighbors that the time of a quiet, peaceful life had ended. It was a well-made toy designed to withstand harsh performances by a restless toddler. I loved that xylophone so much and several times broke its sticks by getting carried away with my musical inspirations. My first experience with a musical instrument opened my young, primitive mind to the endless boundaries of its potential. It would take many more years, however, before I actually understand the real power of music.

The "Truth" About the Rest of the World

It was the peak of the Cold War and our Communist propaganda was telling adults and children that we were the best country, in the whole world, and that everything outside of our Socialist camp was bad and horrible. These teachings came from all sides: TV, radio, movies, journalism, and books. The Iron Curtain protected Soviet people from a realistic knowledge about the life outside the boundaries of the USSR.

In that kind of society, where the media and everyone were saying the same things, it was very easy to make small children believe in whatever we were told, and we all did. I recall one of the children's books I had in Russia, which I believe was titled *S.O.S.* It painted us as humans and those in the Western world as terrifying, wild predators, and it was a good example of what kids were being taught about the rest of the world at that time. The book told the story of a Russian fishing boat that got in trouble in the ocean and sent out an S.O.S. via three characters, Russian children who flew around the world seeking help from all the nations. Obviously, no one from the Western countries wanted to help, especially the "Fashistman" from a New York skyscraper. He sat idly by on bags of gold dollars with a swastika band on his arm, and he was the last one to say "No" when they asked for help. At the end of the story, our 'brothers' from Cuba helped the Russian ship. This compassion from Cuba, of course, embittered all Western nations about our friendship with Cuba, and this book was a typical Soviet presentation of what our children should expect from the Capitalists.

The horror stories about our 'ideological enemies were very elaborate, often with the clear intention of blaming our own problems on the Western world. We were told Capitalists were using airplanes and dropping bags of insects onto our crops to cause bad harvests because they were allegedly jealous of our success. Perhaps most terrifying at all in the ears of Russian children were the rumors that the Westerners wanted to bring war and steal our happy lives. These tales would be chilling for any child, but to hear it from the adults we trusted meant they were more than just idle threats or propaganda; we took them as testaments of truth, and we all believed what we were told and feared and hated the Western world because of it.

Strange and Distant Paris

In 1969, my Aunt Valentina and her husband had a chance to peek behind the Iron Curtain. It was almost unheard of, a stroke of luck that could only happen to a chosen few in the Soviet Union. They were able to get tickets for some "International Friendship People Exchange" and traveled for one week to Paris. These type of programs was designed on the West to promote peace and freedom by the interaction of people from the USSR with other nations.

The odds of this happening for someone at that time were as slim as winning the Mega-lottery three times in the row. For many Russians, just to travel to Socialistic countries like Poland or Hungary was a rare and difficult accomplishment. The only people who had more chances to go abroad than others were elite government officials, top athletes, musicians of the best Soviet classical and folk ensembles, and sailors. Many of those who went to the West often preferred to stay for good in the so-called 'rotted' Capitalistic world and their names were forever erased from the Soviet society.

It was, without a doubt, a very unwise decision for Soviet officials in general to agree to these exchanges and allow ordinary people a look at the real Western country. The Soviet initiative was a prideful one, however, there was a temptation to bring French people to the USSR to show them our achievements. So they sometimes allowed such exchanges for this reason.

My Grandma, cousin Valery, aunt Valentina, my mother and I.

The attention, excitement, and vanity surrounding my relatives' travel to Paris were utterly overwhelming. Everybody was talking about it, and many of our friends were very jealous. My aunt was incredibly thrilled. I had been taught that life outside the USSR was bad and dangerous, and I could not understand why everyone was so happy about it and why my grandma did not want to stop them from going. I was curios and asked about it, but they only smiled and laughed at my sincere concerns for the safety of my aunt and uncle.

After they left, everyone began counting the days to their return, anxious to hear about what they saw beyond the reaches of our world. When they returned safely and unscathed from France, I grew even more puzzled. No one bothered them or tried to kill them while they were in Paris, as I had expected. In contrast, they were much happier than they had ever been. Their friends would not leave them alone and constantly attacked them with a barrage of questions about their trip, as if they had traveled to the moon. The frenzy surrounding their return from France seemed to stretch city wide. But they talked only to our family and close friends, sharing nonstop about the beauty of the Eiffel Tour as the astonished listeners drooled over the fancy scarves and blouses that my aunt was lucky enough to bring home from France.

At that time, it was a standard practice for all those returning from visits to foreign countries to have a chat with some "special" authority officer, who would give them "explanations", "advice", and "recommendations" of what to talk about after the trip and what to keep to themselves. I am sure my aunt and uncle also had this kind of debriefing, and for that reason only talked about the trip to our close friends and family members.

The hysteria surrounding their return did not make any sense to me, and I was completely confused when I received the present from the country of degraded Capitalism. My aunt brought me a small Formula-1 car of incredible detail and colors. It was strange to me that our superior Soviet toy stores never sold anything like that. In fact, I did not even know what F-1 cars were, and I began to wonder why our superhero, Lenin, didn't drive one. We obviously never saw anything like that in our lives. Car racing, like many other sports, was considered a kind of Western propaganda, and it was never broadcasted on our TV stations or spoken of in sports reports in our country.

I asked my aunt and uncle what other toys they saw in France, but they only answered me vaguely, saying they were all as good as our toys. I did not understand yet how difficult it was for my relatives, who had to be sure not to brag too much about the life of our enemies, while all the time they were dying to tell the story about their rare opportunity to see the world abroad. The adults understood what was going on, but no one would even try to explain this to a child.

The picture of life in a Capitalist world could remain only a fairytale if it existed only in vague stories and a few small souvenirs. Their story was also supported by short eight-millimeter films. Uncle Igor was a photography and film enthusiast. He'd spent a fortune (by Soviet standards) and tremendous effort to get the best amateur cameras manufactured in Russia at that time and made even bigger efforts to take his camera to France.

After a long wait for the film developing, the day many of our close friends and relatives had been so anxiously waiting for had arrived. We gathered at my aunt's house to see the movie, the short film about France was our first uncensored chance to see life in the Capitalist world. While some Western movies played in the Russian cinemas showing foreign people on the screen, they were strictly censored and were old or mediocre examples of Western cinematography.

For almost every frame of the shaky amateur film, there were excited comments from the audience. We had never seen the Western life so up close and in person, and it was really very different from what we'd been hearing from our government. I noticed that the people in France were not wild-looking predators at all, and they actually looked normal. Their streets were busy with cool cars like none I'd seen before. I was a child though, and in spite of the excitement of everyone around me, the lack of toy stores in the film sent me into a bored nap.

The Nuts and Bolts of our Soviet Toys

The teaching of a humble, conservative lifestyle began at a young age in our country. The story about the French toy is a good example that we were never spoiled with good toys. In fact, we were never spoiled with them in general and seldom received them at all unless it was on our birthdays or New Year's, as I've mentioned. I remember most of my favorite toys in the Soviet Union, and there were not too many of them. One of the reasons was financial. Parents could not afford to spoil their children with lots of toys and wouldn't allow others to buy them for their children either, knowing that everyone was financially burdened enough already. Hand-me-down toys were common, inherited from older sisters, brothers, cousins, and even parents. Most of my toys were inherited from my older cousin Valery, including my beloved beige bicycle.

Gomel on the vintage postcard. Reads "Hello from Gomel".

It is interesting to note that our toys had different meanings in our young lives than the toys given to Western children. While most societies use toys as simple playthings, distractions, or rewards, they served a much greater function for Russian children of that time. Sharing toys with others was our norm and often a rule. If someone had a scooter, for instance, it was almost guaranteed that every kid in our large neighborhood would get to ride it. Through toys, we developed friendships and even learned how to make deals and fair trades through their exchange. Broken toys taught us to find someone who could help us fix it, and missing toys were the object of many neighborhood searches. Because our toys were few and far between, we learned the value of them and thought of them as precious, and we were taught to care for them and keep them neat and organized in boxes and burlap bags.

Girls played with dolls, and boys enjoyed racing cars with each other or playing war with miniature solders. Toys helped us unveil very valuable aspects of human character, and we all lived much closer to each other than children in today's modern world.

Another priceless benefit of living without too many toys is that we learned to make many of them ourselves. They were much cooler than the ones sold in stores, where the selection was limited. We could customize them and make them any way we wanted. The most common and handy toys for boys were guns and rifles. Older kids who had already picked up some skill at making them from the planks of wood passed their toy-gun-making skills on to younger generations. The materials came from fences, broken boxes and local construction sites that were all great places to find wood—even for adults who needed it for projects.

Most of our toy-making tools came from the kitchen. We were lucky if we found a tool with a folding knife in it, but most often they were dull from many decades of use. I had a knife with a green handle that my grandmother liked a lot. An older friend of mine taught me how to sharpen it against the cement stairs of our house, and that technique came in very handy many years later. We shared our tools and our skills, and if someone had a saw, everyone used it. We all learned to do it from each other.

For us, begging our parents to buy this or that toy was a waste of time, so making our own toys was a more appreciated opportunity than it would be today. Our guns were very primitive, but very cool, probably because we created them ourselves. Often it was much more fun to make them than it was to play with them. I enjoyed making pistols and frequently did not even play with them before I started making something new.

Whenever our attention and hype over war games shifted to something else, we would make different kinds of toys. In the spring, we made small sailboats and ships out of tree bark. It was very easy to carve them using a knife, and we poked small twigs in the middle to hold up the paper sails that would propel the boats through a puddle of spring water.

I also remember making airplanes that we used for air battles by swinging our planes around with twine attached to their wings. Our opponent then did the same, and the planes would collide. The winner would be the one whose plane still had its wing and the body stayed together. The broken ones were later rebuilt and flown again until they were destroyed beyond repair in another air battle.

As time went on and kids grew and materials became more "advanced" and more readily available, much more complicated toys were created in our neighborhood, like carts on ball bearing wheels. To start with, we had to gather the main components for it, large ball bearings about four to six inches in diameters. To get them, all we had to do was go to the nearby ball bearing factory. It was a sight to see a dozen or more kids from four to ten marching to the factory without any fear of getting cut or being in big trouble. We didn't have to worry about tearing up our clothes either, because our dirty clothes, with many stitched patches on the knees and elbows, were classic children's outfits of that time.

The factory was not actually the place we were interested in as much as the trash dumpsters there. The premises of industrial facilities were not isolated and controlled locations as they are in most places today. In a society of a ruling working class, the fences around USSR factories were commonly crummy or not existent at all, often present only near the main entrances. Many

Soviet factories were surrounded by a large mass of its product debris or waste. Their neglectful disposal of refuse and lackluster security allowed us to pick up whatever we wanted without any hassle.

Once these main components were obtained, the rest of it was a mere formality of building the cart frame from common wooden fence planks. It was a very simple but quite ingenious design, with a triangle frame and two bars/axels with ball bearings on each end. A primitive seat was made from anything that could support our small bodies, and then the fun would began. We had wild races through the streets or down the hill at our local park. The carts were powered by one or two kids pushing from behind, and we had the ultimate fun to the point of a complete exhaustion.

My favorite rare Sunday treat - rented pedal car.

To keep our young spirits up and our excitement at its maximum, we sometimes made our versions of rockets. The fact that Russians were the first into space inspired us and gave us confidence in what we were doing. The most innovative rocket design we ever came up with required an empty toothpaste tube. The old paste tubes were made out of metal, and it was very easy to open them at the end and stuff them full of shredded pieces of nitro plastic. Many toys and school items were made from this material, so we never had a shortage of this fuel for any of our pyrotechnical projects. Once the rocket was loaded with fuel, we closed the end and attached it to a stick or simply placed it on a brick. The fire set under the tube heated the whole rocket, and shortly after, it flew into the air screaming, clouds of smoke blowing from its paste exit. It was a lot of fun, but as is the case with many fun things, there was some danger involved.

The story about the creative Soviet childhood would not be complete without discussing its artistic craft side. It involved some knowledge in metalworking and casting, and we did it with the most primitive tools ever. Nobody knows who came up with this idea, but it was so popular amongst many of my friends that we did it every time we had the right ingredients for it. All we needed was a broken car battery, clay, an empty food can, a bucket of sand, and a pile of wood. If we could find a car battery in a dumpster, everything else was readily available. The battery had to be broken with all the lead recovered from its container. The rest of it came with the help of clay, which we knew how to use from many hours of messing with it at our daycares. We created anything we wanted out of clay; some kids made cars, some pistols, and others even skulls with bones... The next step was to place our clay creations into the wet sand in order to make a cast. The lead was stocked into the empty food can. The fire was started with a can in it, and the lead-melting process began. I loved to see how the lead grew softer and finally became a bright liquid. We then took the wooden sticks and used it to pick up the can from fire and fill the sand cast with liquid lead. After all our objects were done and cooled, some kids, myself included, insisted on filing them to give them a smoother surface and a finer look. Surprisingly, we learned very quickly how to use a file, often by the time we were five years old, something many kids today do not even know how to hold even after years in school.

We didn't have many TV channels, and video games were nonexistent. For such entertainment we were able to watch only a half-hour of cartons on Sundays, and there was a ten-minute show called "Good Night Babies" on TV at eight fifteen each night. Two channels on Soviet TV mainly broadcasted political shows, movies about the working class, and boring folk and patriotic music concerts. It was an interesting era when Soviet society unintentionally forced its children to learn irreplaceable human and practical values, provided in a bigger spectrum on the streets than from our television broadcasts. The limited goods, toys, and TV entertainment allowed for us to develop unique personalities and grew our creative individualism.

This was not what our Socialistic society planned, however. Individualism was not a part of our teachings, and we were told that from the early ages. The USSR was attempting to groom children to be a future Proletarians, working class people, and fighters for Communism. We had to be ready to join a society of collective efforts, 'all like one and one like all'. We were prepared to be a part of a huge machine building a "bright future", and any creativity had to be applied only to our universal Socialistic plans; there was no room for individuals. All teachings, including crafts skills, led by the Communist Party of the Soviet Union, were supposed to be just stepping stones to ready children to be later utilized in our factories and fields.

The role of toys and interaction with other kids is impossible to separate from the games we played in the Soviet Union. As in any other element of life in Russia, even the games on the street had political or patriotic substance behind them, an ulterior motive, of sorts. When we played war games, everyone desired to be Red Army heroes, and no one wanted to be a Nazi. Characters and stories were borrowed from movies and children's books, most of which had Soviet thematic elements. As soon as a new movie on any military story was shown, we all ran outside to recreate the drama. One of the many popular military games we played was the reenactment of the battles of our Civil War, started after the Bolshevik Revolution. The 'bad guys' were always the Whites, the Tsar Army followers, and the 'good guys' were the Reds, the freedom-fighting Bolsheviks. We all believed the Bolsheviks were good heroes to idolize, and the Whites were destined to lose.

We lived in a residential community that combined several five-story buildings, and there was a large number of kids in our area. We played late into the darkness of night, until our parents called us home through the open windows. It was peaceful, with almost no crime time, and rarely would anyone be concerned about the children's safety. Riding bicycles on the streets and neighborhoods was a daily routine, and we spent many hours without our parents even knowing where we were. When we were not in daycare, we were practically out in the streets all the time.

Chapter 2

"What's inside?": Life in the Village and in the Town

As any child, I had toys I loved more than others, but my favorites were the ones I could take apart and look inside. If I had no toys for it, I would disassemble anything that had screws and bolts to twist. I was very good at breaking apart things, but putting them back together was a challenge for a kid like me.

In one of my childhood books, a little boy was chasing tiny crew members that he believed lived in a model ship that stood on the armoire at his grandmother's house. He eventually broke the beautiful tugboat, only to discover a few specs of dust inside and no traces of any of its crew members. That was also what I found in most of the items and toys I took apart, but my curiosity pushed me over and over again to explore the internal life of new objects.

Some of the interesting items that often drew my attention and sparked my desire to take a peek inside were clocks and watches. We had a few of them in our house. The era of quartz and battery-operated timepieces had not yet conquered the world at that time, so all the big and small necessities of life had mechanical movements that not only clicked and ticked, but also had plenty of parts moving, jumping, and striking. To me, closed in cases, they looked like little castles full of hidden secrets living within their mystical, mechanical insides. Taking a peek inside them was almost like a journey into a mysterious world. There were some I would only open to the point where I could not go any further and simply admire the golden array of spiky wheels and springs moving back and forth. Some of them, however, would not let me even get them open without a struggle, and some would play a punishment game with me for my violation of their privacy.

One day, I eventually picked a wrong item to be examined by my young crafty hands and here is the story of what happen next...

We had a small, elegant wristwatch, a Pobeda (Victory) that used to belong to my grandmother's husband Mikhail. It had a simple design with a white dial, golden hands, and art deco-style numbers. It was manufactured after WW2, and any watches at that time were somewhat of a luxury. Mikhail only wore it on holidays and at parties. After he passed away grandma treasured the watch, promising to give it to me in the future. The watch was kept in a gray cardboard box, along with a few other items that held sentimental value to her and my mother. I often asked my grandma to let me look at the watch and even wore it on my small wrist for a few minutes. Every time I did that, my curiosity started to climb, and the desire to take a look inside the small timepiece began to swell. I knew asking my grandmother to let me take the watch apart was very unrealistic. She would only let me hold it in her presence, so if I was going to satisfy my obsession of exploring its construction, I had to do it while she wasn't home.

One bright, early morning, just after we had breakfast, my grandma said she was going to the store and would be back by lunch time. My mom was out of town, so I considered it a great opportunity to see what was inside that small wristwatch. When the door closed behind my grandmother, I jump up and scurried to the bedroom. First, I had to find the key to the big wooden dresser where the box with the watch was kept. I found it very quickly under the stack of bed sheets and, in a hurry, opened one of the heavy dresser doors. With a familiar *squeak*, the door swung open, spilling out the smell of old perfume and time that belonged to the antique furniture. I grabbed the box, which was sitting on the top shelf, set it on the floor and started anxiously looking at the watch, wondering how to get inside of this little treasure. When I noticed a small lip at the edge of the back cover, I ran to the kitchen, found a knife, and wedged its blade in to pry the back open. Nothing happened. The cover was very tight and stubborn. I wrestled with it for a long time and almost gave up on it, but suddenly it popped up, and the cover flew through the air. In front of me was an intricate silverfish swarm of moving parts. I moved a short lever that had a +/- sign on it. Nothing happened. The watch kept ticking, and a small spring inside of it continued rotating back and forth. A few reddish dots were spaced randomly here and there in the movement, and they reminded me in color of the big red ring Grandma wore all the time. The inside of the watch was like a jigsaw puzzle, and I had no tools small enough to take the microscopic parts of the watch apart. I could only admire its beautiful precision and the interesting pattern of the movement parts.

Suddenly, I noticed time had flown like lightning, and it was already almost lunch time. I had to put the cover back on the watch quickly and hide all traces of my operation. When I tried to press the cover closed, it did not work. I tried again, harder this time, but it still did not budge. I began pushing it with all my force, but nothing happened. My heart started to race, and I began to panic; the clock on our round table moved effortlessly forward to lunch time without mercy. "Grandma will be back any minute," I said to myself in fear. I realized that I had gotten myself into trouble. Nothing good would come out of it if my secret mission was discovered, so I tried even harder to get the cover closed. It felt like it did not belong there anymore, and my effort was going nowhere. In despair, I decided to tap the cover with the help of some bigger tools. I found a hammer and placed the watch on the rug on the floor and tapped the back cover with a light blow. I heard a snap and picked up the watch. Finally, the cover was closed, and relief rushed through my mind and body. I flipped the watch over to put it away, only to see a much worse nightmare. The crystal was smashed to pieces. I was shocked, and as far as I knew, that was the end of me.

Seconds later, I heard the click of a door lock when grandma arrived back at home. I dropped everything on the floor and ran to her in tears. She lifted me up, fearing something horrible had happened to me. "What happened? What happened?" she kept asking as I panicked.

I shouted through my tears, "I broke the watch!" I was already prepared to get an instant severe punishment for my misconduct.

She hugged me very hard and said, "Don't worry. It's just a watch." I was hanging on her shoulder feeling so bad about my mistake and the watch that I broke. Trying to comfort me and telling that nothing had happened worth such distress, I was happy to be in her hands when I should have been spanked and grounded. She was the best and loved us more than life itself, definitely more than some old watch.

Of course I was not rewarded for what I'd done, but my sincere confession and sorrow was enough. I learned a tough lesson about obedience. As far as the watch's fate, we took it together to the watch repair shop down the street, and the crystal was replaced. I am looking at it right now as it rests on my nightstand. It still runs flawlessly well, just as it did so many years ago, and the tiny ding on its back cover from the hammer blow is still there, reminding me about my wonderful grandma and that day of my "adventurous" childhood.

The Village: Now and at War

My mom worked all day and went to a Communist night school, and my father was not around, so the responsibility for my care and parenting mainly rested on my grandma. She dropped me off at daycare in the morning and picked me up afterwards. She also took care of the cooking, the grocery shopping, and other duties around the house.

Occasionally in the summer, we would go together to see her sister, Dunya, who lived in a small village called Krasnaya Buda, about thirty miles away from our city. Often, we stayed there for a couple of days or even longer. For me, those days were full of wild sensations, and they will forever stick in my memory.

It was very easy to get to Dunya's village. Most of the traveling in the USSR at that time was done by railroad. Buses were another option, but they would travel no more than 300 miles. The local train ran twice a day to our village, and it took about an hour to get there with frequent stops and its slow movement. The Soviet railroad system was huge. I believe it's still the largest in the world, and so are the trains themselves. To a small kid like me, the locomotives and large train cars looked enormous. I loved everything about them: the smell, the look, and the noise they made. Every time we waited for the train to arrive at the city station, I loved to watch its slow, clumsy approach. The steam blew from the locomotive in all directions, increasing with every foot of its approach. When the train passed in front of me, I watched the huge pistons full of grease and oil, pushing the big red wheels forward. At that time, they still used the same train engines that were used in WW2.

Riding inside the train was fun and adventurous for me. Passengers of all levels, but mainly farmers, traveled regularly to the city for shopping. Most of the people chatted with each other, joked, and played cards. The smell of cigarettes, beer, and the old passenger car itself was very unique—an aroma that could only be experienced on our trains.

My grandma knew the atmosphere very well because she had once worked as a train car tender. She traveled on the main passenger train going from Gomel to Moscow. Because of her experience working the train for many years after WW2, her knowledge of railroad systems was incredible. She had an answer for every curious question I asked her, no matter how difficult they were. She told me that after the war, every train car was beautifully and passionately decorated on the inside, and all of them had portraits of Stalin, even the front of the locomotives. "People loved Stalin," she always told me. "He won the war and cared for people." She occasionally raged, "Khrushchev dragged Stalin's coffin from the mausoleum of Lenin. It was so evil!" I had no idea what she was talking about when she said that, so I just quietly stared out through the window of the train car, watching the trees and houses fly by on our way to Dunya's village.

Visiting any Soviet village was a true journey back in time. Cultural life had not changed a lot there since the Bolshevik Revolution in 1917. The economical status of Russian villages, on the other hand, changed drastically. In Tsar's Russia, we were not an industrial country, but our agricultural strength was legendary worldwide. Villagers at that time worked very hard in the fields of high-hierarchy farm owners. In contrast, they did not have much land for their own needs. Lenin promised to every village family that they would get their fair share of land, which would be confiscated after the Revolution from what he called 'rich exploiters'. "Factory to workers! Land to farmers!" stated the Communist slogans. And, for a short time after Bolshevik coup, poor farmers got the land they were promised. However, as soon as they started making good profits and living better, they became known as "Kulaki" (fists), enemies of the revolution. Kulak was described by Soviets as a greedy peasant farmer who got a lot of goods and money from his harvests, which he kept for himself instead of sharing it all with the rest of our working class. Simply put, some hardworking farmers became 'rich' in the eyes of the new Proletarian dictatorship, a status that is now forbidden by Bolshevik's dogma. Soon after, all private land was confiscated, and the Communistic practice of collective farming, "Kolkhoz", was invented. It was the end of agricultural prosperity for Russia and the beginning of a new era of Soviet collective farming—a method that failed to deliver enough food to its citizens for over seventy years.

Kolkhoz was simply a farm which united all village workers into one large agricultural production enterprise. Everyone had to participate in Kolkhoz, despite proclamations that it was a voluntary organization. As with any other Soviet invention, every *Kolkhoz* had a name honoring Soviet leaders, heroes, or just a slogan like "Red Leader" or "The Victory of Communism". All products—livestock, crops, gardens, or any other produce—were raised collectively and delivered to the government. Everyone who worked there was just an employee with a fixed low salary, and they were often paid in the past only with goods their Kolkhoz was producing.

Small pieces of land were issued to each family by Kolkhoz's so they could grow whatever they needed to support their limited livestock and feed their families. This land was not an extra bonus from the government or an additional source of whopping profits. Everything they produced on their own land was normally consumed by their families within a year. Their land served as their grocery store. Villagers also had to support their crops, gardens, and livestock practically without access to any developed infrastructure or supplies to help them do so. After all, they could only care for their own farms before and after they worked all day in the *Kolkhoz* fields. The government did allow village farmers to sell their extra produce at city farm markets if they had leftovers from their harvests. Eventually, the farm market began to deliver more products from the small private lands than all the ineffective Kolkhoz agricultural systems of the Soviet Union combined.

Going from the city to the country at that time was a real cultural shock. Krasnaya Buda was a very small, typical Russian village with about 100 houses in total. It was a quiet, peaceful corner of our beautiful European nature with flat, rich soil. Upon arrival, a short stop at the improvised station allowed people to quickly drop their luggage down and jump off the train. On one side of the track was a forest of mixed trees. On the other side was a large field with Kolhoz's farm animals scattered across it, lazily eating the grass throughout its endless green boundaries. To get to the village itself, we had to walk through that field for about another half-hour. If we got lucky, someone would come in a horse-drawn carriage to pick up a friend or relative, and we could hitch a ride without even having to ask. As long as there was room, anybody was always welcome to jump in.

On the way to the village, going by the dirt road, the smell of hay, crops, and the fresh air was always pure and rich. It was rare to see any vehicles, with the exception of the occasional *Kolkhoz* truck or a tractor making its way through the dusty road.

Here and there along the way, poking through the grass and bushes, we could see the rusted remains of old farming equipment, neglected and ownerless. It was a sad reality of the *Kolkhoz* system. As we passed the various machines, I always had a dream of getting inside of them and explore their contents. I asked my grandma one time if I could, and she said with a deep exhaling, "All the good stuff from it has probably already been stolen, Yura."

The main and only street in our village was a dirt road going from one end to the other. In the summer, it looked like a dusty canyon, and in the spring, like a river. The old houses in the village looked like those in the movies we watched about the Russian Civil War, with the exception of the presence of electricity. Other amenities like bathrooms, running water, or heating sources hadn't changed since their design in ancient times. The water for the entire village came from a few very old manual wells. A little wooden cabin in the corner of the garden served as a bathroom, and heating was accomplished by the brick "pechka" - a large firewood stove. The only phone in the village was the one in the Kolkhoz director's office. There were no police, no school, and no doctors. All local people dressed the same as those who lived hundred years before them, but they were simple and kind and always greeted and cared for each other throughout their difficult Soviet country lives.

The main entertainment in the village was a single TV set in one shabby house. All villagers went there to watch the movie or news. Doors were always been open, and everyone was welcome. I went with my grandma there once and was surprised to see a crowd of about thirty people watching a movie on tiny TV. The clouds of cigarette smoke and the stench of strong moonshine hung like a wall in the air. We didn't enjoy the strange gathering very much and quietly left.

There was not much of a young population in Krasnaya Buda. There were only a few kids, and they had to travel five to seven miles every day on bikes or horses to get to a nearby village to go to school. Life was boring and not promising in the country at that time, and after graduating, all the kids wanted to escape this lost and forgotten world. That was a difficult task, however, because the Soviet passport regime required all citizens to remain either where they were born or where they lived with their families. Exceptions only applied to school and college students. So, this is exactly what youngsters at the villages did: They fled to trade schools and colleges in the cities as soon as they could. The ones who could not do that for one reason or another were forced to stay home and work in the fields of the Kolkhoz.

The Old Country Life

Babushka Dunya lived with her husband Gregory in a little white painted house almost at the end of the nameless main street. They had a son named Andrew. At that time he lived in out city as well and we kept close relationship with him. After serving two years in the Army now he was attending college, so he only visited his parents occasionally. He was the only male adult close to our family that I could rely on after old Mikhail past away. I liked Andrew a lot, and he was very nice and kind to me. Sometimes when he went to visit his mother, he took me with him, and it always made for a great trip. Holding his arm, I often pretended he was my real father, and I walked proudly beside of him.

I loved to be at Dunya's house. They had a cow, a pig, chickens, little chicks, and a very sweet cat. For a city boy, being around the animals was a special and rewarding experience, and I had a lot of fun interacting with them. They also had a fruit orchard and a vegetable garden. Outside the garden, they had a small crops field where they grew potatoes and corn. It may sound as if they were wealthy, but these were just the typical family assets of most villagers at that time. Like everyone else, they were very nice, simple people with only the bare necessities, living a difficult country life.

The basic tasks such as making food or washing your hands were so different from what I knew in the city. While the house itself was small, it felt roomy and very cozy. There were no fancy furniture or luxuries. They only had the bare essentials: a table, two beds, a couple of chairs, and a large dresser. In the corner there was an old Christ icon hanging, and I was little surprised they had it in the house at all. No one wanted to talk to me about it, and I did not press anyone to give me the answer.

To a little child, time in the village can get boring very fast. After exploring everything I could, I usually entertained myself with the objects I found, much different from the city life amenities. The old hand-operated sewing machine was the premiere item in their house. I loved to play with it, making the wheel go fast by pushing its large iron pedal. Gregory did not like it, and I knew I had very little chance, if any, to look at the internal workings of this fascinating machine...

No house in a Russian village could survive without their pechka, a giant firewood stove. It served as a food-making place, as well as a source of heat in the winter. It was constructed out of bricks, and it had a large platform on the top to sleep on, especially in winter time. The heat stored in its walls and radiated back into the whole house, making the sleep at night very comfortable. I spent hours lying on its warm surface, accompanied by its regular visitor, the family cat. The only time the pechka was not in use was in the hot days of summer. During those warmer days, all cooking was done on the revolutionary device that helped our farmers, a kerosene primus.

I will never forget the taste of the food on our trips to the village. Everything tasted so good and fresh. Vegetables and fruits, milk, and corn had a flavor we could not taste in our city meals. The fresh, natural, homegrown produce was delicious. On top of that, the undeveloped and technologically poor Soviet agriculture ironically enhanced the quality of the food int the villages. There and then, our food was not exposed to such a vast spectrum of pesticides, hormones, genetic alterations, and artificial preservatives like what is used today. Everything was natural. Cows ate grass and hay, chickens were fed with seeds, and the fruits and vegetables had to be collected, delivered, sold, and eaten before they rotted. Milk never stayed in the house for more than a day because it spoiled by morning, and bread would grow rock hard after a few hours of sitting on the table. It was a rare, almost comical situation because the life of the Soviet people here benefited from our dragging feet agricultural chemical industry.

Most of my time spent in the village was occupied with exploring the garden, picking berries and mushrooms in the forest with my grandma, and running through the dust on the main street. I enjoyed chasing chicks and watching the pig as he sloppily ate his lunch with his foot practically in his food. Few objects at Dunya's home however, held more of my interest than the animals. It was the small barn that served as a shelter for a cow, the pig, and the chickens. The wooden log barn was actually an old house built before the Revolution, a place where they lived for a long time. Though it was almost completely decayed and sagging to the ground, it had a mystique feel about it, a kind of charm. I had my best times in that barn while visiting Baba Dunya. There was a room in there full of old household items. The things people pay large sums of money for today in antique stores were scattered about and considered old junk back then. Some of it was made over 100 years earlier and had been in the family's possession for many generations. From old twine-making machines and kitchenware to an elaborate irons that worked on coal, they had it all. There were big boxes of old rusty tools luring me to dive inside of them and search for something extraordinary. In the recent past, living as a Russian villager required producing almost everything fore oneself. Even fabrics had to be made, and grain had to be ground to bake bread. The 'old junk' I found in that barn were actually once irreplaceable tools of our people survival. I was picking through them and not once turned everything upside down, what upset Dunya's husband somewhat, and I was often asked to keep my explorations at a minimum.

Traces of War

While I always wanted to check out things that had spinning or moving parts or things that were just unique and unusual, I was also intrigued with the idea of finding some items from the WW2. I was confident that Gregory had hidden some old guns or bullets somewhere, leftovers he found in his fields after the war. I could never find anything, though, so one day I simply decided to ask Gregory, "Do you have any war guns or pistols?"

In loud laughter, he replied, "Even if I do, you would not be playing with that, but we never had that stuff. However, I can show you what we have left behind by a Nazi." He took me outside, and we walked to the corner of the courtyard. "Here," he said, "you can have this." He picked up a water bowl for chickens. When he turned it upside down, I realized it was a German solder's helmet!

I was so blown away that I grabbed it and ran into the house to my grandma. "Look! Look what I got!" I shouted in excitement.

She stared at me strangely and asked, "Why do you need this old trash?"

"Trash? This is a *real* World War Two helmet, Grandma!" I replied in euphoria.

"Come here," she said, "and let me tell you what I know about this war." After that, she told me the story about a day that might have been the last for her and my mother…

In 1943, German troops were retreating from our Soviet Belarus Republic, which was under attack of the Red Army. As they moved through the villages, they burned and destroyed everything that got in their way. The Nazi soldiers were searching for people through the houses torturing and executing them, including some in our village. When Nazi squadron came close to where Grandma lived she grabbed my mom and her sister and hid under the house floor in a cellar. She heard the sound of heavy boots walking into the house, and after a short search, one of the men moved to the cellar handle ring, usually attached to one of the floor planks. He stopped there and started lifting the floor cover. To my grandma, it was the end. In tears, she clutched her children to her heart, kissing and hugging them for what she though would be the last time. The hatch opened, and a German soldier, wearing a helmet just like the one I held in my hands, glared down at my grandma, pointing a machine gun into her face. She ducked to protect her kids, ready to take the bullets in their stead.

At this moment, someone from outside called the soldier and asked him something in German. "Nichts!" he shouted back to his comrade.

My mom and aunt Valentina. Photo from 1942.

My grandma looked at him, still staring at her. He got up, took his gun, and threw it over his shoulder. The floor cover dropped, and he walked away.

She said she could not remember how long she sat there, but when they came out, it was dark. The flames from a few burning houses lit up sky, and there were no more Germans in the village. Belarus suffered greatly in WW2, and every fourth person of that Republic died in the war. Almost every household lost someone at that time, and our family did not escape this tragedy.

I asked Grandma if I could take the helmet home. To her, it was probably a sad reminder and after kicking it around the courtyard I left it eventually in the village.

Going back home from the village was always a long-awaited time for me. While I enjoyed visiting the village, the slow and primitive life there could not keep me entertained for long, and I started missing my home and friends, who were always active and fun to be around. The old train took us back to the city, and like most of the other passengers, we were loaded down with baskets of mushrooms, berries, apples, and corn.

Under One Roof

My mother was worked an average of twelve hours a day, and often I could hardly see her for a whole week. She was always employed either by the Regional Committees or a Communist organization at the factories. Her dedication to work and the Communist Party was incredible. She was absorbed with an honest passion and believed in all of the Socialistic teachings. Everything she studied and learned about Marxism and Bolshevik theory, she tried to apply in her life. She worked mercilessly, sacrificing her time and life to the causes of our ideological dogmas. That was real Communist living, and she followed that concept with a true dedication.

When I was a child, I once asked my mother what Communism is? It was an acceptable and common question from children because while we were told about the bright future more often than anything else, we were ironically never given a true, clear definition of Communism. At that time, according to our teachings, we lived in "Accomplished Socialism" We were told we were building a future of prosperity - Communism, but the plain definition of its simple concept for our population was very vague.

My mother at age of 16.

My mom told me in Communism, everybody would be so honest and truthful that there would be no crime, no wars, and no hungry people in the world. People would work for free because they would do their jobs just for the sake of contributing to society, and no one would have any need of money. To achieve that, she said we would have to build Socialism as a first step in the whole world. I could hardly even picture people going to the store and taking things for free, but my mother told me people would have a new Communist spirit and would not take more than they needed when they went shopping.

It was the clearest description of Communism I had ever heard from anybody during my life in the USSR. I knew my mom would not lie to me, and I was hoping to one day see that bright future. The sad truth about this ideology was that it stole so many minds and lives, as well as parental time from our citizens and children. It is sad for me to admit that I was robbed by this idiotic dogma many times myself. It was my stolen time with my mom, and ultimately even sacrifices of our family wholeness for the causes of the Communist Party doctrines, that my mom lost when she was dragged into it by the Bolsheviks.

A Place to Live in the USSR

My mother was one of the strongest believers in these teachings that I met, and she was a very loyal and dedicated follower of the Communist Party. What separated her from many other Communists is that she did not join the Party for any personal gain or benefit. She never used any special goods and food supply channels for Party leaders and Elite authorities. At that time, many people thought becoming a member of the Party would be a door to better living, even part of a planned strategy for their corrupted plans. Mom, on other hand, suffered greatly from people who were trying to get a back door deals from her, expecting her to use her job position and status to further their own agendas. When she refused to get them a special request or favor, she was viewed as an enemy and became the subject of harsh and undeserved ridicule.

One good example of her loyalty and uncorrupt principles was the situation with our apartment. To understand the level of difficulty in obtaining apartment in the USSR, you have to picture the living standards in Soviet Union at that time. From the time of the Bolshevik Revolution, the government took over the whole responsibility of providing living spaces for our working class. The construction of new houses was a tough challenge for our industrially undeveloped nation. The situation in the villages, however, was not as bad since not many people wanted to live there. Houses could be purchased for nothing or abandoned ones were simply overtaken and given away to anyone who would come to work at Kolhoz. Construction of the city apartments was the legendary struggle in Soviet Union, right up until its total collapse in 1991. It was a slow and difficult task, always falling behind with the delivery of the new buildings.

My Grandma before WW2.

From 1920 to 1930, in order to provide roofs for many needy city families, the government began the program of communal livings, which people called Communalka. It was a desperate and very painful attempt to resolve the apartment problems in our country at that time. In every Communalka apartment, the number of families living there was equal to the number of its bedrooms. In a four-bedroom unit, four families would live there, sharing one kitchen and one bathroom among all its residents. In many old buildings, there was only one bathroom in the hallway, used by many apartments on the same floor, creating long waiting lines of people in the morning. The apartments became nothing more than overcrowded shelters with almost impossible living conditions. These communal living spaces survived through all Soviet history, and I witnessed some of my friends still spending life in these uncomfortable types of apartments.

We were fortunate enough to live in a normal one-bedroom apartment called a Khrushchevka, named after Nikita Khrushchev in memory of his program to move people from the Communalka to better living places. He forced our construction industry to come up with simple, but more civilized apartment buildings. The result were standardized apartment houses usually designed five stories high, but with apartments for only one family per unit. This building design was used throughout our entire nation and while were making different cities looks the same, they became a real Soviet breakthrough in attempt to resolve our decades-old housing problem.

In order to obtain any apartment, we had to qualify for the minimum living standards established by government. At that time, it was something around six or seven square meters of living space per person per apartment. If a family qualified, they could submit a request to city hall and wait in a lifeline. Apartments were granted at no charge up front, with only a small monthly payment thereafter. The wait was sometimes devastating decades and worrisome for people in the Soviet Union. When my mother and I arrived to live with her mom and husband in Gomel, she applied to city hall for her own apartment and the everlasting wait for it had began.

My grandfather Mitrofan.
Lost his life in WW2.

Another way to get an apartment was through the factory or big organization where a person was employed. If there was plenty of money, companies could build their own buildings, and the workers would get an apartment faster than they would through city hall. There were not too many organizations that could do it, and the long wait, as well as corruption surrounded the apartment distribution, was also a part of this process as well. Ironically (to my own future disadvantage), the great deal of tenants in our own building was KGB workers who received their units through this government/organization construction program. Since KGB was only second after the army organized and "respectable" force in our country, they could get to their employees apartments faster than doctors or teachers.

Later, the Soviet government allowed people to build apartments by cooperative effort, but it was an extremely expensive option for normal people, and only a few with prestigious jobs and connections could afford it.

While living in the USSR, we struggled in the same apartment since the days of my daycare, and we continued to live that way for many years. No matter how many of my family members lived there, we were always cramped with someone often sleeping on the floor.

All my mother's life, she was often involved through her job with the distribution and assignment of apartments to people who were waiting for them. With her power and job title, she could have easily gotten a new apartment for herself, but she never did. Her righteous mind and Communistic conscience were indestructible. She was so loyal to the principles of Marxist teachings about truth and honesty that she would never do something so immoral. Because of her potential power to improve someone's life simply by her signature, people often tried to manipulate her into helping them. She never did, and she was well known for that among her coworkers and in our family.

My grandma, on other hand, always complained to her that she was ignoring her own family's needs and avoiding taking the chance to improve things for us. Grandma insisted that she was not asking her to get anything for us illegally, and she wanted her to stand up and talk to her bosses on behalf of herself and us. My mom did not even consider that as an option. Her integrity and pure dedication to Communist principles weighed far above any of her own personal interests. Often, my grandma loved to tell us the story of how she got herself an apartment, and she wanted my mom to follow her example…

It was the difficult time after WW2, and my grandma lived in the basement with my mom and her sister Valentina. It was a damp, dark, cold place, impossible to live in even for animals. At that time, hoping for something better was nothing more than a dream. The country had just started the rebuilding process after the catastrophic war, and many cities, ours included, were still in ruins. Grandma was not trying to help herself at that time as much as trying to take care of her little children. One day, she decided to write a letter to only one person who could help her and who always cared for our working class, Comrade Josef Stalin himself.

She wrote on the back side of a canned food label:

DEAR COMRADE STALIN,

I AM A SINGLE MOM WITH TWO SMALL CHILDREN ON MY HANDS. I SURVIVED THE HORROR OF WAR, AND I LOST IN IT MY HUSBAND. TODAY I AM LIVING IN A BASEMENT, AND MY TWO GIRLS WILL DIE THIS WINTER BECAUSE WE HAVE NO HEAT, NO LIGHT, AND NOT EVEN FRESH AIR. YOU ARE MY ONLY HOPE. PLEASE, COMRADE STALIN, ASK OUR LOCAL GOVERNMENT TO GIVE US A ROOF AND A SMALL ROOM. I AM NOT ASKING IT FOR MYSELF, BUT FOR MY LITTLE CHILDREN.

She folded it in a triangle, typical to wartime, and wrote on its face: MOSCOW. KREMLIN. TO COMRADE STALIN. She placed a postage stamp on it and dropped it into the mailbox.

Time passed by, and she started to lose hope. Then one day, she received a CALL TO APPEAR BEFORE OUR AUTHORITIES. She started wondering what that call could mean. She knew many people who received this type of document never came back from the government building. She also knew most of them were "enemies of the State", "traitors", or "spies". She heard a lot about trials and executions of these thugs from the radio and newspapers. She afraid that by some mistake, she would never make it back from there, but she had no option but to go. She said goodbye to her children and took a small lunchbox and left for the big government building.

Her visit supported and embossed her belief that the only man in the world who cared about and stood behind working women and small children was Stalin. She got a small place to live, and she truly believed it was because Stalin read her letter and gave her a room. She could not understand at that time that letters with similar requests were being sent to the Kremlin all the time from big and small cities by thousands, if not millions, of Soviet people. Most of those letters never even made it out of the post offices and were returned to the local KGB departments. Whether it was just a coincidence or someone in the local government had compassion for her problem and helped her, she still believed for the rest of her life that it was done by Stalin himself. She loved to tell people that story as an example of Stalin's "humanity" and "understanding of the little people's needs". She always loved to pitched this story to my mom as an example of how to act when there is nowhere to go for help. In her mind, if there were still any real Communists left in the Party, they would have helped my mom get a bigger apartment, just like she was certain Stalin gave to her.

Considering all the backward realities of our lives, full of special treatments, back door deals, and corruption caused by our political system, Mom abstained from these flaws all her life. She was a wonderful person, accepting wholeheartedly the Soviet moral and ethical teachings, living her life by the rules of our Socialistic society, but also by the rules of a universal human righteousness.

Yes, my mother at that time was in love with our Communist Party, but after all she loved us more than her spiritual guiding light and cared for us like any good mother in the world. Throughout my whole life, whenever we needed any help or were in trouble, sick or pain, Mom was always by our side.

A Surprising Return and Lenin's Anniversary

When my grandma's husband Mikhail died in 1968, I had to live without any older male in our family living—just with my mom and my grandma. My friends often spent time with their fathers on the river, fishing or just simply playing around, and that was something I always wanted as well but never experienced. Often, I asked my mother if I would ever have a father, but I never got the answer. At that time of low divorce rates and stronger family ties, having no father was rare occasions and somewhat embarrassing fact. What I didn't know was that all this was about to change, and it would become one of most exciting times of my life.

In December of 1969, the doorbell rang in our house, and a tall man walked in with a whole pile of bags, boxes, and a giant accordion in a black case. There was much commotion and many happy greetings and hugs being exchanged. The man walked in the living room, and my grandma asked, with a big smile on her face, "Well, Yura, do you know who this is?"

My father at young age.

I replied with shy skepticism with a question that was hard for me to ask. "Are you my father?"

"Yes I am," he replied.

I ran into his arms with my heart jumping out of my chest in happiness and excitement. It was one of the best days of my life. After years of absence, my father returned to our family—a dream come true. I felt complete and normal, a kid with my own father who would now take care of me, go with me to the beach, play with me, and be my own hero and protector. I no longer had to tell anyone that I had no father or be ashamed about that. The level of happiness at that time was overwhelming, and I recall plans instantly flying through my mind about how we were going to spend our next summer and our future time together.

I could not wait to share this exiting news with all my friends in the neighborhood and at the daycare. To some, it was a big surprise. Many did not care much, but the daycare teacher kept asking me many questions about it, so much so that I didn't know what to say. I discovered later that my teachers simply liked the gossip because when I asked my mom and grandma about their interrogations, they simply told me "It's not their business."

My life had now been changed, and it had something in it that I could be proud of. I had a real father just like my other friends. We often played and shopped together, we went to the beach, and we visited the farm market almost every Sunday. He picked me up from the daycare, and while we walked through the streets holding hands, we planned what we would do the following weekend.

When he returned to live with us, he got a job at the local *Kirov* factory working in the metal shop. He had no college degree and was a simple man of a true working class background. I didn't know that his opinion about the Communist Party was different than my mother's, and he never discussed it in our house. He had a passion for different construction projects related to design, and he loved working with his hands. What he was doing at work at that time I wasn't sure, but

My dad in the army. Inside of T-34 tank.

very often he talked to me about engineering and machineries, something I was too little to understand.

One of the interesting items he brought with him upon his return to us was a big German accordion, a Weltmeister. It was a WW2 trophy that his father had brought home with him from the war. It was a beautiful instrument covered with pearl decorations on its keys and buttons. I loved to mess with it as often as I could, but it was unfortunately huge and very heavy. Every time I wanted to play with it, I had to ask my grandma to drag it to the living room for me. It was very strange to me , however that my grandma always told me to ask my dad's permeation to do that, and she never tried to do it herself. She did not seem to have any warm feelings toward my father, something that could be explained by his past relationship problems with my mom.

Having a Blast

One time I brought home some construction-type black powder shells. I do not remember where I found them, but it must have been during one of my infamous explorations at a nearby construction site. I forgot about them and left them in my pants pocket.

While my mom was doing the laundry, the shells fell out on the floor, shocking her. She was in an absolute panic, assuming they were real military ammunition bullets.

Her discovery was instantly put in my father's hands, and the situation became very intense. I will get punished for bringing them home, considering that playing with any kind of fire or explosive item was not exactly rewarded behavior for any kid.

My dad took the bullets into his hands, bent down toward me, and asked, "Do you know what these are?"

Of course I knew what they were, but to reduce the severity of the judgment, I answered, "I have no idea, Dad!"

"Well, let's all go together this weekend to the forest, and I will show you," he said.

I was extremely exited about the idea, but there was slight fear in my mind that the punishment would be delivered to me in somewhere in the woods.

The following weekend we took food, blankets, and outdoor items and went on the city trolley to the final station of its route. The forest was right at the edge of the city border. The large pine trees and plush wilderness of this forest made it a common destination for many city residents in a search of mushrooms, berries, and a relaxing dinner out in nature.

After traveling for about half an hour, going deeper into the forest, we stopped and set up our blankets and our outdoor arrangements near the little pond. As a rule, we always went with my dad get tree branches for firewood and returned quickly started the fire. He pulled the shells out of his pocket and told my mom and me to take a cover behind the trees. This idea was not welcomed by my mom. She started arguing with my father, telling him that what he was doing was very dangerous. I had no idea what he was trying to do, but because my mom did not like it, I suspected it was something very interesting. My father's wishes prevailed.

We hid behind the trees, and my dad threw the shells right into the fire. When I saw what he did at that moment, I was very proud of him. I felt like he and I had the same spirit, and he was doing exactly what I was dreaming of doing myself. My father ran to us, and the fire pit shortly exploded into a small fireball, blasting ashes and smoke into the air. I was in heaven! My mom, of course, was lecturing him about how childish and stupid it was.

After that, my dad asked me, "Did you see what happened?"

"Yeah. That was cool!"

"Well, son... it was not," he said looking at laughing at my mom, "never, ever try to do it yourself if you don't want to be spanked."

It was one of the most memorable days I ever spent with my father despite its somewhat strange lesson of obedience. We went on other trips and picnics in the summer, but unfortunately, there were never enough of them during my life with my dad. As I would discover later, his presence with me would be far too short.

Lenin's Birthday

In 1970, our nation celebrated the 100th anniversary of Vladimir Lenin. It was the second largest event of the century by Soviet measures, right after the Bolshevik Revolution. The national hysteria of the Soviet TV, press, and public meetings associated with its official Russian celebrations reached epic proportions. Movies about Lenin—everything from fictional accounts to documentaries—were played on television and in the cinemas practically nonstop. The culmination of this holiday, which was celebrated according to our press by "all working class of the world," occurred on April 22 of that year.

It was the most extensive nationwide vanity I can remember from my childhood. All the streets and storefront windows were filled with portraits of Lenin, The central city square, which was occupied by a gigantic statue of Lenin and was named after him as well, was filled with flowers, wreathes, and red banners. Every organization in the Soviet Union at that time was expected to have Lenin's bust, a statue, or a large portrait displayed at their facilities at all the time. His portraits were mandatory decorations on the walls of all executives and directors in any Soviet building, regardless of its functions. Every place seemed to be drowning in buckets of red carnations and banners with Proletarian slogans. To commemorate this glorious event, the USSR issued special awards, trophies, medals, and plaques that were presented to the 'Best of the Best' in Soviet Socialistic achievements. Speeches, concerts, and presentations occupied all parks and stages across our city.

Daycares were not excluded from the list of places that had to pay respect and honor to the so-called founder of our nation. The Lenin portrait that hung in our playing hall at the daycare center was crowned with multiple red vases with flowers and beautiful fabrics. We all had to bring our own flowers and place them under the portrait as a sign of respect and honor. Studio photographer was taking our pictures with Lenin behind us. A special show for our parents and teachers was prepared for this event, songs and poetry recitals glorifying 'Lenin, who loved children direly'. I gladly shouted the poetry loudly about this legendary hero, and I was proud to have the privilege of opening our concert.

A mandatory picture in daycare.

In those days, I once I asked my mom, "Would we live better if Lenin were still alive?"

She answered, "We would already have Communism in the whole world, son. It would be glorious!"

"Wow," I told to myself. "We would have better toy cars than the kids in France, for sure."

At that point, we all loved him and honestly regretted the fact that he was no longer with us. Little did we know then that after collapse of the Soviet Union, we would read the truth about this person, this so-called hero, who invented concentration camps, destroyed churches, killed millions in civil war, and produced the system known as Gulag, where unknown number of innocents died, including parents of children not much older than us.

Chapter 3

My First School and Our Teachers

By the time Soviet children had to go to school, we had to go through the basic learning course of education. It was similar to the kindergarten preschool program in the United States, the only difference being that it happened while we were still in daycare. During our time in daycare, our games and playtime were often replaced with learning letters and numbers. We were required to learn to count to ten, as well as all the letters of our alphabet.

Like any other child, I wanted to be a grownup as soon a possible, and the approaching first day of school was an indicator that the time was coming. Anybody who could do more than we had planned for the day was rewarded with extra time to play, and deep down, as much as we wanted to be grownup, that was our deepest desire.

I personally loved this period and tried to be ahead of other kids in our education process. The tasks were relatively simple, and during our last year in daycare, some of us learned to count all the way up to 100 and recognize simple written words. As always, the great examples of smart children were brought to us from our rich Communist history. Of course, we were told the smartest child who ever lived on Earth was Vladimir Lenin. Imitating him and trying to be like him was the guideline for all children. He was constantly placed as example of the perfect student for us to follow, and among the first letters we studied were the precious L-E-N-I-N, often before we even knew how to write our own names.

Every year on September 1, all the children of our nation celebrated the symbolic Day of Education, the beginning of a new school year. On this day, streets and alleys filled with kids in parade uniforms walking to the schools with flowers in their hands.

Living now in the United States and having my own children who attend school, I see how different our school system was compare to the one in USA. From the buildings to the schooling process to the obviously differentiating ideological views, school in the Soviet Union was a totally opposite world compared to the schools in the West.

Soviet schools required six days of attendance, with Sunday being the only day off. We had three week-long breaks throughout the year: one in autumn, one in winter, and one in spring. The longest break took place in the summer and lasted exactly three months from June 1 until September 1. Once we were admitted to a school, we stayed at that school until graduation. Our first four years in school were considered elementary, and the six others could be broken into four years of middle school and two years of high school, but unlike schools in the U.S., where kids might attend several buildings during their academic lives, ours were all combined in one building, with all grades under the same roof. In order to complete our diploma and graduate, we had to remain in our school for ten years; the only other option was to leave after the eighth grade to attend a trade school. Because we had to attend all of our school years in the same building with the same group of classmates every year, all our classmates bonded into one large family, and strong relationships developed that would last an entire lifetime, far beyond our school years. The school system in the U.S. has its advantages today, but I think it lacks the ability to promote the feeling of unity, and time-tested friendship.

I was very exited to go to school and like all other students had to go with my parents and buy me a uniform. It had gray jacket with pants and a white shirt under the jacket. Girls wore brown dresses with black small aprons on top. The uniforms were mandated by law, and everyone had to wear them. Even though the outfit was not very attractive, it had its own style, providing a small child with an air of distinguishing status in society, something we could not get at the daycare. After WW2, boys were also issued military-style hats and a big belt that was later dropped, probably due to a big cost for families. Schools were also segregated for boys and girls until the sixties, when Khrushchev decided to make our society more civilized and started unisex schools for all Soviet children.

Our schools attempted to follow the principles of our society that dictated that everything best should belong to our children. After personally going through the course of the Soviet education system, I can describe it in one simple phrase: the good, the bad, and the ugly.

In contrast to American schools, our schools were built like fortresses. Usually several stories high, they had all the necessary amenities including large classrooms, a library, gymnasium, and concert halls. Some even had pools and stadiums. Every classroom had extra large windows with desks that sat two students each. Most of the schools had parquet floors and large lunch rooms with their own kitchens. Educational displays on the walls and hallways were rich and elaborate with samples related to the school programs as well as (of course) Socialistic teachings. Everything was done with careful planning, and nothing was spared to show care for the 'future builders of Communism'.

As a rule, all school entrances were required to house a bust or large portrait of Lenin. In concert halls, the pictures of our leaders hung on the walls, surrounded by red flags and Proletarian slogans. Every school also had some kind of museum or wall of fame dedicated to the heroes of our nation or young Communists. Most schools in the cities also had bomb shelters designed to hold all students in case of a nuclear attack.

The situation in the country schools wasn't so glorious. Usually, children from several villages went to one school located at the largest village nearby. Traveling long distances and sharing sometimes few grades in one classroom was the norm for kids in the country. Many of these schools did not have concert halls or stadiums, and the level of education quality was much lower than in the cities. On other hand, children in village schools had much simpler and more humane treatment, with less political concentration and less stringent discipline.

Many parents were eager to send their children to school. "Wait until you go to school," they would warn. "They'll discipline you when you get there." To some degree, it was true. The school had an ultimate power to give children all spectrum of education, including discipline and right behavior, with its own approaches to its enforcement and punishments.

You might consider our whole society at that time as a place of education for children. A child could be given a remark or notice from a total stranger on the street if he behaved inappropriately. It was the norm in our country, and schools were taking that concept even further by taking the responsibility of moral and ethics education away from parents. It was a superior machine, delivering good theoretical knowledge to the young population of our country, along with the tough, dominant presentation of Soviet ideological doctrines and Socialistic beliefs.

It is impossible to vision a school without school supplies. Unlike kids in the USA, we had special briefcases called 'portfel' that we used to carry all our notebooks pencils and books. The backpacks (often just portfels with attached straps) were called ranets, and they were heavily promoted by government as the best bags for the body development of the students.

All school books were purchased at the local bookstores, and the government gave us a huge discount on them. This practice was later replaced with just an exchange of old books for the new ones for the next grade. It was a convenient system that also helped parents financially.

My preparation for school was very busy. To purchase everything we needed, we sometimes had to stand in long lines at the stores. I was excited as I looked at all the pencils, notebooks, and other school supplies, with great anticipation to finally use them for the first time in the classroom.

First Day of School

It was September 1, 1971 when I proudly walked into School Number 10 with my mother and father. The school carried the name of Russian poet Alexander Pushkin. It was in the center of our city and was well known as one of the best schools in town. Local government buildings and Communist party headquarters were within walking distance, and many children from the families of our city leaders attended my school as well. I enrolled into this school not because of my mom's job or position, but simply because I leaved within its district.

It was not the largest school it town standing not far away from our city's river. The building itself was four stories high, with a big red star at the top. Before you enter inside of it you could see the plaque at the entrance staircase indicated the year of its building construction - 1939.

In the front of the school, a large crowd of kids were gathered with their parents, waiting for the opening ceremony of the New Educational Year. The school marching band was blasting patriotic songs and young Communist anthems. I stood among the other first-grade kids with mixed feelings of intimidation and excitement. In an old Soviet tradition, at the school year opening ceremony, the tenth graders welcomed the first graders with flowers and little presents. A tall high school girl gave me huge bouquet of flowers, which I gave to my mother, and a set of pencils, which I put straight into my portfel. When the ceremony was over, we all were escorted to our freshly painted classrooms.

Every grade had three classes on average, assigned in alphabetic order. On average, there were about thirty students in each class. I got into the classroom and sat down at the desk together with another boy. Shortly, the teacher walked in, and after short introduction, she started calling children by names. I realized my name was not called, and I was hoping she simply missed me. The teacher started talking about our school and how big we were, all grown up, already first graders. Suddenly, the door into the class burst open, and another teacher peeked her head in to ask if there was a Yura (my short name) Shishkov in the class. Somehow I managed to wander into the wrong classroom. It was the first day of school, and I was already late to class and had to be found by a school staff. Ironically, I had to be introduced to my original classmates as the 'new boy in class'.

I sat at the dual desk with a boy named Gena. I liked him right away, but not much later, the teacher started reassigning our seats. As a rule in Soviet schools, until the high school years, only a teacher could tell students where to sit. In most cases, boys had to sit with girls. I was reassigned to sit with a little girl named Luda, my "desk's comrade" for four years while we were in elementary school. At that time, I thought the teachers were picking on us or just trying to make us look silly because it seemed they paired the students who were complete opposites. The short boys were seated with tall girls, and chubby boys had to share desks with skinny girls. In my case, I was a skinny kid, and my desk comrade was… well, opposite.

The first couple of sections, which lasted forty-five minutes each, were just an introduction to our school and the rules that we 'big children' now had to obey. Some kids tried to wander around the classroom or play with toys they brought from home. When they were told to stop it, some of them would cry, begging to go home.

The coolest thing about our first day of school was the introduction of the bomb shelter. With the short reminder from our teacher that angry Capitalists wanted to destroy our happy lives and at any time might bomb us with a nuclear device, we proceeded to the bomb shelter, which was located in the basement. We walked through the huge steel door with a heavy handles and locks on it, right into the shelter itself. The shelter was enormous with multiple corridors and passages. Stations for medical treatment and corners to sleep were simple but also somewhat comfortable. There were enough gas masks for every student in the school, and some of us were even brave enough to try them on. The teacher told us the walls were several feet thick. The smell of old cold air coupled with the surrounding complete silence felt very creepy and chilling. On the walls hung many instructions of how to use gas masks and help the injured. We were also told a sad fact about our school. At the time of WW2, the building was used by occupied Germans as headquarters of their military operations simply because it had the best bomb shelter in town.

Many of the educational posters were from the WW2 era and showed airplanes bombing the city. There were diagrams and charts indicating the coverage area and potential damage power of the nuclear explosion. It all looked scary, and I'm sure it was deliberate—that this was our first planned lesson in political content.

The day was going very fast, and after four hours in school, we were free to go home. We were spilled outside screaming, shouting, and running into our parents' arms. They were as happy as we are, excitedly greeting us, though some kids were not as excited about the first day of school and were crying that they would never go to school again.

My first grade class.

A Soviet Student

Our school system reminded by its structured a military type organization, and not only because of its uniform and strict discipline. Schools are universally designed to be not a vacation resorts, but ours had more dominance over students performance and obedience than on the West. Children had to obey all teachers' orders, and teachers had the power of punishing students with their own methods. The class and homework were done in the twenty-four-page notebooks that we had to keep in perfect order at all times. Our grades were often announced loudly by the teacher before she returned the notebooks to us. Placing kids in a shameful and embarrassing situation was a part of the educational process and was designed to boost the children's effort for better performance. There were no concept here of "publicly hurt feelings" for our kids, same as practiced in the army. To see a teacher smacking a kid with a ruler or a long pointer was not a rare occasion in our schools.

Very often, we had a morning black board, an all-school gathering (or lineyka) at the front of the school or in the large courtyard. The reasons for this ranged from honoring our Socialistic holidays to rewarding classes or students for achieving great results to publicly humiliating the degraded kids like those who were caught attending church.

In the USSR at that time, school work was graded on a scale of one to five, with five being the highest. Receiving score of five was a difficult task, requiring not only correct answers in your work, but also a superb execution in cursive style and spotlessly clean presentation. To score a one, we would have to practically muck up our assignments altogether, perhaps draw funny faces instead of answers. A score of three often meant your parent would be holding a belt in his/her hand but would not quite give you a lesson with it yet.

My mother loved to keep everything simple and organized, and she taught me to do the same from an early age. With few books and an old mushroom-looking lamp on the table, I had a clean small study area to do my homework. In the left corner from the desk was an old tube radio/ turntable, a Minsk R-7 that we used for the parties we threw at home. On the right was our sewing machine with two holes on its wooden cover, left from the era of a last war. Several times I tried to take that machine apart. I am glad I never did, because we will be using that machine for many more years to come.

Working on my homework never took me a long time. My study place was set up at our desk in the bedroom right under the window. I could see mature trees outside in a reddish gold outfit of the autumn leaves. When the wind was blowing, the noise coming from the trees sounded like the crash of sea waves—at least that's how it sounded to me, despite the fact that I had never been near the ocean. I often listened to this music of nature while doing my homework, dreaming of distant countries surrounded by the mysterious ocean. After finishing my homework spending about a couple of hours after school, I was already running outside to play.

While school made me feel a bit more grown up, I still played games and enjoyed outdoor fun like any other kid of my age. Only now, I had much more time for doing that. I loved to go to school just for that reason alone. We had the same games and activities as daycare. Riding a bike and climbing trees and top of buildings was still fun, and this habit kept my exploratory spirit busy until dark.

My grandma never had to keep up after me about doing my homework or force me to prepare for my next day of school. She still saw me as a little child doing what was natural for my age. My father worked and rarely checked how I did in school. My mother, on the other hand, wanted me to be a perfect student with practically no "fours", let alone embarrassing "threes" grades. Trying to keep my mom happy and enjoying first year of my education, I was a great student from the start of the school.

Soviet Teachers

Just like any teacher in the USSR, ours was considered our second parent, at least during our four elementary years. This was not only limited to the time we were in school. As a standard practice in the USSR, schools could intervene if they knew of problems in the family or with the child's welfare, and they were also personally responsible for the safety of the children who were in their care. An interesting fact about the obligations of Soviet teachers was discovered shortly after my beginning of school.

One day, late after dinner, some one rang our doorbell. We opened the door to discover my teacher standing there. She had come for a surprise visit to see how I prepared for the next day in school. She was greeted with a warm hospitality and invited in for a cup of tea. She politely declined and asked my parents to show her where I studied and if she could see my finished homework. My parents were so happy to show the superb quality of my attention to study time and the place where I did it. My mother was in heaven. She was very proud that I kept everything organized and that her Communistic reputation was not stained by my irresponsibility. This kind of visit was common and often caught kids off guard if they had not finished their homework before dinner. The punishments in this case went both ways, at home and humiliating discloser of your crummy dedication to the school study in the classroom.

While our teachers had a great deal of power and control over children's lives, it was some time not easy work for them considering the nature of our culture and unusual circumstances. For instance, one of my friends had a less than perfect family. His father often loved to go out drinking after work, consuming a great deal of vodka before he came home drunk and started arguments over anything he was not happy about. It happened that on one of these days, when he consumed too much alcohol, the teacher visited his house to check up on her student. When the door opened and a drunken father saw a stranger harassing his son over unfinished homework and neglected study area, he rushed to defend his child. The teacher was outraged by his actions and began criticizing the drunk—a big mistake. The drunk and angry father was happy to start a little war with intruder and began his favorite dance with the furniture, chasing the teacher around the house. Leaving behind her belongings and school items, the teacher ran down to the staircase in cover. Shortly thereafter, all her items were flying down from the balcony, while the drunken father was rocking the neighborhood in casings. I relatively certain my friend's father was no hero at his workplace after that. This kind of misconduct was reported immediately to the employers by the child's school.

Ironically, our teachers, whose job was to educate us and bolster us for building a bright future, were at the same time the underpaid working class. The Soviet teacher's life, in general, was pitiful compared to the life of an educator in the USA. It was a very difficult job with practically no limit of working hours, six days a week. Teachers never had any assistants or volunteer workers or support to help them in preparation for school, assignments, class work, or inspection of children's homework. We often saw teachers going home with big binders of our notebooks, all of which had to be checked by the next morning. On top of the normal education aspects such as reading, counting, and other basic learning disciplines, they also had to teach all of the Soviet ideologies and doctrines. To keep their knowledge on these topics up to date, they had to constantly attend meetings and classes of the Communist education and know the latest Party initiatives. The worst part of their jobs (and the major difference between them and the teachers in the West) was the fact that they were greatly underpaid in contrast to other our working class. There is no clear answer as to why such unfairness existed in a country that declared the best of our society belonged to our children. To understand the logic behind this, you have to consider a very twisted and somewhat corrupt approach to salary grading in Soviet Union at that time.

In the 'Land of Victorious Socialism', the most privileged class, by our definition, was the Proletarians (after children, of course). Because of that, many hardworking occupations like coal miners, factory and construction workers, and other hard labor jobs were paid much higher than people who worked in offices, or as engineers, doctors, or middle management personnel - the "cozy" jobs. The only people who could gain more income than our working class were elite executives, Army generals, professors, Communist Party leaders, and heads of major organizations. Teachers fell into the category of office workers or "clean jobs", and because of that they were underpaid as compared to those who sweat in the coal mines or told people how to build Communism around the world. There was another hidden reason why certain jobs paid less than others. The access to limited goods, services, and conveniences at work played a big role in the salary. Despite the low pay, these jobs were hard to get. In our country at that time, with so many products in deficit, its low quality, widely spread back door deals,"connections", and power mentality, the place of work often offered more benefits than the salary it paid. Here are two basic examples of that:

To be a worker at the glass bottle recycling station or selling beer from the giant barrels on the street was a "gold mine" for many since it allowed a limited amount of waste, breakage, and spills. All these were manipulated and turned into cash in pockets of these workers and their bosses. These people had the lowest salaries because the government knew about the job's true potentials, but ironically, they did nothing to eliminate the problem.

As another example, the workers at the goods warehouses and stores had the first chance to grab the deficit product and food before it reached the shelves of our supermarkets. It was often sold by them on the black market at a price several times higher than its cost, thus making them "rich" by Soviet standards. The government also knew about these benefits of people who worked in supply infrastructure but also did not do anything to stop this corruption. Simply, we paid them several times less than we would an oil field worker in Siberia.

So, what could our teachers gain at their jobs with so many hours of work and practically no any chance of any additional compensation to their low salary? The answer was simple: a three-month vacation every summer. Most of the workers in the USSR had a floating schedule of vacation time that could be in inconvenient winter, fall, or spring. Often, they had to wait several years before they had a vacation in the summer. With all adults in the USSR working, it was sometimes nearly impossible for some spouses to have vacation together in the summer. Only teachers were always guaranteed summer vacations almost three month long, as compare to twenty-one to twenty-eight days in the off seasons for any other worker in the nation.

Whether a job gave the benefit of access to household valuables, services, or a vacation length, the government took it into consideration when they graded the job salary compensation. This practice of backwards and undermined ethics of salary grading was an ugly reality of our Socialistic system which was impossible to eliminate.

Hippies and Other "Creatures"

The Western world at that time was swimming with hippies and popular culture, but Soviets were still living under the guidance of the Communist leaders, meticulously shaped according to the unique Socialistic ethics. As I've mentioned, our government tried to protect us from exposure to Western culture behind an ideological Iron Curtain, using every fathomable resource to minimize the chances of its penetration. However, it was impossible to completely shut off the breeze of freedom that was seeping in from the West.

As soon as I went to school, I was surrounded by a new atmosphere and cultural developments slowly crawling into our lives. It seemed as if everything for me was rapidly accelerating into a totally different and exiting era.

I had already heard in school about young people in the USSR called "beatlas" . It was related to the Beatles band, but in a different manner. Most of our population had not even the slightest idea about that band. At the same time, Beatle-mania was already penetrating Soviet cultural borders, breaking into the language and stereotypes of ordinary people. The government did not like it and intentionally tried to label, deform, and portray pop culture as something ugly and foreign to our society. The term beatlas was obviously a distorted name of the famous British band, and it was purposely used in the USSR to muck our progressive youth. I was already noticing this type of youngsters on our streets. They looked wild for a Socialistic society, and people often gave them a hard time or made insulting remarks. Most of the time, they wore pants with very wide "trezer" or "klesh" at the bottom, unbuttoned shirts, cross pendants, and dark sunglasses. These youngsters also had outrageously long hair by our standards, and they often carried guitars and were armed with a portable short-wave radios. They loved to call themselves hippies. To soviets and young children they were sharing the level of clowns and monkeys by its intelligence.

To our Soviet officials however, these people were a stain on the clean Proletarian society. They resembled something Stalin had years earlier called a "worshiping of the Western culture." For that, our government had sent people to the Gulag. But fortunately, the time of severe cruelty had already gone, and killing over these behaviors was not a popular solution anymore. The new ways of dealing with those who did not want to listen to marching bands and folk music had been invented. When the criticism and explanations did not work, the law was used to make our streets free from the foreign-to-us culture...

Anyone in the USSR could be jailed for fifteen days without any warrant or court sentence. The drunk on the street, domestic dispute suspect, or even a dirty-looking bum could be a target of the police and might spend a couple weeks behind the bars simply on an officer's orders. Public work was assigned as a punishment, often street and toilet cleaning. It was a law of convenience, permitting our system to deal with true troublemakers. It was also used on people who had to be warned about the real problems they might face if they did not obey the rules.

In the case of 'beatlas', new Russian hippies, the violators were usually snatched up on charges of "public disturbance". Their guitars were destroyed, their shades confiscated, and their long hair shaved bald. The priceless treasure reflecting its cultural preferences as a hairdo was their biggest loss in these arrests. The unmistakable signature of a fifteen-day imprisonment was a head shaved down to nothing. The only people with such an unpopular hairstyle were new Army recruits, small children, and seasoned prisoners. Unless you belonged to the military, your shaved head in the USSR was a blemish on your person.

Spending fifteen days in jail was just the beginning of troubles for many of our homegrown flower people. Going back to work or college afterwards would involve apologies, public humiliation, and often civil punishments. In some circumstances, they could lose their jobs or be demoted. This was the Socialistic treatment of the so-called Western heresy, and these people were forced to endure it.

Costly Cartoons

This wave of a new culture was impossible to stop. It was labeled by Communists as psychedelic, demonic, anti-Soviet, and even as a product of the CIA. Ironically, one of the first references to the hippie culture was delivered to our population by our own television—and even more than that, into the minds of our future builders of Communism, the Russian children.

In 1969, television screens across the USSR aired a musical cartoon called *Bremen Musicians*. The main characters in this movie were touring as a music band, promoting freedom, love, and peace within the Bremen kingdom. They played electric guitars, an instrument practically unknown to most of our citizens. The main hero and the group leader, Troubadour, was in love with the princess. They eventually ran away together from the royal life to the freedom of love and peace. The music and style was completely extrinsic to our lifestyle and imitated the rock 'n roll of the West. Long-haired, outrageous, hippie styled cartoon heroes had nothing to do with our Soviet understanding of the music arts. I would say the most dangerous part of the movie for us were the lyrics to the songs. Lines like "The beauty of palaces will never replace us a freedom" could be viewed in our country as anti-Soviet sentiments. It is still a puzzle to many how the cartoon managed to make it to the TV screens under a government in such total control. Perhaps it was someone's neglect at the censor department, or perhaps it was the lack of understanding of the potential harm of this cartoon to our ideology. It did not take long, however, for the Soviet government to react and place the movie on the shelf, banning its broadcasting for some period of time. The popularity of this musical, however, forced it onto televisions occasionally and even allowed for the production of a sequel many years later.

The heroes of "Bremen Musicians" offered a positive image, but we also had animations in which other long-haired guitar-carrying characters had been completely mucked and displayed as an unintelligent pinheads. In one of them called "Just Wait"!, the troublemaking wolf had a loose hippie-style personality. Carrying guitar on his back was already enough for him to be viewed as a hooligan. To make it worse and to enhance his idiotic image, he was occasionally played songs poorly imitating rock 'n roll.

Another cartoon of that time about hockey, called "Revenge Match", had an ice dancers who were entertaining the crowd at the break time and acted like a long-haired rock trio. They were shown as stereotyped Soviet "beatlas", people worthy only to be clowns on the rink. All this mockery, however, had an opposite effect amongst our children. The long-haired characters were actually becoming real public heroes, especially for the young generation.

The Soviet ideological machine at that time had been working hard to stain any modern Western culture product. They made the mistake of talking about it too much, unintentionally delivering to our people a forbidden fruit. The missing information on the new pop culture of the West could now be obtained simply in bits and pieces from our own media, even though it was heavily criticized.

In Soviet Union, on the streets of our cities, the long-haired guys were began popping up here and there often accompanied by girls wearing funky skirts. Walking with a short-wave transistor in hand, a guitar on your back, dark shades, and wide pants was for us the act of an outlaw. The fact that they were drawing the attention of crowds only made the government more angry. The music and songs blasting loudly out of their radios was usually in English, indicating that these folks were not too shy to say what culture they enjoyed.

Soviet Electrified Music

As a counterattack on this totally non-Proletarian movement crawling into the Bolshevik society, the Soviet ideological machine tried to create its own Socialistic version of pop culture. Small jazz bands and individual singers were now allowed to have slightly looser styles of music, as long as they kept their lyrics within the limits of the Communist dogma. It went a step further with the creation of our own vocal and instrumental ensemble (VIA). These music ensembles were the first government-approved versions of Western rock bands. The ability to play on electric guitars instead of balalaikas did not come for our musicians without inconvenient side effects and compromises. To put some distance between them and real Western rock 'n roll groups, they had to have a wind or folk instrument in their entourage. The VIA groups were also required to have at least seven members in order to keep them further away from the common four- or five-person rock band structure. None of them were allowed to use word 'rock' or call themselves a 'rock band'. The lyrics had to maintain the Soviet and patriotic nature, but love songs were permitted, and most of these bands tried to stick with that genre rather than glorifying the Communist Party in their repertoire.

The early VIA were equipped with instruments that were very unpopular with Soviet officials: electric guitars. It was probably a very difficult decision for Russian authorities to let our performers flash on stages and TV screens with the main "weapon of the Western propaganda". Sadly for them, there was no other option in this style of music since the accordion bands proved to be very unpopular among our youth.

The government controlled all cultural life in our State, and the first VIA also had to have a proper government-approved names. The choices had to be neutral and abstain from Westernized words. Bearing these limitations in mind, the first Soviet groups named themselves in a very banal manner: "Flowers", "Gems", "Streaming Song", and "Bluebird".

Considering there were only a handful of these bands that the government could allow to exist, they were a limited choice for Russian people. It was our only alternative music option to the dominating patriotic genre. Not surprisingly, these bands became extremely popular among the young and the older population.

As a child, I heard these groups on the radio, and some were even played at our *dacha* through the loudspeakers hanging from the trees. Personally, however, I was too little to understand anything about that kind of music and my attention to it only stopped at the level of Bremen's Musicians cartoon.

The touring shows of the VIA had tremendous success, and they were always sold out long before the arrival of the band into the cities. While the members of the groups became Soviet celebrities and gained a star status, they had a distinct difference from their Western cohorts. Rock bands in the West often made a fortune playing music. In contrast, our musicians were paid so little that they frequently had to save money to buy food when they went on tour. At the same time, the Ministry of Culture was profiting in millions of rubbles received from the concerts and records sales of the VIA groups. Soviet musical groups fell into the category of people who (by government opinion) were gaining something more than just a salary. In their case, they had popularity, an easy job, and flexible working hours—all things the government felt they did not deserve on top of a good salary.

Our system quickly recognized the influential power of rock 'n roll and started using it to its own propagandistic advantages. Every band was expected to produce songs that would inspire our people to pursue working heroism. They had to glorify the Socialistic achievements and even mobilize us on the new government projects. One example was Baikal/Amur (B.A.M.) railroad construction, a gargantuan Soviet mission in the 1970s to connect the uninhabited terrain of Siberia to two distant regions of Baikal Lake and the Amur River. The effort of mobilizing a work force into this extremely difficult job located in very harsh conditions was a problem for USSR from the very beginning. The main recruiting targets of the Soviet Union were our young and energetic people. Musicians of all genres were called by the government to promote this massive railroad construction. From the screens of TVs and national radio, the romantic songs about B.A.M. started luring our population to cold Siberia. No one worked harder in this effort than Soviet popular music bands. They not only played charming ballads and dynamic beats from the broadcast studios, but they were also sent to that bitter region to inspire and entertain construction workers. Performing from the roofs of the train cars and buses, bitten by mosquitoes, and suffering in the freezing cold, they played Russian rock 'n roll without any compromises. The propaganda machine was working. People were flowing to the distant *taiga* to construct the largest railroad project of Soviet times.

The rewarded effect of VIA in these cases was valued by our government, and it forced them to accept the necessity of such music genres in the USSR. Soon, the factories in Russia started producing equipment and electric guitars for a new breed of Russian musicians. The government organizations, schools, and colleges began receiving these primitive but priceless ammunition of rock 'n roll for our performing working class.

Little Bolsheviks

The school progress was advancing to more complex assignments and lessons. Each day we had four forty-five-minute classes. After that, we were free to go home or remain in a special group for kids who needed to stay and do their homework in school. It was necessary if someone's parents had to work and could not trust their child to do the homework in their absence. This situation happened to me several times as well.

Usually, my grandma took me home from school, but every time she worked, I had to stay in the extended class. It upset me because it limited my playtime and I was also forced to perform additional school tasks that were not part of our homework. The only benefit I reaped from this special class was doing craft projects after I completed my assignments. It was my first chance to learn basic principles of work order greater in difficulty than what I had at the daycare. While nothing extraordinary could be produced in those classes, the use of measuring tools and advanced materials was teaching me something new every time we did it.

Among the basic education in the first grade, the early serious steps of ideological tutoring began to be implemented into our school program. To make children a part of the Socialistic plans established by Lenin, we were honored to become members of October Organization, to become an "Octyabryonock". Named after the October Revolution, this was an effort to make children feel they were an undeniable part of our society, loyal to our Communistic principles. We were told that to be an Octyabryonock member was a privilege that children in other countries could only dream of; we were told we were the lucky ones. While it was such a "fortunate" favor for all of us, this membership required mandatory participation.

In one of the windy days of Russian autumn, I'd been going to school with pride pounding in my heart. I was about to become a member of the largest youth organization in the world containing children from ages seven to ten. The first graders were lined up in the school concert hall for the official inauguration ceremony. Among all the red flags, banners, and portraits of Lenin and other Bolshevik leaders, we were greeted by old Communists and school teachers. The patriotic speeches glorified our Communist Party while our marching band played revolutionary themes and songs. From the pulpit, pedagogues proclaimed our goals and commitment to the Soviet principles and beliefs. The culmination of this massive ritual was the children swearing in as Octyabryonock. Every one of us received a small red star with a young Lenin portrait in the middle. We were told to carry this symbol of Communist loyalty and always have it pinned on our jackets or dresses, next to our hearts. Every one of us wowed to do our homework and perform better than ever in our schoolwork so that Lenin himself would be proud of us. We were also asked to commit that priceless symbol of youngest Communists in the world would now be guarded by us better than it had been in our own lives.

Most of the kids were filled with joy and pride. I had no clear understanding, however, what special duties and obligations I would now have in contrast to my pre-Octyabryonock life. My homework and school attendance had always been outstanding, and I was told about the importance of good scores all the time as well. When I asked my grandma what I should do as an Octyabryonock, she said I should eat everything I was given for lunch and keep my shoes nice and shiny. Her answer was quite clear, and I tried to fulfill these duties to the best of my ability.

If in a short distant past the poor grades and our shabby homework could be simply reflected in low scores, now it was more than that. The students' lackadaisical approach to the assignments were being considered neglectful to the principles of an Octyabryonock spirit. Placing a child in a front of the class for lecture and humiliation had been an ordinary practice used at our schools. I enjoyed the learning process and did not have to endure such torturous procedures.

On the flip-side, the kids who were doing everything in school to keep the teacher, their parents, and of course Lenin happy were rewarded with special treats. These awards existed in the form of a simple recognition resembling the rewards granted to our workers at the factories. Presented as banners, certificates or plaques which had to be honored and properly displayed, our school achievement trophies also were the objects of the same warship and respect. For example, anyone who received a score of five three times on the raw scores was prized with a red notebook binder embellished with pictures of Soviet heroes or patriotic relics. Having this award granted a student special fame as someone who was dedicated to our Socialistic principles. I scored many times with such honor and having the red notebook cover with Lenin or our heroes pictures on it was a delightful treat for my parents, especially my mom. Stepping in the right direction as a young builder of Communism however, will be not such dedicated journey for me after all.

Chapter 4

"Let's buy a baby!" and Crafty Places

Some of my friends at that time had sisters and brothers. I was watched them interacting and always wondered why I didn't have any siblings to grow up with. I often asked my mom this question and was given strange answers: "The store that sells babies is back-ordered," she said, or "The waiting list for new kids is far too long." Our education on where babies really came from did not exist in Soviet Union, especially for children. In fact, it did not exist at all, except in the doctor's office. The knowledge of how babies are born and what spurns such a birth was happen never discussed in our schools or national media. It was a medical left to private talks between adults and their doctors.

In November of 1971, my mom said she had to leave for a business trip, and I was relieved because I could relax a little from homework pressures. About a week earlier, the annual October Revolution parade had stormed again through our city, leaving nonperishable memories of joy and excitement.

It was a day of a typical drizzly, gray-sky November weather, and the trees had completely lost their last golden leaves. My father told me news I had never even dreamed about. He said we were going to the store where they sell babies. I dressed as quickly as I could, in complete euphoria. Then I realized it would be unfair to go shop for a baby without Mom.

"Relax," my dad said. "She is already there waiting for us." It was great! I asked him how much the baby cost, and he told me, laughing; "One ruble. Here, take this and give it to the salesman in the store." After saying that, he placed in my palm a metal ruble coin.

The whole process of maternity and baby delivery in the USSR was drastically different from the one in the Western world, especially the USA. Cultural and even ritual beliefs played a role in these precious moments of human birth. As a rule and Russian custom, the pregnancy time had to be spent in a quiet, obscure life. Going public when the visible evidence of the expectancy was obvious had to be limited. It was not a shameful aspect of that rule, but rather a protective measure for a child as well as the mother. The general opinion and cultural believe was that pregnant women needed special care and should limit their activity to the minimum. This included early maternity leaves and all throughout the birth process as well.

Unlike in the USA where the delivery happened in the regular hospitals, the Soviet Union had a special medical facility strictly dedicated to this purpose. At the end of her pregnancy a woman would be placed in this "Delivery hospital". She might remain there up to many weeks from the day of her admittance. The visits to this hospital were not permitted at any given time, not to mention bringing video recorders to the delivery room as is common practice today. When mother and her newborn were in good enough physical condition to go home, they would be released.

All medical help and services in the USSR at that time were free of charge, and the "Delivery hospitals" were a part of this system as well. It was well-organized care for our women. However, later in my life, I heard that many Russian mothers would have preferred to deliver their children at home rather than in these hospitals. The suspect of this desire was probably the overcrowded and less than perfect conditions in these institutions.

As we were walking to the hospital, I asked my father if we were going to buy a boy or a girl. He said all the girls were already sold-out and we would have to get a boy. I could not be happier about having a brother, and I couldn't wait to play with him and spend time together like two friends.

In the waiting room, there were a lot of people with flowers and balloons, other happy folks who came to "buy" an addition to their family. Shortly, a nurse appeared holding a little baby wrapped like an egg roll in the blankets. She was escorted by my mother.

"Go give her your ruble," my father whispered into my ear.

I ran toward them while shaking a big coin in the air shouting, "We want that baby! We want that baby!"

Astonished nurse were taken by surprise and took the ruble right after my dad took my new brother from her. After that, the four of us happily went home.

It did not take very long to think of a name for him. My father allowed us to pick the name in honor of old Mikhail, whom we all loved so much, and our unanimous choice was its short name Misha.

Life had definitely changed. There were now five of us living in a one-bedroom apartment. Things got tighter in the house, and we moved our furniture around several times to get the best arrangement for us and a baby.

Living in the USSR without the existence or knowledge of diapers as we know them today, large white sheets were constantly hanging across our apartment on suspended ropes. Many other conveniences know in the Western world that help mothers to raise a baby were not available in the Soviet Union as well. It was a difficult time for my mom and grandma to live in these conditions, but no one complained. Many families in our country lived that way, and it was just a part of life.

I was patiently waiting for my brother to grow up, but it was not happening as fast as I wished and I realized it would take a long time before we could actually have a chance to play together.

Using Hands for Something Good

My interests in taking objects apart was rising to a new level. I was not happy anymore dealing with small and hard to pick inside small items and became interested in the construction of something bigger, like our washing machine a turntable/radio. My parents had to do something to keep me away from my harmful attention to the household appliances. They came to a conclusion that my free time needed to be more occupied by some true creativity, and the opportunity presented itself very quickly.

One day in the toy section of our general store, there was a display of a plastic Mig-15 airplane model. Small kits like this were rare in our stores, and most of them were expensive and came from Eastern Germany. They were high-quality models in elaborate packaging, with many details and components. Finding the less expensive miniature airplane kits in stores was even more challenging than building them. The Soviet model, designed as a basic kit, did not cost much and was a perfect first project for a little boy like me. My dad gladly purchased it for me, while my mom was very skeptical that I could finish it without spilling glue all over the floor.

After spending couple of days behind my desk working on the airplane, I was proud to present the completed project to my family. It looked great. There were a few smeared fingerprints on the wings and a slightly rough paint job, but it was striking. My mom was proud of me for not giving up on the project and for not leaving a mess. My dad was also happy that his investment of one ruble and ten copeyka had not been wasted.

It was my first model, which got me very interested in more complex and advanced creativity. My parents also recognized this pursuit and decided to sign me up into one of our construction clubs, an organized effort of the Soviet Union to provide children a chance to develop their construction skills. As a part of the care initiative for the young generation, it was a good government program that kept children occupied and inspired when they were not in school. For the USSR, it also provided another token of superiority in comparison to the Western world. These facilities were called "Station of the Young Technicians" or "Handy Hands" clubs, and they were available in practically every big and small city of the USSR. In our town, we had several of them, some standalone shops and others in the "Palace of Pioneers" and also at our regular schools. The clubs were free of charge, and many parents forced their kids to admit to it simply to keep them away from troubles. For this reason, the number of students often surpassed the clubs' limits, closing the doors for new applicants.

The "Handy Hands" shop my mom chose for me was not far away from our house. Located next to the city's railroad station, it had been the part of the biggest "Culture Palace" in town bearing the name of our father, Vladimir Lenin.

When we came to this place for a first time we found the group consisted of about twenty children from seven to sixteen years old. The little boys kept busy with simple projects as compared to the teenagers, who made rockets, trains, ships, cars, and airplanes. On the walls were completed and in-progress projects. The finished models around the shop looked stunning—something you couldn't buy in the store or make yourself at home. Everything had a factory-made look and quality. I stared at all these masterpieces and could not wait to construct something like this myself. Many of these models had next to them displayed award plaques and prizes achieved in the local and regional exhibitions. I recognized couple of military ships and radio-controlled cars that I had seen during my daycare years. It was a tradition in our city to display the best work of kids from these kinds of clubs. Usually the small exposition was set up in the front windows at the central book store on the boulevard of Lenin. This improvised collection drew large crowds who wanted to see the fine work of our creative children. Every time we passed by this expo on the way to my daycare, I glanced at these incredible miniature models.

The clubs had the support and sponsorship of local factories that supplied scrap materials and chemicals for the shop functions. No any "of the shelf" model kits were used here stimulating children's ability to be creative and developing crafting skills making projects from scratch. Usually the teachers in these shops were mainly retired engineers or designers with great experience and skills. These technical organizations for kids existed from the 1920s and was something what Soviets could be truly be proud of. Handy Hands clubs' contributions to the engineering world in our country was quite significant. Many talented and famous constructors in the Soviet industrial fields, especially military and airplanes, began their careers in such clubs. At one point in their young lives, people like Kalashnikov, Korolev, Tupolev, Ilyushin, and Sukhoi were a part of this very beneficial education.

The desire to make something incredible truly overwhelmed me. In the air was a smell of hide glue, chemicals and wood. The noise of hand tools in this working atmosphere was new to me in which I instantly fell in love with, and I felt like this place had the endless possibilities for me.

After short introductions and meeting the group, I began to work on my first project. My intuition told me I would make something as beautiful the other models I saw around the shop. This hope was quickly ruined when I was given a drawing of what I had to build. It was an ugly car model that didn't even looked like an automobile. I had to cut out its silhouette using a jewelry saw and then attach it to the rectangular base with the wheels. To me it was hard to accept such primitive assignment, but our teacher, Maxim Andreevich, told me this was what I had to start from.

I said, "I want to make something like that," and pointed at the models shining in bright colors—the ones that looked like miniature real cars and airplanes.

"It will take several years before you'll start making that type of work," he said.

I had no option and began working on my first creation. Many tools and instruments were totally new for me. The jewelry saw and different shapes files were not hard to learn how to use, and on my first day, I made good progress.

Going to this club twice a week was not too bad, but when my friends were playing I wished I could have stayed with them instead. The discipline and atmosphere at "Handy Hands" reminded me something of our school. Listening what my teacher was telling me, while I was trying to do it my way was hard and when I secretly did it any way, I was lectured for disobedience like in the classroom. It was after all not a grammar spelling and when my own approaches to the tasks producing better results than the one's I was taught, my teacher started paying more attention to what am I was doing. While it was a prospect of potential involvement in some cool projects, my patience was not ready for a very long wait.

After a few visits to the club, I had completed my assignment and brought it home. I did not like it at all. The design was absolutely horrible, and the end result was a primitive two-dimensional mock-up instead of a nice-looking model. It was made from thin plywood and painted with a brush. It could not be displayed attractively, no matter which way we turned it. The wheels were made out of thin metal sheets and rested on nail axels, and they looked terrible. I hated that car and was absolutely disappointed in the whole project. It looked so bad that I knew I could make a better car at home if I'd had the right tools and materials. At the same time, my parents were bragging to all our relatives about its beauty.

It was Sunday, and I was on my way to my construction class without any enthusiasm. I wanted to create something incredible and not wait for it many years. It was my young, impatient nature, and I could not understand yet why I had to start from something small and ugly first. Because of that, I was not happy with my classes and wished I could simply do this kind of project at home. My problem, however, resolved by itself. When I arrived at the shop, the doors were closed, and several kids were already leaving. I waited for a while and than decided to go home as well.

When I returned, my mom was not happy about it. Suspecting that I simply didn't want to take these classes anymore, she grabbed me, and we went back to the "Handy Hands" again. The door lady at the "Culture Palace" told us there was no class that day. For some reason, it made my mom very angry. She started lecturing her, saying, "This is a study class, and no one ever closes the school if the teacher cannot come. It should be like that here as well!". My mom also mentioned the Proletarian spirit and true dedication to work, something she wasn't seeing at the club. She asked to talk to a manager or any other executive, but was told they didn't come in on Sundays. At that point, she got very upset. "This club is not what it should be, leaving children on the street in the winter, while this club administration are sitting at home," she stated with an academic *Bolshevik* phonation, and we left.

On the way back home, I knew my mom was not happy about "Handy Hands" anymore. It gave me a chance to start selling an idea to do projects like that without wasting my time in useless (by my understanding) classes. To my surprise, she quickly agreed with me, and I was walking on the crunchy snow thinking of what I could make to prove my point. Nothing was coming into my head at that time and after lunch I went playing hockey with my friends leaving this dilemma for the future.

Missing a Chance

When I was in the first grade, my interest in music was not a very big one, if I had any at all. Many children had taken accordion, flute, or piano lessons, but it was mainly done by the will of their parents. I'd been fortunate that my parents had not pushed me into those sorts of classes. My regular education in school had already been enough for me.

Like any kid at that age, I was influenced by news events, movies, and other sources of inspiration. I did not expect music to be attractive to me anytime soon. However, something changed after our TV broadcast a new movie called Polonez Aginsky, the WW2 story. The main character in the movie was a little boy who lived in occupied Nazi territory. He was helping his older friends and comrades fighting an ambush war against the German Army. The boy was also a violin player. Throughout the movie, he played "Polonez - Farewell with Motherland" ," written by Polish composer Aginsky, which he learned from a local organist and a Nazi fighter. While violin was not a main part of the story, it instantly grabbed my attention.

I do not know why the image of violin made such a big impression on me after watching that movie. Maybe it was the "Polonez" melody, which we had a record of and played very often, or perhaps it was the elegant lines of violin itself. Whatever it was, I became obsessed with the idea of learning how to play that beautiful instrument.

It was my first serious interest in the study of music, and I started asking my parents if it would be possible for me to take classes. My desire was not driven by impulse, which any child has no shortage of at a young age. I had a firm interest in violin study for a long time. No matter how I tried to get the lessons, though, it did not work. My mom told me I was too young for it because it can be an extremely complicated and difficult instrument to learn. It was not easy for me back then (nor is it today) to understand why I would be refused an opportunity to even try something like that. The financial side of the study was not an issue because nearly all music classes were free of charge and could be taken in schools and other special facilities across the city. In many cases, even the musical instruments were provided for beginners at no cost. This remarkable approach to music education in the USSR was another part of our children education program. It did have its own limitations and preferences, like the absolute absence of the study of anything "alien" to us such as genres originating in the West. Folk, classical, and patriotic music was promoted and supported by the government on an enormous scale, and the results of those efforts were known worldwide. Many great modern composers and talented musicians like Stravinsky, Rostropovich, or the Bolshoi ballet became a huge success on stages in the Soviet Union and abroad.

The commitment of our system to the artistic developments among children was not only out of love to little one's. It also was founded on propagandistic grounds as well. The coincided goal was to display to the whole world the advantages of Socialism and what it can deliver to masses.

Despite this hidden ideological concept, the music education had unprecedented support and priceless value for anybody who wanted to dedicate his/her life to music.

My effort to convince my parents to allow me to take violin lessons seemed to be a losing battle. I think my mom saw me as a future engineer or constructor and was very skeptical about my genuine interest in music. Considering that I seemed to have a passion for crafts and loved to work with my hands, the final decision of my family was that I would not take violin lessons. It was a sad reality for me that my desire was free of childish spontaneous encouragement.

The irresistible beauty of the violin sound with its graceful lines has captivated me for my whole life. Many years later, I would pay respect to the magnificent contrive of human creativity by building an electric guitar in the form of a violin.

He Left for Good

It was May of 1972, the time of a blooming Russian spring with the awakening nature after our long, cold winter. Everything on this warm day gave off a sense of refreshing motion penetrating the air and the feelings of people. I was about to finish first grade and had been looking forward to spending three month of our school break with my father. I could not wait to go fishing with him and maybe even escape for few days on a picnic somewhere in the wilderness. I had so many plans and ideas in my head for the forthcoming summer that it seemed we would never have enough time to accomplish them all. Little did I know that all of my plans would soon melt like ice after winter, leaving only a sad reminder of their existence in a puddle of grubby water.

On one of these sunny days, I rushed home from school. Another finished day of the semester meant I was one step closer to the upcoming summer. With an uplifted mood, I ran to the third floor, where we lived. The door to our apartment was open. My grandma was sitting in the kitchen, looking at the window. She asked me if I wanted something to eat, and I noticed she was very sad, as if something terrible had happened. My grandmother did not know how to tell me the bad news that would turn out to be one of my biggest fears: On this day my father left us again, this time for good.

I do not remember how I reacted to what she told me. I do remember that not long before his final departure, the relationship between him and my mother seemed very strange. They had practically stopped doing anything together, and I was often accompanied only by either one of them. Occasional arguments in the kitchen were something I never been concerned about or understood as a potential danger. Whenever I asked my grandmother why they were arguing, she would tell me it was because the soup was too salty or they were just talking loudly. All of their problems were hidden from me, as is the case for many children.

My brother and I became two more victims of the selfish priorities of adults who choose to destroy their own families with divorce. My father left that day and took everything with him, including the big accordion I loved so much. He never said goodbye to my little brother or me. He just packed up his belongings in a friend's company truck and drove away.

It was a Russian custom and an established rule that in divorced families, children could never see their father again, and they always stayed with their mother. There were no shared hours for parents and children and the father only had an option to be involved in the future life of his own children. In many cases however, the desire of a father to see his daughter or son had to be approved by the mother. In my case, my dad never expressed this kind of wish. The next time we saw each other was many years later in a different house and under different circumstances.

The Camps, the Flukes, the Sports, and an Old Tradition

My first school year was over, and after my dad left us, I did not expect anything truly exciting to happen in the summer. Things got quieter around the house, and the dull emptiness seemed to be taking over. My mom wanted me to stay organized and under more control through the summer break. She believed the street might be not the best place for me to be around on for the next three month. For that reason, she made the decision to enlist me for one month in "Pioneer Camp", a Soviet version of Boy Scouts. My older cousin Valerie had already traveled to these Young Communists summer camps in the past. I had a chance to visit him once and see for myself what it was like. I knew the camps were not much different than the *dacha* we had in our daycare, only with more sophisticated rules and discipline. Having sour memories about that place, I had very little desire to embark for a month to the place that reminded me of my daycare life. I had been hoping for something bigger and more mature after school's end, but now, with my father gone, I had not many options.

The Pioneer Camps were designed to keep kids occupied and under control while in the summer school break. Parents were happy to send their offspring to the forest for a one or more months stay. Many used the whole summer package to take a long break from the kids. The camps were sponsored by our union organizations, and because they only charged a small nominal fee, they were an easy kid's vacation solution for many parents.

I had no desire to go to this camp, but no one asked my opinion, so I grudgingly climbed into the crowded bus full of other unhappy kids who didn't want to be shipped off to the wilderness for a month.

The camp was located about thirty miles from the city in the same region of our daycare "dacha" called Chenky. It was actually a compound of many different such camps, each with its own name derived mostly from the Communists lexicon. Our Pioneer Camp, "Salute", had about a dozen mobile home-style cabins with roughly twenty occupants per unit. We were broken into age groups, with kids ranging from seven to fourteen. All kids in a unit formed a brigade with its own name chosen by the whole group and approved by our adult leader, Vozhatiy.

In the middle of the camp was a large plateau on which all brigades marched every morning after breakfast. This gathering was called a "lineyka", meaning "a ruler." After a patriotic ritual and salute to the red flag flying on the tall mainstay, we were told by the camp leaders how, what, and where we would spend our day. As an established practice of the Soviet educational method of public humiliation, this was also the place where the failed ones were brought to shame. The kids that had some problems with discipline and performances on the campground were called there before all brigades and punished in the Soviet style of exposing their flaws in front of other young comrades. The winners of all kinds of competitions and drills were also presented there with trophies, banners, and award flags.

After this daily manifestation, which was hated by all the campers, we had miniature lineykas for our own brigade. The routine now was repeated on a little smaller scale. Everything slightly imitated our factory and military structure with a scheme of implemented ideological doctrines and procedures.

It was not only the time for drills and propaganda, but we also had a chance to play sporting games and go to the forest and occasionally the river. At night time after dinner, the older kids had dances, accompanied by our traditional accordion player. Unfortunately, all these minutes of joy were the least part of our activities. The mandatory patriotic song practice and marching rehearsals dominated the greatest portion of our time.

It was my first experience at Pioneer Camp, and after that trip, I had a strong aversion to those kinds of gatherings with commanding tasks and established duties. I could not wait to get out of that place and often referred to it as a prison camp in its own right. My mom and grandma visited me every weekend. I begged them for mercy to let me return home early, but my mother's strong principles and beliefs forced her to keep me there for my own good. It was my Aunt Valentina at the end who rescued me from the cold clutches of miserable Pioneer Camp. She came few days before our official departure and picked me up, and that was the best day I could remember on that trip. I came to find out that it was my mother's plan, but she did not want to do it herself because she did not want to show herself weak in the commitments to the principles of the Soviet obedience teachings. No matter who took me home after all, I was happy to be again around my family and wanted to forget about this trip.

English Lessons

Throughout my life, I often had an opportunity to obtain something valuable that would prove to be a priceless commodity for me in the future, even though at the time when these events occurred, I didn't see their positive potential. Looking back, the serendipity of it all is almost comical. The biggest positive fluke in my past afforded me the chance to master English language.

In addition to the regular schools in the Soviet education system, there were also those that offered intensive learning programs. Some focused on mathematic, others on athletics and sports, and others on cornerstone subjects. It just happened that School Number 10, which I attended, offered a vigorous curriculum of studying English, starting in the second grade.

In reality, for most Soviet people, the chance or necessity to use English was very slim. Traveling abroad was an unrealistic dream for most, and free communication with foreigners was nearly impossible under our regime. The rare visitors to our country were mostly non-English speaking folks, and most of them could only be found in Moscow or Leningrad. So, why did our teachers waste time to bother teaching Russian children such a "useless" language? There are a couple answers. First of all, we'd been taught that in order to successfully fight any enemy, it was essential to know their language. After WW2, Soviet school curriculums switched from German to mainly English lingo studies. Our so-called "potential adversary" was now across the Atlantic Ocean, and we would have to pick a few words from their lexicon before "they started a war".

Another explanation had something to do with the location and proximity of my school. Nestled right in the heart of our city, School Number 10 was considered the best educational facility for kids in town. Most of the local Communist Party leaders and city hall officials lived in that area, and their children attended my school. If anyone in life would have a chance to go overseas, it would be the offspring of our bureaucrats. For this reason, they placed such a convenient education preference' into our school curriculum.

When we began to study English in the second grade, I was very interested in it. Every day, we studied English for one or two class periods. The learning curve was rather simple until we moved deeper into the linguistics and grammar studies. We were still quite young, and trying to grasp a foreign vocabulary before we even had control of our own dialect was a challenge. As a result, I began to slip and stumble in my studies, but I blamed the English language itself for my slow progress. I told my mother, in no uncertain terms, that the people who came up with such a "tongue" had no idea what they were doing. I also complained to her, certain that my chances of ever needing English in my lifetime were about as great as me flying into space. This skepticism, however, did not prove very prophetic, as my own future would prove me wrong in the end. With a little effort and studying, I could speak near-perfect English by the fourth grade, as could some of my classmates, though I didn't see the point of putting any effort into it. Little did I know that it was one of the greatest mistakes I would make in my childhood, for I had no idea the important role English would play in my later life.

Elevating the Youngsters' Spirits

Compared to other pedagogic places in our town, we also boasted very hideous traditions on top of our special privileges. It had something to do with the fanatical obsession of our teaching staff with the Communist ideology. It was, by far, the worst place to be if you did not support and enjoy Red propaganda. I remember frequent pumped-up meetings and assemblies glorifying new resolutions and doctrines of our Party. In most cases, small children my age had no any clue what in the world the speakers were ranting about from their pulpits. Never ending commitments to the Socialistic beliefs and Bolshevik plans and agendas bombarded our minds. In one particular instance, just before the National Convention of the Communist Party, we were all brought to the concert hall. The pedagogues and principal read the school petition to Brezhnev, exalting our achievements on the ideological front. The rhymed paraphrases and patriotic slogans were shouted by coached kids in cheering frenzy. Not only were these cavalcades confusing to young minds, but also very annoying to our ears. Many of us began to dislike these kinds of manifestations, but any sign of unrest or boredom on our parts rapidly drew the attention of teachers who gave us short lectures, claiming that our Octyabryonock spirit had to be elevated to a "proper" level with the help of a few classic Communist remarks. I trusted our teachers and tried to believe everything we were told; however, the bothersome rallies reminded me of the Pioneer Camp with its similar forced red-flagged jamborees. I considered them a waste of time, and they left a feeling of confusion and diversity in my young soul. I began to develop skepticism and aversion to these teachings, slowly losing trust in our doctrines, and a couple of my friends in class shared this outlook. We always stayed together and occupied ourselves during these kinds of congregations with practical jokes and gags. Keeping these actions not too obvious was the key to maintaining a peaceful existence with our teachers and parents.

Subotnicks

The Soviet Union performed many interesting practices not found in the rest of the world. Some of them were purely for political purposes, and others were designed simply for good contributions to society. One of these positive Soviet inventions was "Subotnick", a day of a volunteer participation in organizing and improving our neighborhoods, schools, factories, and other parts of our communities. The name itself comes from the day of week, Saturday, on which this "holiday of work" occurred. Without exception, everyone in our nation went out into the streets, parks, and city squares to contribute. For many, it was simply an additional work day, only without any compensation. While it was considered a volunteer effort, this wasn't a reality. This Subotnick, as a matter of fact, was a mandatory task, and ignoring it brought severe punishment. The roots of this tradition went back to post-Bolshevik Revolution time, and it was established on the ruins of the Civil War. Trying to mobilize the population to build new society turned out to be a difficult venture for Bolsheviks. The young Soviet government lacked everything, including money and incentives for people to work. Calling for Proletarian patriotism and support of the new working-class government, Communists tried to accomplish their goals without any investments on their part. Anyone who was unwilling to participate in this day of labor awaited the severe punishment of Red justice.

This ancient tradition was not forgotten and was used in the USSR all the time. Surprisingly, it had a positive effect on our society and beautification of the country. The general opinion about these "work-for-free" days was diverse. Many believed in its good purpose, but there were those who hated to drudge an extra day at no pay.

Even children were not excluded from participation in this proceeding. Our little contribution to Subotnick was to pick up litter in the school courtyard, paint, and scrub the classrooms. As always, we were reminded that the founder and first volunteer of this event was our esteemed Vladimir Lenin. In almost every school, you could find the famous Sokolov's painting Lenin on Subotnick, in which our founder was painted within a group of comrades, holding together with them a giant wooden log. This magnificent work of Soviet art was meticulously studied in class, teaching us every detail about it and what it depicted. Lenin's hardworking attitude was brought to our attention and was meant to serve as an inspiring example for us in our daily lives.

Contrary to these teachings, however, there was a legendary anecdote that told a different story about Vladimir Lenin on the day of free service... "Lenin came on Subotnick, climbed on the horse carriage, and proclaimed, "Comrades, Subotnick has been canceled! Trotsky has stolen my inflatable wooden log!" The inflatable wooden log he spoke of became the undeniable butt of Soviet jokes on all the Subotnicks to follow. This type of joke, of course, was considered a serious offense against our precious history and its founders, and telling jokes or listening to them was a sure sign of trouble. Nevertheless, people found humor in them and loved to hear them. We never had a shortage of a similar controversial tales about our leaders, our government, and its history. All these anecdotes reflected the true public feelings within Soviet society among the majority of the Russian population, and children were not isolated from it. On top of being very funny, they gave children a different perspective, a new glance at our reality.

Athletic Education

One of the distinct differences in the life of a Soviet child as compared to an American was access to participation in sports. The main difference is not so much in number of choices but its availability, ease of participation and absolutely free of charge cost.

The strength and success of Russian sportsmen in the world has historically been widely recognized. Soviet athletes have maintained top positions in many competitions in the USSR and abroad. The fact that our Olympic teams have dominated in most of the Games since the 1950s is the result of the exceptional national sports education program. Athletics was probably one of the most privileged children's programs in our country, receiving funds and generous support. Nothing else in the Soviet Union was given as much attention and care as youth sports clubs.

Since the time of Stalin, the call for a healthy working class established countless athletic organizations and institutions. The need for a strong, well-developed generation of Communism builders brought for every kid in our country the opportunity to fulfill this agenda. The Red Army also expected good, strong soldiers for its arsenal. Because of this, all schools began to promote sports and athletic participation. Physical education was mandatory, from daycare right up to college. Recognizing the direct connection between regular exercises and good health, all were encouraged to involve Soviet parents kids in sports clubs and unions.

Our government also could not deny the tremendous political gains by taking part in such programs. The benefits from great achievements in competitions were not only sports related, but they also had a propagandistic gain and purpose. It was a way to show the Soviet people how much the Communist Party cared about its young generation. Delivering such statement to the rest of the world through Olympic Games, however, was priceless.

As soon as a child was admitted to school, he or she became a target of recruiting attacks from athletic coaches. Usually, the first who would try to drag us into some kind of group or sport club was our PE teacher. Every school had at least one sporting hall. Many large and privileged schools had their own small stadiums, Olympic-sized indoor pools, or even ice rinks.

Athletic organizations were everywhere. Every big and small town had a countless arrays of choices for anybody who wanted to get into sports. Like any other education program in the USSR, membership in such clubs was free of charge. On top of that, the great results and perseverance of the athletes was compensated even in the form of payments and benefits. For many adults, it became a career and a source of income. It was a normal occupation in our country to have a position as a paid professional sportsman, and those on the USSR Olympic team were leaders in this field. Though they were officially registered at the factories and colleges, they never had to report to work or classes. In most cases, athletes did not even know the locations of job sites, though they received regular monthly payments from them. On top of this, successful sportsmen were given a chance to travel abroad to competitions, a priceless benefit that anyone would have cherished. The lavish financial rewards however, similar to the Western champions, were never granted to our athletes and they could only rely on fixed but substantial salaries.

When they stop bringing medals to the Soviet Union, they had only two options of how to live in the future; work as coaches, or at the factories which they never attended while they were fighting for the world records. Going to the factories was the worst case scenario for "celebrity" athletes and no one would dare to try to fit into our working class environment. Many could not find or settle with a job of a trainer after having a glorified life of champions and became an alcoholic or joined criminal gangs. Only few well know famous sportsmen in the USSR raised to a level of a respectable and established coaches. For many others lives went upside down after finishing their sport career.

I never considered myself an athlete, but trying to escape the strong recruiting arms of the intimidating coaches was a daunting task. Every boy in our class joined some kind of club, the most popular being soccer. Soccer was so favored that the number of participants was always limited. To get into one of the soccer clubs, we had to wait for an open spot when someone grew tired of soccer and move on to a different discipline. The least popular types of sports had the most energetic coaches when it came to enrolling kids. They would often enter our classrooms in the middle of a period and start advertising and promoting, trying to tweak our interest in sports like wrestling, ping-pong, or weightlifting. They were very persuasive presentations, and many children signed up for sports they had never considered before. In my youth, I participated in several of them, though many of them I only joined because my friends signed up.

Making the team was a rather easy task, and in most, cases coaches did not force children to get involved in the heavy practicing like professionals. It was often a relaxed introduction to the discipline without any intrusive push. On many occasions, we simply showed up, fooled around with the sports equipment, climbed on the walls, or watched other kids practicing. The coaches did everything in their power to keep us involved in any fashion. For those who were skilled athletes, however, life could become very different.

Once a student began to show promise in any sport, the trainer would practically take over his/her life. The value of every potentially successful athlete was enormous for our government. Coaches were given ultimate power to interfere in the personal life of the young athlete and control their destiny. If a promising athlete missed one practice, they were in trouble, and practices often took precedence over other things. Coaches and trainers were even given authority to remove a student from school, or worker from their job for the sake of athletic practice. The personal life of athletes was required to take a back seat to bringing medals and glory to the Soviet government. Successful athletes of the world class level were destined to become simply national property.

Joining and changing sports clubs was a normal practice for elementary school children, and I was no exception. During my school years, I was a member of several different clubs, spending my longest time in a kayak club. Since the early years, I had a love and passion for water, and I always enjoyed doing anything in the outdoors. Even sitting in a hot bathtub was fun for me as a small boy, and I remember playing with toy boats until the water grew cold and my grandma had to drag me out of the bathroom. After school, I took swim lessons for a while, though I never really learned out to swim. Nevertheless, going to the beach was one of my favorite summer recreations, and whenever we traveled to village or went on picnics, I'd always ask if there was a lake or a river nearby.

Fortunately for a water lover such as myself, our city was situated on the banks of the fairly large Sozh River. It was the place where the whole town went for entertainment, particularly on hot days, but even in the winter they enjoyed ice fishing and winter swims. We often had parties in the wooden area behind the beach, and with a small campfire, it was our unforgettable hideaway.

All kinds of water sports clubs and associations gathered along the shore of the Sozh, including water skiing, canoeing, kayaking, and many other physical marine activities. I joined a team called "Red Flag", along with my friend Grisha. We were best friends and classmates, and we looked forward to being a dual team on one kayak. We had very nice light wooden kayaks with different colored nylon tops. Some of them, as well as their respective paddles, had to be repaired, and we did the repairs ourselves right in our club storage area. The masters, those who achieved certain classifications and scores, practiced in very high-quality cool mahogany boats—the dream of many of the boys. To accomplish such a feat, we had to not only work very hard and practice as much as we could, but also achieve competition victories.

We attended practice twice a week, basically joy rides on the river. Until we gained proper confidence on the water, our coach Vasili Ivanovich ('Vaska'), was not very tough on us. After a while, we decided to split and each take our own boat. This way, we could race each other and would not be affected if one or the other could not make it to practice—though we didn't miss practice often or Vaska would call our home or school to see why we skipped. Any sign of disinterest in any sport was treated with discipline and seen as a flaw, and it was promptly brought to the attention of our school teachers and parents. The only way we could quit a club was with permission of our mother and father, and even then, it was looked down upon. Nevertheless, I saw my membership in the kayak club a good thing, and I loved to participate. It was a lot of fun, and the possibility of having a nicer kayak in the future kept my spirits up.

Competitions for us were rare, and even when they did occur, it was typically only the more experienced boys who got to participate in the races. During one of these local contests, several of our members were pitted against other teams. A couple of guys did not show up, and the option was given for volunteers to take their place. I immediately volunteered with great enthusiasm—something that would prove to be a big mistake.

After arriving at the small river gulf, we lined up against our rivals for a one-kilometer race. I was a little boy at that time without any experience and barely sticking out from the boat. The start signal was given, and about twenty of us plowed our paddles into the water. I was pushing hard for about five minutes before I began to realize that everybody was accelerating at a much faster pace than me. My friends and teammates were slightly ahead of me, but the gap between us was growing at a faster and faster speed. I was doing all I could, pouring in all my strength, but it wasn't enough. Soon, I could barely see the other kayaks. The escorting boat was right behind me, and from its deck the coach was shouting, "Harder, harder! Don't give up!"

I did not give up, though I feared capsizing would be worse than finishing last. I hoped everyone who was ahead of me would eventually get tired and begin to fall behind, but it never happened. I could already see many of them finishing the race and paddling to shore, even though I was only halfway to the finish. It felt like I was not going anywhere, as if the paddle could not push my kayak forward. After a long struggle, I crossed the finish line. The referee waved the flag marking my completion of the race, and everybody was screaming as if I had beaten the world record. To my astonishment, the crowd was cheering more fore me than for the much faster winner. My coach was even shouting something about my great job and was congratulating me. I thought they were all making fun of me, but they were not. Everybody was impressed with my dedication to complete such a hard race. It was a small victory on a different scale for me, and from that I learned a lesson of perseverance.

Fishing Incident and Sport Camp

Besides that, the most memorable time of my involvement in kayak club was our trip to a summer sports camp. Such camps existed alongside with the summer vacation program for kids but was organized by the sport education Ministry. Many different clubs had this kind of recreation combined with athletic practicing and our "Red flag" was also one of them. When I was told about the upcoming voyage, I was a bit uneasy about it, having unpleasant recollections of my experiences at Pioneer Camp. I was rather gloomy about it, and my first reaction to the trip forthcoming was simply "No." I could not shake off my disturbing remembrances of the marching drills and the annoying Lineykas, and I did not want to include such an excursion in my summer plans again. It took a while for our coach to convince me that the tyranny of the Pioneer Camps did not exist in sports camps. I eventually gave in and was ready to embark on a forty-five-day trip to the wilderness.

Two weeks before our departure, I decided to go fishing with my friend Sergey for a few hours by the boat station on the river. There was a floating dock for big and small boats where passengers could board to make watery journeys to the towns and villages located on the river shores. It was a large, two-story facility, and it reminded of a train station, containing all the common amenities of a transportation service.

It was a popular fishing spot, and many other kids and adults fished there. The shore was rugged, with plenty of rocks and all kind of debris in the water, so finding a safe place to stand was not easy. Normally, people climbed on the pontoons and little boats anchored under the overpass to fish from them, and we did the same. It was a beautiful day. My sports club friend and I were having a great time. Because it was the middle of the week, we were the only people around the station. We sat on one of the pontoons and tried to make a catch, to no avail.

Suddenly, a rather disgruntled station worker appeared right above us on the overpass. "Hey, boys," he shouted, "grab the end!" and he dropped down a thick rope.

I thought he wanted us to help him drag the pontoon closer to the dock. Trying to grab the end of it, I reached toward the man. At this moment, he pulled the rope back, and with a mad casting tried to whip me in the face. I ducked, and he barely missed me. He was drunk, shouting like a madman at us to jump in the water and run.

Sergey threw himself on the rocks, and I stumbled into the water until it was up to my knees. I had to fight the strong river current as I tried to make it to the shore, and then I noticed that the water behind me was intensely red. Ignoring it, I managed to climb on a nearby boulder, and there I saw the reason for the red water: My left foot was covered in blood. I suddenly started to feel an enormous pain and hopped to the sidewalk with the help of my friend. As it turned out, my pinky toe was sliced almost in half, and blood was gushing from the bottom of my foot like a fountain. I lay down on the ground and tried to hold my leg up in the air to stop the bleeding, but it didn't work. Sergey began to panic, thinking I was going to bleed to death.

Fortunately, a passerby noticed us. The young man picked me up and ran into the river dock station. He was trying to keep me calm as he ran, assuring me in a trembling voice, "It's going to be alright! It's going to be alright!"

On the way, we passed by the drunken madman, who was still standing on the overpass, watching what had happened. I was holding my leg up with both of my hands tight around my foot. The blood was running toward my neck, covering the young man as well, who also began to panic.

Fortunately, the station had a small first aid room that was open. I was dropped on the bed and began to pass out. The nurse plunged an injection into my arm and was screaming at me to stay with her. She wrapped my foot to stop the bleeding and told me that everything would be alright. Soon after she administered first aid, I started regaining consciousness. After that, she tried to call an ambulance to pick me up so my foot wound could be stitched properly.

The nurse took my phone number and called home. My biggest fear now was the reaction of my mom when she heard what happened.

"Hello. This is the nurse from the river dock station calling," the nurse said when my mother answered the phone. My mom later told me she nearly dropped dead when she heard that because this was the kind of call someone would get if a loved one drowned while swimming at the beach. The nurse had enough foresight to know the call would not be a welcomed one and immediately started assuring my mother that nothing that horrible had happened. "Your son is okay," she continued. "He just sliced his foot by stepping in the water on what looks like a broken bottle. I called an ambulance, but it will take an hour or more for them to get here. You should take a taxi ASAP and get him to the near by clinic for a tissue repair."

Ambulance response in the USSR was never guarantied within a specific timeframe. Because it was a free service, like all medical treatments, people called for it often without any urgent reason, meaning ambulances were very often arriving with a long delays. My mom took a taxi, as the nurse wisely advised, and in fifteen minutes, we were already at the medical clinic.

After sitting in the waiting room for about half an hour, my mom got irritated and felt no one really care about us. She stormed to one of the doctors and gave him a short lecture in her well-practiced Communist fashion. I was taken to the medical room immediately after that. My foot was sliced severely on the bottom, almost in half, and the doctor said the stitches may not work there except on my little toe. He decided to give it a try and promised me it would feel like nothing more than a mosquito bites. He lied. Local anesthesia was mainly used in our hospitals and only at the time of open surgeries, so I did not receive any. Over thirty stitches in total were plunged into my foot. The fishing day was done and with my unforgettable catch, it was already dark when we got home.

Because of my injury, my plans to go to sports camp had to be canceled. It was somewhat of a bummer for me because all the other kids from my club and my pal Sergey went. I wanted to go as well, and the accident on the river felt like a big misfortune for me. Coach Vaska said I could go as soon as I felt better and that I could be excused from practices and exercises. This lightened my mood, and I could not wait to get together with our club members out in nature.

I stayed in bed for a few days and quickly began to hop around the house on one leg. Getting crutches was not an acceptable option for me, and I was hoping that in a couple of weeks, I would be fine. At one point, I got a fever and pain in my foot, so a doctor was called to come and take a look. He didn't have good news; I had a severe infection in my leg's wound. His fear was that it was too late to do anything about it, and it would require amputation.

Mom called a taxi, and we rushed to the hospital. I was so ill that I could not even feel what the doctors were doing. Soon, I was back home with both of my feet still attached, right where they belonged. I had to take medication and get shots twice a day, as well as dressing changes by nurses who came to my home, but shortly after that, I began recovering fast and was still counting on going to sports camp.

Three weeks later, I had my stitches removed, and I was limping pretty well around the house and our neighborhood. Still refusing to get crutches, I had only one plan in mind: to join my friends at the sport club's campground.

The same unfortunate river station was where we had to board the boat to depart for camp. Even though I had missed most of the forty-five days, I was still very intrigued to go. Sports practice and training seemed much more alluring to me than the political requirements and orientations of Pioneer Camp and I was looking forward to meet my friends.

My time at the sports camp was my favorite time spent in such an establishment as a child. Despite the fact that the camp took place on the campground of Pioneer Camp, we were spared from all its annoying routines. In my case, I only went on the water to practice for a couple of times at the end of our trip, but having my fishermen friend Sergey and other friends along added to my small voyage in a big way. Though I still walked lamely, even with their help, it was still better than doing it by myself.

Having an opportunity to enjoy nature and taking simple walks to the river without anybody babysitting us gave me a sense of a freedom and true pleasure, but our coach was a leader and took care of us from the early workouts to the nightly dancing at the nearby camps. For a young boy like me, dancing wasn't all that interesting, but it was good for a laugh to see our coach Vaska dancing.

The most pleasurable thing about sports camp was complete separation from the main Pioneer Camp polices and rules. Even though it stood in the same territory, our little house felt almost like a freedom fortress. The kids who were there for Pioneer Camp were openly jealous that we were exempt from the morning Lineykas and marching rehearsals. We were playing soccer and badminton in our cool sports uniforms while they had to sweat in senseless practices of the patriotic plays. When everybody else had to go to sleep, we began setting up a campfire that would illuminate their envious faces as they stared longingly at us out of their cabin windows, looking like prisoners of a so-called 'happy summer camp for children'. Even though I was glad to be part of the sports camp and not stuck in Pioneer Camp again, it was a sad example of how the Soviet system chose to selectively reward some children with a tiny bit of a freedom simply for participation in the powerful lure of sports, just more Bolshevik propaganda.

Unfortunately, that was the last summer of my membership in the Red Flag kayak club, as the facility was leveled to make space for a new shoreline development. The Red Flag club was never given a new place to meet, and I didn't bother enrolling in another club because at that point in life, my interested moved another direction. The nice mahogany kayak would remain nothing more than a lifelong dream for me.

Soviet luxuries and Time In and After School

Life in Soviet Union had unparalleled differences in terms of qualities and values, especially as compared to the United States and European nations. The fundamental moral teachings of our society promoted a humble life, honoring spiritual values above materialistic. These principles were coached to us at school and presented side by side with our Communist dogmas. Even within our strict Socialistic options, the chase for lavish life was criticized, an alien ideal to our Proletarian spirit.

Hypothetically speaking, of course, the Russian government did not want us to live in the Stone Age, but there was no denying among our people that we did not have access to the same assets and attributes as those in the West, due to our inefficient economical system.

We were told we were the best nation on Earth and that no one lived a better life than us. With the inability of the most Russian people to travel around the world and compare the differences for ourselves, many had to believe to our propaganda. The primary example they used to portray the supremacy of the Socialistic economy versus Capitalistic was our amount of produced oil, coal, and minerals. We were often reminded that the USA developed much less of these, and it was on this point that they tried to make us think we were living in a heavenly world. Why we were making horrible home goods from these ingredients was never discussed, especially in contrast with the United States. Such values as freedom of speech and democracy were seldom used in our country unless they were accompanied in our country by the words 'Socialistic' or 'Proletarian'. The Iron Curtain erected in the USSR was a real symbol of our so-called freedom and democracy—a far cry different from the way these moral principles compared to the rest of the civilized.

Regardless of the teaching and dogmas in our society, people were still sought a better economical and social life. With limited goods, a noticeable deficit of many products, and poor services, improving our living conditions was a daunting task. The salaries in our country fluctuated within insignificant margins, and no one made enough money to become rich—at least not by Western standards. Despite these limitations, we still had a 'luxury life" and "wealthy"'items surrounding us on a daily basis, depending on your view of what a luxury was.

In the Communist USSR, a luxury might be an extremely expensive item, maybe even government-granted services and privileges. For example, when I was a child, having a telephone was considered as a luxury, a privilege. No one could buy a personal telephone line. Similar to the way apartment distribution was handled, everyone had to stay in line to get a connection, and the waiting list was up to ten years long. Of course, for government officials, military, or KGB, this "luxury privilege" would be connected to their houses in no time. We were lucky to wait only six years and had to share the phone with our neighbors; anyone from our apartment building could come and ask to make a call. Many of them gave their friends our number, so we often got calls from strangers asking for someone from our neighborhood, and we would have to go and get them. Refusing to do so would have been regarded as an unfriendly jester that would render us an enemy to the requestor for the rest of our lives. Everyone obeyed the rules of Soviet hospitality, as it was our normal way of life.

Having a TV wasn't necessarily a luxury unless it was a color set. This was because they cost five times more than a black and white unit. Color TVs were priced almost four to five times that of an average monthly salary. People saved up for years to buy them, and even when they did manage to save the money, they often went store to store and still couldn't find one because color televisions were on a long list of deficit items. One would have to have a "connection" in an electronic retail outlet or somehow get some prior knowledge of where and when they would be sold. Those who were lucky enough to find that out had to go and sleep outside the stores to be first in line to buy a set. This was exactly how we got our Raduga (Rainbow) 714 color TV, and it was the most expensive purchase we ever made in the USSR.

Many other hard-to-find items were obtained in the same way. These ranged from furniture, electronics, appliances, clothes, and food delicacies. Practically any household item of high quality or popularity became a target that people dreamed of owning.

Jewelry was the most valuable commodity and held a special place in our list of luxury items. It was also a convenient way to invest our rubles into something precious. Buying gold was a very popular option but was too pricey for low-income families. Making an investment in gold was only possible for those who had prestigious jobs or tried to hide their illegal profits.

The Soviet system did not offer banks for the public, at least not the conventional banks used in Western society. It was impossible to get a loan or any type of credit because these things did not exist in the USSR. Those who wanted to buy things they could not outright afford in cash up front only had two options: You could opt to purchase it on layaway and have the funds automatically deducted from your salary; or, you could borrow the money from relatives and friends. All salaries, purchases, and transactions in the USSR were processed only in cash.

If anyone wanted to create a savings, there was only one way to do it. The government-owned "Sbercassa" (Saving Bank) would give 2 percent annual interest on savings, but only a handful of people used this service. Many feared the government might confiscate their money for any reason or that they might become the subject of scrutiny if their balance looked suspicious. Mattresses and socks were our oldest and most popular way of stashing cash, and most people considered them safer options than putting their money in government hands.

The symbol of ultimate status and prestige in the Soviet Union was the possession of the two most precious items one could own: an automobile or a dacha. In the USSR, a car was not categorized as a source of transportation but rather a prime luxury, a trophy of sorts.

The infrastructure and communication networks in Russia had been developed at the very good level, and there was no need to have a personal vehicle to travel around town or to any remote destination. Buses, trolleys, and subways took us from any location in the city to practically anywhere. All grocery stores were built within walking distance of apartment buildings, and unlike in the USA, shoppers couldn't afford towering piles of food. Because of that, we didn't have to go to the grocery in a car.

The only practical need for an automobile would be to deliver potatoes and vegetables to houses for winter eating. These were purchased in large quantities and were stored in root cellars and kitchens by many Soviet families because buying these products in the winter time at stores was very difficult. Vegetables and fruits were bought in village farm markets and brought back to homes, and this was a difficult task for anyone who did not have access to an automobile.

Like most of the merchandise in the USSR, we produced our own automobiles. There were no foreign brands and makes to serve as alternatives to our poorly made clunkers. Despite the shabby quality, they were still prized possessions to be gloated over. Cars bore astronomical price tags, and to buy one of them was not only a financial challenge, but another typical Soviet routine of waiting in line as well. While most of our population saved for a dream vacation on the Black Sea, some people dreamed to buy a car. It was a bit surprising that even though few people could even save ample wealth to buy a car, the Soviet Union could not seem to make them fast enough to satisfy all potential buyers, creating a waiting list several years long. The general public opinion was that one had to be a criminal, a corrupted crook, or a high-ranking government official to buy your own automobile. This belief was not too far from the truth, and possession of a car was the number one reason for government suspicion of anyone's source of income.

Among my all relatives, only Uncle Igor and his wife Valentina owned this regarded item of luxury. It did not belong to them completely and was shared between Igor's brother and their parents. The Zhiguli-2101—a copy of the Italian Fiat—was the first model of this very popular Soviet make. The USSR decided to produce it as a "people's automobile". Despite the fact that it was not one of the most prestigious models we produced, it became an iconic symbol of opulence.

Igor's mother took all of her life savings and purchased the automobile in 1972 in order for them to enjoy comfortable rides to the country. It was a monumental event among my relatives, as Soviets often threw big parties in celebration of any major purchase. This one was called a 'wash it'. In cases of such monumental buys as a new set of wheels, the celebration could only compete with weddings. Igor's family did not avoid this almost religious tradition.

I remember the birthday party of my cousin Valeriy that year. One of the treats for all kids was a ride in the brand new Zhiguli. About six of us jammed in the car and drove to our local highway for a fast drive. It was incredible. For any child at that time in that place, to take a spin in the car was a rare and exiting opportunity. Uncle Igor loved to drive fast, making us fly with all windows opened, everyone enjoying the unforgettable jaunt. It was also memorable because one of the kids, who never in his life traveled that fast, got dizzy and barfed on the brand spanking new upholstery. Igor was very upset, to say the least, and so were the rest of us. We felt sorry for our friend and for the nice new car as well.

People cherished and cared for their priceless possessions in those days. That Zhiguli survived many little accidents, and old Igor is still driving that vintage automobile to this day. Keeping them safe was not an easy task though. For anyone who lived in the city, it was a big challenge to store a car under the roof. Like everything else, the problem was availability, and attaining a garage was not a simple task. Again, we had to wait in line. The units were usually located on the edge of the city, built as a large garage compounds, meaning it was a long bus or trolley journey to get to your car. Traveling to any destination involved sometime a half-day trip just to the garage itself. In spite of this inconvenience, people felt privileged to own a car and accepted this annoyance as part of the package deal.

Another prime luxury item you could possess in Soviet Union was a dacha, the Russian version of a summer house or summer retreat. The small land parcels were distributed at work and by government organizations to fortunate families. The prestige of owning a dacha was undeniable, but it also depended on its location, the size of the land, and the structure of the house on it.

The amount of issued tracts was so limited that it created grounds for speculation and a gray market. Purchasing dacha land was as equally prestigious as owning an automobile, even more. The ability to resell dacha, which were always in demand items, fetched an enchanting gain for many Russian people. Everything in the Soviet Union that was labeled as a deficit (and many things were) could be treated as an investment. These included cars, small transistor radios, and large dacha.

Obtaining land was one challenge, but establishing a building on it was another. All materials and construction supplies were only distributed amongst government organizations. We did not have stores and resources for civilians to buy building supplies to construct a house or a small cottage. Approval had to be granted via permit by the authorities to purchase materials from industrial supply factories. This involved a tremendous amount of bureaucracy and hassle, and these rules created grounds for corruption growth within government and material distribution sectors.

For many, the dacha became a provider of additional fruits and vegetables to their tables. People more frequently went to their summer houses to work than to relax and it often resulted in calling dachas a "Sunday work".

My aunt and uncle were fortunate to have a small place like that on the Dnieper River, about thirty miles away form our town. Igor's mother received the tiny land when she was a leading, hardworking nurse at the military hospital. For many years, it remained as a grassy field until, through the collective efforts of her children, the small house about of 400 square feet was built in the late sixties.

Several times in my life, I became lucky to travel to her dacha. It was in the most beautiful location in our countryside, a place called the "White Shore". The crystal clean white sands along the big river gave the name to this prestigious location. We always traveled there in Igor's car, and the trip felt like royal treats for me. Going fishing and running along the river was a simple but wonderful pleasure for me at the same time. The adults were always working in the garden, crawling on their knees all day, eagerly picking home-grown berries and vegetables. For them, it was typical Soviet dacha "recreation", and they loved it. Bragging to my friends about my trips often made them jealous, despite the fact that the visits there were only day-long journeys.

These two glorified luxuries in the Soviet Union—the automobile and the dacha—were the legal limit of the lavish life for those who could afford it. Possessing two of these items in your family without a high rank job allowing your to own it, could triggered the investigation of your income and the source of funds used to purchase them. I recall a community meeting in our neighborhood when the local police officer briefed us on safety and talked about protection of the property, but he somehow drifted to the subject of wealth and luxuries. The sheriff became unwound at the end of his speech, bawling in anger that everyone who owned a car or a dacha should be in jail. He shouted with uncontrolled wrath and fury, "To earn enough money legally to buy this stuff is impossible in our country, my comrades! These people are all criminals!"

Art and Labor Classes

I was already in the third grade, and the most interesting subjects in school at that time for me were my art and labor classes. Practically all my classmates and friends loved these periods, too, partly because the atmosphere was always relaxed, and the teachers were friendly and funny.

The art class was taught by Katyka, a short lady, who wore massive glasses and had a deep voice. She also ran our school painting workshop. In art period, we usually made simple drawings of various objects and studied Soviet and Russian painters' masterpieces. A large print would be brought to our class, and Katyka began talking in excitement, using terms that were strange to us: perspectives, compositions, angles, and so on. Quite often, class was boring as a brick, especially when we had to study the paintings of Lenin and Socialist art. The hard working or proclaiming a speech in the Kremlin Vladimir Lenin, coal miners or steel melting plants were presented to us in its full exaltation. The beauty of hard labor was glorified and painted as an ultimate goal of life. Dominating red color in our art always reminded us of Soviet classicism and was honored as the only true form of artistry.

The painting workshop, which Katyka advertised tirelessly, was available for anyone after school hours. Since I had always enjoyed drawing, my mom forced me to join the study. I did not mind gaining some knowledge in art, but I was only interested in painting cars, tanks and airplanes. The classroom itself was nested within our school and was a true artists' shop. Large and small statues, paintings, and easels were everywhere. Different special tools hung on the walls. Sticking out from the jars and vases were various brushes, looking like colorful bouquets of flowers. The smell of oil paint gave the room a final touch of mystique and a working atmosphere. It was hard to believe we were still inside our school.

For my first assignment, the small group of us was told to make a sketch of a cube in three dimensions. This project immediately put me on alert, and I began to wonder if the workshop was going in the same path as the Handy hands club. I was reluctant to accept the idea of making drawings of balls, triangles, and leaves for a long time before I could paint a nice bomber. This strategy was not for me. The energy and desire to get everything done as fast as possible was a ruling force in my spirit. I didn't mind working on something for a while, but to do something I found absolutely uninteresting was too hard for me to swallow. After a few more visits, my art education was terminated for good. I was free again to roam around the neighborhood on my bicycle, scaring the pedestrians and enjoying my after school time.

The atmosphere in labor class was much better and closer to my fascination. We had a well-equipped workshop with everything we needed to construct any project out of metal. At first, the teacher was our regular class pedagogue, and since the third grade, the tutoring was done by our school principal who loved to teach kids this kind of stuff. He was an old man, a war veteran who carried a lot of wounds from that era. Because he was a good mechanic, he introduced us to the basic tools for working with metals. The older kids in high school learned how to use mill and lathe machines. Everything was set up so that right after graduation, we could go straight into factory work, practically without any additional education.

Located next to our school's garage, the workshop was big enough to have for about twenty people to work on various projects at once. Two rows of large vices were affixed to steady benches and separated by a thick acrylic glass. The lathe, mill, and grinding machinery were placed against the walls, making the room look like a miniature factory.

At our main stations, we were introduced to real tools and techniques of metalwork. Multiple banners and safety warnings decorated the walls, along with the typical inspiring Proletarian posters. Later in my life, I often recalled this classroom, comparing it to the totally different rundown and neglected workrooms at our factories.

The most common assignments we had to deal with were fabricating and finishing hand tools. Very often, we received very rough pliers or other hardware component casts and have to file them to completed shiny parts. Some of us sneaked to the giant grinders and tried to blast the bulk of work on the stone wheels. Often, without any experience in how to use the machinery safely, these attempts ended up in disaster, ruining the entire part. Our goal was to present the result to a teacher by the end of the period. I always did my work with extreme enthusiasm and passion. The concept of executing a project in only forty-five minutes was a perfect strategy for me. I loved this kind of procedure and working dynamics.

Many of us had blisters after we were done, but it never discouraged us, and we were always told it was a sign of a hard work, typical for a real Bolshevik. The shiny finished parts went back to the factories and were sold to the public. Today, it would be considered child exploitation or illegal child labor, but in the USSR, it was a "labor education".

While we were hammering metal sheets, the girls from our class took their own lessons right above us on the second floor. For gals, this education involved the typical future responsibilities of women. They learned how to cook, stitch, and using a sewing machine as their general assignments. They loved this part of our education as well. Very often after these lessons, when we got back to the classroom, the girls served to us the cookies they made in class. It was a lot of fun. We promised to make them some shovels so they could use them on our next Subotnick.

After School Fun with My Buddy

At that time, a couple of my best friends were in class with me—the kind who become lifelong pals. Grisha was my closest buddy. A lot of people considered him an eccentric boy, but in reality, he was just very energetic. He was also very outspoken. I was often asked by teachers and my parents why I was friends with him and what we had in common. They didn't know a lot about us, especially our friendship. At that time we already shared a common dislike for our annoying ideological education. Despite being such young children, we saw the hypocrisy and utopia of what we had been taught. We were not the only kids who recognized it, but we were the ones who could not accept it and were constantly irritated by Communist propaganda .

He lived not far away from me, and we often went to school and back home together. By the third grade, no one had to escort children anymore. Crime (especially against children) was extremely rare, and the only concern parents had about their children's journey to school was crossing the streets safely. Normally, we were instructed to seek out an adult to help us see the intersections clearly. Very often people volunteered to accompany kids across the street to be sure we were safe. It was a cultural custom, and many families relied on these old unwritten law.

In the morning, we frequently took a bus or a trolley. It did not give us a lot of advantage time wise, but it was a sort of joy ride. Tickets were not really required for kids of our age, so we took the trolley as often as we wanted. The shortcut to school on foot was a much quicker route, and we preferred to walk only on the way home, when the half-hour walk could be stretched to couple hours' journey. Very often, we went on excursions through every store along the way, fooling around at the big and small retailers. We made fun of clothes and shoes and tried them on, deliberately selecting the most oversized and ugliest items. Many salesmen knew us by name, and some of them blocked us from going into their stores. The hats departments were our favorite, along with the toys and school supplies. Placing toys and dolls in funny and strange positions aggravated store staff and often resulted in us being booted out the doors. We sometimes went into the school merchandise sections and with straight faces asked for a third grader's ink or a map of the North Pole in Mozambique language. The goal was to have as much fun as possible, and we never had a shortage of that. A few of the workers at the stores seemed to really like us, probably because we lightened their dull day. We were always thinking of new funny and elaborate practical jokes, fearlessly incarnating them on our next voyage.

Sometimes we finished our long trip home from school in a jumping on the bushes competition. Our newly established blue uniforms could not handle the dirt and dust as well as the gray one, though, and when I returned home covered in dirt, my mom and grandma wondered what in the world we did in school. I had to lie to them and say we had a tough project to do in labor class.

Occasionally, we truly did have rough days in class, especially during the times when we had to collect paper or metal scrap for our government recycling mega-projects. The paper gathering was an easy task, requiring us to walk through the neighborhood and ask people for used books and newspapers. The metal scrap collection was a serious assignment involving dragging rusty junk to the school. We stormed the local factories and their surrounding junk yards in search of precious extra kilos of iron. This endeavor was done in the spirit of Socialistic competition, fighting all classes for the best results. The large billboard chart hung in the school hallway and displayed the amount of scrap each class gathered. At the top was a slogan saying something like "Children's iron for the Soviet B.A.M. railroad construction!" or "Strike with Proletarian recycling against the waste and languish!" The winning team was usually rewarded with a red banner embellished with Communist insignia and slogans. Displaying this trophy in your class symbolized a true Bolshevik spirit for the children who possessed it.

Grandma's Work and Lunches

Every time my grandma worked, she wanted me to stop at the hotel on the way home and have a lunch with her. On the first floor of the "Sozh" Hotel where she worked was a very large restaurant. Allow me to clarify that in Russia, restaurants were not just any places to eat. We had "stolovayas", "pelmennayas", "pirozhkovayas", cafés, and other similar establishments with simple and often poor menu options. They were analogous to the USA fast food chains, and these low-quality eateries were never referred to as "restaurants" in the USSR. Our restaurants, on the other hand, were the best places, and though they offered sometimes limited selection, the delicacies they served were well prepared and gourmet.

At that time, Soviet rules prohibited admission to the restaurants for anyone who younger than sixteen years of age. This was logical and smart decision for our country. On one hand, children were not exposed to the heavy smoking and alcohol consumption, and on the other, the adult diners were not annoyed by crying or tantrums of little kids. Restaurants were where people could have a meal, alcohol, and music served in relaxed atmosphere. Though we, as a nation, had trouble producing enough food for everyone, we knew for sure how to party. The bothersome propaganda was exempt in these places, probably the only institutions in our country free of political brainwashing. A large jukebox played popular Soviet tunes at night time, and it was a famous place to visit after long working week or for a decently cooked lunches. Because my grandma was employed at the hotel, she could treat me to a nice lunch despite the strict anti-kids policy at the restaurant. The doorman knew who she was, and the one ruble gratitude always worked very well to let us be seated.

Grandma and I in 1973.

I will never forget the smell of Russian restaurants —a thick aroma of food, beer, and cigarettes. The atmosphere in there was surprisingly different from every other place in our lives, and many people loved to be there. Despite the expensive night rates, the lines of people waiting to get in were always very long.

The interesting fact in our system was the subconscious reaction of people in odd situations and observations. Noticing a man served without a wait in line or a kid eating at the restaurant always triggered a stereotyped exclamation that it must be a someone "important". No one ever reacted to or questioned my presence behind the table among adults, who were drinking beer and smoking cigarettes.

My grandma had a lot of friends at work, and they would often join us for lunch. One of her good friend was Olga, and she had an interesting personality resembling a tough Bolshevik lady from the 1930s. She was very tall with black curly hair, and she almost never pulled the cigarette out of her mouth. Every time she saw me entering the hotel, I heard her exclaim, "The professor is here!" I still don't know why she said that, considering that my grades didn't really reflect any sort of academic genius. She had no problem offering me a couple sips of beer, which she called "a good appetizer." My grandma always tried to interfere to protect me from her wild behavior and consistently tried to sit between us.

Chapter 5

Jewels and Getting Closer to Soviet Realities

When I became obsessed with working on these small craft projects, little did I know that it might have ultimately determined my future occupation. It was definitely my first true passion, and it grasped my imagination and enthusiasm. I felt nothing could stop me from pursuing and achieving this to proficiency. This new fascination was so strong that it overshadowed and replaced a lot of my other childhood diversions. It suited me as a comfortable, quiet mastery that required not many tools and very few materials. I was falling in love with the projects, and no one knows how it would change my life if it had not ended so abruptly in such a unpredicted fashion.

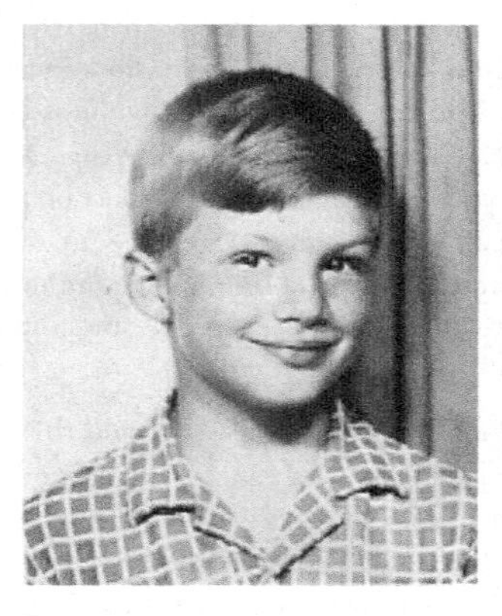

At Ten years old.

I was almost ten years old when I got my hands on a large bag of old buttons that had been kept in my family for many decades. It held a wide array of different colors and sizes of shirt, dress, and coat buttons, as well as something that I found much more enticing: a handful of broken vintage jewelries. None of the pieces had real precious stones or metals, but the colors and shapes were too intriguing to pass my attention. I wiggled the broken broaches and earrings in my hands. Suddenly, I began noticing that many of the gems could be incorporated into parts and pieces from other broken jewelry. I started visualizing what might be created if I could separate their parts, combine them with others, and rebuild them as new pieces.

All I needed were the right tools to break away selected gems and the technique to join them into an original form of art. I learned that all the stones were situated in crown settings, so puling them out would be a bad idea. They had to stay together. To separate connected mounts from each other, I used a steak knife with small, sharp teeth. Sawing soft brass using this kitchen utensil was easy, but when it couldn't fit it into the small openings, I had to use manicure scissors and nail files. It took some time and a lot of effort—not to mention abuse of my mother's accessories—to remove the desirable gems out without destroying the settings.

On the streets, the cold winter invaded our town, delivering long and dark evenings. The snow fell silently outside my window. As I concentrated on my intricate work to get it absolutely perfect, all I could hear was the ticking of our table clock. The craft was such a relaxing diversion that I could do it for hours without getting up from my desk.

I made floral shapes and geometric designs from brass jar covers, dulling up all the sharp cutting tools in the house in the process. When my arrangement was ready to be attached to the base plate, I realized that the glue cement from my airplane model kit did not hold it well together. It also did not look as clean as the original jewelry. I had to solder all of them in the same manner as they were originally made. My cousin Valeriy showed me how to use a soldering iron, and I began attaching them on my brass forms, wires, or directly to each other. With a little practice, I managed to create almost seamless joints, smoothing out all the rough soldering with sandpaper and nail files. They were touched up with gold paint from my modeling projects, and I worked patiently to make them look like new.

My mother never owned very expensive gold or jewelry. Growing up without my father and lacking substantial family income, we had no such luxuries around the house. Therefore, my new hobby became an opportunity for my mom to have something different to add to her daily outfit. She loved how the jewelry looked and started wearing it to work. My little crafts gave her a lot of joy, and she received several sincere compliments from her coworkers about the beauty of my projects, though she never told anyone they were created by her son, with good reason. It was a very sticky situation in that time to mention that your child could make something that could be used by adults because people were reluctant to say anything that might be interpreted wrong. Secrecy and suspicions was ruling our lives, and my mother knew it was best to observe these rule as well.

One time, I completed a cross pendant using pear-shaped ruby-colored stones and several diamond-looking gems. It was a very attractive piece. The style and arrangement turned out absolutely perfect. I showed it to my mother and told her I thought it was one of my best pieces so far. She looked at the cross with admiration and told me it was beautiful, but I had to put it away. As a Communist Party member, she could not wear it to work or anywhere outside our home. Reluctantly, I did what my mom said.

A few weeks later, I found a nice chain in our box of keys and hung the cross on it. It was a perfect match. Deciding I didn't want such a beautiful thing to go unused, I put it around my neck and wore the crucifix myself. For a long time, no one ever saw it, even when I wore it to school.

One day, I was standing with other kids in the classroom, talking to my teacher. Suddenly, she stopped and said, "What is this?" and pointed at my shirt.

I looked down and saw that one of the buttons on my shirt had come loose, and through the opening, she could see the silverfish chain with the cross hanging on it.

She grabbed and ripped it off my neck. "Follow me!" she exclaimed in anger as we walked quickly to the principal's office. I knew then I was in real trouble.

The next day, my mother had to report to school. Our fierce official hatred toward anything related to Christianity had an opportunity to be unleashed now with its full power. We were standing in the empty classroom, and teacher was doing her job of preaching the Soviet anti-religion propaganda. As an ultimate goal to oppress the soul and will of a child, she screamed at me in attempt to receive a tearful repent with a cry for forgiveness. She didn't know that I made that cross myself and that could of cost me even much tougher punishment.

I sobbed and repeated over and over, "I will never, never do it again," and I never did. I never touched or made any jewelry projects for my mom or anybody else, but I still wore my cross every time I went to school.

That was the first time I received an unjust punishment for something not associated with my behavior, but on ideological disobedience. The cold realism of our life made its premiere introduction. I certainly did not regret what I had done, but this desolate incident left an emotional scar on my soul, big enough that I wanted to quit this fascinating craft for good. The next time I would put my hand on gems and stones would be only over thirty years later, and it would not be in Russia or to create a fashion jewelry.

Pioneers, Foreigners and Things to Collect

In order to keep Soviet children in line with the mandated political doctrines, we were all required in third grade to join the All-Union Pioneer Organization. Leaving the Octyabryonock membership behind, it was the next step in ideological obedience and education. Like many other ventures in USSR, this one also had a mandatory participation requirement, despite being officially proclaimed as an "optional choice" of children.

My opinion about our Socialistic teachings was already in opposition to what we'd been taught. Living with my mother, who was a Communist Party member, I still could not grasp the clan-like concept of our political organizations. The never-ending Lineykas, meetings, and rallies with red flags made no sense to me and contributed nothing to my soul. Not only were they boring, but they seemed annoying and vain. Even a child could see the insincerity of what was preached to us by our teachers. The constantly repeated slogans, praises to our leaders, and Communist doctrines lost their power when they were used nonsensically day after day. Sometimes, we felt the only reason for our existence was to worship our Bolshevik Party for everything we had. It was almost like going to someone's birthday and the master of the house forcing us to glorify him for the served dinner—and if we did not comply, there were consequences. The mandatory participation in what was supposed to be an optional choice became the most convincing dishonest farce of our system.

I asked my mom if I could abstain from being a Pioneer. She was very upset and angry with me for even suggesting it and started lecturing me in the same manner as our teachers did in school. My mother told me about the solidarity of all Soviet children and reminded me I should be part of it as well. I could not understand why, in order to learn mathematics, do crafts, or even ride my bike, I had to be a Pioneer. In my opinion, I could do all of that perfectly fine without been a member of some annoying organization. Still, she did not want to listen me, and I had no option in this situation. The only saving grace was that my friend Grisha had the same situation at home as well. His opinion of the mandatory membership was even worse than mine, but just like me, he lost the battle against his parents in his little fight for freedom.

Similar to our Octyabryonock official inauguration ceremony, we became the members of the All-Union Pioneer organization at a swearing-in ceremony. To make this celebration more memorable, old Communists and heroes were brought to our observance. The teacher of Yuri Gagarin personally placed red scarfs on our necks and then asked all of us to praise the new members call: "For the fight of the Communist Party causes, be ready!" and we all had to reply "Always ready!" saluting with the right hand across our forehead. Now, we were the "Young Communists, the future Comsomolets, the builders of Communism." The class was no longer a class anymore, but a Pioneer Detachment. We all had to wear the red scarfs to school, and they became a part of our mandatory uniform. Not having a scarf around our neck meant we weren't allowed to enter the school building, so kids who wanted to skip the day made sure to conveniently forget their scarfs. The rule was so often broken that it was later replaced by simply calling parents for their children's negligence to the principal's office.

Our teacher was appointed the Detachment Commander. She also selected the leaders of the several squads that formed our Detachment. It was almost a miniature military army. We had our own policies and rules, emblems, and drills. A drummer and a bugle now accompanied all marching practices. The discipline and the performance in the class became the mission and the objective of the young Pioneer's life. Any failure in these duties was classified as non-Pioneer behavior, and anyone accused of it was exposed as a bad example of our patriotic organization in front of the entire detachment. The squad leader would also be held responsible for the squad member's lack of perseverance.

Couple times a year, all Pioneers from our school met in the main building of the young Communist, the Pioneer Palace. Located at the old castle of Lord Paskevich, it was a cultural, educational, and craft center with the main purpose to emphasize the greatness of our political system.

The obligations and responsibilities of Pioneers were no longer limited to school ordinance obligations. Now, we also had to serve as active volunteers for other patriotic community observances. Countless youth brigades and clubs were established since the Bolshevik Revolution made it a goal to promote Communistic teachings to our children. The Timurovtsy Squads and Sledopyty were among the most dynamic of these coalitions. These were "volunteer" groups that functioned mainly after school hours. We had meetings with old Communists, helped retired Bolsheviks at home, and investigated the Socialistic past of our country.

One of the duties of the Pioneers and its sister after-school organizations was honoring the memorial places and monuments to the Soviet leaders and heroes. Dressed in parade uniform, kids had to stand in salute for hours next to the statues of Lenin and Revolutionary fighters. The World War II memorials and obelisks were also patrolled in the same manner and famed as preferred places to pay this kind of tribute. To me, the war heroes and those who died fighting Nazis were also always stood as true patriots of our nation.

Not becoming a Pioneer was impossible, but was it possible to be discharged or expelled from this assembly? In my memories, I do not remember anyone who ever lost their Pioneer membership. I know for a fact, however, that to receive such punishment, a true crime would have to be committed. Anyone convicted could risked not only losing their Pioneer tie, but also expulsion from school and possibly being sent to a "colony"—a prison-type youth institution. Often, teachers and even parents threatened kids with this place to stop their bad behavior or poor performance. All we heard was how horrible a place it was, and we were honestly afraid of going there.

It is chilling to me now to remember all these intense effort to fabricate a "new man" with programmed, undeniable belief in our doctrines. I feel sad for wasted time, resources of Russian government, and the lost and corrupted youth of the children. By the end of our school years, only few children who left were loyal to those teachings, and even less by the time they became adults. It is also unknown how many other dedicated followers of our Proletarian dogmas truly believed in all of its concepts. Only God knows how many of them simply realized the potential benefits of the Communist Party membership and joined the "club" to take advantage of those perceived benefits.

Pathetic Nonsense

The Soviet Union tried very hard to make us look completely different from the people living in the West. We could not see much of the other side of the Iron Curtain. However, some images of Western life still penetrated our TV reports, sports program broadcasts, and limited Hollywood "B" movies rarely played at the cinema. The fashion and lifestyle had to be completely contrary from those of our so-called "enemies". Not only did the Soviets try to make us look different, but also to think and act like a special breed of humanoids. Telling us some pathetic nonsense was helping Soviet government to shape our "proper" view on the world.

I remember we were told completely absurd exaggerations about the appearance of foreigners. For example, the long hairstyle of the hippies was supposedly a result of their inability to afford haircuts since they were unemployed and could only dream of living like we did. We were told denim jeans were a symbol of the poor class, and wearing the pants sold in our stores would be a luxury dream of any American worker. Any details of human constituency, which could be identified as Western origins, was criticized and deformed.

Even chewing gum, regarded as a symbol of Capitalism and tried by many of our people, was targeted as an alien and dangerous products. In television hockey broadcasts from overseas and some American movies, we saw the athletes and actors grinding their jaws with the classic treat, and it was difficult for our leaders to convince our people they had a shortage of food in their stores or lack of money to buy something to eat. Soviet authorities called this chewing an "animal instinct", an "ugly attribute of the Capitalist culture". Any student caught with chewing gum instantly regretted it, because on top of losing the precious indulgence, we could be the subject of a disciplinary punishment as unworthy our moral standards. For all these reasons chewing gum was never produced in the USSR, and only in 1980 did the Baltic Republics begin to manufacture this product, which rarely made it to the store shelves. The old classic Soviet slogan "Traded the Motherland for Chewing Gum" was a beloved label placed on our immigrants and dissidents.

Meeting a Foreigner

No matter how much the government criticized the so-called anti-Soviet lifestyle, our people could not get enough of it. Jeans, gum, music, American cigarettes, and other "Western poisons" were being sold on the black market at an unstoppable pace. The source of such products became a mystery to all people, as well as their almost unlimited quantities of supply. It was the underworld retail of our country, the dark side of the Soviet Union corrupted fidelity.

The nature of our closed society restricted the travel of people abroad, but also the amount of visitors coming in from other countries. Chances to see or meet citizens of other nations were extremely rare. In our town, with nothing remarkable to admire compared to Leningrad or Moscow, we could not count on a tourist invasion. The only foreigners occasionally spotted on our streets were students from countries loyal to the USSR. Considering Soviet education was much cheaper, if not completely free of charge for our "friends", young people from Africa, Asia, and Cuba began to enroll in Russian colleges. Our city education organizations were also a part of it...

One day, my grandma came home after work and told us a man from Mozambique was staying at her hotel. I had never personally met any foreigner, and it was a super rare opportunity to meet someone who came from a mysterious, distant world. I asked grandmother to take me with her to work so I could see him for myself. As always, she was kind enough to make such arrangement. When I told my friends in class what I was about to experience, the jealousy and resentment raged in their souls. Talking to someone from another country was about as exciting as meeting an outer space alien. I was excited to shake the hand of a man from such an exotic place and to be the first in our class to score this close encounter of the first kind.

On the assigned day, I rushed after school to my grandma's hotel and eagerly practiced as I ran: "Hello. My name is Yura. How are you today, sir? How do you like our city?" I was very concerned about messing up my English and sounding stupid.

The doorman at the hotel opened the doors with a salute and shouted "Welcome to the "lunch paradise"!"

The always-smoking receptionist, Olga, also greeted me with her classic line, "The professor is here!"

I stormed to the third floor, where my grandma worked as a floor manager. When she saw me, she told me to sit in the chair and wait until the African man came out of his room. The minutes ticked by very slowly. I was restless and thrilled about such an opportunity. One of the doors squeaked opened, and a tall Black man walked out of his room. I got up and marched toward him.

He had a big smile on his face, revealing bright white teeth. "Hello. My name is Roger," he said in nearly perfect Russian.

I was slightly shocked and surprised at the same time with his ability to speak our language. In brisk confusion, I shook his large hand and glazed at him. He looked totally different from us. He had dark skin, a friendly smile, and an unusual outfit.

Roger asked me about my family and school and said he had come to study geology in our university. Finally, he said, "I have something for you, and I think you are going to like it." Out of his pocket, he pulled a package of chewing gum.

My grandma was smiling, and I instantly sensed she had something to do with the surprise.

Despite the fact that I did not get a chance to show him my English, it was a very memorable evening, ending with a tasty trophy in my pocket which I shared with my pals in class. To see and talk to a person who lived so far away from us in a different world was a rare adventure I could have without leaving my own town.

What We Collect

While children in the United States collected baseball cards, comic books, and Hot Wheels, Soviet boys and girls had similar hobbies of their own. Unlike our Western contenders, however, we collected more classic items like postage stamps, pins, and numismatic coins. I was a collector and shared the hobby with a couple of my classmates. As was the case with so many other facets of our lives, the dominating factor in these hobbies were Soviet themes. Stamps and pins representing our history and places in the USSR were considered the most valuable among serious collectors. Nothing else was considered worthy for trade or valuable. Unlike other kids, I had a slightly different view on what was good to collect and what was not. I saw nothing cool about pins or stamps exhibiting our monuments, cities, and attractions. Old tractors, historical events, anniversaries, and other similar themes seemed boring and absolutely uninteresting to me. In my short participation in these hobbies, I set my own standards and rules of what was truly collectible. As a result, my small portfolio looked almost insulting compared to truly valuable compendium. It was filled with the most bizarre contents, and no one admired it or was willing to trade with me. Adventure, foreign lands, and science were my world, and to find what I really liked was not an easy task. For some reason, the postage stamps from other nations were mainly represented in our stores by Mongolian printed sets. Because all of them had Russian Cyrillic lettering, they looked like Soviet stamps, where only the Mongol Shudan sign indicated their foreign origin. The dinosaurs kit was my favorite, and despite its absolute worthlessness from a numismatic point of view, as far as I was concerned, it was the coolest Mongolian page in my stamps album. Pins were the most challenging items to collect since the Bolshevik insignia and red flags dominated most of the designs. For this very reason, I wasn't all that interested in collecting pins like some other kids I know.

People who collected coins, in my opinion, were a special breed. Usually, they were grownups or elderly men. As always, the true academic theme of this trade were Soviet coins graded by the year of mintage and condition. In my opinion, it was the most featureless form of hobby, with the exception of a few collectors who had some pages of foreign coins in their catalogs. On those coins, you could see the seals and design of different nations, and I was eager to look at them, to have a small opportunity to explore remote places and unknown-to-us worlds. Many of the coins came from the lucky sailors or those fortunate Soviets who had the unique chance to travel abroad. Some coins were very rare, particularly those of Capitalist nations. In the USSR, there was only one legal way to possess foreign currency, and that was in small collection form. To have a cash on hands from other countries was a crime and considered very dangerous offense that was closely monitored and tracked by our KGB. Unfortunately, one day I will learn how hard to deal with this aspect of our life on my own skin.

Chapter 6

The Sound that Rocked My Soul

My first experience and introduction to the rumbling sounds of the VIA was in our school. The need for a more modern way to promote propaganda and the fear over the developing of the underground rock bands forced our government to allow such form of art to exist in Soviet schools. To keep up with the new cultural craze, the USSR started production and purchased from our ideological satellites all the necessary equipment to create such music. Practically every educational institution began receiving electric guitars, amplifiers, and speakers for their own VIAs. Supply and demand were developing a gap, and innovative kids started to adapt movie projector equipment and self-fabricated guitar pickups for their stage gear.

From second grade to fourth, we attended school during later hours, the second shift. We started at two o'clock. This schedule not only allowed us to sleep longer, but also to experience things that had been unknown to us before. On a certain days, we heard booming and stomping noises coming from our school concert hall. As we passed by the entrance doors for recess, many of us tried to take a peak at our brand new school band. Usually, that entry was always closed. We would stand next to the concert hall and play on air guitars, mimicking those on stage. The privilege to play in the band was astronomical, and everyone knew it. The lucky guys who made up our school music group ranked among the most popular. Everybody knew their names, and it was considered a very cool thing to be friends with any of them.

I wondered what was involved in making such loud noise and how those guys controlled their equipment. There was little chance of getting a close look at our school band since they always kept the doors closed at their rehearsals. All band members were several years older than us, and none of them would be interested in talking to little kids. The opportunity, however, to catch a glimpse of them in action came to me with an unpredicted circumstance.

My cousin Valeriy also attended the same school. He was five years older than me and was obsessed with all kinds of electronics projects. He spent most of his free time making radio-technical devices that I found rather strange. Fortunately one of the band members was his classmate and a good friend. One day, a guy from the band asked my cousin to fix his broken amplifier. When Valeriy went to their rehearsal to do the work, I made up an excuse to see him and knocked on the concert hall door.

The doorway slightly opened, and through a small gap in the door, one of the band members asked, "What do you want?"

I told him "I need to see my cousin Valeriy."

His tone rapidly changed, and he said, "Come on in..."

Instead of going into the auditorium, I followed the guy upstairs to the small room where the rehearsal was taking place. It was a movie projecting shop filled with amplifiers, drums, and other musical equipment. There was practically no space to walk, and I had to squeeze my way through the pile of interesting objects.

The guys were smoking cigarettes, and a cloud of smoke hung in the air like a wall. I knew it was a serious violation of the school rules, and someone told me right away, "Don't tell anybody what you saw in here, kid."

My cousin was crouched over an amplifier with a soldering iron in his hands. As soon as he noticed me, he said, "What happened, Yura?"

I said, "Nothing. Mom wants to know if you are coming for a lunch on Sunday. She's going to make kholodnick soup."

"Yeah, I am coming," he replied without pulling himself away from his work.

Without further delay, I asked, "Can I watch what are you doing guys?"

"Alright," one tall guy said, "but do not touch anything." It was Dima Rutto, and everyone knew him. He played guitar in the band and was also a good friend of my cousin.

I observed the stacks of speakers and other strange equipment. On the top of one large speakers rested an electric guitar. It was the first time I had seen one up close, and I gently strummed its strings but didn't hear any sound coming from it.

The guys were busy talking about the songs and smoking cigarettes like chimneys. They noticed me putting my hands on their stuff, and someone said, "Hey! Go sit down over there before you break something. We have enough work already without you causing trouble."

Everybody laughed, and I quickly jumped into the chair that sat in the corner of the room.

"There you go. All done," my cousin said and started closing the amplifier cover.

Everybody began moving around, grabbing guitars and taking positions by the microphones.

"Alright, guys. Let's do "Lady Madonna" one more time and keep it clean," said Dima.

"One, two, three, four!" shouted the drummer, and the loud blast of music exploded in the small room.

The shocking sound was so loud that I instinctively stuck my fingers in my ears. It was overwhelming and beautiful at the same time. The guys were singing in English, strumming guitars, and playing a steady, dynamic beat. I had never heard anything like that in my life. It was a powerful, body-penetrating phenomenon. I crouched in the chair, pulling my knees to my chin and occasionally taking my fingers out of my ears to let them hear the phenomenal performance.

When they finished the song, I realized it was time for me to go. The next period had already begun, and I had to come up with a believable excuse for my tardiness. I was ran to the classroom through the empty hallway. Excitement and the fear of being caught by one of the school executives were coursing through my veins. The smell of cigarettes was noticeable on my uniform, and that caused me some worry.

I walked into the classroom and said, "I'm sorry," I said. "I lost my keys in the courtyard."

"Did you find them, Yura?" the gullible teacher asked.

"Yeah!" I replied, pulling the bundle of keys out of my pocket.

As I sat at my desk, the thrill of my experience was still pumping my heart. I turned around to my buddy Grisha and whispered, "I'm going to tell you something very, very cool after class!"

"What?" he asked curiously, jumping toward me.

"Quiet!" the teacher shouted and slammed the long ruler on her desk.

I could not wait the end of the period to tell everybody about my unique and privileged experience. When the bell rang and we all ran out of the classroom, I was surrounded by a whole bunch of guys from my class. They knew my key story was a phony alibi that only a teacher would believe. "So, what happened?" they began to quiz me.

I proceeded to tell them the story of my lucky opportunity to see our school band rehearsal. I went on and on, unfolding the tale in small details about everything I saw and heard in the movie projecting room. They looked at me as if I had just come back from visiting a spaceship. I told them everything except the fact that the musicians were smoking like locomotives. Some of my friends were noticeably jealous, while others quietly walked away, displaying little interest in my story.

That was the beginning of my curiosity about rock music. I was highly intrigued with the song they were playing and what made it sound so loud and powerful. This little event also triggered my friends' interest in such music, and it was a fascination we would share in.

Our Music Teacher

Playing in the school band was considered a great honor, but the fate of young musicians hoping to become one of the members rested in the powerful hands of our music teacher whom we called Geshka. He was a tough, older man with a somewhat unstable temper, and all music programs in our school were under his personal monopolistic control. Despite music lessons not ranking among our most regarded disciplines, he made everyone aware that his teachings were to be respected at the highest level. He had originally been a trumpet player, and it was that musical instrument he used to accompany our singing lessons once a week. Joking and behaving poorly in his class was not only risky for our academic marks, but also for our health. Geshka would not tolerate any disrespect to the musical education he provided, and he was quick to react with an angry outburst whenever any student showed the slightest lack of attention. If anyone gave him any reason to exercise his right to punish, he rapidly transformed into an uncontrollable entity. When he slowly placed his trumpet on the desk, that was the signal to his victim to get up and run. His face usually turned purple, and if he was able to catch the kid in the chase, his unlucky prey was lifted off the ground, shaken, and physically thrown at the door. It was only in his class that we might see a teacher chasing a student around the classroom. If the victim was fortunate enough to land on his feet, he had to run before Geshka used the boy's head to open the door. Ripped school uniforms and head and shoulder bruises were not uncommon in the musical genius's class.

This legendary display of intimidating discipline was well known by everybody, including other teachers, but no one even considered doing anything about it because Geshka was considered a truly valued asset of our school. Besides showing us how to read notes and displaying his dominance, he was also in charge of our marching band, an extraordinary ensemble. It was the best school marching band in our Republic. Because he led the marching band to so many victories in multiple competitions and tournaments in our city and elsewhere, Geshka was deemed untouchable as a talented orchestra conductor and get away with his abnormal personality.

Every summer, on the first day of June, as an annual ritual to celebrate the end of the educational year, the entire school marched to the largest movie theater in our city. We were the only organization that was granted the right to rent this prestigious facility, which was named after Bolshevik Kalinin. In the front of the procession always marched Geshka, with the orchestra right behind him, blasting patriotic youth tunes and Communist anthems. All traffic was stopped to yield to this fanfare and cavalcade. Our red-flagged, forcefully cheerful column bombarded streets and sidewalks, entertaining pedestrians with loud chanting, accompanied by our tireless musical team. It was almost an identical rally to the festive May Day and November Seven parades with one fundamental difference: Only one marching band took to the streets on this occasion, and that was the Geshka Band.

The success and glory of our orchestra was based more on common fear of its intimidating leader than on the band's high musical faculties. Everybody in the marching band was afraid of its conductor and regretted the day they joined, although often, it was not optional. Geshka recruited his members by walking down the aisles as we sang. If he noticed anyone with musical talent good enough to be a candidate in his band, there was no way to escape his monstrous grasp. At that moment, a boy's desire to join the band or not join the band was irrelevant. At first, the Geshka talked to his chosen candidates in a friendly way, tempting them by painting a glorious picture of the musical life. If this didn't work, the powerful Pioneer leverages of our system, along with the help of our school administration, were activated to play on the boys' carefully instilled sense of patriotic duty. The final punch to break young wills and force a student to participate in the orchestra was the promise of access to the highly regarded VIA band of which Geshka was in charge as well...

The majority of kids knew almost all of Geshka's promises were as empty as campaign promises from eager politicians—just a way to sweeten the pot to convince them to become one of his marching band musicians. We all knew that once a boy signed up for the gig, it was a one-way ticket. There was practically no chance to leave his band. Geshka had multiple options to stop anybody who tried to desert or dismantle his little musical kingdom.

All rehearsals were conducted in very harsh, extremely disciplined environment. He treated his marching band as a military division and expected everyone to obey and respect the general. Even the option of choosing the instrument to play in the orchestra did not exist. He personally appointed each student to specific instruments. In spite of the difficult conditions, the result of it was truly the best orchestra of its kind. The iron fist of Geshka propelled our school band among the top in the nation, garnering favor from all local Communists for his style of music.

I definitely did not want to play any type of horn or tuba or waste my time smacking a giant drum. Those kinds of instruments never appealed to me, and I only associated them with May Day parades or other triumphal Bolshevik celebrations. Every time Geshka listened to our voices while he was accompanying us with his trumpet, I deliberately corrupted my tone, knowing that being forced into his band would be a terrible nightmare.

There was another reason why I never liked the marching bands. The orchestras also played for much grimmer occasions - funerals. Many times during my childhood, I was awakened by the gruesome tunes of a final farewell being played to someone from our neighborhood who had died. This kind of morbid procession could last for a couple of hours, and the creepy, sad music continued until the coffin was loaded on the truck and everybody moved to the cemetery. The funeral band players always looked terrible and disheveled, as if someone told them to dress for digging graves. Their often messed-up hair and unshaved faces seemed fitting for such a depressing arrangement. I did not even want to affiliate in any way with such music bands. Even the glorious opportunity to get into the school band was not enough to convince me to want to be part of Geshka's marching orchestra.

Our school's music education program was, in many ways, a mirror image of the way our society worked. Unless we were willing to participate in a very unappealing program, we would not have the chance to taste our dreams. In our case, without surrounding to the will of a brutal tyrant, the chance of ever playing in the esteemed school VIA was less than zero.

Soviet Vacations and the Welcome of the Black Sea

For me, the time of Pioneer Camp was over, and despite occasional propositions from my mother to visit one of them in the summer, I did not even want to hear about them. My dream now was to go to the Black Sea, the best vacation destination in the USSR for summer breaks and family excursions. Observing the beauty of giant waves and an endless horizon over the turquoise sea was only possible for me from our TV screen. To see it in person was a fantasy for many children in the USSR, me included. Some of my friends had already visited the Crimea or Odessa, and some were planning to go in the future. I was hoping that one day, I'd be lucky enough to see that region and step in its clear and mysterious sea waters.

My mom worked a lot and seldom had time for breaks or vacations, and any talks about going to a relaxing retreat in the summer ended with sorry excuses about lack of money and/or time, as if a pleasurable family vacation was not even an option. As far as I knew, it would stay like that forever unless my grandma took the issue into her hands. Fortunately for me, that's exactly what she did.

In the summer of 1974, Grandma decided to take me to Sochi, the "crowned jewel" city on the Black Sea. Surrounded from one side by the peaks of the Caucasus Mountains and washed by warm sea water from another, it was the very best place for vacations in the Soviet Union. Our summer trip to Sochi was an extremely exciting excursion. The thrill of going to see the sub-tropical paradise for the first time was a true adventure for me, definitely a dream come true.

As with any vacation, the costs associated with this type of getaway depended on the level of quality we wanted and what we could afford. It all began with how we wanted to embark on our trip. Considering our limited choices in the USSR, we had a surprisingly good selection of scenarios of how to spend summer vacations. Our widely developed government system of social programs and healthcare offered us many benefits unknown to those in the West, but the availability and access to these conveniences were another dark side of the story.

Places like Sanatoriums, prophelactoriums and pansionates, were designed to accommodate people going for a vacation, particularly for health rehabilitation. It was a wonderful system with only one drawback: It was nearly impossible to get a package to go there in the summer or to be admitted into a very popular accommodation. As always, back-door deals, connections, and corruption were taking place in order to get the priceless admission into one of these places. For my family, this was not an option, so all that was left for us was to travel as dikhars ("savages"), similar to backpackers in the West. It was a simple concept of taking your luggage and traveling to the chosen destination, hoping to find a private room or a bed once we got there. Reservations and transportation arrangements did not exist in the USSR for ordinary people like us, and hotels were only for elite, high hierarchy authorities or those with "connections". All a working-class person really needed to get to the Black Sea was a train or plane ticket.

The summer season in the Soviet Union could be detected not only by the warmer weather and the rise in alcohol consumption, but also by the long lines of people standing at ticket booths. Despite all government efforts to minimize the mass exodus of people between May and September, there was a surge of voyagers during these months anyway. There were two ticket offices near our house, not far away from each other. One sold train tickets, while the other across the street sold airline tickets. There was always a bit of drama involved in getting summertime travel tickets.

The long lines to these places usually formed the night before they opened. By morning, the sleepless crowd was eager to get seats, and they guarded their places in line as if it were their own private land. Occasionally, the ticket sellers checked the names against a waiting list in a usually futile attempt to create some order. When the gates finally opened, there was a flood of chaos. As everyone rushed inside, civilized ethics were forgotten, and a brutal stampede marked the beginning of ticket sales. Often, fistfights erupted as people tried to cut in front of one another to get to the ticket agents first. Broken front windows and benches were commonplace, and torn clothing and missing shoes were considered a fair price to pay to claim the victory in the battle for tickets. Rude and arrogant intruders who wanted to get inside without waiting in line were frequent, and the justice, along with the punishment, was often served on the spot. Broken teeth and black eyes were the regular casualties in the war for travel tickets. Police were occasionally called to keep the rowdy crowd under control, and when everything was over, the lucky ones strolled quickly home to prepare for their upcoming trips.

Flying in the USSR

The opportunity to go to the Black Sea also afforded me the chance to fulfill another lifelong dream: flying on an airplane. When I made the small kit models, I always wondered how everything would look inside of one of the incredible flying machines. More than that, the flying experience was something that could not be duplicated or tried without taking a seat inside of a plane. Always the thrill seeker, the feel of soaring above the ground would certainly prove to be most intriguing for me. Up until that trip, I had only once in my life had the chance to look inside a real airplane...

It had happened a couple years earlier, when I completed few miniature models and asked my father if we could go to the airfield and take a look at the real planes. One day, he grabbed a bottle of wine, and we drove to our small city airport. When I asked him why he brought the wine along, he said he needed to give it to someone as a birthday gift. When we arrived at the airdrome, my dad told me to wait for him by the fence while he went to talk to the mechanics who were working on the airfield. In a few minutes, he returned, without the wine, and I asked him if we were going to a birthday party with those guys. "No," he replied, "they will party without us, but we are going inside the plane to check out the cockpit."

We checked out one of the most popular planes, an AN-24 flying machine that served most of our routes between big and small cities in the USSR. The name of the one and only airline, Aeroflot, was painted on the plane body and a red flag on its tail. Accompanied by one of the mechanics, we climbed the shaky metal ladder into the cabin. We passed by the rows of seats, and I peeked through the round windows outside to watch another plane take off. It was the first time I had seen the process, and I was instantly intrigued by its powerful departure. When we got into the cockpit, I was shocked to see countless instruments, switches, and knobs around the pilot seats.

My dad told me that if I continued to be a good student, I might fly such a plane someday, and I instantly replied, "Will I be able to fly anywhere I want?"

The mechanic standing next to me answered, "No. You can only go where the passengers want you to!" and laughed.

After that visit, I could not wait to experience the thrill of actual flying. Though it was more expensive to fly, the trip to Sochi by train would have taken three whole days, so flying was a better option for us. After typical routing at the ticket booth, my grandmother managed to secure a pair of seats for us on the Gomel-Donetsk-Sochi flight. Flying and going to sea would prove to be incredible experiences, almost too much excitement for me to handle. I anxiously packed my little suitcase with provisions for our upcoming trip, and then all there was to do was wait for our day of departure.

Flying in the Soviet Union at that time was considered potentially dangerous by our authorities, though this assumption had nothing to do with the safety, construction, or reliability of our planes. The government was more concerned with military and political ramifications. For this reason, taking pictures on any flight—especially of the lands and fields below—was strictly prohibited. Airports were treated in military and strategic fashion, and our spying paranoia created many overprotective rules for travelers. The other so-called danger of traveling by air was the potential for hijackings. For that reason all pilots were armed with guns which they carried openly like police. There was strict security in place, as well as tight scrutiny when it came to screening passengers before they boarded any plane. Despite all of the security measures, lack of equipment and a yearning desire for freedom led to occasional desperate incidents of airplane takeovers. Our press never discussed any such cases, but people talked about them and were painfully aware of this problem.

The worst case of this kind in the Soviet Union was the Ovechkin family tragedy. A mother and her ten children, a jazz band family, smuggled on board TU-154 hunting rifles and knives concealed in their musical instrument cases. They unpacked their hidden weapons and demanded that the crew land in London. Instead, the plane flew to a military airport, where, in a poorly executed attempt to free the passengers, ten people lost their lives. The Soviet desire to maintain complete control of Russian borders led to a massacre. In this tragedy, both sides were guilty of committing a crime against humanity; the USSR violated human rights, and the Ovechkin family used hostages as potential doors to their personal freedom. This kind of horrible incident would have not have happened in a truly free society where such desperate measures would not have to be taken by either side.

At the Soviet Sub-Tropical Paradise

Finally, the long-awaited day of our departure arrived, and it was a day full of excitement and anticipation. We took the bus to the airport, and after we arrived there, we waited to board the plane. When this process started, everybody rushed to the terminal gate, pushing each other in the fight for the first seat. The post-9/11 security measures in the United States today are almost identical to those of the Soviet Union at that time. To board, all adults had to have an ID, which in our country was the Internal Passport. Carry-on items were screened through X-ray machines, and any suspicious passenger could be subjected to a body search. Being a young boy and not really understanding the reasoning behind this procedure, I enjoyed every part of our departure. I knew that eight hours after takeoff, we would be landing on the shores of our Black Sea, and I was absolutely delighted.

Once we boarded the plane and settled into our seats, someone at the front began arguing about a situation with double bookings, and the problem escalated into full hostility between the two passengers. In the end, the airline decided that the lucky passenger who got in the seat first could keep his seat, and the other gentleman was escorted off the plane without any compensation except a promise of a replacement ticket that would be issued to him only upon availability—an unrealistic hope during the busy summer travel season. The recurrence of this problem left many people with ruined vacations and plans. In an effort to be compassionate to the victims of these types of mishaps, the crew occasionally allowed people on short flights to sit on the floor. Violating safety rules was common in these instances, and many duplicate ticket holders occupied the plane galleys as a result.

My first trip to the Black Sea remained as the most memorable in my life. Our journey on the airplane was a joyful and fascinating adventure for me. While many people felt uncomfortable and sick during the turbulence that rocked and jolted our small prop plane, I thought of it as a roller-coaster ride and enjoyed it just as much. The same kind of small round window which I had looked through on my visit with my father to the airport now displayed the beauty of puffy clouds and tiny houses sitting below on the Earth's breathtaking landscapes. But nothing was better than the takeoff and landing when the acceleration forced me into the seat and landing against the safety belt. For a kid my age, this kind of traveling was truly a joyful pleasure.

Upon arrival, my grandma decided to get a room in the nearby Sochi town of Gagra, which was not too far from the airport. After our long flight, she wanted us to take a rest and spend some of our vacation time in Gagra. I did not care where we stayed as long as we had access to the beach. It was rather easy to find a room. In contrast to our undeveloped hotel infrastructure, townspeople who were ambitious to make an extra ruble offered room and board for dikhars like us. These rooms were often as small as closets or were glassed-in porches and balconies that only provided a place to sleep. The home owners loitered around airports and train stations to find renters, so there was never a shortage of this kind of service in our resort cities.

Grandma found an elderly lady who had a tiny room for rent in her basement. As soon as we were settled, I tried to drag Grandma to the sea. I couldn't wait to see it, and despite traveling for a whole day, I was eager to step into its waters before sunset. As usual, my grandmother could not resist my persistent pleas.

We arrived at the small beach at the time when most of the crowd had already baked enough under the scorching sun and were leaving. The endless blue water stretched beyond the horizon as far as I could see, and palm trees and mountains complemented the magnificent view. I was in a rush to plunge into the water, and I ran so fast to the shore that I forgot to remove my socks. Grandma yelled a warning to me about the big waves and rocks, but I ignored her in my anticipation to enjoy my first swimming experience in the Black Sea.

After staying in small Gagra for a couple of days, we decided it would be much better to spend the rest of our vacation in much larger Sochi. It was a very well-developed city with plenty of attractions and its own lofty harbor that satisfied my lust for all things related to bodies of water. Besides the regular daily beach routine of most vacationers, after we settled in I convinced my grandma to take me to the harbor so we could see large ships and other vessels.

The boats resting in the Sochi harbor were much bigger than those in the fleet on our Sozh River. Massive cruising vessels and smaller boats were something I could look at for hours. My fascination with the nautical world was overwhelming, especially when I was close to these crafts.

In Sochi.

There was one interesting difference between the Black Sea fleet and the vessels back in my hometown: Nothing in Sochi belonged to the private owners, even a very tiny one's. I wasn't aware of that at first and asked our host family if they or anyone they knew owned a boat. They told me no one was allowed to possess a watercraft on the sea. Of course, these restrictions had a purely political motive. I did not realize it at the time, but this was because the Soviet government didn't want to take the risk of citizens having even a faint chance of crossing the Black Sea into Turkey. All our seashores were considered borders of the USSR and were treated with necessary regulations in mind, including limitations on private watercraft ownership.

It's a Black Sea

One type of sea vessel in Sochi interested me more than the others: the giant hydrofoil excursion boat. Similar types of ships cruised along our river back home, but those were much smaller in size and only traveled between villages and towns as a transportation service. The one I saw in Sochi was used as a tour boat, taking passengers on two-hour shoreline tours. I begged my grandma to take me on a ride, and she could not resist.

It was a rare gloomy day when we decided it would be the perfect time to take a short tour on the hydrofoil, the "Kometa". The boat was packed with about 100 passengers, and I could not wait to blast through the waves on the very fast "water rocket". I ran through the galley to find the most desirable seats at the front, with large windshields to provide a great view of the seascape. Everything inside the vessel reminded of the airplane cabin. There were large, comfortable seats, and the streamlined interior was very futuristic; it felt like we were on a spaceship. After departing from the harbor, we slowly began accelerating, and the gentle rocking of the waves gradually put us into a smooth gliding motion. The whole craft began to rise, and the same exhilarating sensation I had experienced during our airplane takeoff coursed through me. I was having a great time. We moved along the shore and beside the steep Caucus Mountains, which were a sight to see. Ahead of us was the black surface of water so typical for the weather, which ultimately gave the Black Sea its name.

About thirty minutes into our trip, everyone began to notice the waves rising higher and higher. The choppy water started violently breaking against the boat, splashing on the windows. The sky turned muddy gray, and the boat captain made a wide U-turn to make an early return to the harbor for safety's sake. A couple minutes later, the rain started pounding on the hull. In an instant, the joyful atmosphere inside the cabin became one of worry and concern for our safe return. The waves changed to large swells, and in addition to going very fast, we were also making twisting, rocking jumps and jerks. Many of the people began to get seasick from the commotion, and they moved to the rear of the boat, where the tossing was not quite so intense. I, on the other hand, was glued to my seat, still enjoying the ride. I had no worries, even when my small body was literally thrown in the air when we plummeted downward into the tossing sea. It was a lot of fun, at least up to the point when the captain ordered over the loudspeaker for everyone to grab a floatation device. At that point, it was not so funny.

In the rear of the boat, someone began howling in fear. My grandma took my hand and assured me everything was going to be alright. The harbor tower was already on horizon, and the captain began to maneuver the boat to enter the harbor. At this moment, the vessel started violently rocking from side to side on the rolling swells, and I became very frightened. Several people standing at the stern fell down, and panicked screams echoed through the galley. Fortunately, the harbor was only about a mile way from us, and once our captain managed to get the boat in the harbor gates, we began to stabilize. Ten minutes later, we found ourselves on the shore while the tumultuous storm rained down on Sochi with rumbling thunder and lightning. The trip was obviously the most remarkable part of my vacation, a forever reminder of nature's unpredictable power.

During my life in the USSR, I would eventually visit Sochi numerous times and in the 1980s, I journeyed to the Black Sea on my own on a trip that had nothing to do with recreation.

Staying Close to Relatives and Music

Family ties in Russia are traditionally strong, and even distant relatives maintain close relationships. As long as one can trace the genealogy and common lineage of kinsmen, connections will be permanently bonded. Historically, visits and communications with Russian relatives are common during a person's lifetime.

Unfortunately for me, my line of relatives on my father's side was completely cut off from me. I never even met my paternal grandparents. Despite that, however, we still had plenty of our nearest and dearest kin spread out across our vast country—an almost tribal unity extending from Belarus to Ukraine, Rostov on Don to rural Siberia.

My grandma kept in constant communication with relatives, some so far out on the branches of our family tree that there wasn't even a legal term for their relation. Seasonal greetings, birthdays, and anniversaries were never forgotten and were congratulated with a seemingly endless stream of postcards and letters. We shared our happiness and sorrows, life difficulties, and changes in an old-fashioned manner, relying on snail mail in a time before the existence of the Internet or even well-developed telephone services. Long letters were written, page after page describing close and personal affairs and happenings. It often took a few weeks for the long-awaited loving correspondence to be delivered. If urgent news had to be delivered, a telegram was sent, but only in three common cases. A telegram might have been a message about an arrival, such as "Coming June 11. Train # 53. Tosya." They sometimes contained a sad message such as "Ivan died. Funeral on 22nd. Garick."

The third use for telegrams was somewhat unique to our country and reflected the outdated technological level of our communication networks at a time when it was impossible to make long-distance phone calls from homes. At established telephone/telegraph facilities, two parties could be connected via a special phone line that served our entire nation. Several times during my childhood, we went there to talk to our relatives from other cities. For us at the time, it was a seemingly modern and very exciting process. To arrange such a service, a special telegram was sent by one party with something similar to the following text: "Long-distance call. Kiev. September 12. 21:30 hours", alerting the other party when to be at the telephone/telegram facility. Several phone booths with heavy wooden doors were installed in the lobby, and there was nearly always a long line of people awaiting their turns, sitting in chairs along the walls. The operator announced over the PA, "Kiev, 21:30. Cabin 6," and all the family members would rush to Booth 6 to hear their relatives, who were hundreds or thousands of kilometers away. The time was set to limited number of minutes and when it was coming to the end, you would hear the voice of operator, "Your time is up. Please finish your conversation." Very often, the call arrangements were interrupted or canceled due to connection problems or delayed by several hours. The calls seldom happened on time. It was still worth the long wait, as it allowed us an opportunity to speak to loved ones we might not see for many years. Considering its complex and expensive nature at the time, most regarded this primitive communication method as a luxury, and it was thought of as such until in-home long-distance calling became a reality in the mid 1970s.

While letters were certainly appreciated, distant and close relatives were also excited to send and receive packages, not only on New Year's, birthdays, or other holidays, but also at other times as well. Life in the Soviet Union was difficult and created a need for people to send items or receive them from loved ones in a way that would never have been necessary in the Western world. The available food supply, for instance, differed greatly between varying regions of our country. The geographical location, distance from supply centers, and agricultural possibilities determined the quality of meals people had on their tables. In one part of the nation, we had a good selection of certain produce, while those same crops were considered rare delicacies in other parts. As a result, the long-established tradition of sending food and goods across the country was practiced by most families, ours included. Usually, these heavy packages shipped in plywood boxes came as surprises. I loved to receive them and always went to the post office to help drag them home. Based on the contents of the box, it was almost possible to determine the sender without even looking at the return address. Dried fish, sunflower seeds, and seasoned food were common gifts from our relatives at Rostov on Don, while salty pork fat and homemade sausage were dispatched from our Ukrainian uncle and aunt. To return the favor, Grandma stuffed the boxes with condensed sweet milk, grains, and other goods to send back to our kin.

Because tight relationship bonds between relatives were so common in ancient Russian tradition, all celebrations of life—as well as heartbreaking tragedies and losses—were shared among family members far and wide. Skipping any ceremonial event or abstaining from participation was only acceptable with a serious and legitimate excuse.

Russian Weddings

We were once invited to the wedding of a remote nephew of my grandma's. The familial relationship to Grandma was so slim that to trace it was a tedious task of genealogical investigation. But still, my grandmother eagerly took me with her to the traditional Ukrainian wedding ceremony, which consisted of several old rituals, customs, and procedures. In our culture at that time, weddings were considered the most lavish, luxurious of all celebrations and all family members were expected to attend. Preparing for such an event in any country is a mass undertaking involving many people and services, but in Russia back then, life savings and many generations' inheritances were often sacrificed to make it a forever memorable observance. In the Soviet Union, the quality of the reception and its brilliance was judged by the level of hospitality, the richness of the food, and the variety of entertainment. It was the gathering where everyone was expected to have more than enough of everything, from dancing and meals to interaction and alcohol. Lasting anywhere from one to three days, weddings were our most intense celebrations.

We arrived in the small Ukrainian town of Bachmatch a couple days before the beginning of the festivities. It was the first wedding reception I'd been to. Despite my disinterest in all things romantic, I hoped I'd enjoy it anyway.

Soviet weddings originally encompassed traditional bride and groom routines, but the religious nuptial traditions were banned after the Bolshevik Revolution and were then only performed by a few in complete secrecy. The ancient church rituals were replaced by the formal signature exchange at the ZAGS, the Bureau of Acts and Civil Status. After the proper forms were signed and processed, the decorated taxi cab with the newly married couple inside it cruised around the city, placing flowers on the statues of Lenin and our Motherland heroes. When all the civilian necessities were completed, the reception ceremony began with earthshaking jubilee.

A huge tent was placed in the courtyard of our relatives' house, and a large U-shaped table was constructed to accommodate about 100 guests. The old tradition of "selling of the bride" to a groom marked the beginning of the party. In different regions of the USSR, this symbolic step was performed in different ways and at different points during the celebration. In the case of this wedding, the groom could not take his bride to the table until he "bought" her from "the merchants", who, for some reason, had to be two teenage boys. One of my distant cousins and I were the only two candidates suitable for this task.

As soon as the groom entered the house, he exclaimed, "So, who is here is selling the bride?!"

We came forward and told him, "We are!"

"And what is the price today on the market for something like that?!"

"Twenty rubles, sir!"

"So much?! She must be very good for that kind of money!"

"Oh, she's just fine, sir!"

"Why don't you show me what you've got?"

At this time, we ran to the bedroom, where the bride was peeking through the window at everything that was happening. We escorted her outside, one of us on each side, and presented our "merchandise" to the groom.

"She is definitely great!" said the man and gave us twenty rubles.

We each put ten rubles in our pockets, dropped her off to the groom, and ran into the house. For us, ten rubles was a lot of money. I had never had so much cash on hand before and was already thinking of how I was going to spend it when we returned back home.

At that time, the sparkling celebration began. Vodka and moonshine filled all guests' glasses, and loud toasts and clanging of glasses came one after the other, each cheering for the newlyweds and their parents to join the kissing competition. The gourmet food was piled on the tables, and at that event, no one would have ever thought our country had a food shortage of any sort. Within a couple of hours, the dancing began, accompanied by loud accordion music and kicking clouds of dust in the air. When someone started singing, others picked up on the tune and joined in, the whole crowd crooning, prancing, and roaming around to pull others into their happy throng. The whole event began to look like a giant singing and drinking contest. The chanting and rumbling celebration rocked the whole neighborhood. Curious passersby were invited to join the party, and even unknown strangers quietly joined the overjoyed chaos. The reception continued in the traditional old Russian hospitality, and in spite of social and economic difficulties, the parents of the bride and groom went to every effort to ensure that it was the happiest of all celebrations. I would forever remember that day and that wedding, a cherished province of our rich Russian culture.

To Read, or Not to Read?...

Entering fourth grade in the USSR at that time was similar to entering middle school in America. From that point on, we had a classroom teacher that served not only as a teacher in our selected discipline, but also as our permanent supervisor and mentor. Alla Vladimirovna ('Allachka' to us) was assigned to lead our class until graduation, and she was responsible for teaching us the complexities of the Russian language. She had to monitor our performance, and all discipline and communication with our parents was now her responsibility.

At that point, our literature education took another step to a new, intensified level. Russian language was a mandatory discipline in the USSR, regardless of Republic nationality. All fifteen States of our Union studied this language, and students were educated almost exclusively in Russian. The Russification of our country was an important goal of our government. Speaking in Russian was not only important, but it was also mandatory in our Socialistic economy system.

Allachka was a zealous advocate of written works such as novels and poetry. She was obsessed with reading and imposed her passion on us mercilessly. The main core of our literature education consisted of the works of Soviet writers and excerpts from Bolshevik writings. To instill a patriotic spirit in the new generation, the reading of these books was imperative.

The works of Maxim Gorky, Nikoloi Ostrovsky, and Alexander Fadeyev were studied as the pillars of the world's greatest literature. These authors dedicated their lives and talents to glorify Communism and its doctrines. It was the ultimate dream of our education system that we would follow the paths of the fictional Bolshevik heroes exalted in the canons of these authors. Reading such books was mandatory, and they made a crucial impact on my overall outlook on literature. I had no interest in reading these kinds of books and could not grasp the politically penetrated stories and boring victorious Communistic agendas. I found the works not only bothersome, but they also developed within me a dislike for literature in general. I began to associate all reading with something stupefying and authoritarian to my soul, even the adventurous stories of Jules Verne, which I had previously enjoyed. The imposing pressure of our Soviet classics polluted the joy of any of my readings. Gradually, my interest in books narrowed to technical and historical texts. The blatant practice of using narrow-minded literature as a tool to shape people's political orientation corrupted my outlook on reading for the rest of my life, and I didn't know if I would ever be able to enjoy a book again.

Listening to More Music

Inspired by the school band rehearsal tunes, I became more and more interested in popular music. All my knowledge and experience with the dominating official sources of our entertainment made it clear to me that I could not expect them to ever deliver anything in that genre. While chatting with my friends in class, I was pleasantly surprised to learn that some of the music that intrigued me was available on few Soviet records. I was determined to find out what the music was and who had any of the records on hand, and fortunately, this task was not too difficult. My buddies Grisha and Peter happened to be familiar with some of the bands because of their older brothers interest in such music. I also got in touch with my cousin, who was much older and more experienced in this field than my friends' siblings were. Before I knew it, the music I was looking for was just within reach.

7" Soviet record.

As it turned out, in an effort to turn a profit and also trying to keep our international image relatively civilized, the Soviet music industry had produced several interesting records. They featured artists who were completely foreign to us in a cultural and ideological context, including a few songs by the Beatles, Credence Clearwater Revival, Deep Purple, and the Rolling Stones. These records were released by our one and only State-owned record label, Melodija. The small 7" vinyls, usually with two songs on each side, gained enormous popularity among our youngsters, and to find them in the stores was practically impossible. It was a limited but powerful chance for our people to meet the real Western artists playing rock 'n roll.

In this case, the USSR did not feel bad for taking advantage of making an easy profit on products created by our ideological enemies. To date, it is still unknown if the records were produced in contract with the original record label, but regardless of where they came from, it was obvious that if anyone was making money off of them, it was the Soviet music industry. The strict copyright laws and business ethics of the West did not exist in the Soviet Union, and fair financial dealings with foreign artists would be the last concern of our authorities.

It was also a typical example of Soviet hypocrisy. Officially, our government never promoted or advertised these records, trying to avoid uncomfortable controversy in the public eye. Despite quietly producing the works of these artists, the authorities made sure we were never exposed to the musicians, except in very short television segments, where they were displayed as wasteful displays brought forth by the seedy Capitalistic entertainment underworld. While cash registers filled up with revenue from record sales, the official media continued to badmouth Western pop culture on TV screens and in printed publications. The most ridiculous statement ever made by our officials was that rock music was conceived deep in the basements of the CIA to undermine the ideological strength of Soviet youth. Yet all the while, they were financing their propaganda from sales of the rock music itself.

My friend Peter's family owned a stereo phonograph, a very cool, modern-looking Melodiya-101. His brother also had a small collection of a few of these "poisonous" vinyls. We occasionally stopped at his house after school and played the so-called "wild" music, changing the small records one after another. Our favorite was the Beatles "Happy Birthday." It was the craziest one, as far as we were concerned, and we played it dozens of times in a row. My pal Grisha and I pushed his stereo to the limits, cranking the volume all the way up. Peter always tried to turn the volume down, but we were relentless. While one of us held him back from reaching the stereo controls, another commenced with air guitar and lip synching. Every time we promised Peter we would be careful not to disturb or irritate his neighbors, we reenacted our miniature Woodstock hysteria again anyway.

Soviet radio/turntable Minsk R-7.

It was at that point that rock music started slowly crawling into my life. It was an ordinary interest at first, not any different from other kids and adults at that time. However, I began to feel a certain magnetism with rock 'n roll, lured by songs played so freely with such energy and power. The style and sound of the foreign bands were much better than our Soviet VIA music. Catchy melodies and aggressive tunes bursting off of the small records made our Russian bands sound like children's groups. I liked everything about it, but I had only one problem: I could not enjoy this music at home.

Our radio/phonograph, a Minsk-R7, was so old that it only played records made for steel needles. I was told playing vinyls on it would cut a hole through them, and I didn't want to risk damaging such precious commodities. All our records at home were 78s from long ago. They were thick and as heavy as the kitchen plates, but they broke very easily. None of them offered music even slightly close to what I was interested in, and to buy what I liked from the stores was simply impossible. On top of that, the radio itself was broken.

To make matters worse, my mother was not too thrilled about my piqued interest in rock 'n roll, and she was rather concerned about it. She had always liked music, but she was not too sure about my curiosity about something so unpopular amongst Communists. The testing of the waters regarding that matter conveniently came about at a family gathering...

Bringing Home the Music I Loved

One weekend, we had to go to my Aunt Valentina's party. Both her husband Igor and her son Valeriy loved to listen to all kinds of music, so, for this particular occasion, there was no shortage of sparkly rhythms and beats echoing from their house. Igor had a stereo phonograph called "Symphony", which, according to him, was the best one you could by in the USSR. Two large standing speakers blasted dancing tunes, and Igor kept bragging about the incredible sound. He attributed the phenomenal sound quality to "some kind" of tubes inside of the phonograph. He cranked the volume up and down to display the full potential of its power, and I had to admit, it did sound amazing. The bass boomed so strongly that it vibrated the floor, and loose little objects in the house rattled. Then it happened: Someone suggested, "Let's play the Beatles!" Valeriy rushed to his bedroom and returned with an album that looked very familiar to me—a miniature Soviet record containing the songs "Here Comes the Sun" and "Something."

I watched my mom's reaction when Igor placed the record on the turntable and cranked the volume up. Everybody loved the music, and my mother did not leave the room as any Communist would have when exposed to such Western blasphemy. In my eyes, it was a very good indication that she might be tolerant of rock 'n roll after all. On the way home, I started probing my mom as to what she thought about the party. She said she loved it, and when I asked her about the music, she said it was very good.

Now I was confident I could bring rock 'n roll under our roof, but there was still one problem. I knew my parents would never buy a new record player. They cost about one to three months' salary, so it was out of the question. I had to find a solution that fell within our limited budget if I wanted to have greater accessibility to this alluring type of music, and there were not too many options.

I shared this dilemma with my pal Grisha, and he was practically in the same situation. While his brother had a small portable record player, the limitation of music choices that we could play on it made his system almost useless. The only feasible choice in our situation was short-wave radio, and ultimately, it was this device that would become the symbol of our cultural freedom in the USSR.

There were no more than a dozen Soviet records released with the foreign rock 'n roll bands, and I had heard all of them too many times. I memorized them to the point of knowing every minuscule nuance, and I began to yearn for something new. However, the Melodija record label was clearly in no hurry to put out more of this kind of music. It was disheartening to think the limited dosage of the "forbidden fruit" had already been released to the public, and there were no indications that our government wanted to continue the process.

In our country, there were two types of radio broadcasting. Besides standard airwaves with different bands like in the rest of the world, we also had our own unique type—and maybe the first of its kind—cable radio. It was our official "blow horn of information" connected to every house in the nation. This Soviet innovation dated back to the first years of the new Soviet government. Desperate to deliver Bolshevik propaganda to the masses, the then-modern technology of radio played a major role in getting people to understand and accept Soviet ideas. The plan of delivering all programs by wire was an ultimate solution in this case. In every new building construction, it was mandatory that radio service lines be installed. Every old house was retrofitted to keep its residents connected to the voices of the nation so they could stay on top of our political agendas. It was a colossal task of Soviet indoctrination. All cities and remote regions received centralized broadcasts of news, political speeches, and patriotic music from Moscow and regional centers. Single-channel broadcasts went through a self-powered line, which was amplified in homes with primitive speakers and volume knobs. Radio was our ears to the world—the Soviet world. By the time I left the USSR, nothing had changed since the times of Stalin, and the variety of channels was still limited to only one, still harping on the same old Bolshevik political themes.

Expecting any other music from our "cable radio" besides folk, patriotic, or overused Soviet VIA was a fantasy. I knew if I was going to have a chance to listen to new music in the genre I was learning to love, I had to gain access to a short-wave radio. Production of these receivers, also known as transistors, was surprisingly steady. Our store shelves were always stocked with a few models, and the good ones cost about one month's salary. The production of these units had nothing to do with the effort of our government to improve our population's knowledge about the rest of the world. Many remote regions of our huge country could not be reached by the week signals of FM and AM broadcasting, so the need to deliver information to every corner of the USSR forced the industry to create what they perceived as a potentially dangerous short-wave radio option.

At that time, the most popular portable short-wave radios were the VEF-201s. Produced in Latvia, this portable transistor was our most reliable device for listening to Soviet audiophiles. The transistors delivered enough power that in the rural regions of Russia, people used them for dancing in the absence of other musical accompaniments. My friend Grisha family owned one, so we decided to surf the airwaves on our quest for interesting music. It did not take long to find several rock songs that were being broadcast from foreign nations.

I was convinced that somehow, I had to get my own transistor. Knowing my folks would not even consider buying it, I decided to take a chance and ask anyway.

"What do you need it for?" asked my mom.

"I want to listen to the English language on it to help me in school," I fibbed with a poker face.

My mother paused and replied, "No way are we going to buy such expensive item, but we can occasionally rent one for you if you need it."

It was better than nothing. The rental facility was half a block's walking distance from our house. It was a common service in our country, where many could not or did not want to buy household items like TVs, vacuums, or other electrical and daily use devices.

Located in the moldy basement of an old building called the "Communa house", the rental service always had plenty of customers. The most popular rentals besides camping gear and record players were portable radios. With the price of only fourteen copeykas per day, one ruble allowed one to enjoy the transistor for a week. This option seemed promising to me under the circumstances. At that price, about once a month, I was allowed to rent the radio. It was the beginning of a new chapter in my life, and my obsession with rock music officially began on a rented transistor.

Tuning to the "Enemies" Stations

Every week when I had my rental VEF, I could not wait to get home from school where my radio awaited me. After finishing my homework fast as I could, I'd go to the bedroom or a bathroom and sit on the floor with my transistor, cranking the tuning knobs to try to find something appealing. As soon as I found something cool, I called my buddy Grisha and told him what I found. He then turned his radio on, and we listened to the tune simultaneously, digging the wild pleasures of the music forbidden in the USSR. Usually, it was a random search without any systematic or particular stations as a target. Many times, the songs were not even played in English, but it was still fun to listen. Receiving the signals from all over the world, the wide array of nations spanning from Australia to Japan and India broadcasted pop and rock songs. Only our country was hesitant to join in. Quality was obviously low, and to understand what the DJs were saying amidst the static of a short-wave radio was an impossible feat, but not knowing who played the tunes and what the name of the song was did not bother me at all. As long as electric guitars and drums were kicking the hefty beats of rock 'n roll, it was all good to me—even if I could barely hear it.

Ultimately, during my random meandering through the shambles of short-wave kilohertz, I stumbled upon a Russian-speaking female DJ. When the song was over, she announced, "There you have it! That was Led Zeppelin with "You Shook Me", and we will close our "Concert of Popular Music" program on this note until next Thursday. See you then. Have a great day! Tamara Dombrovskaja and the Voice of America."

Right away, I called my pal and told him what I had just heard on my VEF receiver. While talking about it, we realized that all of us had already heard about this radio station at school and in the Soviet media. We were warned that our ideological enemies in the West were trying to destroy our lives with all the possible ammunition they had. The name of "Voice of America" was mentioned as the forerunner of the anti-Soviet propaganda machine barricaded in the United States. Supposedly, it was designed to broadcast lies and fabricated stories about our lives and the Soviet political system. Rock music, in my understanding, had nothing to do with that, despite that it was allegedly produced in the basements of CIA. Even if that was the case, at least the American spies played their guitars much better than our professional musicians did.

I wrote down the location of Voice of America, and the next time when we rented the radio, I tuned to it right away. The signal that day was horrible and hard to accept. It was very annoying and when my pal Grisha told me that it was our jamming signals trying to suppress that station broadcasting, I stopped blaming our Soviet radio quality for that. Strange noises and a roaring squall were situated right atop the station, so all my efforts to get the transmission without any interference were unsuccessful. Through the rumbling jam of such a tumult, I could barely hear the news report in Russian language talking about some kind of political dissidents, KGB, and arrests in Moscow. Eventually, the whole noisy clatter absorbed the station's broadcast entirely, and it felt like an intentional effort to suppress the Voice of America transmission. I was persistent, though, and kept listening, and I was able to hear someone say "pop… music concert" poking through the irritating, squealing jam. However, it was almost impossible to hear the music. After several frustrated attempts, to no avail, I grudgingly turned my radio off.

Nevertheless, the rented transistor became my once-a-month source of rock 'n roll, despite frequent poor listening quality. The half-hour program of Voice of America music program was very short, but when I was able to clearly hear its transmission, I found it very informative and exciting. The story about the bands and their music was delivered in unobtrusive, clear style by the charming voice of Tamara Dombrovskaja. Some time later, I discovered another gem on this station: a forty-five-minute production called "Dancing Program" that played every Saturday at eight fifteen p.m. It was hard to pass on that show.

Not having the radio for the most of the month, I had to go to Grisha house to tune in on his transistor to listen to my favorite programs. His parents were not very happy about our passion for this music, and listening to it over our "enemies" radio stations gave them a great deal of concern. My mom was frightened as well when she caught me tuning in to the Voice of America. Despite knowing that all I was listening to through the receiver was pop music, she warned me I would lose the privilege of renting the radio if I continued to listen to the Voice of America. I tried to argue that all I cared to hear were the rock 'n roll songs, but she was even upset about that. One time, she screamed at me, "That music is as dangerous as their lies and the misinformation about our lives that they're preaching there! I don't want to lose my job because my son insists on listening to the dirty Capitalists on the radio!"

After that, I had to promise to her I would stop listening to Voice of America music programs, and I had to play my radio at minimum volume, rapidly changing the station whenever my mom came within close proximity. Grandma, on other hand, couldn't care less what I did with that receiver. As long as my homework was done and I ate everything she fed me at lunch, I could have rock 'n roll riots at home.

I was not in total disagreement with my mom about strange information coming from the Voice of America programs, as they did speak of violations of human rights, troubles, and totalitarian ruling in our Soviet Union. Young and naive as I was, I could not clearly see any of that in my world. From the time I was very small, we were told the USSR was the best nation on

Earth, offering more freedom and democracy than anywhere else. Hearing all of these accolades every day at school, from our media, and from my own mother, I had little chance of doubting they were telling me the truth. The only part I could not understand was that if everything those in the West were saying was a bunch of lies, why would they be so concerned if people heard it? I couldn't help wondering why they went to such trouble to jam transmissions and cover up all things from the Western world if they were really just liars and enemies and a nuisance to the USSR.

Home Life, Cigars, and Fishing Drama

Life in my family was moving along without any big changes or significant events impacting our long-established routines. By this time, my mother was working at our Regional Council, office running the Department of Economical Planning. Her high level of responsibility in the job made her to work twelve to fourteen hours a day, and I only saw her in the mornings before school. Grandma always complained about how little we saw her. Not only did we suffer from limited family interaction, but her absence from the home forced many of the household burdens onto my grandmother and I. When my grandma had to work and could not take Misha to daycare, I had to fulfill her duties at home. Cleaning the house, scrubbing the floors, and even doing laundry were not unusual tasks for me. The latter of these tasks was certainly not my favorite since our washing machine was always broken, and I had to wash the clothes by hand with an old-fashioned washboard. Some of my friends had similar chores, and few of them ever earned an allowance or any special rewards for their hard work. It was considered a duty—not a heroic act—to help around the house, and it was also part of the necessary learning curve to teach us to be responsible, self-sufficient, mature adults.

Another errand young family members were often called to do was to buy groceries. I do not remember at what age I went by myself for the first time. It was not because our family was in distress or had a shortage of hands. Very often in our country, children as young as four years old would be sent to fetch necessities like bread and milk from the store—a common routine practice in the USSR. It was a way to teach good behavior from very early on. Even if kids could not count, they took their parents' money to the cashier, who was always very honest with them and only took the right amount from their little hands and gave them proper change in return. No one feared that a child might be cheated by store clerks because even though dishonesty was surprisingly common when it came to money exchange, fooling a blind person, a handicapped person, or any child was considered a sin, even for and by hardcore criminals. If anyone was cheated by stores, it was the children's parents. In addition to children being treated honestly, they were also rushed through the long checkouts without any wait.

I often had to visit the grocery for my mother and grandma on the way from school. Dragging home bags full of heavy cans and bottles and loaves of bread, along with my school books, was not always an easy task. Knowing that I always had better things to do than grocery shopping, my generous grandma often told me ignore my mother's request and she would go to the grocery herself. I always respected Grandma's kind consideration of my energetic personality, as she allowed me to delay the dull routines of adult life.

My little brother Misha was growing, and he needed more attention than when he was an infant. Fortunately, we had plenty of my olds toys, which he liked to play with around the house. The age difference between us did not lend itself to common interests, and I no longer wanted to play with blocks and pyramids, which was mainly what Misha enjoyed. On the other hand, I played with him simply because I loved the fact that I had a brother. He was a wonderful child, and unlike many other toddlers his age, he never gave us a hard time with bad behavior or a cranky personality.

In addition to being his playmate, I also had to serve in some respects like the father he had only heard about—and not necessarily good things. Once he was old enough to go outside to play in our neighborhood, I always watched him and protected him from troublemakers. I was never too shy to discipline anyone who was older than Misha and made him cry. The "street justice" in our country gave us a better understanding of good vs. evil than any injunctions and lectures ever could. I loved my little brother, and Misha knew he always had the same protection as other children who had a father to look after them.

My grandma began to talk of retiring. She had worked in the hotel for a very long time, and dealing with floating day and night shifts schedules becoming more and more difficult for her. On top of taking care of all our family members and her own older sister Dunya, she had to bear the burden of organizing all our big and small parties. She possessed the remarkable gift of being a welcoming, loving woman and always gathered around herself people who were not even close to us. She was also a wonderful cook. All her meals were not only delicious, but also unique and memorable. It was just as much a joy for her to have visitors as it was for them to stop by. She loved to see old and new friends, close and distant relatives, and she would be the first to offer to sleep on the floor, giving up her own bed to accommodate any guests who came to visit.

Even people who had to move far away stayed close to my grandmother for many years. Some of her late husband Mikhail's coworkers visited her often, even years after his death. A few of them remained our dearest friends until they're own last days. One of these was a friendly, good man named Nikolay, who had worked with old Mikhail. He always brought chocolate bars for Misha and me, and he spent hours in our house talking to grandma about our lives. For over twenty years after the death of his best pal, my grandma's husband, he continued to visit. When he passed away, grandmother cried, remembering our good old friend and the days when they were together with her husband. She was a loving woman and was also loved by countless people who were a part of her life.

Along with the delicious eats she prepared, Babushka always had something nice for visitors. To everyone's surprise, she was an extremely talented maker of our traditional "beverage" -moonshine. Making moonshine was considered one of the oldest and most perfected "arts" in Russia; however, it was also considered illegal. Nevertheless, people continued to manufacture it for couple of reasons. First, it was much cheaper to make moonshine than to buy vodka, and second, the government's attempt to squelch alcoholism left only a limited supply and of hard liquors in certain regions and stores. Love for this homespun alcoholic concoction was common in our villages. The vast availability of the required ingredients and the shortage of alcohol supply made our urban population experts in the field of moonshine production—and no one made it better than Grandma. She claimed she had very unusual recipe that produced moonshine of unmatched quality, as was evidenced by the constant compliments from our friends about its outstanding taste and absolutely clear consistency. It was not her favorite "hobby" though, and she only made it on special occasions to reduce the cost of party expenses, but when she made it, she went to great trouble to make it well.

My mom, brother Misha and I in 1974.

Unlike the standard procedure of making this product, which involved some sort of tubular complex devices, Grandma did everything right in the kitchen. With nothing more than a kind of dough, a few pans, and some boiled natural components, she accomplished this task with a low-tech approach. I could always tell when she was making it by the funky smell coming from our kitchen. When she was finished, she relied on me to do some "quality control"—though it did not involve drinking the product. She gave me a spoonful of the finished batch and let me carefully light it with a match. If it burned with a barely noticeable bluish flame, it was ready. Time after time, our friends asked for her secret recipe, and she answered, "I don't think this is something I should be proud of. There is no secret. It's just a drink." Grandma was ever humble, and she viewed herself only as a servant to make everyone else happy, even when she received so many compliments. Regardless of the occasion, our guests always left our house well treated, fed, and embraced by her hospitality—and sometimes far from sober.

"Who do you want to be?"

As is the case for any child in elementary school, I was often asked at home and in class what I wanted to be when I grew up. It is a common question asked by parents, teachers and relatives of children worldwide. The answer to this question is often somewhat wishy-washy, depending on children's constantly changing feelings, hobbies, and interests at the time. Every child has many different occupations in mind while growing up, and trying to remember them all today for many would be not an easy task. The most common answer at that age was usually an honest "I don't know" or "I'm not sure." It was not so in my case.

As a rule, the majority of real jobs adults do is totally different from what kids dream about doing when they grow up. Boys in my time typically wanted to be astronauts or pilots or dreamed of being a military officer or the captain of a mighty ship. Becoming a firefighter or a diver were common fantasies for children in those years as well. Romantic and adventurous jobs have always intrigued children. Kids dreamed of flying high in the skies or deep underwater, but if this was not possible, many would choose to follow in their parents' footsteps, especially if the parents were passionate about their jobs or if there was a longstanding history of such work in the family, creating a desire in the child to continue the family legacy. I had no such influences on me, as my dad had not lived with us long enough to inspire me in anything in life, and my mom saw nothing wrong with me working a mundane factory job.

There was not much talk in our house about me ever going to college, though this had nothing to do with finances since all education in the USSR was free to Russians, including college tuition. In fact, students were even paid small amounts for attending universities and other after-school educational institutions. The reason my mother never considered college for me was because of my obvious dislike for studies in general. I was not a horrible student, but my attention and respect to the disciplines in school were not at a promising level that would lead to college success. A very educated person herself, my mother knew I would not enjoy or be able to tolerate the difficult academic studies and standards. She had realized in my early years that it would not be a good option for me. My curiosity for mechanical and construction projects indicated to her that at the best, I would be very happy working in some kind of manufacturing or construction industry.

My personal dreams were not in line with the Proletarian approach of my mother to my destiny. As I remember clearly, besides pretending to become a pilot, train engineer, and truck driver, I had more sentimental and romantic jobs in mind. My love for nature had led me to believe working as a forest ranger would be a great career. "All I would have to do is roam around the forest to be sure everything is okay," I told myself. "I might even get a shotgun." For me, this one benefit alone made being a forest ranger an appealing option. There was, however, another occupation that intrigued me, one I thought would be even cooler.

My love for visiting the Sozh River allowed me to learn much about the river itself and the people who worked on it. While attending my Kayak Club, I often had a chance to observe the guys on a little power boats servicing on the river buoys. Used to guide all floating traffic, the triangular-looking pontoons glowed with lights that were manually turned on in the evenings to steer night boats and barges from the shallow waters. In the morning, the lights had to be turned off. The job was rather simple, and to perform their tasks, they used cool little boats to slowly dock at the buoys and do their work. They lived in tiny houses on the shore all summer and prepared river equipment throughout our long winters. Living in this small cute cottage right on the river was the most romantic lifestyle I could have dreamed about.

Cigars in the Trash

My admiration of this job was shared by my neighbor Kolya. He lived in our apartment building, and we spent a lot of time together on the river, fishing and exploring local dry docks. Despite that he was the same age as me, he still felt he was quite grown up. One of his grownup habits was smoking cigarettes. Children's addiction to tobacco in our country was common, and some kids began smoking as early as six or seven years old, though at this time, Kolya was just starting. Cigarettes in the USSR were only legal to buy for those sixteen and over, though, so Kolya had to collect cigarette butts from the streets and finish them when no adults were looking. He was often caught and received swift physical justice from his mother, but he didn't care and continued his dedication to the bad and unhealthy habit. Sometimes we went to tobacco store, where Kolya tried to score some luck and buy a pack of smokes claiming the cigarettes were for his father. Surprisingly, it often worked.

I never liked to smoke, but going to the cigarette store was actually fun for me. I was especially fascinated by the bundles and boxes of Cuban cigars. At the time when simple packs of cigarettes were often a shortage in supply, the lavish and elaborate selections of products from Fidel Castro's nation always dominated the store inventory. Excessive surplus of this product was the result of Cuban government's debt to pay the Soviet Union back for our military and industrial support, and they had nothing to offer but tobacco products.

Smoking cigars in the USSR was as rare as riding a donkey's these days. Most smokers didn't like the taste, the look, or the heavy doses of nicotine from the thick smoke. The style and culture of smoking cigars was unknown to us, and besides the fact that it was a symbol of Capitalism, it had little to no value among our smokers. The cigars, however, were used by some of our most crafty people. By the entrance to the store, piles of brand new cigars could often be found in the trash. It was not because they were defective or damaged but because people bought boxes of them at eight cents per cigar and dumped them out right after leaving the store. The precious box and the cigar ring were the only items people were interested in. Nicely decorated and elaborate trunks of these Cuban products were converted into a beautiful jewelry boxes with unique foreign lettering and logos. With a little finish on the surface and a velvet lining, they became the prime accessories on the mirror desks of our Proletarian ladies. As far as the bands that wrapped Romeo and Juliet's, Punch's, and Cohiba's, they were used to make men's jewelry. The whole ring was unwrapped and glued on a piece of thin metal sheet. It was cut out later and converted back to a round shape before being covered with the lacquer. Selling these beauties for five rubbles a piece was a good "business", and many of our gentleman's fingers were decorated with these fancy bands.

Our tobacco stores had the smell and aroma of reach quality cigars, but the always tired-looking crowd of customers, desperately trying to grab the rare packs of cheap Prima or Belomor cigarettes. I enjoyed looking at the boxes, which were decorated with strange names and symbols, filled with huge brown cigars that the people in line made fun of.

As an experiment of curiosity, my pal Kolya bought one of these stogies to taste so he could feel like a 'fat American millionaire'. It did not take long for a sales lady to be convinced that the large ring Cohiba was purchased for my friend's father. A few minutes later, the huge cigar was in Kolya's mouth. The trial did not go well, and after couple of draws, he almost passed out, dizzy to the point of barely staying on his feet. The taste of smoke from it was very sweet, though, and every time I smell that scent now, it reminds me of that, my first experience with a fine Cuban cigar.

Foolish Decision While Fishing

One of the favorite places of my friend Kolya to smoke without any fear was on our fishing trips. This was never something we had to make elaborate preparations to enjoy. All we needed to have fun on the water was our fishing rods and a few worms we dug up. Spending usually only few hours on the river was never enough, especially for us, since we loved the water so much. We practically could have lived there and been completely content to do so.

In the autumn, the weather could quickly change from gently warm to spiky cold and rainy. Golden brown and reddish burgundy colors wrapped all the trees in a beautiful tapestry, and we found fall time irresistible. It was one of the most beautiful Russian seasons, and we called it '*Babiye leto*' ("Babushka's summer"). Still, pleasant and sunny days dominated this short part of the year, and we picked a Sunday to finish the fishing season with a trip to the Borovaja, a very popular destination for picnics and outdoor excursions, located on the shore of our Sozh River. There were no villages or Kolhoz's nearby that we knew about, and the main attribute of this location was a giant complex of Pioneer Camps. On the very last day of August, all of them closed their doors until the following summer when the noisy crowds of Pioneers would awaken the sleeping forest with their mandated patriotic songs and chants.

We got on the early hydrofoil boat, and in less than an hour, disembarked with our bags and fishing gear on the shore of Borovaja. Several groups of picnickers and single fishermen were strolling along the river, trying to catch anything and enjoying the last warm days of the year. We broke a little camp, and after short breakfast, we began what was supposed to be a one-day recreation. The day went by pretty fast, and without any significantly sized fish in our possession, we simply relished the pleasant atmosphere on the river. The last boat going back to the city due to come around six o'clock, and we began to pack our ammunition and get ready for our return home. We felt bad leaving this beautiful corner of nature, knowing that it would be a year before we could return.

Being the thrill seekers we both were, the yearning for a short adventure rushed through our minds. We decided to get some feel of being on a deserted island and try our hand at sleeping in the forest like savages. I do not recall which one of us first had the idea to skip the six-o'clock boat ride and return home in the morning. Both of us were immature enough to come up with such an irresponsible and just plain stupid proposition, but regardless of who thought of it, the decision was made to make up an excuse about being late for the boat, and we began to make our sleeping shelter. Branches and tree trunks were gathered to create a sort of tepee.

We stood on the steep end of the river shore and watched the departure of the last hydrofoil, and then there was no one left but us. We began to run around in joy of complete freedom and the sensations of been true adventurers. Not long after that, the sun went to bed behind the horizon, and we had to start the fire. The last provision of food and snacks we had, we devoured with a great appetite. Even our not-so-tasty canned beef was delicious, and we wished we'd brought more of it.

Our little sleeping shelter was very cozy, with the smell of pine and freshly cut leaves. We climbed inside and began to prepare for a dark night in the wilderness. The wind began to pick up, and shortly we heard the first drops of rain knocking on our small tepee. It grew colder very quickly, and the raindrops started dripping through the branches and leaves of our makeshift shelter. The rain quickly rolled into a full-blown storm. First, lightning brightened the sky, and rumbling thunder shook the air. We covered ourselves with our backpacks and crawled around, constantly trying to find a dry spot to sit on. In half an hour, everything inside was drenched. A few branches of our roof were blown away by the wind, and the water gushed inside, rendering our shelter absolutely useless. We went outside and ran under a nearby tree for better protection than our demolished shag. Within an hour, the storm had passed through, and we were absolutely wet, cold, and devastated.

There was no chance to start the fire. We could not find our matches, but it wouldn't have mattered because the pouring rain had soaked all our firewood and tree branches. We knew we had to find dry place to sleep. Using the final bit of our flashlight power, we found a little old boat resting upside down on the beach. We peeked underneath it and found that it had well protected the sand from the rain. We were quick to roll under its hull.

Our new refuge offered us protection from the violent wind, and we tried to warm up, even though our clothes were saturated with wet sand. We both realized we had gotten ourselves in this mess, and sleeping was simply impossible. Shaken from cold and feeling lonely, we talked about how we would corroborate our story about missing the boat.

At the same time, the people at home were in a state of all-out panic because we had gone missing. The police gave our folks very little help, as they would only begin a search for us if we were missing for forty-eight hours.

Back in the forest, we crawled out from under the boat with the first morning light. Having had a little sleep and being slightly warmed, we mustered enough energy to start gathering our belongings. We found our box of matches in a plastic bag and decided to start a fire to dry our clothes, as everything was still wet and damped. We ripped the bark from pine trees and slowly started a little flame burning, throwing all we could into it to keep it going. Once we got warmer and gathered everything that was strewn everywhere from the stormy night, we cheered up. The first boat was to arrive around eight o'clock, and we sat on the beach tired and sleepy, waiting for it with great anticipation. Unfortunately, that boat never arrived.

At this moment, by the river dock, our mothers were feverishly checking the schedules of the hydrofoils going to Borovaja. All commutes during the weekdays were now postponed for the autumn schedule and would be traveling only two days a week, on Saturdays and Sundays. It was now Monday, so no boat was going to come for us.

We were seating on the shore of our Sozh river. The slow-moving river body was flat with black, gloomy water to complement our somber mood. By noon, we got very hungry, but there was still no any sign of a hydrofoil boat. In fact, there were no boats on the river at all. It felt like all life had ceased to exist and we were the only two people on the planet. Hoping to leave later in the day, we began looking for something to eat. There were absolutely nothing left from our edibles, and we went back to our fire pit to search for potato and grilled pork bacon leftovers. Digging through the pile of ashes, we found few pieces and crumbs. In spite of the sand grains and burnt ashes stuck to the food bits, our aggravated hunger convinced us to eat them. The empty beef can was filled with river water, so we boiled it and drank it to help satisfy our growling bellies.

By the time the day had started to come to an end, the boat had still not come, and we began to get very nervous. We were in the state of a complete isolation and despair. In fear for our safe return home and inevitable consequences for our Robinson Crusoe-like adventure, we strolled along the shoreline, hoping to see a hydrofoil or any boat at all that might come to our rescue. But those hopes were never fulfilled, as we saw no one. We were alone and hungry, and night was returning.

As the day came to an end, it seemed we would have to prepare for another night on the river. Practically starving at this point, we were trembling and were willing to eat just about anything we could find. It was the first time in my life that I had felt the immense wretchedness of a hungry man. A few meters away from the shore, we noticed a slowly drifting chunk of sausage, probably discarded or used by bait by some fishermen. Without a second thought, we grabbed our fishing poles and tried to pull the precious piece of meat closer to us. When we jumped in the water and grabbed it, we were pleased to find it did not look rotted; indeed, it was quite fresh. We ate it with almost animal obsession, realizing only later what we'd done.

At the same time, our parents were in the process of begging the police for help to find their missing sons, but it had not been forty-eight hours yet.

Completely exhausted from hunger and our bitter situation, we decided it was time to try and sleep and wait for tomorrow with complete uncertainty. We climbed again under the boat and shortly began sobbing. We could not blame anyone but only ourselves for our tragic state of affairs, and now we only wanted to get home alive. The darkness overtook the beach, and everything grew quiet except for the occasional lapping of waves upon the shore. We tried to fall asleep, but our growling stomachs and fear kept us awake.

Suddenly, we heard howling somewhere in the distance. While we were trying to determine if it was a dog or a wolf, the beast howled again. We had never heard a wolf howl before and were not sure what to think. It was a split-second mutual decision to run. We did not know exactly where to go, and we ran in any direction, away from where we believed the howling was coming from. Tripping over the tree roots and branches, we fled toward the Pioneer Camps, about a mile away from us. We knew the buildings were abandoned and locked up, but we hoped we could stay safely on a roof of one of them until morning. We had almost reached the first compound when through the trees we noticed a dim light. One of the little houses on the camp premises was crowned by the single vivid beacon. We looked around, and through the dark we could see the silhouettes of the camp cabins illuminated by the moon. Suddenly, the silence was ripped with the loud howling coming from right in front of us. We jumped to run back, and at this very moment, the howling changed to a bark. We heard the sound of a chain rattle echoing through the forest, and the door to the little house opened.

The man with a shotgun stepped outside and exclaimed, "Who's that?"

In half an hour we were sitting there drinking tea in the cabin of Pioneer Camp security.

"It is your lucky night, boys," said the man. "I am here only once a week, and you would have missed me if you'd come here tomorrow." He called police, and they contacted our frantic parents.

As we waited there with him, the peace and happiness for our survival soothed and relieved our minds. Nothing at that moment could have felt as good as the roof above our heads, the warm tea, the safety of the walls, and the peaceful end of our self-inflicted adventure. We slept on the floor like little babies, wrapped up warm and toasty in ram trenches.

In the morning, my mom got together with Kolya's parents and for a pricy cost hired someone with a private boat to pick us up from Borovaja. Standing by the river, we saw her coming in a green watercraft. She was standing and agitatedly scanning the shoreline. It was the end of our monumental act of childish indiscretion. The story about being late for the hydrofoil didn't matter to my mother. She was crying, happy to see us alive, ignoring the nonsense we were mumbling.

"We will never, ever do it again," we promised, crying for our forgiveness. We were forgiven, but it was the last time we ever went together fishing in our lives. It was one more lesson I learned about tough consequences for irresponsible decisions, often at a very high emotional price.

Chapter 7

My First Guitar and Underground Rock Lovers

The first time I took an electric guitar into my hands and actually understood its functionality was almost accidental.

I was trying to find something to do after finishing my homework when the doorbell rang. It was my cousin Valeriy, stopping by for lunch on the way to see his friend Dima. I asked him what they were going to do, and he said he was going to help him to fix his tape recorder, a rare and expensive device in our country. Repairs were not only costly, but also an annoying process of dealing with mending services. If you knew anyone who knew anything about them, it was much better to ask that person to help. Despite being a teenager, my cousin was well-educated in this field. Dima's parents were lucky to have him help them with their recorder problem.

The first time I had seen such an amazing machine was at my Uncle Igor's party. His brother Alick just purchased a new tape recorder then, and we all were entertained by its magical ability to record anything on thin brown tapes spooled on bobbins. Using a microphone, everybody at the party had recorded something and loved to listen to their voices coming through the speakers when they were played back. It was absolutely incredible to us at that time. A couple of other kids shouted funny noises into the microphone and nearly died from laughter when they heard their own recorded sound effects. At that time, I had examined the thin tape, trying to see anything written on it; for the life of me, I could not grasp how the tape recorder worked. The principle of magnetic recording was a true mystery not only for me, but also for many adults.

Not having anything interesting to do around the house, I asked Valeriy if I could go with him. I promised to sit quietly in the corner, and the deal was sealed.

We arrived at the Dima's family's apartment, and as promised, I sat down peacefully in the chair. The cover of the tape recorder was taken off, and they began to remove the internal components. I noticed a black electric guitar lying on the table, and I couldn't resist asking to take a look at it. There was a short pause, and Dima said, "It's heavy. This one is from school, and if you will drop it, Geshka will kill me!"

"I won't drop it," I replied almost automatically and took the guitar from the table. It was very cool. There were knobs and switches all over its thin body and on the headstock it had a logo: FORMANTA. I sat in the chair by the table and strummed the strings, forcing a barely noticeable sound.

"You have to play it with a pick," said Dima. "Also, it needs to be plugged into the amplifier, but I am using this junk at home." He smacked his tape recorder, which at that point, had few tubes pulled out of its belly.

Poking something inside of it with the soldering iron, my cousin said, "I think I found the problem."

With everything still disassembled, they took a cable and plugged one end of it into the guitar with another connected to the recorder. Dima grabbed the guitar and turned up the volume. The loud sound filled the room, and I got the real taste of its amplified voice. "Hey, its working!" he exclaimed with joy. "You want to try it, Mr. Hendrix?" he said while laughing and prodding the guitar toward me.

I didn't know who Mr. Hendrix was, but I didn't care. "You bet I do," I said, jumping from the chair and taking guitar from his hands. It was alive! All the sounds from moving my hands along the strings and clicking the switches was transforming through the recorder speaker. Not knowing how to play, I strummed the strings as best I could, and clear, brilliant notes loudly resonated through the room. It was beautiful.

Dima gave me a guitar pick and said, "Here, you need one of these."

It was a teardrop-shaped piece of plastic. He showed me how to hold it, and I rolled it gently over the strings again. This time, much brighter sound came out from the speaker, and in excitement, I did it few more times, every time playing louder and louder.

"That's enough, man," said Dima and was about to take the guitar out of my hands when my cousin said, "Hold on! Let me show him one of these tunes."

It was a simple two notes that had to be played on the first string. Pressing and releasing my left finger at the second fret was not that easy. The string was hard to press down, and after doing it several times, I already had begun to feel a little pain.

"This guitar is garbage," said Dima. "You can break your hands fighting with it, but this is the best we have."

In my opinion, it was marvelous, and I was digging it. I thought it was the coolest thing I'd ever held in my hands. The sound was coming strong, and despite having difficulty doing it right, the primitive two-note tune was coming alive in its probably worst-ever performance. I was ecstatic. My love with this instrument was practically instantaneous, and I didn't want to let the guitar leave my hands. The magical transformation of my playing through the tape recorder was incredible, and I felt thrilled by this musical instrument's capabilities. I held in my hands the worshiped and idolized item of our youth, and I was not just simply touching it, but also privileged to say I played on it. It was the first day of my new true passion that took me from that moment to the unexpected Proletarian road to Rock'n Roll.

Dreaming About Guitars

For me, from that point, the whole concept of music had totally different meaning. Not only was I intrigued by modern rhythms and popular melodies, which were starting to be more and more prevalent, but I was equally impressed by the ability of electric guitar to deliver it in such incredible form.

I went from being a passive listener of music to someone interested in performing it myself. The idea of learning how to play guitar became my biggest dream—much bigger than any old stereo or tape recorder. However, in the Soviet Union, this would be a more problematic goal than in other parts of the world. Not only were guitars very difficult to find in stores, but they were not even close in quality and standards as compared to musical instruments available in other countries. The absence of our ability to collate them to any reputable models meant the product was ignored, and the popularity of it did not grow as quickly as in other nations.

If owning a guitar at that time was not a privilege, it was at least an admired and desirable achievement in our society. It was not only a popular musical instrument, but also a symbol of modern lifestyle—and for some, a humble form of a social protest against our stubborn political system.

Possession of one, however, did not necessarily mean the owner was a guitar player. While buying a guitar, like many other popular items, was a difficult task, learning to play one was an even more challenging mission, especially in the Soviet Union. It was practically impossible to get any kind of lessons or classes to learn how to play a steel string guitar, unless you'd enroll into a music school to learn flamenco guitar. Literature, books, and any other forms of guitar education in the USSR were Stone Age at best. I could not even recall one decent book that taught chords and primitive guitar techniques. Trying to find explanation and logic in this educational vacuum was pointless considering that you could easy access a knowledge of how to play on rare ancient instruments. It's hard to believe, but the fear of rock 'n roll was the ultimate reason to keep our musicians in darkness when it came to a modern guitar education. The only option was for people to be self-taught and learn to play from one another. Several different chords were shared and learned, but the level of Soviet guitar-playing skill remained practically unexplored. With the absence of reputable sources of new techniques, our guitar players served mainly as accompanying musicians instead of features.

Life was also more pragmatic at that time, and without confident assurance of prevailing success, nothing was moved forward, including getting involved in the difficult task of obtaining guitar. To find one in the stores is another tedious journey.

New Friend with Guitar in Hand

My passion for music was growing with increasing desire to at least learn some simple guitar techniques. None of my friends or classmates had one at home. The closest person to me who owned one was my cousin, and I hoped it might help fulfill my dream of learning to play.

It was very old acoustic guitar, typical for that time, with seven tuner keys but set up with six strings. Unfortunately, it was in extremely poor condition. The frets were made of brass and were worn to the point of being completely flush with the neck. The body back was ripped off; Valeriy told me he did it to improve the sound, but it unfortunately worked the other way around. He could play couple of chords, but all my attempts to pick up anything from him proved unfruitful. Even if I thought I had learned something well, by the next time I came to see him, everything was lost from my memory, and I was back to square one. It was no fun, and I knew if I was going to master the guitar, I had to take another approach. I had to get one of my own.

Knowing how difficult to find them in our retailer's, I was very skeptical that I would ever have my own guitar until one day when I met our new neighbor Sasha. He moved to our apartment building a couple months earlier with his father, mother, sister, and grandmother. For them, it was a long-awaited dream to upgrade their miserable living conditions in the communal house, where they were all cramped into a one room for many years sharing same apartment with other families.

At that time, Sasha was headed to the sixth grade in school, which made him 'old' by my standards. Despite the two-year age difference, though, he was kind enough to interact with me and other much younger kids. The first time I talked to him was when he showed us a very nice pin with the face of a hippie on it. When he said he made it himself, I immediately considered him totally cool. Shortly thereafter, we became fast friends. Since he lived only one floor above us, it was a convenient arrangement for us to see each other practically all the time.

Very often, we played with clay, making little cars, spaceships, and American Indians figurines —the things that intrigued us most. Watching movies about so-called 'cruel white Europeans' conquering America and eliminating its native residence, was always an epic event in our cinemas. After watching these films, we played like crazy in the streets, and everybody wanted to be one of the good guys, the Indians. Homemade bows and tomahawks were created from our old fences, and no one made them better than Sasha. He had an incredible talent when it came to reproducing objects with other materials. Not only did is clay toys look like tiny realistic copies of people and cars, but he could also create true masterpieces using other more complicated materials. Once when I visited his house, he was working in the kitchen, fabricating a small knight statue from a thin sheet of metal. As he soldered all the meticulously tailored pieces together, I found it absolutely incredible to see the arms and body parts come together in his able hands. In the end, it was a true masterpiece and was displayed at the school expo. He was a very talented young craftsmen, and I always admired his skill, though this is not what I ultimately learned from him. Though I didn't know it at the time, Sasha would eventually become the man who would truly change my destiny. Without him, I wouldn't have the life I live today, and I cannot emphasize enough my appreciation for his positive impact on my fate.

Sasha could also do something better than everything above... He could play guitar, and as cool as I thought he was before I knew that, this fact placed him, in my perspective, at the highest level of respect. My longtime desire to learn how to play guitar had now moved one step closer to reality. Sasha promised to teach me all the playing techniques he knew. Once I discovered that, the only remaining obstacle was the lack of my own guitar. Understanding the difficulty of the learning process without having this instrument, I had no other option but to somehow buy one.

Soviet Guitars

For those lucky enough to purchase one, it was a memorable and rare event. They were sold in three different types: steel, classical, and electric. Steel guitars had our own original design. They mostly had seven strings in the traditional 'gypsy' style and construction. These instruments were the work horses of the younger generation. The seven-string playing technique was not only unpopular, but also hardly known to us. Everybody removed the lowest string to convert the instrument into a regular guitar with normal tune and playing style. They were cheap in quality and produced nationwide at our few outdated musical instruments factories. Despite their cosmetic and constructional flaws, steel guitars were our only truly affordable option.

The classical (flamenco) instruments were in extremely limited supply. Usually made in Bulgaria or Eastern Germany, they were much higher in quality than their Soviet-made counterparts, but they were nearly impossible to buy without any connections in the retail system. These were the only kinds of guitars recognized by our academic musical education departments and the only kind anyone would be taught to play. Classes and schools were popular and always full, and the style and orientation of the music that was taught was only classical. Blues or rock was not even regarded as a serious style and was completely ignored by our education system.

Tonika. Soviet Electric guitar. Played as bad as it looks.

The third type were the much-sought-after electric guitars. They were totally unique in every way, and the fact that they could be sold only to a government institutions made them almost a museum-quality display at our music stores. Access to one of these rare musical wonders, these treasures, was only possible at our officially organized VIA and orchestras at selected schools, colleges, and official organizations. The majority of them were made in the USSR, and they ultimately possessed the reputation of being the worst musical instruments ever produced on Earth. From aesthetic design to feel and construction, it almost seemed they were purposely designed to be hated instead of loved and played with joy. The enthusiastic youth of our country did not care much about these shortcomings, though, and were very happy to deal with them instead of only dreaming about music. The limited quantities of electric guitars from Eastern Europe were so much better by comparison to the horrible Soviet instruments and were used on a professional level. Guitars from Czechoslovakia, Eastern Germany, and Bulgaria were something that even performing paid musicians dreamed of having. The world-class instruments like Gibson, Fender, or other established brands were not only unknown to the general public, but they were not even in the sights of our top Soviet musicians.

Getting My Own Guitar

I was eleven years old, and my dream of owning my own guitar sent me on a journey to search out the precious cargo in our stores. The chances of finding one on the shelves at that time were very slim, and only persistent and periodic visits to our retailers would afford one a chance to catch one before it was gone. After a long time hunting, my perseverance paid off. Right across the Street of Victory, the small store called "Music" was selling everything from books to pianos and trumpets. There was also a section with accordions, percussions, violins, and balalaikas. Electric Guitars were only represented there with a displayed sign on Soviet electric guitars: SOLD ONLY TO THE ORGANIZATIONS. On that day, among all this array of crummy products, I saw her: a two-tone sunburst, seven-string acoustic guitar, one of only a few such models manufactured in the USSR at that time. The cost was only fourteen rubles, but that was still a lot of money for me. Despite finding the guitar, there was no assurance I could buy it.

I ran home as fast as I could and flew to our apartment on the third floor. My mom had gone on vacation for the first time in many years, and I had to promise grandma a fortune and accept all conditions in the world so she would give me the necessary funds to buy my dream. As always, she was sitting in the kitchen and with a smile listened to me as I changed promises of good behavior. I begged for her money in exchange to be a perfect boy in school and at home. The last bargain in my negotiation was the usual advanced purchase for my birthday, which was still few months away. She got up from the stool and left the kitchen. She was silent, and I did not know if I had won her over or not. I worried my dream had ended right there in our kitchen. She returned shortly holding in her hand fourteen rubles and told me with a big smile on her face "Happy birthday, you great grandson!"

I could not have been happier, and with my heart jumping from my chest, I ran back to the store, hoping my guitar was still on display. I could not even imagine the foul drama of missing the chance to buy it. Everything that was difficult to buy in the USSR (which were many things) had to be snatched without any delay as soon as they were found, and this situation was a good example. I stormed into the music store and found the guitar still situated on the wall. I felt like I had won a prize, and it truly was a birthday for me—the birthday of my new life.

It was a simple instrument with features only available on Soviet models. It had many potential problems besides its shabby cosmetic appearance. With the steel string attached, as on flamenco guitars, the bridge could be ripped off from the top. The adjustable neck angle was controlled with a single bolt driven through the heel and secured inside of the body. Adjusting the neck pitch was easy, but it was unstable and prone to cripple the alignment. With flat fingerboard and usually high action, it was not the most comfortable guitar to play. Despite all these unusual characteristics, it was still a pleasure to have it in our house, and I felt fortunate to own it. I already loved what am I getting involved in and on my guitar's headstock I scribed with the screwdriver "Rock is my life".

Without any delay, I surrendered to my friend Sasha to learn how to play it. My feelings and emotions were overwhelming just to own the guitar. Not only did I possess my own instrument, but I also had the chance to master it with Sasha's help. The failure in learning was not even an option in my case. My enthusiasm and desire kept me committed to succeed in this, and there was no way I would suffer the embarrassment of failing such a task before my friends.

Just like everybody else, I removed the seventh low string and began my learning with the first step of how to tune the guitar. We had no tuners of any kind at that time. If you could not use a tuning fork, your chances to become a musician were very slim. In many cases, one could go no further in their music study without having a properly toned ear. Sasha checked this important ability right away. After few attempts, I was able to tune the guitar with ease just by listening to the sound of one note from his. Everything indicated I should have no problem and would soon proudly call myself a guitar player. Before that happened, though, I had to go through the most difficult part of establishing my fingers' ability to play without a pain.

Anybody who is familiar with this process knows how hard it is for a beginner to press the strings down without driving them into your skin. I was impatient, and my first few days were quite painful. My desire to start playing as soon as possible pushed me to spend most of my free time with my guitar. I locked myself in the bathroom where no one would bother me, and I practiced for few hours every day. I was told that I would develop little calluses on my fingers, but after that, pressing the strings would be much easier. Not only did that not seem to be happening fast enough, but I also had to play what I thought were senseless scales going up and down along the neck. I did not like it, but it was bad idea to argue with my 'teacher'. Sasha said that when I stopped complaining about the pain, we would start playing some music together so I could learn how to play chords, and I could not wait for that time to come. He was my hero at that time, and I listened to everything he told me. I didn't want to give him any reason to give up on me. After all, my dream of learning to play guitar was taking off, and I needed him.

Obtaining the Music Through Underground Sources

As time progressed, our never-sleeping black market began to react rapidly to the growing interest in Western rock music in our country. It delivered an almost unlimited supply of anything that was produced in the genre. Vinyl records of the Beach Boys, Pink Floyd, The Who, and many other bands were flowing into our expanding community of audiophiles. As with anything else on the black market, the prices on these records were astronomical by Soviet measures. Fetching almost half an average month's salary each, they were only affordable by a limited group of hardcore rock 'n roll fanatics. As with any other attribute of Western culture such as jeans, electronics, or magazines, albums were coming at a rate and quantity too high to be imported by our limited tourists and sailors. Later discoveries proved that well-organized underground import of these records was work of our corrupted government officials, who bashed rock music all day while orchestrating the trafficking of the 'contraband' behind the scene.

Music records were not only expensive, but considered dangerous anti-Soviet propaganda. The reaction of police to any large possession of it could ultimately lead to a questioning session in the basements of the local KGB. As a rule, anybody who needed to take a record somewhere always wrapped it in a newspaper, plastic bag, or a briefcase to conceal it. Possession of such a record was highly acclaimed and considered trendy and fashionable. Walking on the street with the music wrapped a paper was considered classy. The chance of getting stopped by police in this case to inspect your wrapped item only served to add a little adventurous spice to your passing fancy vogue.

Concentration and availability of them was greatly dependent on your loop of connections, knowledge of the right people, and also the place where you lived. The most diverse and largest selection of rock music records was in our capital of Moscow. All big and small underground dealers of this product made regular visits to the capitol to bring fresh and specially requested albums. Practically any new release of your favorite artist could be purchased on the black market. The only limitation was one's budget. All people who had a chance to own these forbidden forms of art in our country were in tightly disguised groups. With the referenced protocol of new participants and associates, the fear of a conflict with our authorities kept these syndicates in complete isolation from our society. To penetrate its loop or get in contact with these people without introduction was nearly impossible.

For those who could not afford these ultimate examples of pop culture freedom, the growing availability of tape recorders was the only feasible solution. This type of equipment was coming into our lives in increasing numbers, and arrival of cassette tape recorders was practically a revolutionary gift for those who could afford them. Unfortunately, the design and quality of Soviet electronics was another enemy against rock music lovers, embodying constantly failing components and jamming cassette tapes. Despite all of that, though, it was still an intriguing and exciting way for Soviet youth to get their first tastes of rock music, and that taste developed an appetite. The ability to record practically anything you wanted allowed a little freedom to listen and share with each other music that was in short supplies or even banned.

The closer your relationship with the elite group of our audiophiles, the better the quality of your tape recording will be. As always, there were paid 'services' for those who were desperate for a clean recording of Nazareth, the Beatles, or the Rolling Stones, but most had no access to such people. For a few rubles, you could get someone to tape it for you through the underground channels.

Ordinary people made recordings from each other's rock music albums, and most of these free recordings were poor quality due to countless re-recordings. Barely recognizable voices and muffled sound were common, and instrument clarity was almost impossible.

Probably known only in the Socialistic world, another type of music sharing developed and began to gain a footing. The 'music recording kiosk' was a newly invented form of our "customer service". Located usually in the mass gathering places like bus and train stations or markets, they provided small records made on thin plastic film. Many people called them 'bones records' because the plastic film was sometimes made from medical X-ray copies.

Using primitive equipment to duplicate the songs from the records or tapes, these places provided a large list of popular Soviet music for your choice. Surprisingly, if you looked carefully enough through the list, you could always find the 'lost' or often deliberately misspelled songs of your favorite British rock bands. Written in Russian translation, the names and titles were only understood by the crowd who was 'in the know'. They were obviously unauthorized and illegal songs, yet loved by many people. The uneducated and clueless authorities rarely caught these banned tunes, and a little extra profit went into the kiosk workers' pockets.

None of these options to listen music were within my reach. My age and family financial situation did not permit me to even think about such luxuries as a record player or tape recorders. But the rental radio was not enough for me. The poor quality of the broadcasts and limited access even to those were not fulfilling my curiosity and developing love for music. Unfortunately, I had no other options. All I could do was continue to expand my music knowledge in an already established manner with the help of my friends, relatives, and an occasionally rented transistor. Any talk about purchasing a stereo or recorder was absolutely unrealistic, and I did not want to irritate my mother with such an absurd idea. I continued my radio rental routine once a month and occasionally invaded my pal Valick's house for some improvised rock concert jams accompanied by his stereo.

My situation improved a little when my cousin received a Soviet cassette tape recorder "Electronica" for his birthday. It was a flagship of our technological abilities at that time in musical equipment. With the price tag of more than one monthly salary, it was a treasured item not only for him, but also for his whole household. Because he knew a lot of guys with good connections, his collection of Western records began to grow, and every time I visited him, I did nothing but listen to music. Rock bands like Queen, Deep Purple, and Led Zeppelin were among my favorites and I dug it with joy, exploring many other artists while expanding my knowledge in rock music.

First Chords, My 'Stereo', and Sasha

As soon as I became comfortable playing guitar and the pain in my fingertips had diminished, Sasha began teaching me more advanced techniques. The tablature of basic chords was written on four pages ripped from a school notebook, providing me with all the basic and fundamental chord charts. He wrote several explanations and notes about their names and definitions, which gave me a better understanding of what each chord meant and how it should be played. They didn't look all that difficult on paper, but it was a much more difficult task to actually execute them on my guitar, and my first attempts were not all that impressive. My progress on the instrument was not going as fast as I wished, and my virtuosity at mastering the chords was not improving at desirable pace. I was struggling with it, occasionally wondering how in the world Sasha could play on my guitar with such ease when I could not even do a fraction of what he could. I was irritated and discouraged by this, having always had a general sense of control over my studies. My difficulties with the guitar were somewhat of an unexpected surprise for me. I thought part of the problem was that I had very small hands, making it difficult to grasp the neck properly. Another possible culprit in my poor progression, ironically, was my own impatience with myself. I wanted to master it right away, ignoring constant reminders from my teacher and parents that it always takes time to learn any skill, especially mastering a musical instrument. I had dreamed of becoming an expert guitar player in a week, but that didn't happen. Eventually, I accepted the fact that it would take time and diligence to get me where I wanted to be, and I had to set more realistic goals for myself.

My finger placement on the proper strings was not the most tiresome part. The problem was with the way I was holding the guitar. It was a constant battle and a physical struggle for me. I tried to adjust the neck to correct the problem, but it became somewhat of a tail-chasing ordeal; every time I resolved one issue, it only created another. The guitar was poorly made and not professionally designed, making it painful to play on, especially for beginners such as I was. There was no easy solution. The only thing that kept me going was realizing that I was not the only boy in the world that was facing such a problem. This kind of thinking helped me to stay on track. My enthusiasm was overwhelming, and it helped me to move forward, building up not only my experience, but also a level of improvement in my learning course. I kept my guitar lessons and their humble results a secret from my friends. I wanted to wait to share my achievements when there were something worth sharing.

In spite of my impatience with myself, my mom and grandma were very happy about my dedication to this new hobby. The only concern they had at that time was that it might interrupt my attention to my school studies and homework. I promised them it would not adversely affect my grades and would even help me to learn discipline and patience. Of course, I thought this was just a way to get them off my back by telling them a bunch of verbal rhetorical nonsense. I had no idea that my empty promises were the absolute truth.

Loosing Faith in School

In my mind at that time in my life, nothing was more important than learning to play my guitar well enough that I could show off to others without fear of error or ridicule. School was becoming less and less meaningful to me, and I had trouble making it a priority. My personal perspective on everything that was happening there was the same as many of my friends. Our education was becoming more oppressive, and dominating Socialistic doctrines that were constantly being pounded into our psyches were keeping kids from enjoying school at all. "I hate going school" became a common complaint, not only from kids who struggled with academics, but even from those students who had always has been good examples of exceptional performance. If any student showed an outstanding level of academic prowess, the political side of school life had to go alongside with their grades. These unfortunate brainy kids had pre-tailored futures and were destined to be involved in leadership or influential positions tied to Communist agendas and teachings. Excellent scores and superior accomplishments in school were not something I felt important, and the constant pressure to be on top, coupled with the Socialistic dogmas, was beginning to turn me off altogether. I felt I had already been taught everything I would need to know in life. In my opinion, they were just trying to occupy our minds with anything other than our own interests. I was not alone in my opinion about this, as my best friends had identical feelings about it, and that only strengthened my opinionated stance. The only thing that mattered to me – the only thing I wanted to learn – was playing my guitar.

Making Progress in Playing Guitar

Despite my slow progress, Sasha began to play some music with me. He was certain that doing so would help me develop better playing skills and gain some experience. Sasha directed me to play simple 'solo' tunes while he accompanied me by playing chords.

I never learned how to read notes since I could never quite understand how the strange written symbols could be connected to my guitar strings. They were like hieroglyphics to me. So instead, I simply played all music by ear. Sasha was a good teacher but an impatient one. He didn't hesitate to give me a hand-slapping education if I didn't play correctly, and while it may sound cruel in today's perspective, the old school technique surely helped enhance my concentration at the time.

When everything was in order, we sounded great. I slowly became very proud of our accomplishments, and it wasn't long before we moved our practice sessions out onto the street. With dozens of mature trees and little cabins where people loved to relax after work, our neighborhood looked almost like a small park. The benches where we held our repetitions became improvised attraction spots. It was an amazing and unexpectedly joyful experience. Even though I didn't think what we played had any interesting parts, our sessions drew the attention and curiosity of many our friends, as well as folks we didn't even know. We played the songs of the Paul Mariah orchestra, The Beatles, and popular Russian tunes, and people seemed fascinated to listen. As always, I plucked out the single-string solos, and I was surprised to see that our audience seemed to enjoy that part as much as (or maybe even more than) Sasha's more advanced chord accompaniments. Very soon, our improvised shows had become a rather well-known neighborhood attraction, and we had developed quite a following.

I was eleven years old, and Sasha was only thirteen when someone gave our duo a name: The Sergeants. The locals dubbed Sasha 'Sergeant' and me 'Sergeant Junior'. Playing guitar on the street at that age in the USSR was not only rare, but it was almost considered a hooligan trend by Soviet standards. There was nothing criminal in it, but the Soviet stereotype of this kind of amusement associated it with the rock 'n roll outlaw crowd. Youth who were prone to playing guitars or listening to their transistors in the late evenings often became targets of local police raids. Because the police knew most people did not agree with the limitations being put on music that was not 'Soviet approved', the police used the excuse of public disturbance to destroy or confiscate precious guitars and transistors. It was not so easy for kids to be considered shameful by most standards, but being cast as proponents of rock 'n roll was an image that stuck to us almost instantly.

It was probably not so much the skill and quality of our music as it was our young ages and the unusual style that drew curious onlookers. It wasn't long before older guys were asking us to bring our guitars outside and play popular songs. For one reason or another, they liked to laugh and drink while they listened to us, and when the beer or wine took effect, they began to sing along with us. Teenagers from our neighborhood loved us and gave us an assurance of protection from anybody who would dare to give us a hard time. It was quite intriguing to earn such respect from our peers just because we could play guitar. Guitarists at our young age were unique prodigies by Soviet measures, and we also performed music many adults never heard of. For me, all the attention was absolutely unexpected, especially because I thought we were just having fun. I had no idea we could become so famous doing something we loved.

With great dedication and patience, I mastered my chord-playing skill and strived to play as well as Sasha. It was a very interesting and exiting time. I could already pick the songs I liked using chords, and our little improvised street shows gained a much better repertoire and level of performance as I improved. Our guitars traveled everywhere we went, even to parties at Sasha's house or anywhere we were invited. I simply could not live without my instrument. I was absolutely in love with it and considered myself a dedicated guitarist for life.

By the time I turned twelve, I had an ultimate goal in mind: to play in a real band someday. I wasn't sure how it would happen or if it ever would, but one thing I did know was that I would never join the school band led by Geshka. Enjoying my own guitar was better than any dream at that time, and together with Sasha, we continued our spontaneous miniature gigs, much to the delight of local fans of "The Sergeants".

"Are we getting a new stereo, Mom?"

It was never a welcomed event in Russia when an appliance stopped working properly. Our old Minsk R-7 turntable was completely busted electronically and mechanically, so there was no way for Grandma to listen to her collection of old records, which she loved. When I began playing guitar, the rental radio was not the best choice anymore to assist me with practice because in order to pick up melodies and chords, I had to be able to play the songs repeatedly. Bearing all this in mind, the time had come to try to talk my mother into buying some new audio equipment for our house, but I knew convincing her would be no easy task.

I absolutely admired Valick's stereo system, a Melodiya-101. Having visited Valick often, I was quite familiar with the stereo's functionalities, and I loved its modern and sophisticated look. It had a built-in multi-band radio and stereophonic turntable. Two square tubular speakers gave the unit its charming sound capability, and they didn't take up much space. I knew one of these would be a perfect addition to our household, as it was the most modern technology available besides a color TV. I told my mom about my idea of purchasing a new stereo like Valick's, and the battle lines were drawn.

As always, my grandmother was willing to help. She was always an open-minded person and saw nothing wrong with living a civilized lifestyle with modern conveniences. Her influence on my mom was probably more convincing than mine, and it wasn't long before the purchase of a new Melodiya-101 phonograph was officially approved by my mother.

Now I had to find this stereo in the store. Considering that my returns from school almost always included senseless visits to the shops with my buddies, the search for this phonograph was an easy project for me. In one such trip to a department store called Univermag, I found just what I was looking for. The next day, Mom promised she would buy it at lunch and it would be waiting for me when I got home from school.

To commemorate such a great event and to share my excitement, I told my friends in class about the upcoming arrival of a brand new stereo into my life. Valick was the best candidate to help me to unpack and set up the stereo, and I was thrilled when he offered to come home with me after school. We ran home as quick as we could, eager to find a box at my house and waiting to be opened. All the way home, we could talk of nothing but music.

I had no idea what embarrassment would befall me in just a half an hour. Even the complete absence of new phonograph at home would have been less devastating than what I was doomed to encounter.

As soon as we got in the door, I excitedly asked my grandmother, "Grandma, Grandma, did Mom buy the stereo?"

She said with a happy face, "Yes. It's under the bed."

We ran to the bedroom and peeked under my old bed. I knew instantly something wasn't right. The box that was sitting there was way too small for what we were expecting to see. I pulled it out and read, 'Monophonic record player with two-band radio. Serenade-304'.

"Is this is it?" Valick asked, almost laughing.

I was in a shock and had no idea what to say. Why my mother had bought something totally different than what I had asked for was irrelevant. I only knew that I would now be the brunt of continuous jokes in school. "Yeah, this is it," I said with a poker face. I began to open the box and asked my friend to help me take the mysterious unit out, all the while trying to think of some logical explanation in my mind for this surreal embarrassing predicament.

We pulled out a horrible-looking small phonograph. It was of the poorest quality, made of cheap plastic parts. It was so hideous it would even have been an insult to display it in a poor old village house.

"You said you were going to get a stereo like mine," Valick said, confused.

Trying to come up with a believable and logical answer, I shouted back, "It was a joke! This phonograph is perfect for me and will fit right here next to my desk." I was sure he didn't believe me, but it was worth a try.

Valick had brought a test disc, and we played the small Soviet record with some Soviet songs on it. It sounded horrible, no better than our crappy wall radio with the ridiculously small speaker. To avoid further embarrassment of the delusional psychodrama, I told Valick I had to start doing my homework before mom got home. He left, and I went immediately to Grandma to see what in the world happened with the stereo we wanted to buy. She knew nothing. All we could do at that point was wait until my mother got be back from work so she could explain what happened.

As it turned out, it was my mother's lack of knowledge in electronics that had caused her to purchase and bring home such a piece of junk. She had made the mistake of asking another shopper in the store about which stereo was best. Some backward-thinking tool told her what she wanted to hear, "They're all the same," and naïve as she was, she believed him. As a result, the purchase was made based on the cheapest price tag. I now owned a piece of electronic garbage, and I looked like a fool in front of a good friend. My grandma could not believe how in the world her daughter, with such a good education in economics, could make such a foolish decision. Even she saw that the joy of listening music would be hard to extrude from this small box of electronic parts and plastic knobs.

Product returns was unheard of in the USSR, and all items were sold as-is. Even if something was taken home and then discovered to be defective, you were stuck with it. The only option consumers had was to try and take advantage of the manufacturer's warranty, but that process was more disturbing than having a root canal.

So we were stuck with the ugly little monster, but thankfully, due to its horrible quality, not for long. It may sound comical, but it was truly pleasant and remarkable day when our Serenade performed its final note, a true statement of its fine craftsmanship. Heavy smoke accompanied by an awful stench billowed out of its belly when we tried to listen some of our records. As the songs slurred and smelly clouds of smoke filled the room, it looked like some dramatic epilogue shot for a movie.

Right after it happened, the lecture in economics education was presented by my grandmother to my mom. She was seriously mad at her for wasting money on such an obvious piece of trash and for listening to the advice of some buffoon in the store instead of common sense. "You got what you paid for," she exclaimed time and time again.

The lesson had been learned, and became a new family goal to get a newer, better stereo that would be worth the money. A couple months later, I accompanied my mother to the store to serve as an advisor and inspect her shopping practices. The Melodiya-101 phonograph we bought was like a hard-earned war trophy, and our house finally had the chance to welcome the long-awaited addition to our little entertainment world.

Buying Music From Our Stores

Now I was completely equipped with all the necessary tools to grow as an amateur musician. I had my own guitar to practice and a stereo to play music and listen to radio. The new problem arose that I wanted to expand my musical awareness, but the assortment of Soviet records containing foreign and Soviet VIA recordings was very limiting. Even borrowing vinyls from my friends and a cousin was no longer helpful because I had already heard everything in our collective music collections.

Albums of Soviet bands and even Eastern European artists were the best I could hope to find in our stores. As with anything else that was in high demand in the USSR, this became a challenging mission. The inventory and genre of music represented in Soviet retail outlets only reflected government-approved selections. There was never a shortage of folk music, patriotic songs, and symphony varieties, as these were the prevailing preference of our authorities.

The only way to tell when something interesting had hit the shelves was to pay attention to when hordes of customers gathered and fights and wrestling ensued. Any civilized behavior and polite ethics would only earn you the most boring music. The barbaric, arrogant attitude and force had to be implemented if one was to get their hands on any music worth the effort. I was still too young for such battles, so the only time I could buy any good records in these situations was when I could squeeze my small body forward through the bickering, greedy crowd.

Listening my new phonograph in high quality was not only a pleasure, but also very loud. Such noisy amusement was not welcomed much by my mother, but when she wasn't home, I blasted my favorite tunes and radio broadcasts with the stereo volume all the way up. I loved the feel and energetic punch coming from the speakers. It was like having a little concert in the room, and I often played along with my guitar or trashed our books by using them as makeshift drums. Grandma periodically knocked on the door and warned me that the whole neighborhood could hear me 'studying and doing homework', and I had to scale down these recitals.

My friend and teacher Sasha was a common visitor in my house to join me in the music exploration. Listening to records and radio was not only fun, but also a truly joyful experience for him. He had no radio, turntable or any other electronics beside a black and white TV set in his house. Living in fairly simple and unsophisticated world, his parents never strived to enhance their cultural life, despite making good money working at well-paid factory jobs. They had few interests, so most of their money was spent on booze and occasional hunting and fishing excursions.

My Friend's Family and School

A lot of our neighbors used our phone, and Sasha's family often visited for this purpose. Drunken disputes and fights between his parents often forced his mother over to our house to call the police and beg them to arrest his father. She seemed to enjoy calling to tattle on him, but she always refused to let the authorities take him into custody when they arrived. Sasha visited us for shelter from these awkward and painful situations, and we frequently went out on the street with our guitars so he would not have to be involved in his parents' drama. For Sasha, music was an escape from his less-than-perfect life. He suffered a lot from these domestic disturbances, which affected his entire family. I felt sorry for him because he was left to care regularly for his little sister and grandmother while his parents were working out their own problems.

School Number # 28, which Sasha attended, also like mine had an intensive education. Music tuition was introduced there on much higher level, and students could choose their studies from a wide array of options. Musical instruments and vocal programs were offered, with the exception of guitar lessons. Unlike in my school, where the English language was a mandatory requirement, for Sasha, it was only optional to participate in music education. Nevertheless, my friend was signed up to the accordion class by his parents, and he considered his music classes as a minuscule torture. As popular as it was to play guitar in my country, it was just as unpopular to be caught playing an accordion, something considered ludicrous, particularly by the youth. It was almost an idiom of a mockery among teenagers in our country to call some one an accordion player. Sasha's parents obviously did not know or care about this, and he had to obey their will.

He had to practice his accordion at home, but playing boring music was simply not his style. I brought my guitar over, and together we played songs like "Shocking Blues," "Venus," or "Smoke on the Water" in never-heard-of accordion and guitar duets. Still, this did not help him love the accordion and only made him crave his guitar. It completely deteriorated his last drops of his effort to play the sorry instrument, and soon the accordion was under his bed and the embarrassing time of this unpopular music education was over as far as he was concerned.

Guitar Care

By the time I was twelve years old, my relationship with my guitar was already permanently bonded into a lifetime of devotion. Not only did I have that guitar in my hands practically all the time after school, but I also stood it by my bed so I could play it quietly before going to sleep. It seamed the two items I could not live without were my bicycle and guitar. I cared for both of them with my all dedicated passion. I took care of my bike by keeping it clean and maintained, as it was my main transportation for practically my whole life in the USSR, and I protected my guitar from all unwanted harms. Changing strings and doing adjustments on it became a normal and necessary procedure to keep it in playable conditions. While tweaking this instrument was simple and not a complicated task, replacing the strings was somewhat of a pain simply because it required drudging through the stores to find replacements. Yes, even guitar strings were difficult to find in our country. For this reason, we didn't only use strings until the sound quality deteriorated, but until they would break – and sometimes even beyond that by tightening two ends together with the small nail securing the nut from slipping. Sasha was very good at making sailors' knots, and that enabled strings to be usable even if they broke in the middle of the neck. For this reason, winding the entire string on the tuner shaft gave us extra length, which could be used in its repair when necessary. Since low strings were much harder to break, they served almost the whole life of our guitars unless the coiled part broke in pieces and caused severe rattles.

Because they were so hard to find, it became necessary that we not only bought strings when we needed them, but on any rare occasion when we saw them in the store. It was difficult to find individual strings, especially the first string, which was the most commonly broken. Strings were usually sold in a seven-string acoustic guitar set. Sometimes, fishing line or a transformer wire was used to replace a string if it was rendered unusable and irreparable. For anyone who had access to industrial steel wires, broken guitar strings were less of a problem.

Electric guitar strings were represented in one gauge and type of sets. Flat-wound and heavy, they were made to last and were expensive alternative in case of an emergency. These were also used when your guitar was already impossible to keep intonated due to the random and odd-looking strings. They were so thick and stout that using them on our dinky acoustic guitars might cause severe damage. Ripped off bridges were the most common problem for those who tried to test their instrument's strength or endurance with these kinds of strings. If you were going to use them, you had to be careful. I remember when I broke my first string beyond repair. I had to invent a story so I could buy this pricy set and was absolutely amazed to see how immensely tough they were. Later in life, we even bought them to use as light bass strings.

Nothing was easy for guitar players in the the USSR, and maintenance and repairs of the precious instruments were left in the hands of guitar players themselves.

"Now my pal is even cooler!"

Sasha was my good loyal friend and partner in music. We shared songs and kept our extraordinary gigs around the neighborhood alive. Very often, we were asked by older guys to play when they were bored and wanted to hear something like Alice Cooper or Black Sabbath played in funky style by little kids. Sasha could also sing, and this talent was not wasted. He knew all the lyrics to all the Russian popular songs that were major hits in the USSR, and because of that, he was often asked to sing and play. He was dedicated to his passion and had an uncompromising personality. He was not only demanding on himself, but on me as well. As any child, there were days when I did not feel like practicing or learning some new song that he had just picked up. On these days, I simply hid from him or pretended I was too busy to join him. We were such good friends that he could almost read my mind, and he would follow me around the neighborhood until I would give in and go home and get my guitar. It happened often, and I never regretted it in the end. It was always fun, and if he wanted me to learn something, he knew I was going to like it... and he was always right.

One day he was very excited and dragged me outside, promising to tell me something very cool. I wondered what it could be, because he told me to leave my guitar at home. He was absolutely on fire about it, and he said I probably wouldn't be able to keep it to myself because it was such great news. He walked around our huge courtyard for a while to find just the right spot to make his astonishing announcement. Finally, he shouted with indescribable joy, "I am going to play in our school band!!!" The guitar player's family from his school had to relocate, and it opened a spot in the band. He was the best candidate for the open position.

I was in utter disbelief for a moment, and I did not even know what to say. A surge of inexplicable joy and delighted contentment for my good friend rushed through my body. I was almost as grateful and happy as he was because my best friend was going to have the coolest experience any one of us could have only dreamed about. The news was not only for Sasha to celebrate. I knew that somehow, it would also bring more interesting changes for me as well. Just talking to him about his time with the school VIA was enough to give me a taste of what it was like to be involved with such an amazing adventure. I was sure he would not forget about me. We were the best of friends, and I knew his pride would never get in the way of our relationship. And I was not wrong about that.

The Joy of Playing, Soviet's Animosity to Rock, and the "Cage"

As soon as Sasha started his VIA rehearsals, he began educating me in basic knowledge of the band functions and equipment. The differences between bass and guitar amplifiers, microphones, and drum sets were explained to me in great detail, but visualizing it all in my mind was not so easy. Even when he tried to draw illustrations for me of what they had in their musical arsenal, and despite his best efforts to tell me what they did in rehearsals, I still wanted to see it in person.

Access to VIA practices was restricted not only for kids from other schools, but also for anybody who was not a member of the band, even within our own school. The schools were not so concerned about interference and discipline, but their desire to maintain internal security meant the restrictions were universal across the board. Among all crimes and burglaries that occurred in colleges and other learning centers, the most common items that were been stolen at that time were electric guitars and other VIA instruments. Because Sasha's school offered intensive musical education, they were better equipped than many other education faculties. For that reason, they were very selective and careful about visitors to the school, particularly anyone who came to their rehearsals. While casual visits to band practice were not possible, I still held out hope to someday see my friend play in the VIA.

Meanwhile, I could still occasionally enjoy the taste of what he was dealing with at the rehearsals. Sometimes he brought home electric guitars they used in the band, and I could not wait to see and touch them. Sasha brought home two similar guitars, the only slight difference being their shapes and the configuration of their knobs. Unlike the electric guitar I had seen at Dima's house, these instruments looked a lot nicer and were of a much better quality. Made in Czechoslovakia, the Jolana brand was one of the best available in our country. The beautiful red guitars with white pick guards were not as heavy as our Soviet instruments, and their high level of craftsmanship compare to our Soviet surrogates made them very desirable and popular among our musicians.

Sasha was not allowed to bring instruments home very often, but he told me their music teacher, Senya, was an easygoing man who was not very hard on the young VIA musicians as long they did not abuse or neglect the school's property. The band guys borrowed his nickname from Western terminology and called him 'Boss', and it perfectly reflected his personality. Apparently, from what Sasha told me, he was an interesting character who was not so intrigued by Soviet dogmas. He was a proponent of modern pop culture, and that made Sasha's participation in the band all that much more pleasant and joyful.

When Sasha was able to bring home a guitar, he brought it over to my place, and we plugged it into my old Minsk phonograph. The only function that still worked on the Minsk was the external input, and after sticking to wires into it, we could play the guitar with amazingly loud volume. Sasha had told me about the benefits of tube equipment and how much better it sounded, but I was skeptical. My old radio proved me wrong, blasting the excellent tone and sound through its eight-inch speaker. The old technology truly was a wonder from the past.

Every time I had one of those shiny electric guitars in my hands, I felt privileged and indescribably happy. They not only looked great, but were also very easy to play compared to the instrument I owned. For all I knew, I may never have the chance to own one of those amazing electric guitars, so I was forever grateful for Sasha to give me a chance to experience such good times.

Whenever I asked Sasha what they played in rehearsals, he always seemed less than euphoric about it. The folks in his band had very little knowledge of what Sasha and I played at home. The most 'progressive' music they knew were Soviet VIA hits. A couple Beatles songs were the 'hardest' pieces in their repertoire, but for some reason, they did not feel the need to expand the variety of what they play. There was intense pressure placed on school bands to only play strictly patriotic music. When Sasha told me their Boss did not care much what they were playing, I urged him to play more rock songs in their band. Sadly, even with his vast knowledge of Western tunes, Sasha could not convince his colleagues to diversify what they were playing. The Russian songs were enough for them and still made the crowds dance like crazy.

Practically every month, their school had some kind of event or celebration, accompanied by my friend's VIA. However, to go and see them playing there was also impossible. In addition to not being a student of the same school, I was also only twelve years old, too young to attend such events. Every time they had some kind of party or dance, I tried to go with my friend anyway, but I was never allowed inside, regardless of my 'connection' with one of the members. Whether it was for misbehavior or the same reasons of mine, many other kids were also banned from the parties. For us, the only option was to stay outside and listen to the band from the street.

The large concert hall was located on the second floor, so it was impossible to see what was happening from street level, but it was not a big problem for us. All what we cared about was hearing the sounds of a modern band. I could hear Sasha singing practically all the songs, and sometimes I could not believe I was fortunate enough to be one of his friends. I gathered with other curious guys below the open windows and enjoyed the loud music. The rain often dispersed our little gathering, but if I could find shelter and room under a nearby tree, I stayed and listened until the party was over. When the band stopped playing, there was a long wait before the band members started leaving the school, and while that was somewhat of a drag, I did not want to leave before I had a chance to share with my friend everything I'd heard outside. I also wanted to hear anything interesting he had to tell me about what happened at the dances. A swarm of kids always followed the band members home, and I strolled proudly behind Sasha, watching him been attacked by girls like he was some kind of rock star.

When winter came, it was more challenging to loiter around outside the dances, but there was no way I could miss the New Year's celebration at Sasha's school, the biggest celebration of the year. The dance lasted much longer, and the music was much more diverse. I put on as many warm layers of clothing as I could and joined the other misfortunate kids and teenagers outside in the snow, jogging in place to keep warm as we listened to the free music concert.

It was not so uncommon in our country for these kinds of gatherings to happen outside of concert halls and dancing events. The fascination with doing so could be easy attributed to the limited availability of organized entertainment in the USSR for teenagers and young adults. Still, even though I was not alone in my efforts, it was no substitute for real participation in the event, not to mention really playing in the band. I was dreaming about the moment of joy when I could not only step on the floor to hear the band in its full glory, but also be a part of it.

Hatred Toward Rock n' Roll

The negative Soviet opinion of rock music was very irritating, and the difficulty with obtaining information about it or records was very frustrating. I could not understand the reasoning behind it. The logic of the governmental aversion could not be explained in any sensible way, and the attempted ideological justification only created more questions than the answers for me. I could not connect the dots as to why beautiful music could be considered harmful or anti-Soviet or how they saw songs of The Beatles or Pink Floyd as dangerous and alien. Just because the music did not come from Soviet composers, it was somehow considered hazardous. Our authorities hated the music just because it was not an innovation of Communistic production. According to the principles they had been teaching us since we were small, we should have banned everything that what was invented outside of our land, including TV, radio, and even glass bottles. Wearing pants and dresses should have been outlawed as well since they were not part of the original Soviet conception. I could not understand what kind of political system we lived in where a few simple songs could destroy our foundations and "happy life". The frustration was intensified by propaganda and idiotic statements from our government about the alleged political agenda behind rock music and its authors. In some warped way, we were supposed to view John Lennon or Simon and Garfunkel as CIA employees and their music and lyrics as a strategic plan to destroy Soviet Union. Still, it was double-talk, because at the same time the Soviet authorities were labeling these artists as stained, they were quietly producing their works in the USSR to bring good profits to the government. This Utopian logic was a true torment for me. The intentional restriction of all means of Western music and influence was doing much more harm to the Soviet Union than the imaginary conspiracies they accredited to rock 'n roll. I was not the only one to have my doubts. People were asking the same questions as I was, and the plan was backfiring; the only thing being planted in Russian hearts was a genuine aversion toward our political principles and oppressive government.

My love of rock music had a profound effect on me growing up where I did because it triggered me to question and lose my belief not only in our Socialistic principles and dogmas, but also cast doubt on everything we were told by our official propaganda. Despite my young age, though, I knew that openly making any statements about personal conclusions could be harmful, so for the time being, I kept my opinions to myself – except amongst my friends and classmates, who mostly agreed with me.

"Kletka"

Every summer, at our central park - a former Paskevich palace estate, beginning in May, there was a most popular attraction for our young population in a place called "Kletka" ("the Cage") in the courtyard. Places like that were practically in every Soviet city. Surrounded by centuries-old trees, the dance floor was fenced by a wrought-iron wall that looked like a cage, ultimately giving the facility its nickname. Every night, with exception of Mondays, hundreds of teenagers and young lovers gathered at the hot spot to do some dancing. What was actually more popular, though, was to stay outside of the Kletka to listen to the onstage band. The band could still be heard from the surrounding extremities of the facility, and this allowed listeners to save money on tickets.

People from all over the town visited the Kletka, though some for other reasons than listening to music. Some went there for dates, and others went to resolve the mindless regional disputes by fist fighting.

Because of the variety of people who visited the "Cage" and the motivations behind their visit, the place was a perfect sampling for psychological observations and even scientific studies of human interactions and behaviors. Surrounding the facility, there was always a swarm of people moving in a counterclockwise direction, as if some mysterious centrifugal force was rotating the entire mass to the beat of the accompanying music. Watching this strange spinning human carousel was entertainment all its own. Standing by outside its orbit were observers, represented in an even much larger crowd of youngsters.

Every time Sasha went to see this attraction, he invited me along. At that time, he was fourteen, and I was twelve. It was not illegal to roam around the city after dark at that age, but police could stop you anyway (just in case) if they had nothing else to do. They were particularly fond of hovering around the Kletka to spy on youngsters. For this reason, going to the park and 'under Kletka' was a bit of a risk, but as far as we were concerned, that only added some adventure and spice and intrigued us all even more. Wearing his father's jacket and putting a cigarette in his mouth, Sasha could easily pass as a sixteen-year-old guy, so police would ignore him. In my case, however, there was nothing that could possibly make me look old enough, so I had to rely on pure luck and my legs to run away from any trouble.

We stayed close to the older guys from our neighborhood. Knowing who we were and respecting our Sergeants duo, they always offered us protection and a little shelter in their clan. Because of them, we were able to quietly sneak around in what we considered to be a very adult world.

In the bystanders zone at the Cage, certain rules had to be obeyed, many of them unspoken. For instance, we had to stay with the crowd from our own neighborhood, and no one was allowed to be a smart ass. Watching for cops was our biggest concern at that time, though they were not only the authorities who could take us to the police station. There were also volunteers called 'Druzhinnick' who had similar power to patrol the place. They dressed in civilian clothes but wore red bands on their right hands to indicate their power to act on behalf of authorities. Armed with just a whistle and patrolling our streets usually in threes, these guys were sometimes more irritating than cops themselves. Trying to capture a hooligan or score a serious bust, they sniffed around like dogs in search for adventure. Recruited from the Young Communists Organization, they usually hated rock music and anyone who loved it. Breaking youngsters' guitars and radios was one of their favorite assignments. The Kletka was the perfect spot for them because the music listening crowd gave them plenty of candidates to arrest or intimidate. Every time we went there, I tried be invisible and hid behind big guys as soon as police or 'Druzhinnick' appeared to be in close proximities.

The only reason we risked being around that place was to hear the playing of the band inside the "Cage". It was a very good VIA, and their skill gave us a lot of reasons to listen their performance. They ranked among our local celebrities, and playing with that band was considered a very cool gig indeed. They played there every season for many years and were practically set up for life, not only doing what they loved, but also getting paid for it. Sasha and I knew being onstage at Kletka was an impossibility, so we didn't bother dreaming about it. It was such cool job that no one would volunteer to give it up for any reason. Just to be there and listen how older guys were playing was enough for our entertainment and exploration of the music knowledge we so badly wanted to obtain. It was almost like a nightly retreat for us. After playing our own guitars at home, these trips to the city park were adventures that gave us a small feeling of being part of the musical life.

Chapter 8

Knock on the Band

My dream to play one day in some kind of band was constantly swirling in my mind, but the reality was, it seemed a dead end – at least at that time in that place. The band in my school was under the oppressive regime of Geshka, and the road into it was blocked by mandatory participation in his marching orchestra, which I wanted nothing to do with. I was too young to play in any VIA anyway. Playing around the neighborhood was my only alternative at that time, and the alluring fantasy of playing in a real band someday began to feel like a permanent deception, until...

I will never forget one warm May day when I was given the taste of this dream. Sasha had a startling revelation that sent me on an emotional roller-coaster. The school band he played in was going to be losing a bass player due to his upcoming graduation, and his spot would be vacant the first of September. "You can join our band!," my friend told me in a most intriguing voice.

I thought I was dreaming and could not even move for a moment, completely overwhelmed by shock and euphoria.

"There is only one problem," he said. "You have to be a student at our school."

And just like that, the dream was over. There was no way I could change schools. It wasn't that I had any feelings for School #10, which I attended, but I knew that convincing my mom that I had to be transferred would be absolutely impossible. School transfers were rare and almost never happened unless it was because a family relocation. It was required that a student lived within a certain proximity of their school district, but going to Sasha's school would not violate this regulation. Regardless of that, I knew telling my mom "I want to change schools so I can play in the band" would sound like a clumsy joke. I knew she would not even listen to me and worse, I worried she might start thinking my guitar playing was having a negative impact on my education.

Despite my strong pessimism, though, I approached her with my proposition. My skepticism was quickly confirmed. Not only she did not even finish listening to me, she also said that I should never repeat my ridiculous request again. I had to come to terms with the fact that the incredible experience of playing in a school VIA was probably nothing more than a fantasy, a romantic dream that would never come true for me.

While I wasn't one to give up so easily, I didn't know what to do and was looking for some kind of solution in this case. Trying to convince my mom to transfer me to another school was much harder than convincing her to buy a new stereo for our house. Even that required the old phonograph to quit working to make her give in and buy a new one. This time, I was certain that even if my school burned to the ground, she would still make me to go there and continue my studies on its ashes.

I knew that such a drastic change would require drastic reasons, and playing in the band seemed like a childish reason to my mother. After all, she considered my obsession with guitar a temporary hobby. She knew that becoming a professional musician in the USSR would require more credentials than playing in some school band. She was convinced that learning to play the guitar would not be as valuable as learning the Lenin's teachings. As all mothers do, she wanted great things for me, and she imagined me going into my life after graduation with my guitar stuffed in a box of old childhood toys. She never saw it as a tool I might use to support myself, and just like others in the older generation, she considered playing in a VIA a less promising venture to positively effect one's future destiny than collecting post stamps. In their opinion, a 'real' job would require a college degree or some time at trade school, not wasting time on rock 'n roll. My mom was like so many others in our society when it came to her tastes, ideas, and stereotypes. I had nothing in my arsenal to win this battle with her, so I began to lose hope of ever getting my foot in the door of Sasha's school or their band room.

ПОЧЕТНАЯ ГРАМОТА

One of my mom's many Awards for hard work.

While I was practically defeated at home with my proposition, I still strongly desired to get an inside look at Sasha's school band. We decided Sasha would practice a couple songs at home with me so I could at least try out as a potential band member at one of their rehearsals. Our plan was not let the band teacher know that there was a less-than-zero chance that my mother would relocate me to his school. We just wanted to see if I would even be accepted into the band, and I knew in advance that regardless of the outcome, I would love everything about the opportunity to get an inside peek at how the band worked, and I could not wait for that day to come.

We used my guitar to practice a couple of Russian popular tunes that I could play for my audition, until Sasha brought the bass guitar home from school one day so I could get a real feel for it. I had never in my life played a bass guitar. In fact, I had never even held one in my hands. All I knew was that it had four strings, and it was larger than a regular electric guitar. The one Sasha brought home was a huge semi-hollow body bass electric guitar made in Eastern Germany. It already showed some signs of age and extensive use, but the old Musima instrument was built to last – or at least it looked like it to me. Everything was big on it, from its fat strings to its length and body shape. When I hung it on my shoulder, it felt like an upright bass suspended on my little body.

After several attempts to move around the room and pretend I was onstage, I got the taste of it and started plucking my part. It was a very awkward and unusual feeling. Compared to my acoustic guitar that I was used to, this bass felt like a giant monster. Everything changed, though, as soon as we plugged it into my old Minsk-R7 phonograph. The low, deep sound filled up the room. The powerful, dominating resonance was so overwhelming that I couldn't even hear Sasha's acoustic guitar. He turned my volume down so we could have a more balanced, productive rehearsal, and it was an unusual jam. Despite my uneasy feelings about the behemoth bass, I grooved around, playing the right notes and enjoying what I could at that time. Still, though, it was bittersweet; I knew that even if Sasha's Boss loved my playing skill, I would never get a gig without admitting into that school. Considering that it would be my first and last chance to play in their band, I wanted to get the most out of every minute of it.

The Audition

My audition was scheduled, and in anticipation of the most unprecedented episode of my life, I felt much like an astronaut awaiting his first launch into outer space. The only difference was that my fame and glory wouldn't be as noticeable. I was nervous about my first liftoff since I'd never played together with the band before, and the last thing I wanted to suffer was a 'crash landing'. On other hand, I did not expect anything more from this event other than a chance to play only once. Knowing that falling flat on my face onstage might put an end to my frustration about being unable to play with the band in the end helped alleviate some of my worries, as anxiety as it was. Really, I didn't have anything to lose but a chance I wouldn't have in the first place.

On the walk to Sasha's school the day of my big gig, he kept reminding me to watch him and stay in the right rhythm. "No matter what, do not stop playing," he lectured as we walked into the school. "Stay calm and listen to everybody. I brought you here and put in a good word for you, so don't let me down," he coached as we ascended the school's stairs.

On the second floor, Boss was giving his students a trumpet lesson in the small classroom. Sasha knocked on the door, and after short conversation with him, we began moving all the equipment into a concert hall from a locker.

Other band member Andrew showed up, and after short introduction, we began setting up all the gear on the stage. Everything looked old to me except for two giant speakers of a "Harmony" amp and the electric guitars. We hooked up several amplifiers, and Sasha was showed me how to connect everything. He acted like a true leader in his band. With swirling cables on the floor and all the equipment arranged toward the large ballroom, the stage came to life when amplifiers were turned on.

The drummer, Andrew, finished setting up his drum kit, and in spite of the fact that it looked very shabby, he made amazing sound from it. A tall girl named Lena, the keyboard player, came last. The giant black grand piano she used was completely personalized by generations of school kids, covered with graffiti and etchings consisting of students' names, slogans, and all kind of profanities.

Semyon, a.k.a. Boss, then came onstage. He was a short man with black hair and was dressed in a nice suit. I could tell right off that he had a totally aristocratic personality. He lit a cigarette and said, "So, what we got today?"

"This is Yura. He wants to be our bass player next year," Sasha said, pointing at me.

"Have you ever played before?" Semyon asked me blowing cloud of smoke into the air.

Before I could open my big mouth and blurt out that it was the first time I had been onstage or played with the band, Sasha shouted, "Oh yeah! He plays a lot. He can show you now what he can do with the bass."

I knew at that point I needed to correct my friend and explain that my performing career was limited to wiggling around our neighborhood on guitar and playing at home with Sasha, but the bass was already in my hands, and everybody was waiting to see what I could do.

Boss had moved to the middle of the hall and shouted, "What do you know, Yura?"

"How about 'Let it be'?" I shouted back.

"Let's roll," he said. "One, two, three, four!"

Elena began the piano part, and its amplified sound charged the entire ballroom. Sasha began singing into a microphone, and when we all came together, the music poured loudly from the speakers, shaking the stage floor. It was a heavenly sound, surrounding me from all directions. Guitar, drums and all the band were rocking like a dream. I had to balance between enjoying our performance and playing the right notes. The experience was overwhelming, and realizing that I was a part of the sensation only elevated my enthusiasm. I did not play a single wrong note, and in my opinion, the whole performance was incredible.

"Not bad, not bad," said Semyon when we finished. "Now how about something a little faster?"

Sasha again interrupted me before I could answer. "We can do the 'Shoemaker'."

The song was a popular Russian tune we had practiced for the gig, but it was not one of my favorites. This time, Lena sang. As soon as we started, I realized I was losing my track and was playing all over the place. Sasha was staring at me, somewhat unimpressed, so I decided to follow his advice and just pretend I knew what I was doing, even though the notes I was playing weren't right for the song.

"What was that?" Boss asked me when we were finally finished.

"I was improvising," I said without hesitation, hoping a joke would lighten the tension a little.

To my surprise, Semyon said, "It was good. I liked it!" as he walked onto the stage. I did not know if he was being truthful or sarcastic, but my gut was telling me that even a deaf could hear how bad I had been flailing around during the performance like a real amateur. I couldn't believe it when he continued, "Well, if you come to our school next year, you're welcome to join our band."

While it was very kind of him, the words couldn't have hurt me more. While it was something I'd always hoped to hear and I was completely flattered, his statement felt like a knife pierced into my heart. The joy I had experienced just moments earlier was replaced instantly with the sad realization that my transfer to his school was not even a subject for discussion at home, and there was no way I could join the band without that transfer. As the rehearsal continued, I sat in the corner to listen as they played. The happiness I saw in them as they played was somewhat excruciating for me, because I knew that I had no hope of joining them.

I knew it would be difficult, but I didn't realize that the one-time deal to play in the band would be so impossible to accept. The thrilling experience of been onstage and becoming part of the music creation had an almost instantly addictive impact on me. I was hypnotized by the whole process, from the setting up equipment to tuning and preparing for the play. The evolving process from assembling large and small speakers, connecting wires, and hooking up the gear transformed at the end into wonderful music, played by few enthusiastic guys, and I was among them... but only for a moment. I felt like someone who had purchased a winning lottery ticket and then lost it, and now I had to go back to my normal life with my rock band dreams crushed. Truth be told, I was almost angry that I had even gone to the rehearsal, and in that crushing moment, all I wanted to do was go home and ride my bike. As much as I loved music, in that moment of shattered dreams, the melodies only mocked me and left me feeling empty and hopeless.

In Deep Forest

Going back to normal life after my band audition was not so easy. Sasha was just as upset about my situation as I was, and he even wanted to talk to my mom about it, but he didn't want to risk his good relationship with my family by upsetting her uncompromising, stubborn,

Communistic personality. Despite the fact that my transfer to Sasha's school was not even a subject for discussion, I felt satisfied that I had at least been invited to be a member of the band.

For a couple of weeks, I did not even look at my guitar. As the school year came to an end, I became sad as I pondered returning to the same school again the following year. One day while thinking about this, I took my guitar and started playing. I realized that while I had no chance to be a VIA member, I could still play as I used to and no one could take that away from me. My guitar had become a permanent friend, a companion for life; it was not just a fad or some temporary amusement for me. After my brief hiatus away from it, my guitar sounded so good that I ran to Sasha's house with it to practice the last songs we had learned.

When I got to Sasha's place, he had just returned home. He told me he was going to be attending a summer camp of what he called "work and leisure." As he told me stories about the romantic life they would experience living in the tents and all the fun they would have in spite of their "light-duty working activities," I couldn't help but think back to my days at Pioneer Camp. I asked him if he really wanted to go or if his parents were simply trying to get rid of him for the summer.

Unlike Pioneer Camp, Sasha's camping trip had nothing to do with the government. It was a purely a school initiative to let kids see what it was like to live in the wilderness without access to civilization. There would be no Lineykas, no marching recitals with drums, and no Communist praising circus involved. Everything would be laid back and relaxed, and the only goals were to cook on an open fire and sleep in tents for a month and do once in a while "labor education".

After Sasha explained all of this to me, it sounded incredible, and I wanted to go with him. I was afraid of the answer, but I asked him, "Do I need to be enrolled at your school to go on the trip or not?"

Sasha looked at me with a little pause and said, "Let me find out."

The school was a bit more lenient about this than they were about the VIA, which they operated as if it was an issue of national security. However, to be sure there was room in the tent for me, Sasha had to tell a little white lie – that his "younger brother" also wanted to go on the trip, and he promised to keep an eye on me all the time. Unfortunately, he hadn't put a lot of thought into this excuse, for some people at school knew all his family members – so they knew I was not his "little brother". Still, he told me to be sure I used the same last name same as his when I filled out the forms for camp. Since our last names were so similar (his was Shishkanov and mine is Shishkov), we had a bit of freedom to manipulate it for our benefits.

The plan went flawlessly, and a couple weeks later, we were in the back of a large covered military truck, taking us deep into the forest for a wildlife experience. The most precious items we took with us were obviously our guitars. Playing songs on the way to our destination situated us to serve as entertainers during our one-month adventure. Most of the crowd were high schoolers and enjoyed singing along, and that only enhanced our excitement in playing.

The truck stopped in the middle of a dirt road surrounded by mature pine trees.

About thirty kids and few teachers disembarked and started gathering all the gear. Tents and bags of canned food were loaded on our backs, and we trekked deeper into the forest. The smell of fresh air and pinesap was almost too much for us after enduring the polluted fumes of our city. Eerie silence and faint noises of whispering nature were new sounds for some of the city kids, and the deeper we went, the wilder the atmosphere became.

When we reached a small, open area, we began making camp. A creek ran nearby, and it became our water supply for the rest of the trip. By evening, we had our tents set up, and little improvised kitchen was established where we began to prepare our first meal.

I met two of Sasha's good friends from his class. Petrukha and Dimos were certainly characters, but they were good guys who deserved to have a good friend like Sasha. The four of us stuck together, and I decided to stay with Sasha and Dimos in the same tent while the more adventurous Petrukha insisted on his own little sleeping shelter. And just like that, our short time of living the savage life had officially begun.

It was an absolutely incredible and unforgettable experience for me, probably the most informal and free organized venture I ever had in Russia. While we were supposed to exercise some kind of labor participation, the only such endeavorer we ever participated in was debris removal at the new Pioneer Camp construction site a few kilometers away from us. Beyond that, going every day to collect firewood and gather wild berries and mushrooms was considered labor enough. The teachers who chaperoned us on the trip had a great time, too, occasionally having drinking parties and enjoying the outdoors. For them, as well as for us, this was an exotic vacation, a time of rest, refreshment, and relaxation, and they had no intention of treating it like a structured school activity.

The Sozh River was not far away, and it was one our favorite excursions. The nightly swimming jaunts were a favorite among the bravest campers, and for some reason were very popular among our girls. Surprisingly, for such an isolated and tribal lifestyle, there was plenty to occupy us. Playing volleyball and participating in other group activities were not the only fun part. It was just as entertaining to spend time in the outdoor kitchen and take part in taking care of the camp. None of it felt like work, and no one complained because even the chores seemed fun and exciting.

At nightfall, everybody gathered around a huge bonfire and sang Russian popular songs, with Sasha and I serving as accompaniments. There was even a talent show, of sorts – an improvised concert where everyone got up on the grassy 'stage' to show what they could do. One of the teachers even brought his accordion for "entertainment".

Occasionally, the campers had dancing parties, and this helped spark some of the older kids' summer romances under the stars. It was all in good, clean fun, though, as no drugs or wild sexual activities were ever involved. If anything did happen, young couples were not so apt to kiss and tell in society so set on maintaining purity in our youth.

Petrukha had brought along the coolest radio I had ever seen, a Japanese Sanyo multi-band transistor. His father, a military man, had brought it home from one of his stints working in our "friendly nation" in the East. Every night, we took the radio in the tent and listened to it until very late, enjoying Voice of America and other stations that played music. The signal was much better than in the city, and many of the campers – guys and girls alike – loved to join us as we listened.

At one point during our trip, Sasha had some kind of dispute with his friends and even went to stay in someone else's tent. I was stuck in the middle of the argument. Since I got along so well with Dimos and Petrukha, I could not voluntarily stop hanging out with them when they hadn't done me any wrong. Sasha got mad at me for that and decided to punish me with his isolation. It did not take long, however, before he came back to make peace with the three of us. Sasha was a peacemaker, and he always wanted to resolve things. He was not good at holding grudges.

Everything was going well until, one day, I became a victim of our less-than-intelligent plan to get me on the trip. I was serving my turn on kitchen duty when one of the teachers came to me and said, "So you are Sasha's brother?"

"Yes," I lied without any concern.

Picking his teeth with a match, the teacher replied to me, "Well, I know his father, and he never told me he has two sons."

I was not prepared for such an unpleasant revelation and immediately started to look around for Sasha, who was nowhere in sight. Not knowing what else to say, I complicated the lie further. "The truth is, I am his cousin... but I really wanted to go on this trip!"

"Hmm. So that's it?" he said. "I understand. I was just wondering why his father never told me anything about his second son." He jostled my hair a bit and walked away laughing.

Even though I had escaped that minor problem, our concocted story about my relationship with Sasha was becoming somewhat complicated, and we had to do something about it. Very soon someone else made a comment about our bloodline, and others who were just trying to start trouble began even asking about my real last name. Something had to be done, and Sasha again took the matter into his own hands. He never had a problem looking trouble right in the eye.

He confronted one of the teachers with a confession and told them everything about our plan to bring me along, but to soften the anger of the school authorities, he also told them about my desire to enroll in his school the following year. Everything worked out great; the teachers even admired our perseverance and galvanized friendship. Many people encouraged me to join the school, but the soured memories about my lost battle with my stubborn mother over this issue surfaced again in my mind.

The forest trip soon was over. Dusty and savaged after long depravation from city life, we returned home. Everything felt different as we returned to the chaotic, noisy streets and smells of modern life around us. It was a bit of a culture shock to return to something that was so in contrast to what we'd just experienced, so to ease the transition, after taking a short rest and shower, Sasha and I headed underneath the Kletka to have a little fun.

Escape from Reality

The summer passed so fast that it seemed time had simply vanished. In just a few days, I would be returning to school, but my usual excitement to see my friends and classmates wasn't there anymore. My heart was elsewhere: in the band room at School # 28. I could not accept the fact that such a rare and perfect opportunity was slipping away right before my eyes, and there was nothing I could do to change it. In my mind, there still lingered fresh memories of my audition, and the sounds of that beautiful music we made still rang in my ears. I was sure that those memories, those sounds would just become a permanent collection of unrealized dreams. I had given up hope of any alternative, and I tried to prepare myself for another year at School # 10.

It was a cold and rainy September. Everything felt dark and reprehensible – inside and out. To make this anguished state even more desolate, our school imposed a new set of rules that made it even more difficult to tolerate that place. It seemed our teachers and district authorities were coming up with a never ending list of 'innovations' to try and impress our local Communists with new ideas and regulations. On top of being the strictest and most demanding in performance, our school had now become an experimental playground for maniacs in the educational field.

The newly imposed polices turned the school into an almost prison-like establishment where kids were the inmates. The doors were closed the moment first lesson bell rang, and anyone who wasn't inside – even if they were only a minute late – was sent home. There were absolutely no exceptions, and kids who were locked out had an absence placed on their record. The doors would remain closed until the end of the school day. There were no more recess periods outside, no outdoor time at lunch, no early dismissals, and no going in and out. Only teachers or kids with medical emergencies could exit the school early.

Even making us sit in the classroom all day was not enough of an 'improvement' to satisfy the totalitarian minds of our administration. Someone decided that for kids to do homework at home was not a very productive approach. It was determined that all schoolwork had to be done at school, so the number of class periods was simply doubled to dedicate some class hours to giving homework equal time. While we used to spend six or seven hours a day in school, we were now there a whole day. It was the most insane concept ever conceived by our educational council. The goal was not to improve our performance or to give us a better education; it was simply done to maximize control of our lives, leaving practically no time for us to do anything on our own. It was a way for the government to teach us from a very early age that we had to surrender to them and their doctrines with complete obedience. The authors of these rules were viewed as truly zealous followers of this ideology – and sadly, as national heroes.

I was not the only one who was unhappy about our new school regime. No one appreciated the so-called 'improvements'. The unanimous opinion of practically all students was total outrage; someone even scribbled 'Mad House' on the school entrance (and no, it wasn't me, though I agreed wholeheartedly and got a good laugh out of it).

The reaction to the drastic changes in school was greeted at home with a little surprise. Grandma was more straightforward about it. Her biggest disappointment was that I could not be home for lunch. Also, she could not believe I had to study there all day and come back home only to sleep. My mother, on other hand, viewed it as another opportunity for me to learn a discipline, though she did show a little concern about my prolonged days in school and hoped they would consider revising their rules a bit. Her hopes were pointless, because no changes were being made.

Irritated children and their parents confronted school authorities about the lack of extracurricular activities since the children were in school too long to participate in things like sports or art classes. Temporary reliefs and early dismissal permission slips were issued to the most outspoken families to keep them quiet. I had no such after-school activities except for playing my guitar, and a hobby did not qualify me for an excuse. It was absolutely horrible. Having practically no time for anything after school, I was boiling angry inside. This new, unexpected life change was not a welcomed one, and while all my friends were playing outside, I was still sitting in the classroom. This gave me good reason – more than just playing in the band – for me to talk to my mom again about switching schools. I tried to approach the subject gently, but I got the same reaction as before and was told to forget about it for good – again.

My hatred toward my school reached the highest level, and I intentionally began arriving late just so I could be sent home or skip to spend the day walking in the park or around the city until dark. I knew the teacher would call to see why I was absent, so I had to disconnect the phone as soon as I returned home. When I was finally busted doing that, the atrocity of this conflicted situation came to a head.

"I am leaving..."

The one and only cure in this case was to get out of School # 10 (which I had began to refer to as 'Prison # 10') so I could have normal life again. I did not even care anymore about where I would be taken as long as it was not there. I felt so helpless and oppressed in the situation that I knew I had to do something outrageous, so I decided to run away from home.

It was not an intelligent plan. In fact, there was no plan at all. It was merely an outburst of frustration, and I did it without any concept of how I would proceed or even where I would run to.

I picked Sunday to make my disappearance less noticeable. My mom went to the store with my brother, and Grandma was working. This gave me time to pilfer some simple food and emergency items from our home into my backpack. I found everything I needed with the exception of one important item: money. All I had was some pocket change, only enough to buy a ticket on the bus or local train, but it was not enough to buy food for even couple of days. Nevertheless, I had made my decision, and I was planning to leave before my mother returned home.

Right before I was ready to go, someone rang the doorbell. At first, I thought it might be best to ignore it, but then I quickly realized I was making too much noise to be heard outside, so I opened the door. It was my uncle Andrew.

"Hey, Yura! Where are you going?" he asked, walking into the house and taking his coat and hat off.

"I am going to a movie," I fibbed with a short pause.

"And you're taking a backpack to the movies?"

"This? It's actually not mine. I have to drop it off to my friend. I have to get going. You can watch some TV. Mom will be back in a bit."

"Alright. Do you have money for the movie?"

That was exactly what I did not have, so I was glad he asked. "I have some, but not enough for candy or ice cream." Uncle Andrew was a great man and loved to spoil my little brother and me. He never said "no" to anything, and this time was no exception.

"Here," he said as he shoved a large ruble coin with Lenin's embossed profile on it into my hot little hand.

"Thanks!" I said and began to retreat from the house before anyone else had a chance to stop me.

On the way outside, I stopped at our mailbox. The previous day's newspaper was still in there, so I slipped a note inside it for my mom and grandmother. It said: "I am fed up with my school and all its stupid rules. Don't wait for me because I have run away and will never come back home! Yura."

Now I was a free man, but it was not so easy to figure out where I was going or how I would get there. I decided to go for one night somewhere where it would not be easy to find me.

I knew I could hide at the summer Pioneer campgrounds in the Klyonkie village where I spent my summer trip with the Kayak Club. Whatever I did, I wanted to be sure I punished my school and my mother for making me go there.

The sky was gray, and the black water of the river was slowly moving around the boat as I was riding to my secret hideaway. There were only a few people onboard besides me, and it gave me more confidence that everything would be alright. There were no witnesses and no sneaky adults to ask too many questions. The plan looked promising.

We docked, and I immediately hiked the familiar trails toward our old Pioneer Camp. In half an hour, I was standing in a front of it. Everything was quiet and deserted. The only noise came from the wind that swayed in the trees and a few crows cawing somewhere above me. The place felt like a ghost town, was and it was somewhat spooky. I walked around and looked at every cabin, hoping some of them would have open doors. Unfortunately, all the buildings were closed, so I decided to explore the other campgrounds. There were plenty of them near by.

A light drizzle began to sprinkle me, and I had to find the shelter before the real autumn rain poured hard on me. I went to the next camp, and after several attempts to find some kind of open building, my effort was rewarded when I found a broken lock on one little cabin. A few steel spring beds were standing in the room, and I crashed on one of them. I was already hungry and started nibbling on my few provisions. As the sky grew darker, I finished my lunch and lay on the bed to think about my next steps. A light rain tapped on the thin roof while I tried to concentrate on coming up with some kind of logical plan. I couldn't think of anything practical. Instead, I was slaughtered with memories about my own home. As I thought of my family, my anger at the school softened. I began to wonder what Mom, brother and Grandma were doing at that moment, and I began to feel foolish for trying to punish them for not giving me my way. I also remembered my fishing journey with Kolya, and I knew the overwhelming drama of a search for me was about to begin again – only this time, my mother would worry because of a much more stupid, selfish reason. It was obvious that what I was doing is not going to help me get what I wanted. There was no reason to make my family suffer and worry. I started to miss them, and in my heart I felt very guilty. My selfish plot was ridiculous, and when logic took over, I knew it was time to go back home.

Suddenly, I recalled something: "Yes, it's Sunday! The boats are on the fall schedule, and they will not go back to the city until the next weekend!"

In a panic, I jumped out of the rickety cabin bed. I ran to the small river dock, desperately hoping I had not missed the last boat. The day was almost over, and the darkness of the approaching night was quickly closing in. The small waiting room at the dock was empty. I looked around, trying to find any information on commute schedules. All kinds of old washed-out safety and Pioneer posters adorned the walls. Among the signs was posted a schedule of the riverboat departures and arrivals. The last commute to the city would be at six o'clock. I reached into the pocket to check my watch, but then I realized I had left it at home because I was in such a hurry to escape Uncle Andrew's interrogations. I peeked through the moldy window to try to determine the approximate time, but it looked much too dark to be any earlier than six. I sat down on the floor, feeling defeated.

A single light bulb was hanging from the ceiling, slightly swinging from the gentle motion of the dock. I stared at it and began wondering how I would get back home. The railroad bridge across the river was nearby, and I knew people sometimes rode their bikes over it back to the city. The long country road on other side went through the deserted fields, and it would take me the whole night to walk home if I went that way. Not only I did not know that road, but the rainy weather and the dark would make the voyage even more treacherous. I decided to wait until morning and sleep at the dock.

It was getting cold, and I tried not to think about what was going to happen at home when I got back. I knew that this time, my foolish decision might cost me much more than a screaming lecture and a few smacks on my head. The metal floor did not make for the most comfortable bedding, and my mind was tossed about with thoughts of how I would explain this all to my mother. I sat on a welded, rough stool and opened my backpack to grab a bite to eat. Just as I was starting to chew, the silence of the place was broken by a subtle engine noise, and the darkness was illuminated by the wonderful glow of navigation beacons and cabin windows. The boat was slowly sailing to the dock station, and I was greatly relieved to see and hear it.

As soon as the boat arrived, I hopped aboard and ran into the corner of a warm cabin. "Maybe everything is not so bad!" I thought to myself as I tried to surmise how I would handle my arrival back home. The runaway note popped in my head. "What am I going to say about that? Maybe the mail still will be there so I can get it before they see it. Or I could just play dumb and pretend I did not write it or just say that it was a joke". I thought through one story after another all the way back to the city, and in less than an hour, we were docked. It was time to face the music...

Hungry, cold, and anxious to see if the mail had been picked up yet, I ran home as fast as I could. The door to our apartment entrance was swaying from the wind and shutting it behind me as I rushed to the mailboxes. The papers were picked up, and the box was empty: not a good sign. I knew now I would have to make a convincing presentation about my absence from home.

I opened the door and walked into the house. The delicious smell of dinner lingered in the air as I sneaked into the bathroom and began emptying my backpack. I threw all my provisions and supplies under the bathtub until it was safe to put them away without being noticed.

"So, where have you been?" my mom asked as soon as I walked into the room.

"At a movie with Kolya, and then I went to Gena's to help him fix his bike. Can I eat and go to sleep? I am tired," I mumbled as I quickly went into the kitchen.

"Of course, Yura," said Grandma while looking straight at my mother.

I was just waiting for the moment when the showdown would begin. The fear of my runaway note being waved in front of my face gave me an extra boost to devour my meal as fast as I could. I wanted to finish dinner and get safely into bed, where I hoped they'd just leave me alone.

It was intensely quiet in the house – eerily quiet. The TV was off, and Grandma was stitching something on the couch while my brother played on the floor. On the round table in the living room, my mom was ironing shirts. I hoped none of them would start any conversations with me. In a hurry I gobbled up the remainder of my dinner and quickly departed to my room.

I knew that at some point, I would be interrogated about the note. I was sure of it. But it never happened – not that day, not the next day, and never after that. It was never discussed or mentioned, as if no one ever got it. What happened at my house on the day of my running away from home was a mystery to me, but I decided it must have had something to do with my grandma's involvement. In extreme situations, she always had ultimate power and the final say. In my opinion, the reason no one ever talked about it was simply because my grandmother was the only one who knew – and she thought it best to keep it our little secret.

"Am I going to prison?..."

The next week did not look very promising. I knew any immature attempt to make explanatory statements was going to backfire on me. Something was going to change in my life, though I didn't know what; I could feel it. I feared my guitar would suddenly disappear or that – even worse – my parents would sent me to a School-Internat, where I would study and live all the time except for an occasional weekend. The strange silence at home only made me feel more endangered. I expected the silence to be broken eventually, though, and I was not looking forward for any conversations with my mom.

Sure enough, a couple days later, when my mother returned from work, she said, "Son, we need to talk."

"This is it", I thought to myself. "Now I can kiss everything goodbye".

"I am going to your school tomorrow to talk with teachers about your future," she said with a cold voice.

It was at this moment I experienced the deepest regret for trying to run away. I was sure she knew about it, and I wished I could have taken it back and not done something so stupid. "Why?" I asked, hoping I would at least not be sent to a correctional youth institution or Internat.

"I need to talk to your principal," she said.

Fortunately, I was briefly saved by the ringing of the phone. As Mom talked to the person on the other end, I began to rationalize that I should confess and plead for mercy as soon as she came back. A half an hour later, she was still on the phone, so I decided to wait for her in my bed. She still hadn't come when I drifted off to sleep, and when I woke up, breakfast was already waiting for me. Mom wasn't home.

"Where is Mom?" I asked Grandma.

"She went to work and will stop at your school on her lunch break."

"What is she going to talk about with my principal?"

"I don't know, but don't worry about it. Eat your breakfast," said Grandma.

I did not want to eat or go to school that day. My grandmother telling me not to worry gave me a little hope that she knew what was going on. She would never lie to me, so and I counted on her statement that whatever happened would certainly not be the end of the world.

My mom arrived at my school right when we were finishing up one of our regular periods and preparing to do homework and studying. She had to wait by the closed doors for a school clerk to let her in. This little delay aggravated her, and I knew she would be easily very upset now about anything. While she talked to my teacher, I stood far away but tried to detect what they might be discussing. My mom was asking a lot of questions, and I was sure that at any minute, I was going to be reprimanded by both of them, for my sins at school and home.

Moments passed, though, and they never called me to talk to them. Instead, they both started walking to the principal's office. At that point, I knew something major was going to happen, and I feared I was in big trouble. Curious, I followed them and stood outside the office counting planks of the parquet flooring to overcome my anxiety about what was going on inside.

About ten minutes later, the door opened. My mom stormed out of the office with an angry look on her face. "Let's go, Yura!" She grabbed my hand, and we walked toward my class. "Do you want to go study at another school?" she asked me in a bitter tone.

I did not know why she asked me that, but I was afraid she was talking about the horrible prospect of living in a correctional institution, so I answered with a groan in my throat, "I don't want to go to Internat!"

"Not Internat!" she said, jerking my hand. "I'm talking about School # 28."

In disbelief and utter shock, I answered, "School # 28? Yes, Mom! this school is horrible!"

"Go to your classroom and grab you stuff. We are going home," she said with a well-practiced dominance.

I still didn't know what happened behind the closed doors of the principal's office or what was said to make her so angry, but I did not care. It didn't seem my running away had anything to do with it. Whatever played a role in her decision, I was very happy for it, and all my worries were put to rest and my disappointments were solved.

Later that night, the mystery was revealed. The door to the kitchen was slightly ajar, and my mom was talking to Grandma about my school. It seemed she had discovered that all my complaints about the new idiotic, prison-like rules were true, and when she approached the principal about them, she did not like what he had to say.

Grandma listened intently to her, and when Mom was done, she said, "I told you to go and see it for yourself. The world will not collapse if he studies at another school."

My runaway attempt was never mentioned in that conversation, and I was excited that the incident would be forever forgotten as I stepped into a new chapter of my life, thanks to my mother's intervention and my grandmother's kindhearted silence.

Chapter 9

My new School and its Band

It was still hard to believe all my hopes and desires had such an unexpected resurrection. On one hand, closing the door to my old school for good was a joyful proposition, but in some ways, it was a sad event in my life. Mostly, though, it was a relief, and I considered everything that happened as a miracle that opened to me exciting and unknown new prospects. I was exhilarated at the chance to try something new, but leaving friends behind who I had known for years was admittedly difficult. Until that time, I didn't know I had grown so close to my classmates. My good friend Grisha felt awful that from then on, we would be apart. He did not appreciate the things that were happening in School# 10, and he tried to convince his parents to transfer him from there as well, but he was in the same situation I had been in, and he was stuck there – at least for the time being. My farewell to my classmates and the school itself was full of mixed emotions, feelings of unavoidable loss and my own dubious future.

School # 28 was much smaller and older than my previous one. It stood behind the railroad tracks, not far away from the train station. It was hidden in the old part of the city, which mainly contained single-story old houses. Most of them were built before Bolshevik Revolution, and that whole region seemed more like a large village than part of a modern industrial city. The new school was such a drastic change – as if I'd gone back in time.

Being the new kid in class always comes with strange and outlandish feelings. My new teacher was an elderly lady, a hardcore disciplinarian. Maria Petrovna not only taught my Russian language class, but she also turned out to be the mother of our school band piano player, Lena. I was greeted my first day in school with her presentation to the class: "Kids, please meet our new classmate, Yura Shishkov, and don't forget to wash your hands before you shake his hand because Yura is also our new guitar player," she said with some detectable sarcasm. I instantly realized my relationship with her would be more than strictly educational.

The class welcomed me, and couple of guys volunteered to give me a short tour around my new school. It was an old two-story building, completely different from the one I attended before. Everything was simple and very old. There was no parquet flooring, so we did not have to change our shoes upon arrival to the building. At the corner of every classroom was an old-fashioned wooden fire burner, used in the past to heat the building in the winter. The only part of the school that was modern were the impressive concert hall and gymnasium, which had been recently added.

In contrast to my old school, there were no bathrooms on each floor – only one old 'village style' toilet outside to serve all the kids and teachers. Some of the kids told me they occasionally dumped kilos of yeast into the bathroom to make it overflow. When such a prank was pulled, children were sent home, and an emergency truck had to come to pump out the toilet and clean up the nasty mess.

Behind the small transformer building was a hideaway spot for kids to smoke, something kids at School # 10 wouldn't even dare to try.

The atmosphere and life there was quiet different from what I had to deal with in the past. There were no extended school days or brutal Communism proceedings. It was still a regular Soviet school with all the same political teachings, only there was no fanatical obsession like I had endured at School # 10.

Now, my companion on the way to school every morning was my good pal Sasha. He was almost as happy as I was about my transfer, and the potential for changes in the school band with my arrival was one of his biggest hopes.

At Last, I am Playing in the Band

To become a member of the school's VIA was not only a dream come true for me, but also one of the biggest events in my life, which at that point set the course of my future destiny. I did not know this guitar-playing hobby would become a never-ending adventure that changed my lifestyle and even later my country of residence. All I wanted to do was play in the band. At that time, that was the ultimate goal of my life, and my enrollment at School # 28 made me feel I was accomplishing that goal.

My first rehearsal was practically a monumental experience. On that day, I was not going to sit and watch someone else playing or dream about holding an electric guitar in my own hands for joy and admiration. I was going to be part of the band – to absorb myself in the long-awaited fixation.

We began practicing songs for our upcoming school dance. The other band members were not only enthusiastic about bringing a new member into the band, but some new songs as well. There were only four of us: Sasha, me, Andrew on the drums, and Lena on the keyboard. I used the bass guitar because it was already familiar to me, and I began to pluck the strings to learn some new songs. Sasha occasionally switched instruments with me to show me some licks and moves on the bass. I loved to play his red Jolana guitar, and since Sasha didn't have any great preference on which guitar to use, my friend often let me play some songs on it while used my bass. The new tunes we learned moved much faster forward because I was more familiar with the guitar than with the bass. I was in heaven, and every song I played seemed like a little treasure to my soul; I cherished every performance.

The band equipment was quite old, and as I familiarized myself with it, I began to realize there were plenty of items we needed to improve our stage sound. The problem was, getting new equipment was a difficult task for any band, our school band included. The production of amplifiers, speakers, and other gear was about as advanced as the invention of the wheel era in our country, and considering its limited supply, it was very difficult to acquire regardless of its often shabby quality and high price. Since all the gear was sold only to government organizations, every one of them used their own back doors and connections to obtain it. Schools were not in the position to have major leverage in this acquiring game, so they always had to take a place in the back of the line to get their musical equipment. They used whatever they could as band gear. Even blow-horns that hung from streetlights were used as speakers in Soviet VIAs. The most popular amplifiers among our musicians were "kinaps", movie theater power-amps that were the most powerful Soviet tube equipment ever produced. To buy them was simply impossible, so when an old movie theater was demolished, refurbished, or renovated, the lucky new owner of an obsolete amp could make a fortune by flipping it to any musician. Sasha told me it would be a dream to climb into our movie projector room and snag one of them for our band. Knowing about this plot in my friend's mind, Boss told us if we tried to execute such a wild idea, we'd be promptly expelled from band and quite possibly the school.

My guitar and our VIA became my obsession. They completely absorbed my free time and had a direct impact on everything else in my life. I would not have been able to dedicate so much energy to it if my educational obligations had been too demanding, but fortunately, the assignments in class and the amount of homework was much lighter than in my previous school, allowing me the time to occupy myself with music. If we were not having band rehearsals, we would bring our electric guitars home and spend our after-school time with Sasha playing on them through my Minsk-R7 radio and sharpening our skills.

Our rehearsals were scheduled a few times a week. Since we didn't have Senya babysitting us all the time, we could pick the days ourselves and practice as long as we needed. We took advantage of such freedom and worked as hard as we could to practice for the upcoming dance.

I began playing almost exclusively on guitar. The few songs I could play on bass, my friend could still play better than me. Every time I had to play the bass guitar, I sat on a chair or held it like an upright bass. It was a huge instrument to me, and when it was strapped to my shoulder, it felt like a wooden log. Sasha chased me onstage, forcing me to play it the right way, so I hung it on my neck and began to act like a clown with it. The new chase would begin, and the whole rehearsal turned into a circus.

In a few weeks, we had completely finished practicing our program, and I could play my parts without any blemishes and flaws. The time had come to introduce to our band a lot of songs Sasha and I only played around our neighborhood. For starters, we played a few Beatles tunes to soften up the backbone of our stiff repertoire, and after few practices, we moved to what most Soviet ears would consider heaver: Deep Purple's "Smoke on the Water," followed by songs of Pink Floyd, Nazareth, and Led Zeppelin. This kind of music was not completely unknown to many high school kids or teenagers; it was simply never played to the audience in school band performances. We knew it was somewhat risky to have them in our program, and we were concerned about what the school administration would think. More than anything, we were concerned about the reaction of our own Boss, Senya.

We had just finished practicing Alice Cooper's "Black Widow." Unbeknownst to us, Senya had been listening at the window. "What was it, guys?" he asked.

Sasha yelled back from stage, "It was Alice Cooper!"

Boss started coming toward us, and I began to think he was going to turn our amplifiers off and send us home. "It was nice, guys. Just little more attack and sing it in two or three voices," he said, passing by to walk back to his classroom.

It was the seal of approval. We had a green light to roll more heavy tunes from Western rock bands into our repertoire.

What was happening onstage while we played had to be an odd, remarkable, and pathetic scene at the same time. While we were doing our best to play exactly like the bands we were imitating, our equipment and youth could not deliver the power of a true rock band. On the other hand, it must have been the amazing play of a good quality from four dedicated and passionate kids. We were unforgiving to any flops and errors in playing these songs. Everything had to sound clean and as close as possible to the originals. Nothing was considered unimportant, with the exception of the song lyrics.

No one spoke English at that time well enough to understand what we were singing. As long as the main lines sounded close to correct, everything else was pure fantasy and a pile of mixed English words and phrases. Sasha was a genius in doing this part, and when he screamed into a microphone this English language 'salad,' it was hard to tell the lyrics were not real. I also stepped into help singing to make our play more realistic and colorful. Being a vocalist was not my favorite part, but singing backup and shouting wildly through the speakers became my trademark. We all yelled senseless phrases into our microphones; In our opinion, we resembled the crazy rock music we tried to imitate. It was often a chaotic, bizarre scene we would not want our parents to see.

Getting Songs

Our mutual friend Petrukha helped us gather songs for our repertoire. His family had a bobbin tape recorder, and in his collection were plenty of Western bands, which he taped from everybody who would let him do it at no charge. For this reason, the quality of them was far below desirable level, but as long as we could hear the melody, the unrecognizable lyrics did not concern us very much. Since he lived not far away from our school, we often stopped at his house to rip every song which possible to use for dancing. We swiped everything we could, mainly from

British bands, even when we didn't know who the bands were. The goal was to get the tunes that would be the most shocking to Soviet ears.

Some of the concert recordings gave us some insight as to how the audiences in the West reacted to the music. For us, it was wild. In contrast, all performances in the USSR had to be civilized according our moral standards and out of respect to the artists and the audience. No one ever screamed, whistled, cheered, or danced. Regardless of the artist or music, everyone behaved as if they were at a fancy opera or piano concert. Any outbursts beyond clapping politely or shouting "Bravo" would be considered unethical and would guarantee a police escort out of the concert. When we listened the screaming audience at the rock concerts on the tapes, we wanted our music to have that kind of impact on the kids at the dance. All we needed were the right songs – the kind the crowd could sing along with or play back to the band. The concerts like "Slade Alive" and Deep Purple's Japan and Europe tours were perfect examples of what it will take to make the audience stand on their heads. We knew it was risky and that the school administration might shut us down, but our adventurous spirits had to try. We picked few tunes for this purpose and began practicing them. Rehearsing these songs was already enough to spread rumors across the school that we were preparing something beyond an ordinary dance.

The First "Show" and its Outcome

The day of my first performance arrived, and I was quite anxious and a bit nervous. I had never performed onstage before, and I was concerned what the audience would think. Sasha tried to calm me down and promised it would be no different than playing for drunks in the neighborhood.

For the program, the concert hall was converted into a large dance floor. The chairs were shoved to the rear, opening up the room enough to fit the entire high school student body. Only eighth-grade students and older were allowed to attend, so I was the youngest person to witness what was happening at the show.

We got our equipment onstage, and after everything was ready and all the instruments were tuned, the door opened to let the crowd in. For a short time, we returned to our small equipment storage locker. For some reason, a lot of people wanted to squeeze into our room. A few of Sasha's friends and some kids from the tenth grade managed to sneak inside. In anticipation of a fun night, girls and boys were knocking on the door, asking how soon the dance would begin. Cigarette smoke filled the room, and someone pulled out a bottle of wine. A few older kids started sipping cheap booze straight from the bottle, and the atmosphere of the upcoming party was already underway. It was not that much of a shock to me, but I had never known teenagers at school could act so liberal and so adult.

Sasha was definitely our leader, the mastermind behind all the band's decisions. He always had a plan for everything. Every song was strategically put in order to make the crowd slowly unwind toward the last part of the spicy songs. It was his plan, and we counted on his leadership and wisdom. "Let's go," Sasha commanded, and we all ran onstage.

In the concert hall, the transformed crowd of girls and boys were dressed in fancy dresses and shirts and were quietly awaited the beginning of the dancing. The first chord of my playing career was strummed, and all anxiety and worries instantly despaired. In a few songs, I was enjoying the play as much as the audience on the floor. We sounded great. One after another, girls came to the stage and asked us to repeat this or that song. The warmed-up crowd cheered after each dance. I looked at my three friends across the stage; they had helped me realize my long-awaited dream.

After playing for almost two hours, we took a short break. We went to our gear closet again and locked the door behind us, hoping for a few moments of silence. Our pumped-up fans were smacking on the door, and Sasha openly told them to go to hell. "That's the only thing they'll listen to," he said, and he crashed on the desk to relax.

Once they left, we talked about the first part of the concert, which we all thought was absolutely incredible. I was on fire and still could not believe everything that was happening to me.

About fifteen minutes later, the second half began. We had only played a few songs when the fist fight on the floor broke out, a typical occurrence at Soviet dances big and small. It was usually for a silly reason like someone saying something or a dispute over a girl, and the teachers were quick to take care of it. After the brawlers were thrown out, the party continued.

After playing for another hour, Sasha told me, "The crowd is ready" and called one of the guys who was standing in front of the wall of people. "Go turn the light off, and we will play some "zaboy", Sasha said to a guy in a short purple pants. Everybody knew this slang word, which described something insane – what might be known today as hard rock.

We waited for a minute, and as soon as the lights on the floor were extinguished, the crowd exploded with ovations and cheering. Two dim projectors brightened up the stage, and the whole atmosphere changed to a truly crazy party.

"And this song is for our friend in purple pants!" Sasha shouted into a microphone, and the first chords of "Smoke on the Water" ripped through the air.

Someone shouted from the horde, "Deep Purple!!!" Everybody jumped to dance in hysteria, and we were doing our best in complete euphoria.

In the middle of the song, a teacher turned the lights on, and an overwhelming throng of booing filled the hall. We could see from the stage the arguing in the corner by the main switch box and shortly the teacher had mercy on the begging kids. The light turned off again, sending the happy teens into a frenzy.

When Sasha called the dancing pack to sing after him, they roared back "Smoke on the water!!!" with such power that we broke laughing in disbelief of such generous participation. Everything at that moment was so different from anything we'd ever experienced. The excited crowd and fun music made the dance incredible for everyone.

One of the teachers climbed onstage and announced to everyone that if another fight broke out, the lights would be turned on and everyone would be made to go home. From that point on, the kids knew that controlling order and peace was in their own hands. This message was also made clear to any punk that if he started a fight, the whole crowd would be angered for the loss of such a great party. Everything was smooth and perfect from that point.

Time flew. We played song after song, and a few tunes were played several times at the request of the electrified audience. At eleven o'clock, the sad announcement of the end had to be made. The light was turned on, and I looked at the dance floor, where exhausted and happy kids were heading to the exit. From the walls, the uptight faces of our Kremlin leaders gazed at us from the portraits, and the whole feeling of a party had an almost unrealistic feel at that point. Everything around us seemed contrary to what we'd just experienced. The dull, hypocritical perception of our twisted reality, the red-flagged auditorium, and our surroundings convicted us for having fun. It was hard to believe that we could play this kind of music under stiff oppression of this genre by our Communistic authorities.

We began to dismantle our stage and talked about the highlights of our performance. Having so much fun and experiencing something totally different from our typical Soviet-organized entertainment was overwhelming. We could hardly comprehend what we'd just been a part of. It was not an ordinary dance, as we knew them. Instead, it reminded us of the rock concerts we heard on underground tape recordings. We were practically intoxicated by the experience, addicted to it, and we knew we could never play music in any other way in the future.

The oldest guy in our band on that day was Sasha, and he was only fourteen. In spite of his youth, he encouraged us to play with dedication and passion on that incredible night. Personally, it was the biggest night of my life, my mind-blowing first performance. The adrenaline pumping through me was almost too much, and I could barely concentrate on unplugging our equipment.

Our Boss Senya showed up and asked us how it went. We hadn't even noticed that he had missed the party. The teachers also lacked quality time to relax, and the compensation for this deluge was to send them to school dances so they could have a good time themselves. It was no secret that many of the teachers spent these nights alone in their classrooms drinking. So, Boss had missed the show doing the same.

On the way home, we still talked about our show. We were so excited that we began to dream up more extravagant presentations in the future. What we didn't know was that our loose behavior and rowdy reputation would eventually cost us some casualties.

Some Couldn't Handle It

The very next rehearsal brought news we never expected. As soon as we set up our equipment, Senya came to talk to us. We were still waiting for Lena to come while we did our final adjustments and tuning. Boss walked on stage and told us we should not wait for Lena. "She is will no longer be playing in the band, kids," said Senya. "Her mother was outraged by your performance at the dance and said her daughter cannot be a part of such a distasteful ensemble."

Now we wondered what was going to happen to us and our show and who would play the keyboards for us. Also, who will sing some of ABBA songs which we learned just before the gig.The biggest concern was obviously if we will be still allowed to play what we liked. We even worried that this might disperse our band completely.

"I can't help it if her mother doesn't understand this music. It's her own problem," said our Boss. "Now we have to find a new keyboard player and move on."

The whole outcome of this case, despite losing one of our members, wasn't as bad as it could be. Senya was on our side, and this fact allowed us to offer new Western songs that a lot of people knew but never got to hear live.

It was sad that Lena would no longer be with us. Having a girl in the band was a big plus, considering that some songs were sung with a female lead, and we would not be able to play them anymore. Also, she knew our entire program, and to teach someone from scratch would take a while, not to mention we needed to find someone who fit in with our band on a personal level.

My own concern was from another angle. Since her mother was our classroom teacher, I knew this would affect our already crummy relationship. She had enough hideous comments about our band, even when her own daughter was playing with us, and now she could picking on me out of hatred toward the music we were playing. My fear was confirmed shortly when I turned in a less-than-perfect class assignment. She connected to my VIA participation to it and threatened to ask the administration to remove me from the band. In my eyes, she became a living symbol of the official state propaganda machine, badmouthing something she knew nothing about and painting musicians in evil colors simply because she didn't like the music we played.

At the next rehearsal, Senya walked in together with a short guy and said, "Here is your new piano player, guys. Please meet Valentine."

I knew Valentine was from one of our parallel classes, but I would have never thought he could have played any musical instrument. Fortunately for our band, I was wrong to assume that. He was not just an ordinary piano player. By the age of twelve, he had already won several awards and music competitions, and he was a true prodigy. We were lucky to have him and soon the time will prove it.

This change brought nothing but more positive results for our VIA. Valentine was not only easy to work with, but he also had a remarkable memory and learned our entire program on the fly. Because we were now an all-boy group, practical jokes and childish pranks infiltrated our rehearsals quite often. Boys will be boys, and musicians are no different.

Music, Fun, and Freedom

It was a great time of unforgettable moments. Everything we did seemed to provide a laugh. Sasha was always kicking me for making fun of him onstage or for starting a jokes that often derailed our rehearsal goals. I was the equivalent of the class clown, eager to ridicule and laugh at any situation. Andrew, our drummer, was my partner in crime, and if I needed assistance with any kind of joke or prank, I could count on him to assist me.

I always picked the worst time to crack jokes, and even when I couldn't pull them off, I would chuckle to myself about them. Senya would shout at those moments, "Yura, what the hell are you laughing about now?!!" He knew I would always approach the most serious matter with a great sense of humor and repeatedly avoided talking to me about it.

It was nothing new. I had always had a great sense of humor and smiled practically all the time. In rare Soviet photographs, which were typically very serious, I was often scolded for smiling before the shot was taken and throwing in the air the two fingered "V" sign (an anti-Soviet jester by Communist's definition) . I had uplifting feelings about my life and was a genuinely happy kid. The cloudless sky of my childhood at that time was reflected in my daily mood, and I often recall those days as the most joyful, happiest of my Soviet life. I was playing in the band and had a lot of good friends who shared my interests. The bonds we created in Russia were unconditionally, lifelong ones.

The music we played at that time and the feel of freedom to do it without anybody bothering us gave us a sensation of paradise. We did not need much in those days, and having a chance to play the songs that were officially banned in the USSR was a wonderful and rare opportunity. It was truly unbelievable that any professional musician who would dare to perform from the Soviet stages anything remotely resembling what we played would be written up, lose their job, or be interrogated and lectured at the KGB office. It is still a mystery to me why we were never forbidden from playing foreign rock music at our school dances. This strange phenomenon must have been slipped through some kind of flawed school regulations or by permission of the KGB, who – for one reason or the other – may have intentionally allowed kids to be exposed to the political and cultural influences of other lands. Whatever the reason, the decision to close the authorities' eyes and ears to what kids were playing in schools definitely did not work in favor of any government plans. Not only did we learn the music of other cultures and nations, but we also built an understanding of freedom and the beauty of language that had no limitations or boundaries – the language of music, with its unlimited frontiers of love and peace.

Marching With the Band and New Friends

I think there was something sacred about marching bands in our society. It seemed none of the Soviet organizations could survive without them. They were present in nearly every institution, regardless of its size, and orientation was almost mandatory. Even when there was not enough staff for it, they at least ample musical instruments to organize a band if such an opportunity would come about. All government organizations, from cheese factories to constriction groups to sewer plants had bands, and schools were the most active participants. The main purpose of their existence was to support our political gatherings and parades. The next of these celebration days on the horizon was the Bolshevik Revolution anniversary.

Our School, # 28, also had an orchestra, and while no one would ever outperform the team of Geshka in style, quality, aggressive presentation, we had a good marching band, with our VIA boss at the helm. Unlike School # 10, which practiced colonial approaches to recruit its members, our small orchestra consisted of true volunteers, reflecting its liberal rules. While it was someone embarrassing for a rock 'n' roller like me to be involved with such a group, it seemed to be my destiny, and even changing schools would not allow me to avoid it. Senya asked all of us to help him in the upcoming parade and fill in for missing musicians in his marching band. He promised that we would only be helping temporarily and would not be required to become permanent members of the band. I could not say "no" to him, and neither could any of my friends. My only concern was the absolute absence of knowledge about wind instruments, besides my trumpet-destroying experience in daycare. These worries were evaporated, however, when we were told the only people the orchestra was short on were percussionists. That cheered us up a bit, though we still were not too keen on the idea of participating. Senya knew we were not looking forward to the gig and told us we would only had to go to rehearsal once, so we decided that instead of grumping about it, we would look at the parade as an opportunity to have some fun and joke around.

Andrew, Sasha, and I began to debate which instrument each of us would take. The enormous bass drum was so big that I would almost drag it on the ground before me, so Sasha – a bit larger than me – was chosen to take the burden of carrying the monstrous instrument on his shoulder. Andrew and I decided to rotate the small drum and cymbals between us. I had few moments at our VIA to sit and practice behind the drum set, and after Andrew showed me the basic drumming principles, I quickly learned how to tap rhythm and beats. I had to do only a small part of it, practically the same routine I had heard over and over again at our Pioneer Camps.

The Parade

November 7 that year was cold, gray, and gloomy. Our entire school assembly was filled with red flags, banners, balloons, and other Bolshevik-glorifying regalia, and everyone gathered outside early in the morning. Some had less than enthusiastic feelings and could not wait to fulfill our mandatory participation in this ritual and go home. High school kids at that time considered themselves adults, and once they left the school premises, in the chaos of this extravaganza, it was practically impossible for the teachers to control them. Many of them could not wait to march through the streets, taking a few sips of wine along the way from the beverages they had stashed in their pockets.

We were about to proceed into the center square of our city, the place where we had to deliver our best performance for our local leaders. The whole congregation began moving slowly, and the first marching tune detonated through the cold autumn air. Our boss, Senya, was walking in the front of the band, only giving us occasional rhythm gestures. Dressed in a long trench coat and looking like some kind of mafioso from right out of a gangster movie, he was the least enthusiastic among all the teachers about this masquerade.

Marching while simultaneously playing patriotic anthems and hymns was an awkward and bizarre experience for me. I never would have thought I'd find myself doing such a thing, but I considered it as paying my dues, and I kept right on drumming, alongside my friends.

All three of us were slowly getting into the groove of having fun in this strange endeavor. Every time it was my turn to strike the cymbals, I could not help almost bending backwards under their heavy weight. I had to hold my elbows against my stomach to keep my balance, and I probably looked quite comical, as evidenced by the laughter of the kids behind us. My friends began to play loosely, striking unnecessary accents and blows into the drums as a sort of musical practical joke. Our comical improvisations sent all of us into hysterical laughter. Senya looked back at us a couple of times but didn't say anything besides ordering us to play one tune after another.

I am drumming at one of the school's parades.

Glorifying slogans were shouted through the streets on megaphones, and we yelled back, "Hurray!" with a rock 'n roll growl in our voice. The Central Square of V. Lenin was within a short distance, and Boss commanded that we prepare for a "March of Aviators" tune to be played when we passed in front of the city authorities. Standing on the massive granite podium crowned with gigantic statute of Lenin, the local leaders waved little red flags as the procession went by. Senya raised his hand, and we started the song. For some reason, we realized it was the perfect moment to really put on a performance of our own. We began making jazzy accents and strikes, and the mockery of the patriotic song began. We almost derailed the rhythm of the whole orchestra, and in agony, Boss tried very hard to conduct us and keep us playing together. The officials at the podium were gawking at us, wide-eyed and open-mouthed. Bending backward as much as I could, I slammed the cymbals together above my head in an array of solos, accompanied by the drumming chaos of Sasha and Andrew. We could not look at each other for fear of laughing and only the finished song prevented us from completely falling on the ground in hysteria. After the parade was over, we did not want to talk to Senya. We knew he was not pleased with our antics and would not compliment us on such a rebellious performance. He also kept his distance, knowing his own temper and realizing he'd easily blow his fuses and go into a rampage at us. We happily headed home, knowing the day was not wasted, and in the end, we had much more fun than people who were marching in the column with flags and banners.

As displeased as Senya must have been, that was not our last time to participate in the orchestra. Many other official school meetings and ceremonies required our accompaniment. Every time Senya asked us to help, he begged us not to repeat our "experimental" percussion stunt that we had performed at the November 7 parade. I loathed taking part in such festivities for many reasons, particularly their political orientation and ramifications, but out of respect for Boss, I never declined his requests.

Friends Who Could Do Anything

Getting involved in my school band expanded my circle of friends a great deal. Because I was spending so much time with Sasha, his classmates and people that were helping us to obtain new songs for our program also became close to me. I was spending more and more time with kids a couple years older than me, and they became good role models for me in my youth. Some of them were very disciplined, and others exhibited loyal, unconditional friendship. Most of them were Sasha's old friends, whom he had known since he was seven years old. I became very close to them, sharing many common interests in music or admiring their creative characters.

Petrukha was one of these mutual friends. After spending time together at the last summer camp, I learned that he was an incredible craftsman – too good for his young age. He lived in an old, small house that was built by his grandparents decades earlier, and he had a rare ability to build very interesting stuff right in his own back yard. Using only hand tools, he constructed small furniture and made repairs around his property. I loved to go to his place and watch him working on projects. He was eager to show me what he was doing and was very passionate about his work, and sometimes he allowed me the chance to take his projects into my hands and finish them. One of his most ambitious undertakings that truly showed me a good example of perseverance and diligence was his construction of a catamaran. It was a project big enough for several adults, considering the complexity of design and limited materials and tools he had at his disposal. He took the drawings from some hobby magazine and was so absorbed in this project with such enthusiasm that several other guys from his class so Sasha and I got sucked into the venture with him. Petrukha was only fourteen years old, but he took on more work than any of us, and he exercised fanatical dedication and overwhelming commitment. By recycling old plywood boxes and wooden scraps, he finally finished that catamaran.

We all carried that giant monster through the streets for several miles to the river. After sailing for about half a day on it, we noticed that it had begun taking water into its plywood pontoons, so we quickly maneuvered it to shore, where it sank right before our eyes. It was sad to see the loss of such an irreplaceable vessel, but the sense of accomplishment of such enormous project was a great reward for all of us, and I was glad I had played at least a small part in it. Petrukha stood as a good example before me as a man of indestructible devotion, and his accomplishments have frequently brought him to the forefront of my mind during the most challenging times of my life.

New Year Madness and Other Gigs

A few weeks later, we had to play the biggest party of the year: The New Year's celebration. Our program had to be at least four hours long. To understand the vanity surrounding our New Year's festivities is impossible unless you consider that it was the only holiday with origins not based on the Bolsheviks. It was not politically driven, so there were no hypocritical feelings about it, and people could happily enjoy it in spite of Soviet politics and mandates. It didn't require holiday postcards bearing Communistic slogans or glorifying our totalitarian lifestyle. For this reason, New Year's was truly the favorite observance for all Soviet folks, and no one loved it more than kids and teenagers.

At our school, a great deal of preparation always went into our New Year's masquerade, the best and longest dance of the year. It was going to be my first year playing in the band for the extravaganza, and in preparation for the upcoming long night and our expanded music program, we decided to throw a little show onstage and dress for it in a wicked outfit. Our plan was to wear a shocking ensemble that would look completely different from the boring medieval masks and snowman costumes typical for this event.

When the night of the party arrived, we were behind the large stage curtain doing our last-minute adjustments. In the middle of a concert hall, a giant New Year's/ Christmas tree was erected. Everything was decorated in snowflakes and winter themes, making for a festive, casual atmosphere without any political attributes to dull it down. There were no official ceremonial speeches and lectures prior the dancing this time, much to our relief, as this was commonplace. It was nothing but fun and dancing, a special night indeed. Crowds filled the dance floor early, and kids began to clap in anticipation for a great night of fun and music and dancing. The curtain was raised, and instead of everybody seeing the band playing on stage, there were nothing there but our lonely equipment. A few minutes later, everyone began chanting for us to come out.

One of Sasha's classmates announced on the microphone, "Dear friends, unfortunately, our school VIA could not come to play for this party, and we had no option but to invite musicians who have never played together before." She was so convincing in her false announcement that the crowd believed her entirely and booed. "Allow me to introduce... Cavemen!"

In complete shock of the crowd Andrew ran out from backstage, dressed in a goat skin, with his face covered in black ashes. He had a club in his hand and climbed behind the drum kit to start playing a fast beat. Right after Andrew, Valentine came out in a tuxedo, with a monocular in his eye, a tall hat on his head, and a large cigar in his mouth. He had a huge portfolio of note sheets, which he showered all over his piano and then sat behind it like a cartoon character of a Capitalist, placing his feet on the keyboard. "Mister Twister!" the girl introduced him.

Our school band before New Year party.
From left: Me, Andrew (top),
Valentine and Sasha with his bass guitar.

Under escalating beat of drums, Sasha came out in completely trashed outfit with ripped-up pants and a long blond wig covering his head. "Please meet Lost Hippie Boy!" she said under the loud laughter of the crowd.

Andrew was beating harder and harder on his drums, and the energized audience could not wait for the music to start.

"And now, our last guest from the uneducated Western world, Dumb Student!" the girl said, trying to overpower the crowd.

I came out in super high-heeled women's shoes and pants completely covered in pins and attached ropes. My inside-out jacket was torn and sliced in pieces. I had a bright red wig and dark glasses to complete my outfit. I held a Russian language textbook in one hand, upside down, and I greeted everyone by making a V with my fingers.

"Happy New Year!" the girl shouted into a microphone.

After the extra-long drum prelude, we plummeted into Led Zeppelin's "Rock and Roll." The audience went absolutely nuts. Usually we never began our show with a foreign songs and always left them for the end of the dances. We weren't sure how they would react, but our calculations were perfect, and the party took off before we even started to play. It was by far the craziest night we ever had in our school band experience. It lasted almost until two o'clock in the morning, and even the teachers did not want it to end, as they were enjoying it as much as the kids.

Everything on that night was remarkable and unforgettable, from our music to the stunts and costumes onstage. In spite of the fact that they were somewhat comical, we looked and acted wild, playing music no one was even allowed to listen to in public. My upside-down school book was a message to my teacher, and she knew that when I came out on stage with it. She adored it in her own way, and it wasn't like our relationship could have gotten any worse. We left school that night exhausted and happy, filled with memories that will never be erased for any of us who were there.

See How Others Played

At that point, I already had a feeling music would undoubtedly be a major part of my life. I dedicated all my spare time to it, from listening to records and radio to playing guitar. I loved picking up new songs, and when I ran out of songs to pick apart to find chords and licks, I started to experiment with pieces of classical music and popular melodies. I chose the easiest tunes from Tchaikovsky or List and tried to play them in my own finger-style. It was very difficult at first, and I could not understand how all flamenco guitar players managed to combine the melody and accompaniment chords to play simultaneously. Slowly, I discovered how to manipulate the chords and notes to produce the sound I'd been looking for. With practice, I learned few classic tunes and shortly learned how to play some rock ballads and songs in the same manner. It was fascinating for me to discover almost endless playing potentiality of the guitar as a musical instrument. When we had no chance to play together either at the band or with Sasha, this unusual technique gave me an opportunity to stay busy and be occupied with my guitar almost endlessly.

Going to concerts was not only entertaining, but also educational for us. However, it was not that easy to do. Bands rarely visited our city on tours. This was due not only to the limited number of VIAs in our country at that time, but also to the fact that they preferred to play in big cities where our Gomel was not such a candidate. Even if any Soviet band would come to our town, it was difficult to get a ticket for the show. The music was so censored that it had nothing to offer the rock 'n roll enthusiasts. We did, however, manage to find a vey convenient alternative.

Besides working at our school, Senya, our boss, also had a part-time job as a band manager of the VIA that played nights at one of the city RDKs (a Soviet "Regional Palace of Culture"). This center was specially dedicated to entertainment, cultural, and informational purposes, and public dances were held there two or three nights per week. Every RDK had its own VIA, which employed amateur musicians for a nominal monthly pay. To play in one of them was almost as prestigious as being onstage at our Kletka, except the RDK operated year-round, with the exception of the three summer months. The same rules applied at RDK: You had to be at least sixteen years old to be on the dance floor. In our case, we had a perfect connection, as Senya not only helped us get in to listen to his band play, but even encouraged us to learn something new from them. Boss did not personally play in that band, and he rarely showed up to watch them rehearse. He was, in my opinion, fortunate or talented to gather around himself musicians whom he had no need to show how to play every note, and this allowed him freedom and limited headaches with his students.

Since we were still far from sixteen, we made sure to arrive at the RDK earlier. The band members let us hide in their gear locker until they finished setting up the stage and the dancing began. Watching those guys playing was an incredible experience for us. They sounded awesome. From their stage presence to their skill, they gave us a lot of good examples to imitate and learn from. Usually, we sat at the corner of the stage and enjoyed the show. The songs they played were not as wild as ours, for it would have been too risky and dangerous for them to openly perform rock music that authorities had banned at that time. They still played Beatles, Rolling Stones, and Credence, but they did not want to risk including bands like Black Sabbath or Led Zeppelin in their program. We were somewhat happy that our band was more "progressive," and they laughed in disbelief when we told them what we played at our dances.

At one point, Sasha scored by being allowed to play and sing few songs with those guys. To see him perform together with skilled adult musicians was very impressive. I hoped I'd have the honor of doing the same some day, but at that time, I was more concerned about not provoking any curiosity of cops who might come around asking why I was there so late at my age.

We visited that place with Sasha practically every weekend, and even when my friend didn't feel like going, I went there by myself. I never regretted it until someone tipped off the authorities that a minors were sneaking into the dances. When Sasha was caught there by a cop, he told him he was sixteen but even holding cigarette in his mouth did not help him prove his lie, and he was promptly thrown out an I spent couple hours hiding in the gear locker. Once everyone left and the last piece of equipment went back to the storage, the band guys let me out. Later the band members were questioned, and when Senya heard about it, he told us never to mention his name if we went there again. We learned our lesson and stayed away from that place – at least for a while.

Playing for Other Schools

Occasionally, we were invited to play a dance at other schools. We had to do these jam sessions in which we provided music for less fortunate schools that did not have their own VIAs. At that time, every party had to have a live band, and there was no such thing as a DJ in the USSR. If live music was not available for people to dance, a turntable (and later tape players) served this purpose, but this was considered an embarrassing surrogate of live entertainment, something only used by poor village people. Dancing to records would only gather a fraction of the crowd compared to a music band, and not many people wanted to participate in such a savage type of dance. Live musicians guaranteed a more lively, happy crowd, and the shortage of bands in the city kept any ensemble busy, helping others to have fun. Since only a handful of schools had their own organized bands, we became rather well known across the city as guys who could put out quality entertainment for others. Often, our rehearsals were replaced by gigs somewhere on the other side of the city. Sometimes we had only a few hours notice, but we had grown accustomed to that and had learned how to get all our equipment loaded on the truck so we could be ready not only for playing the dance, but also to practice new songs on the way to the gig. It was often enough for me and Sasha to play chords in the car, and Valentine. would then know what he had to do behind his keyboard when we arrived. Andrew's part was always easy, and having played drums for a couple of years, our talented drummer could pick up almost any song with a simple hint of any given rhythm.

Playing at other schools' parties and dances was always an intriguing experience. We enjoyed the chance to observe new audiences and see the reactions of people who had never heard a live band before. The most common question we were asked was, "When you will come again?" We were slowly gaining a reputation of being a quality band, especially because of our "progressive" repertoire. We played songs that put kids in hysteria and teachers in shock, and for that, we received overwhelming compliments. It was also interesting to see the differences in rules and policies between different schools.

Some of them reminded me of the stiff authoritarian dominion I had experienced at School # 10, where kids were uptight and always looked over their shoulders, trying not to behave "inappropriately." The worst place we played was a few months later at a place called the Sport "Internat". It was one of those places where kids lived and studied all week, with the exception of optional weekends and breaks when they could go home. This compound was designed to grow professional athletes and sports enthusiasts. It did not take long for us to realize that they had no other interests in life besides building a sports career. When we began to play at our gig there, it seemed no one wanted to dance, and their angry-looking teachers were marching around the floor like a police squad, making this slow party even more frigid. Everything seemed unwelcoming and over-controlled. The dance ended right on time, which was not typical at all. At Sports Internat, the military-like discipline and gorilla-looking teachers forced kids to run back to their rooms the minute the dance was over. It was sad compared to what we usually experienced.

When the last kid left the ballroom, we were still sitting on stage. Sasha came to a microphone and said, "And now, this goodnight song is for little children who don't want to sleep," and whispered to us "Highway Star." We gave our best performance of the popular Deep Purple tune, and it reverberated from the empty concert hall through the corridors of the Internat with awesome power. We knew we could be heard in every corner of the building, and we knew it would anger the militant teachers. I still cannot believe how loosely we behaved at our gigs, and if we were unable to make a crowd unwind, we at least always made sure to make it fun for ourselves.

Proper Equipment and Its Care

The importance of having quality equipment could not be underestimated when playing in the band. While our guitars were better than other Soviet examples that were nearly impossible to play, our other equipment reflected on the overall poor quality of "Made in the USSR" products. At any given moment, we were at risk for equipment failure, and nothing was worse than when it happened during or right before our gigs. Smoking amplifiers and blown speakers were true obstacles for us, especially when we were in full swing at school parties. It was always embarrassing, even though we had nothing to do with it. In order to save face and keep the party going, we had to act or react right in these challenging situations. As always, our "master" and savior in these unpredictable scenarios was our leader Sasha. I was always caught off guard onstage when these kind of problems happened, and my instant reaction to smoke billowing out of the amplifier was to turn everything off and tell everyone that the party was over. It was not even an option with my pal Sasha. In countless situations like these, on the fly he threw the cables from one amp into another, often combining the bass and vocal. It didn't make for the best sound combination, but at least the sound was still there. If the microphone suddenly went silent, he would not stop playing and grabbed it from the piano as he continued to sing as if nothing was wrong. He was always declaring, "The show must go on," even when we had multiple gear failures and had to combine everything into one surviving amp. Sasha wanted us to play despite delivering distorting and cruel sounding music. It was painful to my ears to hear all this and act like nothing was wrong, but Sasha assured us, "Most of these people on the floor are not sure how we are supposed to sound anyway. They'd rather dance to a bunch of clanging cans than to have to go home." And he was right. The quality of our music was not really a concern for our audience. Even when our Soviet-made amplifiers failed at the worst possible moments, the crowd was happy to see that it did not keep them from enjoying the dance floor.

The struggles we faced with our equipment were nothing new, and malfunctioning, poor quality products were part of the Soviet life. We lived knowing that things would one day break; it was never a question of if, but when. We learned at the young age to cope with unexpected hassles in the Soviet life, and we learned this lesson well when it came to our band equipment.

Repair services were not only slow in getting the job done, but it was also a drag to deal with them. It was no one's job but ours to take our faulty equipment to the repair facilities and check on when they would be ready. The repairmen seemed to hate having to watch us kids drag our heavy amps into their shops, and they always greeted us with sincere condolences for our troubles, but in spite of their compassion, the work still seemed to take forever to get done.

Partly because of the long wait, it was always a great joy to get our repaired amps back, like long-awaited ammo delivered to the battlefields. Nothing was more delightful, more fulfilling, more pleasing to us to have our amps working in full spectrum so we could make high-quality music.

Chapter 10

First Music Competition, the Fame, and the TV Performance

Winter was at its peak, and piles of snow were everywhere across the city. Frosty windows in our concert hall sparkled under bright, sunny light, and we were slowly setting up our equipment for a scheduled rehearsal. When we saw Senya walking onstage, we were surprised to see him coming. He usually only came onstage if he needed to tell us something important, and it was no different this time. "Alright, guys," he said, clapping his hands to get our attention as he roamed around the stage. "The city has invited us to participate in the youth music competition, "Red Currants" (a symbol of Bolshevik Revolution). Today, the school has decided to give you a chance to show the quality of music you can deliver because you may be able to score high among other schools with a great performance."

Upon hearing this exciting news, we went nuts and began jumping around like little kids, shouting in exultation about what we could play to destroy all the potential competitors. From popular Soviet love songs to Beatles and Pink Floyd tunes, the suggestions were thrown into the air.

Senya stopped us with a raised hand. "You guys are crazy! This is not a dancing party. It's an official State music competition, and I have already picked what you are going to play." He sat down behind the piano and opened his notebook. "You will play 'Red Cavalry'," he said and started playing an awful racy song.

We stood around him and looked at each other, quietly chuckling. "I am not playing this", I thought to myself. It was absolutely terrible. Just the title itself was an insult to our rock'n roll spirits. Not only would it be embarrassing to play such silly song, but even to announce the title onstage. We all had the same feelings, but our boss knew what he was doing. He had no any illusions about the beauty of this song or its propagandistic thematic. He was not on a mission to impress young girls and boys. His job was to make us succeed before the official city judges, who knew nothing about rock'n roll beside that it was the "product of our ideological enemies."

We had only couple of weeks to get ready for the competition. If we could win it, we would move on to the regionals. After that, it would be the all-Republic finals—the prestigious event that was our ultimate goal.

Without any delay, we began practicing our "Red Calvary" song. Senya demanded perfection and got after us for every minute deviation or minor mistake. No one liked the song, but it was not up to us to decide, so we submitted to our wise boss and worked like we were on some grueling treadmill.

Senya was dead serious about the competition and made all of us sing. I knew it would be a personal struggle for me to sing the silly propaganda without giggling in the middle of it, and that's exactly what happened during rehearsal. Senya flipped out about this and asked me if I would be willing to keep it to myself and pull off the song without laughing during competition. I was honest with him and told him I could not promise that. My honesty meant the end of my singing part for that performance, but that was a great relief to me. I just wanted to play guitar.

For some reason, the competition was very important to our school administration. Our principal stopped in at our daily rehearsals, and he complimented us on our playing. Even our teachers were instructed to expect and excuse our earlier dismissals from classes if we needed to practice. We were pretty sure this was because the competition and its outcome had something to do with the school's financial budget, and school employees would benefit from our success in this event.

We were ready for our first battle onstage with only one minor problem: Our band did not have a name. At that time, every VIA below the professional level adult band was simply associated with the place it belonged or attached to. Even if some adult band from the factory or a local Palace of Culture came up with its own name, everybody called them the "Brick Factory" Band or "Palace of Chemistry Workers" Band or something like that. In our case, it was different. Senya said we needed a name, and we started throwing out great-sounding ideas: Coliseum, Shockwave, Speed of Sound. Many of the names we suggested were in English. Senya covered his face with hands and shook his head, mumbling, "You guys want to lose this competition before you even get on stage? Do you? Your band name is going to be "The Friendly Fellows."

"What?!" we all said with sour faces.

"There will be no arguing!" Senya replied and left the stage.

We felt awful. Not only did we have to play a song fit for the 1920s (which we were well past) before a cavalry army, but we also had to go onstage with a band name fit for a kindergarten dancing group. In spite of the honkey entourage he was forcing us to be, we had to succumb to what we felt was our boss's humiliating plan.

Despite having not very appealing band name and a totally "un-cool" song to perform, we were very exciting about our upcoming contest. The thrill of a true competition against other performers and the chance to advance to a higher, more interesting venture was keeping our spirits high. I felt very fortunate that all the changes within last year had brought me not only to my dream of playing in the band, but also to taste the interesting aspects of our unusual music life.

My parents were happy about my new school and my participation in the band. I was obsessed with music, and my strong dedication to the band with regular guitar practice made them satisfied and proud of me. My grades were good, and I never complained about anything. Life felt better than ever, and I often compared it to the days when I was a School # 10 student. I felt like an escapee from captivity, given a new chance for freedom and joyful changes. I was sure those days were the happiest of my life, in spite of the primitive, humble Soviet reality around me. Everything ahead looked very promising and optimistic.

Taking the Stage

The truck came early in the morning to take our equipment to the Palace of Pioneers, where our first (and maybe last) round of competition was going to take place. Everybody was nervous, despite that we were prepared very well and had to deliver only one song.

All kind of music groups—from choral and folk ensembles to individual singers—gathered from around the city to represent their schools in the competition. Everyone was broken down into groups, and we waited for our audition while we watched our competitors go onstage one by one. We could not resist the temptation to comment the lousy execution of songs and music onstage and quietly showered the performers with hideous jokes; it was far too easy to mock and ridicule the other bands. Senya was trying to keep us quiet, but he could barely keep from laughing himself at what we were saying. "Let's see how well you do up there," he whispered to us with a great deal of seriousness, and it instantly woke us up and forced us to sit quietly.

We climbed onstage, and after everything was set up and ready to go, we realized it was not as easy to look at the full concert hall and judges and play as casually as we had always done at the school dances. When the first chords were strummed, everything went back to normal. Costumed in identical gray and blue suits, we delivered a smooth, balanced performance of our "Red Cavalry." The song felt like had no end. While it was a fast and dynamic song, we all felt it played four times longer than at our rehearsals. When it was over, the short pause was broken by applause. The only people who had no reaction seemed to be the judges. We left the competition tired from stress. No one wanted to talk about our performance, and despite that Senya was very happy with what we'd done, he cautioned us that in this competition, the judges were the ones who would make the final call.

The Judges' Deliberation

We had to wait another week before the results of our audition were sorted out and the final decision was announced. When Senya came to our rehearsal, his expression was stiff and not very encouraging. He did not know how to deliver the news and decided to play a little game with us. We thought we had been outperformed, and for a moment, were in a state of shock. Finally, Senya broke the news to us. Along with a few other competitors, we had passed the audition and advanced to the next regional round of the "Red Currants" competition. The joy of victory filled our young hearts, and we were ecstatic. There was something fabulous about our achievement that gave us another level of confidence in our performances.

After our win at that first stage of competition, the school administration was absolutely delighted. The first harvests of a true appreciation for our hard work began to outpour on our heads in ways we hadn't dreamed. First of all, we were granted as much time as needed for rehearsals, and there was unlimited time off from classes to accommodate our practice. Of course, we put this privilege to good use every time we simply wanted to skip the class or have a short school day. Friends and classmates were jealous when we were rocking the stage while they had to entertain teachers with their homework and tests.

The funds for our band equipment were allocated to new amplifiers and anything we needed for a better-sounding performance. Buying all this stuff was not so easy though. It was our job to find what were looking for in the stores and then deal with the bureaucratic Soviet purchasing system for schools and government organizations. Piles of documents had to be filled out for this purposes. Sasha was the leader in all of our affairs, and this was no exception. We searched everywhere, even raiding the inventories of shabby music stores. A big green Fuzz/Wah pedal was one of my trophies from these hunts, and it afforded me my first chance to get the sound out of my guitar that I'd heard the real rock bands used on the tapes I'd listened to.

The powerful amplifiers and speakers were only available through the special distribution system for government organizations, and the only ones we could buy outside that system were either not suitable for our needs or of extremely poor quality. Despite these limitations, we used the opportunity as an excuse to skip school again, claiming we were on a "chase for a band equipment" while we were really out watching the latest movies in the cinema.

Going to the Second Round

After our first success, everyone was even more dedicated to helping us succeed. Our school, teachers, and our boss Senya were definitely behind us. He decided to bring in two extra guys to sing with our band, and he promised we would sound as good as British band Queen. After auditioning dozens of candidates, Senya chose Sergey and Andrew T. to join us for the next round of "Red Currants" competition.

This time we were allowed to add one more song to our program, and Senya picked a wonderful song called "Grass of Childhood." The flowing melody and touching lyrics of the World War II thematic was a perfect counterbalance for the speedy "Red Calvary" song.

The never-ending rehearsals had begun, and what Senya had promised to us began to slowly emerge from our hours and days of tedious singing practice. He made all six of us sing, and before long, we did sound somewhat like Queen's "Bohemian Rhapsody." He fought with us to make sure every note sounded exactly as he wanted, and we trusted that Senya knew what he was doing. It was hard but very rewarding. Not only had we mastered that song to proficiency, but we also developed the confidence to use our collective singing to elevate many of the songs we'd used in our regular dancing programs.

The day of the regional competition arrived, and at the Palace of Lenin, the best young musicians, folk, and choral groups gathered to perform before thousand of visitors, friends, and judges.

For a Soviet Union concert hall, it was an enormous building with an incredible stage and lightning system. Just to stand on such an impressive stage was intimidating and nerve wracking. When we finished our performance, the whole audience got up out of their chairs to give us a standing ovation. Elderly spectators and World War II veterans were touched by the emotional song "Grass of Childhood" and wept while they exclaimed, "Bravo! Bravo!" We really did deliver a great performance, thanks to the days and hours of intense rehearsals. All of us, including Senya, were extremely happy about it.

A week later, we received incredible knew that the judges had chosen us among a few who would represent our region at the Belarusian State finals in its capital Minsk. For our band, it would prove to be an unforgettable journey.

Ups and Downs of Little Popularity

Playing in the band was not only big-time fun and a passion for my friends and me, but it was also a lifestyle unknown to many people in USSR at that time. The status of celebrity in our country only existed for a select group of Soviet-approved elite artists. No one knew the personal life details of those bands or treated them in the way typical for the Western World. It did not apply to kids in the school, where everything had its own rules and expected behavior. The school band always had celebrity status, regardless of the quality of music they delivered. In our case, we were also the most popular guys in school. To be our friend or sit at the same desk in class with any of us was an honor and a privilege. The success at the music contest brought that status to a much higher level. Yes, we all had girls chasing us, and secret notes asking for dates were passed to us almost on a daily bases. Our personal lives were not under paparazzi-style scrutiny, but our phone numbers became public domain in school. Kids knew where we lived and also a lot about our families. Some kind of miniature Hollywood-like vanity surrounded us, and we were often more irritated by the attention than flattered by it. Being in the limelight was fun, but to deal with it every day eventually became annoying. As is the case for any teen, the rejected girls grew angry, and the school hallways were often filled with gossip and completely absurd stories about us. While everybody wanted to be our friend most of the time, it was impossible to tell if they had true intentions of friendship or if the "cool factor" was playing the major part in their infatuation with us.

A few girls in my class had crushes on me while I played in the band, but unfortunately, they were often not the ones I wanted to be with. The blind dates and secret phone calls became a routine part of our school life. It was all childish fun and games until a girl became a stalker, which happened occasionally. It was not easy to put a stop to such behavior, and the actions we had to take to do so were often regretful and not always kind. The price we paid for our small local popularity came in all forms, and there were no precedents or established protocols as to how to deal with something like that in our society. The craze was noticed by teachers, and they didn't help matters much. Most of them were either jealous or atrocious toward us and insulted us in class with nasty remarks about the band. We had to take it all: envy from the teachers and tears from the girls who had crushes on us. Sometimes we wished everything could just be back to normal, but those were futile wishes.

In many cases, just passing through the neighborhood streets was not an easy task for me, mostly because the local youngsters knew us only as musicians. They enjoyed dragging us into their houses to entertain them with our guitars while they drank booze. Not only it was irritating, but it was just plain dangerous. Playing a few songs was not always enough for many. Following Russian tradition, it was a sign of disrespect to refuse to drink with the "master of the house." Some people had no problem honoring this ancient tradition, even if it meant shoving full glasses of wine or vodka in the faces of twelve- or thirteen-year-old kids.

Going on TV

When Senya told us we had been invited to perform at the local TV station, we did not even know if we should scream, cry, or break our equipment in euphoria. It was our first of several TV appearances, and the chances were something like winning a mega lotto. It was, without a doubt, the most prized and rewarding achievement for anybody in Soviet music, considering even professional musicians could have had a lifelong career and never have been afforded the luxury of appearing on television. In fact, at that time, the idea of television itself was still something somewhat magical, so being on TV was a stamp of great honor and respect. It was also time of Soviet-style broadcasting, in an era without MTV or cable channels. Local stations in cities like ours had only few hours of programs a day, and only a handful of those were dedicated to music and art; those who were lucky enough to play music on television were usually playing accordions and balalaikas in their hands. Standing in the front of TV camera in those days with electric guitars was about as common as a celestial eclipse—a true rarity—and to be invited to do such a thing in our country would instantly mean true celebrity status.

It was not only an epic event for us, but also for our school and those who would be watching us. We were, without question, the first teenage group in our city who was honored with the chance to play at our local TV station, and the avalanche of delirium about this flooded our minds with anticipation.

Everything about this experience was new and mysterious for us. When we arrived at the local network facility, we had no knowledge of the studio recording procedures or anything related to a TV play. We brought a truck full of our equipment, only to find out that a couple amps were needed to record the instrumental tracks. The microphones and studio mixers were so impressive looking that we felt like we had stepped into some futuristic space rocket control room. First, we had to record our instrumental part, without vocals, and were told to be ready to dedicate a whole day to doing that. Two of our vocal guys had to go home, and we began the excruciating but exciting process of recording, which last almost till midnight.

In front of TV Station before audio recording. From left: Valentine, Sasha, me and Andrew.

Everything there was not only mysterious and sophisticated, but also seemed somehow sacred. Considering that television glamour was granted only to a few select chosen ones in our country, the studio felt unique and priceless, enveloped in a museum-like mystique. We touched and rubbed everything we could, and as was common for us, we dedicated plenty of time to practical jokes. A few priceless pictures were taken in front of the studio and inside it, complete with a lot of childish and funny poses.

When the video part of our performance had to be recorded, we arrived at the studio in our gray and blue suits and baked under the bright heat-emitting lights for several hours. Playing only a couple of songs and spending so much time and effort for it was a new and unexpected experience for us. We were happy when it was over, and all we had to do was wait for the day of the program broadcast.

Inside TV Station before Video Recording. From Left:
Sergey, Andrew, me, Senya, Valentine, Sasha, Andrew T.

Reunions and TV Broadcast

One of our annual Soviet school gatherings was a reunion party, in which old students and classmates could get together and see each other many years after graduation. The well-established tradition consisted of a long-lasting dancing night, and everyone looked forward to it with great anticipation.

The predominant difference between the reunion and regular parties and dances was that it was not open for the current school students. Only graduates and alumni were invited. However, it was practically impossible to tell if the attendees had ever even attended our school. It obviously became a problematic issue. Depending on where students lived, they might not have been able to take part in the regular dances, so the reunion became somewhat of a free party for everyone in the neighborhood, presenting the school administration with multiple challenges in controlling and regulating who attended the event. Many who claimed they had attended our school could barely find its location and brought their friends from every corner of the city when they did.

Andrew and me rocking "Smoke on the Water". The covering ears hairdo was "hot".

These parties were always packed to the legal limit, and the doors had to be closed to retain order. Because the participants were not students or kids and no longer had to obey the school staff, the teachers had a difficult time controlling these reunion parties. Not only that, but many of them attended simply to resolve old disagreements they had with other former students. Police presence was practically mandatory, and the nasty fights between groups of old rivals kept them busy. In one such situation, the party had to be stopped early when several people got involved in a fierce battle using bike chains and knives. The bloody clash forced our school administration to stop the festivity and an angry crowd had to go home.

Playing for this party was not as fun as playing for our regular school crowd. Not only were most of the audience unfamiliar to us, but they were also less enthusiastic on the dance floor. For us, it felt like playing for "old" people, in spite of the fact that most of them were only in their mid-twenties or older.

It was, however, interesting to see the reaction of the older guys to our performance. We received constant comments about how well we played, and we made sure to perform certain songs from their past multiple times during this nights. Playing for an audience with such a different reaction to our music was very beneficial for us. Not only did we get a peek of the different styles and interactions of the other generation on the floor, but we also learned how to play for older folks who had a different attitude than the normal high school crowd.

Still, I personally did not like these gatherings so much because of their violent and unpredictable flow. It was way better, in my opinion, to play for people I knew, without the company of police cars around our school at the time of the party. Nevertheless, it proved to be a good learning experience for me—one that would prove beneficial later in life when I played at weddings, which were, by far, the wildest of Soviet parties.

TV Broadcast of Our Performance

When the day of the TV broadcast of the show with our performance was announced, the whole school was informed about it by a special school bulletin and an announcement at our newsstand.

We got together with Sasha and our parents to watch the show. It was absolutely surreal to see ourselves on the TV screen. We laughed about the fact that the television versions of us did not look like we did in real life. It was without a doubt an unforgettable event for our parents to see us reaching the highest honor in Soviet entertainment media.

In the dressing room at TV Station.

We knew our TV appearance would bring a load of different reactions from our classmates, teachers, and friends. What we didn't know was that the outcry of interest about us would come from much further distances. Letters started coming from girls who wanted to meet us, asking for our phone numbers and contacts. Many of them sent photographs of themselves, and every time we received more fan mail, we were eager to see what girl it was from and what school or class was interested in us. It was a very bizarre experience, and it gave us a lot of good laughs. We did not know what to do with all the letters we received. There were some we wanted to reply to with some ludicrous comments, but when the amount of incoming mail grew too large for us to read it all, we began opening them up just to see the girls' pictures. Some of them were very nice looking, and there was sometimes a dispute as to who would write back to them. It never evolved into anything more than curiosity, as far as relationships went, and no one ever went to meet our correspondents. The "romances" consisted of only a few exchanged letters, but the craze died down a couple months later. After that, life went back to a normal pace for us, and we were able to focus once again on our popularity within the walls of our own school.

Chapter 11

Young Bolsheviks,Bizarre Bedlams, and Jeans

Every time I had a chance to listen the radio, I opted for either music stations broadcasting in Russian language or the U.S. and British political programs. They talked a lot about human rights violations in the USSR and our political prisoners. I wondered if their speculations and observations were true. When the topic concerned something we all knew about—like lines in stores or restrictions on international travel and our access to foreign culture—we needed no proof because those were things we dealt with on a daily basis. The fact that Soviet propaganda labeled those radio programs as a bevy of lies caused me some doubt in trusting our own information sources. Another question that ate away at me was why our government insisted on jamming the foreign programs if they were not telling the truth. One thing I knew for sure was that Communism allowed no freedom of choice in your personal opinions, and there was no liberty granted for political viewpoints. An excellent example of that were the upcoming changes that all teens in the Soviet Union had to go through in our schools, and I was no exception.

When we reached the seventh grade, our Pioneer membership automatically expired, and it was time for us to become Komsomolets, members of "All-Union Leninist Young Communist League." This was, for all intents and purposes, nothing more than a Communist youth organization that extended the less aggressive ideological teachings of the Pioneer school organization. The process of becoming a Komsomolets was quite different from the automatic age level-based participation in the Pioneer Youth League. It was not a mandatory practice, but all children were encouraged with irresistible force to pursue this goal. As a result of these rather forceful persuasions and coercion, practically all students in seventh grade pledged the oath to serve the nation as young Communists and follow the "older brother," the Communist Party of the USSR, to build the "Bright Proletarian" society. We were taught that we should sacrifice for it our own interests—if need be, even our souls. A little red flag pin with Lenin's profile was issued to every new member, along with a membership book. This was to be guarded and carried by your heart at all times. Paying the monthly dues and participating in regular patriotic meetings and drills was considered the "proud duty" of every Komsomolets.

In the official guidelines, only the best and truly dedicated Communist children could join the political organization, but the reality was very different from that. Practically anyone could become a Komsomolets without any problem. A formal application and a short meeting of the school Komsomol leaders was all it took to be granted a warm welcome into another Soviet brainwashing organization. Recruiting new members was the obligation of every Komsomolets. When the pool of volunteers grew then, the comrades of the organization began to apply heavy pressure to those who had no interest in joining the League. The moral and patriotic cards were played before potential victims of this Communistic trap. Only degraded characters with horrible grades in school and criminal records were considered unworthy of this so-called privileged, and everyone else was relentlessly pressured, even threatened, by the Komsomol leaders to join the organization.

"Thank you, no Komsomol please."

The time came when I became a target of teachers and our Komsomol heads to join the League. My opinion about the Soviet system was already well established, and to participate in anything related to Communism or its organization was not a viable option for me. I was aware of the consequences of openly refusing to join the Komsomol and did everything I could to stay out of it without revealing my true opinion of Communism. The easiest way to escape membership was to state, "I'm really not ready morally or spiritually for such privilege." Playing this game would not buy me a lot of time since everybody knew I was not a criminal nor a slacker in school and that I was most certainly ripe for the picking. Even more than that, the fact that I participated in the school band only encouraged them in their pursuit of me, because they would have the patriotic-looking benefit of having one more Komsomolets onstage. I did everything I could to brush off the constant recruiting attacks of my annoying teachers and the League leaders. I made every excuse, even telling them I had no money to pay the membership fees and making jokes that I wanted to remain a Pioneer for life. Surprisingly, in the end, I prevailed. Suddenly everything stopped and no one bothered me anymore about Komsomol. It was a bit strange and unnerving when the raging recruiting frenzy stopped so bluntly, and what or who was behind this sudden change will remain a mystery. Someone obviously told them they were wasting their time bothering me about it. As nice as it was that the pressure stopped, I knew that as part of Soviet life, even something like that could mean that a "note" about my firs resistance to participate in Komsomol was sent to "higher" authorities .

"How about drums?"

My interest in the band did not stop at playing guitar and learning new songs. Just as a curiosity, I began practicing drums and exploring sounds of piano. The drums gave me a great deal of fun. For some reason, I found them to be very energetic and stimulating. Andrew showed me many tricks and basics, and when it was possible, I played some songs on the drums. Over time, I learned them well enough that I could have played practically our entire program on the drums if I'd had to. I loved to play guitar, but the ability to play more than one instrument was very beneficial, especially in the USSR at that time.

While my attempt to master drums was quite successful, I didn't do so well on the piano. I was unable to read the notes, and while I did pick up some chords from Valentine, I could not advance into a more serious level of play on this magnificent instrument. I never tried to take any classes or make an effort to study music notes. Because I chose to pick up songs by ear the same way I did on guitar, my piano skills were limited to learning a few simple songs. This was not so upsetting for me, though, for I dedicated most of my time to playing my beloved guitar.

When It's Never Enough

One of the most bizarre, unusual ways Sasha and I entertained ourselves was our improvised band "practicing" at home. I am not even sure who came up with such a peculiar idea, but what came out of it was the strangest and most fascinating amusement.

My old Minsk R-7 radio/turntable was broken for a long time, but at one point it was repaired by my cousin just as a "challenge" project, and I now could again play my records on it. It was not even close to the quality of the stereo we had at home, but it delivered a very loud and punchy sound. Still, it served us well as a home guitar amplifier, and we decided to do something similar to what had been known in the West as a Karaoke, sing-along entertainment.

We began playing some of our few small Soviet records like the Beatles, Rolling Stones, Credence, and Deep Purple, which I had at that time. At the same time, we plugged our guitars into the Minsk R-7 and began to play along, balancing the sound of our instruments and records. It made for very loud and interesting music. After doing that just with our guitars, we started singing, as well assisting by adding some of our own vocals. To give this idea a more pronounced feel, we later made a little change. With my newfound ability to play drums, we took cymbals from our school set to create an improvised drum kit, in conjunction with few boxes, pots, and buckets. I beat into them without mercy, and Sasha played bass, cranking the volume all the way up on my Minsk R-7 radio. We blended nearly perfect with the original record songs. The bright, loud sound of cymbals made everything sound fresh and natural.

We truly wreaked havoc in our house. With our accompaniments, songs like "My Lady from Tokyo," "Can't Buy Me Love," and others shook the floor and penetrated our apartment building with piercing sound. It did not take long before my neighbors were at the door with non-negotiable demands to stop. After that, we moved to Sasha's apartment, but the result was the same. No one, including our parents, could tolerate this madness. The solution came with a brilliant idea of moving everything to Sasha's balcony. Since passing cars never bothered residents with their noise, we assumed our music would be a delight for pedestrians to hear, particularly in comparison to the rumbling trucks. There were no limits on the balcony to how loud we could sing, play drums, or crank up the music. We did it with passion and the almighty power of my radio, and it was wild. Not only did no one complain, but some folks even came out on nearby balconies to listen to our ridiculous musical innovations. Some of them even shouted and applauded after we finished. It was an incredible amount of fun. My poor Minsk R-7 was working in overdrive, reaching distorted levels of sound to make the whole makeshift concert a real bedlam. Bypassing pedestrians looked up to try to understand what was happening up on the balconies. Many of them stopped and after listening for a while, either laughed or walked away shaking heads. We had a great time. We did it practically all the time as long as the weather was not cold and rainy. This extravagant form of fun gave us a chance to stay in touch with the music between our rehearsals or on school breaks.

Jeans

Despite all the efforts of our government to block it, it was an era when popular youth culture and fashion was penetrating our closed society. One of the most distinctive visual symbols and glorified fashion trends at that time was jeans. The popularity and overwhelming desire to own a pair surpassed anything our nation had ever seen in the past. The quest to obtain the denim pants, which weren't produced in the USSR, reached legendary levels of hysteria. In the eyes of our ideological leaders, the casual fashion trend was a true symbol of Capitalistic society. To say it openly to the public, however, was not such an easy task for Bolsheviks. It was nearly impossible to convince even the not-so-sophisticated part of our population that jeans were associated exploiting Capitalists. Everybody knew just from our TV news about Western world problems, and practically all the protestors and unemployed people in the USA wore these jeans like a uniform.

Despite the fact that such foreign clothing was never officially imported into our country, there was no shortage of them, thanks to the ferocious black market. It will probably forever remain a mystery how a society with completely closed borders, barbaric laws, and limited access of civilians to the outside world, jeans were purchased and worn. To buy a pair of these was limited only by one important factor: the price. On average, a pair of Montana, Lee, or Wrangler jeans fetched a price that was comparable to one or more of the monthly salary of a Soviet worker. Not many families could afford such luxury for their kids. However, even for parents, it was hard to avoid the hype. For those lucky enough to have a pair, they were the ultimate gift. In the USSR, it was so much more than a fashion trend or a status symbol; it was a cultural orientation expressed openly in public. Anyone who possessed these pants was usually better familiar with everything else the Soviet Union was trying to block from coming into our country, such as music, fashion, and beliefs. Of course, you would never see a Communist or government leader wearing jeans, but being loyal to their hypocritical nature, they were first in line to provide this "spit of Capitalism" to their own kids.

When the overwhelming madness surrounding jeans could no longer be ignored by the Soviets, our clothing industry was given an order to produce our own version of them. Like everything else we tried to imitate or reinvent in response to our 'enemies' merchandise, Soviet jeans were an ugly parody of what they were supposed to be. Not only were they shapeless and deformed stylistically, but the fabric itself was not even close to real denim. It was the worst product the USSR ever tried to imitate, from every point of view. To wear these humiliating fashion examples was impossible without putting yourself in a most embarrassing situation. Soviet jeans became nothing more than a mockery. They were affordable and were purchased only by those who could not afford the real American version, and... I was one of this people.

I did not even try to convince my mom to buy me a pair of jeans. It was way too expensive for us, and as far as I was concerned, buying a pair of pants that would have cost as much as a Soviet moped was an absolutely ridiculous idea.

The biggest problem with Soviet jeans was the shape and abnormal proportions. The length was cut in only two patterns, "large and tall" or "short and skinny." There was no option for more particular sizes. My pants had to be short, almost up to my knees, to fit me right everywhere else, so I had to come up with an interesting solution. All I had to do was buy a pair that would fit well on me without looking like a prison uniform. The length could be compensated with a clever idea. Following a stylish trend at that time of rolling up the extra length at the bottom of the real jeans, I asked my mom to sew this imitation extension to my ugly Soviet jeans. Using contrasting light-colored material, it looked practically normal when it was done. One problem with Soviet jeans, in my case, had to be solved before they could be worn in public. The color of these jeans was far from the originals. Not only was the color horrible, but they were not "stiff" enough, so the texture was loose and uncomfortable. To kill both these birds with one stone, I decided to try to paint them with aerosol paint. The challenge was to do it consistently and evenly. I knew nothing would work better than to do it while they were on the human body. It did not take long before I was standing with half of my upper body wrapped in a newspapers while Sasha sprayed my jeans with blue aerosol paint. It dried almost instantly, and I could feel the coldness of it against my pants. After about a half hour, the jeans looked near perfect. They did not look as good as the real thing, but they were much better than before, and my friends complimented my efforts. A couple weeks later, I was asked to visit my friend Gena to paint his Russian jeans in his house, right out on his own balcony. Gena could not wait to walk about the streets, flirting and proudly wearing our own version of this "symbol of pop culture".

Journey to Minsk's TV Station

Our advancement into the final round of the all-Republic "Red Currants" competition was by far the biggest achievement in the history of our school. Everyone was extremely happy about it and looked forward to our trip to the Belarusian capital, Minsk.

The trip was to take place during the early weeks of March 1978. After a long and snowy winter, everything outside was still frigid, with no sign of spring on the horizon. Standing at the school entrance with all our gear, we waited for the bus that would take us to Minsk. By noon, we finally saw it slowly entering front courtyard of the school. When it made a turn and stopped, we were surprised to see that we were not going on the voyage alone. The bus was already full of other kids from our region who were going to the same competition. Someone at the school district did not realize that taking few members of the school VIA would also require taking their gear. Our first reaction to this was that we could not simply go because there was no room for our equipment, which was vital to our performance. That idea was instantly rejected by Senya, and he briskly ordered to us to begin loading all our stuff anyway. Just getting our speakers and equipment into the bus was a challenging task. The narrow doors and aisle between the seats were not designed to transport anything besides people. Forcing our largest speakers into the cabin and stacking them in the aisles, we made our way deep into the crowded bus. When everything was loaded, there were only two seats left vacant. We hopped on our equipment and squeezed between each other in the most uncomfortable positions and prepared for the six-hour drive to the Belarusian capital.

Short stop in the forest on the way to Minsk.

It was the wildest trip we had ever been on. During the long journey on snow-covered roads, the kids from other schools began practicing their chorale singing. We did the same, and the whole ride became a rehearsal studio on the wheels.

After the long and exhausting trip, we arrived at the small athletic sports camp near Minsk. Located in the rural village of Ratomka, it was surrounded by a large forest of mature trees and was practically empty of any visitors. After unloading all our gear and getting situated in a large sleeping room fit for about twenty people, we crashed and fell quickly asleep.

Recording

The next morning was bright and sunny, though big piles and drifts of snow still made everything look like it was the middle of winter. The bus-loading routine had to be repeated again, and after another hour of driving, we came to what we believed to be a central TV station, but it wasn't. At the top of the giant old building was a big sign that read, HOUSE OF RADIO. It was our first day of audio recording, and for some reason, it was to be done there instead of the television facility. Struggling again with all our gear, we took it inside of the building only to encounter a little surprise.

A tall lady with a fancy hairdo, dressed like she was ready to go to some sort of royal ball, said, "Why did you bring your equipment, guys? We have everything you need, and we cannot use your crummy stuff anyway. All you can take to the studio are your guitars."

After dragging, punching, beating, and loading all our gear time and time again, we were now ready to burn it. But instead, we frustratingly stuffed it back into the bus and went inside the House of Radio.

Everything in the studio was very intriguing and unusual. The large hall was designed to record everything from folk duos to full symphony orchestra music. All kinds of musical instruments and equipment was stashed allover the floor. Harpsichords and harps, grand pianos, and wind instruments were everywhere. We were told right away not to touch anything, but true to our established rebellious natures, we accepted this warning as nothing more than an invitation to explore whatever and wherever we wanted. Many of the instruments were truly antique, and it was incredible for us to see them with our very own eyes. It was the first time in my life when I could gently touch and play items most people could only see in the movies or on television. It was a fantastic experience.

Amplifiers with foreign names stood in a specially isolated chamber. We plugged our guitars in them, and the familiar process of audio recording of our propaganda songs officially began. When everything was finished, we had a few hours before we went back to our small resort, so we decided to take a stroll through the city streets. Everything in the town was big compared to our humble Gomel. The buildings and stores, streets, and a new subway were amazing to see and experience. It was our first of a couple of visits to the capital of Belarusia as a school band, and it provided us with unforgettable memories not only of the city itself, but also of what we encountered there.

The next day, we went to the TV station for the Red Currants video shoot. It was an enormous new facility with the ability to broadcast and record TV programs in color, something still fairly new in USSR television.

All styles and genres of music were represented there. Solo acts, folk orchestras, choirs, and other VIAs fought for the nomination of best in their genre. The show recording was in the full thrust, and one after the other, contestants from other regions took their spot in front of the rolling camera. Everything seemed to have a strange preprogrammed feel, and lip synching had to be done in front of the judges, who were composers and movie actors. Several times, recording had to be stopped for various reasons. Kids grew tired of this quickly, and many got bored with the dull process and all the setbacks.

As for us, though, we were seldom bored. As we sat to create an improvised audience in the studio while we waited for our turn, we quietly commented and joked about what we were observing. I held my guitar and strummed the chords quietly, but Senya asked in a raging whisper, "Can you stop that, Yuriy? Do you see anyone else playing their instruments while they sit here?"

In a joking sort of mood, I loudly whispered back, "No, but they're not playing because they don't know how!" to which all of my band mates erupted in loud laughter.

The show director on the floor exclaimed, "Cut!" He looked at us disapprovingly, but we couldn't stop giggling. It was one of those situations where something quite innocent can make you die laughing, and he looked none too happy about it. Senya tried to make some lame apologetic excuse for our behavior, undoubtedly regretting his attempt to boss us around.

Happy Birthday!

When all the recording was finished, we had a chance to walk around the city. On this day, there was one more reason to have a good time besides visiting TV station: It was my fourteenth birthday. We couldn't resist the opportunity to celebrate it at our resort. The proposal has been made to get some wine and do it "in style." Senya said we could do whatever we wanted as long as there was no trouble. Everybody swore we were doing it just for symbolic reasons and assured him we would maintain peace and order while we celebrated this milestone birthday. Buying alcohol in USSR was legal at the age of sixteen, but they weren't so strict about it. If a teenager even looked remotely close to sixteen, getting booze was no problem at all. Two big bottles of Cuban rum were picked up at the liquor store, along with the traditional "zakuson", a simple canned food, sausage, and other snacks to complete our celebration menu for the night.

Having our own equipment with us was a major plus in this situation, and it guaranteed a good time at the improvised birthday party. After few toasts and finishing the first bottle of rum, we were ready to set up our gear and throw a free concert for all the occupants of the sports resort. Senya asked for the leftovers of the second bottle of our booze and disappeared into one of the rooms with it, joined by a couple of music teachers from other schools. Energized with good feelings about our day and the warm atmosphere, the dancing party began at the large hallway. No one was prepared for the songs we chose to play. After listening to our mellow propaganda music at the TV competition, the other contestants were shocked to hear the resort halls filling with the sounds of Led Zeppelin, the Beatles, and other foreign tunes. Not only did we play things many of them had never heard before, but our full vocal band that we had at that time made us sound like a professional rock band right out of the West. In half an hour, the party was shaking the whole building. Even though we were from different schools and regions, everyone loosened up and merged into one happy throng of dancing teenagers. There were no school administrators there to tell us how long to play or what to do with the lighting. It was our party, completely under our own control, and everyone had a great time until the party ended around two a.m.

When everything was over, we went outside to get some fresh air, and a little incident happened between Valentine and Sergey. While the two were trying to relieve themselves, there was apparently not enough room for them to find privacy in the wilderness, and Valentine came under fire of Sergey. This was what started the fight. Sergey did not even try to engage the much shorter and younger Valentine, but Valentine was mad at him, and after few kicks, he stormed into the darkness of the forest, which was still covered with a thick blanket of snow. He ran off without any warm clothing or even a hat, and we knew he would not survive out in that "tundra" for even a few hours. A drunken Senya showed up and, after learning what happened, ordered everybody to chase him. We dressed quickly and ran in the direction where our friend had departed. Senya and all of us were shouting through the silent cold night, calling for Valentine, but he was nowhere to be found. Trying to see his steps on the snow was absolutely impossible in the dark, and all we could do was head toward the distant lights sparkling through the trees. About twenty minutes later, we arrived at the local train station, where we found our friend sitting on a bench, shivering from head to toe.

Posing in Studio with my guitar in front of TV camera.

When we returned to the sports resort, Senya said he would talk to us in the morning. None of us—especially Valentine—looked forward to that lecture. Our "Friendly Fellows" band had a little crack in its image, and we knew that even sincere apologies would not ensure a peaceful meeting with Senya in the morning.

The options of what might happen to us after this incident were endless, but the expected punishment never took place. Senya was not in the mood to deal with it the next day, or at least he'd lost his sense of anger over the dispute. Presenting everything as an accident and misunderstanding, we all promised him that it would never happen again. We also swore that our band would never drink that heavily again. Senya quickly cut the conversation short after we mentioned the rum and told us, "I don't remember anybody drinking there." We all promptly agreed that it never happened, and that was that.

Our bus came to pick us up after lunch, and after loading our gear, we packed the buss with a whole bunch of new friends. The return journey home from Minsk was long and bumpy. The first warm days of spring had melted down some snow, and the muddy, wet roads forced our bus to go slow with frequent stops. Tired and exited at the same time, we arrived back at our school after midnight, and a couple hours later, we were all safe and sound back in our homes. We had enough of memories and stories about our few days in Minsk that we could share them with our friends for many days to come. It was a unique, memorable experience, and we could not wait to tell everyone about it or to see our color television performance on the TV show a few weeks later.

Little Recognition

Shot of our performance from a TV screen.

By the end of the school year, our VIA band was being carried on little waves of a fame and glory. After the broadcasting of the show in Minsk, we began to earn recognition from our local authorities as a fine example of Soviet youth that could be used for any propagandistic or official entertainment purposes. The government's list of "approved" artists was not an easy one to get on, but if a band or musician found themselves among the governmentally accepted, gigs in shows, concerts, and TV programs were almost guaranteed. This was also the case for our band, and we were invited to play at all kind of gatherings and official concerts in our city and region. Whether it was a dancing party for kids or any sort of patriotic gathering, the organizers could count on us as a reliable and "tested" entertainers. We were also invited to perform on TV programs that had nothing to do with "Red Currants" or political themes, and this allowed us to record few neutral songs with banal, naïve lyrics, the songs we often played for dancing. This made us even more appealing to our audience, though we were nowhere near celebrities or of legendary band status.

Our gigs on TV shows earned us even more recognition, as well as much more correspondence and fan mail from our admirers. Before, the letters came mostly from young girls and beginning musicians, but now we started to receive them from old veterans and Soviet heroes, telling us about their feelings and appreciation for our music and songs. They were often touching, emotional letters that we passed on to our school administration, who would display them on the school bulletin board for everyone to admire. In our gear locker, we had another billboard with dozens pictures of our female distant mail friends. It was an absolutely unbelievable time, and all of us felt we had accomplished great things in such a short time.

I was absolutely confident that my life would always be somehow involved in music. For that reason, I was not looking forward to graduation because I could not imagine working as an engineer or government employee or any other job without a connection to music. My guitar became an extension of myself, my constant companion in all kinds of situations. I was extremely happy that my destiny brought to my life Sasha, without whom I could not have this incredible passion. My participation in the school band was the greatest, most memorable time of my life in USSR. It allowed me to feel free with our yet unusual and limited ability to play the music we loved. I couldn't imagine being happy without being part of the band, and if I had to leave the band for any reason, school would have seemed utterly senseless to me. Everything was so perfect for me while I was part of the band, and I didn't ever want it to come to an end, but life sometimes has a way of getting in the way of your dreams and changing your plans.

Trip to the Wilderness

The summer came so fast that I could not even prepare for it with some kind of plans or ideas of how I would spend it. The only available recreation for Soviet teens of my age was the dull Komsomol working brigades and participation in the Bolshevik patriotic clubs. None of these brainwashing exploitation camps interested me or my band mates. All we wanted to do was have fun in the sun and spend time with our friends. After long debates with Sasha about what we should do for the ultimate summer break, we decided to go with Petrukha on an adventure. The plan was to spend one week living in the wilderness in the tent, surviving only on bread, canned food, and whatever Mother Nature and God would provide from the river and the nearby forest. We decided to go to the area where our last school summer camp was.

It was a very ambitious plan. Not only we were too young for such an outing, but none of us had any idea what we would do there for such a long time. It was more of a test of our willpower and courage, a chance to see what we might encounter in the middle of nowhere. My biggest concern was actually getting approval from my mom and grandma to go on such mission, considering my less-than-perfect record on such excursions.

The striking difference between the Soviet Union and United States recreational activities was that we were not limited by strict regulations as to where we could go. In this regard, places in the USSR were far more open to the public because no one privately owned large parcels of land and the natural areas belonged to the government, or "to the people," as we were told. On some levels, this was true. We could picnic, for instance, anywhere it was convenient. The only area where these places would have to be assigned or specially dedicated to such a purpose were within crowded city limits, but everything in the nature was opened for exploration, fishing, and adventures. National forests and preserves did exist, but besides shabby signs on the side of the road, no restrictions or controls were really enforced. Camping and fishing required no special licenses, tickets, or fees. As long as our voyage did not involved commercial tree-cutting or fishing with large nets, we could truly enjoy our beautiful nature anywhere we wanted. Many Soviet citizens took advantage of this freedom as an escape from our Communistic reality. For us, it was going to be an adventure to test our endurance and to live in the wilderness—to see if we could survive the unpredictable weather and primitive conditions. We were filled with confidence that we could tackle it like pros, and we were excited to give it a try.

I looked forward to that trip with a lot of anticipation. The fact that we knew the area where we were going gave us a sense of assurance that we would have a safe, fun excursion. With our backpacks containing a simple tent, food provision, and survival tools, we headed off, eager to spend one week on our own, away from home and our families. Everybody was concerned about our wellbeing on such a bold, ambitious journey, of course, and Sasha and Petrukha had to swear to my folks that they would watch over me and bring me home in one piece, safe and sound.

My pal Sasha and I.

We took our provision and all gear and after couple hours of drive our bus stopped on the side of the road. Even though there was no bus station there and no signs or markings, everyone knew it was the Novaya Guta village stop. The village itself was located few kilometers away on another side of the road. We get off the bus and began walking toward the forest with our heavy gear in tow.

The Russian wilderness is a vast, powerful place, full of forests, lakes, and fields, but after looking around a bit, we recognized the area where we had spent our school summer camp. As we moved deeper into the woods, the rich smell of the mixed forest trees ventilated our mind and souls, a welcome change of pace from the crowded city atmosphere we were used to. Further away from the road, the sounds of nature became more prevalent. The wind in the trees and cries of wild birds intrigued us and encouraged our adventurous spirits. After we'd walked about twenty minutes, we realized our trip to the river would take much longer than we had anticipated. There was only one way we could move faster, and that was to dump half our gear and come back for it later. Someone had to stay to guard our supplies, and I was chosen to be that someone. We decided that two of my friends would go toward the river to find us a place. Then, one would come back for me and the rest of our luggage, while the other began making camp.

Near the tall wooden fire observation tower was a perfect spot for me to stay and await Sasha's return. I sat on our backpacks and watched the slowly drifting clouds. The weather was beautiful. After a while, I got bored and decided to get a closer look at the tower. It was very old construction assembled from the large pine logs, about 200 feet high. The ladder that led to the observation platform had a lot of missing rungs, but it looked safe enough to me. I stepped on few of them at the bottom and decided to continue going up. The ladder spiraled around the square perimeter, and the higher I got, the more deteriorated the wood looked. At one point, I realized it was covered with mold and rotted by woodworms, and it did not look safe anymore. Where the cross steps of the ladder were missing, I climbed along its rails, heading higher and higher. As I neared the top, the tower gently swayed and creaked, and it began to feel very dangerous, but I was only about a fifth of the way from the platform, and I wasn't going to give up, for I desperately wanted to see the view from the top. A couple steps later, though, the rotted wood broke under my foot. I managed to stick my bent knee onto the next step to stop myself from falling, but my heart was racing like a motor. I looked down and could not believe how high I was from the ground. Holding tight in this position, I had to come up with a plan to get down. Just then, I noticed Sasha on the ground looking for me. "Hey! I am up here!" I yelled out to him.

"What are you doing up there, you idiot?" he shouted back.

"I think I am kind of stuck here!" I replied, still wondering how to get back to the ground safely.

"Hold on a second!" Sasha shouted and began to climbing up.

I knew my friend was larger and heavier than me, and there was no way he could help me without putting himself in grave danger. "Wait! Don't climb up here! It's all rotted and decayed, and you'll fall!" I started yelling at him. I quickly decided to slide down the rails without stepping on the unreliable rotted steps. To make my decent as fast as possible, I juggled my hands in agony down the rail, sporadically stepping on decayed steps and snapping a few of them on the way down. With scratched hands, elbows, and knees, I practically rolled down in cloud of dust at the tower base.

"How was the view?" Sasha asked sarcastically while I tried to wipe myself off and make sure nothing was broken.

"It was great," I lied without hesitation.

"Well, get the backpacks, and let's do some swamp walking," said my friend, loading the big bag with our food onto his back.

After getting all our remaining bags, we went through the area where our little school camp had been stationed. After about ten minutes, we found the spooky trail leading through the swamp close to the river. It was a dangerous path, but it would greatly cut our walking distance. I had never had a chance to walk through a swamp before. Someone had thrown a bunch of thick tree branches across the loose soil on top of the water to give a little more support to the nasty, soggy walkway. The path was surrounded by bushes and small trees, and everything wiggled every step we took. I held a long stick out in front of me and poked the ground to make sure I wouldn't fall through into murky brownish-black water. Sasha constantly telling me to simply follow the barely visible trail. Through the openings, we could see pools of dark water that seemed to lead down into the abyss. The croaking, chirping frogs made us feel even more uninvited. In spite of the difficulties, though, another benefit of dragging ourselves through this risky trail was that it would take us to the bank of a river, where we will be even more isolated from the rest of the world.

By the time we got out of the swamps, I was not looking forward to marching any further with our heavy provisions beating down on my back. We took a short break and let the light wind and scents of Russian summer soothe our minds. Lying down on the grass was so relaxing that we nearly fell asleep. Soon, though, Sasha got up, poking me on my side with a fishing rod, forcing me to wake up, and after about twenty more minutes of walking, we had arrived at the shore of the river.

Petrukha had not wasted his time while we were gone. He was a true handyman, and when we arrived, he was already working on building a table and benches with the help of an axe. By the evening, we already had a fully functional little camp that would keep us alive and well as long as we had enough food.

Walking through the swamp.

My friends knew what they were doing, from cooking to preserving the meal and perishable provisions. Fortunately, my job was less complicated, and I was glad to keep myself busy with just trying to catch fish to make Ukha soup and walking to the forest to get the firewood.

We had the greatest time in the wilderness. We were alone with our own agendas and plans of how to spend the day, and we enjoyed it like true adventurers. After we ate dinner that we cooked on our fire pit, we would stare at big, magnificent starry sky. In the city, we never saw the overwhelming beauty of the nighttime sky view. It was first time in my life when I saw the Milky Way with my own eyes. Out there, far away from our town and its pollution, we could feel the power and the unparalleled grace nature.

We had everything in place to stay safe and out of trouble in practically complete isolation. The only fear we had was the common occurrence of local hooligans from the village shaking down campers for booze. It was an unfortunate problem, and people from the city, like us, were practically powerless against savage raids of gangs of bored country teenagers with nothing better to do. We knew the easiest way to protect ourselves from such pillaging was to have a bottle of vodka or a couple bottles of wine on hand to bribe them to leave us alone. Booze was the necessary part of provisions for any trip into the unknown in our country. It was always carried for emergencies, to be used as a warming-up or medicinal substance, and we were sure to bring it along. We knew there was a real chance, albeit a slim one, that we would encounter some of these teen gangs, and the outcomes of these types of encounters were absolutely unpredictable, from friendly drinking with uninvited guests to fierce, bloody fights or even murders. It all depended on luck. The raids were always known to happen at night. We hoped our distant, isolated location would give us a well-protected shelter from such invasion, but we were wrong.

Having lunch.

Uninvited Guests

One night, we were sitting around the fire, enjoying the calm summer night. In the distance, we saw flashlights slowly creeping through the field in our direction. We hoped it was not someone looking for a free drink, but our fears were confirmed when four drunk, cocky teenagers yelled at us before even getting close, "Do you have any booze?"

Petrukha took the axe in his hands and replied, "Anything you find is yours."

I was holding the large blade from an old bayonet in my hands, and Sasha was twisting a giant stick in the fire, ready to take action if it became necessary, but we knew we did not stand a chance against them in a fight. They were much older and much bigger than us, and drunk to boot, and we knew that even if we tried to beat them with burning fire logs, we would never escape alive.

The gang realized the search through our stuff would be too complicated and simply asked us one more time, trying to sound kinder, "We have some food and fresh vegetables. We'll make a trade. Your booze for our "zakuson". How about that?"

We knew that even if we could convince them to leave or fight them off, they would return with half their village to level our camp. Drinking with the bastards was a better alternative than starting a risky fight. The offer was accepted, and in about ten minutes, we were opening the bottle of a cheap wine to reluctantly share with our intruders. Drinking with the bums was creepy, not to mention dangerous. At any moment, we knew they might slam a bottle across one of our heads, and the friendly pack of strangers might leave us beaten and robbed in the middle of nowhere. If that happened, there wouldn't even be a police investigation; more likely, it would be conducted by the uncles, brothers, or even parents of the thugs. All city folk knew about the so-called justice of the rural regions of Russia.

I am fishing

Slowly, our visitors mellowed out, and after they were completely drunk off of our provisions, they were ready to go back to their village. They had about an hour of walking through the field, forest, and—if they were stupid—through the swamps. They felt good that they were welcomed to drink with us, since most city people always tried to avoid that. They left after midnight, and we could see their flashlights for awhile lingering through the field.

We sat around our dying fire and started asking ourselves why we simply did not let them have the wine and send them away but insisted on drinking with them. We could not find a logical answer and decided to go to sleep, hoping they would not return again, and they never did.

In a few days we returned home without fish or mushrooms to our happy parents, but full of great wilderness experience.

Last Year in School and Sad Events

I knew my last year in school would be a new and different kind of year with a lot of intriguing and sad changes.

The Soviet school system at that time allowed kids to choose to stay all ten years or leave after eight years of studies to obtain a trade education. Andrew chose to leave after finishing eighth grade, leaving us without a drummer. We had no luck finding a replacement, so the decision was made to give the position to me. After all, I was the only one in the whole school who knew how to play drums, so I had no choice but to switch instruments. I could still use my guitar at any time, including taking it home, and Andrew offered to play at dances with us even though he left school.

Riding on a Soviet bus. 1978.

Since I moved to drums, we had an open guitar spot. To fill it, we brought onboard the guy who lived in the next apartment building over from ours. Oleg (a.k.a. Slon) was always riding a fancy folding bicycle around our neighborhood, and we had no idea he knew how to play guitar. But Slon went to our school, and when he approached us with the request to be in the band, we were pleasantly surprised.

Once we had all the positions filled, we began practicing with the modified band crew. It didn't take long for me to pick up enough skill on drums and I did almost as well as Andrew. Occasionally, our former drummer still came to our rehearsals to give me some tips and pointers. I truly enjoyed my new role in the band, and the drums were slowly becoming my second passion.

We looked forward to our musical adventures, and the first dances we played went perfect. Not only did we have a great team, but because Andrew missed us and sometimes came to play at our parties, the extra man allowed us to rotate the instruments and sometimes gave me the chance to go out on the dance floor to see what it was like to be outside the band. The girls always begged me to dance, and when they did, I felt like a fish on sand. It was common for musicians to abstain from such entertainment, and none of my friends who played in the band enjoyed dancing either.

New Boss

Everything seemed to be going well. We were looking forward to more exciting times with our band, but then everything suddenly changed when we received the surprising news that our Senya, our "boss," was leaving the band behind. His excuse was that he was too overloaded by other responsibilities and had no time to work with us, but we had our suspicions that something else was going on.

When the replacement band teacher was announced, we realized that life was not going to be the same anymore. The conductor of our folk music orchestra was appointed as our new boss. Yakov was a stiff, pale character of little personality, and he was obsessed with his folk band. He reminded us of a clown; he wore a giant mustache and glasses that were too big for his face, and his hair was done up in a sort of afro. Even at our very first meeting with him, we knew we were not going to like the changes he wanted to make. He decided the keys to the storage room would be in his permanent possession, and our rehearsals would be under his constant supervision. That wouldn't have been so bad, as he at least promised not to touch our music program, but what truly threw us into the curb was when he decided that in order to continue to have the privilege of playing in our band, we all had to agree to play in his folk band as well.

To understand the level of embarrassment and humiliation associated with this, you have to imagine our four young rock 'n' roll spirits trying to play dull folk music. The whole idea was so insulting and absurd to us. It was like asking a renowned artist to paint the bathroom walls in a prison before he was allowed to touch the real canvases. It had nothing to do with music; his reasons were purely selfish. The folk music he wanted us to play was presented to the masses by the government as an alternative to modern pop culture. So much of it was so forcefully injected into our lives that it was impossible not to develop a hatred for it. Accordions, balalaikas, mandolins, and other folk instruments no longer truly represented our reach culture, but they were used as weapons to wage an ideological war against "Western propaganda". After making our youth hate our own folk music, to be a part of it was not only embarrassing for me, but also somewhat unethical.

Yakov's conditions were very clear and very real. None of us wanted to lose the advantage of being in our regular band—the only passion we had at that time. I caved and forced myself to go to the folk orchestra rehearsals. We were assigned instruments, and mine were folk percussions. It was absolutely horrible for me. Not only did I hate what I was being forced to play, but Yakov made it clear that he disliked me. He constantly picked on me and made sarcastic and personally insulting comments. Our mutual aversion for each other was aggravated by the horrible play of my parts which I hated. He suspected I was failing intentionally in order to get out of it, and he eventually expelled me from his folk band. I was relieved and hoped he would leave me alone, which he did—but at a higher price than I could possibly comprehend, for I was also expelled from my beloved position in our VIA band.

Uncle Andrew

It was rainy, typical, very gray Russian autumn. At this time, there were practically no leaves left on the trees; they had been torn away by the windy storms. The trees stood like naked skeletons, often shaken in the rain, reminding everyone of the long winter that was on its way. It was a desolate season in the villages, with the air turning misty and nature becoming dark and lifeless.

On one of these gloomy days, my grandma's sister, Dunya, was sitting by the window in her house, looking out toward the end of the long, lonely field. She did this every Sunday for many years without fail. At this time, the train would drop off visitors and village residents to the curb of the railroad. They would slowly move toward the Krasnaya Buda village, and she would look for her son Andrew, coming to visit her from the city. He never missed the Sunday visits, and she always awaited him with great joy.

The train arrived, and a few minutes later, its loud whistle announced its departure. Dunya knew it would take another fifteen or twenty minutes before the tiny human shadows on the horizon would be visible from her house. She was anxiously looking through the hazy mist, but she could not see her son coming among the others. As all the visitors moved down their own paths, only one woman, dressed in all black, headed toward Dunya's house. Immediately, Dunya knew who it was. My Aunt Valentina had only visited her one time, and on this day, she was there to deliver a dark message.

When Valentina arrived at Dunya's house, neither of them said a word. They just stood together and cried. Dunya knew with in her heart that she would never see her son again, and Valentina's dark clothes only served to confirm that harsh reality. My aunt was a strong woman, and she bore the responsibility of telling Dunya that her son had fallen victim to a tragic, senseless incident.

My Uncle Andrew was twenty-eight years old when he died, and it happened just two months before his wedding. Sadly, it happened after he attended the reception celebration of his distant friend. No matter how much Andrew's fiancée begged him to avoid the party, he insisted on being there. On the way home from the village where the festivities took place, he decided to take a nap in the rear of a bus—a nap he would never wake up from. The carbon monoxide gas from a faulty engine design killed him quietly while he slept.

I had never experienced the death of any close relatives before, with the exception of old Mikhail passing away in 1968.

This time, my mom called me from work and told me about the tragedy. I could not believe it. I had just seen Andrew the previous week when he had stopped by with his fiancé Irina and brought me and my brother two bars of chocolate. He had been in such a happy mood then, and his broad smile was still fresh in my mind. His death was surreal, almost impossible, and I was in denial. He had been my closest male role model I had during my childhood. He interacted with me like I was his own son, and he was a strong comfort to me during many of my trying times. The loss of my Uncle Andrew seemed even more unfair since he was Dunya's only son. Without his help, it was going to be very difficult for the elderly woman to survive the old-fashioned, un-modernized village life, but now she was left alone. Andrew's bride-to-be was so upset about his death that she vowed never to marry; though she did many years later and named her first son Andrew, after her beloved deceased fiancée.

It seemed everything around was spinning in the wrong direction. I was expelled from our band, and the man closest to me had died. It was unthinkable, unimaginable misery, and things looked so much darker than they had only a couple of months earlier, as if someone had snuffed out all the bright parts of my life. Life is full of colorful pages, though, and the dark ones were not excluded from my life story.

My Hometown and a Little Victory

Since I left Leningrad as an infant, I had never had a chance to go back and see the city where I was born. The so-called "Northern Capitol" of Russia had always captivated my imagination, as well as the interest of many others. Its legendary past, museums, and architecture attracted people from all corners of Soviet Union and few lucky ones from the West. The city was glorified by our government mainly for its remarkable beauty and art heritage. For the ruling authorities of the USSR, it was known as the "Nursery of Revolution," where Lenin and his comrades formed a Bolshevik coup in 1917, a time remembered more than any other time in Leningrad history. Therefore, instead of being known as the "City of Peter," St. Petersburg even became known as the "City of Revolution and Lenin, or Leningrad." The historical happenings associated with Imperial Russia were often viewed in a negative light, but the revolutionary background of the city was given an elevated reputation by the power of Soviet propaganda. Even battleship names such as "Aurora" and "Smolny" were used to imbed these ideas in the minds and souls of the Soviet people from their childhood, to promote the script of the revolution itself. When it came to Leningrad, though, this was not something that interested me. I wanted to return to see the architecture and museums, some of which, like Hermitage, was considered the best in the world. I wanted to witness the incredible beauty with my own eyes. I asked my mom if it would be possible to make a short trip to Leningrad, and the idea intrigued her since she had spent her youth there and still had friends in the area.

We arrived in Leningrad in the middle of autumn, when the weather was cold and rainy, not the best time to see the charm and beauty of the northern town. Booking a room in a hotel was never an easy task in the USSR, and getting one in Leningrad was practically impossible at any time of the year. Fortunately, my mom's friend welcomed us to stay at her house in Lomonosov, a small town not far away. As soon as we arrived, I could not wait to go sight-seeing, as the historical places were very inspiring for a teenage boy. I found antiquity very appealing, so Leningrad had plenty to offer me around every corner.

Walking through the streets of Leningrad, I was blown away by the unparalleled architectural beauty of this city. The palaces and cathedrals were magnificent, and I could have stood in front of them forever admiring the intricate details and breathtaking craftsmanship. Many of them were obviously decorated with memorial plaques that told the story of Lenin and other legendary Bolsheviks during the Revolution. The questionable red flags, banners, and statues to the "founders of the Soviet Union" seemed odd placed among the true works of art created by artisans hundreds of years earlier.

Leningrad's art before Revolution.

My mother, a true Communist, was eager to see the honorable places associated with the revolution and its history. She decided it would be great to see Lenin's "Shalash", the hovel he used to hide from the Tsar's authorities prior the Revolution. I had absolutely no interest in this attraction, but the trip required us to travel the Finland basin by boat, which was very exciting. We embarked on this excursion on a rare for Leningrad sunny day.

The greenish-brown water outside our boat seemed to mirror my own feelings about visiting the "Shalash". It was indeed the most boring trip we took during our visit to Leningrad. We walked into the memorial center where the whole Lenin's saga at this place was exhibited in a large scale. Elaborate display showed Lenin working hard on the plan to overthrow the Russian government. One exhibit at the visitors' center pictured him seated on a tree trunk writing his plans for a coup, but none of the displays were very intriguing to my taste. The "Shalash" itself, made out of hay, looked almost factory manufactured and was obviously not original. All of the displays attempted to convince visitors that Lenin lived like Robinson Crusoe while he planned the most significant event in Russian history, but they all seemed ridiculously dull to me.

Leningrad's art after Revolution.

As I gazed at the replicas of Lenin's relics and historical documents, I wondered how different we would have lived had the Tsar's police discovered Lenin. These were not questions anyone would answer or even dare ask, and I dared not mention the thoughts and doubts swimming in my head about what we'd been taught about Lenin in our country.

We returned to Leningrad and spent the rest of our trip visiting much more interesting places than Lenin's picnic spot. The most memorable was our trip to Petergof (or Petrodvorets), the fountains and palaces of the Russian monarchies. It was an extremely impressive place with hundreds of unique sculptural wonders. Created in the baroque and renaissance styles, the lavish gold-plated statues and small and large winter houses of Tsars and royal family, displayed grand examples of pre-Revolutionary artisan craftsmanship. According to the guide, the artisans created these wonders "with sweat and tears under the tyranny of their masters, while living in poor, decaying conditions." It was an honorable statement on behalf of our government, but it was questionable what kind of prosperity these "poor artisans" obtained after the great Bolshevik Revolution, not to mention what kind of 'masterpieces' they were later allowed to create.

It was soon time to leave the "City of Peter," and I hoped that some time in the future, I could return to visit Hermitage and many of the other incredible places that made the city famous, but unfortunately, I never returned.

Back to the Band

My expulsion from the school band not only affected me, but also the other band members. They were not sure who they would get to replace me. In order to find some one, they auditioned several people, but either they were not able to play drums or were impossible to teach. After many unsuccessful attempts, Yakov declared that the guys would rehearse without a drummer and he would ask an old drummer to join them at the dances. After long thinking, Andrew had no option but agree to help to his old friends.

No one liked what happened to me, but Yakov refused to even entertain the idea of bringing me back. He was a stubborn and very unreasonable person. He turned our band from a very happy, successful VIA into a group of hostage kids playing under constant fear. Sasha threatened to quit the folk orchestra as well, but Yakov made it very clear that he would go further with the punishments against anyone who would dare to sabotage his boring folk orchestra.

Despite the fact that I was unable to play with my friends in the VIA, I still played guitar at home with Sasha and dedicated all of my free time to listening and learning new songs. I really had no desire to participate in something controlled by such a maniac teacher anyway. The band had changed so drastically under Yakov's leadership that I didn't consider it much of a loss; it was sad, but not a catastrophe. I knew that one day the situation would resolve itself.

It was the biggest party in the school, the New Year's celebration. Knowing that the band was missing one of its main members (me) and that it was under new leadership, everybody was wondering how the event would go. Andrew said he could only play for an hour or so, since he had to be at the his own Technicum (low-grade Soviet college) party. Yakov had a Plan "B" that he thought would be a wonderful solution: He brought a record player with a pile of Soviet pop song vinyls. We knew this would turn the crowd off in seconds since they were used to live music. What he didn't know was that the band members had a little plan in mind for him as well.

The New Year's Ball began, and after about a half-hour, the crowd began requesting that the band play their favorite songs. Sasha kept telling the crowd, "We can't! Yuriy is the only one who knows them, and he got kicked out of the band!" The angry mob turned their fury on Yakov, demanding to know why in the world I had been expelled from the band, and standing by the window biting his nails he had nothing to say in his defense.

Twenty minutes later Andrew announced that he had to go. When Sasha announced that the live music was over and the turntable would now replace them, the audience exploded with a loud boos and hisses of disapproval. For the kids on the dance floor, this was the worst possible news, because they didn't want to dance to records like our village people. It was also the worst thing for Yakov, because not only did the students refuse to dance to the crackling, pathetic records of old Soviet music, but they also refused to leave. New Year's was supposed to be the biggest, longest party of the year, and going home after only an hour was unfathomable. The pressure and outrage was mounted, and no one was happy about the music arrangements. The girls seemed more angry than anyone because the hours they had spent finding just the right special dresses and primping in front of mirrors were now wasted. It was also the last New Year's party for many of the students, and to have their celebration ruined in such horrible manner was unthinkable.

As always, Sasha had everything under control. Turning all our equipment "off" and unplugging amplifiers the plan was to convince people that it was not a joke. When everybody saw it and was bagging him not to leave, he diverted the angry crowd to the source of the problem. "Go talk to Yakov," he said. "He's the only one who can let Yuriy back onstage so we can play the songs you love all night long!"

A dozen aggravated boys and girls, fueled by booze, saw me and literally threw me onstage, screaming, "Play for us! Screw Yakov!"

I knew it would cost me more than a meeting with the principal if I dared take my seat behind the drums. I was standing onstage, looking into the distant corner, where Yakov was being attacked by swarm kids who were demanding that he not impose upon their New Year's fun. I could see the party lights glistening in the reflection of his thick glasses. After a short pause, he gestured to me that it was okay to go ahead.

"Hotel California" rocked the walls of the school ballroom. The lights were turned off, and in complete non-Soviet fashion, the happy crowd began screaming in hysteria, dancing the night away.

So, we had won the battle because of popular demand, and I was reinstated in the band without any official announcement or discussions with Yakov. All he had to say to me was a warning not to be late for rehearsal, and he assured me he didn't need my help in his folk band—and I was just fine with that.

Goodbye School and Our Final Performance Together

I only had a couple months to make a decision as to what I would do with my future. I had the option of leaving school after eighth grade, and I wasn't sure if I wanted to stay the additional two years. Sasha and our new guitar player, Oleg, were ready to graduate, which meant I would be stuck there by myself to deal with Yakov. I was not even sure if anybody in the school could step forward to adequately replace all our leaving members. Not only I did not want to be in this situation, but I also wished to be done with school in general. I had no idea what the next chapter of my life would entail. All I knew was that I could not picture my life without some involvement in music. My intuition told me I wouldn't fit into the proletarian worker system, and I had no interest whatsoever in enrolling in any of our Trade Schools.

The best option for me was to try to pass the exam that would allow me to enter the music school of Sokolovski. It would have been an ambitious idea even for someone with a strong background in musical education and knowledge, and I had nothing in my repertoire that would even qualify me to attempt such a challenging endeavor. My guitar playing was good enough for the band, but I was nowhere near ready for a music school admissions audition. I did not even know how to read notes properly, and the few classical tunes I had picked up myself would be not enough to impress the judges. The only option I had, in my opinion, was to try out for percussions, my reasoning being that drumming didn't require much reading of notes, and I was already better at that than our previous drummer, Andrew.

The chances of being offered admission to either of the two musical institutes in our Republic of Belarus were extremely slim, even for those with much experience and education. In my case, the idea was so unrealistic that my own friends laughed at me and called it ridiculous and absurd. I knew, though, that if I never tried, I would have no chance to become a professional musician. Even if I failed the exam, I still had nothing to lose. Bearing all this in mind, I made my final decision to graduate after eighth grade.

When the last dance party and graduation ball was played together by our band, I said goodbye to my school and in the summer of 1979, I sent in my documents to apply for the percussion exams to enroll at the Sokolovski music school.

The Final Play

Incidentally, our band's last school gig was not the one we played at graduation. It was almost meant to happen, as if something was willing us to play just one more time, and our last time to play as a school band happened to be my first wedding gig

Someone was looking for an affordable band to entertain the guests at the reception, which was to take place at the Teachers Union Clubhouse, the "Teacher's house." At that time, Soviet celebrations of that kind were held in places that didn't seem quite suitable. Most commonly, wedding banquets were held at restaurants and eatery chains. After that, factory clubhouses, union buildings, or anyplace that could accommodate a couple hundred people were acceptable. As long as food and music could be delivered to the festivities and the price was acceptable, the party would be underway.

Our reputation as a great little band was already well known outside of our school, and the request for us to play came from a friend-of-a-friend kind of connection. At that time, playing at the wedding was one of the best sources of income for musicians—a pretty hefty chunk of cash, on average about the amount of one month's salary.

It was an intriguing proposal for us, and the fact that we could play on much better equipment provided by the Teacher's house was very attractive. Everything was great about the offer except that the payment was going to be far less than we expected. The party hosts decided since we were kids, we should play in exchange for food. We reluctantly agreed, though, considering we were curious about the opportunity and enthused that we were one of the youngest party bands around to be given such a rare opportunity.

We came to find out that for bands, a Russian wedding was a difficult, long, and tiresome gig. Starting at around five or six p.m., the dancing went on until the guests literally fell under the table, with only short breaks in between. The musicians were treated often better than anybody who was invited, though, because it was traditionally believed that well-fed musicians would deliver the best music, while an unhappy, hungry band would deliberately make the crowd bored. The separate table for musicians was always stocked with plenty of food and drinks, and it was someone's sacred responsibility at the party to make sure the plates and bottles of musicians were never empty. One bottle of vodka per person, two bottles of wine, and unlimited bottles of beer were the minimum to keep the musicians happy. Weddings usually continued into the next day, but the party we played was only set up for one night, so we looked forward to having a great time.

When we arrived at the place of my first of many wedding gigs, our table looked like it was set up for government authorities. The equipment was very good (by Soviet standards), typical for a union culture palace. The guitars were not the best, but still playable. It was the last time our school band would get together: me on drums; Sasha on bass; Oleg on guitar; and Valentine on keyboard. When the crowd began filling the room and looked onstage, we knew we had to wow them, and we did exactly that. When the first chords of music ripped through the auditorium, everybody got up and ran to dance. Not only were the guests surprised to see that kids played so well, but they were also hearing music none of them had ever heard or had never dreamed they'd see played live.

After two hours, the alcohol began taking effect on the crowd, and some all-too-friendly guests began flocking onstage, telling us how great we were playing. It was really just typical behavior for a Soviet wedding for the musicians to steal the attention away from the bride and groom. At most weddings, band members would often leave with girls, but we were too young for many of the young women to flirt with. Still, with the alcohol releasing their inhibitions, several of the female guests began grabbing our hands and butts. We had a great time, though, and everything there was far more entertaining than anything we'd witnessed at the school dances. The crowd, being completely drunk, was easy to manipulate and entertain. Just for fun, we played foxtrots and polkas, which allowed us the chance to see drunks dancing with chairs or ladies doing belly dances on the tables. It was a wild time.

By the end of the party, we were ready to start opening our own bottles of booze. As the vodka and wine filled our glasses, the party began to grow quiet. The chaos of the reception was coming to a conclusion, and old wasted guys sat at our table, telling us their life stories. One of them poured vodka into his beer and said, "Try it this way. It's much better." He was unable to explain already why it was better, and by the time I learned what he meant, it was too late. I was severely sick to my stomach the next day, and my attempt to convince my mom that I had gotten food poisoning at the wedding was not very believable.

I will remember that first reception gig for the rest of my life. Every time I played such an event after that, I took my vodka home instead of drinking it "at work", and never since have I mixed it with beer.

Chapter 12

A Surprise Enrollment and My Friend's Departure

I had little knowledge about the school I was hoping to attend and didn't even know what would happen if I were lucky enough to be offered admission. Young graduates like I was can sometimes have naïve, foolish ideas about how perfectly easy the future would be, and I was living under the delusional impression that if I got into that school, the world of music opportunities would just fly open to me. At the same time, I knew that there is a chance that it all could be different and tried not to think about it too much until I got more information. My next step would be the admission "filtering" process and to get through it I had very little clue of what it will take to concur. To pass my exams all I could do was rely on God's intervention and do the best I could to impress the professors and teachers that would decide my fate.

Of course, there were far more students trying out than there were available spots. This fact alone told me that the school had to be a good place, since students would rather go there than to the trade schools that tried to lure kids off the street with all kinds of promises... A student could walk drunk and half-naked, completely illiterate, into one of those trade schools and still be accepted. Not only did that the trade schools offer admission to anyone without exams, but they also provided free uniforms and campus boarding for students from other cities and villages, as well as a monthly financial stipend. For kids from the country and villages, attending trade schools provided them a loophole to escape the "passport regime" that usually kept young villagers from being able to leave their places of residences. Because they were only allowed to leave their villages to pursue educational opportunities in the city, they filled our trade schools by the millions, leaving their birthplaces behind. Nothing like that was happening at the Sokolovski Music Institute; there were no free room and board, no free uniforms, and no free lunches. The Soviet system of so-called fair treatment balanced the compensation between trade and music schools with a true Proletarian approach.

Music School

When the day of my first exam came, I was not even sure of what exactly would be involved during this process. For me, it was more of a personal exploration than a competition with the other, more qualified candidates, and I had little hope of outshining them. My only hope was that no one would ask me to play or read any notes; to my surprise, no one did. The quizzes, interviews, and tests mainly involved showing our ability to hear music well and pick out the different rhythms. It wasn't difficult, in my opinion, but many left the classroom with sorrows. After the exams each day, a list of passing applicants was posted on the bulletin board. I never expected my name to be there, but it always was. When the final lists of the passed candidates was displayed, I was sure my name would not be among them. It took me a while to realize the unthinkable: Somehow, in spite of all the odds, I was among those accepted for admittance to the school. It was more than a dream-come-true. I felt like a hot air balloon hobbyist who had been called to be a fighter pilot in the air force.

I did not even know how to deliver the amazing news to my parents and friends. It was the biggest achievement of my life at that time, and it would be an unexpected shock to everyone. Not only I was one of the lucky ones who would proudly attend one of the most prestigious institutions in the city, but I also had the advantage of knowing my future in music was secure.

I was showered with euphoria, praises, and congratulations from relatives, friends, and old school teachers. Everybody thought I was some kind of hero. It was indeed very difficult to get into that school, and my lucky accident made everybody believe I was worthy of such an honor. Unfortunately, hysteria and naïve excitement can sometimes turn into great disappointment, and this was no exception.

When Friends are Leaving

A couple moths later, my friend Sasha was scheduled to move to Kostroma city to attend a Technikum. In his opinion, it provided a good education that would guarantee him a well-paying job in the future. He also did not hide his desire to get away from home us8ing this approach in education. While his parents drank nightly and fought bitterly, he had to care for his grandma and sister, who also still lived with them, and be a problem-solver around the house. It was too much responsibility for someone so young, and he was glad to be getting away from it.

Still, his relocation was a sad reality for him and me. We had grown very close over the years, almost like brothers. I will never forget the warm summer nights when we hung out with our guitars, and unforgettable time at our school band.

My Music School and a Little Reward

On September 1, my first day of study in Sokolovski, I arrived at my new school with a lot of enthusiasm. Located right in the center of our city, the school was nestled among many famous places and well-known attractions. That fact alone was quite uplifting for me.

Everything was new and strange when the doors were opened and our group of about twenty-five gathered together for the first time. The other students and I would be studying different music majors, and our classes would consist of varying music disciplines and general high school courses. It was a nice atmosphere for learning. The teachers were very polite and addressed us in the same way the addressed other adults. There were portraits of mainly Russian and Soviet composers hung in the classrooms, and their music was played in every corner and classroom of this school.

I was amused by this new world, which was so different from anything I'd ever experienced. As soon as we began our first lessons, I was quick to realize I was the worst prepared student in the school. Not only could everyone in my group read notes and understand the basic music theology, but all of my classmates had already been playing musical instruments for many years.

I was the only percussion major in my grade, and my background didn't even compare with that of the others students my age. Within a couple days, I knew my worst fears were going to come true: I would not be able to catch up or keep up to the caliber expected at the school. I was expected to already know how to read notes and to have a good grasp of music theory, and learning all of that in the blink of an eye was absolutely impossible. Though the school offered introductory courses, they were done at an accelerated rate because they assumed all the students already knew the basics. To give you a better idea, it would be similar to giving a yacht hobbyist just a brief introduction before throwing him into the captain's seat of a submarine and sending him off to war. It was very difficult for me to understand and learn the terminology and the music language basics, and I felt I was drowning beneath all I was expected to know.

But even that was not the worst revelation about music school. My dreams of becoming a professional musician after graduation began to crumble when I realized that after completing my four years of study, I would more than likely end up as an elementary school music teacher. The chance to become a professional musician was less than slim and would only happen for a few lucky graduates who were good enough to join an orchestra or concert team. "We do not make talents here," said one of our pedagogues. "If you are not one of them, then you will be working to find them like needles in the hay as a teacher." At that time, when someone finished trade school, college, or university, they were usually sent for four or five years to wherever they were needed, and this was determent by the government. I had no desire to dedicate my life teaching kids in the rural school how to sing hymns to Lenin, but it was the practice of the Soviet educational system to send graduates wherever there was a shortage of people in certain occupations. A graduate could be sent anywhere, whether it was in some town not far away from your own city or a little village in the Siberia. It was a mandatory procedure in our country, and only the lucky ones or graduates with connections would end up in the best places after graduation. Music education organizations were not excluded from this practice and once I realized this, my hopes for my future after Sokolovski school melted down. If that would have been the only disappointment, I suppose I could have made it work; I would have found a way to realize my dreams even in a rural village. But, the other shocking discovery was that my drums and percussion education included nothing like the music I had played with our school band. It was a classical music learning center, and anything outside that genre was simply banned from the institution. My main musical instrument of study was the xylophone. When I was told to buy one, I could not even tell my friends about it because I was too embarrassed. I had only seen one as a toy when I was a child, and I had no interest in it at all.

The eye-opening truth about the world I've had surrendered myself came quickly in one of our music theology lessons. We were studying all genres of music in the world. When we came to the final classifications of styles during the study, rock music was introduced to us as well. I was ready to hear something logical and intelligent presented to us by our professor—something that might explain Rock as an evolving genre from the all previous forms of music styles wrapped into a modern bundle filled with technological movements and expressions. I assumed that within these walls, I wouldn't have to hear propaganda purporting that rock music was some evil tool of the CIA, but I was wrong. Rock music was classified as "psychopathic music," and that is what they forced us to write in our notebooks. Jazz and blues were also excluded from discussions altogether. After that, I had no more hope of ever being truly and logically educated about the music I so enjoyed. Still, as much of a letdown as it was, I had to accept what I'd gotten myself into and just try to go with the flow.

The Tape Recorder

As a reward for my enrollment in music school, my mom bought me a bobbin tape recorder called a "Nota". It was the cheapest of its kind but very popular in the USSR at the time. It was really an attachment, as unlike a few other models that were produced in our country, the "Nota" had to be connected to a stereo system because it had no speakers or amplifier of its own. This made my tape recorder somewhat more reliable because there were less parts that could potentially break. People who understood the value of electronics truly loved it and thought it a great invention. The majority of the population, however, still wanted something that would play the music through its speakers. While everybody was after "Yauza" and "Kometa" recorders, people who had some kind of stereo at home were fortunate to buy the little "Nota" without going through major battles for its alternatives in the stores.

When we got our tape recorder, I knew my world of music would leap to another dimension. The beauty of having it at that time was that you could expand your music collection to practically unlimited size. You were no longer limited to a few Soviet records to play or to listening to crummy quality of foreign radio broadcasts. All I needed with the Nota was a good source to record the music from. The options were not many unless you had some kind of connections with the underground and black market world, but it was also possible to obtain copies of some rock bands that had been rerecorded dozens of times. People shared those without any issues, but if you wanted to get a fresh recording from an imported vinyl record, you had to know someone and have plenty in your wallet to bribe them with. I was fortunate enough to know folks in our neighborhood who had some of these priceless "Western propaganda" records. Now, I wanted to hear something new and more diverse than the Pink Floyd, the Beatles, and other bands I'd already heard. My first tape recording was made at the cost of two rubbles for the album "Funny Adams" by the British band called Sweet. To me, it was wild stuff, and I played the heck out of it. Grandma asked me why I had to blast it so loud and play it so often, and I answered, "Because I love it and this is how it meant to be played live!" Besides that, I had no money to buy any other recordings.

Fortunately, at that time, my good friend Oleg, from our old school band, began getting involved in collecting records and tape recordings as well. Having such a hobby required a great deal of financial support. Somehow, Oleg managed to get money from his parents, who were well situated in the system, and several pricy records already stood in his collection. I recorded everything I could from his collection. It not only allowed me to increase my knowledge of rock music, but I also met many new friends of Oleg's, and they also shared with me whatever they could.

The diversity of styles and level of music quality that we listened to from those records was astonishing. Dozens of new rock groups came to our knowledge. We were ultimately exposed to bands like "Yes", "Genesis", "Supertramp", and "Rush", music we'd never heard in the USSR before. Not only did this avalanche of music entertain us, but it also exposed us to culture from the Western world and showed us the results of a society of liberty and freedom in which people could express themselves. All we could do at that time was dream about the era when we could also have a chance to play what we wanted and buy everything we needed for it in the stores. While these dreams seemed like science fiction, a future that would never dawn on Soviet soil, the light at the end of a tunnel began shining with the arrival of something no one ever expected in our society.

First Soviet Rock Bands and Catastrophe with the School

The world of underground tape recordings exploded with the first homegrown rock bands in our nation. It came to us as a bombshell delivering the statement of independence and freedom that swept the minds and souls of our youth like a hurricane. Coming from the Leningrad and Moscow, these new bands wreaked havoc not only on the hearts of our population, but also on our government. Everything about these groups was different than the official censored VIAs. The music, lyrics, and even the names of these bands were a shock to our carefully programmed Soviet understanding of proletarian art. At the forefront of this movement was the rock band called "Time Machine". Without the doubt, "Time Machine" had as much influence on music in our country as The Beatles had in the rest of the world. There was true "Time Machine" mania going on. The groundbreaking lyrics were bold, and if listeners listened between the lines, they could hear that "Time Machine" was freely expressing their ideas, exposing our society's faults and problems. They played new melodies and styles, leaving official pop music to die in their wake.

This music, like everything else in USSR that was different, fresh, or considered out of the box, was held back, prohibited, and outlawed. We did not see "Time Machine" or other bands like them on TV or hear them on official radio broadcastings. Recordings and albums of bands like "Time Machine", "Dynamic", and "Aquarium" were distributed through trusty underground channels and began filling the tape players and minds of our young population. It was indeed a cultural revolution that inspired and provoked the growth of hundreds of new Soviet rock bands. The concerts of these artists were held in undisclosed locations, where only a carefully selected audience was lucky to see them play live.

A lot about these rock bands was a mystery however. We didn't know how they managed to record their music, where they got their equipment from, or even who they were. Like many groups of that era, they had evolved from the school bands or the little clubs where government officials failed to enforce such ideological control over kids. Those boys then grew into true underground celebrities, overtaking not only the crummy Soviet world of music, but even overshadowing the fame and glory of many Western bands among our young population. It was the beginning of a new era in Soviet and Russian rock music.

The government officials tried to ignore the existence of the new phenomena, but the so-called "problem" became much bigger than our authorities anticipated it would. After some time, it could not be longer been ignored, and they demanded that something had to be done to stop it. They didn't know, however, how to fight the uncensored rock bands and were afraid to simply start throwing musicians in jail, for fear of counter-attacks, so a chain of very ineffective and unsuccessful Soviet attempts began to take place.

It became obvious to our authorities that the biggest threat to our population from unofficial music was coming from its liberty- and freedom-driven lyrics. To divert the attention of young population from these bands, many authorized and approved artists were instructed to produce some Western songs in Russian language. Records with this surrogate music were released in immense quantities. In an effort to overshadow and destroy the popularity of groups that the government could not control, the Soviet record company named Melodija put several albums on the market by groups like ABBA, Smokey, Elton John, and a disco band from Jamaica called Boney M. Some of them, like Boney M, were even invited to play concerts in Moscow. This strategy did not turn out as they hoped; in fact, quite the opposite. It only sparked more interest in rock music, including Western music and the underground rock in Russia. There was an unstoppable natural desire to listen to music not only in our language, but about our problems in Soviet Russia.

Dealing with my Music School

At the same time as these cultural struggles and changes were going on, my own struggle at music school continued. As I delved deeper into my education, I had a great deal of difficulty keeping up with overwhelming load of studies that I could barely understand. My absence of knowledge in reading notes and music grammar was my biggest enemy. While many other students had a previous education in these field, I lagged behind in every major. Learning how to play piano was one of the most difficult faculties for me. Not only was this study extremely intense, but I was unable to read notes and follow my pedagogue. All of my studies proved very challenging for me, and I grew increasingly disappointed with the whole concept and the potential rewards of getting that education, which were going to be lesser than I had naively hoped. At the time when everybody around me was looking at me as a good example of a young man establishing his life, I was just trying to survive at music school. It was getting to the point that I began to hate being there and regretted my decision to go.

On top of very difficult lessons that I found somewhat dull, we all had to participate in our school musical ensemble. This was mandatory, and no one could escape it, even if they were not interested. Like in my previous school, I was again forced to take part in a marching band. My musical instruments in the marching orchestra were drums and other percussion items, which led me to a permanent abomination of those types of music.

The music school band was very different than the one I had been in before, at a much higher level since it was practically the official city marching band orchestra. It was made up of students who were believed to be the best musicians from our region, unequalled in talent and forced to serve our city authorities on demand. Every week we had to play at some kind of official gathering or celebration. Learning the hymns and patriotic tunes took up most of our rehearsals. Whenever a big official or foreign proletarian delegation arrived in the city, we had to play Soviet and visitors' anthems at the airport or train station. We played every event that local bosses thought might require our fine music. Eventually, I had to participate in my worst fear of that time and play at the funeral of an old Communist party member.

Unlike in my past, I could not even dream about playing in the school VIA because, despite being the center of fine musical education, the Sokolovski school did not have one. They considered VIA music foreign and demoralizing, and so it was banned. Apparently, this was true not only for our school, but all music education colleges in the USSR at the time.

"Do I really need this?"

In this situation, I tried to find a solution to survive my difficult studies and the grim outlook of my discouraging future. In the midst of all of this misery, I looked to my xylophone teacher as an example of a so-called "successful musician". I wasn't sure I could have a life like his, though, regardless of how I finished at school. He was living the life of a typical Soviet pedagogue, but in many ways, he was very a fortunate man by our standards. He taught people like me during the day, but he had a real job which was far more profitable. Almost every night, he played at one of the city's big restaurants as a drummer. At that time, it was one of the best-paid occupations for musicians.

To work in a restaurant band was one of the most prestigious jobs among musicians at the time. There was very little fame and glory in it, but it was extremely desirable because it was so well paid. Truly, it was just a part-time occupation, but a restaurant musician only had to play a few times a week, late in the evenings, to make good money, even with days off work. To become a member of a restaurant band did not require much of a musical education. While it was always a plus, the main key to getting a spot in this highly desirable job was good connections, and sometimes a good amount of money. When a rare opportunity came along and a band member wanted to step down, he could sell his seat in the band for thousands of rubles to a potential candidate. It was one of those unique jobs in the USSR where the real salary came not from the official payroll, but from the money made on the side. Musicians could sometimes pocket the equivalent of a monthly salary in just a couple of days by playing requests. When weddings were celebrated at the restaurants for a whole weekend, the profits for band members skyrocketed. For any musician who could play drums, guitar, or keyboard, it was a paradise position to be in, a dream for anyone who wanted to make money playing music. The Soviet system tried to stop this source of illegal profits, but small payoffs to the restaurant administration and law enforcement personnel made this entertaining business a money-making heaven for guys who could play sleazy tunes for a drunken crowd. I realized that my xylophone teacher's work at the restaurant was not reliant on his education, and he even told me himself that having good connections would give me better opportunities in music than a prestigious diploma.

At the time, while all my friends and relatives were jealous and proud of my participation in the music school, I was wrestling for my survival there and even questioning if I even needed to bother with the struggle after all. I knew that when the semester exams and tests came, I would not pass them. Without a doubt, I had lost my desire to even try. I was not only disappointed with the school program, but also with the concept and the lackluster opportunities I would have after my graduation. It was even hard for me to share my thoughts and concerns with my classmates because all of them came with music education experience and mainly did not care much about what they were going to do after getting diploma. Not many of them were into rock music, and none of them seemed to mind that they wee going to have low-paying job after graduation. They were just happy they wouldn't be working in factories and would have cleaner work than that, even if it did mean the boring life of a music teacher in an elementary school somewhere.

Leaving School and Mother's Reaction

When I made the announcement that I had quit Sokolovski school, it may as well have been a nuclear explosion. My friends could not believe it and kept questioning me about what I was going to do next. I honestly had no any idea myself and was hoping that something would come along.

My mom, however, was not as patient as I was. First, she tried to make me go back to school by setting up a meeting with the principal. When she realized even that wouldn't work, she tried to take total control of my life. To say she was angry over my decision to drop out of music school would be an extreme understatement. She was absolutely enraged, and I was afraid all my musical toys would be smashed and tossed out. It was even more aggravating to her that I had an absolutely reluctant view on all the Soviet principles and an outright dislike of anything related to Communist perspective on education. My mother disagreed with me and wanted me to follow the established official proletarian life guidelines. By that time, I was old enough to understand the good and evil of our Soviet system and did not hide my opinions about it from anybody.

This drove my mom into revenge mode, and she told me that she knew better what I should do with my life. She said she found a place for me and that I would go, whether I liked it or not.

One of the biggest factories in our city was "Gomselmash", which produced heavy agricultural machinery and employed a good portion of our city. It was so big that it even had its own trade school. That school was where my mother decided I would go. One snowy morning in the winter, she forced me to go with her for an appointment she had set up with the trade school principal. I had gone from the heights of a most prestigious music school down to the lowest place I could be—a factory trade school that would take anyone from the lowest grade characters to seasoned bandits into its classes. I knew I was in trouble but could not resist my mother's angry persistence.

We arrived at the school when all the kids were in their classes, and as soon as we set foot in the door, I could tell it was a tough life here. There were Soviet propaganda posters on the walls, and it was a cold, official-looking environment. I knew if I went there, I was going to hate it so very much. When we were called to the principal's office, we were greeted by a large man with good personality and traces of rough life experience on his face. We sat down, and my mom started talking about my recent music school experience. Suddenly, the man asked her if he could talk to me privately. My mother was caught by surprise, and I could tell she did not want me to talk to the principal alone, but she cooperated and left the room.

When the door closed behind her, the man began talking to me like to a friend. He told me about the school and what they did there. I listened quietly until he asked me a flat-out question: "You don't want to be here, do you?"

"No, I don't," I said, looking him straight in the eyes.

He called my mom back to the office and told her they unfortunately didn't have any vacancies for me at that time, but if I want to come back in September, they would talk to me then. My mother was completely shocked. She knew something had happened in our private talk, and she knew there was no such thing as "no vacancy" when it came to trade schools that large. When we left that dreary place, my mother was stone cold and quiet, but I was walking on air, feeling as if I'd just escaped a prison sentence.

Another School and Speed Affections

The Soviet system we lived under had rules and laws pertaining to practically every aspect of human life. One of the most controlled and regulated areas of enforcement was the education of the young Russian population. The one fundamental requirement in which there was no leeway or concession was that everyone had to complete their high school education. That meant no one could have less than ten years of school studies in the USSR. This requirement could be met by finishing at a regular school or by attending other special facilities such as trade or "techniqume" institutes. Once that requirement was met, we could attend college or university or go straight into the workforce. Leaving school after eight years and do nothing could have meant facing criminal consequences if you were caught by the government. It was a situation I found myself in, and as a result, I had to enroll in the middle of the school year in some kind of educational place. Not only was it our law, but it was also my mother's requirement. There were very few options, especially considering my absolute disinterest in any trade school, which prepared kids to work at the factories or construction places.

We did find one option that seemed like a compromising solution: "Evening" school. The schools had been established many years prior in our country for people who had a sudden interruption in their high school completion. In the war era, all industries in the USSR suffered greatly from a shortage of labor, and students were often sent to work to fill the gap, interrupting their educational progress. Later in life, many of them wanted to get a college education, but in order to meet college entry requirements, they had to attend evening school to make up for the high school classes they had missed. These places were also for criminals who spent time in jail at a young age instead of being behind their school desks, forcing them to fall behind academically and make up the work in their adult years.

One of the main requirements for evening school was that students had to have a daytime job; they worked during the day and attended school in the evening. If your shift was at night or after lunch, you would be in this school in the morning. It also served as a temporary shelter for those like me who needed to be under the control of government until the end of a school year without working or enrolling now in a trade school.

A block away from our house, there was one of these schools. It was very small place located on the first floor of an apartment building. This school was designed more like an office facility, with about a dozen classrooms scattered here and there. It was not considered very classy to be enrolled in such an education center and it was the least prestigious way to earn a high school diploma. I was not thrilled to be there, but I knew there was no point in arguing with my mother about it.

Year 1980.

When I walked into my new school, I knew immediately that it would be very different from anything I'd seen before. I was right. The classes were small, and there were no more than ten students on any given day. However, I quickly learned that it was an easy academic situation. It was not designed to provide a great education, but rather, it was basically the place to get a piece of paper stating that you'd completed Soviet educational requirement.

Attendance at the school was poor, and those who did show up really didn't care to participate very much. Most of them were adults, with families of their own and many responsibilities outside of class. Teachers did not enforce the rules very strictly, unless a student completely disappeared altogether. Very often, good grades were given just for showing up in class. Answering questions even remotely correctly would gain you a great score. For anyone who did well in school, it was paradise, because the school was so easy. On the other hand, though, it was basically a phony education, and teaching was done at the lowest possible level. Trying to enroll into a college after graduating this place was a equal to going swimming into the melted iron.

After a few weeks, I began enjoying my new school. There was nothing exciting about the education I was getting there. It was simply the ease of participation and lack of homework that I found attractive. The periods were also only a half-hour long, and since there were only a few a day, I could be in and out of the school in a couple of hours. Since I had no job, I had to attend the school in the morning; this allowed me to have almost a whole day at my disposal. At the same time, my friends were barely making it home from their educational institutions by five o'clock.

Love for Speed - (Soviet Style)

Such a luxury gave me plenty of free time for everything I loved to do. At that time, I was obsessed with rock music and bicycles. To say that my love with two-wheelers hobby was the same as it was when I was ten would be incorrect, but for me, bicycles were just a substitute for something I could not afford and could only dream about: motorcycles.

Nothing is more exciting and thrilling for a teenager as moving fast. I was very interested in racing, but this sport was presented in the USSR in such limited availability that it remained somewhat primitive for decades. Many world renown racing programs such as Formula-1, Moto-GT, or Prototype Cars were unknown to the Russian population. Despite our political belief that it was a Western show-business type of sport, alien to Soviet people due to its so-called "violent" nature, there were more logical explanations as to why the USSR duped it. Most of the racing sports required technological sophistication and support, and our society could not sufficiently produce automobiles and motorcycles with the quantity and quality to satisfy just the general demand. Neglecting these types of sports, however proved impossible, if for no other reason than international embarrassment, so many years ago, the clumsy Socialistic solution was invented: the "DOSAAF," short for the Russian term for "Volunteered Association of Supporting Army, Navy, and Air Force." Everything in the USSR had to have some kind of links to our Communistic goals or be affiliated with the Red Army. Somehow, the racing and the auto-moto sport in general became a branch of our military machine, despite the fact that there was nothing military about it. The limited and very unsupported clubs that united its few lucky members was involved in internal USSR racing competitions. Our Soviet street automobiles were converted into Rally cars, and Russian Urals, Czech Jawa, and CZ motorcycles to motocross bikes. They were horrible, as was the level of our sportsmen in these fields. It was the lowest quality sport in our country compared to our glorious Olympic world-dominating disciplines. Everyone was aware of our lackluster racing performance, and the USSR racing teams never even competed abroad in a world class competitions for fear of embarrassment.

Despite that, getting into any of the racing clubs was extremely difficult due to its very limited numbers. And like everything else that was in high demand in the USSR, these type of clubs were also infected by the corruption of our almighty government. Getting your foot in the door of these clubs often cost dues or at least required good connections. For everybody else, the citizens who had moral standards and were not good at finding back doors, these shabby clubs were a dream. It was a dream for me as well. For many years, I hoped to one day own a motorcycle, but they were a low-level luxury, and my friends and I could only look on with envy as folks rode them down our streets. The most speed we could get at that time was racing each other on our bicycles.

Our bike racing obsession in those years was also fueled by something we discovered completely by accident. At one of the recycling paper gathering raids in school, someone found a Czech magazine called "Svet Motory". That magazine had a nearly explosive impact on our minds. It was filled with pictures of racing cars and motorcycles, absolutely mind blowing to us. Packed with Hondas, Porsches, Ducatis, and all kinds of images and information about the racing world, we considered the magazine almost anti-Soviet. You could not buy these magazines in our stores, but we found a nice little loophole in the subscription system that allowed it to be received from our friendly neighbors in Czech Republic. It did not take long before the magazine started coming to my mailbox every few weeks. Its effect on all of my pals and me was ground shaking. Not only was the magazine exposing us to the contrast of USSR motor sports to those in the West, but we also learned something else. The realization that it was unthinkable for the magazine to be published in the USSR but it was okay in other Socialistic nations struck us, and it revealed to us the level of censorship in our country; it was like nowhere else in the world.

Fueled by never-before-seen auto-moto material and photo reports from worldwide high-speed races, my friends and I could only dream about watching such sports live with our very own eyes. It never happened in our Soviet life. All we could do back then was enjoy looking at the pictures and hope that one day we would be able to buy a Soviet- or Czech-made motorcycle. Meanwhile, our bicycles were getting a facelifts; we tried to make them resemble motocross bikes by painting the names of Western motor brands on them. It became a great activity for us, and transformed our bike-riding to somewhat of a social cult. We imitated everything we could from what we saw in the "Svet Motory" magazine. It was very hard to replicate motorcycle life on our bicycles, and we used our great imaginations to make our bikes as close as possible to something that was well beyond our reach. We made jumping ramps and did wheelies all around the neighborhood, putting our poorly made Soviet bikes to the test. The bystanders and pedestrians were amazed by some of our tricks, and we often had to deal with broken frames and bent wheel rims.

Not only did we dream about having motorcycles, but also about joining the shabby motocross club that our city was fortunate to have. It was a typical Soviet venture with all attributes of bribery and back door business. Becoming a member involved more than a raging desire to do so, and we knew that very well.

Riding my bike.

Riding our bicycles across our city to the club was an almost daily routine. We loved seeing the outdated Jawa and CZ motorcycles; they made a lot of noise and smoke while their fortunate riders constantly adjusted their ever faulty engines. Looking at the mechanical beasts was far more than fun for us; we were awestricken. We were not the only ones who stood in the club courtyard, digging the Soviet mockery of a motocross club. Occasionally, some of us had the good fortune of being asked to clean the riders' motorcycles in exchange for a chance to sit on them. Despite the childish reward for getting our hands dirty, we considered it a cool opportunity—the closest we were going to get to the sport none of us could ever reach.

I was absolutely ecstatic about thrill of speed, and pedaling my bike downhill in the parks and the cross-country were the fastest rides I could hope for. It was the thrill that I could only compare to playing in the band, and later in life I would come to understand why rock 'n roll and high speed are a perfect union.

While motor sports were becoming a great passion of mine, our Soviet government had quite an opposite opinion of it. Just like rock music, it was partially banned and neglected, and even if it did exist, it was only in a primitive form and was used as yet another tool of propaganda. I began to believe that anything I enjoyed or cared about, my government tried to oppress or did not promote. But I was not the only one. Millions among our population suffered in that so-called "utopia," living in a world where the government was telling the Russian people that their interests were criminal or Western or evil or foolish. For decades, we were told that these activities were foreign and alien to our Socialistic culture, and far too often, this put an end to questions and open discussions in our society.

Good News From a Friend and the Moscow Olympics

When the end of the school year was near, I had to come up with some kind of plan for my future. There was no option for me to stay any longer in the evening school since I could not get a job at my age. The only choice I had was to go to a trade school, which would give me some technical education and a high school diploma at the same time. There was an overwhelming array of options when it came to trade schools. Not only were there plenty of schools, but there was also a full spectrum of choices when it came to occupations. The only problem in my case was that none of them appealed to me. I still believed that somehow, I could find the way of sustaining my life in the music field. It was a dream which would not leave my mind, despite the failed attempt of going into the music school. But I did not know what other options I had to get to that point. The choice had to be made before my mother would drag me again back to the Gomselmash factory trade school. I had a full summer ahead of me, and I promised my parents that I would find a place to go and actually complete it.

Meanwhile, my good friend Sasha was writing pitiful letters home from his distant education at the technicume in Kastroma. It was sad to read about what he had to go through while living on that campus. The school itself was pretty bad by his description, but the living conditions were even worse. It was a well-known fact in our country that some regions of the USSR offered better living standards than others. Demographical differences played a role in how wealth was distributed throughout the nation, and many places were much less privileged than other areas of the Soviet Union. Kastroma city was one of the locations that had a shortage in supplies; there was much disparity between it and our town. Whether it was the result of a faulty Soviet distribution system or the lack of local infrastructures, people there suffered from a shortage of even basic goods and quality food practically all the time. The solution in Sasha's case was quite gruesome and reminded me of some kind of rescue effort for starving people in poverty. His mother sent him packages with canned food and other provisions so he would not be hungry most the time. Cigarettes were also in short supply, and shipping them by the case guaranteed my friend not only a smoke, but a good way for him to barter for other things he needed. He often traded his cigarettes for toothpaste and other basic daily necessities.

Not only did he hate the deplorable living conditions, but also his school as well. It was hard not only for him, but also for his family, who felt like their son was off in a war zone. When he said he could not take it anymore and wanted to return home, his parents did not resist. For me, it was a great news: Knowing that we could soon rejoin and get some music band going again was very exciting and uplifting. He also missed the fact that all we had experienced was abruptly stopped and disappeared without any hope for a future. In his letters, he wrote a lot about it and could not wait to finish the last few days of his school attendance so he could be free from his nightmare.

Finally, life did not seem as dull or hopeless. Because my good friend, my guiding mentor, was coming back, the prospect of going to get the required education at some shabby trade school (or so-called GPTU) wasn't such a big drama anymore. I knew that regardless of what GPTU I went to, music would be the most important part of my life again. With Sasha's proactive personality, it would be a very realistic prospect.

Olympic Games

When the 1980 Summer Olympic Games was held in Moscow, it took the nation into the biggest propagandistic event we ever experienced. Despite the flop with the Soviet presence in Afghanistan and the following boycott of the Games by many Western nations, USSR still took the opportunity to display our Socialistic system in its full "glory" and "superiority." It would not be so easy, though, without a massive facelift. This involved not only cosmetic construction renovations of Moscow, but also some social adjustments and improvements. The brushing and cleaning of the Soviet capital went to unheard-of extremes. Former criminals were ordered to leave Moscow for the whole summer, and registered alcoholics were dispatched to the closed rehabilitation centers or labor brigades outside of our capital. Bums that lurked around train and bus stations in spite of claims that they were a "symbol of capitalistic society," were swept to jails on false charges of solicitation just so they wouldn't be an eyesore. Everything had to look like the propagandistic posters of the Soviet Union. We had to be a clean society without any flaws in the eyes of the Western world.

The cosmetic beautification and Moscow's crowd "pest control" was not enough to make the visitors of the Games believe that we were superior or somehow isolated from the rest of the world. Coke machines and fancy ice cream kiosks were placed throughout the cities where any Olympic competitions were taking place. Western products had to be introduced in some stores —a shocking sight for many Russians, even in limited quantity.

Spice It Up With Some "Modern Music"

The picture would not be complete without showing to the rest of the world that military marching bands and balalaika trios were not the only art form that our "modern Socialistic society" could produce. We had to throw a bone at anyone who would dare to question that our Proletarian "freedom of speech" did not allow people to play any music they liked. To make it some what believable, not long before the Olympic Games, our government created the first, one and only official Soviet "Youth music" festival in the Georgian capital of Tbilisi. The location itself was far away from Moscow, hand picked in order to have a better control just in case things got out of hand. It was probably the most difficult event the Soviet officials ever had to organize. The government had a full and open hatred of rock music, so placing all the underground bands in one place and letting them have a good time was true torture for our officials. Nevertheless, it had to be done for the greater cause of propaganda, so the festival took place despite the "ideological danger" they claimed it held for our young Soviet minds.

Many homegrown bands like Mashina Vremeni, Autograph, Integral, Aquarium, and few others had a chance to present their programs to the audience without any fear for the very first time. Organizers elected a jury to choose the winners of the festival, but the government opinion mattered little and was not a respected choice among the young audiophiles.

Despite this lavish gesture from the Soviet government to even allow such an event to take place, ruling authorities were still reluctant to refer to our musicians as "rock bands." The standard "group" was still used in all big events and any media coverage.

When the Show is Over

When the Olympic Games were over and the propaganda machine could stop trying to make us look civilized, all the rock bands were sent back to their underground world. Life back to normal meant closing the doors on everything that had been even slightly liberalized at the time of Olympics. As was often the case in Soviet life, the temporary corrections and adjustments that were made to give us credibility in the world came at the expense of severe backlash. Not only were the rock musicians banned from performing openly before the crowd, after being approved by our government just a month prior, but all Western attributes and brands were pulled back from Moscow's streets in order to maintain the "proper Socialistic manner" of our society.

The so-called "cleanup" did not stop with the people who lived inside our borders. Anyone in the world who was unhappy with the Olympics or who made any negative remarks about our country at that time was blacklisted as an ideological enemy. Many politicians, civil activists, citizens of other countries, and even entire governments were demonized by our official media for supporting the boycott of the Olympics as an outcry against the Soviet presence in Afghanistan. Among of them were quite a few musicians from the West. Swedish group ABBA and Greek singer Demis Roussos were among those on the "no play list" in the USSR for supposed remarks about the Afghanistan situation. In many cases, association was enough; if the government even saw someone talking to or being around known anti-Soviet persons, they were doomed in the Soviet Union. As a result, these musicians were wiped off of our television screens and radio waves as if our government wanted to erase them from the Earth altogether.

The pressure on enforcing the strict Proletarian regime was coming with more intensifying force. It was important for our government to tighten what they felt was a "loose feeling" after the Olympics so they could make people to understand that nothing should be more important to Soviets than the "purity" of our Socialistic life. For many residents of our country, it was very understandable that when the "show" was over, everything would go back to normal. But for some, the old machine of grinding human souls into the gravel of a senseless obedient crowd was not working as it did in the times of Stalin. People's imagination and interests had been piqued, and they wanted to know about the life outside of our camp. They yearned for better living conditions in their lives at that time, and they were growing weary of promises for some allegorical future that never seemed to come. More and more, the younger generations in the USSR were becoming interested not only in music of the West, but also in all aspects of life abroad. The Iron Curtain was weakening, no longer able to shield the desire of people for knowledge and freedom, but the totalitarian machine's response to these threats was to implement even more elaborate oppressions. Our longstanding Socialistic society was approaching its fading state of existence, and the agony of the dying political system was in the final phase of its cruel attempt to survive. But before a change for the better would occur, I would have to live through some of the worse years of the Soviet regime that I had ever experience; the beast fought hard when backed into a corner, and we all took the brunt of it.

Chapter 13

Friends, Construction Brigades, and a New Band

I lived in a world that was making changes very slowly, if any. Things were happening, though, in all aspects of our lives, including our social infrastructure, long-established taboos, and customs. More than anything, it involved relationships. For Soviet people this aspect of life was by far the most valuable. During the time of my residence in USSR we all mainly lived in the same places without moving around, often for our whole lives. This stationery kind of life was not actually our preference or choice; it was a reality established by our system and laws. Relocating or moving from place to place was hard for many reasons, most of them having to do with tight restrictions and apartment shortage. While no one was happy about it, this part of our political system had one positive side effect: People grew very close to each other, and relationship bonds were long lasting, sometimes for a lifetime.

All our neighbors and relatives were more than just people we knew. They were a part of our life, and we shared with one another, whether we were in pain or happiness. The relationships stood through many years of tests and trials, and we all knew our friends well enough that we trusted each other with our deepest secrets and knew we could count on one another. Not only was it common to have dear friends who were closer than relatives, but it was the norm. The friends we met in kindergarten and daycare rarely left their old residences and stayed around for a very long time. The buddies we met later in school and others we met in social circles only added to this ever-growing loop of friends. The one significant fact about Russian culture of that era was that friendship was valued as one of the most important aspects of our life. To call someone your best friend was much greater than a respectful jester. It was powerful title, and one that wouldn't simply be given to just anyone you'd known for a long time. Betrayal or unfaithfulness was regarded as the lowest, most unethical crime, and it was unforgiven if it was committed against a trusted friends. There was a universal code of moral standards in Russia, but friendship was treated in a much more sensitive manner due to our very close spiritual bonds. Lifetime relationships were the most prized treasures we were harvesting in the USSR. The sad irony about this is that if we had not lived it ourselves, we never would have known such closeness could exist under the tight thumb of a political system that kept us closed off to the world.

Like many other kids in Russia, I had a lot of friends. In fact, the house was practically never empty of them. We would often sit on the floor since there wasn't a lot of room or furniture in the house. Our apartments became a hangout, and even if the resident left for a while, the friends would stick around and make themselves at home. Sharing all we had was part of our culture, and we did it without a second thought. We lived in a non-materialistic world in which friendship was our greatest commodity. To a certain extent, we could not survive in our society without true friendship. I was blessed with a lot of beloved people in my life, and not once was I ever betrayed by anyone close to me. However, I only had couple of true best friends that I felt I could trust with my life—a reality in any country regardless of its political system.

Youth Construction Brigades

When the summer of 1980 was in the full bloom, the time of Youth Construction Brigades was at the top of the government's agenda. Not only were these used to keep our young generation occupied, but also politically in check. The brigades were organized by trade schools and colleges to "help" our comrade workers in the construction fields of our nation. Simply put, it was an easy way to get cheap (mainly free) labor and prepare the young generation for hard work and government obedience. The main reason however, was a desperate need in a workforce to compensate our unproductive economical system. At the time when child labor was prohibited in our country, the summer Construction Brigades were promoted as an "educational venue." Groups twenty or thirty kids aged sixteen and older were taken to construction sites and lived in the portables or campers while they worked for a month with adults. The kids were volunteers, and they were promised that they would make money, though most of them came back home without a penny in their pocket. Everybody knew it, but just as people are driven to hope against the odds for a lottery win, and enticed by the thought adventure, thousands signed up to go. Many of our teenagers were attracted by the advertised romantic challenge and a chance to get away from boring city life in the summer. Somehow, my friend Sergey lured my good pal Slava and me to go on one of these so-called adventures, and it was definitely an interesting experience.

Building a School

Our bus took our brigade to a rural area a few hours away to help with a school-building project. Upon arrival, we were admitted to a newly finished small apartment building, and the next day was supposed to begin our first day of work.

In the morning, we were told that the food and our beds were prorated and would be deducted from our salary. We were promised to be paid at the end of our trip, though they never told us how much we would make per day. While this was the normal practice in our country, I already felt something fishy about the whole scenario. All we could do was wait until our work was evaluated and graded.

As soon as we settled, the first thing on the agenda for many kids in the group was to get booze. Having drinks for teenagers in the USSR was a common habit, and these kind of trips were also a perfect escape and chance to have this kind of fun. Controlling this bad behavior was very difficult since the people whose job it was to be on top of it frequently drank with teens at an even faster pace.

Like everything else promoted by the government, the advertised Construction Brigade had little to do with the reality. We were taken there not so much to learn any skills and trades, but rather to serve as a clean-up crew at the construction site of a new school. The most shocking thing to us was the fact that this school was built by criminals on probation. Besides their term in prison, they were also sentenced to work on government projects. Needless to say, our parents would have never let us go had they known we'd be around criminals. It was a typical Soviet solution: No one in our country would want such a job, so the kids were an easy and naïve solution to getting the tasks completed.

When the work began and we started moving piles of trash from the construction site, the wild-looking workers simply stopped working and stared at our girls. After few days, they began making advances on the teenage ladies. For the convicts, it was the best entertainment imaginable. Fortunately, the criminals were escorted on separate buses to special prisoner camps, and that kept our girls safe.

Working all day in the dust and dirt was not only tiresome but boring as well. There was nothing interesting about moving construction waste around, and when we asked for something more intelligent to do, our supervisor told us we could learn now to use a jackhammer. It seemed like a more exciting task until we realized that the only reason they assigned it to us was so we could break up the huge concrete mountain that had been dumped by the truck in the front of the school. The criminals showed us how to operate the giant compressor and use the 100-pound jackhammer. It was loud, monstrous equipment only suitable for people who had enough strength to handle it. We wrestled with that project until many of us strained our backs and hands. The job was more than we could handle, and it didn't take us long to realize we'd been duped into doing the task our criminal co-workers did not want to deal with. Considering their absolute lack of interest in any kind of work, it wasn't really surprising at all.

At the end of the day, we still had energy left over to have some fun. Our main entertainment consisted of singing together and drinking beer. Some of the teenagers coupled up together for a little romance, but our puritan education overrode their hormones, so teenage pregnancy was not usually an issue. Despite all the difficulties and the strange working environment, we enjoyed the little adventure and hoped for a good, rewarding end to our trip. As always, I took my guitar with me, but it was not that easy being the only one in the group who could play. The drinking parties sometimes lasted until late into the night and since I had to entertain everyone by playing popular songs, I could not leave the party was over.

Proletarian Effort and its 'Reward'

When we were asked to do something very shabby and dangerous, I started questioning the integrity of the construction site leading personnel. In the basement of the school, the floor was very uneven, and the crew wanted to level the foundation by creating something they called "umbrellas." We were told to build a floating plywood floor that would stand on bricks and wood supports. On top of that, we had to pour concrete, and that would bring it to more level position. When we asked if it was going to collapse later, we were told with laughter, "Yes it will, but we won't be around!" Like any and all workplaces at that time in the Soviet Union, the building of that school was hailed with positive propaganda, banners that screamed falsities like "Our love to children through our proud labor!" or "Best in our country... to children!" Looking at those slogans—those lies—was pathetic to me after I learned of how that school was really built and by whom.

We worked on that project for a couple of weeks, and when the time of our evaluation came, we could not wait to see how much money we already made. The long list of senseless data was read to us by our field supervisor, and when the numbers came down to the earned wages, we were told that every one of us owed twenty-four rubles! We could not believe it and asked if it was a joke... but it wasn't. They told us we ate their food, slept on rented beds, and used their fuel and time to be driven to the site, and in the end of their funky and absurd calculations, we made less money than was spent on us. How it was done we could not understand since we worked all day long and never sat around doing nothing. In the end, we were advised to work overtime and help the crew of criminals deliver bricks to the fourth floor using wooden crates. They told us this would bring us more revenue.

After the meeting, my pal Slava and I went for a walk. We realized that this little government scam, these Construction Brigades, was a good source of not even cheap, but free labor. The decision was made that it was time to go home before we owed even more money, though that was not an easy task. Leaving without permission meant an official complaint would be issued to our educational institution, as well as some other consequences and complications. In my case, it was not an issue, since I was already out of my evening school and had not enrolled elsewhere. My friend said he didn't care about the "complications". So, in the morning, we left notes on our pillows stating that we weren't going to work for free anymore and were going home. About an hour later, we were already on the local train, taking us with empty pockets and tired back to our city.

A New Band

The return of my good friend Sasha was a great relief and an exciting time for me. The idea of putting together a band was finally a reality again, and we could not wait to implement this goal. In those days, it was practically impossible to establish such a concept on your own unless you had a lot of money and connections to obtain all the necessary equipment. Even if we managed to do that, performing before the crowd without the government's permission was absolutely impossible.

We were not even thinking at that time about playing any kind of original music and simply wanted to do what we had done in our school. The only solution was to try to land a gig at one of our culture palaces. Owned by unions or cities, they were the only places where ordinary people could practice all kinds of performing arts. They hosted everything from official patriotic meetings to amateur and professional concerts and dancing, and in general, they were not a horrible concept. Still, though, the activities there were heavily controlled, and enrolling in some of the most popular could prove to be a challenge. It cost nothing to participate there, but the spots were limited. For VIA bands spots, basically was the toughest one to get.

One of these cultural clubs for proletarian constructors was located not far away from our house, and we decided to build a band and present ourselves to its administration. Our program options were limited to what we already knew, and the main task now was simply to get our school VIA members together. We had to notify Valentine, our keyboardist, and our drummer Andrew so we could start tapping into the culture palace. While Valentine was excited about this idea and was ready to go for it, Andrew was already involved with the band at his trade school and could not join us. Since we had no other drummer, the only option we had was to bring our pal Oleg from school to be a guitar player so I could take over on the drums. It was just a temporary solution, and I hoped to soon have an electric guitar back in my hands. But our first priority was seeing if we could gain interest and a place on the palace roster.

We knew they already had some VIA band at the "construction palace", and that meant we had little chance of squeezing our way in. The plan was simple: We would walk in and tell the administration who we were and see what will happen. When we walked into the "palace", we were told to see Stas - manager and also the lead man of a band that was already playing there. This fact already gave us little hope to get a gig under this roof. When we met him, he was very skeptical about our abilities and said he first wanted to see if we could play, and we could talk after that. We were a bit surprised that he did not send us home and got exited.

In the small rehearsal room, there was plenty of equipment, and it looked much better than our school's beat-up amps. Even though it was a cheap imported one, the Amati drum set looked like a masterpiece compared to what we used in our band, and I found it stunning.

We grabbed the instruments, and Sasha commanded, "Burn!" The Deep Purple hit blasted through the building.

Stas got up on his feet and was in complete shock at what he heard. As soon as we were done, he said, "Alright. I think we need to talk."

Twenty minutes later, we were walking home cheering in excitement that it was so easy for us to grab one of the most desirable spots in town to play. The deal was made that we would play all dancing and promo concerts while the old band would concentrate on "important stuff". What it really meant was that they would play whenever they wanted, including the high-paying weddings, and we would be the palace workhorses. It was totally fine with us, though, and we were thrilled about the rare opportunity.

It was the beginning of another band journey for me; my Soviet life would offer me quite a few. I was hoping we would not be stuck in limbo trying to find a drummer, but all the efforts to find a replacement were to no avail. I stuck with the drumsticks but was still happy because it was better than nothing, and I also enjoyed playing drums. The guitar was still my favorite instrument, and I would occasionally switch with Oleg when he could play something simple on drums.

Our performances were technically the same drill we have had in our school. The repertoire, though, had to be slightly muted, since all the wild stuff we had done in the past was not appreciated by our new club administration and authorities. The closer we were to the general public, the more censorship and control was placed on musicians. Playing songs of Led Zeppelin or Beatles at dances was still possible, but the balance of Soviet and imported music had to be in favor of our homeland tunes. All official concerts and patriotic celebrations had to be completely pro-Soviet. Any attempt to violate this rule meant immediate termination and a possible audience with authorities. Knowing what to say, to sing, or to show was becoming a natural instinct for every Russian performer, and these rules came naturally in life. No one questioned it, and all just simply obeyed and accepted it as a part of our reality. We did the same and played by the rules to keep our dream alive. Our band was in the situation where all our energy was concentrated on playing the best we could without taking any chances that might result in tragic consequences.

The main purpose and goal of the culture palaces was to "deliver culture to the masses". "The culture belongs to people," stated the red banner above the entrance, and this message was delivered with a questionable results. But the palace could not escape the need for revenue, and the dances that occurred a few nights a week were not free of charge. Making money on the events they hosted was essential, the main profit for this type of organizations. Technically, musicians were employed as part-time staff and paid a minimal salary, but in our case, this part was dedicated to Stas and his band. If they ever showed up for a gig, it was for fun and a couple of songs. They were our staff band and were the "enthusiasts". We were okay with that, and we understood that it was the only reason we were allowed to be there. It was better than nothing, and many musicians in our country were in the same situation. To be in the VIA band was not a choice; it was a privilege, and we totally understood that.

Trade School and Helping Comrades on the Field

When the time came to pick my next educational place, I was absolutely baffled about it. I did not want to go to any of them. The whole concept of a trade school would limit me to working in a factory or, at the very best, in construction. It was mainly the lowest level of education we could get compared to a technikume or college. For many reasons among our population, the abbreviation GPTU, which stood for "State Professional Technical School," was ironically reworded as "God Help Stupid to Settle." There was a bit of cruel truth in this mockery, pointing at the contingent of its student body.

I had no option but to choose one of these places to complete high school and to be inline with the protocols of Soviet life. A couple of my friends from our neighborhood had just finished their eighth grade year and had to find a place to continue their education as well. Most of us had no preference as to what trade school we should enroll in. As long as the prospect of going to work somewhere at the factory or construction site after graduation was not in the picture, we were okay with it. I wanted to be sure that my future job would at least give me some flexibility in the choices of where I could work. The School of Electrical Technicians fitted these parameters, at least in our opinion. Since this occupation would be high demand in any area with electricity, it was the most flexible occupation we could find.

Three of my friends—Slava, Igor, and Alex—and I submitted our documents, and on September 1, we showed up at our new trade school. There, we would learn the basic majors of high school, and half our time would be dedicated to skills training and trade education. In three years, we would graduate with diplomas, certified as qualified technicians, but before that happened, the thirty of us students had to go on our first "potato trip."

When the Agricultural System Flawed

Every September, students in every college and trade school, as well as most of the factory workers had to go for a few weeks to the fields of our agricultural organizations to work. It was a mandatory obligation of every Soviet proletarian to help our comrades in the country to harvest potatoes, cabbage, and any other farm produce. These junkets were called "potato trips." The flawed system of our agricultural infrastructure could not survive without the support of our students and city workers. The government used all elements of the propaganda machine to boost the moral and patriotic feelings of our people about this never-popular obligation among our society.

City workers was gathered in the first days of September from their workplaces and loaded on the trucks to be taken to unknown destinations, villages and farms. The pay was simply their regular work wages: Whatever they made at the factory or science lab where they worked, they made the same in the farm fields.

It was a nonnegotiable duty for everyone except executives and authorities. Hospitalization or the death of a family member was the only accepted excuse for not showing up on potato trips, and the punishment for absence was severe. While losing one's job was one of the consequences, in most cases disciplinary actions was also taken against the no-shows, including withdraw of their pay and public humiliation. Privileges like summer vacation time or one's spot in line for a new apartment would be taken away. In the past however, the punishment would be much more worse... At the time of Stalin, citizens were even executed, accused of "sabotaging the Communist Party agenda".

Taking students into the fields was the easiest and most productive way for the government to accomplish this task. Teens could be easier manipulated and yelled at, and they worked harder out of fear, since they knew they would have to withstand disciplinary trial upon return to their schools. Millions of our young population worked in kolkhozes and farms every year, hoping they could at least return home with a bag of potatoes.

When our truck loaded with boys and girls from our school stopped in the small village, we felt we had truly traveled back in time. It was the most neglected and rundown place I'd ever witnessed in my life. About forty shabby houses stood along the dirt road, and the eerie silence pierced our ears. It was not even really a village, but a khutor, one of the most scarcely populated places in the country. A bunch of khutors like this, were united together into one collective farm or kolkhoz. The local kolkhoz director, who was riding an old horse carriage, told our teacher and group leader that we would be living with the village families, a standard practice. The hosts volunteered to house the workers, but if they hadn't, the kolkhoz administration could force it if the household didn't agree. Any family who had "proper conditions" would house two or three students for a short stay. All they got as compensation for this obligation was grocery produce or salt and matches. Some people truly welcomed the young workers from the city and shared their house in very warm Russian hospitality.

When I walked into an old single lady's house with my friends Slava and Igor, we knew life there would be very interesting. Her house was a tiny log one with a wood stove, two beds, and a table, and no modern utilities other than electricity. The old lady turned out to be a true character, and she openly disliked people from the city. She told us she had never seen a train in her life and had never visited a large city. The stories she told were quite chilling at times. When she told us the Nazis were very kind when they occupied the village, we knew there was something wrong there.

Every day we had to walk to the large field of beetroot and dig it for eight to ten hours a day. We had to harvest a certain tonnage before we could go home, and that amount was carefully calculated to keep us busy all day. At noon, lunch was delivered to us by horse, and many of us fell asleep right after finishing our meal. A short while later, everyone was awakened and crawled to continue our proletarian duty. When we noticed no kolkhoz workers on the field and asked about it, we were told that there was no one left in the village who could work. A few alcoholics and elderly people were the only inhabitants of that forgotten place, and that was why they so badly needed our help.

When we returned from the fields, we had to use a heavy axe to split firewood for the stove to cook dinner. The old lady took advantage of our stay and demanded more and more wood every day. She had us put it away in the little barn and told us it needed to be preserved in case of rain.

It was enough of it for the whole winter, but we kept chopping more. On the weekend, we went to her backyard to dig potatoes that she told us were for dinner, but when we brought back our mini-harvest, she stashed them in her cellar under the floor and said they were "for the future."

Despite our very hard work in the fields and the cruel treatment of our babushka, we had enthusiasm to go out late in the evening to have fun. A few teenage romances occurred with the girls, and ongoing social drama between the classmates was typical for these kinds of voyages.

There was little to choose from when it came to entertainment in the village. No one there even had a TV. The radio worked once in a while during the week, and we felt like we were living in the eighteenth century. Drinking moonshine was the only amusement for those who were still living there, and they cheerfully shared it with us. I understood the reason for the great level of alcoholism in our countryside and villages after visiting that place. It was truly savage, completely detached from any form of civilization, modern conveniences, or even current manners and etiquette.

There was limited space in the old lady's house. There was only two beds, and others had to sleep on top of the wood-burning stove. Food was just as limited. We never felt like we had enough to eat, and we constantly asked our host if she could feed us a bit more, to which she always answered, "People don't eat much in the village." We tried to cook ourselves, but it did not work out well, and we often drank raw eggs to keep our energy at good working level.

In the middle of our trip, we wanted to go to the city on the weekend to get some food and have a shower. To do that, we had to walk eight miles to the closest train station and from there go to our town. Despite the long trip, the walk was nice. We journeyed through the fields of crops that were ready to harvest and traversed narrow dirt roads that cars only traveled once a week to deliver the mail and basic needs. It was a calm and beautiful time in September, and seeing the picture-perfect scenery and natural beauty of such an isolated part of the world was truly unforgettable. It was the only place in our country where there was no political influence and daily Soviet propaganda. We quietly walked among chirping birds and listened to the soothing whisper of the wind through the branches and leaves of trees.

We reached the train station at the regional center, and by evening we were already back home. After two weeks of living in the time-forgotten small village, the sounds and energy of our city roared at us with all attributes of modern life. Our parents told us that we looked like we had come back from the war. Tired and thin from working so hard and eating so little, all we wanted were two days of rest with plenty of food and nice shower.

When we returned to the old woman's village with bags of provision, the brown fields of beetroot were waiting for us to harvest and clean them. Good old Babushka cheered us with a new supply of provisions, but later we saw only a tiny part of it on the table. "The rotted bread must be eaten first, boys, and then we will go to fresh food," she said when we asked her about the meal she stashed away from us. We took pity on the old crooked woman and felt she needed it more than us.

After two more weeks, our first trip to the kolkhoz in three years would come to an end. We finished our job and were congratulated by the teacher for our brave effort in supporting the government, but that was the only reward we got for such hard labor. Students always did the job for free, and since no one told us we owed money to the village for food and our stay, it was a good outcome. The only payment we received was one bucket of potatoes from the old lady's garden.

We hoped such an odyssey would never happen again, and they never did, but the following years were not without more adventures in the name of Soviet agricultural trips. There would be no more babushkas. Instead, we faced bloody fights with local drunks, sleeping in our coats and boots at the freezing village school, and having our teacher deserting us in fear of a local massacre. Adventures like these were become common in our lives, even though they were often unheard of in other nations.

The Trade School Band and a "Special" Performance

Trade school didn't turn out to be such a big drama after all. There was no pressure on us from the teachers to earn outstanding grades, and we had much less stress to deal with. The institution was meant for people who had already decided that this was the last stop on their educational journey. Future college plans and university classrooms were not in minds of the school attendees, and the teachers understood that. Most of us were just trying to get the required high school diploma "the easy way" (compared to a regular high school course), and the atmosphere in the classrooms was mainly carefree and laid-back. Teachers were aware of that, and they also knew that enforcing strict educational diligence would be a waste of their time and effort. Everything was standard practice, which had been established throughout the years. Students merely had to show up and act in a civilized manner; that was all it took to gain respect and decent grades from the teachers. It was similar to evening school, only with a much higher level of notoriety.

The only courses that were intense at all were our trade disciplines. That made sense, given the fact that it was the main reason we were all there. I was not thrilled with the idea of learning about the complexities and working in the electrical world, but while the technical aspect of it was a bit of a drag, it was must-have knowledge at the time. Giant transformers, wire cables, and switchboards were extremely boring to me, and it was difficult for me to pay attention. I was not alone in this, as most of the students shared a similar disinterest in these dull topics. To say that all of us would attain a practical trade skill would have been a falsehood, as it really only applied to those who were very interested in an occupation as an electrician. Those dedicated students were not within my circle of friends. Most of us only spent a half-day in class to keep the government happy and then went home to busy ourselves with our true hobbies and affections.

One day after classes, I heard a familiar noise coming from the concert hall; the school band was practicing for the upcoming dancing. I was pleasantly surprised to know that we had such music activity in our trade school. Usually, such a luxury was reserved for colleges and other higher education institutions outside of regular schools. For some reason, our school garnered generous support in this from the administration. I entered the concert hall to listen the band and was instantly appalled by the brutality of music someone was trying to play. It was absolutely horrendous. None of the band member could decently play with the exception of a singer and a drummer. They were from the third level of our school and acted like they knew what they were doing. When they stopped playing, I asked them if I could get onstage. When we started talking, they asked me if I could play an instrument and if I wanted to try it out. At the corner, a semi-hollow body guitar drew my attention, and I grabbed it to give it a try. It was the first time I had seen such an instrument that was manufactured in the USSR, but it looked good and seemed to be of decent by Soviet standards quality. It was an old guitar from the sixties, but I knew that with a little tweaking, it could be a great one to play. I tuned it and asked them what they wanted to play. The popular song at that time, "Mashina Vremeni," was picked for a test, and we began. I played all parts and sang together with the lead vocalist, and it sounded very good.

When we were done, the singer, Igor, asked me to step outside. He told me everything upfront. "Look...we need someone to keep this band alive. If you will join us, I will take the bass, and we can finally have decent band."

I told him I was already involved with the construction palace band, and it would be hard to balance the two group gigs. He said he would take care of it by planning the school dances around my other band practices and performances. It was a very tempting proposition, and I could not resist the chance to play guitar again. "Can I take this guitar home today to practice if I agree?" I asked Igor.

"I will give you the case for it right now," he replied and disappeared in the gear locker.

Now I was busier than ever with music. Playing and rehearsing in one band on the drums and on guitar in another took up practically all of my free time. It was challenging, but at the same time it was an exciting scenario. I desperately tried to find a way not to overlap rehearsals and gigs, and I always planned everything in favor of my old band, where I played with Sasha.

Playing on a Disclosed Location

By that time, our "Construction palace" band was already covering a lot of different events by traveling around the local destinations and entertaining everybody from factories to kolkhoz farms. It was part of our duty to "deliver art to the masses," and we were doing that with a lot of joy. Every time we went on those types of gigs with some kind of propagandistic brigade, or in honor of our Soviet holidays, our band was the dessert on the menu of such occasions. People were always amused to see young teenagers playing music not only a high level of expertise, but also with the capability to play songs by requests, even those only few knew or remembered. We had plenty of tunes at our disposal. Back when we were playing in our first school band, our teacher Senya told us there is no such thing as too many or very bad songs. He said, "People will ask you one day to play something very stupid, but they will hold a banknote in their hands, and if you don't know the song, the bill will not be in your pockets." He was absolutely right, and we took that lesson into account and never regretted it. Those kinds of requests, however, did not come as often as we wished. The majority of our performances had little to do with making money. It did, however, almost always involve a lavish lunch or dinner, according to the tradition of treating musicians.

Very often we covered many performances where the table after the gig was a long-awaited treat, the only one we received. Every event was different, and the food was usually specifically chosen or delicately prepared for each purpose. Treating your guests or a performer in Russia always involved hard-to-find produce, but the traditional social protocol insisted that the custom was honored at all costs. We experienced plenty of those meals during our performing life. However, the most unusual we ever had was at one of the Red Army ballistic missiles military installation.

One day we were told by our heads at the palace that we were going to play on the weekend and had to bring our passports (which you receive at age of 16) with us . The reason behind this request was not explained to us, and we assumed it was just to verify our ages. When we were already on the bus, we asked where we were going, and we were only told, "You'll see very soon." It was both intrigued and alarmed. We weren't sure what to think, but we really did not want to perform at a treatment plant or prison.

After driving down the long road through the forest, we stopped at the huge gate with a red star on its face. Military crew rushed into the bus, and the red-faced officer asked for our passports. He disappeared behind the gates, and at that moment we understood everything. Ten minutes later, the gates opened, and a dozen soldiers in a prancing jog rushed into the bus. The red-faced officer followed them and with established punctuation shouted, "Your equipment, comrades, will be unloaded by this squad. They're at your disposal for all future orders!" He saluted and stepped down from the bus.

We rolled into the manicured military base, which had mainly barracks and windowless buildings. It was the most organized place I'd ever seen. The painted curbs and groomed bushes made it seem as if it was maintained by the most skilled Japanese garden gurus. Everything was clean and decorated by the army, including many patriotic banners and displays. When we stopped at the building where the concert was going to take place, our new squad started grabbing all of our equipment and dragging it inside. It was a relief for us that this not-so-enjoyable task was done by someone else for a change. We felt like real rock stars with our own stage crew! When were ready to perform, we did not know if we should dare to a "psychological attack" on the generals and blast a few Black Sabbath or Scorpions songs. We'd done a lot of outrageous and risky stuff onstage in the past, but this time, we knew our passports were in the hands of military personnel, and we were afraid they might keep them for a while if we provoked them by doing anything insulting to our Red Army. The classic Soviet tunes and few popular

Russian hits were played, and we received a standing ovation from our young soldiers. When the show was over, we were loaded on the bus by our makeshift stage crew, ready to go home.

Right before we were ready to depart, the officer told us to follow him. Again, we weren't sure what to think. We walked the short distance to an unmarked building and strolled behind him down the narrow, winding corridors until we entered a large hall, the main officers' lunchroom.

"Please enjoy our humble military lunch, guys," the officer said, smiling as he showed us to our table.

There were white, crisp tablecloths on a few of the tables, and when we sat down, two soldiers began serving food to us. It was one of the best meals I ever had during our band travels. Not only was everything delicious, but the gourmet courses were served one after another, and we could not believe we were at a military base and not at a five-star restaurant. Everything was prepared in such a wonderful manner, so atypical to primitive military provisions. The "humble military lunch" was obviously reserved only for the commanders of the base, and we were honored to partake of it.

Vodka and wine were offered as well. After a few shots, we started joking around, asking soldiers to join us. "Come on, guys! We'll tell your generals to be quiet. Otherwise, we can sing 'We Will Rock You', and your missiles will self-launch in horror!" The poor soldiers tried desperately to hold back their laughter.

After taking too many shots of Stolichnaya one of our "smartest" band members suddenly asked a general , "Did you get all this nice food from Americans? If so, you should aim your rockets away from the States!" It was not a funny joke, and the general did not even crack a slight smile. We could always spoil any situation with our childish and often smart-ass attitudes. This was a perfect example, as joking like that at a classified military base was just plain stupid. Now we had to leave before they started getting upset or asking questions.

We finished our meal and thanked our hosts for the truly outstanding food. It was already dark and we could not wait to get our passports back and get out of there. We were worried that our drunken jokes might backfire on us, but it was not the case. The officers continued to thank us for the great show for our soldiers, and we returned the appreciation and gratitude for such a wonderful meal. The last comment we heard from our military friends was, "You are funny guys. Just be careful."

We sank into the bus seats, thinking about all we had just experienced. The bus drove us back to the city from the military base, which we were probably only civilians ever visit.

"Freedom of Speech" and New Friends

At that time, the Soviet Union began to experience spontaneous lack of basic supplies, which threw our population into a rampage of mass hysteria. No one could explain why certain items suddenly disappeared from our store shelves, especially when many of them were never considered as a deficit items. Such disruptions in supplies came one after another, from shortages of salt to the complete absence of matches and toothpaste. As a result, violent clashes often occurred in the stores whenever products in shortage went on sale. In a panic, people tried to stockpile items for themselves, grabbing kilos of salt and big bags of matches, only worsening the already dire situation. Like all other aspects of our flawed system, the media ignored this situation. People had to rely on speculations or rumors as to why it was happening and who could be blamed. Since no one ever received any clear explanation from the government, the most popular theory was that there was a conspiracy within the supply chain to spike the prices and divert the items to the black market. To some degree, it was the truth, as anything we could not find in regular stores seemed to be available in the black market, but always at astronomical prices.

When cooking butter completely vanished from our grocery stores, people did not know what to think, especially since it was one item that no one was selling on the black market. Long lines at the stores and the limiting of the product per person angered a lot of people. For Belarus Republic, fairly stable in supplies compared to other regions of the USSR, it was a very uncommon anomaly. Stores were shaken by the storming crowd of people trying to purchase just a stick of butter. At the same time, on our TV screen and radio programs, the government raved about our emblematic industrial and agricultural "achievements on the road to Communism." All this canting hypocrisy was seen by our people, but making negative conclusions about our internal problems was not acceptable. Everybody complained about it at home or among close and trusted friends, but making any kind of assumptions or public outcry was risky business. Everyone knew the unspoken rules about when to criticize the flaws of our system and when to be quiet about it. However, even at home, I could not really talk about it without my mother defending our socialistic society. In her world and her bolshevik opinion, all difficulty and troubles were the result of "lazy people or natural disasters" and "started by the Western world Cold War." Talking about the issues or debating them with her was about as useful as screaming at the television. She was dedicated Communist, and she honestly believed everything her party was preaching. She always warned me to never say in public the things I told her at home about my view on our problems and USSR polices in general. I tried to heed her warnings, but I could not silence my outrage at the dishonesty of our system.

At our trade school, we had a class called Political Economical Studies. It was probably the worst class in our whole education program because it attempted to teach the students about the alleged superiority of our socialistic economical infrastructure. It was taught to us by a teacher who was highly dedicated to Communistic dogmas. I could not stand to listen to such biased trash coming from someone who was either brainwashed or blindly following our leaders. One day, the teacher was going on about the so-called "prosperity" our agricultural system allegedly delivered to the people in our country. When she finished her long monolog and stopped, I made a remark and said to her as the class listened in complete silence, "Don't tell us you're not fighting in the stores for a stick of butter and piece of sausage."

She did not yell at me or try to make any comments. She only said, "Well, we can talk about it if you want, but not right now."

We did eventually talk about it...in the principal's office. I was suspended for a week and not allowed to attend the class until my mom came to school for explanations. On top of that, I was expelled from the band and not allowed to play there until I graduated. The latest punishment of course, was the most brutal to me, but the outrage of my mother was by far the worst I'd seen from her in a long time. I had received my first big lesson about the Soviet version of freedom of speech.

Choosing Friends Wisely

Living together with my mother, grandmother, and brother in our little apartment, felt like we would never be apart. We tried to manage in our tight living quarters, but it seemed as if our space was becoming smaller and smaller. My brother and I needed more privacy, as we were fast growing into teenagers and young adults. Somehow, we always managed to find the way to keep our three generations under one roof in peace and harmony. Despite sometime tension in my relationship with my mother over politics, we loved each other, and she tried to help us establish good lives for ourselves, using all of her strengths and resources. For my part, I did everything I could to keep from upsetting her with my criticism of Socialism and USSR policies.

My dislike of the Soviet system only grew with more cruel evidence of our "justice" and "superiority," which only contradicted the daily avalanche of official propaganda. I began listening to Russian-speaking Western radio stations, broadcasts like "Radio Liberty" and "Voice of America." I knew everything they were saying was the truth and not just capitalistic propaganda, as our leaders would have us believe. I realized there would be no reason for Soviets to jam those stations if they were actually telling lies and plain falsifications. The violation of human rights, economical outages, and false utopia of our political system was exposed by those radio programs. Many events and untold facts about the situation in our country could be only heard on those media outlets, and while I was skeptical at first about the credibility of the information I heard, it soon became evident that our own media was actually the source of lies and fabrications.

At that time, I bought from my friend a very old tube radio just so I could listen the programs. Jamming of the Western stations by our government at that time was probably at its highest peak. For some reason, though, tube radios had better resistance to this Soviet blockade of free radio waves. Every night, I turned the volume down to a minimum and placed my ear near the speaker so no one at home could hear me listening radio. My mom knew I was doing it, but she was tired of fighting over it. Only my grandma occasionally made remarks, saying, "Why are you listening these lies?" to which I answered back with love, "Because I love tales and science fiction."

New friends started to come into my life, and they shared the same views and opinions about our political system. Some of them were plain angry about our reality, and some were truly ready for fight against our regime. No one in the Soviet Union could take a stand without ending up in prison, a psychiatric hospital, or placing their life at risk. Many well-known human rights activists and dissidents like Andrew Sakharov or Natan Scheransky were under severe pressure to keep quiet from KGB in our country. The only place where you could hear about them was on short-wave radio stations broadcasting from the West. The USSR did not admittedly and officially have political prisoners or even people who were against our system. No one at the time would ever hear about anti-Soviet feelings among the Russian population, at least not from the official media. The only elements who could question the righteousness of our government were foreign "enemies of our happy lives" and "traitors." Any celebrity or person of notoriety who dared to betray our dogmas or did not return from a visit to the West was publicly condemned and erased by our authorities from Soviet history. Many of our athletes, artists, performers, and scientists made the difficult decision to leave their country and their roots in exchange for freedom. For people who wanted to make our nation truly free and democratic, the fight of our Socialistic system was the mortar path in an unfair war. Many of these brave people would end their lives in our Gulag system or unmarked graves.

I chose my friends carefully, knowing that among people who loved rock'n roll, there were also those who still believed in Soviet lies. I surrounded myself with those who had a clear understanding of the hypocrisy of our system. One such new friend was Anton, a second generation true anti-Soviet activist. His father lost his life after undying battle against our political regime. When all measures of oppression were exhausted by our authorities, a single bullet stopped his desperate fight for freedom in our country. Anton took the hard path of his father and became a regular guest of our local KGB organization. We grew very close, and his very outspoken and fearless personality enabled him to condemn our political system every time he had a chance to. Going through all stages of a dissident's life, he was locked up many times in mental institutions, harassed, and interrogated by the KGB. Eventually, he was thrown to jail on a fabricated case of assaulting a bum at the train station. Only four feet tall and incapable of harming a fly, Anton had to endure a closed trial where the verdict was read by a district judge without any defense or evidence being presented. He was sentenced to four years in prison and two years of hard labor for telling the truth about the Soviet version of democracy. He was another victim of the system, which did not tolerate any anti-Communist opinions.

School friends and I.

Losing Anton was a stinging reality for me to face. I was doing everything I could to keep myself away from upsetting our authorities, afraid I would meet the same fate as my friend. Cases like his not only affected the victim of the repression, but also his family members and close friends. Anyone who complained too much about our issues would cause a mighty throng of dictatorship to ambush his household. I could not afford to risk the welfare of my brother, grandma, and mother, and so I sought a shelter from our utopian socialistic life in music.

It was absolutely torturous to live in a society governed by those who so openly lied about everything happening to us and around us. At the same time, it was impossible to fool the entire nation about our life, and many, having no other solace, turned to alcohol and isolated lifestyles to try and block out the painful and unsolvable reality. The majority of population, though, did not want to dig into the causes of our problems, or else they simply believed the propagandistic lies.

Rather than alcohol and isolation, rock music was my personal escape from that socialistic existence. I listened to as much music as I could on the short-wave radio and my tape player. I also began to buy vinyl records on the black market. It was a very expensive hobby, but the occasional weddings we played helped me earn a little money. I had very few priceless examples of Western music, symbols of freedom, but they inspired me to be creative despite living in very totalitarian society. I was influenced not only by the music, but also by the record album cover art. For us, every new album represented more than just another release of music. They were symbolic windows to a world in which no one would tell us what music to play or listen to or even how to dress. We did not have that kind of freedom in our world, and we were just happy to see that it did, in fact, exist in the world of others.

My Own Rock Group and "Salad" Bands

We lived our entire lives under the constant control of the authorities. Soviet people were practically coached from childhood to follow our rules and do only what we were told or allowed. Expression of individual views and beliefs was only tolerated through the censorship of our system, and not many people even considered doing anything that was outside the boundaries of the established cultural protocols. Lives were so tightly governed that trying to be an individualistic person was simply a violation of our principals. In our country, rock music was more than entertainment or an expression of teenage angst and rebellion; it was changing people's minds, their perspective of all of the dogmas that had been drilled into our heads since our youth. It became an avenue of social protest against the totalitarian system that oppressed us, and for many of us, it was the only way to express our true feelings.

After being expelled from my trade school band, I began thinking more frequently about having my own band without anyone to control us and tell us what we could or could not play. It was much bigger than a dream; it was an idea that I wanted to pursue. To do it without equipment, a rehearsal place, or any kind of public venue for playing was a challenging hurdle though. There was only one encouraging factor that convinced me to try. I had two friends, Victor and Leon, my old friend since daycare. We had the same dream, and we were sure that if Rush could play with only three members, we could do the same. It was more a freedom-driven desire than a music-making venture in our case. The concept of having something independent without government control and regulations was more intriguing than playing music for the crowd.

We did not have electric guitars or a drum set, not to mention amplifiers and other stage equipment. One thing we did have was our band name, "Emergency Exit". Very often we gathered in the stairwell of my apartment building. We brought our two guitars, and Leon used a makeshift drum set comprised of a couple boxes and books. Pursuing an image of individuality, we tried to develop our own songs. After few weeks, we realized it wouldn't really work unless we found a way to get our hands on some real musical instruments.

I was absolutely reluctant to bring our "Emergency Exit" act to the culture palace out of fear of disclosing our secret project, but the chance to have an audience without public knowledge soon came up. My pal Leon had a connection with our old mutual friend at the "Teacher's house". The place that gave our school band our first wedding gig was available for practice a couple of nights a week, whenever we wanted, in exchange for a bottle of vodka. It was an ideal scenario, and our old friend Vladimir was so kind to help us. We were happy that someone could share their equipment with us, no matter how crummy, without any fear of getting busted for something suspicious brewing. The Soviet system did not provide us with many valuable lessons through its doctrines, but one thing it did inadvertently and unintentionally teach us was to help each other to survive the ideological turmoil and strict social limitations. Our band, "Emergency Exit", therefore began its short-lived musical history, and we were thankful for the opportunity to try.

Soviet underground music gave a stimulus push to every rock enthusiast in the USSR, showing us that even in our totalitarian country, creativity could exist and thrive. Our small band was making our own small steps, doing something none of us had ever tried before: playing original songs. The joy of playing original music that was not just a regurgitation of someone else's work was an exciting, intriguing adventure, albeit a risky one. It was such a common practice to play only popular and well-known music that the concept of creating an original song seemed to be taboo in the minds of most. What we tried to accomplish had nothing to do with following in the footsteps of our underground established rock bands, making some kind of recording, or becoming famous. We were not naïve enough to think any of that could happen anyway. All we wanted to do was express our emotions in music. It represented the first taste we'd had of free expression, and we enjoyed playing what we'd created ourselves without anyone, especially the government or authorities, to stop us.

After practicing for a few weeks, we had several songs with our own lyrics, and everyone who had a chance to hear them at our rehearsals liked them. Since we had no plans of what to do next, we continued to create songs that would have been considered provocative by Soviet standards. The power of song lyrics was overwhelming at that time. Not only was it dangerous to make any attempt to openly criticize our political system, but we also risked scaring or upsetting the friends who allowed us our practice space. In those days, underground music skillfully delivered messages between the lines of its lyrics without coming out and bluntly saying what it is we were trying to say. It was the only way to avoid being crushed by our government or sent to jail for "staining" our lives. Our band utilized the same clever strategy of encrypting messages between the lines so that we did not draw unwanted attention from authorities. We still had no idea what we were going to do with all the music we were creating, but keeping it to ourselves seemed a somewhat senseless concept.

Trying Out the Stage

Living in the city of few musicians (we had nowhere the number of them that places like Moscow and Leningrad had), we pretty much knew who was playing, and where. Everyone in our small musical community seemed to know each other, whether they played at Culture Palaces, factory clubs, or dancing facilities.

One of the VIA bands we knew very well played dancing gigs at the Culture Palace of Lenin. We often went to different places to listen other bands, and the band from "Lenin's" was among them. They knew about our little underground project. One day, when all three of us went to watch them play, they asked if we would be interested in taking the stage and trying a couple of our tunes. It was an unexpected request, and we were nowhere near ready for such a performance. However, it was an intriguing proposition, and it was very tempting to have a chance to see how people would react to our music, since we'd only played it for ourselves and a few people we knew. The "Lenin's" group leader, Ivan, introduced us as a "band well known in limited circles." It drew some attention of the overhyped crowd, and when we finished playing our tune, "Melting Time," everyone cheered and applauded. We weren't sure if the audience was simply being polite or if they honestly were complimenting us, but it was still the most exciting moment I'd experienced in a long time. We were overwhelmed with pride because the song we'd performed was all ours, original and created by our own souls. That meant the audience appreciation was for US, not for a rendition of someone else's work, and that meant a lot to us. We left the stage a new band, thrilled that we had achieved something in our lives without any kind of government intervention or permission, and that was a great feeling of inspiring freedom for us.

Every time we visited the dances there, the band allowed us to play a couple of our original songs—until someone noticed that our lyrics were a bit "controversial." After that, we seemed to be ignored when we visited the place. There was a simple unspoken message: You are not welcome here anymore. It was then that we realized that playing what we really wanted to play was going to be a much more difficult obstacle than we initially anticipated.

Soon, we were told by our Teacher's House friend that it would be very difficult to make time available for our rehearsals. Even an offer to increase our vodka "payments" did not help in this situation. It had become a typical case of people not wanting to take the risk of dealing with our authorities when awareness of what we were doing began seeping outside of our small circle of friends. The "Emergency Exit", our band, had no option but to cease our existence until better times.

My Music World Limitations

As if the short life of my first underground band was not enough disappointment, very soon our Construction Palace group also faced the same fate. My good friend Sasha was called for two years of army duty, forcing us to find a replacement, but we did not even know where to begin looking for one. To make matters worse, around that same time, our keyboard player, Valentine, had plans to enroll at the university. We lost two major players at the same time, leaving only Oleg and me to fight for our survival. Even that did not work out, because Oleg decided to dedicate his time to playing strictly weddings and his goal was to find the same type of musicians for a new band.

Deserted by my band mates because of life circumstances and left alone, I had only one option: I had to start looking for a way to build a new band from the ground up. I thought about bringing Emergency Exit to the Construction Palace, but I knew that was a dead end. Neither of my two friends had any desire to play dances or entertain kolkhoz farmers or factory workers. The members of our "Exit" only wanted to create pure, independent, creative music of their own, and they had no desire to adhere to the agendas at the Construction Palace. This would never happened under that roof and I knew it as well.

While I waited for my next band to be born, I could not stand to live without playing music, so I looked for occasional gigs. When someone could not make it to the play at some band in the city, there was an urgent need of a replacement musician to fill the spot. This happened frequently. You could get a call from someone you knew or from a complete stranger, asking you to come and play for a dance, wedding, or some kind of promo concert. Weddings were always a paying gig, but the other performances were just a matter of musicians helping each other in tough situations. Very often, these kinds of emergency replacement gigs were called "salad," named from the fact that the band was made of a mishmash of musicians who had not played together before. Complete strangers or musicians you had met only once played weddings in these salad bands, or when a local factory had to hire a VIA for some kind of a celebration. The equipment in these cases, as well as the available instruments, was also a complete salad. Expecting something of a good quality was a naïve dream, and weddings were the worst. Because it was low-quality Soviet-produced gear, that only intensified the difficulty of a musician's tasks. Some lucky guys had their own Russian- or Eastern Block-made instruments, but most did not. We all dealt with crummy broken drums or guitars, having no other option.

The only people who had the luxury of using higher quality gear were those bands who played at restaurants. Since musicians there were making good money, they could afford to buy better equipment. Ironically, all that the government provided to the band at these places were only the power outlets on the wall. One time, I was asked to replace a restaurant's band drummer for a week while he went on vacation. The atmosphere, food, and pay there was a true representation of the rumors I'd heard about restaurant gigs. It was the only time I ever had the chance to play in an "elite" place for our musicians.

No matter how weird or bizarre the play could be, it was always fun to be around people who shared your love for music; there were often good laughs and sometimes a few rubles of pay. I loved those experiences, but I could not wait to have a band of my own again, whether playing on guitar or drums. After dealing with horrible instruments at the "salad" gigs, I also dreamt of one day owning my own electric guitar.

Chapter 14

Death of Brezhnev and the New Mood of the Nation

It was autumn of 1982, and my good pal Sasha was sending me letters from the barracks of our Red Army. He was experiencing life in a completely different world, and it was hard for me to understand, being on the outside of it. He was already detached from our old affections, constantly talking about his gray, difficult days in the army. On our end, we were also crossing the threshold of a new, even gloomier era of our Soviet life, which could be objectively described as the "dawn of Socialism."

November 10, 1982 was almost like doomsday for many Soviet people. When sad music began playing on our radios and TV programs changed to an old patriotic shows, we all knew something horrible had happened in our country. We were right, for our leader Leonid Brezhnev had passed away. When the announcement was made, many Soviet citizens truly believed a World War would start at any moment. Fueled by many years of propaganda, a lot of people thought the USA would promptly attack the USSR while our nation was in a time of crisis. For some, the death of Brezhnev was a "worldwide crisis."

Brezhnev's passing was a true shock for many, who could not picture Soviet Union without him. He was associated with our mighty power, leadership, and glory and it was unthinkable in many citizens' minds that our nation could go on without him and his "care" for us. We were born and raised in a world where the Soviet leader was always glorified as an irreplaceable, almost immortal ruler. We were brainwashed to think that Brezhnev was the "brain" of our country, and without him everything around us would simply collapse. When he died, the most common question among the people was, "How are we going to live now?"

The last leader who had passed away while in power was Stalin. His funeral created mass hysteria, and hundreds of observers died that day in street stampedes. Fortunately, history did not repeat itself this time. Things were more under control, and there was not such a rampage from the crowds. There was, however, still an extravagant and monumental week of burial ceremony. Half the nation was in tears, and my parents were among those weeping. Having truly believed that Brezhnev was "protecting" and "caring" for all Soviet citizens, my mom and grandmother watched the funeral on our TV, in absolute tearful grief like so many others.

Surprisingly, or perhaps not surprisingly at all, there was no sign of any impending attack on the USSR. Instead of planning a sneaky attack on us while we were down, as they were accused of plotting, hundreds of world rulers paid tribute to the desisted leader of the USSR during the Red Square funeral procession. Life continued without Brezhnev, and the apocalypse did not take place like many believed it would.

One near-apocalyptic outcome did happen afterwards, however, shocking the minds of many Soviets and sending fear among that people and even those abroad. The person who replaced our leader was the former KGB head, Yuri Andropov. We never had a democratic election system in our country; all our rulers were appointed by the Politburo, a group of political leaders in Kremlin. When Andropov was placed to run the USSR, it sent the message to our people and to the rest of the world that the Soviet Union would be taking a more oppressive, hard-line course. Not only would this apply to our foreign policies, but to the control of people within our borders as well.

It did not take long before the new so-called visions and ordinances were issued by our Communist Party. "Discipline enforcement" and "obedience of laws" became the new government agendas. Many Soviets viewed this as simply a wave of new political repressions of anyone who was unhappy with our system. The "cleaning" was not only taking place in the dissident world that was so invisible to laypersons in the USSR, but also on the surface. Our media and entertainment was completely overhauled, and anything and everything that was "alien to our Proletarian spirit" was removed from existence. Many TV shows, books, and entertainers were put on hold, reorganized, or discontinued in an effort to reflect the new government policies. Our Rock musicians always suffered most among all genres of art since their music was directly connected by our authorities to the "Western propaganda". Now they became even a larger target on the of Soviet ideological battlefield map.

With the placement of Andropov, the power of the KGB received another boost and more control over Soviet people life. Everybody felt its dark, penetrating, authoritative force on our minds and lives. The uncontrolled mightiness of the KGB organization, which now had its own leader in charge of the whole nation, made no jokes and exercised little tolerance when it came to enforcing our Soviet doctrines. Everyone knew that life would never be the same for anyone who had an opposing opinion about the Soviet rules and dogmas and agendas.

Our only source of information about what was really happening in our country and its onslaught against human rights was to listen to Western radio stations. The news about upcoming changes in government control for us was not very uplifting. More arrests and home searches were conducted against dissidents in Moscow and other cities of the USSR, all while the official Soviet-sanctioned media touted and trumpeted about "nationwide support and welcome" of new doctrines from Kremlin to enforce "discipline" and "order" in our country. For the majority of our people, it simply meant we had to think even harder before we said anything bad about our Communist Party.

Stepping into an Adult Life

Life became far more complicated. Stepping into an adult life meant leaving behind everything what life was given to you when you were a child. Many of the doors that were open to me as a kid were closed; even that version of a "happy childhood" was now gone. The replacement of all of it now was the harsh reality of our Soviet system. With the more obvious level of hypocrisy and dictatorship, it was very hard to imagine how to live the rest of our lives in that country. I often heard on the Short Wave radio about many desperate attempts of our people, risking their lives trying to escape from the USSR and other Socialistic countries in the West. I completely understood their motives and drive, but they took a great risk. Most of them ended up in Gulags or were shot while tried to cross the border. The mystery still remains as to how many people lost their lives in these attempts. The few lucky ones who managed to make it to freedom were mentioned on the Western radio programs. The majority of those who escaped were those who had been traveling abroad and simply refused to go back to the USSR, as well as a few miracle escapes on the boats or through the mountains into Turkey.

The gruesome feeling that our society would never truly change for better was the source of much hopelessness in our lives. Reality was grim and inescapable for most of us, pouring into our ears and eyes from every corner. No part of our lives was free of the political dogmas and teachings. We could not turn on the TV or open a newspaper without being force-fed mountains of propaganda or brainwashed about our so-called "bright life". On top of that, the never-ending "education of masses" bombarded us at work, at school, and in all public places.

Year 1982.

The government did not want us to forget about our Communist Party and Socialism, no matter where we went or what we did. Giant posters, slogans, and banners were everywhere on our streets. But by over-glorifying Lenin, the party, and our leaders, they were accomplishing quite the opposite of their intended purpose. People were choking on what they were being forced to quietly swallow, from those red-colored manifestations screaming at us from every corner, "Glory to the USSR! Glory to the Communist Party! Forward to the victory of Communism!" No one took it seriously, and the government was aware of that. Their solution was as foolish as the original concept: They decided to make it even more prevalent and rampant in the hopes that eventually, everyone would simply have to accept and believe it. Billions of our country's monies were wasted on that senseless propaganda, while many more important Soviet infrastructures suffered from lack of funds.

We called the USSR the "big jail," where even a lavish cell and a golden bed would not replace the crummy shag and a sleep on a dirt floor in the freedom. Immersed in all of this, I looked at the future with little to no enthusiasm. I only hoped that my disdain and outrage would not lead me into the jail or the morgue.

The falsities of our so-called Utopia became more obvious and irritating to most, but everyone had an opinion about this new era of the Soviet Union, one way or the other. Those who saw nothing but the desperate attempts of Communists to turn more to the glorious hard-line past in our country could not speak about it openly. On other hand, there were those who welcomed the strong regime's efforts to clean house and rid our society of the Western influences and cultural changes that had slowly taken place in recent years. Those people were the ones who turned the other way when innocents were executed during the time of Stalin and falsely accused their neighbors in order to save their own hides from any suspicions of the KGB. The sad reality was that I saw a lot of people like that in my own life, and many of them made my existence a true hell on Earth. As was the case with followers of Hitler and Stalin and the like, the supporters of such crooked ideals suddenly disappeared from the public spectrum and quieted about their past as soon as a new free era came to pass.

Another Band and "Time Machine"

Even though I didn't yet have my own band, I still could not live without playing guitar. I practiced all the time at home and picked up various tunes by playing finger style. Over time, I managed to play many classical pieces in probably every obscure style and ordinance. It felt good to be able to lead the bass and rhythm at the same time while I plucked the main tune. Since I had no formal training and no knowledge of how to play guitar by notes, I had to come up with my own style and techniques. It was very strange and probably completely against all fundamental principals of a classical guitar style execution of the songs, but everybody who heard it told me it was sounded normal. Trying not to insult the world-famous classic composers with my fantastic and rare approaches, I drifted into playing in a jazzy and romantic style, picking up songs of artists like Sinatra and The Beatles, as well as making up my own simple tunes.

While I was waiting for a chance to play in a band again, I went occasionally to the Construction Palace . The old band, Stats, often asked me to play drums at some of their gigs when their own drummer was out of town. It was a good experience for me, and I always took an opportunity to stay busy with music.

There was once a theater performance at the palace, and onstage I met Igor, a bass player and singer with the same "unemployed" status in music as mine. He was working as a stage technician, moving around the decorations before and after the play. He was overjoyed to share with me about his desire to play in a band. We talked about the idea for a few days, and a couple of weeks later, we arranged to meet with Gena and his friend Victor, keyboard and guitar players. And just like that, a new band was formed. I was again left to play drums, but despite my longing desire to go back to guitar, I submitted just for the chance to play. It seemed my time on the drums would never come to an end.

We approached Stats to see if we could replace the broken-up band I had played with a few months earlier. The deal was made, and all we needed was a solid program to entertain our working class.

After a few rehearsals, we were ready to hit the road or handle the regular dances at the culture palace. The only difference this time was a strict protocol of what we were going to play. Music could not be picked anymore in such a loose manner, according to Soviet terms. As in the past, the list of all songs we intended to play had to be submitted to the palace administration for approval. We knew the people in the office would have no idea what the name of every song meant, so translating the titles of Western songs into Russian, we fooled the bureaucrats, and they were clueless about the true content of our program. Playing a lot of non-Russian music, however, was not an easy task anymore, and even though the administration did not know the classic rock 'n roll tunes we played, the presence of the English language made such performances suspicious. We tried to keep our ratio of Soviet tunes to others within range and play along with the new and more stringent Soviet censorship rules.

Playing with Igor and Victor was a lot of fun. Not only did we enjoy our touring gigs and the dances we played, but we also shared the same view on everything that was happening in our country. The closer we became to each other, the more we got to know about our lives and personalities. Our rehearsals often ended with long discussions, tearing apart our political system. It felt like we could no longer stay in the environment we all existed in without at least talking about it. Every one of us came from very different social groups, but regardless of who our parents were and what education we had, the difficulties we faced were shared among all. To survive in the closing jaws of our political system with its constant control of our everyday life, we needed a good helping of healthy laughter, and we had plenty of that. The new laws and regulations coming from the Kremlin was nothing to laugh about. However, we make fun of them and deliberately inserted stupid Soviet propaganda songs (which we knew even authorities hated) into our programs and laughed about it. Our band was united not only by music, but also by our views on all the senseless principles of our system. When you are surrounded by people who share your opinion about the world, it makes your life less problematic and softens your feelings about the future.

"Time Machine", or Soviet "Beatles"

The so-called cleaning of our cultural fields by new Soviet visions and doctrines reached every corner of our performing arts. Most of the underground bands that were temporarily released at the time of Olympic Games from the shadows of our hidden subculture had already dispersed back to where they came from. The only band that survived and was officially touring our nation was Mashina Vremeni. Eventually, they had to follow others back to the underground world, when the government realized they were doing "too much harm to our ideology." Even the fact that our government was making an astronomical amount of cash on this band while paying them a standard workers' salary did not stop the authorities from shutting the group down.

Soviet Rock band "Mashina Vremeni"

Before that happened, the most famous band in our country came to Gomel to play couple of concerts. For any musician, missing such a historical event would be an absolute tragedy. Not only were they the best and most popular band in the USSR, but their songs reflected many of the feelings of the people at the time. They attracted millions of music lovers from all demographic levels of our society, despite never having been promoted by official media and press. Having listened to them on tapes made only underground, everyone knew their songs, and the opportunity to see them playing live was an epic event in every city they visited. Igor and I learned that they would play in our stationary circus amphitheater, we ran to fight for our tickets. We were lucky to get those precious passes in the sweaty fight and even grabbed few extra ones for our friends.

When the day of concert arrived, the mass hysteria around the circus amphitheater was at it highest peak. The sold-out show drew a massive crowd of people looking for an extra ticket to the show. It was by far the biggest gathering of an uncontrolled crowd to ever take place in our city. The police were greatly outnumbered by people who wanted to get inside, and when the show began, the angry folks without tickets stormed the glass doors of the circus. The tempered glass shattered, and the rampant crowd rushed inside amphitheater. How our authority managed to push them outside still a mystery, but the wave of rock lovers was defeated and pushed back to the streets and into the police cars.

At the same time, we enjoyed the concert. At that time in the USSR, Mashina Vremeni (Time machine) was even more popular than Western rock bands. I took my little brother Misha, who was still an elementary school student, and for him the concert was an unforgettable event. People looked at him in complete shock, probably thinking he was the son of some high official since he had a ticket to such a prestigious event. No one at that time would bring a child to a show for which the tickets could be sold at the door for a fortune. Such a privilege was typically reserved for true diehard audiophiles or high-ranking officials' children, whose parents strangely didn't mind their kids seeing such a show, even after bashing the bands all day long on public.

The concert was absolutely incredible. To taste something that was not officially fabricated under the laws and regulations of our Cultural ministry was inspiring, bathing all of us in the spirit of freedom.

"Let's see it again!"

We could not get enough, and my pal Igor and I decided to try our luck next day to somehow sneak into the show again. The odds were so slim that we even had a backup plan for when our little adventure failed. Standing by the crowded entrance where people searched in agony for that elusive magical ticket was a waste of time, so we went to the back of the building, where the service entrance and loading docks were. In about five minutes, a short guy approached and asked if we wanted to see the show. We obviously told him we did, and he told us how he could help us sneak in there for just ten rubles. A few other folks jumped onboard with the proposition, and the plot of penetrating the most guarded place in the city at that time was revealed. The short man was the driver of a little hatchback truck that delivered food to the circus amphitheater, and all we had to do was to hide inside the truck, which was just a block away. He promised he would take us straight into the heart of the amphitheater through the guards after a short drive.

When he took money from about ten other teenagers and stuffed his pile of cash into his pocket, we ran to climb into the truck. The door shut behind us, and we were in complete darkness without any ventilation or windows. The stainless steel walls and floor were instantly wet with sweat, and as we crouched under the low ceiling, we could not wait to get out of there. We drove for about five minutes, and when the truck stopped at the gates, we could hear the driver talking with the security crew. At that moment, all our plans were up in the air; we had no idea what would be the outcome. We could hear our heartbeats, but when the truck started moving again, we knew we were safe. As soon as the engine was turned off, we were all ready to burst out from the truck. Sweating profusely and having difficulty breathing, we could not wait for the doors to open, as they were locked from the outside. The driver got out, and we could hear his steps leaving the truck. He was not walking to the rear of the truck, and when his steps grew silent, we knew there was something wrong.

Few minutes later, we could no longer breathe without gasping at the thick, steamy air like fish out of water. Someone lost the patience and yelled, "Open the door!" In our misery and fear, we had nearly forgotten why we were there in the first place, and we wanted get out of the truck before we lost consciousness. The situation was growing more intense every minute, and we started pounding the steel walls. We heard nothing on the outside, so we began to desperately smashing the door with our feet. One girl started crying in panic, and at that point, I felt the situation was out of control and growing very dangerous.

Suddenly the door opened wide, and the short truck driver whispered, "Sorry, guys. There were two cops walking around the dock, and I had to take them back to the storage room to have a smoke."

The angry guy who was yelling in the car grabbed the driver and raised him into the air. "Do you know we almost suffocated in your stupid car?" Then he threw him to the ground. Everybody at that point was relived about the relatively happy ending, and our guide showed us safe passage to the auditorium.

Blended with the crowd, we climbed to the staircase where the real ticket holders were sitting, prepared for the show of the century. As soon as the music began to play, we quickly forgot about our almost fatal attempt to get into the concert, and we began shouting in hysterics as soon as "Mashina Vremeni" took the stage.

Trade School Walkouts and the KGB's Eye

My trade school was the only place in the USSR that I managed to enroll in and graduate from. It was not that I liked it so much, but I simply had no option to go elsewhere. Not only was it a boring place to get an education, but providing a "good Bolshevik spirit foundation" to the students was one of the main goals of every Soviet school. The political agenda was very tiresome and irritating for me and several of my classmates, enforcing Socialistic doctrines as part of our occupational studies. After coaching us in the classrooms about the ideological side of our responsibilities at work, they expected us to show our "Proletarian enthusiasm" during our occasional labor "practice hours." This was done either at the local factories or in the construction fields. It was very reminiscent of my experiences in the summer Construction Brigade. We never did anything related to our electrical studies and were often stuck cleaning or doing hard manual labor or dirty work. Everyone hated it, and we were all painfully aware that it had nothing to do with the occupation we were trying to learn. It was just another way for the government to assign laborers to the hard tasks that no one wanted to do, and the same tactics they used to force children into labor were used on the trade school students. It got to the point that every time we were told we were going out on a practice assignment, several of us would claim we were too sick to go. When those false excuses failed to work any longer, we simply began walking away. Our refusal to cooperate angered our administration greatly. Since they could not and did not want to expel anyone from the school, they punished us by placing all kinds of limitations on us and forcing us to take on "special assignments." For Soviets, breaking the students' will and teaching blind obedience was a much higher priority than allowing anyone to have any say-so in his or her own education. Unfortunately, when we began making mass walk-outs from the so-called practice assignments, it caught the attention of someone much higher in rank than just our school principal.

One day we were called one by one into the office and had chat with a man who was presented to us as an "education specialist from the Trade Union." We knew it was a lie, and when he asked us for the names of the initiators of the walk-outs and told us to keep quiet about the conversation, we all got scared. Being interrogated by some unknown official was an omen in the USSR. No one wanted to catch the attention of the KGB, and realizing that the walk-outs could potentially lead to a real interrogation at some other location, we decided it was best to stop our boycotting activities. In my case unfortunately, it did not help...

The Consequences

In our country, it was normal for everyone to simply be like everyone else. No matter how outraged we were about the doctrines that were forced upon us, we could not make them vanish from our lives, and since we could not change the system, we often had to settle and change ourselves. The ultimate goal of the Soviet political oppression strategy was to cripple people and force them to submit. Since no one could freely leave, there were really only two options: 1) become a "loyal Proletarian" by becoming another bolt in the huge machine of the Soviet Union; or 2) finish your life in pain and suffering.

For me, it was no longer a matter of human rights violations or repression. I was seeing the harsh reality before my own eyes, and it was not a dream or some fictional drama. It was a nightmare from which there was no escape. If we could not change the life we were immersed in, it would eventually change us, whether we wanted it to or not. My always-smiling personality began to reflect the world in which I was living. The sad realization that we were stuck in such a society for life affected many people, and adapting to the never-ending "battle for Communism" was a challenge for millions of Russian citizens. I handled it the best I could, as I did not want to end up in a Gulag just for having a different opinion than our Soviet officials. But I could no longer lie about my feelings about Socialism and the reaction of our authorities.

The colorful side of Soviet life cannot be apprehended unless you lived through it yourself. Many of us took the dogmas of our political system as reality of our destiny and simply quietly followed the paths predetermined for us by our Russian leaders. Others were boiling angry at the stupidity and cruelty of our totalitarian regime, throwing fists in its face. Those were the people who knew our proletarian dictatorship would grind us to dust without anybody coming to our defense. If we did not take the side of our Communist Party and accept their doctrines, we were proclaimed an enemy of the state, and there were dire consequences. There was no room for second guessing when it came to our Socialistic doctrines and dogmas, and we had no options for viewing the world in any other way. I did not want to view things that way and disagreed with much of what our political leaders were telling us and was becoming more outspoken about our regime and system. Slowly I was entering the time when I would have to accept the rules of our Socialistic empire and become a slave of the system or be at peace with my soul. I could not choose the side of our hypocritical society, and the results of my dissatisfaction and doubt would manifests themselves very soon in the form of with tragic surprises, betrayals, and personal dramas.

When I was questioned the first time by a KGB officer about my "behavior", it was clear to me that from now on I will never have normal life in this country. After few minutes of talk, I realized they knew more about my persona than I could have imagined. Of course they were aware of what I'd said in public and over the phone to my friends, but they even knew about private conversations I'd had with my mom and my closest pals. They also knew what short-wave radio programs I was listening to and how I debated them with my friends. There was a reason that the KGB let me know what they knew about me: The psychological effect of such a tactic was tremendous. When you begin to suspect your best friends and even your own family members of reporting you to the KGB, you become more careful and suspicious and are less likely to share your true feelings. It was very difficult after that for me to simply talk to anyone I knew; there was always the suspicion that they may pick up the phone and report on me.

The chances of our apartment be bugged, in my opinion, were very slim. I was not in any way a "big fish" in the dissident movement, nor did I possess any classified information or share secrets. There was no reason for me to attract attention. Still, I did not know how far the control of our population really went and who the authorities were really listening to. Many of the apartments surrounding ours housed active KGB officers, so there was a high chance that someone would be listening in. The KGB neighbors looked like any other normal person, and they always had charming personalities and were well-liked in the neighborhood. Suspecting them of spying or bugging the walls seemed to be a ridiculous notion. I said hello to them almost every day, and we even shared household items, which was a common practice in our society among neighbors. It was a known reality that they were in the KGB, but we could not just approach them and ask, "So, did you bug my apartment, Uncle Dimitry?" or "How is your neighborhood spying project going, comrade?"

It wasn't long before I learned from some of my friends how far the paranoia of our government went in tracking the citizens it deemed unreliable. After they returned home from military service, some of my close friends informed me that my letters to them had been confiscated by the army's KGB officers; however, those letters had absolutely no anti-Soviet value. I was not so naïve and foolish as to bash our system in my messages to friends while they were in the army.

Those who worked for the KGB were very educated and were psychological experts. They were completely different from the stereotypical KGB as portrayed in Western films and media. Trying to fool them was a dumb idea, and if they asked a question it was always wise to assume that they already knew the answer and were just trying to play mind games to put people at unease.

Our "secret police" went to great effort to make citizens believe they were "friends" and that they could help people avoid life complications and guard them from "very bad elements". These "elements" were simply people who wanted normal life for our citizens without tyranny and oppression. For those whom the KGB decided were disobedient, the complications included the banning of many privileges, such as overseas travel, reputable and managerial jobs, or the chance to serve in the army or law enforcement. These limitations would be enforced through many official channels with the help of KGB, blaming ethnic origins, alleging criminal activities, and fabricating medical disorders and illnesses. The unfortunate victims of this were basically blacklisted, labeled with an invisible lifetime seal of defective. Some of my friends were already victims of this kind of treatment, and I soon joined them.

After my first questioning by the KGB I was so traumatized that I did not even tell my mother about it for over a year. I didn't know if she would be angry or feel sorry for me. Either way, I knew she would be very upset, and did not want to see her reaction, regardless of what she would have really thought about it.

Church, my Guitar Modification, and Finishing School

The only institution that was officially "separated" from the government in the USSR was our Russian Orthodox Church. Since children were filtered by police at its entrance or chased from churches under pressure from the school, we had to wait until we were old enough to go inside without the fear of being spanked or punished by adults. Still, if you were not an elderly person and attended the church in the USSR, you were considered "not normal" by our authorities.

The only church in our town was the St. Nicholas Cathedral, built in 1914. It stood by the railroad tracks in the old part of our town and was surrounded by single-story houses, gardens and trees. After the 1917 Bolshevik coup, every other church in Gomel was closed, destroyed, or —like St. Peter and St. Paul cathedrals—converted to a planetarium. The secluded location of St. Nicholas, distant from the center of the city, may have been the only reason that it survived the atheistic war of our government. From my early teens, I loved to go there to ride my bike. I watched for police patrolling the entrance and sneaked inside when I could. During weekdays, there were usually no police around it, and I made trips to the church after school or during summer breaks.

The whole atmosphere inside was very peaceful and full of love. Centuries-old icons and paintings decorated the walls with Biblical images, though the stories behind them were absolutely foreign to me. We received no Biblical education and had no resources to learn about the history of Church. The Bible was considered prohibited literature and was not available to us. It was the most known "unknown" book in our country, though it was impossible even to purchase Bibles at the church.

Despite the fact that the government claimed the church was separate from the state, the Soviet Union still controlled the function of the church and its activities. One of the main restrictions of our regime against the church was on the production of any publications. The privilege to publish any material belonged only to Soviet authorities. The fear and suspicion of our rulers that people might begin printing anti-Soviet literature meant no one was permitted to publish any documents. Those restrictions also applied to the church. Only once during my life in the Soviet Union did I have the chance to read the Bible. When a friend of mine from the dissident circle told me he had access to a copy of it, I asked him if I could borrow it for a week. It was small, pocket-sized edition, printed thin onionskin paper with the text fonts so tiny that we had to use a loop in order to read it. Those Bibles were printed by evangelical organizations in the USA and Europe with only one purpose: to deliver them to Soviet Union. They were smuggled in either by tourists or athletes visiting our country, and they were considered contraband. Bibles were banned from import in any form or language, and they were immediately confiscated by customs if found in luggage. For any Soviet tourist or person who traveled overseas, a Bible found in their luggage upon their return to the USSR would easily pose an arrest and interrogation by KGB.

Soviets referred to religion as "opium for masses." For seventy years, the Soviet Union waged the war on faith, yet people still believed in God despite threats of prosecutions of the Church and atheistic propaganda. A love for God had grown in my heart since I was a child, and the pressure against it in our society only made me want to more frequently go to church. Not only did it represent spiritual replenishment for me, but also a chance to connect to our millennia-old Russian culture and traditions. There is nothing more beautiful than Russian Orthodox liturgy with its heavenly singing and ceremonies. The harmony of architecture and church processions could not be better introduced than at our cathedrals.

Despite anti religion war in USSR, all major Christian holidays were celebrated with big crowds of people at the church. It was very exciting to see such a massive gathering of faithful and fearless people. Every January, the Baptism of Christ was celebrated in our church with the blessing of the Holy Water. Even those who didn't attend this Orthodox event were reminded in the streets by people carrying traditional milk canisters called "bedon", full of blessed and venerated Holy Water from the church. The old ceremony was usually performed by priests not far away from churches, at locations where there was an excess of water. Rivers, ponds, and creeks were the most common places, but in the cities, the ritual was done at the churches, when water was brought in with large barrels. The cold Russian winters always made this holiday very special. When the blessing of the Holy Water took place outside the church, the bright and snowy surroundings became even more beautiful with the chiming of the church bells. People would get the water from the venerated barrels; despite the freezing temperatures, the water was warmed by all the excitement and from being moved through the crowd.

The significant difference between regular water and Holy Water is that Holy Water have spiritual value and holiness, as well as healing powers. While the atheistic experts would deny this, they could not explain why the blessed Holy Water taken from rivers and ponds never rotted and contained no bacteria that caused it to go bad. In our house, we always had bottle of the Holy Water that stood on the shelf for over twenty years. During all that time, it remained crystal clear and had absolutely no foul smell or residue at the bottom. Even more interesting, just a few drops of Holy Water could be added to regular tap water, and that would make it holy as well, with the same power and properties.

I loved that celebration. Carrying bedon was a chance to show everyone, including our authorities, about its purpose, especially when we traveled with it on buses and trolleys. People often asked for a drop of Holy Water, so the bedon would be half-empty by the time we returned home. Those who were too afraid to take part in the celebration waited not far away and would fill bottles and jars with tap water to have a few drops of Holy Water added to it. Sharing with neighbors and relatives was always a part of that holiday.

Despite that many of our citizens were unable to go to church, they always respected our Orthodox religion, and keeping a Holy Water in Soviet houses was almost a universal practice. Everyone participated in that holy sacrament, including many government officials. The hypocrisy of Soviet politicians was obvious through their camouflaged observance of the Orthodox beliefs and principals. Members of the Communist Party and Soviet authorities kept Holy Water with a great deal of secrecy while officially claiming to be zealous atheists. However, it was very hard to conceal their double standard life during family members' funerals. Crosses were erected on tombstones, and there could not be a more obvious statement of their faith.

Living without God in the Soviet Union was very hard unless you were willing to accept all Bolshevik's utopian dogmas. For many people, God was the only escape from our harsh reality. For me, God and the church were a home to turn to during my most difficult moments.

Electrifying My "Rock is My Life" Guitar

There were some years when many of my friends were called to the army, and only those who were enrolled in some educational institution were exempt. The time came for two our band members, Gena and Victor, to join the Red Army, bringing another of my bands to a crashing halt. Igor decided to go to music college in the Belarusian capital of Minsk, and I was again left alone without a group to play in.

All I could do was wait until my pal Sasha returned from his military duty so we could try to establish our own band again. Music still was my main interest and shelter from our Soviet utopia and I could not leave anymore without it. Until then, I had to live with playing occasionally in the salad groups.

Since I still did not have my own personal electric guitar, I had to play at home on the old instrument my grandma had bought for me. It was already well beaten up from hours of practice and from traveling to all kinds of places with me. I loved that guitar to death, but one thing I wanted was to be able to play through the amplifier, or I should say my old tube radio.

The Soviet Union produced only two acoustic guitar pickups that could be installed into the guitar sound hole for an amplification. The only problem with them, besides their awful appearance, was the fact that they sounded absolutely horrible. It never occurred to the designers that they would not work well in correlation with brass acoustic guitar strings. The tone and output were way off balance. They were not popular with musicians, due to their poor quality, so they practically collected dust on the music store shelves. Everybody knew they were useless, and I decided to come up with my own solution.

Studying at the Electrical Trade School may not have given me a lot of knowledge in circuit boards and transformers, but it did help me resolve my guitar amplification dilemma. I came across an item during class that made me wonder if it could be used as a guitar pickup—the window security sensor in the shape of a one-inch round tablet. Two wires from it were supposed to be connected to the security line. I decided to plug it into the radio input and see what would happen. The sensor made a loud noise when I rubbed my hand against its surface. I knew it would work, though I wasn't sure how well it would sound once it was mounted on my guitar. Using children's playing clay as an adhesive, I stuck the sensor right on the top of my acoustic guitar bridge. I plugged the wires into my radio and was astonished with the full and powerful sound that came from the speaker. I did not realize that the piezo-sensor pickups already existed in the West, and I assumed I was the first to use a non-magnetic pickup. The only little problem with "my" innovation was that I could hear every little move and touch beside the strings. The sensor was doing what it what supposed to: conducting every motion on the surface it was attached to. Despite this little inconvenience, I enjoyed the makeshift electrification of my guitar. With the volume low, it was a very pleasant sound, but the rest of my guitar quality somehow also had to be improved.

Playing on my guitar.

The feel and comfort of the instrument was far from any, even Soviet-made electric guitars. The huge, bulky neck was oversized, and the fact that it was made for a seven-string instrument made it even more uncomfortable. Having played on it for several years, I had adapted to it, but every time I played on an electric guitar, the feel was far better than what I was used to at home. There was only one way to correct this issue: I had to completely reshape the neck, removing the top portion where the seventh string had been. It was not an easy task to conform the guitar to a much more slender profile. The frets could not be removed, and I had to shear the top portion of the neck while the frets were still attached.

We had a big metal box with tools left from old Mikhail. It was kept under the bathtub, and most of the contents were completely rusted. From it, I took a couple files and a hacksaw and began my guitar renovation in our bedroom. Once I started the process, I realized that it had to work, or else my beloved guitar would be ruined. I worked slowly so as not to damage the frets and filed the top portion of the neck. The next day, I began shaping its profile. After spending all day with rusted files and a few small pieces of sandpaper, I finally got the neck to a comfortable grip for my hand. I could not wait to attach it back to the body with the single bolt and see the result. The first time I played it, it felt very awkward; it did not really feel like mine anymore. Nevertheless, after about a half-hour, I began to enjoy the new feel of it, and by midnight I could not put it down. It felt absolutely perfect. The thin, slender neck profile felt great, and the silky, open wood surface was fast and incredibly smooth. Playing it through my radio was a very exciting, inspiring experience. It was not a true electric guitar like the ones I dreamt about, but it was the closest I could make out of a Soviet instrument and a security sensor. I was thrilled with the results and showed it to a couple of my friends. Everyone loved how it felt and played, and the ease of getting security sensors made it even more of a blockbuster.

So Long, Trade School

By the end of my term at the trade school, the prospect of working as an electrician was absolutely out of my picture. I learned practically nothing about the occupation I was studying, and I had no desire to be electrocuted on the first day at my job. Students were usually distributed for four -five years to different workplaces after graduation as a mandatory term. Fortunately for me, the electrician occupation was not in high demand at that time, so the distribution of students to jobs was not necessary to be implemented. My diploma would be issued, and my job allocation would be in my own hands. I knew the teachers were aware not only of my primitive knowledge in the electrical filed, but also of my rebellious attitude toward the Soviet regime. Recommending me to our industry as a product of the school was not in their best interest.

The graduation exams did not involve anything extraordinary. Basic high school tests and evaluations were much simpler than those at regular Soviet schools. The exam was very easy, and electrician certification was simply a matter of preparing cheat sheets. All of the students did so, and the teachers knew about it, but they did not try to openly police us. They were only concerned with showing the system that our qualifications were completed at the highest possible level, so the cheating made everyone happy—the government, the students, the teachers, and the authorities. Like many other things in USSR, the only thing that mattered was that everything looked good on paper.

It was the end of my educational life in the Soviet Union. A couple of months later, we all received our diplomas. We had no assigned places to work, and we were free to get involved in adult Soviet life.

Chapter 15

Techno Wonders and My First Job

I was constantly surrounded by music and very attached to it. In fact, living without it seemed impossible. Since I still had no permanent group to play in, I had to compromise and listen to as much music as possible on tapes and records. All the money I made playing occasional weddings was spent on black market vinyls as I expanded my interest in different styles of rock. The influx of a new breed of Western music, heavy metal, brought to our land the works of Iron Maiden, Saxon, Motorhead, and similar artists. This style was very popular among us, and we were overwhelmed with the wide varieties of bands coming to us from our underground rock suppliers.

While I did enjoy heavy metal, I still listened to all styles of rock and pop music. In fact, I always enjoyed any genre, from classical baroque and jazz, to hard rock and Church choral singing. I played my Supertramp, Yes, and AC/DC, turning our apartment into a never-ending rock concert. My grandma always asked (as grandmas often will) why I had my music up so loud. I tried to explain to her the concept of rock 'n' roll and the fact that it was designed to be played at high volumes. Since no Western bands came to Russia to perform concerts for us, all we could do was play their music at home, trying to duplicate the way it would have sounded onstage. My grandma received a lot of complaints from the neighbors about the noise, but I could not help it; I continued enjoying music as often as I could. Whenever I hear a classic rock tune today, it takes me back to a flood of memories. It's a unique and incredible sensation to associate Western music with my Russian upbringing, but I discovered rock 'n' role in my homeland.

The eighties brought to the world many new technological wonders for music, and some of them made their way to our black market. One of them was the portable tape player, like the Sony Walkman – a device that allowed a person to be completely isolated from the surrounding environment and wholly consumed by music, no matter where you were. For such a small gadget, the portable tape players had a hefty price tag for most music enthusiasts, about two to three average monthly salaries. They were definitely a luxury, and those who owned them loved to flaunt them in the streets as a status symbol or an item of modern fashion. Anyone who owned one was considered more of a show-off person than a music lover. I never owned a Walkman or any such device. Not only were they completely out of my reach in price, but the inability to record on them made them seem impractical to me. Besides, I wanted the music I listened to to be heard by my entire body – not just my ears. In my opinion, the sound should penetrate and affect all of you when listening your favorite artist; this is the closest thing possible to actually experiencing a concert firsthand.

Another technological advancement of the 1980s was late in reaching our country. The revolutionary media of compact discs (CDs) was delayed for more than a decade in the USSR. Few underground audiophiles could afford CD players, for they were sold at an astronomical price the equivalent of more than the average annual salary – far too expensive for ordinary people. On top of that, availability of music on CD was in the infant stage, not only on Soviet black market, but also in the rest of the world. Many simple, helpful modern conveniences that were ordinary to those in the West remained unknown to our population until the collapse of the Soviet Union, and CD technology was one of them. While living in the USSR, not once did I see a compact disc in person.

Nothing, however, did as much damage to our ideology or impacted the masses as much as the introduction of the video cassette recorder, the VCR. When the first models of this truly incredible device showed up on our black market, it marked the beginning of a new era. It was by far the most expensive item ever sold by our underground entrepreneurs. For an average person, a VCR would cost as much as four to five years' salary. Despite its enormous price, though, people were desperate to see what everyone around the world was watching, and VCRs were the only item at the time that would enable that. The whopping price tag on VCRs took the life savings of many Soviet people, but nevertheless, they began to show up in Russian homes, and when they did, they changed everything our people knew about the world.

Of course, there were a couple of limitations when it came to using a VCR on a Soviet TV. One of them was the system by which our TVs worked. At the beginning, our government chose the least common broadcasting TV platform, SECAM. This was likely intentional, so that we would not be able, under any circumstances, to watch TV shows from Europe, which was played in PAL. The TV sets in Russia offered only SECAM signal broadcasts, but all the imported VCRs sold in the black market were set to European PAL. As a solution, thousands of electronics enthusiasts in the USSR began offering on the black market an "upgrade": adapters that allowed Russian televisions to work in conjunction with Western VCRs. Even people who did not own a VCRs wanted the upgrade on their television sets, just in case things might change in the future.

Another limitation was the complete absence of videotapes in our stores. Everything associated with VCRs was only available on our black market. Somehow, this enormous, truly independent world existed side by side with our monopolistic Socialistic system and was delivering to the masses everything the Soviets did not want us to have. VCR Western movies, cartoons, music videos, and even adult shows were available on the black market on an unprecedented scale. Every movie was translated into Russian, and the list of titles was endless. The fortunate ones who were able to purchase VCRs turned their houses into cinemas for their friends and relatives to enjoy; some people even charged strangers for the privilege of watching movie at their houses, but that soon became too dangerous for fear of the government and criminal elements. Movies like "Rambo", "Commando", and "Star War"s were the most popular titles in our country. The "Indiana Jone"s and "Back to the Future" series were watched dozens of times by many Soviet people. It was an utter cultural shock, a chance for our nation to see what the world looked like on the other side of the Iron Curtain, without any Soviet propaganda. People began copying each other's videotapes, and the number of available copies in the cities was spreading like wildfire. While the quality of the copies was not so perfect, they were still the best entertainment we could get our hands on.

The VCR outbreak was one of epidemic proportions. The government was so overwhelmed with the scale of this technological invasion that they had to surrender; they did not even tried to fight it, knowing there weren't enough KGB force in all of Russia to concur it. However, authorities could not ignore the fact that people now had a chance to watch whatever they wanted, without official approval or permission. Everybody in Kremlin understood that underground market of VHS recorders and movies was undermining our Socialistic beliefs and dogmas. The widespread use of them, though, was impossible to stop with the government's limited prohibition measures and capabilities.

The Soviet Union decided the best way tot tackle the out-of-control video-mania by producing their own VCRs. The goal was to make a statement that technologically, we were not behind other nations, and that Russia was also capable of producing complicated electronics. Despite its outdated design, its shabby quality, and a one-year's salary price tag, the waiting list to buy one of these Russian VCRs was about eighteen months long. Another agenda was to establish official Soviet video rental facilities that offered only government-approved or USSR-filmed movies to the public.

Watching Western movies and music videos was a special event for my friends and me. We often rotated viewing places, and whoever owned VCRs would sometimes bring them from one house to another. We would watch videos until morning, all the movies any of us could buy, borrow, or trade. There was another priceless value of the VCR in USSR... For us, it was also our first chance to see our favorite rock bands on the TV screen. There were dozens of bands that we knew only by their music, so seeing them for the first time on video was like seeing them live. For the first time, we witnessed those fancy guitars and all that wonderful musical gear. It was absolutely unreal. Every time I watched those music videos, I dreamt even more about playing in a band again and having a real electric guitar of my own.

Getting My First Job

After graduating from trade school, my top priority was to find a job. Walking the streets without having any official place of work was simply illegal and punishable by law. I had very little idea of what I wanted to do and was simply looking for a place where no one would bother me with our Socialistic competition at work. I still had absolutely no desire to work at a factory or on a construction site.

In theory, it was easy to find a job in the Soviet Union. Our government bragged all the time that we were the nation where "Socialism achieved the unthinkable for Capitalistic society." To some degree, it was true that the USSR did not suffer from unemployment, since all the workplaces had long lists of available jobs. It was very easy to control the situation by simply creating more jobs than society really needed. This was of great benefit from a political standpoint, but the fact was that ten workers produced only as much as five could. As a result of this practice, our society was constantly haunted with empty shelves in stores and a frequent deficit of products.

When given a closer look, the job choices were not comprised of unlimited options. Hard and dirty jobs were at the top of the "Help Wanted" lists. In my case, the pay rate did not matter to me as much as finding a job that would allow me to work in quiet conditions without so much Soviet propaganda being forced into me while I was working. Factories and construction places were known for this. The only jobs that did not use these "motivational" tactics were low-paying janitorial or clerk positions. I quickly realized that these jobs were very hard to get. Boiling room operators, night guards, and kindergarten technicians were dream jobs for people like me, and I was not alone in searching for them. Ironically, our society was full of artists, poets, and musicians who were making a living by doing these jobs. They did not want to be pummeled with too much government influence, and the only places where they could find relief were in janitorial and clerical jobs.

I knew that spending more than one month without a job could potentially land me in jail, so I was desperately trying to find something before my mother sent me to the factory to keep me out of trouble. The search was a far more complicated task than I could have imagined. All of the good, peaceful workplaces were completely full, and "Help Wanted" signs had been removed from their walls. The pressure was building with the time running out, and I had no option but to go to a toy store where they needed a temporary loading dock worker.

It was my first official job in the USSR, and I had simple duties and responsibilities: get the new toy shipment unloaded and store it in the tiny back room. There was nothing exciting about such an occupation, but it did teach me how to organize in small spaces. Stacking boxes of toys in the small store was like solving a jigsaw puzzle. Doing it fast and in a practical order gave me a basic knowledge of what one can do with the limited options. It wasn't long, however, before my first temporary job was over, and another odyssey of search for a place of work began.

In my hunt for another job, I began observing strange situations with my potential employers. The retaliation of the system for my dislike of Soviet polices became a reality. I realized that the warnings issued to me long ago by authorities were no joking matter. There were no job interviews like those in the West; all we usually had to do was sign the documents and show up at work. That was not the case for me. Even when I was lucky to find the right place to work, I was given a variety of ridiculous excuses for why I did not get the jobs I applied for. The most common answer was that the job was "on hold" or "temporarily not available," yet when I returned a week later, I was still told to "come back later." It felt as if someone was telling potential employers to deny me a chance for employment. Eventually, I had to blame the same people who had warned me to stop criticizing the state policies and keep my mouth shot.

Clearly, the Human Resources offices were in the business of doing thorough background checks in the USSR. One thing I knew, though, was that my ability to fix a doorknob or patch the wall on the hallway in daycare was not under question. When I was denied the job, there was only real reason: my political "unreliability." I was paying the price for my so-called disobedience, and I had to do what the government was pushing me into or end up in jail for "tuneyadstvo", intentional avoidance of work. Our officials knew there was no better place to reshape the minds of alleged rebellious elements than force them to be a part of some kind of factory team, where all kind of political organizations from Komsomol to Union and Communists could "help" them become a worthy member of our society. For me, that was not an option.

The clock was ticking, though, and I realized that the matter would never be resolved without some official involvement. The only way to fight our system was with its own weapons. The only person I could trust and truly count on was my own mother. Since she worked at the Regional City Administrative office, she had the power to intervene in any situation, including the background checks that were being run on me. All I had to do was tell her about the job that was available, and despite of hate to do it, she promised to make necessary contacts with that place so I would be hired. When a draftsman position opened up at the local Office of Mineral Resources, instead of going to fill out application, I told my mother about it. A week later, I had a permanent job drawing endless numbers in the reporting charts and columns.

This took place in the time before computers and printers. Even overhead projectors were rare technological wonders for us. All presentations at workplaces were done with simple cardboard, illustrations and charts drawn by hand. This was what I had to do all day. It was a very boring, low-paying job. For me, being stuck behind an office desk with seven other people every day was a complete drag. I knew the gig would not last. It reminded me of my first grade school assignments, practicing writing my numbers. It was a total pain in the neck for me, and the humdrum, monotonous atmosphere in the office made my days there feel like an eternity. I knew I had to somehow deal with the job since quitting would absolutely kill my mother and I would be on my own trying to find another place to work. So, I surrendered to the boring "calligraphy" exercises while I waited for my friend Sasha to return from the Army so we could finally establish our new band.

Life After Andropov's Death and My Last Band

In February of 1984, sad music and patriotic movies began playing over our radios and television broadcasts. We knew another prominent Russian figure had died, but we did not expect that it would be our leader, Yuri Andropov. It was a short ruling term for him, and many people hoped that his departure would lead to some democratic changes in our country. Everyone knew that no one could run the nation with such intense totalitarian policies as the former chief of the KGB. With the arrival of Konstantin Chernenko as our country leader, many Soviet citizens became optimistic that the dark shadow of the secret police was going away, and we could breathe more freely. It did not take long before everybody realized that nothing would change, and in many cases, things would only get worse. No one expected the implementation of such harsh policies in our cultural world, and the biggest target was rock music. More Western artists were banned, and TV programs were taken off the air or decommissioned under Chernenko's lead. To our surprise, even playing at the dances couple songs of Rolling Stones or Beatles which were released by our own record label was also now a tabu. Movies, books, and even children's "inappropriate" cartoons like "Bremen musicians" were placed on the shelf one more time.

The fact that our nation was no longer in the hands of a former KGB leader made a lot of people in the West believe Chernenko would not follow his predecessor, but this was not the case. The doctrines of new discipline and order were enforced with even more intimidating power. Our pro-communist and hard totalitarian ruling received another charge of reinforcement under the new regime. The most memorable acts of the new dictatorship were Soviet raids to enforce the discipline and attendance at work and schools.

In the middle of a day, at bus stations, movie theaters, and entertainment facilities, police and people in civilian clothing would block the exits so that every person of a certain age and profile could be interrogated on the spot. The raid was targeting on anyone who might be skipping school or work or was simply "tuneyadets" (not working). Every suspected individual had to produce documentation, the name of their workplace or educational institution, and the reason why they were traveling or entertaining themselves instead of being at work or school. All information was later verified and submitted to the workplaces and schools. Anyone without documents was escorted to a nearby bus and then taken to the police station for further questioning.

These kinds of raids sent a wave of fear and panic among the people, many of whom had no reason to be accused. When people had vacation time or were out of work or school for valid reasons, they often stayed home instead of going out, because they did not want to have to explain their presence elsewhere and risk ending up in the police station. It was an outrageous act of human rights violations against absolutely innocent people. It was absurd of our authorities to think the raids would minimize the loss of work hours in factories or force kids to stay in school. The moronic efforts did nothing but anger Soviet citizens even further, even the most loyal among them.

Another so-called enforcement of justice was the war on "illegal" profits. This attempt to eliminate any off-record income affected absolutely everyone, from black market music dealers to taxicab drivers. How effective these efforts were is very difficult to say. It sure sent a lot of people to jail, but the underground economy was barely touched by the new enforcement. Ordinary people were the most common and easiest targets for our police in these cases. The old babushka selling flowers on the corner, waiters and servers at restaurants, and taxi drivers who gathered tips were considered disgusting and greedy by the USSR. As a result, they lost their jobs, and old babushkas were dragged to the police stations, forced to pay enormous fines.

Another target in this war on illegal profits was our musicians. Playing weddings and taking tips in restaurants became a dangerous act. Musicians were often raided, and these sting operations usually involved an undercover cop paying a few rubles to the band to play his alleged favorite song. When the musician took the money, he was immediately handcuffed, and for that moment, the dancing was over.

Everybody who played weddings at that time knew it was best to ask the family who hired them to pay upfront to avoid any chance of being caught after the gig. In many cases, people had to lie to authorities that musicians were playing for free because they just happened to know the newlyweds, or something to that effect. It was difficult to fight this tactic, and the government came up with several strategies of stopping bands from playing weddings for an uncontrolled fee. After a while, all bands who wanted to play weddings had to be registered at a special office, and any family who was looking for a band had to hire them from a list of registered bands. The music program of these bands was censored, documents had to be submitted, and labor records had to be made. Paying the band members only a fraction of what the family was charged for it, these agencies became a profit centers for government, but more frequently they were sources of corruptions. No bands were interested in playing weddings for such low pay, so the heads of these offices sold "official" documents under the table to musicians, stating that the band was conducting business legally. It was just another example of the Soviets trying to fight corruption, while even more corruption grew right out of the soil of our ineffective economical system.

The Last Band

Nothing in my life at that point was more exciting for me than my hopes to someday play in a rock band. I was no longer interested in entertaining factory workers with a popular Soviet songs or playing dances for college students. To me, music meant much more than just standing onstage and pretending to be a rock star. Our underground bands shared that same passion. No one was dreaming about making money or playing at the large stadiums; we just wanted to express our feelings and thoughts through our music without governmental intervention in our art. We knew that any attempts to achieve that would not be possible without going through the authorities that hated rock music. No one wanted to deal with that, so we had to settle for our homemade albums of the rock bands we loved.

When my best friend Sasha returned from the Army, though, we did not wait. Immediately, we went to everyone we knew, hoping to build our band and play our own original songs. Unfortunately, most of the guys in our social circles were interested in making money, but we were looking for members who wanted to make music and be more than just a dance band. It was our most serious attempt to put together the best group we could, and we did a great job accomplishing this. Before long, we had five guys in our band: a singer, two guitarists, a drum player, and a bass player. The only two I knew were my pals Sasha and Oleg, our guitar player from school, but my long-awaited desire to play on an electric guitar again was finally within reach.

Next, all we had to do was find someplace where we could safely rehearse. The dilemma of finding a place with decent equipment and administration that would let us practice led us back to our good friend at the teacher's house. We recalled the last situation at that place, when we were kindly ask to leave with our own music, but we maintained hope that Vladimir, the head of the small facility, would cave under our tremendous pressure and box of vodka. In the end, we prevailed; he could not resist our begging or our vodka or our promises that we would not play any music with controversial lyrics.

Within just a few days, we were already honing our first heavy metal-style songs. The five of us fused together into a solid-sounding band. Even though we only had old, crummy guitars and aging, beat-up equipment, we did the best we could with it and managed to squeeze out some decent music. The joy of creating our own music elevated our spirits, and in a few weeks, we had almost a whole album of ready to record songs.

At one of our rehearsals, we heard a crowd cheering outside of the building. We looked down from the third floor of our makeshift studio and saw a pack of teenagers. The news about some "nasty" band at the teacher's house had spread throughout the surrounding neighborhood, so we had an audience. We really liked the fact that people could somehow listen to what we were playing and actually liked it. This fact, however, ultimately led to the demise of our rehearsals there, for not only did the news about our rock group reach the rock lovers in the community, but the authorities' less-than-tolerant ears as well.

Putting our "wild" imitation of "Capitalistic entertainment" out of business was very easy for the communists. That era was by far the worst for rock music and pop culture in our country. Expecting any kind of tolerance from our bureaucrats was a very naïve assumption, and it did not take long before one of our band members was subjected to a behind-closed-doors conversation with the government officials. The message he heard in that conversation was loud and clear: Stop the so-called madness or the leaders of our band would be locked up. I knew I would be one of them, and neither Sasha nor I wanted to put the rest of the band members at risk. In a quiet meeting, we said goodbye to each other and bid our last and best-performing band farewell.

Not only was it the end of my music career, but it was also the end of my hopes of being able to freely express myself. Everything we cherished and had dreamt about was destroyed by the senseless political motivation of our authorities. Hitting the wall in the same manner was a very common outcome for thousands of our artists and creative people. We were not alone in this situation, and considering the aggravated state of the political situation in our country, we had no hope that things would change in the future. The system was mercilessly stomping on anyone who even looked in the wrong direction. I could not deal with that dark life without any light at the end of a tunnel, and it was then that I decided living in my homeland any longer was absolutely senseless.

Shattered Escape

The Soviet Union was one of the most closed-off nations in the world. For anyone who is living in a modern civilized society today, it is very difficult to picture a situation where citizens are forbidden from freely traveling abroad. We had to deal with restrictions on relocation, as well as where we wanted to live, even within Soviet borders; emigrating elsewhere was not an option. The opportunity to even visit the outside world was a once-in-a-lifetime opportunity few people had, and one had to undergo intense scrutiny by the KGB before they would be granted a departure visa for traveling—a document used only in Socialistic nations to allow people to leave the state. People who were denied a departure visa were known as "otkaznicks" (deniers). In the USSR, this status was practically a permanent ban on international travel for life, as well as a way to mark someone as unreliable in the eyes of the Soviet Union. At the top of these lists were ethnic Jews and political dissidents, but anyone who was suspected of any lack of loyalty to our Communistic dogmas would also never leave the nation.

This group of people was treated equally harsh, regardless of the motive behind their request for departure. They were marked as deniers whether they wanted to leave the country for good or just as a tourist, and the Soviet authorities considered them to be the lowest grade of citizens. Not only did this blacklisting serve as punishment for an accused disobedience, but it was also an attempt to stop any negative information about Soviet life from leaking to the West. Knowing that dissidents would not have kind things to say about the Soviet regime during their travels, they were treated as enemies of the state and held in our country like prisoners, without ever having committed a crime. Like so many Soviet efforts, this practice actually did more damage to the image of the USSR than if they would have simply let the unhappy people leave. Of course, there was a question as to how many people would have fled the Soviet Union if the opportunity presented itself. The government knew that the numbers would be in the millions, so they enforced the strictest possible limitations on any travels abroad, fearing desertion if the people they were trying to control realized the grass was actually greener outside those cold Soviet borders.

When our boss at work had to go to Cuba on a business trip, it was a mega-event in our organization. No one really cared about his journey to Fidel Castro's nation, which was friendly to Russia at the time. However, everyone was very interested in the fact that he had a stop-over in England, where he would visit the London airport. We knew our supervisor would have just see a small glimpse of Western life, but we could not wait for his return so he could tell us about his encounter and share his experiences with us. Unfortunately, he never set foot on British soil. The tight Soviet hold stretched beyond its borders, even onto the planes travelers rode. No Russian transit passengers on Soviet planes traveling through this Capitalistic nation was allowed to leave the plane in London. Therefore, our boss spent two hours, along with other passengers from the USSR, observing through the window as planes landed and workers unloaded luggage. Soviet paranoia reigned supreme, no matter where Soviet citizens went, and even when someone left the state, they were often forbidden to see and hear and experience anything the authorities did not want them to know about.

As I've mentioned several times, I was always irritated by the lack of justice in our country, and as time went on and I matured, I became more and more outraged by the limitations on our freedom in the Soviet Union. It limited me in so many ways. Not only did it prevent me from playing the music I so loved, but it also inhibited my ability to express openly what I thought about our society at large. My friends and I often referred to our country as a "big jail" and often shared pained laughs at the fact that even prisoners were freer than we were; in jail, people have a chance to say what they want. It was a very sad but a predominant truth. My patience with the Soviet regime was running thin, and the idea of escaping from the USSR became a frequent fantasy.

The easiest way to depart for good from the USSR at that time was to take an overseas trip and not return. I was aware that I'd already been tagged for life as a denier, so I couldn't even think of ever leaving the country that way. Soviet borders were basically locked, and escaping would mean risking one's life in a bold and dangerous attempt. Anyone who was contemplating the idea knew that it was a most treacherous plot. Not only was it a risk, but it would also require leaving relatives and friends behind; there was little chance of ever seeing your family members in the future, whether you lived or died on your escape attempt. If one managed to make it out of the country without being shot in the back, captured, or imprisoned and made it safely to some Western country, the Soviet government would go to all means to ensure that the escapee would never see any of their loved ones again. There was no chance of them being granted permission to leave Soviet borders, and those who got out would never have a chance to come back home.

I knew about these heartbreaking consequences, but I still could not imagine spending the rest of my life in our big jail. In my heart, I had the same spiritual drive that made many other Russians risk their lives in an attempt to run for freedom. That same drive was what caught people on the barbed wire in the concentration camps of Stalin, forced Cubans to swim to the USA or float there on old doors, and saw people shot dead on the Berlin Wall. Still, I began to consider my options to leave Soviet Union for good in exchange for freedom. So many of them were too dangerous and completely unrealistic. In despair, some of our citizens tried to hijack a plane or simply run across heavily monitored Soviet borders. I even heard about someone's attempt to cross the North Pole on skis to get to the USA. I had to put these types of plans out of my mind, for I knew they were guaranteed to fail or would come to an ultimate violent end.

Considering the enormous size of the Soviet Union, we were surrounded by nations that were loyal satellites or politically neutral in regard to the Soviet regime. We shared a border in our western territory with the Capitalistic nation of Finland. To make a breakaway to Finland through the complex and fortified border was a matter of pure luck, and occasionally, someone made such a successful escape. Unfortunately, Fins were quick to deport any escapees back to the USSR, despite knowing that the deportees would spend the rest of their lives in gulags or Soviet mental institutions.

The only country that did not cruelly eject Soviets back to Russia was Turkey. Anyone who was fortunate enough to somehow make it to Turkey and ask for political asylum usually ended up shortly in the USA. Turkey, however, was very difficult to reach. Situated along the Soviet republic of Georgia on the Black Sea, the border we shared with the country lurked on the other side of mountains that were difficult to traverse. Not only was the terrain a major obstacle, but getting close to the actual border was also very problematic for political reasons. In those days, the small towns or villages located close to the borders were completely controlled by local authorities. Any visitor who was not a resident there had to immediately register at the local police station. Locals were obligated to inform the government about anyone they saw who seemed suspicious or who did not living in the village. In the case of large cities, some of them were simply closed to outside visitors who had no written permission. After long analyses, I realized that the most likely chance to escape to Turkey was by swimming a short distance there by the Black Sea.

One of the largest sea resort towns in Georgia was Batumi, located only thirty miles from the Turkish border. It was, to the best of my estimation, the perfect place for my attempted to escape. Since Batumi was a popular destination for many vacationing people in the USSR, the city had no closed status and required no permit to visit. Obviously, its close proximity to Turkey meant it was under the scrutiny of the most intense border control in the nation.

My plan was simple, but at the same time very difficult to accomplish: All I needed was a lifejacket and some flippers for my feet. Knowing that all the shores and the local waters were constantly monitored by the Coast Guard, swimming to Turkey sounded like a mad idea, but it was the only way to deceive the coastal radar, which would easily detect even the smallest inflatable boat.

Swimming in the Black Sea was a wild and almost intolerable task. Just considering the distance, it would be hopeless to swim all the way, but as far as I knew, it wasn't as bad if one swam from a sailing ship. The city of Batumi had a port from which many passenger water crafts launched to various Soviet Black Sea destinations. I planned to board one of the ships departing at night and drop into the water from its stern when it would be far from the shore (and closer at the same time to Turkey). With my lifejacket, flippers, and a compass, all I would have to do was drift slowly toward South. I assumed I'd be in Turkish waters by sunrise, and from there, if I am lucky, I'd be picked up by their Coast Guard, who would not send me back. The Black Sea was my only ticket to freedom.

In the summer, the water in the Black Sea reaches sometimes seventy-plus degrees Fahrenheit, and I knew that there was a very realistic chance of surviving in those waters for a couple of days if need be. As long as I remained unspotted by the Soviet Coast Guard, I would eventually end up on Turkish soil. While the plan was simple, I knew that to accomplish it successfully, I'd have to thoroughly prepare for it.

I had a small window of opportunity, as I had to make my escape in the summer. For several months, I prepared for my dangerous mission. As I exercised and tried to build up cold water endurance, I also played over in my mind thousands of times every detail and possible scenario of the escape. The plan was to fly to the city of Sochi and take a train from there to my final destination. I knew that going from my town to Georgia on the train was much safer approach than an airplane trip, since purchasers of railroad tickets did not go on record in the USSR; however, I could not dedicate a week on the train for my escape plan, so I decided to risk traveling to Sochi on a plane, like any ordinary tourist would. From there, the train was the safest option to reach Batumi.

Run for Freedom

In August of 1984, I took vacation and told my parents I was planning to visit Sochi for a week. I had a backpack and a bag containing my lifejacket, flippers, and everything else I needed to make my escape. Everything was ready for my life-risking attempt, and it was a very emotional time for me. I looked at my family and realized I very likely would never see them again unless it was in a Soviet court or in Heaven. The worry about the potentially awful outcomes of my attempt filled my mind with doubts, causing me to question if I was doing the right thing. I considered my future in the USSR, and I decided that I could no longer bear to spend my life there – especially since my life was really just beginning. Having to keep my plans to myself, I hid my heartbreaking emotions and said a final farewell to my mom, brother, and grandma, and then I closed the door behind me and headed to the airport.

When our Soviet AN-24 plane landed in Adler Airport near Sochi, I went to get my luggage and found that it was lost. It was an unexpected problem, and I almost aborted my mission because of it. Suddenly, an airport worker showed up and handed my backpack to me. Inside was my lifejacket; without that, I would be like a brick in the water.

Buying a train ticket to Batumi proved to be quite a challenge. Hundreds of summer travelers were boarding the same train to head south, and I was worried that there would be no room for me and I would have to sleep at the train station. In the end, this was exactly what happened. After wrestling with the crowd for quite a while, all I could do was get a ticket for the next day, so I started looking for a corner on the floor where I could rest for the night. I only had enough money for few days' worth of food, so I had to stick to my agenda and conserve all energy and funds that I had.

Sleeping on the concrete floor was not only uncomfortable, but it was also dangerous in my situation. At any moment, I knew I could be asked for documents and be subjected to a search. However, I needed rest for my own personal D-day, and sleeping in town would cause even more suspicion. So, when nightfall came, I wedged between the wall and someone's luggage, and the next morning, I was on the train, rolling through the Georgian mountains on my way to Batumi – to freedom.

The Unexpected

The slowly moving train was jam-packed with people of all ages and different nationalities, most headed to the summer places along the Caucus Mountains for vacation. Several local Georgians sat quietly in the car on the way to their homes in villages and rural towns. As a common practice on Soviet trains, everyone tried to be friendly and make conversation. "Where're you going?" was the standard question to open the discussion, and my story to everyone was that I wanted to see old Batumi. Many asked me where I was planning to stay, and some even offered to give me room and board at their place. Making up answers on the fly, I tried to concentrate on details about my plan, thinking over and over again if anything else could be done to make my escape a success. Sleeping on the train was never comfortable, but I was so exhausted from my worries and travels that I quickly fell asleep and woke up on our approach to Batumi.

The weather was perfect, and that was a good sign to me. Nothing could have been worse at that moment than bad weather and the resulting bad visibility on the sea. I grabbed a quick breakfast at the train station, and after picking up a local map at a kiosk, I headed without delay in the direction of the local harbor.

The streets of Batumi became crowded as I looked at the map to make my way to my final destination in my Motherland. It was easy to tell that I was in a border city because the streets were occupied by many KGB military border personnel, dressed in their classic uniforms. Trying not to think about them, I carefully checked my route and realized I had missed a turn at one of the streets. I instantly turned around to go back. As I lifted my eyes off the map, I immediately saw a man walking toward me. I had a nearly photographic memory, and I recognized him as the one of passengers who had taken the plane ride to Sochi with me. While he was passing by me, I intentionally stared at him, but he made no eye contact and kept looking into the abyss. The odds of him being on the exact same path with me were too much of a coincidence. I didn't think the KGB would see .me as such a threat that I needed to be followed, but the chances of the man being just an ordinary tourist on the same journey as I was all the way from Gomel did not seem to have any logical explanation. I realized then that I might be very close to the end of my escape plan without even touching the water. Slowly, the thought of my luggage's little disappearing act at the airport came to mind, and I had to question it.

To scrap everything at that point would have been a true tragedy for me, but being handcuffed and hauled off to jail would have been a much worse scenario. If the man truly was a KGB spy, I knew my chances to make it onboard the ship were slim, not to mention slipping into the water. I knew I had no option but to go back home. At that moment, I could not be completely certain whether or not I was being followed, but if I was, the road to the harbor would be the end for me. In a split second, despite of a great desire to leave this country, I had to come up with an emergency retreat plan.

I had just enough money left to buy a train ticket and a sandwich, so I began a winding walk through the narrow streets back to the train station. Occasionally looking back, I hoped I was not being followed, and I was already thinking about how to ditch my most incriminating evidence – the lifejacket. To minimize its visibility on the water, right before my departure, I had turned it inside-out and painted green and blue lines on it for better camouflage. Trying to explain that to anyone would be very difficult. At the same time, leaving it behind might arouse suspicion. I decided to take it with me on the train. My main goal now was to leave that border town as soon as possible.

As I neared the train station, I had to suppress the excruciating desire to turn around and go to the harbor. I could not picture going back to the life I had before, and I was upset that I had to abandon my escape plan at the very last minute. Still, common logic and the enormous risk of going to Gulag prevailed, and I comforted myself with the thought that staying out of jail would afford me the opportunity to execute some other escape plan in the future.

I hoped getting a ticket back to Sochi would not be as big of a problem as couple days ago. When I approached cashier, the cold-faced woman told me the tickets were sold out on my train. Back in those days, that did not necessarily mean I could not get onboard. If one was willing to pay double the ticket price, passage was often granted. I showed my last ten rubbles to the old woman, and she quietly pushed my desired ticket over to me.

Hiding in the less visible corners of the train station, I kept an eye on my old Pobeda watch. Time seemed to be crawling at a snail's pace. I gazed at every person, trying to detect if I've being followed. The minutes seemed to stretch into hours. When the time to board the train finally came, I walked into the No. 7 car and realized that it was practically empty...

Knowing that I had to dispose of my lifejacket and flippers, I hoped the train car doors would be possible to open during our trip so I could toss it on the tracks. Unfortunately, all the doors were shut tight, and I also realized that someone on the train might see me discarding it, including any possible followers who might still tracking me. I waited until night time, and after making sure no one could see me, I threw my bag on the third level luggage shelf in the next train car. I went back to sleep and prepared myself for any unwanted company that might be waiting for me at the Sochi train station.

In the morning, the train arrived at my destination, and I exited through a different car, trying to minimize my chances of being grabbed. When I safely left the Sochi train station, I began to wonder how I was going to get back home. I had no money left for food, but buying tickets for the trip home was even more problematic. Massive crowds were heading to their places of living, so finding an available plane or train ticket was a great deal of challenge, regardless of how much it would cost. Not only did I somehow have to find the money I needed for my return, but I also had to survive the short stay in Sochi without having to sleep on the streets. The only hope I had at that moment was to try ask one of our old friends for help. When I'd visited Sochi a few years prior with my mother, we stayed with Vladimir and his family in their little house. They were very kind people, and they were my only hope in that moment of desperation. I didn't want to deceive them, but I had no option but to come up with some kind of believable excuse as to how I ended up there without any way to get back home.

After Retreat

When I arrived at the home of Vladimir, he and his family were obviously surprised to see me on their doorstep. I opted for the easiest and most believable story about a stolen wallet, and I told them I had come to explore the Caucasus Mountains. Vladimir and his old mom had no doubt I was telling the truth. The very nice family offered me shelter, and after comforting me for a couple of days, they provided me with the money and a ticket home.

The last night before my departure to Gomel, I thought again about everything that happened. Doubts swam through my mind, and I worried that I might have overreacted and maybe should have tried to pursue my plan to swim to freedom. I couldn't help but wonder if the man was truly following me or if he just resembled the man I saw on the plane. My disdain about having to go back to the life I had tried to escape from fueled me with regret and feelings of failure about the unaccomplished runaway attempt. At the same time, I realized that I had not burned any bridges or created an uneasy situation at home, since none of them knew about my plot and thought I was just going on a temporary excursion that I would return from. I still had a job, so I could return to it after my assumed vacation. No one at home would ever suspect that the story I told to Vladimir in Sochi wasn't true. The only consequences I would have to deal with upon my return was my inner grief and turmoil about my failed attempt and how it would effect my future life. I tried not to think about it too much – to forget everything that happened, as well as the dreams that didn't.

"Let's talk now."

Nothing was worse for me at that time than going back to my hopeless, Soviet-controlled life. After I returned home, everything seemed even worse, if that was even possible. The dull, gray political atmosphere and the new so-called ideological innovations from our regime pounded into us how much harder we had to try to build Communism up to something great. I had to forget about my dream to escape that totalitarian country, but their failure to make any improvements only gave me more motivation to question my decision to abort that mission.

My doubts were soon put to rest when I was, in fact, taken in for questioning by our KGB. During the 'audition', my naïve tale about mountain explorations only made the officer smile. They had found the lifejacket and flippers, so my claim that I was terribly aqua-phobic only served as more entertainment for them. I expected that I would be facing many false accusations and a threat of imprisonment. The most shocking thing they mentioned, though, were not the questions about my recent trip to Sochi. They revealed to me, "It is only one faithful Communist who is protecting you from very serious trouble, and it is only because of that person that you have a freedom you do not deserve." That loyal Communist was: my own mother. The authorities did not care about me, and they would have gladly snuffed out my life with little regret than smashing a meaningless mosquito. All they cared about was the reputation and image of a dedicated member of their party. They accused me of "staining" that reputation with my "outrageous disrespect of the Soviet system." According to classic Communist dogmas, their world, including their families, were supposed to remain pure and clean – free from any form of disloyalty. Typically, if a Communist had someone like me as their son, that loyal parent would be expelled from the Communist Party because of it. My mother was a true patriot of our country at that time, a zealous defender of Communism. Only out of respect for her dedication did the KGB allow me to escape imprisonment and suffering that some of my friends endured.

Living with Hope in God

I came to realize that I simply could not fight the system. It had broken the backbones of millions of its own citizens, any who dared to disagree with the political regime. It was more than a battle with windmills, and I could no longer even think of trying to escape it. The world around me could not be changed, and I had to find the way of somehow living in that vacuum of freedom. I was not the only one in such a dire and depressing situation, and many of my friends were a good example for me that we could find the way to ignore our dictatorship. For me, God and music was my only window to spiritual freedom, and I planned to cling to it with all my heart until the end.

My radio, stereo system, and guitar were my best friends at that time. I still dreamt about playing in a band again, but considering all the negative experiences I had in my attempts to form one, it became too painful to even think about it. Occasional salad and wedding gigs served as an additional source of income and supported my needs for clothing and records from the black market. It was the only option for me at that time if I wanted to have any experience playing, and I carried on with the humble hope that the future might be brighter and offer me more opportunities to practice my passion.

Days, weeks, and winter months crawled along at a slow and boring pace. I spent the evenings with couple of my close friends at home, and we often listened to American radio programs that were jammed even more fervently by the KGB. In long political debates, we discussed the situation in the USSR and the information we heard on the shows. It was our only source of knowledge about how deep our country was going into political and economical crises. The daily television programs on Soviet TV reported an "ever-growing strength and prosperity," but that false presentation of our reality contradicted what was really happening in our state. It became impossible to believe a word of anything we heard from the official media. The world we knew was turning upside down right before our eyes, and more and more people began to mistrust the government that was telling us Western radio programs were citadels of lies.

The system survived by fabricating misinformation, not only about the economical situation in our country, but also about the political problems. Corruption, mistrust, and double standards ruled our lives. It could not last forever, and the seventy-year political experiment in our country had to come to an end. No one knew when and how it was going to happen, but there were really only two options for our future: either reinforce the totalitarian regime and become a Stalin-type country all over again or give up on the Communistic failed mythology. The second option was practically a fairytale, and our political doctrines and policies seemed to be pointing toward becoming a completely closed society once again. It was the most hopeless time of my life, and like many of my friends, I reached a point when I expected nothing better. We had no idea that the world around us would very soon take a drastic change – one that would not come from civilian uprising or outside invasion.

Chapter 16

Perestroika and New Hope

As some of you might remember, March of 1985 became a breaking point in the history of the Soviet Union. When our media announced that the Konstantin Chernenko, leader of the USSR, had passed away, it was rather easily accepted news among our population; it was something we'd become desensitized to. After all, he was the third president of the Soviet Union to die within a three-year period. The frequency of our rulers' departure was probably some kind of a sad record, but it was so common that it became somewhat of a dark joke.

Therefore, no one was really surprised by the announcement of Chernenko's demise. He had not made many public appearances in the months prior, and the issue of his poor health was the stuff of many rumors. Generally, the death of a Soviet leader led to extensive media coverage of the burial and so forth, but this was not the case for Chernenko. Rather, while he was buried with honor, all the media attention was instead placed on a man who was attending the closed meeting of our Politburo to take his place. That man was one Mikhail Gorbachev, and he would change not only the face and destiny of Russia, but also other nations of the world.

In Gorbachev's first speeches before our leaders and Communist Party members, he made groundbreaking statements about democratic reforms in the USSR. He made fresh proclamations and suggested political doctrines that had never been heard before. Some of these were "Glasnost" (free speech) and "Perestroika" (reformation), which were meant to pull our country out of its stagnant political and economical "zastoy" (standstill).

His ability to capture the attention of the masses was incredible. Some people even shed tears when they listened to Gorbachev talk about foreign concepts like freedom of speech and democracy reforms in USSR. It was very promising time, filled with much emotion and hope. Everybody was very enthusiastic about new innovations that Gorbachev was manifesting to the nation. Finally, we had a leader who was brave enough to admit the truth to Russian citizens: As a nation, we were not in good shape economically and politically. To hear these words coming out of our leader's mouth – words that only a few weeks earlier would have seen common citizens interrogated by the KGB or locked up in prison – was a shocking concept. My grandmother listened to Gorbachev's speeches without interest, but when he began to discuss our nation's past and talk about Stalin, she quietly turned off TV and went to the kitchen. My mother, on other hand, was very enthusiastic about the new reforms, though she was concerned about things getting out of hand.

Following Gorbachev's courageous and wise lead, our tumultuous history, the era of repression, and Stalin's life were no longer taboo discussions. Suddenly, the so-called "evil forces" of the West were being called "partners in dialog for peace." Ronald Reagan, then the U.S. president, became one of Gorbachev's best friends, and to see them together on the screens of our televisions shaking hands was like watching some kind of fictitious movie. The hope Gorbachev brought to Russia was overwhelming. Finally, a better life and the relief of political tensions with the West were possibilities in the USSR.

In Gorbachev, everyone saw a young, honest politician of a new breed. For most of us, he was progressive and energetic leader, and people wanted him to succeed in his ambitious plans. In an attempt to reach out to ordinary people and really listen to their everyday concerns, he took several trips to rural regions, where he visited factories and farms. It was a new style of leadership, in direct contrast to our old Communists in the Kremlin, who rarely made appearance in public and then only in staged and carefully orchestrated productions with plenty of forced fanfare. In Gorbachev's case, his surprise visits and spontaneous appearances on the streets added to his popularity and the respect the Russian people had for him. Everywhere he went, enormous crowds gathered. Having a chance to see and talk to the leader of our country in person was absolutely incredible.

Gorbachev spawned a truly revolutionary mindset in the country, and people were overcome with tremendous hope that the oppressive life we had been enduring for the past seventy years would now be changed for better. When our longstanding dissident academic Andrei Sakharov took to the pulpit for a speech in the Kremlin, he made a solid statement about how serious our leader was about making those changes, albeit remaining within the limits of our Socialistic society. Gorbachev however, had no intention of dismantling the Soviet regime or discarding our Communistic beliefs. What he wanted to do was create "Socialism with a humane face." The end result of it was to be something like modern China, where the Communist Party still rules the nation, but society is Socialistic in nature, with its own limitations.

Communistic dogmas and teachings continued to be the foundation of our country, but the government did not view it or talk about it as they had in the past. The priority of Gorbachev and his new cabinet was to make Socialism attractive, and to do so, they had to discard the old approach to promoting its principles. If they were to make people believe in our old teachings, they had to be fresh and inspiring. At that time, Perestroika had to be the symbol of change, promising us not only political improvements, but economic ones as well.

Everyone began looking into the future with a healthy dose of optimism. The press was being granted more freedom to openly discuss our present and past life. All media was still under government control and ownership, but the strict censorship and old style of Communistic propaganda was fading away, with more liberal and democratic themes being presented to the masses.

The Light at the End of the Tunnel

Changes also seeped into our cultural life, slowly but surely. Old movies, books, and programs that had been shelved during the era of the old Soviet regime were brought back to life. New films and stage plays began to blossom, and this represented the vibe and atmosphere of our transforming nation.

During this cultural revolution, something I loved was given a breath of fresh air. Under Gorbachev, rock music was finally legalized in the USSR. After being banned for many years, Soviet groups could at last officially refer to themselves as rock bands, without fear of reproach, suspicion, or punishment. Rock n' roll was no longer a forbidden term, and no one gave bands a hard time for sounding or looking like their Western partners.

My brother Misha and I at home.

Because it had existed only underground before, the evolution of Russian rock music was a bit behind the rest of the world, but once the ban was lifted, it unleashed a bevy of creative musicians to emerge. Our rock artists, however, were still in infancy as far as their musical careers, as compared to popular Western super bands. It was also hard to establish a rock group and began touring, since the old system of concerts and shows was still in the hands of the government, who didn't see the onslaught of new rock bands as a top priority. Everyone knew it would take time for the bands that had been lurking underground for decades to make their way to center stage in our concert halls. For most of the new and already established Soviet music artists, there was only one option: create recordings of music now that there was no risk of being prosecuted for it. Thus, homemade studios sprung up in basements and kitchens, and a new era of music compositions began to take shape. With no ban or restrictions on music-making, our tape recorders were flooded with free albums. A few lucky Soviet bands even got a chance to release their first records under our Soviet label, Melodija. Of course, none of them ever got rich, but the pride and the ability to openly cut an album were even more valuable benefits; record deals in the USSR were a new and treasured concept, regardless how little they paid.

War on Booze

One fundamental change that Gorbachev wanted to achieve was to eliminate or at least minimize the problem of alcohol addiction in Russia. This reform unfortunately had a catastrophic failure programmed into it from the very beginning. Alcoholism had been a problem in our nation for centuries, and trying to stop it at that point was an impossible task. Even the harsh prohibition going back in Tsar's and Stalin's time could not make a dent on the country-wide obsession with drinking. Gorbachev wanted to reach people through education and enforced reduction of alcohol consumption in the USSR. He saw the negative and destructive effects of this problem, not only on people's personal lives, but also on the whole economy of the USSR, and he was right to be concerned about it because it was a massive problem.

The war on alcoholism and drunkenness was rolled out on enormous scale. The sale of liquor was prohibited near factories, colleges, and schools, and even in places where it could be sold, it was limited to only few hours a day, typically not earlier than two p.m. A big part of this campaign was to promote nonalcoholic weddings – a notion that was laughable amongst most people, because vodka and champagne were integral parts of all weddings and were considered a tradition. When people ignored these pleas from the Kremlin to put their drinks down at matrimonial celebrations, a new regulation was put in place to limit the number of bottles of booze at weddings.

To combat the havoc of people buying as much vodka as possible during liquor-sale hours, a coupon system was put into place. Distributed at work, these coupons allowed only one bottle of hard liquor per person per month. Unfortunately, this plan backfired as well, for the selling and trading of these coupons became yet another underground activity.

Even those who were loyal to Gorbachev were angered by the liquor law reforms. When the difficulty of purchasing alcohol reached the point of mass hysteria, private moonshine production went through the roof. This eventually led to a severe lack of its main ingredient from our store shelves, and there was little sugar to be found for anyone. Thus, this created another unwanted problem for Gorbachev. He seemed to be losing the alcohol battle, despite the strict regulations and sometimes absurd approaches to reducing even the visibility of alcohol. The labels on some bottles of Vodka were changed to plain, unattractive printed stickers in an attempt to make the product less appealing. Any film that contained scenes of alcohol consumption in what was deemed an exceeding quantity was banned from broadcasts. This tactic was quite upsetting for cinematographers and movie makers, who had hoped Gorbachev's plans would have given them more freedom to create. No matter what Gorbachev tried, it made no impact in the long-lasting relationship of Russian people with alcohol, and eventually, his anti-alcoholism reform drowned in a sad defeat.

Chapter 17

Making My First Self-Made Electric Guitar

Personally, I observed the changes in our country under Gorbachev's rule with more and more enthusiastic hope than I had ever had before. Nothing influenced me as much as the freedom we had to play the music we loved. My hope of eventually becoming a musician or dedicating much of my personal time to music did not seem to be an unrealistic goal anymore. I still had no any idea how, with whom, or where I would play again, but that was not a great concern for me at the time. I had plenty of friends who were dying to take a chance in our newly liberated rock music life. The bigger question to me at the time was what I was going to play on. My long history of borrowing electric guitars from our schools and culture palaces gave me the motivation to finally own my own instrument. I was inspired by the positive changes taking place in my world, and I was very confident that the first step in my new life in music should be to obtain a professional or at least good quality electric guitar.

Unfortunately, there was still a great lack of supplies and limited manufacturing of musical instruments in the USSR. Not only was the availability unchanged, but in many cases, even some equipment and ugly Soviet electric guitars began to disappear from store shelves with little explanation. Perhaps it was because of the new freedom of musical expression, and people were grabbing whatever they could since they were now free to produce music. There was also a constant fear of inflation in any time of change, so people tended to buy things while the prices were still affordable. In the end, though, it didn't really matter why the junky Soviet electric guitars were flying off the hooks in our stores, for their playability and quality were truly an embarrassment, and anyone who bought them had to have very little knowledge about guitars.

Considering all the changes our government was promising, I hoped that we would soon begin to produce quality electric guitars or that imports of the nice instruments from the West would be allowed. As it turned out, neither of these were the case, and it began to seem like waiting on Russia to catch up to quality musical instrument production or supply was a futile waste of time.

Electric guitars were not the only items that disappeared quickly from our stores. One by one, more ordinary household products became very difficult to buy. The majority of people in the country did not blame it on Gorbachev's Perestroika. For some hardcore Stalinists, however,

Gorbachev was considered an enemy of our regime, and his reforms were at fault for all of the new problems and deficits. Others blamed the "dark forces" who wanted to sabotage the new policies of the government.

Since buying a Soviet-made electric guitar was not an option I was willing to consider, I was left with only one possible solution: the black market. Everything from keyboards amplifiers and electric guitars could be purchased from the underground dealers. The only problem was the astronomical price on these items, rendering them impossible for me to afford. To pick up a Japanese or American guitar through these sources was also not so easy, as there were few options to choose from and limited availability. The majority of instruments were from Japan such as Ibanez, Aria, or Fernandes. The American brands like Gibson or Fender were rare due to their high prices overseas and even more in Russia. If anything was brought to the USSR by sailors or through our shady corrupted channels, it was intended to make a huge profit. Any of these instruments might cost me the equivalent of four to five annual salaries or more. Paying 4,000 to 5,000 rubles for a non-necessity luxury item like an electric guitar was only possible for those who somehow earned very lavish illegal profits – something a lot of musicians had to do in order to own the decent music gear they required. Reselling records and jeans or playing weddings for years was the classic way for many guitar players to make it happen. No matter how I looked at the situation, I saw no solution, and I had no way to obtain so much cash in any near future.

I reached the point of desperation, and I had to find a playable alternative that would be almost as good as an American- or Japanese-made instrument. Playing my old guitar at home one day and enjoying the feel of my retrofitted neck on it, I questioned what would it take to make a whole guitar from scratch myself. The more I thought about it, the clearer the picture became in my mind, and I decided it was the only realistic way I was going to have my own quality electric guitar. I assumed I could not possibly make a guitar as poorly as the Soviet Union was constructing them. By that time, I had a decent amount off knowledge about guitar function and parts, but the construction and building process were something I was in the dark about. In the Soviet Union, we wouldn't have ever had the opportunity to take a class on how to build guitars, and there was no information available (remember, this was long before the Internet came to be!) There were a couple of books released in our country on this topic, but the books were very difficult to get, and some contained the wrong information, touting the "official" approach to electric guitar construction that resulted in the sorry instruments made in the USSR – that was not the kind of guitar I wanted to build.

The Materials the Parts, and the Tools

Another problem with my plan was the absolute absence of materials, parts, and quality tools that I would need to accomplish my task. The guitar materials situation was probably the most problematic obstacle for me. The government did not sell raw materials to the public unless it was related to some kind of construction like a Dacha or a house in the village. Even in those cases, the red tape to get what you were looking for involved mountains of documents and bureaucracy, and the Kremlin had no intention of allowing the government to sell any quality materials to anyone for projects they deemed unimportant and unnecessary. Thus, the government had a monopoly on any type of fabrications and had no reason to let anybody else to have a piece of it. This dilemma could only be resolved by obtaining everything one needed from the factories and construction sites through the back doors.

The parts were another problematic issue since no one produced or sold components suitable for quality instrument building. The only things that ever showed up on the shelves of our stores were cheap tuner keys and useless acoustic guitar pickups. I realized I would have to fabricate some guitar components or have them custom made for me. There were people who could help you get things done. Anyone who worked at a factory in the USSR could produce items on the side for a small fee. Of course it was illegal, but in many cases it was our only solution since official services of this kind did not exist.

Tools were yet another obstacle. Not only was the market for power tools limited to drills and primitive sanders, but even those were so hard to get that searching for them throughout the stores would be a total waste of energy. The hand tools produced in the Soviet Union at the time were as poor a quality as their trashy electric guitars, and whatever few were offered to the public were only hobby-level products at best. To construct my guitar the way I wanted, I knew I would have to make a great effort to find the best tools I could.

My curios idea to make an electric guitar was slowly growing into a carefully calculated plan. I began analyzing every little detail about guitar construction and thinking of ways to gather the things I would need. I could not just limit this list to tools, materials, and parts, as I also had to think about a suitable time and place to work on my project. Since we still lived in the same one-bedroom apartment, I did not have adequate space to set up a little corner for my project. My only solution was the bathroom or the kitchen, where I could do it simply on the stool or right on the floor. When I was going to do it was another question.

Time and Place to Make it

My grandma had retired and spent her whole day at home taking care of the kitchen and working around the house. She wouldn't mind if I would make a little mess or noise; she was already immune to that after living with us her whole life. My little brother Mikhail was already a teenager and was very happy and supportive about my plans. Therefore, there was only one major problem. I worked from nine a.m. to six p.m., so I was technically at work all day, and late evenings were absolutely not an option for my construction project. My mom was at work practically all day, and when she returned home late in the evenings, I knew she would not want to see any guitar-building going on in the house. I had to do something about it, and the only solution I could think of was to find a job that would allow me more free time at home.

I had already had enough of drawing numbers on the cardboard at work and was happy to finally have a good reason to quit my job. I knew my mother wouldn't take the news well, unless I found a new job before leaving my old one. It became my number one priority, and I started vigorously looking for a suitable place to work. Looking for a job that would meet all my requirements was more difficult than I thought it would be. I wanted something with flexible hours, not far away from home, and that had absolutely nothing to do with manufacturing. Finally, I found something that would be absolutely perfect for me.

Our local TV station had a "Help Wanted" ad for a movie projector technician, and it listed that there was "no experience required." I knew I had to try to get the job, and I was already counting on my beloved Aunt Valentina to help me out. She still worked at the TV station, and her reputation and respect there was unprecedented. I knew I would have a better chance at the job if I enlisted her help, but at the same time, I was very concerned that she might be contacted by people who would try to block my employment there. On the other hand, the political changes and the whole atmosphere in the country made me feel as though I was no longer a subject of concern for our government. After long evaluations, I decided to take a risk and approach the TV station management on my own with my request about the job.

The interview didn't seem to go so well, but when the manager learned that I was Valentina's nephew, he changed his tone. "Let me think about it. Come back tomorrow," he said, shaking my hand.

The next day, I had a new job. It was the perfect employment for me from every point of view. Our TV station was located not far from home, and I could ride my bike there in ten minutes. The best part of my job was the dual shift work schedule. I would have two other partners, and we could rotate our shifts from the morning or from late afternoon. It turned out to be a very easy and even a somewhat boring job that required me to operate movie projectors that played reports of our local news programs filmed on 16mm film. After a few days, I was able to handle all the responsibilities on my own, and I could not wait to use my free time for building my very own electric guitar.

"What am I making?"

My first step was to determine what I was going to make and what my first instrument was going to look like. Heavy metal music was on the rise, so pointy, modern-looking electric guitars like Jacksons or Yamahas were extremely popular at that time, like the ones we saw in the dozens of music videos we watched on our VCR. To me, however, the classy look of the electric guitar played by most popular musicians was much more appealing. One of my favorite guitarists, Ritchie Blackmore, had such an instrument, and I knew he would not play on it if it wasn't considered to be cool. I wanted my guitar to be cool too.

I had a snapshot of Ritchie holding his guitar in a perfect position, and I could copy every detail of its design from that picture, with the exception of the headstock, which was cut out. To transfer and scale up everything from that picture with maximum accuracy became more than a single-step procedure. I decided to take a photo shot from this image, load the film into a slide projector and beam it on the cardboard. I borrowed a camera from one of my friends, took the shot, and had the film developed. I pinned the cardboard on the wall of our apartment. Knowing the guitar's standard scale, I drew a straight line on the cardboard in the proper length. I divided the line in the middle so I would know where to put the twelfth fret and the bridge saddles. Then, all I had to do was move the slide projector back and forth until the bridge and twelfth fret on the image met my line marks on the cardboard. When I had it positioned correctly so that everything matched up, I carefully traced all parts of the body and got a perfect 1:1 scale sketch of my new electric guitar.

With the drawing in my hands, the building process was next on the agenda. I was anxious to start construction, but I couldn't move forward until I had all the parts and tools for my undertaking. The hardware, pickups, and other components were absolutely impossible to buy. I knew the ultimate solution would be to find some kind of donor guitar that could be stripped for this purpose. The most challenging part was finding a match for the pickups. Not only did they have to look the same, but I also wanted them to sound better than the ones used on our trashy Soviet electric guitars. I knew which guitar had very similar pickups, and I also knew the guy who owned it. The instrument was made in Eastern Germany, a Musima model that was rarely available in our stores, even considering its mediocre quality. My pal Alexei had one that was in very rough condition, and if I could buy it from him to be a "donor", I could move forward with my building. When I approached him with an offer, he turned me down and said he didn't want to sell it. Instead, he wanted a straight trade on my retrofitted acoustic guitar. Everybody who played on it loved it for its slim and comfortable neck, and Alexei was no exception. I had to think about his offer for some time. It was difficult to picture my life without that instrument. Not only was it my first guitar, but it had so many memories and stories attached to it that parting with it would prove to be a very emotional challenge for me. Alexei had no interest in cash, though, and there was nothing else he would take in trade. After considering all my options, the decision had to be made that I would trade my old beloved "Rock is my life" guitar for parts to build my new one.

Breaking a 'Donor' Guitar

Just a couple days after my old guitar was placed in the hands of my friend Alexei, the old Musima he'd traded me for it was completely taken apart so I could see what I could salvage from it. I tossed only the body, the pickguard, and the bridge. The most difficult and first challenge was constructing – or rather reconstructing – the neck. I decided to save the original neck, since it already had a truss rod, but I wanted to completely rebuild it. It had a funky fingerboard with plastic block inlays and ugly binding that I hated. I wanted the maple-looking fretboard instead, and a slim, comfortable neck; at that point, the huge thing looked like a baseball bat. I also needed frets. No one was selling them, and finding any would prove to be extremely difficult.

I gathered all the hand tools we had in our house and discovered that many of them were badly rusted or not suitable for what I was trying to do. The limited supply of them in our stores didn't help the situation, so I had to hit the doorsteps of my friends, gathering anything people could afford to lend me from their toolboxes. Most of my friends at that time knew about my plan to make a guitar and tried to help with any tools they had. I picked up few files, a nice hand drill, and one very old stapled-together chisel with a cracked handle but an incredible blade. Soviet chisels were made of steel, but it was such poor quality that they felt like aluminum and people had to resharpen them constantly.

Among my inventory of tools and scrapped parts from the donor guitar, I was still missing one thing: the bridge. It was absolutely impossible to find one that looked like or Blackmore's guitar, so I knew I would have to make a very close-looking one from scratch. Since I'd never had a chance to even touch an original guitar like he had with my own hands, I was completely at a loss as to what it should do and how it should function. I knew it was a tremolo bridge, but my goal at that point was not so much to make a clone, but to have a nice, playable instrument. All the fancy features were not as important to me, as long as the instrument looked nicer and played better than the ones I could have bought in our stores.

Despite my burning desire to get my guitar construction underway, I had to be patient enough to have the bridge made to my own specifications. I laid out on paper a detailed drawing of my unusual design, which had the same dimensions as the bridge on Ritchie Blackmore's guitar, only without a tremolo. I wanted it to be as simple as possible, but I was eager to make it happen. It was a wild idea, and I wasn't even sure if it would work, but there was no option other than having it custom made. My good friend Sasha's father was a machinist at the local industrial plant, and for two bottles of vodka (he refused to take cash), he took my drawings to his work to fabricate the part for me.

Getting Wood and Taking Care of Parts

At the same time, I began searching for a good source of wood for my guitar body. Taking advantage of our neglected, disorganized manufacturing plants, I hopped over fences or simply walked into the woodworking shops to ask for scrap wood. I wanted nice-looking wood that was dry. Everywhere I looked, people told me, "Come back next week," or promised to have some dry wood for me in a month. No one cared about my project as much as I did, and they were not interested in wasting their time looking for wood to donate to me. When I finally offered workers a bottle of Vodka, though, they were suddenly more motivated to help me. Unfortunately, even that kind of bribery could not change the fact that good quality wood was not readily available. All I got were soaked pieces or ugly scraps of pine – nothing close to what I needed to fashion the beautiful guitar of my dreams.

While I was hunting for a piece of wood suitable for the body of my guitar, Sasha's dad completed the bridge, and I had to make it ready for nickel plating. Every component was in a rough-milled shape, and the surface of each piece had to be smoothed, as well as holes being tapped with threads. It was yet another challenge to overcome. As far as tools to accomplish this task, I needed small needle files, a caliper, and threaders. These so-called manufacturing tools were not available in stores because our government believed the public had no need in them. For that reason, many people did not even know what these tools looked like. My only option was to buy them from someone who worked in a factory.

During my guitar-building process, I paid the people who helped me with our universal liquid currency—vodka. Considering all obstacles in getting my hands on liquor from the stores, I was fortunate to have an inventory of vodka stashed at home, my reward for the weddings I played. Every musician was given one bottle of it, and rather than drinking mine, I always saved it and took it home. I was glad I had saved it, because it helped me a great deal in my project. Two bottles were paid to friend of mine in exchange for the tools I needed to properly finish the bridge.

After the whole bridge was polished with a small piece of sandpaper, it was ready for nickel plating. How I would accomplish this stage of the process was yet another puzzle. I talked to several people, and I was advised to send my bridge to the railroad car refurbishing factory. It was very old, rugged plant located not far away from my old School # 28, near the city train station. My biggest concern was that I knew no one who worked at that factory. The only option I had was to go there myself and ask the workers to plate my parts.

Getting to the Refurbishing factory was not so difficult. The railroad tracks and partially demolished brick walls around the facility served as the common entrance for its many workers. Once I was inside, I'd have to blend in with the crowd to minimize attention from management. The standard uniform at most of our factories was any kind of rough and dirty outfit, so I used the worst old construction garb that Old Mikhail had left behind. I took my envelope full of bridge parts and headed to the factory in the morning so I would arrive when the workers did.

After sneaking onto the factory premises, I began looking for the Galvanic Department. Everything in the factory was enormous, from the cranes that were lifting railroad cars and stacks of locomotive wheels, to the other machinery and equipment. As I observed this chaotic field of giant objects, I rubbed the little bridge parts in my pocket. I could not picture how in the world someone could plate such small items in that massive environment.

When I finally found the Galvanic Department, I was surrounded by huge, oxidized, rusty bath tubs full of boiling acid. Everything was filthy, confined by century-old dirty brick walls, making it look like some underground sewage chamber. A rough-looking, unshaven man was pulling thick chains to remove plated door grills and huge parts from the brown, foamy liquid. I was afraid to even think about letting my valuable bridge be submerged in that toxic-looking sauce. The chances of my parts being lost or melted in there seemed to be a terrifying reality, considering how difficult it was for me to get and tool the parts in the first place. I was just about to give up on my plan and leave when I was stopped by a growling voice. "Hey, pal. You need anything?"

"Well," I replied, "I was wondering if you could help me plate these parts for my bicycle."

"A bicycle? What parts?"

"These," I said, as I showed him the envelope. "I'm afraid, though, that they'll melt in there in a matter of seconds, sir."

"No, they'll be fine. I plate watch parts in here, and they are even smaller. I'll do it for you for a bottle of ink," he said, referring to cheap wine.

"Sounds good," I said and handed him my envelope of parts.

"I'll drop it off in your department tomorrow. Where do you work?"

I had to make up an excuse quickly. "Uh...I am just here from the trade school, practicing. We are removing trash, so I will just come back here tomorrow with the booze for you," I said, and then I left the creepy place as quickly as I could.

The next day, I picked up the bridge and left behind a half-liter of wine. All I had to do after that was polish the matte silver coating to a shiny, bright surface. How I would do that without a buffing wheel was beyond me; I just knew it would not be easy. The solution came in the form of flat wooden sticks, on which I attached flat pieces of wool and leather. After applying brass polishing compound on it, I buffed all the parts of the bridge to a mirror shine. This was the method I adopted for nearly all of my guitar-making journey. It was my first self-made part for the guitar, and it made me even more excited about the whole project.

Working on the Neck

After the bridge was completed I decided to make the neck, which I was sure would prove to be a bit of a challenge; I was right about that. I had to refurbish the parts from the donor guitar, but the struggle of doing that was at least an iota easier than fashioning a new neck from scratch.

I ripped the old fingerboard off the neck, but to get a little plank for a new one took a lot of effort. Unfortunately, material like maple, which was used for guitar necks worldwide, was not readily available in Russia, at least not in any high quality. You could find it as a raw material, but it was riddled with mineral stains and knots. For this reason, beech wood was used a lot in the Soviet Union as an alternative for furniture and other woodcraft productions. Eventually, I found some beech wood in the basement of one of my friends. To make a fingerboard out of that piece, I would have to remove about 70 percent of its mass. I used a large wooden hand plane and sat at the kitchen table to begin shaving the surface. The work didn't go as smoothly as I would have hoped. Not only was the plane uncomfortable to work with, but it seemed to constantly lose its settings. Even when I was lucky enough for it to stay together, the dull blade hacked away at the wood, ripping chunks out of it. I tried to sharpen it on the special stone, but instead of the sharpening stone doing its job, the dull blade shaved the stone down. Finally, I tried sharpening it on a concrete step, and it worked perfectly. After I managed to get down to the right thickness on the beech wood fingerboard, I glued it to the neck, and since I didn't have a vice or any clamps, I put it under our kitchen china cabinet to press it down until the glue adhered properly.

Next, I spent a couple of days shaping the back of the neck. I needed to keep it in one place while I was working, and I tried all kinds of things to hold it down. I tied it to a stool with ropes and tried using my knee to hold it down while I crawled around it with rasps and files until the back was shaped just the way I wanted.

The next step was to create a smaller radius on the surface of the fingerboard. It was a bit puzzling how I would manage this consistent and precision task. Without any knowledge of how it was done in the real guitar-making world, I made the decision to use a small hobby plane, a piece of glass, and sheet of a sand paper. I carefully shaved the wood and made a gradual radius with a plane. I stopped when it became close but was still a bit rough. I took two sheets of sand paper and taped it to the glass. The neck was placed on it with the fingerboard down, and with a rocking motion, I managed to sand the surface to a perfect radius curve. Already, it felt like nothing I'd ever had in my hands before, but to finish it completely, there were more challenging tasks ahead.

To mark the location where the frets would go, I used the old fingerboard. I had to keep all the lines perfectly parallel, and I was wondering how I would cut the fret slots. I measured the fret's "foot," which sits in the wood, and I concluded that I did not have any saw that would be appropriate for cutting the channel for it. The only tools that might work at all were a small jewelry saw with a giant U-shaped frame and a hacksaw. One of them was impossible to keep vertical due to a massive frame, but the other had wavy teeth in its blade, which would make the channel too wide. I decided to flatten a hacksaw blade with a hammer, and after an hour of beating it while it was sandwiched between a silicon brick and a plane blade, it was completely flat. To start cutting the fret channels, I needed something very narrow that would run exactly along my pencil marks. The awkward jewelry saw was my only option. I knew I could ruin my entire project if the slots were not perfect and in the right place, so I went about the job with extra care and patience. The whole process of cutting all channels with those two crummy tools took me a whole day, but it was worth the struggle. Everything turned out perfectly parallel and clean, and my cuts were the desired depth.

I was about to begin hammering the salvaged old frets into the freshly made slots when I realized that the fingerboard face black markings had to be made first. How to make them quick and clean was another dilemma. Again, I had no any idea what kind of technique a factory would use for this step. The guitar manufacturers might have used paint, stickers, or inlayed pieces, but I had none of those at my disposal. I probably could have found paint, but painting them directly on the wood in a perfectly round shape would have been next to impossible. While I knew my creation was not going to be an absolutely perfect clone of the original, I wanted to create something of a higher quality than some school project. There was no easy solution, so I had no choice but to go through a tedious process to make the freeboard markings from raw material.

The graphite rods were made by Sasha's dad in 6-mm diameter. I cut several little pill-sized pieces from it and decided to inlay them into the wood. All I had to do was drill shallow holes and glue the markings in. If any of it hovered above the surface of the wood, I could sand it flush with the fingerboard. This would give me the perfectly round, clean circles I was looking for. The only problem now was that the drill bits I had were coarse and not suitable for woodwork; they kept walking off the centered marks. To keep them in the right place, I tried to first drill a smaller hole to use as a guide, and the trick worked! Once the holes were drilled, I glued in the black "pills", and the next day I sanded them flush with the surface of the neck. It looked great, and I finally hammered the frets into the neck. It was a very slow, tedious process with many careful steps, but I only had once chance to get it right, and the end result was more important to me than quick completion.

After that, the neck was almost done; there was only one step left before it could be finished, and that was to make the shape of the headstock. The original Musima headstock form was not only big and ugly, but it also had a faux pearly binding that I decided had to go. Since the guitar I was modeling mine after had the headstock cut out on the picture, I made my own design of this part based on shapes that were popular in those days. My goal was make it plain and simple, and after a half-hour of pencil drawings, I had come up with something that appealed to me. After fitting everything in place, I used a jewelry saw to begin trimming the shape to match my design.

While cutting the headstock, I made sure to pay close attention to the perpendicular level of all the edges. A simple right angle metal tool that I found in Old Mikhail's toolbox finally had a purpose to serve after all those years of waiting to be rusted. Working with the wood was a very pleasurable thing for me. I loved how the material could be shaped, cut, and sanded to my desirable specifications.

During the process, I was thinking how this guitar will feel and sound and could not wait to finally have it in my hands to play music. In my opinion, it was the only item that separated me from the ultimate goal - having my own rock band. I believed that everything now was much closer to my dream then ever before.

My neck was getting very close to its completion, and I reached the point where it had to be sanded. However, it was difficult to find the right grit and brand of sandpaper, which wasn't readily available in our hardware stores. It was particularly difficult to find grits that were in high demand. I had to consider myself fortunate if I found any sandpaper for sale, and I would have to buy it regardless of the grit and quality. After a long and unsuccessful search, I found help from the other of one of my good friends. How she got this sandpaper was absolutely unknown to me; that was something people in those days rarely questioned each other about. It was just an unwritten ethical rule that we did not ask anyone where they obtained the items that the government failed to deliver to our store shelves.

Final Details Before it's Painted

I had sanded the neck, but before I could paint it, I had to dress the frets and make sure they were perfectly level. To get it done with ultimate precision, I decided to use the same technique I had used when I leveled the fingerboard on a piece of glass. I turned the neck with the frets facing down, and I traced them on the glass against taped-down sandpaper. Using a needle file, I crowned each fret individually, while holding thin sheet of metal in place to protect the fingerboard. I created these guards from discarded food cans, and I had a set for every fret spacing. Instead of throwing them away, I placed them in the drawer just in case they could be used in the future for something else. They were used again, but the purpose of them never changed.

Since steel wool and masking tape were not available to us, we used electrical tape and brass brushes. I managed to adapt these two items for many different tasks during my guitar-building, but the rarity of electrical tape often complicated my project with hunts for this simple item.

After buffing the frets by hand using a piece of leather and brass polishing compound, the neck was ready for paint. It was absolutely beautiful in my opinion, with shiny frets and comfortable neck shape. Everyone who had a chance to hold it in their hands was very impressed with it, but until the body was constructed, no one could tell for certain if guitar, as a whole, would be the wonderful instrument I was hoping for.

Slow Moving Changes in Life and Guitar Construction

Many days and weeks had passed since I had begun the construction of my electric guitar. Despite the conveniences of my job, it was very boring, and I dreamt of someday having a job I would actually enjoy. I knew that becoming a professional musician and making money playing was a bit of a far-fetched and extraordinary goal in our country. My only hope at that time was the evolving course of democracy, which Gorbachev had been enthusiastically pushing. If we ever got to the point in our country when freedom would truly provide musicians a chance to make a living by playing, then my guitar could truly serve its purpose. But in the meantime, changes in the music field were not happening fast enough. We were still in the mode of making adjustments, and when things would actually come to fruition was really still in question.

In our country, the welfare and development of music as an art was not the highest priority agenda for Kremlin. Since everything was still under control of our government, music had to have the official support from financial to infrastructural perspective. Economical changes and political reforms seemed to require much more attention from the authorities and the media; like many other things, the evolution of rock music in the USSR had to take a backseat. On top of that, most people were distracted with worries about signs of inflation, which could be detected by a growing number of deficit products and escalating prices in the stores and the black market. These aspects of life mainly bothered the adult population though. My only concern back then was to finish my first guitar so I could finally have a chance to start the band and never again have to play on a borrowed "monster" instrument.

Painting the Guitar

Despite having no joy of playing films for our local news, working at the TV station was a true help to me for my project. It was so close that I could ride my bicycle to work in a matter of minutes. I had plenty of free time, and the slow pace of the work allowed me to think about what I was going to do when I got home. When I worked the first shift, I could not wait to go home and continue my project; it completely galvanized me. While I sat in our tech room during my work hours, I was meticulously planning every new step in the process of making my guitar.

I was sitting in our projecting room at work, trying to figure out what to use to apply the lacquer on my finished neck. My options were limited: I could either paint it with a regular paintbrush or try to use an airbrush. The only nitro lacquer that was for sale, NZ-328, was well known for its fast-drying ability and shockingly toxic smell. Without question, it was the finiish I had to use. In my opinion, it was somewhat cruel to brush that substance on my beautiful guitar neck, but I wasn't sure how to go about airbrushing it. I had only seen an airbrush in action a couple of times in my life. Not only was it a mysterious apparatus to me, but finding this gadget in stores would have been most problematic. Still, as I thought about the best way to paint my guitar neck, I decided to go on search for an airbrush kit.

After several unsuccessful days of roaming through practically every store in our city, with no success, I got on the phone and began calling the small villages and towns nearby. My effort was rewarded, for an art supply store in the small town of Kastukovka had an airbrush kit. I told the lady over the phone that I would come the next day to pick it up, and I was very excited about that.

The town was about an hour away by bus, so I had to take a whole day off work to make the trip. It was a nasty day, typical rainy autumn weather. All of the passengers tried to find shelter under a small tent at the bus station as they waited on the bus to stop by. When the bus to Kastukovka finally arrived, we all jammed into the crowded, steamy saloon. After a slow and hectic ride, we arrived in Kastukovka an hour or so later.

I only had one thing on my mind, so I would not come home empty handed. As soon as I left the bus, I went straight to the store and and asked a saleslady for my airbrush kit.

"I don't think we've had any of those for a long time, sir," she replied nonchalantly, picking at her nails.

"That can't be right! I called you last evening, and you told me you have them in stock!" I explained, obviously frustrated. It was an absolutely terrible and unexpected bump in my road. Not only had I wasted my time and a day of work, but the crowded bus ride had been next to torturous, and it was all for naught. I would have to go home with nothing, and it all seemed to be some kind of really bad dream.

"Oh! That was you who called? I am sorry. We put one aside for you. It will be twenty-seven rubles, please," she said, and then went to the back room to get my airbrush kit.

The happy ending to the nearly tragic adventure cheered me up. On the way home, I mentally planned how I would set things up to paint the neck. As I thought about it, I suddenly realized there was still one thing I needed, and that was an air compressor. It was truly in the category of impossible to find in our country. I had never even heard of anybody owning a real manufactured compressor. Everyone who used an airbrush at that time had to adapt a little compressor pump from a dismantled refrigerator. I had to find one of those, so the saga of painting my guitar neck had a whole new chapter to its story.

The odds of finding someone who just happened to have a broken refrigerator was less than slim. I looked through newspaper advertisements to see if anyone was selling an old refrigerator at an affordable price, but I had no luck. Then, a friend of mine introduced me to his pal Vladimir, who was nicknamed "Kholdun" (Shaman). He happened to be a guitar enthusiast and quite a handyman. He was utterly fascinated with guitar construction, but he was only interested in the bass and the electronics. When we talked about our shared obsession with guitars, I shared with him my drama about the painting process and my hunt for a refrigerator compressor. "I have one of those," he said to me. "Twenty-five rubles, and its yours."

It was marvelous! I did not even bother negotiating. It was the cost of a quarter of my monthly salary, but I wanted to finish up my project as quickly as I could. Without any delay, we went to his house, and the little scratchy air pump was riding back home with me on the trolley. As I held that treasured final piece of the puzzle, I glanced out the window. The dark night was lightened by streetlights. Old trees were flying by as the trolley took its course, and I was overcome by a wonderful feeling about the outcome of that day. Everything seemed to be falling into place. I even began to think that my failed attempt to escape to the West was not such a bad thing after all. It seemed that a brighter future was on the horizon for the Soviet Union and for me. Our country was moving toward a better life, and I was making my own electric guitar. When I finished it, there would be no one to tell me I could not play the rock music I so loved.

Under that warm feeling of euphoria, I carried my compressor back home, and I could hardly fall asleep that night as I thought about the my next step in finishing the neck.

The Fumes

Airbrushing was absolutely new to me. I'd never worked with spray equipment before, other than aerosol cans. Fortunately, the miniature, delicate airbrush was not too difficult to operate. After I bought the lacquer from the hardware store, all I had to do was find a place to do the painting. My first option was the kitchen, where there were windows for proper ventilation. When no one was home, I set up the neck on the kitchen table and tried to put the first coat of lacquer on with the airbrush. The amount of spray was so little that I had to open the airbrush throttle all the way. Big clouds of overspray fumes filled up the kitchen. I opened windows completely, but the cold wind was blowing way too hard, and the dropping temperatures began to interfere with the lacquer viscosity. The smell of the paint was absolutely horrendous. It wafted into the living room and lingered there, despite my desperate attempts to clear the air. I knew I would have to change my plans.

The only option I had left was our apartment basement, an underground facility used as a root cellar to store potatoes and canned food for the winter season. Almost every apartment building had one of these small units, about as small as a closet and only big enough to fit a few household provisions. The hallway of the basement reminded me of a World War II underground bomb shelter; in fact, it would have served as such in the event of any air strikes. It was packed with the plumbing and sewer pipes, as well as vents and valves. On occasion, the basement would flood, wreaking havoc on the whole building. While it was free from these common disasters, I could use it for my spraying project.

Located two stories underground, it was only visited by our tenants occasionally to drop off or pick up cans of food or baskets of potatoes. It was chilly down there year round, and it never got above sixty degrees.

By our root cellar, was standing a stroller, left over from my brother Mikhail's childhood. It was filled with my bicycle parts and other miscellaneous items. I made a sort of copper wire frame to attach to the neck of my guitar-to-be so it could be easily rotated around for thorough spraying. I placed the neck on the stroller, which I covered with a piece of cardboard. After hooking up the compressor, I began my paint project. Clouds of misty lacquer filled up the basement, and I had to cover my face with an old shirt so I would not breathe the noxious fumes while a thin, shiny layer of finish built up on the surface of the neck. I completed this process in intervals about a half-hour apart. The airbrush process worked out well, despite its minuscule power.

After a few hours of work and completely filling the basement with lacquer fumes, I ventured outside. The neck was still resting on the stroller, and I wasn't sure if I should keep it there overnight to dry or take it home a couple hours later. I did not want to take any chances of anybody stumbling across it, so I decided to keep it in our kitchen until it was completely dry.

Even when it was dry to the touch, the neck reeked like hell all night, and the dizzying chemical stench of the lacquer was still seeping into the living room through the closed door. Of course, my family had plenty to say about it. The aroma was giving everyone headaches, and I did feel bad about causing my family any discomfort. Thankfully, by the next day, the odor from the lacquer had drastically diminished, and all I had to do was wait until it was completely dry.

The neck looked fabulous! I had never expected the finish to be so smooth and shiny. I knew it needed to dry for another couple of weeks to be completely ready for me to clean up the frets and install its tuners. Now, all I had to do was find the wood for the body of my electric guitar—yet another hurdle I had to leap if I was going to meet my musical goals.

"No, no newspapers." and *Working on the Guitar*

Considering that the TV stations in the USSR were mostly channels of Soviet propaganda, there was no room for TV station employees to have disagreements about internal discipline and political orientations. We all had to obey to any ordinance of our administration and participate in all Union meetings and political gatherings. Most of them were mandatory, so like any other place of work, we could be punished for ignoring or missing those events. I valued my job greatly at that time not so much for its ease (to the point of being extremly boring), but for the convenience that allowed me to work on my own projects at home. I knew I could lose my job if I disobeyed the policies, so even when I didn't agree with them, I followed all requirements at work, including the useless meetings and obligations.

One such obligation, despite our government's proclamations of a new era of freedom, was the mandatory acceptance of periodicals. Every year, all Soviet organizations from elementary schools to nursing homes were obligated to sign up for an annual subscription to newspapers and magazines.

When we went to school, all of us had to read the "Zvezdochka" (*Little Star*), then the "Pioneer Pravda", and then the "Komsomol Pravda" newspapers. There was no option back then; you had no choice and had to subscribe. It was simply a "mandatory requirement of every Soviet citizen." This totalitarian tradition spanned throughout a citizen's entire lifetime, and every workplace and school enforced the propaganda delivery system. The only difference for adults was that we had our choice between three main trumpets of Communistic journalism: "Pravda" (Truth), "Trud" (Labor), or "Izvestiya" (News). The difference between them was about as profound as the difference between vodka, rum, and whiskey; they were really all hard liquor when it came to propaganda. The only minor contrast was absence of occasional naïve articles in "Pravda" about UFOs or snowmen, which began showing up in our media. Everything else was the same, with only minor rephrasing of the main political themes in the commentaries. I never liked any of these papers, and I tried to avoid having to subscribe to them, but that was simply impossible.

I decided, though, that when the next subscription time came, since we were truly supposed to be stepping into a new era of democracy in our country, I would simply refuse to sign up for any government-controlled newspapers. The manager of our Operator Room, an old regime sympathizer who was responsible for this obligation, came to me with the list of options. I told her I refused to sign up for anything I did not want. It was taken as an insult, but when I reminded her that we were no longer living under the Stalin regime, she turned several shades of red. She openly hated Gorbachev and said he would ruin our country and make us slaves to the United States forever. She was so angry that she began to threaten that I would lose my job if I did not subscribe to any of the three main newspapers. After unsuccessful attempts of trying to convince her that I had the freedom to choose, I paused and quietly said to her, "I'm sure you don't know this, but I am actually cannot read." She stormed out of my work area and never returned. I did not lose my job, and no one else bothered me about the newspapers again. While it was only a small one in the grand scheme of things, that little victory was a big one for me in my personal battle for freedom in the USSR. It was also a sign that the old regime was apparently losing a steam.

Wood from a Reliable Source

After a long and unsuccessful search for wood for my new guitar body, I had only one more option: the major wood processing furniture factory located in our city.

Winter had already reached its peak, but the amount of snow was barely visible on our streets. I took advantage of the mild weather and went to the facility, hoping to come back with just the right piece of lumber. I used the same approach to get into the factory premises as I had at the railroad plant, and I found myself standing in the middle of a giant facility under the sky, loaded with enormous logs of mahogany trees. It was quite overwhelming, to be sure. I had never seen so much wood, but finding the piece I was looking for would be like searching for the proverbial needle in the proverbial haystack.

Right in the middle of the factory was a railroad track used to deliver the colossal mahogany trees for processing; it also served as unofficial entry to the factory. I walked along the track, observing the layout and facilities of the plant. Very shortly I noticed that most of the storage racks and pallets were made from that exotic wood. The material was bought from African nations that were friendly to the USSR, for practically nothing, so its value around the factory was obviously lower than that of plywood. Because the luxurious wood was disregarded and so readily wasted at a staggering level, I was rather certain I'd be able to find what I needed. I just had to look for it.

After spending about an hour walking through the place and watching the production and manufacturing process, I noticed mahogany logs were being made into veneer that would later be used as front panel overlays on furniture made from MDF boards. It took a while to find the department where lumber was sawed. By the time I got there, it was already lunchtime, and I noticed a couple guys sitting in the improvised break room, drinking something "better than tea." I knew they might be of great help to me, so I approached them. After I explained that I was looking for a scrap of rectangular wood blank, they told me come back the next day with a bottle of booze as payment for their assistance. They were also very specific that I had to have it there before lunch. I tried to offer them payment in cash, but that was not as popular a concept in those days. At that moment, I hoped that finally, I would get my hands on the wood I'd needed for so long. I wasn't sure about using mahogany for my guitar, but since I had no idea what Ritchie Blackmore's instrument was made from, the idea didn't bother me. As long as I got a clean, dry chunk of wood in the suitable size, I would be happy.

The next day, I returned with my payment and met the men. In exchange for the booze, I was given a perfect, light-colored mahogany blank, and I was very excited. I walked around the factory to see if I could use some kind of saw to cut the shape of my guitar there, but the place was not equipped for that kind of intricate work on smaller pieces. Even such common machinery as band saws, which were readily available in places like the U.S., were nowhere in sight. After my unsuccessful search for anything to cut the body, I still wanted to at least look for any unique materials or supplies that I couldn't find in stores. When I noticed large drums of used sandpaper in the factory dumpster, I was sure I could put it too good use. I stashed all my pilfered treasures in an old bag and headed home in anticipation of starting the work on my guitar body.

Slow and Tedious Work

Cutting the shape of my guitar by hand turned out to be a slow and tiresome task. I had nothing amongst my tools that I could use besides a large hand saw, so I had to make straight cuts into the body horns and then use rasps and chisels to shape it to its final contour.

Without any clamps or vises, I first cut the body on my stool with a saw, holding it down with my knee. As I chiseled out the big chunks, I saw it slowly coming together, moving to the outlined contour. When this rough work was done, I sat on top of it and began to file it down to the right shape. Trying to keep all sides perpendicular, used the right angle to slowly approach the pencil lines I'd made.

Working on my project in the apartment instead of a workshop was not only frustrating for me, but also for everyone in the house. The noise and dust was troubling, but I tried to minimize the impact on my family by working when no one was at home.

Every day when I returned home from work, I dedicated a few hours to my project. I moved it from the kitchen to the bathroom and sometimes did some cutting in the entryway of our apartment. Within a week, the final shape of my guitar was nearing its completion. Not knowing how to make the radius bevel of the body edge, I decided to file it at forty-five degrees in a perfect quarter-inch line around the perimeter and then gradually blended it to comfortable contours with sandpaper. It worked very well, and my guitar was starting to take a refined shape right before my eyes, looking better and better with every passing day of work.

When it was time to undertake the task of carving a neck pocket into the body, I knew it would be a very crucial procedure. Not only did the neck have to be perfectly centered and aligned in reference to the bridge, but it also had to have a very tight fit. All the walls of the pocket had to be perfectly square and smooth. My chisel was not the right tools for this task, and after a vigorous search for something better in the stores, I had to settle on the poor Soviet excuse for these instruments. Their plastic handles were attached to a low-grade steel. I made them as sharp as I could, and even though I had to re-sharpen them every ten minutes, I could at least continue my work.

Moving with a great deal of care, I was carving away wood while sitting on the bathroom floor. I knew a mistake at this point, no matter how small, would be quite costly. After spending so much time finding the wood and making the body shape, I could not afford to ruin it. Slowly, the depth of the pocket increased. I left extra material on the sides so I could make the walls absolutely perpendicular. To finish it, I took a square wooden block, placed it right on the pencil line, and held the chisel against it to trim the walls in a perfect ninety-degree angle. After sanding all the walls this way and finishing with sand paper, the neck pocket was finally complete. I fitted the neck to the body with an airtight tolerance, and I could not believe how well it fit. My guitar could finally be admired and held, all in one piece. The first time I held it with the neck in place, it felt like a dream. Everything—from the balance to the comfort of it—was amazing, like something I've never experienced before. I was absolutely thrilled with the progress, but I knew the more difficult and tedious work was ahead for me before the instrument was completed.

Destroyed Body and Finishing the Guitar

My next step in the process of making my guitar was to carve out the electronics compartment. All the pickups, switches, and control pots had to sit under the pickguard. Without ever having a chance to get a close look at a real american guitar, I was obviously unaware of the internal routings as well. The contour of the pocket resembled a pool shape, and it was the biggest and most complex project, involving wood removal with chisels.

After arming myself with my small arsenal of hand tools, I sat in the bathroom, placed the guitar on the floor, and began digging out the wood. Everything went well, and by the end of the first day of work, I'd made great progress.

A couple of days later, I was very close to completing the entire electronics chamber, but then my doorbell rang. I opened the door and saw our neighbor, Vitaly, who lived right below us. Not only was he our neighbor, but he was also employed by the KGB. "Hi, Yuriy," he said with a sneaky smile. "What in the world are you making, pal?" he asked as he tried to peek through the door.

"I am making a bookshelf," I replied, dusting off my shirt.

"You've been banging around for so long you could have made a whole library by now!"

"Well, it's a bit complicated," I said, trying to close the door before he had a chance to barge in.

"Can you show it to me when it's done?"

"You will be first to see it," I said and shut the door.

Despite the fact that he was a KGB worker, I was skeptical that he would try to cause trouble simply because I'd been pounding on the floor. His wife was a good friend of my grandma's, so I was sure he would not go to the extent of involving the secret police to quiet down someone building an innocent bookshelf. However, I didn't want anyone questioning my activities and having any suspicion that I was creating something dangerous. I had to make some changes to keep myself out of trouble.

The entire electronics pocket was nearly finished, and it was almost the right depth. I still wanted to finish it up that day, but I didn't want to see Vitaly again. To avoid any complaints from him or anyone else about the noise, I placed a thick blanket under my guitar, assuming it would soften and insulate the blows I was making when hammering the wood with a chisel. A few minutes later, I would come to discover that my idea was a big and costly mistake; the thin wood at the bottom of my guitar electronics chamber crushed under strike of my chisel. With only a soft blanket underneath and no solid support, the wood just collapsed as if someone had stepped on it.

The horror that I was observing was very difficult to describe. I was as crushed as the guitar was, hoping it was just a terrible nightmare that I would wake from any moment. All that struggle and hard work was a total waste. I could not stop condemning the blanket, the neighbor, and myself for the foolish mistake. The prospect of trying to make another body at that moment was not even going through my mind. All I could do was sit on the floor and look at all the work I had done and the effort that went into it. "That stupid KGB got me even when I was making my guitar," I was saying to myself, ready to cry out of desperation. I looked at my destroyed guitar and did not even know what to do next. When that catastrophe happened, it was so disheartening that I was on the verge of forgetting about all my music playing dreams.

It felt like the whole project had come to a bitter end, but when I took the neck into my hands, something happened inside of me, and my sadness turned into anger—the same anger that probably fills an athlete's mind after failing to achieve the record score. I considered my unfortunate mistake with an attitude of revenge. I realized that after I'd dedicated so much work to my guitar, I would have to put in extra effort to finish what I'd started. While it was very unfortunate and accidental mistake, I knew it was not the worst thing that could have happened in my life. If I was going to give up on something as insignificant as a broken guitar body, I would never be able to face much more difficult challenges that life would present to me. Realizing this, I packed up all my tools, dumped the body in the trash, and went to sleep.

One More Body and Struggling with Tools

The next morning, I took a day off and went to the furniture factory. I had my liquid currency in hand for the wood for a new guitar body. I repeated my tale at the factory again, and by lunch I was holding a new blank of wood for my guitar. I knew I had to forget about the misfortune that had happened and forced myself not to think about it. All of my concentration had to be focused right on the new body, and I had to pretend the first one simply didn't exist. After the accident, it became far more than a guitar-building project; it became a test of my dedication and patience.

After just a couple of weeks of working on it, I was already back to the point where the disaster had happened the first time. To avoid any trouble with complaints about the noise, I did my pounding with a chisel only in the morning, when our nosey neighbor was busy chasing so-called enemies of the state at his KGB office. The second time, I made much quicker progress, and all the techniques I'd used the first time were refined and improved.

After finishing the electronics chamber, the only remaining step was to carve out the little "pocket" for an output jack. Fortunately, the donor Musima guitar had the same style output as was used on the Blackmore's guitar. The only trouble was that I hadn't the proper tools for making this "pocket". It had to be carved with some sort of scoop-style chisel, and I only had a small quarter-inch flat one. With it, I dug a triangular recess in the guitar body and could not go any deeper. I needed a special cutting tool that I'd never even seen in my life. I tried everything I could think of from my house and the houses of my friends to adapt some kind of instrument for this task, but in the end, I was once again stuck for lack of the right tools for my project.

A couple days later, we were having a family dinner. The traditional grechnevaya kasha had been my favorite meal since I was a little boy. While eating, I could not stop thinking about the missing tool I needed to finish my work on the guitar. As I poked my spoon into my plate of kasha, I suddenly realized, "Yes! I need something this shape—something with a curve on a blade". I looked at the spoon handle and instantly saw exactly what I'd been looking for. It had a gently curved shape with a little concave radius across its handle's width. All I would have to do would be sharpen the end. I flipped it over and realized the scoop part of the spoon sat perfectly and comfortably in the palm of my hand.

An hour after dinner, I was honing the end of a spoon handle against a silicon brick. The quality of the stainless steel was incredible. After working on it for about half an hour, the tip of the handle finally began looking like a professional carving gouge chisel. Without any delay, I began using it to carve a little cave in the body for the jack output. While it still tried to bend in the middle, the spoon helped me carve out that hard-to-reach area of the cavity pocket. When I used it in conjunction with my small chisel, it worked out great, and I was finished in only a couple of hours. The jack plate fit perfectly, and after digging a little deeper to make room for the cable jack, I could finally look proudly at my completed body.

Final Steps in Finishing the Guitar

After locating a bridge placement and drilling holes for it, the neck plate, and the strap buttons, I had to paint the body. Winter had truly gripped us, and the cold temperatures prevented me from being able to successfully use my airbrush, so I began looking for an alternative way to accomplish this step in my guitar-building project. I remembered seeing a paint shop in the furniture factory, and I wondered if they would be able to paint my guitar. Armed with a "liquid cash" inside of my coat, I went to the factory talk to someone who worked in paint department. The plan worked out very well, and in a few days, I picked up my painted guitar from the furniture factory. How they managed to apply the clear lacquer was a mystery to me. The finish looked very even, but it wasn't as shiny and luster like on my neck. Considering that I had no other options, I decided to leave it, because it still looked very nice.

The only thing remaining before I could try my guitar for the first time was to make a pickguard and install all the electronics. I did not expect the search for the simple plastic material for my pickguard to be such a drama, but it was. Taking into account that raw material of that nature was never available for sale, the only choice I had was to fashion it out of some other kind of plastic object.

I had no any preference of color, but I knew white would make for a very cool-looking guitar. Around my house, I didn't have too many items to choose from though. When none of my friends had any suitable material that I could use as well, I decided to reach out to some of the folks I played salad gigs with. One of the guys I knew, had a stash of old electronics in his closet. I got lucky when I came across a bobbin-type tape recorder cover. It was a perfect size, and more importantly, it was white. He proudly donated it to me fore a great cause.

It was not a very complicated procedure to make a pickguard from it, and after I cut it with my large jewelry saw, I began installing the electronics on it.

Everything was going very well, but one part of the pickguard was missing from my version. The pickups switch, which looked like a blade on Blackmore's guitar, made no sense to me. I'd never seen anything like that in my life, and the three-way toggle switch that came with the Musima guitar was my only option. I cut it shorter so it wouldn't stick out so high and installed it, along with the Musima pickups and pots. The knobs and tuner keys also came form my donor guitar, and I was lucky that I was even able to retrieve enough screws from it as well. After fitting everything on my pickguard, the long-awaited process of putting the guitar together had arrived.

My first self made guitar.

Minute by minute my new guitar was coming together, and the excitement of finishing my very own electric guitar had my pulse whirring like a race car. I could not remember a moment in my life when I'd been so happy. After so many years of dreaming and hoping, right there, before my very own eyes, my electric guitar was becoming a reality.

The final setup and tuning took me a whole day, but the second everything was finished, I strummed it with a gentle sway. The brilliant tone of the strings, fresh from the black market, rang quietly through the living room. It sounded as beautiful as it looked, and I could not wait to plug it into my old Minsk tube radio. When I did, it absolutely came to life. The tone and resonance of my guitar was like nothing I'd ever played before. I could not believe I was strumming an instrument I'd built with my own two hands, and it was absolutely magical feeling. The way it played and the comfort of it was far beyond that of any guitar I'd ever held before. Everything about it, from the way it sustained to the tone of it, captivated my mind and soul. I couldn't stop looking at every single part of it, and as I did, I realized that all the trouble I had to go to to accomplish the task was being repaid to me. I was rewarded for my dedication and patience with a beautiful-looking, quality-sounding instrument. I was one step closer to my dream of playing in an independent rock band. I had no any idea, however, that the guitar I'd crafted would truly change my life and would turn out to be something I never expected.

After playing the guitar for a couple of hours, I still could not put it down. My family members could not stop praising my work and craftsmanship, but I wondered what they truly saw in my guitar. Receiving compliments and encouragement from your mother or grandma is the universal norm; I needed the opinions of my friends who knew little bit more about electricguitars, and they could not wait to try it out.

When it's All Done

Everyone reacted to my guitar as if I'd made a time machine. All of my guitar-playing friends were very impressed, but none of them had ever played on a real Western-made guitar or even seen one. For them, my Blackmore-inspired guitar was something from a different world in quality and appearance. I valued their opinions, of course, but I wanted feedback from someone who'd owned or even just played a professional American or Japanese electric guitar, so they could contrast my instrument to the real thing.

I finally found a guitar player in our city who had once owned an Ibanez instrument, and I took my creation to him for a test drive. After few minutes of playing it, he said he really liked my guitar. I was a bit skeptical of his reaction, assuming he was just trying to be nice to me, but when he asked me if I want to sell it, I knew he was serious. Surprisingly, his request sounded a bit disparaging to me. After all the effort and work I'd poured into making my guitar, it was like a child to me, and the thought of selling it seemed to be a cruel notion. I'd dreamt of owning it for so many years and now, not only did I own an electric guitar, but I was on the threshold of another lifelong goal: playing in a real rock band. I took his feedback and his offer to by as a truthful evaluation of my work, and I went home with only one plan in mind. I was ready to start a new music career.

Chapter 18

Chernobyl

Nothing is more frustrating than unaccomplished dreams, especially when no mater what you do, your goal just keeps slipping away from you in spite of your persistence and efforts.

The dream of having my own band was about to come true. I already had people lined up who were ready to take another chance to play the rock music that had, for so many years, been a taboo in our country. I finally had a guitar – one I'd fashioned with my very own hands – and it inspired and influenced me and equipped me to play better. I felt like nothing could stop me from reaching my musical goals. The only obstacles I thought I might have to deal with were lacking a place for rehearsals or maybe personal problems of my future band mates; but alas, as is often the case, trouble came from where I least expected it. I had no idea that I would be a witness to a truly cataclysmic drama, like something straight out of a horror movie, but what happened in the USSR in the spring of 1986 made an impact not only on my plans with the band, but also on the lives of people in our country and abroad.

In one April's night, I was sitting at my good friend Pavel's house, watching the evening news while we played backgammon. When the anchor made an announcement that an "accident" had occurred at the nuclear power plant in Chernobyl, it instantly caught our attention. This sort of news had never been made on our public TV programs. According to the news report, the situation was "under control," and authorities were "working on establishing power and technical order." Even though the reporter seemed to deliver the news in a casual, relaxed way, as if it was just the average run-of-the-mill news story, we knew it may have been a lot worse than he portrayed; it was typical of our media to try and water down tragic events so as not to cause alarm or political unrest.

Pavel was instantly very concerned. "Do you know where Chernobyl is?" he asked, rising to his feet.

"I have no idea," I replied, assuming it was somewhere far off in Siberia.

"It's about 70 miles from here!" he shouted, worried and shocked.

I simply stared at him in disbelief.

The TV news report was intentionally delayed by the government and came to us a couple of days after the incident, an attempt to try and localize the scale of the catastrophe. The only information we had was what we were told in official reports, which were a bit inconclusive. Some leaks of radiation were reported, but we were told there was "no threat to human lives." People hoped that under the new Glasnost reform (Gorbachev's freedom-of-speech initiative), the media would be more honest, so everyone trusted what we were being told.

A few days after the accident, a friend of mine invited me to go on a road trip with his family, sixty miles west to the bordering Russian small town, a shopping trip for new clothes. In those days, the rural areas in the Soviet Union often had a better supply of goods for shopping as a means to lure people to move to the villages and make their homes there. When we decided to take that hour-long drive, we hoped the potential radiation would stay south of us. Of course, that was not the case, for on that innocent shopping trip, we witnessed disturbing things that would forever haunt our memories.

Soon after our departure, we noticed many military trucks and soldiers on both sides of the road. They were wearing anti-radioactive protective uniforms and were hosing down the houses with some kind of greenish substance. Along the road every forty meters were signs warning, "Do Not Pull Over." We realized then that we had made a big mistake by taking that trip. When we arrived at the village, the atmosphere there was so intense that our shopping trip turned into an immediate retreat. The villagers were worried, talking about the military personal and the spread of radiation. Realizing that it was a much more complicated situation than our government was telling us, we rushed back home.

May First parade was to be held in our city, as always drawing a large crowd. We were told that no one should fear radiation in Gomel and that everything was under control in Chernobyl. But at the same time those deceitful words were leaving their mouths, wind was blowing radioactive clouds right over our city, showering deadly nuclear dust on hundreds of thousands of Russians who were cheering and marching in the streets, unaware that they were being poisoned by the very air they were breathing.

At the same time, no one knew for sure what was really happening in Chernobyl, and our local TV station was only allowed to give the "official Moscow" reports on nuclear incident story. If anything was different from the central TV information on this topic in our news from Gomel, it was our short reports about the "positive effort of our government in containing the Chernobyl accident."

The Truth About the Accident's Scale

The only reliable sources of information in that case were the short-wave Western radio stations. Despite all efforts to capture Voice of America, Radio Liberty, or BBC from London, all we could hear was the blasting jam of the major broadcasting companies. A couple days later, at intermittent intervals, the signals could be heard. What we learned from these more accurate and honest reports was that the horror of the massive disaster was taking much more gruesome shape. Scandinavian states like Sweden and Norway, as well as other European nations, reported a spike in radiation levels in their countries. If it was much higher than normal as far as thousands miles away from us, we knew that our city, which was only an hour's drive from Chernobyl, was probably suffering from extraordinarily high and dangerous levels of radiation.

The intentional hiding and glossing over of crucial information in those first days about the situation in our region struck a major blow to the people's newly established trust in Gorbachev and his government. While the official media continued to claim that the scale of the incident was "exaggerated by Western propaganda," people were panicking because they knew the truth. The traditional tactics of Soviet misinformation, tricks, and deceit had to be resurrected to calm public fears. Desperately trying to avoid any chaos, officials fabricated stories about "minimal radioactive contamination around the nuclear plant," even though those who lived closest to the disaster were instructed to evacuate by those same officials.

The situation in Gomel was getting very intense. Anxiety and fear over our safety spawned a variety of rumors. To separate the true facts from gossip was nearly impossible, and everyone hoped that whatever the calmer, gentler story the government was telling us was the truth. People began to fear a "total meltdown" of the reactor that might result in a nuclear explosion. No one knew for sure if this could happen, but when we heard about a secret "emergency evacuation plan" of the entire city, the fears of many people seemed to be confirmed. Supposedly, if the failed reactor were to melt through its foundation and seep into the ground water, there might be a great chance of an explosion, like a nuclear bomb. The validity of these rumors was very difficult to verify, but through our TV station administration, our small crew was told that "all options, including a city-wide evacuation are being considered." If the evacuation was ordered, we would all have to leave Gomel immediately. Everyone would be instructed to go to the city train station, to be boarded onto cargo trains. All private and public traffic would move only in one direction, north, delivering people from their jobs and homes. This contingency plan for the disaster, the government claimed was not dangerous, was never revealed to the public and remained classified in order to minimize the spread of panic.

"Keep the windows closed."

Even though there were no official orders to evacuate, many people who had a chance to leave town did so – in a hurry. My mother and grandmother discussed sending my brother and me to Rostov to stay with relatives. The only problem was that it was almost impossible to get tickets to any outside destination. On top of that, we were still under passport regime residence law in the USSR, so simply moving to another city to take up residence without a permit was impossible. The controlling, prison-like system limited people's migration and prevented many of our citizens from seeking safety in this drastic situation. The only chance for any of us to seek other residence outside of Gomel was if an official evacuation order was to be issued. Until then, everyone who left the city on his or her own would have to return to Gomel or deal with our draconic laws.

While common sense and survival instinct was inciting people to save their own health and lives by escaping the dangerous situation, the inertia of human mentality held many of us in place. Even some of the people who were specifically told to evacuate from their villages and small towns close to Chernobyl refused to leave their homes. In many such cases, it was the elderly citizens who did not want to leave everything that they had behind.

Despite that the danger of a nuclear explosion in Chernobyl eventually dissolved, the fear and frustration still haunted our citizens. The media, still working under official guidance to try and calm down the anxiety, assured everyone that the situation was under control and that the level of radiation was "not dangerous." The radio, and even the TV station where I work, advised the public: "Keep the windows closed, avoid traveling to natural areas, limit your time outdoors, and you will be safe."

It was also interesting to observe how wishy-washy and hypocritical Soviet education of the masses about the exposure to radiation was. For years, we'd heard heartbreaking stories from our government about the nuclear bombing of Hiroshima and Nagasaki by the United States. We'd been told for all that time that even slight exposure to radiation greatly affected the Japanese people, causing them to suffer from long-term health problems and even death. When the Chernobyl incident occurred, our "experts" suddenly changed their story, claiming that not many people in Japan was exhibiting any effects from the nuclear bombing in that country. We did not know which story we were suppose to believe, but the skepticism about the reliability of our media did not allow us to trust them very much. At that time we didn't know that the level of radioactive fallout from Chernobyl was 400 times greater than Hiroshima's nuclear bombing.

In theory, since I worked at the TV station, I should have been closer than anyone to the truth of the situation in Gomel. In reality, though, we knew only a little more than the general public. The only real glimpses we got of the Chernobyl disaster came from the restricted travel of our film crew to the contaminated regions. Every day, we were given a list of places where we could not longer go, and that list continued to grow.

In an attempt to provide answers and comfort to our frustrated viewing audience, our city invited a professor from the capital to do an open-phone Q & A session on the air with our residents. Unfortunately, he only shared the same nonsense about the "exaggerated fear of radiation," yet it was clear he could not wait to get out of our city. When the program was over, many of the staff at the television station asked him about true level of danger in our situation. He looked very uncomfortable and began to sweat, and then he told us, "If I were you, I would leave now."

Dealing with Radiation

People tried desperately to find solutions to prevent their health from being harmed from radiation. Iodine was thought to minimize the risk of thyroid cancer, so it wasn't long before the iodine supply in the city was depleted. Everyone – young and elderly alike – applied it to sugar cubes and ate it daily. Another popular belief was that vodka was the best weapon for fighting the radioactive isotopes, so some took many doses of such "medication." Despite doctors' warnings about iodine poisoning and the nonsense of the "healing power" of vodka, people were desperate to try any kind of remedy to protect themselves from contaminated air and food.

The most distressing reality of life was the lack of "clean" groceries in our stores. Some of the food labels said, "For Adults Only"; these foods were known by the government to carry "a slight level of radiation" and were not supposed to be consumed by children. Shoppers insisted on buying all of the "clean foods". The warnings kept people from buying those particular "labeled" produces, leaving no "uncontaminated" for the children. What was truly happening with the "clean" foods meant for children was anybody's guess, just as it was anybody's guess if it was really having radiation in it or not.

It would be unfair to say that the government was doing nothing to contain the nuclear fallout or was not helping people who were victims of this tragedy. To minimize the risk of radiation poisoning and to give us a chance to know if we had been exposed to dangerous levels, our largest regional hospital offered checkups. I happened to be in that area visiting a friend and passed by the hospital decided to see how the procedure was done.

As soon I entered the hospital premises, I got into a long line of people who were waiting for a checkup. There had to be at least 200 in line, which stretched so far that we couldn't even see where we were going. When I asked if it was the right line for radiation tests, an elderly man turned to me and said, "If you want that done, you should do it now. I was told there were only a couple dozen folks here this morning, but the line gets longer every hour."

Someone behind us shouted for us to make way, and hospital personnel were carrying several children on stretchers. Behind them was a crowd of commonly dressed country people, many of whom were crying and begging the doctors to save their kids. They had just arrived by bus from the contaminated zone, and apparently the whole hospital was full of those poor victims of Chernobyl.

The line to the area where doctors were doing exams moved rather quickly. There was no special office for this procedure, and everything was done right at the end of the hallway. When I got closer to the exam spot, I saw two doctors taking measurements with a tubular device that resembled a police flashlight. They stuck the device in a person's throat and then looked at the display that was attached to the tube by a cable. Once they examined the display, they said either, "Okay," or, "On the left." We had no idea what the normal result of the test was and only assumed it had to be dangerously high to get the attention of doctors. They did not ask the people in line for any names or information. Those who were told to go to the door on the left obviously had a high level of radiation in their thyroids and had to remain in the hospital. I saw only few people going "to the left," and we could see the distress on their faces when they were told to stay.

When I finally reached the exam area, a doctor stuck the metal rod into my throat. After looking at the display she shouted, "Next!" and I ran back to the exit with in great relief. The line was already backed up clear outside of the hospital, and another bus from the contaminated zone, escorted by police, pulled into the hospital courtyard.

When I returned home, I told my family to go and have a checkup done. Grandma and my mom would not even consider it, but they told my brother Misha to have the test done right away. He came back with a good result as well, but the claws of Chernobyl reached him twenty years later when he, like many other people from our region, "lost" his thyroid.

Healthy Food

Sad as it was, dealing with radiation became the norm. People began getting used to current radiation levels being mentioned in our weather reports. In most of these reports, radiation was always"within appropriate level". It became "normal," and the majority of our citizens either ignored it or wished to believe that it was the truth. Gradually, the government found a way to keep the anxiety of our citizens under control. They began releasing bits and pieces of information about the post-accident cleanup and constantly assured people that level of radiation was dropping, and this helped to put a stop to the spread of panic. The fear of radiation among our citizens, however, never fully went away.

The biggest concern of our people was the quality and safety of our food supply, and local authorities were doing their best to minimize the chance of contaminated products reaching our tables. While at the collective Soviet farms and food processing factories it was done with a certain level of a reliable control, the situation in our farm markets was totally different. These places were our most popular source of vegetables, fruit, and garden products, which were brought there for sale by local farmers. The produce came from places where the level of radiation was never checked or areas that were believed to be unaffected. Because the foodstuffs were not checked for safety, people feared that practically everything offered by the village people contained radiation.

Since our stores were not capable of providing enough food for the population, it was economically impossible to ban the sale of all agricultural products at these markets. Unfortunately, no one knew for sure what the quality was of the food being sold there, and something had to be done to get the issue under control. Thus, special "inspection crews" were dispatched to the entrances of the markets, and everyone who went there with items to sell had to allow their products to be checked for radiation. Many popular items like berries, mushrooms, and homemade dairy produce had to be inspected thoroughly before being placed for sale in the open markets.

This at least gave our people some degree of assurance that everything sold at the farm markets was "clean." However, when the rumors spread that inspectors were letting anybody go for five to ten rubles, additional "inspectors" of "inspectors" were sent to the market to verify these claims of bribery. With the high level of corruption that had historically existed in our farm markets, no one believed that every single basket of vegetables and fruits was checked for radiation. Unfortunately, though, some people relied on what the sellers told them: As long as an old babushka said her mushrooms were from the "cleanest place on Earth," she'd have no trouble selling them to those who believed her.

Reading the Radiation Rays

Nothing what we heard from our government about the situation around our erupted nuclear station could be fully trusted. The Western radio stations did not have a lot of confirmed information on the topic, but we still learned much more truth from them than from our propaganda machine. Despite proclaiming "freedom of speech", media was still under the control of government and reported only on what has been allowed. All areas surrounding the incident were blockaded from reporters, so to say exactly what was happening there was impossible. To get some independent information on our ecological situation, people tried to obtain dosimeters, devices used to test radiation levels. These instruments were never sold to the public, and only officers in the Soviet army had access to them. Those who were fortunate enough to be close to military personnel claimed the level of radiation in our city was all over the place.

To verify these claims was very difficult without actually having a dosimeter. People began to construct these devices on their own, and anyone who had such ability could rake in a great deal of money. A good friend of mine, Oleg, was a big electronics buff. After finding a schematic of the instrument, he made one of this extremely valuable items for himself. It was a small rectangular box with an LED display showing the level of radiation when it came in contact with any surface. Walking around the city and measuring the level of radiation proved the stories that the levels were extremely sporadic. In just a matter of 100 yards, there were dozens of different readings. When the dosimeter was placed on the ground or various objects, the levels jumped from normal to hundreds times above allowable limits. Most of the contamination seemed to be in the areas where rain water had puddle. Altogether, though, Oleg's homemade dosimeter made it clear that things were not as "normal" as our government claimed. This fact did not surprise us: Once again, we were assured that information coming from abroad about the situation in and around Chernobyl was much more reliable than from our "reformed" Soviet media.

Life After the Chernobyl Disaster

With summer fast approaching, many schools, daycares, and kindergartens were moving to other parts of the USSR to minimize the potential health risks to children. The government-sanctioned summer camps and resorts served as shelters for our kids and for the people who were evacuated from around Chernobyl. Many Russian citizens also opened their homes to those evacuees who had nowhere to go, and there was a vast emergence of hospitality. Unfortunately, as is the case in any society, some had no compassion for the victims of this disaster and kept their distance, ostracizing them for being "radioactive." It was very painful to hear stories of those who went on the Black Sea and were refused rental places due to the fact that they came from the contaminated zone.

While some people were afraid to even talk to the Chernobyl victims, other residents from our region did not even try to stay away from the harm of radiation. This was mainly due to a low level of education and misunderstanding of the radiation concept in general. The biggest problem was that radiation could not be felt, seen, or observed. For these naïve folks, radioactive contamination was something like dust or dirt. They assumed it would eventually evaporate like smoke or fog. Believing that it could be washed, dissolved, or filtered, they thought they could combat it just by thoroughly cleaning their homes and possessions and bodies. Washing hands and vacuuming a floor was not a viable solution, but many considered this a suitable precaution and thought they were safe from danger.

It was a very dramatic situation where people, and people looked at it with two extremes: Either they thought everything was bathed in radiation and unsafe, or they assumed it wasn't there simply because they couldn't see or feel it – yet. Many even ignored official warnings not to travel to certain areas for fishing or mushroom or berry picking. The tragic reality was that those people were acting based on self-denial of the great danger or reckless negligence. It was almost surreal.

As the result of this disaster, the true scale of the catastrophic accident was at a level none of us knew at the time, living in Gomel. Many years later, after the collapse of the Soviet Union, the horrendous aftermath of Chernobyl was revealed from independent and declassified sources...

In Chernobyl, when the first brigade of fire fighters arrived to extinguish the blazing radioactive fire, they were not even told about the danger of radiation. Two days later, twenty-eight of those heroes were already dead. They received such a high dose of radiation that their bodies had to be buried in led coffins, welded shut.

Sixty percent of all radioactive fallouts landed on Belarusian soil, mainly around Gomel. Countless number of families had to run from the deadly rays of Chernobyl, leaving behind all their possessions in their forever-lost villages and towns. Over 250 villages and towns were evacuated, and many were bulldozed to the ground in attempt to stop the spread of radiation. None of them will be inhabited again for many centuries. Millions of livestock had to be slaughtered and burned due to a high level of radiation in their bodies.

Twenty years later, over 60,000 people who were involved in the liquidation of Chernobyl's aftermath are now dead. The number of civilians whose deaths were directly related to radiation is in hundreds of thousands. An area the size of the state of Connecticut, or 22 percent of all Belarusian lands, is still closed, declared and remaining a dangerously contaminated zone. Today, my Gomel is the home of the nation's largest oncology research center, and the prevalence of thyroid cancer there is 80 times greater than in the rest of the world.

It is difficult to find any family in the Gomel region that has not lost a loved one or been affected by illness resulting from the Chernobyl disaster. For many years, thousands of people in Gomel received free milk as compensation for radiation. Years later, the complete truth about the long-term consequences of the disaster still has not been told. The scale of this tragedy and its effect on public health is still a source of great debates between the Belarus government and independent scientists.

The catastrophe of Chernobyl and how our government delivered information about it to the public had a great impact on my opinion of the changes Gorbachev was allegedly promoting. Our government's refusal to disclose to the public important and vital information about the disaster until few days after its occurrence was proof of their own selfish agenda. The lies and misleading data about the accident were intended to protect the government's interests, its image, and the nuclear energy industry.

Trying to cover up the catastrophe and forcing people to march under a radioactive sky during the May First celebrations was a profound and cruel crime against our citizens. How many lives and people's health could have been saved by simply informing everyone about the true danger in the air? Sadly, we will never know. And even more sadly, no one has ever been rightfully punished for withholding information and for spreading false information about the health dangers in the towns and villages where the Soviet people made their homes. The true tragedy of the Chernobyl crisis was the dishonesty of the government that covered it up because they were too cowardly to tell the truth.

The Soviet Union, at least in my eyes, remained the same authoritarian state with no real freedom of speech. I could no longer trust the libertarian speeches of our leaders after observing the despicable lies surrounding the Chernobyl situation. The system fell short in proving that we were a new nation where human life was the highest priority and concern of our government.

No More Dreams About a Rock Band

Life changed shortly after the Chernobyl explosion, and I felt uncertain not only about a better future life in our country, but also about creating a rock band. All those plans obviously had to stop when the disaster happened, but even after the panic and fear began to subside, the world around us was no longer as we knew it. After that horrible catastrophe, everything seemed like some huge drama that we all had a role in, some theatrical play that would eventually come to an end, and the cold Soviet life we once knew would grasp us again in its icy, dominating claws.

While people tried to adapt to our "radioactive era," our values, priorities, and reasons for living became significantly different after the tragedy. I was still in love with music, but the dream of becoming a rock musician no longer dominated my thoughts. Of course I would have loved to rock out with my new guitar in my hands, but the aftermath and changes resulting from the Chernobyl disaster began to dictate a different path in my life.

Life Moving Along

A few months after the Chernobyl disaster, we all gradually accepted the reality of living with the consequences. It is human nature to comfort ourselves with assurances that in spite of circumstances, everything will get better. That, coupled with our government constantly preaching to us that the ecological situation in our region was improving, many of us began to believe it. Personally, however, I did not feel as confident as some of our citizens were in a speedy recovery after an accident of such magnitude and with such dire troubles. Applying common sense and knowledge about the danger of radiation, I knew that life would probably never be the same again. In spite of my doubts, though, our only choice was to talk about it and move on—to continue living and busying ourselves with our daily routines, much like the way Americans had to after that fateful 9/11.

The same summer, I met my future wife Natasha. We began dating each other, a practice still considered romantic and traditional for such a relationship at that time. We never had shopping malls to walk around in, and we had no amusement parks to have some fun. Serious relationships in that Soviet world involved buying flowers and walking around the city before the sunrise. It was very different time: Girls acted like grownup ladies, adorning themselves in makeup and fancy dresses, and they expected boys to be gentlemen and treat them like grown women. In those days, old-school etiquette was still in place, and men—young and old—would open doors for a woman, help her to her seat, and walk with her arm under his. It was normal to kiss a girl's hand. The courtship we practiced in those days is a thing of the past now, and there were some social faux pas. For instance, it was considered rude to show up on a date without flowers or to ask a girl's age unless we were very close to her. These dating customs may sound outdated and old-fashioned today, but it was how our society functioned, and I followed the protocol when I was dating Natasha.

Chapter 19

Making Guitars is My New Passion and "Business"

In spite of all the changes in my life, and all the ups and downs, the one thing that remained relatively constant was my affection for music. Even though I hadn't yet reached my goal of becoming a rock musician, I played guitar all the time, and my music-loving friends adored, admired, and envied my first handmade electric guitar. They were so persistent in pressuring me to sell it to them that I realized, "Hey, if I made this guitar, why not make another?" I knew I could do it again, and there was something mysterious and alluring in the process of making my first instrument that drew me back to my tools and create it one more time.

I truly enjoyed the process of building it in the first place, even though I had to go through some difficulties and problems to get to that point. The fact that I overcome the drama with my first broken body and managed to make a new one inspired me to take on even more serious and challenging tasks. This time, I wanted to complete the instrument from scratch without any help from a donor guitar. It would be a different approach, and everything had to be prepared methodically. All of my materials, parts, and finishing processes would have to be in place. The idea of making a new guitar for someone who wanted to buy it began building up in my mind.

To people who wanted to buy a guitar from me, I promised to produce it for half of what a Japanese-made instrument would cost on the black market. At that time, the fixed price of 2,000 rubles was equal to about $100, almost double my annual salary at the TV station. My desire to make another guitar had nothing to do with making money; it was more of an adventure and another complicated challenge which I wanted to tackle.

It was a Crime

Considering that my guitar-making venture was now an underground business, of sorts, I knew I would not only have to deliver high-quality work, but also do it in complete secrecy. Such entrepreneurship would have been frowned upon by the government, and authorities would not tolerate it. Regardless of Gorbachev's promises and initiatives, we were still a truly Communistic society, with anti-Capitalistic ideas and dogmas still being pounded into our heads every day.

Thus, any profit made outside the realm of the government's control was still considered a criminal act, punishable by long sentences or worse, as the government had a habit of attaching extra indictments to charges against citizens, even if they were not relevant or accurate. Since producing and selling our own merchandise on an independent or freelance basis went against the constricting grain of our political and moral Communistic principles, it could also be treated as a political crime. No one in the USSR could escape such a charge without serving some jail time.

The only dim light on the horizon that would involved a different form of employment at that time was talk of Gorbachev about limited private enterprise called Cooperatives. First such experimental ventures were established in Moscow, but for our city this new initiative was nothing more than just a media talk.

I had to take a new, much more serious approach to my guitar-building projects, considering all the consequences that could follow if I got caught fabricating my own product with intent to sell. I was not very thrilled about such risk and danger, yet I could not resist a temptation to work on a new guitar and I could not simply "give away" my labour.

Gathering Best Tools, Materials and Making Parts

My first step before I could begin any work was to gather tools, which I was short on while making my first guitar. It was a priority to find very strong clamps, gouge chisels, and a selection of files. I managed to find files and clamps in secondhand markets and hardware stores, but it took a long time to find a gouge chisel that would relieve me of having to use my homemade tool, a sharpened spoon.

Through several of my friends, I was connected to a lonely janitor at one of our colleges. He was a sculptor by trade, and like many other artists in Russia, he had to earn a living doing menial tasks like fixing broken doors and plumbing. He was a very nice young man, and after I shared with him my passion for music and guitar-making in particular, he gave me two chisels and said, "Here. Bring these back if you quit making guitars."

The gouges were quite used, but I was still thankful to have them. One of them was so old that it had multiple cracks on its wooden handle, which was glued together and wrapped with a rope. The blade on it looked like it was centuries old, but the shiny, sharp edge made it evident that the steel was of superior quality. That old chisel would come to be one of my favorite tools, and I kept it in its original condition, with its old handle, polished by time, until I left the USSR years later. I was also fortunate to find a rarely available metal toolbox that had plenty of space for all my tools, except for one large handsaw, which had to be stored in a different place.

I visited stores frequently, always looking through their inventory to find anything that I might be able to convert or adapt to a tool or parts. I particularly liked to look through the kitchen hardware department. One of my best finds there was a large vegetable shredder. On its wooden frame were three wide steel blades, and I was able to take it apart to create a perfect spokeshave for my guitar necks. Plane blades were converted to scrapers, and I sharpened small screwdrivers to be used as micro chisels.

Designing Parts and Components

After gathering all the tools, which took a bit of effort and patience, the next stage in my preparation was a dilemma. I no longer had a donor instrument for parts. Soviet guitars were virtually useless for this, and foreign instruments from the Czech Republic or East Germany were rarely available for sale. In the future, I would buy some loose knobs and jacks from dismantled old electric guitars. My main source of this components, however, would be old broken radios. All of my hardware, pickups and non-wooden parts would now have to be made from scratch or modified from already existing items. As I've mentioned, it was impossible to buy quality guitar parts, and there were none in any of our stores. My only solution was to buy foreign guitar catalogs and brochures on the black market so I could see the details of real instruments up close and imitate them myself.

Before I could begin gathering this reference material, I first had to hunt down everything I would need to make the neck, particularly the most important internal component, the truss rod or an "anchor bolt". This simple device is nothing more than a metal rod that lies inside of the guitar neck and works as a counterbalance against the tension of the strings. However, without it, the neck would bow, rendering the guitar useless. It is secured with a metal plate on one end (the anchor) and an adjustable nut on the opposite side. Even though it only consisted of three parts, none of them could be purchased in our stores. The rod itself had to be a specific diameter and a specific strength of steel. I knew that without that, I could not even pass the first stage in constructing the neck, and I needed to get my hands on one without having to bribe factory workers with liters of vodka. I hit our stores, searching for an item I might be able to adapt or convert into this important part. In my search, which became later a common practice for me, I found tree branch support rods at the garden store. The size of the rods and the hard steel they were constructed of made them perfect for use as truss rods. The other two parts could be found in bulk at factories, so I could finally move on to finding other guitar's hardware.

I struggled quite a bit with obtaining the tuner keys. The only option was to purchase a replacement set of this guitar hardware that fit on all our Soviet electric guitars. There was a reason why these were for sale in our music stores and other electric guitar components were not: The quality of the Soviet instruments was so poor that the tuner keys had to be frequently replaced. The gears were sloppy, and constant slippage was a source of common frustration among Russian musicians. To use such shoddy hardware on my guitars was out of the question, but with a closer look, I found that the most important gear part on them could be modified and salvaged. I realized I could create my own design for the tuner keys using those components, and I could make them function properly and look great. After several days of working on drawings, I had everything ready to mill all the parts for my first prototype set. I gave it to Sasha's dad Anatoly and returned to my hunt for other materials and supplies.

I already knew that most of the components I would need for my guitar production could be made with help of factory people. In the guitar catalogs I bought, I studied the complicated locking tremolo guitar bridges and came to realize that I could not make identical ones. So, I started working on completely different concepts for my own bridges and developed several types of locking and non-locking versions. Some of them had thumbscrew adjustment for the intonation and tuning, while others were of an intricate design, with the whole assembly held together by a single screw. They eventually proved themselves to be reliable hardware, but the limitations with the availability of a casting process did not allow me to fabricate them to look exactly like the Western examples. Still, though, creating them was very inspiring and challenging, and I continually tried to modify and improve all of my designs. Creating the rough-milled parts came to be a part-time job for Sasha's father, but I soon began paying him in cash due to the limited supply of "liquid currency" at my disposal.

Even small items like screws were difficult to find. Most available screws in the USSR were flatheads, in rough condition. They had to be turned in with a hand drill against a file and sandpaper to make them look even remotely normal. However, after chrome-plating, they shined like the ones in the best Western guitar catalogs.

Nothing that I needed for my guitar-making came without a great struggle, it seemed. Some of the materials, like sheet plastic for pickguards and back covers, were extremely difficult to come by, and I made all my friends aware of it so they could help me. I bought anything I could get from them that would be suitable for this purpose, and I had to be strategic about buying as much plastic as I could, as I used it not only for covers and pickguards, but also for making pickups. These electronic component parts were, by far, the most unusual and unique items I fashioned for my guitars. In the beginning, I created them using earth magnets that could be found in our refrigerator doors; they offered a tremendous amount of pull. They were wrapped in the coil of wire taken from old transformers and housed in small black plastic boxes that I created by using records covers: After cutting the plastic into rectangular pieces, I sanded them flat with sandpaper and fused them together into a box shape with acetone. Then, I polished the surface of the boxes, and they looked like the authentic real closed-type pickups of that era. The only problem with them was that the magnets inside them were too strong, causing a lot of distortion.

Many other attempts were made, including retrofitting Bakelite telephone handset speaker drivers to make pickups. The internal bobbins in one pair were exactly ten millimeters wide. I sandwiched three of them in a row to make humbucking pickups and fitted them in the same recycled records plastic boxes. They sounded wonderful, but my supply of old phone headsets ran out when a good friend of mine, who worked at the phone repair service, quit his job. I periodically worked on other concepts for magnets and wires, and at the end of my guitar-building career in the USSR, I began to use the pickups that my friend Vladimir Kholdun made at home. They were incredible pieces, and he put such quality work into them that it was hard to tell they were not professionally made at an American factory.

Hunt for Frets

One of the most important parts of a guitar is the frets, and these were absolutely impossible to make. Obviously, they were never sold in our stores, leaving me with yet another challenge. I knew that gathering them from old broken Soviet guitars was not a professional approach. Besides, those were often made of brass, which was not very durable. Without these strategically crucial items, I knew my project would never lift off the ground. After several days of research, I found that one of the factories that produced parts and musical instruments was located in Chernigov, a city just 100 kilometers away. The voyage there became a priority on my list of things to do, and I simply had to find a way to sneak into its premises.

The trip to Chernigov was truly an eye-opening experience for me. After a short journey on the bus, on one rainy, gray day, I entered the most outdated and poorly managed factory I'd ever visited in the USSR. As I'd done in factories in the past, I walked through the main entrance at lunchtime, trying to blend in with the crowd. I was astonished at the sad scene, and after seeing that place and witnessing how the work being done, I was not surprised that our musical instruments were of such horrible, low quality. All kind of performing type products was made at this factory. It was hard to silently observe how careless the workers were in preparing the mandolin bodies and haphazardly gluing piano parts together. They obviously had no woodworking experience, and the end result of it was reflected in what they were making.

To make matters worse, the product designs were completely outdated, and the technology had not been updated or maintained for decades. Everything looked old and broken and was poorly managed. Much of the work was even done outdoors in the elements, under the cover of nothing more than shabby tents. Nothing they produced had any appeal or quality to it, and to me, it was a pitiful picture of how the USSR wasted materials and human labor.

After walking around the unimpressive place for about an hour, I found what I'd been looking for. In the small, messy building, I noticed a few women operating noisy machines that rolled out various sizes of fret wire. Everything from brass frets for mandolins and large frets for Soviet bass guitars was produced under the roof of that place. Beside the huge bundles of shiny new fret wire, I saw small rolls all over the place. I asked one of the ladies what was wrong with those smaller bundles, and she just said, "Nothing. Just leftovers from the larger bulk. It's scrap!" she shouted over the volume of the growling machine. The fret wire leftovers looked perfect to me, so I picked up about twenty pounds of the so-called scrap metal and cleverly (and admittedly dishonestly) asked her if I could take them for our project in the next department. "Please do," she replied, moving the machine levers with her filthy glove. "Then I will have less to throw away."

I was glad to have found what I needed, but it was no easy chore to get the scrap fret wire out of the factory. Despite the fact that the place was neglected on the inside, the entire territory was surrounded by massive walls, and walking out through the secure entrance with my harvest was far too risky and suspicious. After observing the layout of the place, I decided to throw my loot over the wall and hoped it would land in an unnoticeable place on the other side so I could safely retrieve it. This attempt worked as planned. It was the most important find during my entire Soviet guitar-making career, and the amount of fret wire I gained that day served me for four years without having to replenish my stock.

Root Cellar Shop and the First Order

As impossible as it seemed at first, practically everything for my guitar could be made or found, as long as I put a lot of effort into it. The thing I needed most, though, was not something I could easily arrange: the location. It was not efficient or convenient to file bodies on the kitchen stool, and it was too risky to pound with a chisel in my apartment, as I feared I might again draw the attention of my neighbors. I could not subject my family to the mess, noise, and disturbance any longer, and I did not want to chance being turned into the authorities by one of our noisy neighbors for my illegal production. I needed a place close to home where I could be less visible and free to make noise.

Soviet life did not allow citizens to rent space for such a purpose. In fact, not many people had any kind of spare room to share with others. Everyone lived in very small apartments, and while the majority of citizens would have loved the opportunity to rent extra space, it simply wasn't possible. I was practically out of any options, but there was one tiny space that belonged to us, so I decided to give it a try: the root cellar in the basement of our apartment building. The root cellar itself was extremely small, practically a four-by-four-foot closet. For all of us, the main purpose of it was to store potatoes in the off season. Big bags of potatoes were kept there during the winter, and besides those valuable provisions, the cellar also housed old items and junk that Grandma did not want to throw away.

The beauty of it was that people rarely went into the underground place. Other than the occasional rats or the stray cats that wanted to make a meal out of them, there was really no noise or activity in the place. The walls were thick since the cellar was basically built into the foundation of the five-story building, so no sound would penetrate into the apartments above. The cellar was situated at the very end of a labyrinth-like basement and took a few minutes for someone to get to, so there was a built-in warning system since I could hear the heavy entrance door open and had a moment to hide my work. Of course, there was always the possibility that someone would question what I was doing down there, but it was the only option. Besides, one lesson I'd learned was that without taking risks, it was impossible to accomplish anything in Soviet Russia.

Root cellar 'shop' and all my tools.

I knew that even if I did make a workspace out of the cellar, there were many other issues that had to be taken into consideration. Located deep underground, it was always cold, and there was periodic flooding because of ground water and plumbing failure. To protect their belongings from this harsh reality, people stored their items in raised containers, but even this did not always work. I could handle the cold by wearing warmer clothes and gloves, but flooding was something I could not control or manage. My only option would be to wear rubber boots when the cellar was wet in a spring flooding. Also, I would have to take all of my tools home each day, since cellars were often robbed; even insignificant items like canned food or old and broken bicycles were stolen on occasion, and I did not want thieves taking off with my hard-earned tools and supplies.

Even with all of these factors to consider, this option was much better than having no place to construct my guitars. I was sure that if I convinced my mother that allowing me to use the root cellar would prevent noise and mess at home, she would agree. I talked to my parents about moving their things from the cellar to our balcony, kitchen, or trash, and after the expected resistance and a short interrogation about the purpose for my plans, I got permission from Grandma, the boss around our house, and began cleaning up the root cellar.

After getting everything out from the basement and allocating new place for it in our house, I needed only one more thing to make the place workable: a workbench of some kind. It was not so easy to find something small and tough that would work perfect in my "shop" without modifications. I needed a table that was made out of sturdy wood and not a flimsy particle-board construction that would not hold up to the damp conditions in the cellar, as well as all of my necessary pounding, etc. I thought long and hard about it and finally remembered a perfect candidate I'd seen to serve as my new workbench. It was kept in the little storage shed of my grandma's sister, who lived in the village. Without any delay, I went there the following weekend. Sure enough, it was exactly what I'd been looking for—a little, rigged old two-person kitchen table. I dragged it across the field to the train and brought it back to my root cellar. It was a perfect fit, other than one small issue: It was a bit too low for me to stand and work behind it, but since the ceiling in the cellar was very low anyway, I had to get use to working while sitting, so I made do.

First Order

Finally, everything was in place for me to begin construction on my newest guitar creation. By that time, there were several impatient guitarists who badly wanted an instrument from me. My first customer was a bass player from one of our Belarusian amateur rock bands. He had been referred to me by my friend Evgeniy, who told me that he was dying for a handmade bass. I was not very interested in making basses, but I could not resist the pressure from the guy, who had already heard so many good things about my guitar. When I met him and he talked about his dream bass, I realized it would not only be my first contracted guitar, but also one of the most difficult builds. He brought a Japanese guitar catalog with him and pointed at a white bass guitar. "I want one exactly like this," he said and showed me the picture of a white neck-through bass. Having no idea how to make such an instrument, I tried at first to steer him away from that model, but then I realized it was actually a great opportunity to try something very challenging, to see if I could make something even more complicated. I took a small deposit, and after we shook hands, I began to really think about the construction of such an instrument.

For the duration of my entire guitar-building journey in Russia, I never had an instrument that gave me so many headaches like this bass. The biggest problem had nothing to do with its complexity; rather, it was simply the size of the piece. The neck of the base was not bolted to the body but was actually a part of it that ran all the way through its center—the neck-through construction. When I got the rectangular wood blank for its neck from my "suppliers" at the furniture factory, I brought it to the root cellar and instantly faced a problem. My shop was too small for it, so I had to keep the cellar door open to give myself enough room. Just turning the wood around was a hassle, and wondered if I should just move my work area back to the house, though I knew that was off limits. My family did not want me to make another mess in our apartment, and it wouldn't have worked anyway because I had so much wood to chisel to create the neck shape.

So, I stayed in the cellar and slowly proceeded with creating the neck. It seemed like it took an eternity to chisel the long neck, and by the time I finished the profile, I sincerely hoped no one would ever again order another bass like that. The headstock, which was tilted back, had to be carved as well since I did not want to glue it like on Russian guitars, which suffered from constant breakage. Every neck had to be chiseled out from a rectangular slab of wood and amount of material removed by hand in this case made it the most laborious task in my guitars construction. This feature remained constant in all of the guitars I manufactured in Russia, in spite of the long and tedious work involved.

After digging the truss rod channel, everything else was similar to the construction of my first guitar neck. The elegant shape of a neck began to emerge from the slab of beech wood. The fingerboard was made, the face dots and frets were installed, and the headstock was trimmed and contoured similar to the shape of a hockey stick—a classic for eighties music.

When all of this was completed, I had to glue the sides of the body to the neck, but I ran into another hurdle when I discovered that I did not have any extra long clamps for this procedure. Soviet stores never carried anything of such a large size, so I knew I would have to rely on the help of Sasha's dad to make them to my specs. However, I didn't want to face any further delays, so I decided to use a simple trick I'd heard about. Long rubber belts used for physical therapy were readily available in our pharmacies, and while they were intended for medical purposes, they served me well in the making of guitars. Wrapping the glued-together parts with this material compressed them more-and-more with each wound. It also allowed us to keep everything aligned and centered while gluing parts. Most importantly, it forced a strong glue bond. The rest of the process took me through more tiresome work, but the closer I got to a finished guitar, the more and more it began to look like a professionally made instrument.

The Woodworking Process was Captivating

I treated the guitar-building like a second job, but my regular job slowly began to take a backseat to it. I thoroughly enjoyed what I was doing in our little root cellar, as well as designing hardware and finding supplies. The woodworking process was so captivating for me that I began to show up late for work at the TV station, and when I was scheduled to work first shift, I stayed in the cellar until my grandma had to chase me back home to sleep.

The cold, dark, quiet environment of my crummy workshop did not bother me at all. To keep warm, I simply worked faster, heating myself up by sanding and filing wood. The only problem that I did find annoying was that my hands began to accumulate metal stains from holding cold chisels and tools. Gloves have been a solution to protect me from the cold and the stains, but I preferred to be able to touch my handiwork with my bare hands. There was something magical in observing the transformation of wooden blocks into a musical instrument. Cutting wood with hand tools was its own irreplaceable experience, especially when my freshly sharpened tools sliced through it like butter, creating scrolls and shredded piles of chips. As I built up my experience, I was also developing a deep understanding of the wood properties—something not so easily acquired today, when we rely so heavily upon machines to do our woodworking. There is something refreshingly satisfying about seeing a piece of wood transform by your very hands into a completed project.

Buff the Guitar to a Mirror-Like Shine

It took a while to finish the whole guitar and prepare it for a paint job, but when it was time for that step, I had to make decision of how to go about it. I could no longer rely on some strange, uncontrolled process at the furniture factory. It would have been also very difficult to smuggle that large one-piece neck and body anywhere where it could be painted. From that point on, I had to establish a permanent, reliable, consistent technique, considering that I planned to continue producing guitars. Airbrushing was not a viable option, as it was very slow and caused too many noticeable and hazardous fumes. I had to find a way to paint the guitar in my house, without any kind of spraying hassle.

I looked through the inventory of paint at our hardware store and found several types of paint developed for interior use, including hardwood floor lacquer and furniture paint, some of which could be brushed on. After trying few samples, I found white paint that dried in a thick, hard coat and parquet varnish; while the varnish had a nasty smell to it, it dried with a very clear and durable coating. By adding heat-resistant black paint into the varnish, I was able to create an incredible black finish. The result was so spectacular that practically all of my future guitars were built and painted with black, white, or clear finishes.

After applying a couple dozen coats of the white paint on the freshly built bass, I let it dry for two weeks before I began leveling the rough patches and taking care of some of the parts of the surface where runs had appeared. I sanded it with medium-grit sandpaper to create a well-prepared surface, but the crisscross brushing pattern was too rough for me to get it done flat and fast. Than I tried to use a metal file to start the leveling process, and it worked very well, improving not only the speed, but also the quality of the work. After working with files for a while, I moved on to sandpaper, gradually replacing it with the finest grit I had. When I finished the work, I could still see small scratches on the surface, and I realized I could not buff the guitar to a mirror-like shine with the tools and supplies I had on hand. Since I had no idea what to try next, I turned again to my friends for help. When I told my pal Kholdun about my dilemma, he advised me to stop at his house and said he might have something that could help. He gave me a small piece of sandpaper, about two square inches, with such a fine grit that it felt like ordinary smooth paper. The only difference was that it was a cloth-back type material, and it had to be used with water. I had never heard of such a technique, but after I tried it, I was amazed how well it worked. Unfortunately, Kholdun had given me the only piece he had, and he had no idea where to find more in our city. I treasured that small piece of sandpaper like a prized possession and used it on all of my guitars. By the end of my guitar-making career in the USSR, it practically felt like a piece of old leather.

Making guitar bridge at home.

To buff the finished guitar surface, I had only one available process: by hand. We never had any buffing machines or power-driven tools for that purpose in our stores. The whole process consisted of wrapping a cotton cloth around a closed fist, and using a tube of brass-polishing gel. As I worked the gel into the surface with a circular motion, a glassy shine began to emerge. It was one of the most tedious processes in completing the instrument, and there was no alternative or easier way to accomplish such a result. Even thick layers of cloth could not prevent the blisters from appearing on the palms of my hands. By the time everything was done, though, the hard work and sore arms felt like a worthy price for the beautiful guitar. It was truly a showpiece, and the shiny finish reflected everything around it like a mirror.

Built and Delivered

All hardware was specially designed, milled, filed, threaded, and chrome plated for this bass within the last couple of months, and finally it was ready to be installed on the finished instrument. It had taken several months for the birth of my first custom-made guitar order to come to fruition, and I could not wait to see the reaction of its new owner. Not only was I proud of the results of my work, but I was also intrigued with the process of constructing an item for someone else—an item someone was willing to pay a premium price for. I also felt an indescribable sense of freedom after I created this instrument. I had done it on my own, without anyone telling me what to do or how to do it. I had created an item that no one would ever find on the practically empty shelves of our government-controlled stores. I had constructed exactly what my customer wanted, and I was very happy about the fact that I had created something of a higher quality than our failed system could produce.

I delivered the guitar to my first customer, and the indescribably joy on his face is something I shall never forget. He looked like he had just won a mega-lottery. The look and sound of the bass absolutely blew him away, and he could not stop telling me how much he loved it. His happiness and joy with that guitar in his hands was a much better reward to me than any financial benefit from it, and I knew exactly how he felt. After all, not long before, I had waited many, many years for a quality instrument I thought I'd never have. For him—just as it was for me—that guitar was a dream come true, and I was happy to have played a part in it.

By the time I finished this guitar, I knew I could not stop producing them. It was not the money I cared about, but I had fallen in love with the challenge, and my passion for the instruments and the music they would produce inspired me to continue. I knew that from then on, nothing would get in the way of that passion, and I could not wait to get my hands on another project.

Soviet "Cooperatives" and My Effort to Get One

As i mentioned earlier, one of the new initiatives put into place by Gorbachev at the time of Perestroika was the establishment of small, privately owned and operated businesses known as "Cooperatives." These were not implemented in an effort to move our nation to the free market or open the doors for Capitalism, but rather to support the Soviet economy, which was quickly crumbling. To minimize the outcry of old Bolshevik diehards, who questioned the necessity of such an "alien" form of enterprise in our Socialistic society, our leaders had to revive some of the ideas and propaganda we'd been previously taught. Thus, they reverted to the teachings they had, themselves, condemned, claiming that Lenin made similar reforms during his New Economical Policy (NEP) after the revolution in 1917, in an effort to stabilize the crippled economy. This project later backfired on Communists, in that it revived old forms of a free market economy. The whole NEP policy was then scrapped by Stalin, and the small Capitalistic ventures were closed down, with their owners sent to the gulag.

Gorbachev was very careful to avoid a repeat of these events, so he and his administration limited cooperative reform by allowing only a single person or a few partners to establish such businesses. All functions of the emerging enterprises were kept under the close and strict scrutiny of the government and were required to adhere to a colossal amount of bureaucracy, regulation, and taxation. Our regulations prohibited cooperatives to have an official 'owner', so they were only allowed to have "directors" who earned a salary that everybody deemed appropriate. All profits had to be shared equally among the employees, keeping in line with the Socialistic principles of our nation. None of these policies, however, were possible to enforce and the "directors" technically controlled all the money and power of their businesses.

Despite all the complexity and red tape involved with opening a coop, the number of them in the USSR were rapidly growing. This new initiative, also finally came to our city as well.

Regardless of the difficulties and constraints, people were eager to get involved in what they viewed as a legalized Soviet moneymaking machine. Most "coops" were in the culinary sector and sold foodstuffs like homemade shish kebabs and sandwiches. Slowly, manufacturing cooperatives began to form, and the cheaply made small household products they produced began showing up on our store shelves, offering items similar in quality to those you might find in a modern-day American dollar store. The people who manufactured these products knew that in such a product's vacuum, retailers could profit from just about anything they had to offer, regardless of quality; it was truly proof of the law of supply and demand. As a result, people began to associate cooperatives with poor quality goods offered at a high price. Even food kiosks became targets of common rumors, and people began accusing them of using expired or spoiled ingredients and questioned the sources of their meat supply.

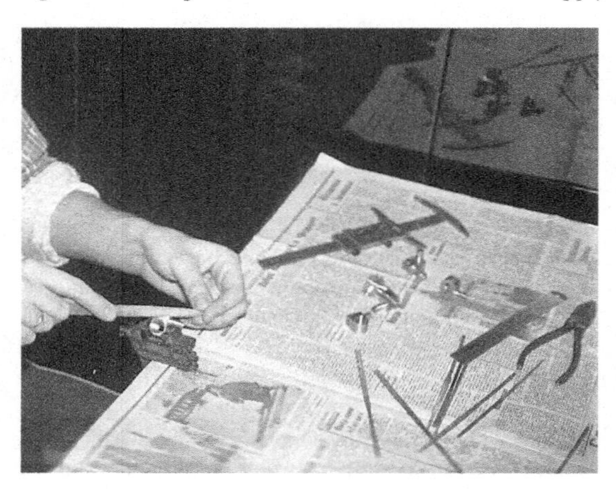

Making tuner keys.

The official main goal of the cooperatives was to fulfill the need for products that our society was short on and to supporting the national economy. In reality, however, those who were involved in the new trend, often criminal elements, began to capitalize on the ventures, focusing only on making as much money as they could. They utilized every conceivable legal and illegal method to fill their pockets, and as a result, from the very start, they began to feed and nurture the worst byproduct of our Perestroika and coop reform: the infamous Russian Mafia. All sorts of creepy stories were shared among our people about the backdoor affairs of our cooperatives. Fraud, tax evasion, and document falsification were normal for these endeavors, and under-the-table bribes to officials and authorities became a common practice for cooperatives who wanted to stay in business.

Competition, which is an important part of any successful economy, was practically nonexistent, and anyone who managed to open a coop was practically guaranteed to rake in a hefty profit. Behind this thin veil of this so-called financial success, however, the ugly consequences was emerging in a frightening way that had not been known in the Soviet Union before. Mafia-type relationships between cooperatives and the organized criminal world came to the forefront of our lives, and the brutal reality of what was happening began to ooze into our culture, from big cities to small ones. Little kiosks and production shops became prime targets for racketeering and extortion. Everyone who was involved in the coop movement was, in one way or another, affected by this new virus of criminal activity, like none the Soviet Union had ever seen before. As soon as a new cooperative opened, it was an immediate target for vicious gangster groups, who demanded dues in exchange for "protection". The first horror stories about the despicable and sadistic punishment of those who were unwilling to succumb to the extortion and pay the dues are eerily similar to tales of the Chicago mafia that mar the archives of the United States. Because they knew that coops made much more money than people who worked regular jobs, criminals shamelessly demanded up to 80 percent of their profits. Those who tried to avoid or could not meet the demanded payments faced terrible consequences. Cooperative leaders and their family members often disappeared or were murdered. There was no remedy, because if a coop director contacted the authorities for help, they were often doing more harm to themselves than good; the authorities seemed to have no power to do anything about the extortion, or else they turned a blind eye, as the mafia had bribed them to do. Even ordinary criminals admitted that the newborn Russian mafia broke all their rules and codes by applying evil and barbaric tactics to their victims.

The tyranny of the gangsters had no limits, and many cooperative bosses had no option but to quit what they were doing. The mafia treated its prey as nothing more than a source of unearned revenue, and they would not allow a cooperative to shut down and leave them high and dry by stopping their business operations. In essence, coop owners became slaves, forced to support the mafia for the rest of their lives. The government never openly admitted existence of organized crime in the Soviet Union, and all stories about any Russian mafia activity was disputed by the authorities. Many people believed the government's suggestion that the stories were false, and they didn't come to realize how wrong they were until they attempted to open their own enterprises and got caught in the cruel web themselves.

Trying to Get a "Coop" License

A few months later, after I finished my first custom-made instrument to order, I was already working on new guitars. New customers were coming at me from all directions, to the extent where I had to stop taking new orders. Since the process of guitar-making was such a slow and painstaking one, I could only produce three or four quality instruments a year.

I was so in love with the craft that I could not see myself doing anything else with my life. Not only did I want to make more guitars, but I wanted it to become my full-time work. To do that, I would have to quit my job, but the law required me to be registered as an employee somewhere. As I saw it, the perfect solution was to legally establish my guitar-making business as a cooperative. I was an idyllic candidate for this type of enterprise, according to all our laws and Gorbachev's vision: I had a high-quality product, there was a demand for them, and there was a significant unavailability of them in stores. These factors were core ingredients for the existence of a coop. Another benefit of opening my own cooperative was that I would be able to set up shop in any of the established factories, as long as I paid rent. The government supported these kinds of enterprises, hoping that energetic, ambitious people could influence and collaborate with Soviet manufactures, which tended to drag their feet. I would have access to machinery and materials, as well as the opportunity to legally buy any supplies I needed directly from the factory, without having to sneak and throw surplus and scrap over the fence and smuggle it home.

Entrance to the root cellar.

Despite the horrific tales I'd heard about the danger of being swallowed up by the mafia, I decided that I would be okay because I was not planning to make a huge production and/or deal with enormous profits. My activities would be clean, without any kind of shady manipulations that were so typical for the coops of the day. The dishonest leaders of many coops avoided reporting their real profits so they become perfect targets for the mafia. Easy money cooperatives often attracted the attention of the criminals: "Video saloons" that played bootleg movies from the West for the public; private toilets at the train stations; and private taxicabs were among the first to suffer from mafia attacks. On the contrary, I would be a self-employed, working-class coop, and every penny I earned would be a result of my hard labor. As such, I assumed I would be last coop that criminals would be interested in. I believed also that working within behind the walls of a factory would offer me some privacy and protection, and I would be well concealed from the criminals' eyes.

After evaluating my situation thoroughly and realizing that making guitars in the root cellar all my life would be impossible, I decided to submit documents to one of our regional Soviet municipal's offices, the 'Raysoviet', for a cooperative license. Gathering paperwork was the first step in the process, and as soon as I started doing that, I faced the ugly reality of our bureaucratic world. Knowing that I could not move forward without all my paperwork in order, I spent many days gathering senseless documents and filling in ridiculously long applications. After everything was ready, I had only one line to fill in: the name of my business. I had no any idea what to call my new guitar shop, so assuming that it should have some music-related name, I wrote "Sustain" on the name line. I believed the universal musical term would be easily identifiable with my activities, so I used it on all my initial applications. After I filed all the documents with Raysoviet, I was told I would be called in a few weeks for an interview.

Caught at the Factory and the "Coop" Interview

The main benefit of legalizing my business was the ability to build my guitars out in the open, without hiding and being confined to the humble root cellar. Not only was it physically difficult to produce underground, but the underground profits I was making were still illegal in the USSR. This fact was reinforced with more severe punishments by our government. I hoped that the bureaucratic torture I went through was worth it for the reduced risk, because every time I went to a factory to smuggle surplus materials and supplies, I knew my mission could result in being caught and thrown in jail. Whether I was trying to get scrap wood or nickel plate my parts, the consequences could be very dangerous, and things did not go smoothly all the time. I still recall one of my trips to the furniture factory that put me to such danger.

Working in the root cellar.

I was "shopping" for guitar body wood, and after getting everything I needed, I was moving along the railroad track inside of the furniture factory, heading to my regular exit, which was hidden by the broken-down wall of the plant. As I passed the main entrance, I walked near the truck gates, secured by active-duty policemen; they were the only reliable way to ensure that there was not a mass exodus of materials from the factories. Their job was to inspect every departing truck to be sure their cargo and documents were in order. I had passed this spot many times before and had never had a problem, considering that the officers were focused on fully inspecting trucks and paid little mind to anyone else. On this particular occasion, though, I noticed that one of the guards was watching me.

As soon as I realized that I had drawn his attention, I began to wonder if he was simply staring at someone behind me or if he was actually curious about what I had in my bag. I looked at him out of the corner of my eye and noticed that he was moving in my direction. I tried to stay calm as I kept walking toward my hidden exit, but I could hear him stomping with his boots, faster and faster, and getting closer. "Hey, sir! Stop right there!" he shouted just when I was trying to make a turn between the buildings.

My mind was instantly filled with horror. I knew I was in big trouble and began to panic about what might happen over the next few moments of my life. I knew if I was taken to the security office, my next destination would be the local police department, where I would be charged for multiple crimes and violations. Without question, I would be going to the jail, because even though all I was taking was unwanted scrap, it was still considered national property. I knew they would not reward me for wandering around the factory, and I had to prepare myself for the worst. There was no use trying to explain that I was only taking production waste because I needed materials that I could not get in our stores. Soviet police officers were promoted and rewarded for hunting down criminals, so even there was no chance to convince them to let me slip by. The air was fresh and breezy, and gray, gloomy clouds slowly moved above me across the sky. I looked around, trying to soak it all in, terrified that it might be the last time that I would see the outdoors for a very long time. I was counting my last seconds of freedom, knowing that minutes later, I'd be handcuffed and dragged away—all for the love of my craft.

When the officer approached me, I was standing still, trying to appear innocent. "What's in your bag, pal?" he asked me right away.

I knew it would be the first question he would ask, and I slowly started pulling the cutoff slabs of mahogany and beech wood from my bag. "Just scrap pieces," I replied, throwing them on the ground.

"Hmm. Scrap, you say?" The officer leaned over and began looking at my material. "What you are going to do with it, son?"

"I want to make an electric guitar, Officer," I replied respectfully and honestly, realizing that the less I lied, the less I'd be beaten at the police station.

"All right. So you want to make guitar out of these?"

"Yes, sir," I said, pulling my hands from my pockets so I could be easily handcuffed.

"You know, this is very stupid," he said, trying to light up a cigarette. "Let me tell you what you should do."

At that point, I wanted to tell him I didn't need any brainwashing about dedicating my life to building Communism instead of guitars, but I held it back to avoid a punch in a stomach.

"When I was a little boy, my dad made mandolins, and he never used mahogany," he said, deeply inhaling his cigarette. "He always used pear wood. It sounded great, and I even tried to play on it, but I had no patience to learn. That was long time ago," he said, gazing up at the gray, blustery sky. He paused for a moment, and I was sure he was going to tell me it was time to take me in for official questioning, but instead he looked at me and asked, "Why don't you ask Svetlana from Warehouse 4? She should have some pear wood in there. There may not be much, but I'm sure you can find enough pieces for your guitar. Go ask her before she goes to lunch." Then he turned around and ran toward the gate, where a truck was awaiting inspection.

In that instant, I felt like I'd just been released from prison or escaped some miserable death sentence. An indescribable feeling of freedom and joy overwhelmed my soul. I gathered all the wood blanks back into my bag and could not wait to get out of that place, praising God for saving my rear end from getting into big trouble.

Despite that frightening experience, I never sought for a second to stop building the instruments. After that trip, though, I was much more careful and disguised when I had to go to the factories, and I always tried to avoid security posts. I knew not all the guards would be as kind and understanding as that one had been.

Cooperative License Interview

When I was called for my "coop" interview, I was very excited. After going through all the paperwork and waiting for such a long time, I could not wait to get my business legalized. Expecting to deal with only some sort of formality, I made sure I had all of my documents, as well as a few pictures of my finished guitars, and went to the Raysoviet. I assumed it would only be a few hours before my guitar-making was considered a legalized business. It seemed there were big life changes on the horizon for me, and I looked forward to quitting my job at the TV station so I could spend all of my time making guitars. Having all my documents and applications in order, I was confident that within a week, I would be putting my new shop together. My future looked so much brighter, and I was sure I would never again have to worry about what I should do to make a living. I would be doing exactly what I loved, and I would be doing it legally, without the risk of arrest.

After arriving at the Raysoviet, I realized I was not the only one there for an interview. A few other folks were standing in the hallway, looking at a long list of cooperative names that was posted on the billboard. All the businesses on the list had been granted their license and the right to conduct business. I glanced at the list, but then someone called my name, and I rushed into the room where my interview was to take place.

As soon as I walked in, I saw five people sitting behind a long table. In the middle of the room was a chair, and I was told to have a seat. Each government official had a pile of papers in front of them, and after shuffling through them, they began the interview.

It was the strangest meeting I'd ever experienced in the USSR. It was not even an interview; it felt more like an interrogation. I realized very quickly that I was not there to talk about the details and nuances of my cooperative plans, but seemed to be standing trial for committing some kind of crime. They questioned me about my past employment and also about what kinds of music could be played on my guitars. Then they asked me why I had given my cooperative a "strange foreign name, Sustain." I tried to explain to them that it was musical terminology and was relevant to what I would be doing, but that was literally a waste of time since none of them had any understanding of electric guitars in general. I knew this was true because they tried to tell me that the Soviet Union was already making "wonderful" and "affordable" instruments; clearly, they had no high level of expertise when it came to guitars if they considered the Soviet junk to be of any value whatsoever.

Working on neck at home when the root cellar was flooded.

The bureaucrats who interrogated me seemed very rude, and the questions were condescending, judgmental, and invasive. They acted as if my plans to build guitars were right on cue with building bombs or explosives. No one even bothered to ask about the difficult process of hand-making musical instruments. Instead, they seemed to focus on the price of the instruments and how I would spend any profits. None of them made any comments about my work or exhibited the slightest bit of sympathy or understanding about what I was trying to produce. I had gone to the interview excited and hopeful, expecting to be granted a business license, but instead, I was only insulted.

One of the women on the panel tried to coach me in what I should do with my craftsmanship ability. She looked and acted like she had just performed at an opera house. She exuded a prideful, dominant disposition that was typical for most of our authority figures. At the end of the so-called interview, she pointed at me with her finger and told me my coop name might be posted on the hallway list when the 'processing' of my application was completed.

I left Raysoviet feeling the same way as if would I exited the police department after a DUI detention. I had envisioned the interview completely differently in my mind. However, knowing that this was how our government usually talked to its citizens, I decided to see how long it would take for my case to be evaluated and decided upon. Sadly, there was no champagne on the table to celebrate the cooperative license, and I had no cool stories to tell my friends and family about the excitement of our officials to allow the very first guitar-making coop in our country. Instead, all I could do was hope and wait.

Denial of License and Lost Hopes

The following week, I wanted to go back and see if those self-proclaimed "musical instrument experts" had posted my name among the licensed cooperatives. My name wasn't there, and it wasn't there the week after that or two more weeks after that either. Every time I checked, I saw names of licensed cooperatives that had just had their interviews, but my name still was not there after weeks. I became very discouraged and began contacting the Raysoviet to ask about my status. Every single time, they told me, "We are working on it."

The harsh truth of why I was waiting so long and what it would take to get my license came to me after I mentioned my Raysoviet ordeal to another cooperative owner. It was already well known to many that the coop movement was drowning in corruption and that it was getting worse every day. One thing I didn't realize was that someone could be sucked into the system even before their business doors opened. Simply, in order to get the authorities to make a decision in your favor and approve your coop, you had to pay someone under the table. Everything was already set up and in place to run this scheme like a well-oiled machine. If you did not get your license shortly after your initial interview, it was to be considered a message that you had to pay your "license fee" upfront. Knowing who you should talk to and having the right amount of money was the key to establishing a cooperative. The amount the government crooks demanded for their approval—for that single piece of paper that would allow you to operate your own business—was astronomical and constantly on the rise. Depending on the scale of the potential operation, it could cost many thousands of rubles. To me, this scenario was not only unacceptable, but also beyond my financial abilities. Paying some corrupt thugs who praised our so-called Communistic morals while taking bribes under the table was absolutely despicable in my eyes. I could not even think about beginning my official guitar-making business by crawling into bed with those selfish Soviet government crooks. My business—my passion—was far too valuable to me to taint it in such a way.

The reality of the license-issuing process hurt my feelings and put another dent in my trust in the Soviet Perestroika. I still hoped to hear something good from the Raysoviet, like that there were at least some righteous people in our government. Very soon, however, my hopes were shattered when I was officially denied the cooperative license. The reasons they gave me were absolutely ridiculous and blatantly biased: 1) Absence of necessity to produce such product (electric guitars), which has no economical benefit for society; and 2) Availability in stores of similar high-quality instruments, as manufactured by the Soviet musical instrument industry. Not only did these sorry excuses reveal that the people who made them knew nothing about guitars, but they also confirmed my suspicions that the purported corruption of those responsible for issuing licenses was close to the truth. Everyone I talked after I was denied permission told me that I was very naïve if I expected anyone in USSR to hand over a "ticket to financial freedom" unless they could get their share of it.

I had hoped that the claws of corruption and governmental control of every aspect of human life was just an exaggeration and that there was some civilized life left in our country, but those hopes were destroyed yet again. I could no longer trust anything our officials told us. I was not a rabble-rouser or a rebel or an upstart or a leader of mutinies. I was a lover of music, and all I wanted to do was make guitars and live a quiet, peaceful life. I had no options left to legally do what I loved, so I decided to literally and allegorically keep my guitar-making business underground. I refused to give up something I loved for a government that I was beginning to hate even more.

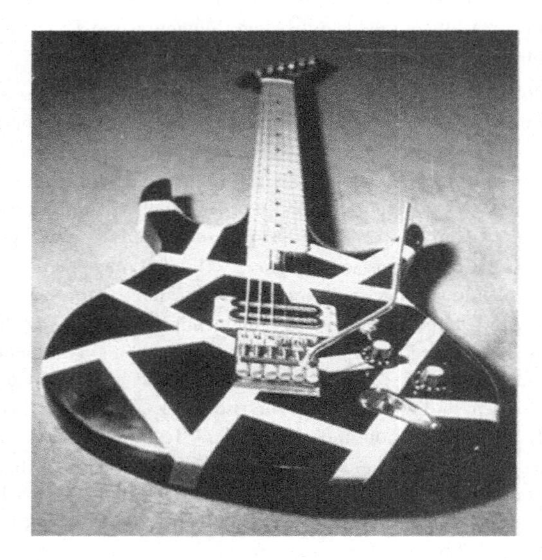

One of my "Neck - Through" 24 frets Guitar concept.

Chapter 20

Family and My Father

My family was getting older, and even though my grandmother had been retired for a long time, she still could not stay home while my brother and I were in school or working. Despite the fact that she was well up in years, she took on part-time jobs at local factories as a receptionist or clerk. People loved her everywhere she worked, and her kind and lovely personality gained her incredible amount of friends. Even at her age, she had the strength to travel periodically to the village, so she could help her sister Dunya with her hard country life. My grandmother dug potatoes, worked in the garden, and picked berries in the forest, and her strong individuality and motivation continued to impress us. My mother was getting close to her retirement as well, and while she continued to work for the government office, she began to lose some of her interest in the Communist Party dogmas. Perestroika opened her eyes to a lot of Communist philosophy, ideals she had trusted for most of her life and principles that had been her passion. A lot was said about our past, and this caused my mother to reconsider her belief in the utopia of Communism. The truth about Stalin and Gulag was a bit shocking to her, and the "clean and holy" halo surrounding our Communist Party was shaken before her eyes by the growing Soviet corruption and dishonesty. She no longer preached to us at home about living in the true Communist society. The harsh realization of our reality changed her perspective on Soviet political dogmas. She continued to do her best at work, but she was closer to her family than to her formerly beloved Communist Party.

My little brother was sixteen years old, and trying to follow my steps, he learned how to play guitar. While he never played in any bands, he was very interested in everything surrounding it, and he was inspired to try guitar-making on his own. He constantly asked me about the process and watched how I went about it. Often, he would come down and practiced in the root cellar, and I hoped that one day, he would truly dedicate himself to this task and take it seriously.

Reunion with My Father

It had been many years since I'd seen my father. After he left us that last time, we hadn't heard from him at all, so it came as a big surprise to us when our grandma told us that he had called her. My mom obviously did not want to hear anything about it, but my grandmother saw it from a different perspective. He left his address with my grandma and said he wanted to see my brother and me. The whole time he was away from us, he only lived in a small village about a twenty-minute train ride away. We didn't even know how to react to such news, but it was our father, and not some distant relative or stranger. We knew that it was important for us to see him, a necessary gesture not only to reconcile our dead relationship, but also to give us a chance to talk to him so he could clarify many unanswered questions from our past.

So, the following weekend my brother and I decided to go and see him. He had a family of his own, a daughter and two stepsons from his new wife's previous marriage. We knew it would be somewhat awkward, but we didn't have any hard feelings toward them and could not wait to meet them.

The train arrived in the small station in the village of Korenevka, and we quickly found their house, which was only a short walk away. That place where he lived, surrounded by large trees and flowers on the curb of a dirt road, looked like the types of places we'd always heard of in tales about Russian country life. Typical for our Soviet rural world, it was small, but it was well maintained and very cozy.

We knocked on the gate, and a lady dressed in country attire answered. When we asked if we could see Feodor, she said, "Of course! Welcome and come on in!" and then showed us into the house.

We were sure it was his wife, but we asked, just to be certain, "Do you know who we are, ma'am?"

She turned to us and warmly answered, without the slightest bit of discomfort, "Yes! I can tell by your eyes, boys."

We walked into the house, and she told us that our father was in the garden. We asked if we could go see him, and when we reached the shady backyard, we saw him approaching. He was a skinny little man, not the giant I remembered from when I was a young child. After warm greeting, we went into the house and spent several hours talking about our shared past.

It was very strange to talk to the man without that close father/child relationship. He seemed like a stranger to us, yet few saw ourselves in him; we recognized his mannerisms, his eyes, and his body language. He told us about his life and begged us to forgive him for leaving us. He blamed everything that happened between him and our mother on some of her friends. We didn't want actually to hear anything about that, though, for after so many years of separation, the last thing we wanted to listen to was a recounting of his old unfinished personal drama.

We wanted to hear about his life, but we also wanted to know about our paternal grandparents, whom we had never had a chance to meet. Both of them had already passed away, but in the pictures, we saw that my brother looked exactly like our grandfather. For us, they were unknown people from an unknown world—just a man and a woman gazing at us from old, brownish photographs. It was a tragedy to miss out on that relationship that could have been, but in Russia, a traditional consequence of divorce was that one side of the family became permanently isolated from another.

He asked about our lives as well. Misha told him about school, and I shared with him about my guitar-making and how difficult it was to practice my passion under the Russian laws. He offered a lot of sympathy, for he had endured his own struggles with the Soviet regime and his own personal wars against its bureaucracy. From the big folder hidden in the closet he pulled a pile of documents and pictures of his little invention that he was trying to bring to life—some kind of adaptor for an excavator that would convert the machine to do all type of tasks on construction sites. My father's folders contained a number of patents and prototype reviews from the industry experts, as well as multiple stamps and seals from various government offices. He was not seeking to make any financial gains from his idea. All he wanted was to have it manufactured and used by workers because he used the device in his own job and discovered that it saved a tremendous amount of time and money. However, the slow, bureaucratic system of our government showed no real interest in his invention, despite the praises of the experts. He had ultimately given up on his attempts to get it recognized and produced. Because I had dealt with similar issues in my own passion, I understood and felt very close to him in his frustration with the stubborn Soviet system that discouraged free thinking and initiative.

We asked him where he was working, and he said he was still an excavator driver at the same construction organization where he had work since he had lived with us. He had done all kinds of work around our region, and he had recently been dispatched to Armenia to help with the cleanup efforts after a major earthquake. His most recent job was to remove soil from fields contaminated with radiation after the Chernobyl disaster. As we listened to his stories of the hard work in the dusty fields, with no more protection from radiation than a dust mask, we got the chills. He had to scrape the top soil layer with his excavator and then dump it on trucks; it was buried not far away in a deep trench. "They even didn't tell us what the radiation level was," he said, "but our bosses would only show up for a minute and did not even get out of their cars. They always wanted to leave the field quickly, and hurried out their instructions so they could get out of there." He was greatly distressed about the whole Chernobyl situation, and after we discussed that for a while, we asked him about his new family and home.

He showed us around, and we learned that he had built the house himself. The garden and the backyard were also the results of his hard labor. He also showed us some projects he was working on. In the little storage area, we noticed a small cart he had fashioned from old plumbing pipes, and a motorcycle motor. His creativity and construction ability was something new to us. I had only known him when I was a very small child, and my brother really hadn't known him at all. Learning more about him, and seeing how similar he was to us, I was overcome with a deep sense of regret that he was living a life completely separate from his sons.

His daughter and two stepsons were just back from visiting the city, and their mother was in the kitchen preparing a country-style dinner. Meeting my half-sister Nataliya for the first time was an interesting and very unusual experience. She had the same dark eyes as all of us and looked like another member of our family that we had never known. Her soft, kind personality was coupled with the hardworking, caring attitude that was so typical of country folk. She was in the process of finishing school, and like my brother, she did not have too many plans for her future. She was only limited to working in the kolkhoz or enrolling in some kind of college. Her half-brothers were typical country boys with a simple personality, and they were obviously not spoiled with city life. They were older than Nataliya and helped my father around the house, taking care of the family's country life necessities.

As we sat around the table for dinner, I made some interesting observations. While we were all strangers, we still felt like a family. Our lives had been broken apart by circumstances, but there was a noticeable sense of compassion for one another, and we were all united—at least in some small way—through my father. In that moment, I did not hold a grudge against my parents for what had happened, even though my brother and I lived without our father while he was close to his other children. We had never even eaten dinner with the man of the house sitting next to us, so feeling the fullness of a complete family was a new experience. We deeply regretted that we had missed those kinds of moments, but on that day, there was a comforting sense of closeness. As I looked at my dad, I was happy we had reunited after so many years, and it was even more inspiring that it was by his choice.

It was already dark when they all accompanied my brother and me to the train station to see us off. The night was quiet and warm, with the rich, natural aroma of country gardens wafting through the air. Nataliya and her brothers were running around with their little dog, and we admired the peaceful place and the wonderful people we were leaving behind. My dad's wife picked a bunch of flowers for us from their backyard; while it was a large and beautiful bouquet, it was a bit awkward to present such a gift to my family. We decided we would tell my mother that we had picked them from the forest. Walking by our side, our father talked to us about the principles of life and his vision of the world. He was very discouraged with the Soviet system, as discouraged as I was. We left the village and promised my father that we would return. On the ride home, we were glad about our reconciliation and considered the event another closed chapter in our lives.

When we got back home, Grandma asked us about our trip. We told her about all we experienced. We knew our mother would not want to hear anything about it because of her personal angst with our father after their bitter separation, so we only discussed it when she wasn't home. After that visit, our father called us frequently and even brought berries and mushrooms that he picked up in the forest close to where he lived. Since my brother and I were seldom ever home, my grandmother saw him very often or spent most of the time talking together on the phone. This strange but wonderful relationship continued between them for many years.

Making Guitars for a Living and Getting Married

In the summer of 1987, I took my one and only vacation and went for a few days to Sochi on the Black Sea. It was a great opportunity to think about my plans for a future life. I was looking for a solution in my situation, as I wanted to make guitars on a higher level, but my ability to do this under legal limitations was not an option. Something had to change if I was going to dedicate myself to this craft full time. The law of registered employment kept all of us under the powerful thumb of our government. All people in the USSR had an "Employment registration book" where all records of previous and current jobs were made. It was always kept at the employer 's administration office. Trying to avoid this Soviet regulation was impossible, so I had to find a job that could be technically registered while I worked in my root cellar all day making guitars. None of the government employers would offer me such a deal, and finding a workplace where I could spend less time than I was spending at the TV station was nearly impossible. I knew my only option was a cooperative of some sort, but landing such a job in those days was not so easy since they usually only hired relatives and close friends. To make it even more difficult, my goal was to work as little as possible so I would have free time to work on my craft. The ideal situation would be to find a place willing to keep my employment registration book so the government would have no any suspicion about my working status.

My own designed bridge and pickups.

After I returned home, I began a search for a coop that would meet these criteria. After several weeks of searching, I still could not find anyone who was hiring. It became a much more difficult task than I had expected, even though coops were considered to be run by easygoing people. Struggling with the limited time I had for guitar-making because of my TV station work schedule, I began to stay even more hours in the root cellar, often long after midnight. It became my world and life, and things seemed to drastically change around me. For one thing, I had very little personal life, if any. I seemed to be departing from the vanity of surrounding me world. While I had always dedicated my free time to my pals, music, and my obsession with playing guitar, my interaction with friends were now being limited to occasional gatherings at someone's house, and playing music had dwindled down to a few wedding gigs a year. All I did was making guitars and playing on my own at home, before I went to sleep.

I could no longer deal with our authoritarian policies dictating my destiny and prohibiting me from doing what I loved. I despised those draconic laws. After many long emotional struggles, I decided I had no choice but to quit my TV job and completely dedicate myself to my beloved craft. When I did that, life became even more confusing and intense. I was terrified of being caught since I was knowingly avoiding the required obligation of every Soviet citizen to be officially employed. The consequences of being busted for not maintaining legal employment would significantly increase if I were caught undertaking my guitar-making activities instead. I hoped to eventually find a coop that would allow me to work part time, and I was even ready to pay someone to keep my employment registration on record to keep me out of trouble. I had only a few allowable weeks without registered employment to find a place, so I dedicated many hours of my days roaming the city in search of a solution. In spite of my efforts, I had absolutely no luck. Running out of time, I had to prepare myself to avoid any and all interactions with government agencies that would attempt to verify my employment status. In that era of life in the Soviet Union, that meant avoiding everything from doctor visits to getting a library card. I had to seem as though I was employed, and I could not expose my absence from work to anyone, not even my closest friends. My presence on the streets and around the neighborhood would draw the attention of those people who were always "on alert" to spot and report so-called criminals. I was getting very frustrated with the difficulty of my situation, and things at home were not making it any easier. My mother was very concerned about me getting in big trouble, and I even considered returning to the TV station just to put my family at ease.

One weekend, I was searching through the help wanted ads in the local paper, and I stumbled across one ad placed by a boat-making coop. Without delay, I called them and scheduled an interview for the following day. The place that was hiring workers was technically the same coop business venture I had planned to start. It was located in the river vessels repair factory, and they were trying to establish production of small sailboats. I shared my own guitar-making coop drama with them, and they had great sympathy for me because they had gone through similar bureaucratic torture. Unlike me, however, they somehow managed to obtain a license for their operation, though I never asked them about the details. I was simply told, "It was more than just emotional pain." After talking to the business leader, I realized that taking a job there would be the perfect solution in my circumstances. He completely understood my situation, took my employment book, and told me to come in and work when I had no guitar orders. It was absolutely remarkable luck, and I was so happy knowing that I could finally work on my guitars full time without any fear of getting caught without legally recorded employment.

"I am getting married."

My love for making guitars was only mirrored by my love for my girlfriend, Natasha. After dating for a long time, we decided in September of 1987 to get married. She was only eighteen at the time, and I was twenty-three. These days, that may sound young to get married, but it was very normal at that time. Most young women were married before the age of twenty, and couples aimed to build their families before they were thirty years old.

Not long before our wedding, I took Natasha to visit my father. We took him an invitation to our wedding, and after my dad met her, we went for a walk into the forest. It was a lovely day, with the first touches of autumn painting the lavish countryside in a palette of reds and golds. We talked again about life, met all of his family members, and returned home after dinner. Before we left, my father apologized and told me that he could not join us at the wedding reception. I completely understood, considering all the hostility toward him from my maternal relatives, and I knew the presence of my mother and father in the same place would make our wedding day a very uncomfortable situation for all of us. Nevertheless, I felt obligated to invite him, and we understood his decision not to participate.

Traditionally, as I've mentioned, weddings in Russia were the biggest and most lavish of all festivities. In our case, though, counting on something extraordinary and glorious was impossible. Natasha's parents were also divorced, so even between our two broken families, we could not afford a fancy wedding. Still, we aimed to do our best to make the event memorable. We booked a small banquet hall at a restaurant, where another wedding was taking place at the same time in a different room. The band would play both receptions at the same time, but before the double-celebration could begin, we had to follow some of our established rituals and rules.

Several taxis were rented for the event, and after I picked up the bride from her house, we headed to ZAGS, where the record of marriages were kept. Surrounded by several close friends and family members, we exchanged rings in a Soviet ceremony. Then, my wife and I had to undergo another Russian wedding ritual. Everyone followed us in their taxis to one of our city's distinguished memorials of honor to place the flowers for those who contributed greatly to our Socialistic life. Fortunately, we had two dignitaries to choose from: the monument of Lenin on our central city square or the memorial in honor of fallen soldiers from World War II. Without question, I had no desire to use my wedding as an excuse to thank Lenin for destroying democracy and freedom in our country and establishing his totalitarian regime on one-sixth of Earth's soil. So, after we arrived at the Eternal Fire Memorial, we placed our flowers on the granite plaques where unknown soldiers from World War II were laid to rest.

It was the last stop on our way to the banquet hall, where the celebration was to take place. Our small group of guests, about forty, were seated in a U-shaped formation at a large table, and we dined on the best food the restaurant could deliver. My closest friends—Sasha, Evegeny, Dimitry, Oleg, and Yuri—surrounded me, and observing my tight circle of the people who were so dear and valuable to me and were a part of my music and daily life in the USSR was a comforting and very emotional experience. They each reminded me of the best days of my life, and I could not thank them enough for giving their friendship to me for all of those years. They were there with me, celebrating the birth of my family, and it was a wonderful feeling. Little did I know that I would never get to share any of their wedding days with them when the time came.

As always, drinks were on the table, and while the anti-alcoholic laws were still in place limiting amount of booze served at such events, we had brought enough with us from home to keep all of our guests happy and entertained. The band was playing loudly for the two weddings happening under one roof, making for a raging, exultant Russian celebration. My wife and I followed tradition and left before midnight, but many of our guests partied on until sunrise.

Living Together and Continuing my Passion

Next on the agenda for my new family was to decide where we were going to live. Since having our own apartment was still just a wild fantasy, and Natasha had been living with her mom, so in the beginning, we decided to live at her place, considering that my house was way too crowded to bring in another person. It was a very unusual concept at that time and in that place, for newlyweds traditionally moved to the groom's place.

Moving into my mother-in-law house, however, required me to rearrange the way I was operating my guitar-making "business". My initial idea of riding back to my old apartment root cellar every day turned out to be a bit problematic, for it was too far of a commute, an hour long on the overcrowded trolley. To make matters worse, I knew that constantly going in and out when I was supposed to be working might draw the attention and suspicion of my grandmother's KGB-affiliated neighbors.

The decision was made to get move all my tools and my little workbench to my in-laws' house. Since my wife's apartment building had no root cellar, I set up shop in the kitchen, a completely new environment for me. It did not take long for me to realize that the setup was not going to work. The mess my work created in the kitchen was very difficult to keep under control. Traces of dust were everywhere in the house, including getting in the food. On top of that, my constant pounding with chisels and hammers resonated from our seventh-floor unit throughout the whole building. People began asking what in the world was happening in our apartment, so I had to make the decision to move back root cellar. Not only did I plan to move my little shop back to its origins, but my wife would be moving with me into my grandmother's place as well. It was a difficult choice, but staying at my in-laws' apartment was no longer an option. If I did not do something, I would have had to give up my guitar-making or face getting in trouble, and I was not willing to do either. So, we loaded our few bags of belongings into a taxi and moved back to my old house.

Despite the obvious inconveniences of living in a cramped, one-bedroom apartment with my mother, brother, and grandma was the logical solution in our situation. Many soviet families spent their lives in such conditions, working out the generational differences under one roof, and now it was a reality for us as well.

My Own Concepts

After we moved back to my house, my guitar-building returned to normal. People who wanted one of my guitars came from all over the place, and word-of-mouth began spreading awareness about my operation. Many of the instruments I sold were created at my own discretion, but most often, my customers had ideas of their own about their dream guitar. Since many of them wanted to copy guitars that were already in existence, I did not want to produce them for ethical reasons, and I tried to steer my buyers toward something original. Unfortunately, few wanted to hear about that and focused their attention on getting a replica of a famous brand. Occasionally, I came up with some of my own radical designs, but those were always the last instruments to sell. Despite that, I still yearned to be more than just a guitar duplicator and continued creating my own concepts. As I considered fresh ideas and designs, I made a couple of instruments with popular eighties attributes, pointy or angular concepts. Fortunately, there were some open-minded buyers out there, and they were eager to buy custom-made instruments from me instead of purchasing their guitars elsewhere.

To make instruments exactly as they looked in the catalogs was not an easy task, mostly due to a lack of parts and adequate fabrication capabilities. Just to make a plane script or logo for the guitar headstock in a professional manner was a tricky process. I had no access to silk screening or other processes by which I could accomplish this. When a friend of mine mentioned to me that one "Coop" in Moscow was selling Western alphabet-style transfers, I made a trip there just to purchase them. It was a wonderful resource for me, for now I could create professional-looking logos on my electric guitars.

Even though I finally had a way of doing things with great elegance and accuracy, not many wanted to see the actual name of the original maker (me) on the headstocks of their instruments. The reasoning behind this is difficult to understand without knowing the mentality of our Soviet culture. For all of us, the symbol of quality could be only represented in "foreign" words and trademarks. People did not look at my guitars as a handmade instruments. They wanted to hold the real-deal axes in their hands, instruments made in the West, but they could not afford them. To most folks, my instruments were considered knock-offs, of sort—a substitute for something they were dreaming about, asking for a famous brand and not my name on the headstocks. Therefore, despite all the praise I received for the quality of my work, only a couple of my instruments were sold with the name of "Yuriy" on them. It did not bother me at the time, for I realized and understood the desperate desire of our people to own a respectable brand. I even felt privileged that someone might associate my quality of work with professional guitar manufacturers. Also, it was not necessary for my name to be out there to generate more sales, and it would have been dangerous for me if the wrong people caught a glimpse of it. If I had put my name on too many, it could have served as self-incriminating evidence, and I could be charged with conspiracy. Ultimately, the process and craftsmanship that I put into my instruments was the most important aspect to me, whether or not my signature was on them. While making copies of famous guitar brands was the least enjoyable part of my work, it gave me a lot of knowledge about instruments' designs and concepts. I learned from it in the same manner as people learning to play any musical instrument by playing some one else's music.

I also tried to create guitars with very complicated constructions. I made a couple of "neck through" instruments that I considered top of the line in my inventory. People loved them, and despite the incredible amount of hard labor involved in their creation, I still sold them for a mere $100 a piece. I knew many people had a limit of what they could pay for an instrument—even one of such high caliber—and I never increased the cost for my guitars, despite growing inflation in our country. The financial reward for my work was not my motivation; It was a true passion, and I felt I could and would do that job, even for free, if circumstances forced me to make a choice between guitar-building or anything else. Without a doubt, my guitar-making affair had turned into a permanent, unbreakable bond between me and my craft, and nothing in the world would separate or destroy it.

My Beloved Dog and the Unwanted Phone Call

We continue to live under one roof with my whole big family, but to my surprise, we even somehow managed to house a collie puppy. We named the black and white dog Tarzan, and he instantly became a beloved family member. He was smart, with a kind personality, and he grew up in our small apartment, surrounded by our love and gave us back even more of his. Everybody who had any interaction with him noticed his striking intelligence, and we were happy he matured to be an elegant, loyal pet. Whenever we had to be away, we missed him tremendously. Tarzan was not the first dog I'd had, for I'd had two little mixed puppies when I was a child, but I never felt as close to them as I did to that collie.

Our dog was so smart that he understood not only the intonation in our voices, but also the impression on our faces. Instead of barging into our bedrooms, for instance, he simply nudged on the door and then waited to be invited. We did not even have to bother telling him, "No," or "Go away," for if we said nothing at all, he would politely turn around and leave.

When we walked him down the street, we were often puzzled about how he could sense things about the people we encountered. If we came across people we knew that he hadn't yet met, he ignored them and stood behind us. If a stranger approached and asked for a cigarette lighter, he guarded us with his deep growling. At the same time, never in his life did he show the slightest sign of aggression, other than growling, even to vicious and unfriendly people. Unlike many dogs I knew, he could walk without a leash without ever going further than an inch away, regardless of the situation.

My wife and Tarzan

We never trained him or taught him obedience. It seemed as if Tarzan was born knowing human language and understood any command from the first time. We often joked that he should read magazines and books, since he could probably make more sense of it than any one of us.

We all loved him to the point that it was impossible to tell who his true master was. He never really showed any of us preference over the other and was always loving and gentle to all of us. Tarzan slept right by our entrance door, as if he felt obligated to protect us from any intrusion. In spite of our attempts to spoil the dog, he refused to sleep on the blanket we gave him .

Caring for dogs in the Soviet Union was probably no different than it had been for hundreds of years, with one exception: Before the Bolshevik Revolution, veterinarians treated dogs differently than a Kolkhoz's cows in the Soviet era. We had only one veterinary clinic in the city, and its main purpose was to do vaccinations and artificial fertilization of farm animals and livestock. Dogs were considered unimportant from an agricultural standpoint, and the government did not feel they deserved the same attention and care as goats and pigs.

Also, dog food was never produced in the USSR. We had a shortage of food for our own people, so even considering providing food for pets would have seemed foolish. Many of us were not even aware that outside of the Soviet Union, people actually produced and purchased food specially meant for dogs. Rumors about such an absurd product occasionally came from the few who were fortunate enough to travel to the West; one bizarre rumor claimed that some of our tourists considered eating dog food to save money so they could buy jeans during their Western travels. In this way, I suppose our dogs were more fortunate than dogs in Capitalist nations, for instead of dry kibble, ours were fed leftovers from our own tables. In this way, Soviet pets were benefitted from our lack of dog food production, and Tarzan was spoiled with table food and scraps. On top of that, because my grandma was such a loving person, she even cooked his favorite blintz and soups for him on occasion. Feeding him in the kitchen gave her a lot of pleasure, and it was very sweet to watch her talk to Tarzan while he was eating.

We loved our dog with all our hearts and souls and could not imagine how we ever lived without such a marvelous creature in the past. He was truly one of our family members, and it saddened us that he was all cooped up in our small apartment with us. Because of Tarzan, I absolutely fell in love with large and intelligence dog breeds, but while I will have more other dogs in my life, Tarzan will always be considered the best dog I've ever had.

"You're fired."

Everything was going well with my established underground guitar production. I began collaborating with more and more people who could provide services to me, such as plating my hardware, milling, and fabricating my specialty tools. After while, I adjusted to my complete underground operation and knew how to behave on public to make my lack of a daily job be unnoticeable. I was not very happy with that disguised and undercover kind of life, but I had no other option and had to continue with my secret and unusual lifestyle.

Realizing that my strange existence could last for a long time, I had no plans to change anything about my guitar-making operation, in spite of the ever-present fear of being caught. I was officially employed at the sailboat "Coop" and assumed my phony employment could at least somehow shield me if I was questioned by our authorities.

Everything seemed to be going smoothly until I received a call from the boat-making cooperative to inform me that the management there had changed, and they wanted me to show up for work full time. That was not part of my plan, and whether they changed their mind about keeping my employment registration book or decided to use my woodworking experience, I could not stop making guitars to work on boats. I tried to talk to them and even considered offering some kind of exchange if they would maintain my employment documents to keep up the façade. There was no solution, though, and I was faced with only two options: work full time or leave... Just a couple of days later, I was already officially unemployed.

This changed everything. I could not stop what I was doing in my root cellar, but at the same time, I could not risk failing to be legally registered at some workplace. The only option I had was to try and find another coop that would work out a similar deal with me and keep me on their employment list.

Troubling Perestroika and a Gloomy Future Ahead

Considering all aspects of my situation, I began a vigorous search for a place that would give me another chance to avoid Soviet employment violation. I walked from one workplace to another and received nothing but denial after denial. The more time I spent searching for a suitable 'employment', to no avail, the more frustrated I became.

One of my "Neck Through" guitars.

That, coupled with my observations of the accelerating decay of our economical state and its infrastructure, had me wondering what the future could hold. More items and household products began to disappear from our store shelves. It felt like the whole system was falling apart, all while we were being assured that we were officially "moving into the new political and economical prosperity." The sense of chaos dominated everyone's minds, and it was obvious that our old Soviet regime officials did not want to yield to the progressive reforms Gorbachev was trying to implement. It was very abnormal for there to be such a disconnect between our local authorities and the new polices released by Kremlin. The political obedience that was so typical in the Soviet hierarchy no longer seemed to be working; in fact, it seemed the actions of our local government were actually sabotaging their own leaders. The slow and heavily bureaucratic machine did not want to change for the new dynamic and productive forms of operation demanded by Kremlin. Instead of eliminating the roadblocks to the more progressive economical reforms of Gorbachev, new local policies and regulations created chaos and bureaucracy in our country. To many people, it was very obvious that the spontaneous disappearance of daily necessities like soap, toothpaste, and salt from our stores was not caused by "production interruptions" or "panicked buying by the customers," but that it was a result of conspiracies of old regime Communists. This created an atmosphere of frustration and outrage about empty store shelves. The economical havoc happening in our country was the result of stubbornness from the people in local power, who refused to change for the better.

Gorbachev's popularity began to decline, as everyone was beginning to get fed up with such disorder—something the Soviet people were not used to. The reform meant to encourage free speech, Glasnost, was beginning to produce unexpected outcries like our country had never known. The first worker strikes were reported in the rural regions of the USSR, where frustrated citizens were desperate for government aid for their critical economic condition. Though Gorbachev was a proponent of free speech, the strikes worked against him, in favor of all who wanted the hard line regime to be reinstated on Russian soil.

The slightly liberalized political control of our people also unleashed ethnic conflicts and separatists, issues that had been bubbling under the surface but were formerly suppressed by our totalitarian regime. Bloody clashes between the Armenians and the Azerbaijani shocked our nation with something the Soviet Union had never experienced. It gave our zealous defenders of the strong regime more leverage and fuel to demonize the reforms Gorbachev was so desperately trying to implement for the betterment of the USSR.

We were definitely living a different country from the one we'd grown up in. Despite the proclamations of improved Soviet life, reality was very different from what the government was telling us. We were slowly sliding into a real economic and political chaos that none of us wanted to deal with. All the positive changes our new leaders were trying to make began to seem like putting a saddle on a cow: They did not fit our core political structure, which was still oriented on Socialistic dogmas. The absence of a true democracy and free market did not allow our nation to move into a stable and economically prosperous direction. What we could expect in the near future was anybody's guess. One thing was known for certain: If were going to spiral down into much more troubled economical and political turbulence, we would more likely revert back to the old strict totalitarian regime.

In such an unstable situation, I could not picture how I was going to raise a family and have children. The future looked very blurry for us, and all we could imagine was living under one roof with our relatives, waiting for history to take another tumultuous turn in ever-struggling Russia. People did not have the slightest idea how we would be living a year later, and that was very unusual for Soviets, who were used to a slowly changing, routine, very controlled kind of life. Enveloped by economic and social chaos, as well as the vile aftermath of the Chernobyl, many people desperately yearned to escape the nightmare. Hope was a quickly vanishing thing, and the dream of leaving the Soviet Union for good became more desirable than ever before; however, such a dream was also much more unrealistic.

Surrender Myself to My Passion

At that moment, I didn't know how to deal with my job situation, or lack thereof. All efforts to find any feasible solution proved fruitless. I was wasting my time trying to find visible employment to hide my underground guitar production activities. After a long search, I began to realize that even if I did get busted while making guitars, the phony employment status would not save me from a prison term; in fact, it could have made the situation worse and even aggravate it, since I would be guilty not only of unlawful operation of my business, but also for fabricating my employment status. Everything was pointing to the end times of Gorbachev's dream, Perestroika, and I expected my guitar--making to be yet another casualty. Whatever was going to happen in the USSR in the near future, the one thing we knew was that our lives would change yet again. When that happened, I was sure no one would be interested in guitars any longer, considering the inevitable harsh backlash that would be unleashed upon everything Gorbachev had allowed, both culturally and politically. Still, my love for the craft could not be thwarted by fear of the unknown, and I decided to surrender myself to my passion and make guitars until my Soviet life led to yet another catastrophic conclusion.

The most dangerous time in my guitar-making full time, without any documented legal employment, officially began. Thus, I had to be much more careful in my actions and guitar operation, and everybody in my close circle of friends was told that I was still working part time making sailboats at the cooperative. Everyone knew, however, what my true job really was, and many of my friends sympathized with me and admired me for my risky—and perhaps even foolish—dedication to my passion.

One of my guitars.

Chapter 21

America's Visas and Taking a Chance

One evening, we invited my good friend Vitaliy and his wife over for tea. They joined us for the small gathering, a common social invitation in those days among Soviets. Little did I know, though, that the casual and seemingly insignificant rendezvous would turn out to be one of the most important get-togethers of my life.

As we conversed about our lives and what lay ahead, the topic came up of people trying to leave our decaying nation. Most of them were Jewish people, who wanted to take the chance to make their escape during eased Soviet restrictions on their departures to Israel. In our case, we could not even dream about attempting such a journey without having any Jewish relatives in our bloodline. As the discussion went on, Vitaliy shared with us a rumor that the U.S. Embassy in Moscow was accepting applications from anyone who wanted to immigrate to the United States. He said he had heard this from someone who had just returned from Moscow.

Of course the information intrigued me, but most of the things people said about the USA, and especially their embassy in Moscow, were merely rumors, and speculation that turned out to be false or inflated, like urban legends, of sorts. Frankly, it seemed too unrealistic to be true. Considering that access to the embassy was always guarded by our police force and undercover KGB officers, I was certain this information was exaggerated or simply untrue. I asked Vitaliy if he would ever leave the USSR himself, and he said it would be impossible considering our cruel emigration laws. He was right about that, but even a minuscule chance of escaping from all that growing turmoil was enough to spark a bit of hope, and that was better than nothing.

Regardless of what other people were telling me, I always tried to find the truth for myself, especially in situations when information could be very important. Not only would it be risky to call the embassy, but it was also problematic for one simple reason: the phone number of the place was never available for ordinary Russian people, and obtaining it through our information service via the telephone company would have been the same as asking it a KGB officer. Since calling was not an option, the only one way to check if what my friend was telling me was true was to travel to Moscow and see for myself. Fortunately, the address of the embassy was known to everyone who listened to Voice of America on their short-wave radios. Its location was mentioned occasionally in news reports, and many of our people memorized it, just in case. I was among those people, so without delay, I purchased a ticket on the next train to Moscow.

By the Embassy

The following day, the train took me to verify most crucial information I might ever learn—information I thought might significantly change my life. When I arrived in Moscow, I bought a city map, and after short breakfast, I went on the subway to my destination.

As I approached the big old building that had been constructed during the Stalin era, I saw a large red, white, and blue flag waving in the breeze above the entrance to the U.S. Embassy. Surrounded by Soviet police patrols, the entrance reminded me of a customs checkpoint rather than a diplomatic residence. Several large American cars were parked nearby, and U.S. military soldiers, polished from top to bottom, guarded the entrance. Everyone who entered the building was required to show their ID to our police officers and to the U.S. military personnel, and only U.S. residents and selected Soviet personnel were authorized to go inside.

As I watched the distinguished-looking Americans, I observed a moment that was rare for us to witness. They were foreigners from a rival nation, the most demonized nation of our state in the recent Cold War. In contrast to the stereotypes and years of propaganda that had been forced into our ears and minds, they looked both happy and very friendly. Even for me, it was difficult to grasp that they were not the angry at Russians monsters they had been made out to be. I expected to see on-alert and cautious expressions on their American faces, but instead, I saw amicable smile.

The whole area around the embassy was filled with people, and I tried to discern if any of them knew anything about applications for immigration. In a few minutes, everything was clear: Yes, it was true that the U.S. Embassy was accepting applications, and they were distributed once daily at the entrance. The problem was that number of people who wanted an application greatly outnumbered the number of people allowed to go to the embassy checkpoint to take one.

The whole situation was reminiscent of the severe product deficits in our stores. There were "volunteers" from the crowd keeping an order to get the applications. They took a headcount of the crowd and gave the list to the police officers. From that point, they allowed small groups to go to the window at the entrance to pick up their applications. When I glanced around at all the chaos, I realized I would be stuck there for days, and in the end, I might not even receive an application after all.

As always in situations surrounding any desirable item in the USSR, there were those who wanted to take advantage of people's desperation and make money on it. A rough-looking, unshaven man approached me and asked if I needed an application. I asked him if he knew someone from the embassy, and he told me, "I don't need to know anybody there." He pulled his coat open and showed me a stack of papers nestled on the inside. "It's twenty-five rubbles for one," he said in a gruff whisper. It was a lot of money considering that I could try to get one for free just twenty yards away, but I had no place to stay if I got stuck there for several days. All the hotels in Moscow were booked ahead for years, and sleeping at the train station was too dangerous, especially considering my lack of an official workplace. I looked one more time at the crowd, and without any further hesitation, I bought two applications from the man. Even though I had to pay a high price for them, something was telling me that those documents were more than simple paperwork, and I held them tightly inside of my coat as I walked back to the train station to travel home.

No One Would Allow Us to Leave

When I arrived at home, the first thing I did was look at those applications. Everything was straightforward, written in both Russian and English. Two pages had to be completed and I began filling them out line by line. I was not sure how to answer the questions about my employment at first, but since I assumed the U.S. officials would not turn my application over to the KGB, I wrote an honest answer: "Guitar-making Business, Yuriy Guitars."

My wife was a bit skeptical as to whether or not anyone would actually read the application, let alone grant us a chance to emigrate to the USA. The other people in my household had the same pessimistic opinion, for they were sure no one would simply allow us to leave our country that easily. The problem stemmed not only from the Soviet draconic laws of international travel, but also from United States policies as well; only a fraction of the applicants would actually be fortunate enough to receive their visa, their walking papers to leave the Soviet Union. We were not simply seeking a tourist or travel visa, but qualification to obtain official refugee status in the United Status. Only those who had political reasons or were prosecuted in the USSR for their beliefs, could qualify for this status. Considering that in our country was impossible to find a person who was not suffering from the backward reality of our political system, anyone could technically claim the right to refugee status. Strangely, none of the questions on the application asked about our political backgrounds or any troubled past with the Soviet regime; those would be discussed at the face-to-face interview. Before an interview could be scheduled, however, these applications had to be submitted in person to the Embassy, so I began preparing for a return trip to Moscow.

Before I left to deliver my documents to the U.S. Embassy, I also talked to few of my close friends, the ones I felt I could trust, and told them about my plan to apply for refugee status and my upcoming trip to the American Consulate. Some of them were surprised that such an option was available. Most of them, however, had no interest in even trying, assuming it was too much of a risky lottery that might rouse the suspicion of the KGB in the process. A couple of my close friends even warned me not to pursue the idea, for they feared I might return from the Embassy in handcuffs. It was the typical attitude of many of our people, but I did not want to hear it. Everyone seemed to be complaining about our lives, but few tried to do anything to change them.

Fear, coupled with lazy inertia, held a lot of my friends captive in the mental state our Soviet system wanted them to exist in. I was a bit surprised at their reaction, but it was my family's future, and I was ready to take what might be our only chance for freedom.

"You will be Number 638."

When I arrived in Moscow to submit our applications to the Embassy, I was not even sure how to go about it. There were no clear instructions or directions, and I soon learned that it was a much more difficult task than obtaining the application in the first place. Every day, only a limited group of people were allowed to submit their petitions inside the U.S. embassy. This process was controlled by our police force, who secured the entrance. They gathered people into small groups and allowed them to enter, escorted by U.S. personnel.

There were more people than I could imagine trying to get through, and I was told to sign up in line near the Embassy, where one energetic lady was making a list of everybody who needed to drop off their documents. Later, they would turn the list to our policemen, who would announce names and gather a group to go inside. I asked the list lady how long the wait would be.

"You mean how many days? You will be Number 638. What's your name, sir?" She opened a big notebook.

"I am sorry, miss, but how many people do they allow to go inside every day?" I asked in total disbelief, looking at the long list of names scribbled in her notebook.

"It depends on the day. It could be forty, or it could be eighty."

I turned around, looked at the crowd, and realized I would be there for at least two weeks, just to turn my applications in. "Can I sign up and come back few days from now?" I asked, hoping I could find a place to stay in Moscow for for some time, or go home and return to Moscow.

"No. It will be your turn at one point to hold this list and write people's name. When and at what time it will happen, I don't know. I am leaving in ten minutes, and this guy," she said, pointing at a bald, sleepy-looking man, "will take his turn. The line can move slower or faster. There is no way to tell. You might be here for two weeks or four days. If you leave, you can lose out on your chance."

It sounded exactly like our waiting lines at the stores when they were selling wallpaper or decent-quality furniture. I had no option, and despite having no place to stay in Moscow, I signed my name in the notebook on Line 638.

I wandered away from the crowd and noticed that the day's last group of people were entering the Embassy. Police and the curious crowd were thinning at the entrance, allowing me to get a bit closer look. One cop was still patrolling the area by the entrance, where the sidewalk was barricaded by metal rail guards. "What do you need, pal?" he asked, pulling the divider guard closer to the entrance.

I wasn't sure what to say, so I looked at the Americans behind him and mumbled, "I have a question about inviting relatives from the USA."

"Well, if you have a question, you can ask it very quickly there at the window," he said, pulling the fence aside to let me in.

I was so unprepared for that that I didn't even know what to do next. After walking to the entrance, I saw a little window, where American lady was checking everyone's ID. Suddenly I brought my thoughts together and pulled the application from my coat. Without any delay, I asked her if there was a way to just drop it off, since I had no place to stay in Moscow for two weeks.

With a very heavy accent and a warm smile, she replied, "You can submit it right now if you want since we still have plenty of vacancies for today. Can I please see your ID?"

I could not believe what she had just said, assuming that a huge crowd was waiting outside in line, and as I pulled my ID out, I watched the cop behind the barrier; he was staring at me as well.

"This way," she said in terrible Russian, pointing to the little chamber where U.S. Marines were posted to once more verify IDs.

Inside of the "Forbidden" Place

I was entering what used to be one of the most heavily Soviet guarded buildings in the country. Historically, the authorities had feared that Russian people would try to sneak inside to ask for political asylum. If I had come to the building just a couple years earlier, it would have been absolutely impossible. For many years, it was an unreachable place for ordinary Soviet citizens, I was so surprised that the true security of the building was no longer a top Soviet priority.

Stepping inside that place felt alien somehow, like stepping aboard a spaceship or some forbidden place. Everything was completely different from what I had seen in our buildings. Assuming it was both my first and last visit to the place, I tried to take it all in. On the second floor, I entered a large room with several windows and a bunch of chairs set up as a waiting area for those who wanted to submit their documents. The crowd of applicants who had been standing outside ten minutes earlier looked energized and happy, as excited as I was to be amongst them.

I took a seat and patiently waited to be invited to the window. One by one, people were called to submit their documents, but I was clueless about what would happen after that. About an hour later, I was called, and I slid my papers under the window and answered the few questions that were asked of me by a young man who spoke Russian very well. He smiled a lot and seemed very relaxed, and I wasn't sure if he was really listening to me or concentrating more on my application form. He asked me nothing specific about my life in Russia other than my reasons for wanting to leave. I wasn't sure how to summarize everything that was pushing me to leave my motherland. I wanted to ask him, "Don't you know anything about life in the USSR?" but I refrained. I managed to describe my motivations to him in a few sentences, though I wasn't sure if he completely and truly understood.

"Okay," he replied. "You will get the package with instructions about your interview by mail."

"By mail?" I was sure he had to be kidding. All mail that came from overseas was checked, double-checked, and, for all we knew, even subjected to chemical analysis by the KGB. I could not believe they intended to send me a package about my refugee status interview via the heavily censored Soviet mail service. It sounded like a joke, and while I understood that they had no control over our postal procedures, I was sure they should have had at least an alternative method for people to receive their documents from the Embassy.

Regardless, I didn't bother arguing or trying to explain what trouble that kind of mail might cause. In spite of my worries about that, I was still grateful I had managed to miraculously turn in our applications without having to stay in Moscow for weeks. On the way out of the Embassy, I picked up a few applications just in case; after all, they cost a fortune from the scalpers outside the Embassy.

Waiting for Papers and Moving Along with our Lives

After arriving home, I didn't know what to expect as a result of my trip to the U.S. Embassy. I was sure my visit hadn't gone unnoticed by our nosy secret police, and I expected a conversation with them about it. Days and weeks went by, and no one bothered me about it. I didn't know if that was because our KGB was too busy with much more important issues or because they didn't have enough staff to chase every single person who had no interest in the Soviet doctrines they were trying so hard to shove down our throats. Whatever the reason, this anomaly was a good sign that I could continue quietly making my guitars while I awaited the package from the U.S. Embassy that would tell me how to proceed with my interview.

Practically all of my close friends and relatives were telling me that expect the paperwork to actually arrive by mail was an unrealistic and naïve pipe dream. According to them, my efforts to obtain a U.S. visa to leave the Soviet Union was "a gamble guaranteed to lose." I was told I was wasting my effort and time, chasing a dream that would never come true and would only lead to disappointment when I waited many months, only to have to return to the dismal reality of our Soviet life. Specifically going to America was neither a dream nor an obsession for me; all I was after, really, was freedom. At that time I wanted nothing more but a normal life for my family, where we could live without being subjected to further cataclysmic experiments conducted by a controlling government on its oppressed population. I wanted to have a chance to do what I loved in my life without risk of being jailed for it, without having to bribe our authorities and racketeers. Unfortunately, my motherland did not allow me that opportunity. The country I loved so much was hijacked by Communists in 1917, and they turn it into an ideological battleship on which I refused to cooperate as a silently obedient sailor. Russia was heading to an unknown destination, and the Communist 'captain' was losing control of the crew, who was ready to throw him overboard. It was obvious that our near future was not going to be as glamorous as we had all hoped when Gorbachev came into our view.

There was no safe or comfortable zone in the USSR where we could find a shelter from the growing destabilization in our country. People have a natural survival instinct, and many were ready to go anywhere to avoid living under a Stalin-era regime or having to withstand a complete collapse of all our economical and social infrastructure. When my friends told me my plans to move to the United States were hopeless, I had to convince myself that the chance was still worth taking. It was my only lifeboat, and I wanted to get as far away as I could from that disoriented, sinking Soviet ship before I went down with it. I would not rest until I had my answer, and as I waited for the documents from the U.S. Embassy, the chaos continued to accelerate in the USSR all around me.

People Were Still Buying Guitars

Despite the deteriorating living standards in our country, people still wanted to buy my guitars and hose who played at the restaurants were in the front line to get one.By nature, musicians have an unstoppable nature to sacrifice even life's necessities to pursue their passion, but there was also another explanation as to why so many were willing to spend their hard-earned money on my products during such a time of uncertainty. Historically, in any time of trouble, our people tried to avoid keeping cash on hand, knowing that inflation would eventually gobble up its value. For this reason, anyone who had savings or a modest income spent it on luxury items in the black market. These items—like gold, Japanese VCRs, stereo equipment, and fancy watches, for instance—were constantly going up in price. These were the most desirable items in which Soviets wanted to invest their money. For musicians, my guitars also fell into this category. They cost nearly twice less than a Panasonic VCR; for a guitarist, this was not only a great deal from a financial standpoint, but also from a practical perspective as well. Knowing that hard-to-find or limited items in the USSR could technically act as "hard currency" that could be resold later for a profit, people were more than willing to dump their ever-devaluating rubbles into them.

This situation worked in my favor, so I kept building guitars in my root cellar as I patiently waited for any word from the U.S. Embassy regarding the interview. The hope of getting this information by mail was very low, but I believed that the Soviet officials were aware that hijacking the mail of thousands of applicants from the U.S. Embassy could potentially damage the U.S.-Soviet relationship that Gorbachev so desperately trying to stabilize. On top of this international political factor, the rising concern of the economical and social crisis in our country kept our secret police occupied with much more important issues than filtering all circulating mail in the nation. We only hoped our documents would not be confiscated by our mail service; otherwise, we would be forced to share that doomed destiny right along with the rest of the Soviets.

Application for My Brother

I had submitted applications for myself and my wife, but not my brother. Considering the situation around us, we all were agree that he needed to apply for the visa as well. Therefore, the application I had thought to pick up on the way out of the Embassy became a priceless trophy. When my brother went to Moscow to deliver his petition, we knew he might be stuck there for several days, so we made arrangements for him to stay if he needed as well. An old friend of my grandma's was still living in Moscow and promised to shelter him for a short time during his trip.

When he arrived, he did not even have a chance to enter the Embassy. In just a few months, due to an uncontrolled and overwhelming flood of applications, they had changed their procedure. The news about a chance to go to the USA had spread like wildfire, and the avalanche of applications nearly paralyzed the Embassy, so the whole process of submitting paperwork was changed. A giant box was placed by the entrance for completed applications, but it was so full that papers were falling out of it and were scattered all over the ground. When one of the newspapers reported that a similar box full of applications was found in a nearby Moscow trash dump, it created a lot of outrage. No one knew if it was the work of a discredited journalist trying to get attention or if it was a trick of our authorities to place a mark of blame on the U.S. Embassy. Only a naïve person would have believed that such a just plain stupid act would have been committed by the official American Consulate. Either way, the method I had used to deliver my applications was no longer an option. When my brother went to Moscow, he saw no drop-box at the Embassy; instead, there was a note stating that all petitions had to be mailed directly to Washington DC in the USA. Many people considered this the end of the U.S. refugee program for Soviets and gave up, not wanting to spend the money or time to mail their forms to the U.S.

My brother decided to mail them anyway, hoping against hope that they would get where they were supposed to go, on time and without being tampered with.

Dying Soviet Union and Checking the Mail

Signs of the decay in government power were reflected in the growing demand by many Soviet republics for their independency from Russia. At first, it was small, spontaneous meetings and protests by people asking Moscow for more freedom in their republics, since they felt that Moscow was controlling every aspect of their lives. Later, these notions became more radical demands for complete separation and exit from the USSR. The first in line with these demands were the Baltic Republics of Latvia, Estonia, and Lithuania. Our Soviet media never commented on the demonstrations and protests, of course, but they were covered by the more sympathetic Western radio station programs. Many people in the USSR did not believe such demands could not possibly really be voiced from any of our own Soviet republics. As far as they were concerned, in their old way of thinking, the Soviet Union was "one and whole for eternity by the will of its people," and it was unthinkable to them that separation might occur, even in the time of Perestroika.

The centrifugal force of the small changes Gorbachev was making in the Soviet Union was enough to inspire everyone to unleash all the frustrations that had been building up within our country for many decades. In April of 1989, a huge demonstration for the liberation of cultural and economic life raged in Tbilisi. In fear of some kind of miniature revolution, the Georgian Soviet Republic sent Red Army troops to the streets to disperse the protestors. During that skirmish, twenty-two people were killed, and hundreds were injured in a bloody shed in the Tbilisi capital. Not only did this tragedy undermine the democracy and freedom claims that the Kremlin was making, but it also shocked the nation when it was mentioned on Soviet media networks. A catastrophic event of such proportions and resulting in so many casualties could not simply be swept under the carpet, and the government had no choice but to tell its side of the story, twisting the facts and exaggerating the tale as it always did., conveniently blaming the so-called "provocateurs" and "separatists." Soviet officials desperately tried to detract attention from their inability and unwillingness to find a political solution. It was impossible to say if the clash between the Red Army and the Georgian demonstrators was the work of those who were sabotaging Perestroika or whether it was done under direct orders from the Kremlin.

For many in the USSR, it was a sign that the government was still operating under the tactics of the old regime to control all the happenings in the nation. For all of us living in the USSR, it was a clear sign that the country we all knew would never be the same again. In spite of all we'd heard from the Kremlin about democracy and freedom, the events in the Soviet republics made it clear that the government was not even in line with its own policies. Whatever little trust we still had in the honesty of our leaders was rapidly dying. The deadly outcome of the demonstrations in Tbilisi shattered the universal belief that our army would never stoop to the depths of shooting at its own people. In order to ensure the survival of our old Soviet system, our leaders were ready to use any means necessary, even if that meant opening fire and taking the lives of disgruntled and unhappy Soviet citizens. Ordinary people were victims of our political struggle, and we only hoped it would not lead to a bloody and violent civil war.

The Yellow Envelope

Checking the daily mail became more than a daily routine for me. We could not wait to hear something from the Embassy. The moment our mail carrier, a lady we knew well, dropped our mail off at the mailbox on the second floor, we ran down to see what had arrived. Several months after I had submitted my application to the U.S. Embassy, we still had heard nothing from the American Consulate, and we began to lose hope that we ever would. But then, the day came when that all changed.

I was working in the root cellar when I heard someone rushing to the basement area. Still fearful of being caught in my illegal business, I closed the door behind me and covered the guitar body I was working on with a jacket and quickly placed a stool leg on my workbench to act as if I was repairing it.

"Yuriy, it's me!" I heard my brother's Misha shouting. "You need to go upstairs to your apartment now!" he exclaimed with a big excitement.

"Why? What happened?" I asked, pulling the jacket off and returning nonchalantly to my work.

"The package from the Americans has arrived!" he said, waving his hands in the air in euphoria.

I dropped my tools in the toolbox, wrapped the guitar body back up in the jacket, and rushed back home with it. When I got there, a big yellow envelope was lying on our round family table. We opened it and started reading information concerning our interview at the U.S. Embassy in Moscow. Clear instructions and dates were spelled out in a short letter, and after several emotional minutes, we started talking about our upcoming trip. At that point, the reality of emigrating from the USSR became more of a reality than a simple dream. We were surprised to see that the information had arrived safely from the Embassy without being censored by the strict Soviet postal service, and this gave us even more hope. We were scheduled to appear before the U.S. Embassy a couple of months later, and we had to offer them a clear explanation of why we wanted to move to the United States.

No one we knew had undergone one of these interviews, so we did not know how they would be conducted or what specific questions would be asked. All we knew was that only very few people were granted such permission, and what that decision was based on remained a mystery.

A brief explanation of the U.S. immigration laws was included, and from that we learned that no nationality in the world was given preference or privilege. When it came to immigrants in the U.S., all were treated with equal consideration. By this we assumed that the annual quota for France would be the same as for Zimbabwe or Mexico; thus, only a limited number of Russians would be allowed to go to the USA, and more Soviets sought solace there than in England. We desperately hoped we would be granted a right to move to the USA. At that moment, we did not want to destroy our hope by thinking about how we would get permission from the Soviet government to leave. We wanted to concentrate only on one agenda: being granted U.S. refugee status.

Going for the Interview

On a cold, windy night, my wife and I got on the train without telling any of our friends about our trip to the U.S. Embassy. We had to stay in Moscow for a day before we were scheduled to appear for our early morning interview, so we rented two beds in a train car that had been converted into a sort of makeshift hotel. These were basically sleeping quarters, and the converted train hotels were operated by a small coop; they were really the only place to find shelter for a night. Moscow was not only chaotic and drowning in corruption, but it was also a place where shady, greedy cooperatives overtook even public toilets, making them pay-for-use facilities. It made no matter to us, though, for our minds were not on our discomforts. We were far too consumed by what would happened at our interview, and after a nervous and stressful day, we managed to get some sleep before what might prove to be a difficult morning.

After spending the night on the train car, were awakened by a worker at six a.m. We had to leave the crowded train car, where every inch of open seating was filled with snoring and strange characters. We used the pay bathrooms, had a short breakfast at the train station, and headed into the most important interview of our lives.

Chapter 22

Interview at the Embassy and OVIR Denial

The whole process of getting inside the Embassy for our interview was a bit strange. Everyone who was scheduled for interviews that day had to present their passport to the Soviet police guards, and the guards took the passports inside of a small station—a kiosk, really—that was set up near the Embassy. No one explained to us what this procedure was all about or why they were taking our passports, and after waiting for about a half-hour, our documents were given back. One thing we did know was that this screening had nothing to do with Embassy security; Americans were clearly aware of who was coming and going in that building, so they had no need to rely on the Soviet police for monitoring that. Once we were inside, the motive behind it became rather clear.

All in all, about forty applicants were called in for interviews that day. Once the passport shuffling and screening was complete, we were escorted into the Embassy. Everyone gathered in a large waiting room, and one by one, we were invited into the special office dedicated to interviews.

In the waiting room, where we were all sitting, there were a few windows where tourist visas were being reviewed. While waiting to be called, we observed the Embassy clerks denying petitions for these visas. They were particularly very strict about any misleading information provided by the applicants, and we understood that somehow, the Americans knew a lot about the applicants' backgrounds. Some of them were openly accused of being members of the Communist Party, though they attempted to lie about it in their applications. At that moment, we realized that if the U.S. Embassy were of details about the people applying for visas, they probably knew much more about those wanting to leave the country for good; it was a bit unsettling to see just how much they knew.

A few hours later, we were finally called for our interview. The small, comfortable office was set up like a living room. We each took a seat. The officer who conducted the interview was very friendly and listened carefully to everything we had to say as we explained our lives and our situation. We noticed that he did not have any paperwork in front of him, and he did not take any notes. To us, this seemed somewhat alarming, and we were paranoid that the Americans have already decided our faith. We didn't really understand the process, and in spite of our nerves, we tried to concentrate on answering his questions without sounding suspicious or stupid. I was a bit intimidated by the whole situation, doubting that we had much of a chance to attain refugee status. In spite of my aversion to some of the political things going on in my homeland, I was not a true dissident; I had not spent time in the gulag or been prosecuted in court for my anti-Soviet beliefs. Yes, I had been kicked around a bit by the KGB, but I was never jailed or tortured like so many human rights activists in our country. I told the truth, and when I was asked what I would do if I was granted access to the U.S., I answered simply, "I would make guitars." The officer laughed, and when the interview was over, we were told the documents bearing their decision would be presented to all applicants outside of the Embassy at five p.m.

We walked out of the building in silence, our minds debating and pondering what we might expect as a result. It was hard to believe that our future now was in hands of some clerk from a foreign nation. Huge crowd were still gathered by the Embassy, waiting to find out where their futures would be lived, just like we were. The applicants were surrounded by friends and relatives, and while there was anxiety controlling most of us, some were already cheering in excitement in anticipation of what they hoped would be approval. Sadly, for many of them, their premature celebration would turn into a desperate outrage when their refugee status would be denied.

It was already getting dark when an officer in a long trench coat came out of the Embassy. He had a large stack of papers in his hand. Standing by the entrance, he asked everyone to gather 'round, and he began reading off last names and passing the results to the applicants. It was quiet, and the tension was thick in the air. We were standing about four rows from the officer. As the applicants looked over their results, occasionally someone would shout, "Yes!" Others looked at their results with forlorn faces and quietly left the crowd, cried, or shouted "No" in anger; we all knew what that meant. In spite of what was going on in the crowd, the officer continued calmly reading off names, repeating in an emotionless voice, like a broken record, "These decisions are final, subject to no appeal!"

Almost everyone was receiving denials, so I prepared to tell my wife not to worry and that we would survive somehow. When our name was called, our slip of paper traveled through a couple pairs of hands before reaching us; a tall, young man finally handed it to me. He looked briefly at the page before he handed it to me, and I tried to gauge the reaction in his eyes; it was one of the few times I ever noticed an expression of jealousy and sorry at the same time. I glanced at the document and saw two boxes, one for YES and one for NO. An X was marked beside the YES, confirming the decision of the U.S. government to grant us the right to enter United States under refugee program. I could not believe it for a second, but once my wife and I grasped the reality of it, we burst into a chorus of cheers. In the end, from among that huge group of hopeful, desperate Soviets, only six were granted refugee status that day.

The doors to United States of America were now open to us, and we ran through the streets of Moscow mindlessly giddy, not even feeling the ground beneath our feet. In a few hours, we would be heading back home on the train, and we could not wait to share the great news with our families. What we didn't know yet was that the battle for our freedom was not over; we had only won the easiest part of the fight.

USSR Still Refused to Open its Borders

No one expected us to return with refugee status in our hands, and the news we brought from Moscow was truly shocking to all our relatives. While everyone was utterly surprised and happy, for it was no secret that getting permission from our government to depart from the USSR would prove to be a much more challenging task.

The next step for us was to visit the OVIR department to apply for a departure visa and our Soviet travel passports. For many years, it was well known that this procedure was nearly impossible for ordinary Soviets. Despite the freedoms promised by Perestroika, the USSR still refused to open its borders and allow anybody to leave the country. This human rights violation fueled long-lasting political confrontations with the Western world, but besides easing the chances for Jews to immigrate, others were still banned from leaving the Soviet Union for good. It was a nearly impossible task just to get an immigration application from the USSR. An appointment had to be set up with an OVIR officer, and an interview would be scheduled, in which we would be questioned about the reasoning behind our decision to leave the country.

The OVIR organization was a branch of the Internal Affairs Ministry, and they worked in close cooperation with the KGB. Decisions about the right to travel overseas for tourism were based on one's loyalty to the Soviet regime. For those seeking permanent departure, the process was even more complicated. For anyone who wasn't Jewish, even asking for a permanent departure visa was considered an act of treason against our country. Because of that, we knew we had no option and would have to face a very uncomfortable conversation at our OVIR.

My wife and I arrived for our scheduled interview at the central OVIR office in the city's Internal Affairs Department. The chief of the regional OVIR was an old general, with his awards and commendations proudly on display; for most people, these were very intimidating. In his large office, he greeted us with very welcoming smile, and after short introduction about our refugee status, he began questioning why we wanted to leave our country. It quickly devolved from an interview into a lecture about loyalty and patriotism to the Soviet Union. He did not want to hear about our desire to have a choice of where to live, and he kept talking about a "bright future" that he claimed had already started to show its "glory" with arrival of Perestroika. I was so infuriated by this that I almost burst out in a rage, "As a result of your so-called new Soviet freedom and the alleged commitment to legalize private enterprise, I am forced to build guitars in a root cellar!" but I knew it was best not to irritate him. His brainwashing rant reminded me of the old propagandistic programs that we used to watch on television. Noticing that we were not very interested in what he had to say about Soviet patriotism, his tone changed to an obnoxious one, and he began to speak in derogatory slander.

Once I had heard enough of his insults and threatening statements, I asked him plainly, "Can we depart from the USSR and live anywhere we want?" He stared at us with a cold, angry look in his eyes and flatly answered, "No."

"Why?" I demanded to know.

Kicking back in his rocking chair in a most arrogant way, he said, "The law does not allow non-Jews to leave the Soviet Union."

At that point, I knew the conversation was over. As I stood from the table, I asked him one more question: "How can the world trust this nation to make positive changes if you still insist on caging your own citizens like birds?"

He was not used to anyone standing up with him, and with confusion on his face, he said, "That is not true. You can go anywhere you want as a tourist, as long as you have a proper invitation from that country."

We left the office completely devastated, realizing that all of our efforts to get our U.S. refugee status had been futile. The ominous predictions of our family and friends were proving true, and we were once again frustrated, feeling like we would never be given a chance to leave the Soviet Union. What we were going to do next, we didn't know, but I could not give up. After all, we had already invested so much time and energy at accomplishing part of our plan, and we couldn't let go of our dream.

Getting Invitations and US Currency

Working in the root cellar on my guitars, I continued to ponder all possibilities for getting us out of the USSR. We had several months before we would receive our departure instructions from the U.S. Embassy, but we had to have our authorized Soviet travel passports in hand before then. Realizing that all legal channels to accomplish this were now closed to us, we knew we had to find some solution, even if that meant a backdoor one. We had to do whatever we could to escape the political and economical crisis that was forever looming over us there.

I remembered what the general at the OVIR had told us: "You can go anywhere you want as a tourist, as long as you have a proper invitation from that country." "That's it!", I said to myself. "We must get a tourist invitation from the United States and leave the USSR as tourists". We already had refugee status. We just had to get out of Russia however we could. It sounded simple, but in order for us to be invited to the USA, we had to know someone who lived there. That was the problem.

The process for Americans to invite Russian visitors involved the invitation being verified and approved by a Soviet consulate in the United States. The document then had to be mailed to the Russian person who was being invited for a visit. Even still, this was not a guarantee that the Russian could visit America. Permission then had to be granted from the OVIR, and the passport had to be issued and authorized. After that, the Russian had to visit the American Embassy to apply for a U.S. tourist visa. To accomplish all of this without a contact person in the USA, an inviter, was more than a problematic task. However, it was only one logical chance for us to leave Soviet Union.

Where to start with this plan I had no any idea. My only hope was to find someone I knew who had relatives in the USA; I hoped I could find someone who would be willing to have their relatives invite us. This option, however, had its own inherent problems. Even if I could find a volunteer for such a favor, the person in the USA would be taking a great deal of responsibility by sending the invitation. It was unlikely that any stranger in the U.S. would invite a Russian to visit, unless you were a Nobel Prize winner of some sort. Since we knew no one personally who had connections in the USA, I began seeking out companies and organizations that I thought could help us. To do this, I needed access to U.S. media and newspapers. Fortunately, I knew a guy who was an obsessive collector of such publications, so I went to see him without delay.

Igor lived in a small a studio apartment with his mother and dedicated his time collecting all kind of magazines, which he bought on the black market. He could not read any foreign language, but he loved the photographs depicting the lives of people living outside of Russian borders. I did not reveal my true motives, but I asked to see the latest additions to his collection.

He had a huge pile of magazines lying around the house, and I began to search through them, looking for U.S.-based businesses or travel advertisements. Among the stack of publications like "National Geographic" and "Popular Mechanics", I noticed a thick Russian language newspaper. Knowing that he never read our papers, I asked him what it was.

"Oh," he said, rising from his couch, "it's an American newspaper. It's called "Novoe Russkoe Slovo (New Russian Word)", for Russian people living in the USA.

I pulled the bulky publication from the pile and began looking through it. It was actually a very interesting paper, but I was specifically looking for information about emigration to and in the USA. When I reached the advertisement section, I found a column titled, "Visas to Russia and Invitations to USA." There were ads for many small firms and lawyers, offering their services. I immediately realized it might be my only hope. I asked Igor if I could borrow his paper for few days. He agreed, and I placed it in my briefcase and ran home. On the way, I thought about how I would contact these businesses in America.

Reaching for Help

I did not even tell anyone at home what I was trying to do. I knew the chances of receiving a technically phony invitation to the U.S. were slim, even using this approach, so I did not want to get anyone's hopes up. The most challenging part of the plan was the first step: contacting the businesses and organizations from the advertisements. They all included phone numbers and addresses. I needed to ask them openly if any of them would help me in my case. Assuming that such a letter would never make it unmolested to the USA, I knew the only viable option I had was to make a phone call. I realized that it was absolutely insane to make the call from my house, considering the "close relationship" I already had with our secret police. I wasn't sure where or how to make the call without it being traced. I did not want to risk being busted by the KGB, so in spite of my burning desire to call from the convenience of our home, I knew I had to be more realistic and go about it in a different way.

In our neighborhood, I had a very good friend named Alexander Sukhorukov, who was a painter. He was much older than me and still lived with his old mother and father. I visited him often to see his work and talk with him about life. Like many other creative people, he was living mainly off side projects like painting icons for the local church. During the day, he worked for the Union of Soviet Artists, creating Soviet propaganda posters and billboards. Alexander faced the same frustrations as many artists in the USSR, where there was really no freedom of creativity and uncensored expression. He was a wonderful man with a broken heart. Divorced, and having no real way to display his own art, which was his true passion, he lived the quiet life of a typical non-established Soviet painter. As a result of his troubled and sad life, he frequently turned to huge doses of alcohol to numb his pain. Very often, he begged me to visit him so he had someone to talk to about his pitiful, soul-shattering life story. His little bedroom also served as his living room as well as humble art studio. On the walls, he hung some of his artwork, along with a collection of very old Russian Orthodox icons. A foldable couch and stool were the only places to sit, and the room was drowning in all his painting gear, easels, paints, and brushes, leaving little open space.

I was going to Igor to drop off his American/Russian newspaper back and stopped at Alexander's house to check on him. He had no any sympathy for the Soviet regime, though he never openly expressed his displeasure to our government. Because of this, I was not afraid to share with him my plans to leave the Soviet Union. When I told him where I was going, I mentioned my dilemma to get permission to leave USSR to the States. He was very sympathetic to my troubled situation. At that time, he was the only person among all of my friends with whom I shared my plans to fool our draconic immigration system. I showed him the newspaper and the ads of the U.S. services that promised to help bring Russian relatives and friends to America. He looked at it and said, "Which one do you want to call?"

I said to him that I looked through the dozens of businesses and if any of them could be trusted, it would be an attorney. There were only a few attorneys listed in the paper, and George Levin had a largest ad among them. "I would call this guy," I said, "but I know if I do, the KGB will come knocking tomorrow to question me about it."

When I showed Alexander the ad, he took the paper and began to read the ad as he chewed on a rice cookie. Having already glass of vodka, he felt relaxed and exited. Then he got up and left the room. I was looking through the book of Salvador Dali work when he returned to the room with a little notebook. He opened the notebook and began dialing numbers on his phone. I was still turning pages of the book of Dali's works when suddenly Alexander shoved the phone into my face and said, "Take it. Mr. Levin is on the phone."

I was so shocked that I almost dropped the book. I was speechless at first when I took the phone from my friend, as I had not expected him to do such a thing.

A deep, steady voice on other end was asking, "Hello? Hello? Is anyone there?"

There was no time to debate with Alexander about the risky gesture that he did for me. I instantly came back to my senses, realizing that it might be my only chance to talk to this law firm, and I began quickly telling him about my situation. The conversation lasted for only two or three minutes, but I gathered all the information I needed to go forth with the plans for the invitation. I hung up the phone and immediately scolded Alexander for his irresponsible act, for I knew he was putting his own security at risk. "If anyone from the authorities contacts you about this," I said, "you must give them my address. I will not allow you to take the blame for this."

"Don't worry, Yuriy," my artist friend said. "My dad is a hardcore Stalinist, and the government loves him, so I'm sure our phone is not blacklisted. If anyone asks me about the call, I'll just tell them I was drunk and didn't know what I was doing. They will believe me, I swear."

It was a more-than-compassionate gesture from my friend, and the fact that he would place his own life at risk to help others was a true reflection of his kind personality. He knew I would never have agreed to use his phone to make such a dangerous call, even if he had assured me it was safe. Thanking him was not enough for what he did for me. He deserved more than words, and I didn't know how to express my gratitude for such a heroic action. At that time, I didn't know it was only the beginning of what he would do to help us depart from the USSR, and ultimately, he would put himself in a very dangerous position in order for us to leave the country. Truly, Alexander was a masterpiece of a friend, just like the masterpieces he put on canvas.

It took me a while to calm down from the shock and stress that came from talking to Levin. When my emotions settled down and I was more clear-headed, I began to consider what my next step should be. The information I received from Levin was simple: I had to send $100 in U.S. currency to his office, along with the names of the people who were to be invited. Then, the invitation would be mailed to the address I provided. It was exactly the kind of help I'd been looking for. That invitation would allow us to get our Soviet travel passports, and with those vital documents in hand, we would be one step closer to realizing our hopes of going to America.

Sending Money to the USA

I spoke with my wife about our slim options. To get this invitation, we had to figure out a way to get the money for the lawyer and find someone who could deliver the letter and money for us. Sending these important items via mail would have been absolutely impossible, and courier services like Western Union for delivering mail and packages overseas simply did not exist in our country. Not only was it nearly impossible to send funds abroad, but it was illegal to possess American dollars in the Soviet Union. While currency could be obtained on the black market, it required a great deal of hassle and knowing just the right people among the black market gangsters. Exchanging our money for U.S. dollars and getting them safely to the United States now became our biggest priority. We knew the documents would be arriving soon from the U.S. Embassy, and we had to act fast.

In the late 1980s, more and more people were leaving Soviet Union. Practically all of them were ethnic Jews, repatriating to Israel under the Israeli immigration program. However, not many really ended up in the Middle East after their departure from the USSR. Instead, they changed course in the European relocation camps, and many Soviet immigrants assimilated in the United States. While the door was slightly open for Jews to leave, our government still often refused to issue departure visas to non-Jewish spouses, splitting up married couples. These spouses were often refused to leave the state under bogus excuses such as "military responsibilities" or "previous access to national confidential data." Gennady, a friend of a friend, was one victim of this Soviet regulation. When his Jewish wife left for Israel, he was denied permission to leave with her, based on some bogus reason; we all knew it was because he was not Jewish, like his spouse, so they forced him to stay behind in the USSR. The couple was split up for a year, and once his wife arrived safely in America, she invited him to visit as a tourist. When we learned that he would be traveling to the United States, we knew he might be our only hope.

We arranged a meeting with Gennady and spoke with him about our problem. We asked him if he could help by taking the letter to the United States and mailing it to Levin's law firm. He understood our situation and promised he would help us. All we needed was $100 to accompany it. Since Gennady was scheduled to depart for America only few days later, we were under pressure to find someone who could exchange our rubbles to U.S. currency; typically, this would have taken at least a week. Fortunately, Gennady had something in his possession that would help us. In exchange for Soviet rubbles, at the OVIR, special government-issued traveler's checks were given to those traveling abroad. The government did this to prevent any foreign currency from circulating among the Russian people. It was impossible to exchange the checks in the Soviet Union; they could only be cashed at foreign banks or turned back to OVIR. They were granted to all immigrants and tourists, and Gennady had already received his maximum allowance of few hundred dollars in checks from the OVIR. Knowing this, we carefully asked him if he would be willing to exchange $100 worth of checks for rubbles at the black market rate. The offer was declined. At that time, the value of Soviet rubbles was falling rapidly, and he did not want to waste his opportunity to have more American money once he arrived in the U.S. It felt as if our chances were slipping away because we had no way to come up with the $100 in U.S. currency in a short time. Our only option was to try to convince Gennady to help us. My wife and I gathered all of our valuable possessions and offered them to him in exchange for $100: Our gold chains, necklaces, earrings, pendants, and rings were collected and placed in a small box. Many of these items were gifts from our wedding, birthdays, anniversaries, and even part of our inheritance. Besides the sentimental value, they had a high face value that was worth far more than $100, and after careful consideration, Gennady simply could not pass up such a great deal. In exchange for our belongings, we had a promise from Gennady that he would mail our letter, along with $100 in traveler's checks, to Levin's law firm. Now, all we had to do was pray and wait—something we seemed to do a lot of during our efforts to get out from under the tight grip of the Soviet Union.

Tarzan, Return of Gennady, and a New Apartment

Waiting for a result from Gennady was a long, tiresome drag. We had no way of knowing if he'd followed through on his promise until he returned from the United States, and even after that, we would have to wait for our invitations to know the real outcome of our plan. As always in such situations, we were overcome with impatience and uncertainty that was difficult to deal with. Only time would tell if we had any chance to move to America, or if we would have to give up on our dreams and face whatever uglier political form the Soviet Union eventually took.

We moved on with our daily routines of life, but it was not a mundane and peaceful existence, because we were constantly faced with changes no one would want to encounter. In such circumstances, we had to try our best to maintain hope and make efforts to divert or fight the upcoming tragedy. Standing before inevitable misery, helpless to do anything about it, is a terrible situation that no one wants to endure, but that was the kind of situation so many Russian citizens had to face every day.

One night while I was visiting my friend Pavel, someone called him on the phone. He answered it and told me it was my mother, calling for me. She had never called me at a friend's house like that in the past, so I wondered what was so important that she had to reach me with such urgency. She didn't sound good and only told me to get home as fast as I could. I insisted that she tell me what was wrong, and through tears and sobs, she informed me that Tarzan, our beloved dog, was dying. I couldn't believe it and had no idea what she was talking about, but I quickly grabbed my coat, bid Pavel farewell, and ran back home. Rushing through the streets, I kept wondering what could have possibly happened to dear Tarzan. I hoped he was only sick and that my mom was just overreacting, as she sometimes did.

When I returned home, though, the situation did not look good. Everyone was crying, gathered around our furry friend, who was lying in the middle of the living room. He was barely breathing and occasionally letting out quiet squeals and whimpers, as if he was in great pain. His eyes were closed, and we knew he was suffering. It was impossible to call a veterinarian since they were already closed, and even if they weren't, there was no way any would come to our house, and animal clinics were not set up for quality diagnostics or surgeries anyway.

I asked my family what had happened to him over the last few hours since when I left, and they told me he suddenly became weak and irritated. When he was let outside, all he tried to do was wander away, which wasn't like him at all. I remembered that when I took him outside after lunch, he was not active at all and briefly started walking away from me, something he had never done in his life. When I called him, he bowed his head down and kept slowly moving away into the distance. At that point, I had thought he just wanted to play or was still a bit sleepy after a nap, but I was so tragically wrong. I found out later that dogs often act that way when they feel they are about to die; they try to go off on their own and look for a resting place where they can quietly pass away.

There was such a lack of concern for pets or veterinary care that we could have stood in the middle of the street screaming for help for Tarzan, and no one would have an answer. Therefore, the fate of our animals often fell to the hands—or paws—of the animals themselves, and only God Himself could save them. We all gathered around our canine friend, our lovable family member, and we prayed tearfully that God would step in and save his innocent life. There was no one to call for advice or even to ask what was happening to our dog. While we desperately wished we had some way to extend his life, we had to prepare ourselves for the inevitable. An hour later, our dog stopped breathing and peacefully passed away. It was a moment of a great despair and sorrow for all of us. We could not stop crying and asking why it had happened to him. Our dog, a joyful, loving part of our lives, lay before us. He was a mere two years old, but he would live in our hearts forever.

The tragedy was not over yet, though, because the next step was finding a final resting place for our dog. There were no any animal services for these dreadful events, so we wrapped Tarzan's lifeless body in a blanket and headed out in the darkness of night to find a place where he could rest in peace. My face was soaked with tears as I carried my dog through the streets, trying to find an uncrowded park or some little patch of secluded greenery that would make for a proper burial. We decided to bury him under a large tree not far away from where we lived, and we began to dig. Everyone was too emotional to speak, and it seemed as if none of our tears would ever end on such a sad occasion as putting a member of our family in the ground, never to see him or hear his bark again.

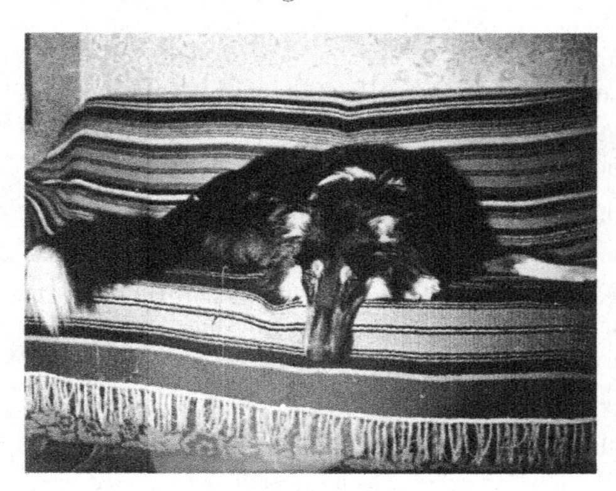

In the distance, we noticed a policeman coming toward us. He instantly realized that something horrible had happened and asked us about it. We told him about our tragedy, and he insisted on seeing our dog's body so he could be sure we weren't up to any misconduct like burying a child or something sinister. We unwrapped his corpse, and the air was filled with our outcry. The cop told us we had to bury him a much further distance away, so we walked another quarter-mile and made a grave right next to the railroad tracks where he loved having a walk. We placed his leash with him and covered him with his blanket and told him goodbye, but we did not have the heart to cover him with soil until an hour later. Once he was buried, the chilly air, a reminder of the coming winter, forced us to return home, and we spent the entire night crying and remembering the best dog we'd ever had. As any dog owner knows, the loss of a beloved pet leaves a lasting memory of horror, and we will carry that increasable pain with us forever.

Even today, we still have no explanation for Tarzan's sudden passing. We have contemplated the possibility that he was poisoned or that he had some sort of a cancer. In spite of the reasons, nothing can take away the pain of our beloved pet departing so soon.

After a Long Wait

When Gennady returned from the U.S., we could not wait to talk to him. As he promised, he mailed our check to the attorney's office, so all we had to do was await our phony invitations. We knew that even though Levin had our money, it was no guarantee. We didn't know whom we were dealing with in the first place, and it is never easy to rely on the honesty of someone who lives oceans and worlds apart from you. Even if he prepared the documents and submitted them to the Soviet Embassy, we knew there were a million reasons and excuses that they might use to reject them.

The biggest gamble in this plot was really the safe arrival of the invitation to our house. We had received mail from the U.S. Embassy, but those were mailed from Moscow and were subject to different mail-screening processes than mail coming in from abroad. We knew that a letter mailed directly from Levin, containing our invitation to the U.S., may never make it to us, especially since wee had already asked the Soviets for permission to leave and had been denied. The chaos mounting in every infrastructure of our government, as well as the censorship of our mail processing, left us very little hope that the letter would actually make it to our door.

While we were awaiting our invitations, my mother received the good news she'd been waiting for for two decades. Finally, she was granted a chance to have her own little apartment. Technically, it was for my mother, my brother, and me, but we would decide later who would live there. It was great news with perfect timing, considering the fact that our chances to leave the USSR were still very slim. We were all very happy about it and could not wait to see the new place. Located in the center of our city, the apartment had been left to the government by a family who had departed to Israel, and considering the overwhelming corruption surrounding the distribution of apartments at that time, my mother was fortunate to get it. It was the same size as the one we were already living in, only it was situated on the fifth floor and had a different floor plan.

So, we had to decide who would live with my mother. Considering the fact that I needed a root cellar to make guitars, my wife and I opted to stay with my grandma because the new place did not have any basements or underground storage. Thus, my brother and mother moved out into a place of their own.

After so many years of living together, it was troublesome to accept the fact that we were now separating. Despite the difficult and cramped conditions we all had to deal with at our old apartment, we had such strong bond that it helped to protect us from the miseries of our everyday lives. Now, my brother, my mom, and our new dog, Ramses, would have their own space and after years of sharing a roof with three generations. It would be more comfortable and spacious, to say the least.

For my wife and me, it was joyful to stay with my grandma. We loved her with all our hearts, and our generation gap never caused any sort of wedge between us. Her charming personality was a true blessing, and I couldn't fathom living without her. We adjusted to our new living conditions, and life began to move again into our unknown future.

Concentrating on My Work, Passports, and the Embassy's Flop

Despite the aggravating political atmosphere in the nation and the blooming major crises, my work on guitars continued. Assuming that we might never be able to leave, I concentrated on what I loved to do for living. There was the ever-present fear of getting caught in my little enterprise, but the harsh economic and social conditions in the country suggested that the government had better things to do than go after someone like me; people was not one of the "hard liners" the Communist regime were going after at that time. I was dedicated to building guitars, as long as people were interested in buying them or until some cataclysmic situation in the country or our departure to the USA would put an end to it. Until that moment, I would never surrender my tools.

Every time I went down to the root cellar, I felt isolated from all the troubles in my life. For me, it was almost therapeutic, as working on guitars had an almost magical and hypnotic effect. It allowed me to disconnect my mind and soul from everything that surrounded me out in the Soviet world. I felt timeless, and I was not concerned with anything other than concentrating on my work, almost to the point of losing the feeling of the ground beneath my feet. The only thoughts that ever visited me when I was making guitars were wishes that I could do exactly that for my whole life, without any fear or the absence of proper conditions and supplies.

I still had no power tools, so when I came across a power drill at the hardware store, I bought it immediately. That purchase carried mixed emotions for me. I loved the fact that I would not have to drill every hole on guitar with an old crank tool, but at the same time, I felt my handmade guitar construction would be somewhat contaminated by the utilization of a power tool. I didn't realize the way I had been making guitars was a method practiced as far back as the seventeenth century. Even at that time, people were adopting water-driven mills and primitive equipment to do the hard labor tasks. My knowledge of the handmade guitar-manufacturing process in the West was zero. In my understanding, "handmade" was to be taken literally; I naively believed that no power tools should ever touch guitar during its construction. Later, though, after my arrival to the United States, I realized how far this mistaken belief was from the reality of modern manufacturing. Until then, I used that presumably evil power drill to speed up the process, and I continued to feel a bit guilty about it.

Getting Travel Passports

When the letter with invitations from United States arrived, we didn't know if it was for real or a dream. It was so hard to believe that the package actually made to our house without any trouble, including approval by the Soviet Embassy in Washington. On the front of the invitation was the name of Marat Fedotov; we were being invited by someone we had never even heard of. According to the documents, our destination was New York. The next step—and hopefully the last—would be to obtain our exit visas and passports from our OVIR.

We knew this was our one remaining opportunity to get Soviet documents and permission to leave the USSR. However, we also knew how risky it was to go through with our attempt. If the Soviet authorities smelled anything fishy about our supposed U.S. tourist visit or its connection to periodic trips to the American Embassy, they could and would deny us our request to travel. At that point, all hope to relocate to the USA would be lost. For this reason, we decided to seek some help from people who had access to the local office of Internal Affairs. Life in the Soviet Union taught the citizens to help one another whenever the system worked against the common people. Many of us did favors for each other, knowing that one day, we would return those favors one way or another. Unfortunately, if you faced a critical situation and did not know anyone who could help, you were forced to pay under table.

We had reached a pivotal point on our quest. We knew going through the doors of the OVIR to get our documents would be not only risky, but quite possibly downright foolish attempt. We had already tried it once, and we had no reason to tap into the failed route again. We spoke to a friend of one of my wife's relatives. That person worked for Internal Affairs and was responsible for documents preparations for travel passports. She had an access to slip our documents through without them being subjected to a thorough KGB screening. She was a bit hesitant to do the task and requested a hefty fee upfront. Considering how far we had gone in our preparations to leave the USSR, no price tag was too big to pay. She was not very interested in cash because it was quickly becoming worthless in our society, but after we offered her many of our personal possessions, from fur hats to our last pieces of small jewelry, she agreed to help us.

After giving her the phony USA invitation and all necessary applications, in a few days we had travel passports in our hands. We had conquered what we thought to be one of the most difficult steps on our path, getting "Tourist travel" stamped on our newly issued Travel passports. The one remaining thing for us to do was to get a U.S. entry tourist visa. We had to make sure that to the Soviet authorities, it looked as if we were just traveling to America as tourists, so we knew we would not pass through Customs at the border showing our Refugee Status documents at the airport.

Considering that we had already been approved for refugee status, we were confident the U.S. Embassy would sign off on our tourist visas without any concerns. The main reason why most Soviet people were not being allowed their entry visas to America was because the U.S. government feared the Russians would not want to return home after their visit. It was a valid concern, considering that not many who had a chance to leave Soviet Union at that time ever wanted to return. Our situation was slightly different, though, so without any delay, we bought tickets for the next train to Moscow.

The Unexpected 'Surprise' at the Embassy

As always, the U.S. Embassy was crowded with people desperately waiting to be interviewed or get their tourist visas. We were quick to discover that the line was already several days long, and there were some sneaky characters controlling who got to go inside and when. The crime that had been happening around the nation in almost every aspect of our lives had reached finally the doorsteps of the foreign consulates. Criminals and shady scandals were taking over in anyplace where they could make a profit on any of our people's needs. Now, they were standing before the U.S. Embassy doing what they did best. They came to Moscow from various Soviet republics, where corruption was nothing less than a dignitary lifestyle. They were on the hunt for easy money, and taking over control of the line at the Embassy meant guaranteed revenue. We did not have to be investigator's to realize that they were not there for Embassy business; it was rather obvious what they were up to. As soon as I got close to one of them, he told me I was Number 745 and that I would have to come back three days later for a check-in call. Then, in the next breath, he whispered, "Or you can go today for a 100 rubles." I knew it was a scam, and all the cops around the Embassy had been paid off by the muggers; otherwise, they would have been mercilessly beaten at the police station. Therefore, it was pointless to complain to the cops or anyone in the crowd. Facing the reality that three days later, I would inevitably be given the runaround garbage from the so-called "line controller," I gave him 100 rubles. When he took our passports and gave them to a cop to escort us to the Embassy, I knew that without paying the criminals, we would have never gotten in for an interview—at least not anytime soon.

Finally, we were only a couple hours away from getting the last piece of approval to go to United States. At that moment, we understood that everything would be a matter of formality, but we soon faced the unexpected. We assumed bureaucracy was a Communist or Soviet disease, so facing it inside the U.S. Embassy came as quite a shock to us. In the end, we were denied our entry tourist visas because we might "stay in America and never come back to Russia." It was really an insane reason for a denial! Of course we would never return to the USSR; we had been granted refugee status, and we were simply looking for a way to legally leave the Soviet Union—something we could not do without an American tourist visa. It was not a secret to the U.S. officials that our government was going to great efforts to prevent the Soviet people from leaving. We were so frustrated and angry that we were ready to scream. After all, the USA had technically already welcomed us, yet they were afraid we might want to stay for good?.. It felt as if we were trapped in some kind of surreal nightmare. It had made no sense and did not follow any kind of logic, but in the end, all our explanations and documented proof were useless. The clerk at the window did not even want to hear what we were saying. It appeared to us that the Immigration and Tourist Departments of the Embassy belonged to two different nations. We could were beyond outraged, but we had no one to complain to about our situation. As soon as our interview was over, we were asked to leave the building.

We stood outside the Embassy, feeling helpless but not wanting to leave. In outrage, we wanted to grab some of the workers and literally beg for someone to be logical and look at our case again. Amidst dozens of others who were also refused their tourist visas, we met a young couple who were in the same predicament, desperately seeking a second look on their case. Since there were no chance to discuss the outcomes and denials, people began sharing their outrage with each other. The young couple told us that they were very angry at the U.S. Embassy's decision. At that moment, we realized we were not the only smart people who had tried to fool the Soviets and leave the USSR on the tourist visa while holding refugee status in our hands. Tamara and Victor got their approval to go to the USA under this program a few months earlier, and after a severe battle with our authorities to let them go legally to America, they gave up on it just like we had. They followed the same steps we did, and after receiving tourist invitations from their friends in the U.S., they were also hit with the wall of bureaucracy at the Embassy. We knew we could share our drama with them, and together we looked for anyone from the consulate who might be willing to listen. Unfortunately, there was no one we could appeal to. The American personnel said the decision was final and that there was nothing the Embassy could do to help. Cops were chasing everyone who was tying to talk to Americans, and shortly thereafter, we were ordered to leave the area around the U.S. consulate.

Victor and Tamara lived in Moscow and said they would return to the Embassy doorstep every day until they were granted a chance to talk to one of the executives. After exchanging phone numbers with them, we left Moscow with the hope they might somehow break the idiotic disconnect of logic at the U.S. Embassy.

Going home without a tourist visa was a catastrophe, and we were outraged because our final chance to leave the USSR had been ruined by the same people who were supposed to be providing us with political shelter. For us, it was the most astonishing blow to our plans to leave the Soviet Union. That kind of unimaginable stupidity was something we expected from the Soviet bureaucrats, but not from the American Embassy. We did not have the slightest idea what to do next.

Documents for Departure and a Desperate Decision

When we received the big envelope from the American Embassy with a detailed documents regarding our preparation for a departure to the USA, we still had no good news from our new friends in Moscow. All their attempts to convince the Embassy authorities to let them go to the U.S. on a tourist visa had proven futile. There was nothing more troubling than having those documents requesting even a medical exams for our safe travel to the USA, while a senseless bureaucratic glitch would not even allow us to leave Soviet Union. It felt like the Americans had teamed up with Soviets to block our departure to the USA and was now cruelly teasing us with shiny applications for entry to the U.S.

A couple months later, we were supposed to submit all the completed forms to a newly created organization called Soviet/Pan Am Travel Effort (SPATE), which was meant to assist refugees from USSR to travel to America. U.S. airline, Pan-America, which was falling into default, was one of the partners in this endeavor. With ticket purchases subsidized by funds from the Ronald Reagan and George Bush immigration programs, the airline would take Soviet refugees from Moscow to America. We looked at the documents with little hope that we would ever be aboard such a flight. The fact that we had gotten so close to freedom and now had no option to overcome our bad luck only fueled our frustration.

We didn't know if we should even bother submitting the SPATE documents, but since we had no obligation to present our travel passports, we decided to go ahead with it. Several pages of these documents were simply duplicates of everything we had already presented to the consulate, but intensive medical exam, including chest X-rays and blood tests, were something we never expected we would have to do for U.S. authorities. The paperwork explicitly stated that no one with any sign of tuberculosis would be allowed to set foot on U.S. soil. The most interesting thing, however, was that they demanded proof of us never having a record at our 'narcological' clinic, a place designated to the treatment of alcoholics. From this, we ascertained that America had no desire to import Russia's legendary alcohol problem.

When everything was ready, I went to Moscow to drop off our documents. Since I was close to the Embassy, I was tempted to talk to some of the U.S. personnel to see if they would take a closer look at our case so we could resolve our problem of tourist visas. When I had a moment to catch one of the Embassy officials, I quickly learned that begging for help was pointless. They had no desire to evaluate my situation or pay me any attention at all.

After leaving Moscow, I thought very seriously about what else could be done in our hopeless situation. Confronting Soviet authorities again was guaranteed to get us in trouble instead of earning us permission to leave the USSR, and bothering the U.S. Embassy would be just a waste of time. It felt as if we would have a better chance for freedom by throwing ourselves on the Berlin Wall, whether that freedom be in this world or the afterlife. We felt we were standing at the train station, watching our train leave, while holding tickets on it in our hands. Some mysterious force was holding us there, not allowing us a chance to move, and no matter what we tried, the train cars slowly departed into unknown destinations without us.

We had dealt with the realities of Soviet life for so many years, and now we faced its worst cataclysmic culmination. It was a terrible scenario for us, especially while we were holding permission in our hands to live in United States. For me, staying in the USSR meant a live no better than the grave itself, and I was certain the inevitable crash of Perestroika would mean an utterly despicable post-Gorbachev future in our country. Everything was at stake: My opportunity to build guitars without any fear and secrecy and raising a family away from Communistic doctrines and radiation were too much to give up without a fight. I knew I had to do whatever it would take to move us to a country, where we would never have to deal with tyranny and inhumane treatment.

When all of our legal and semi-legal options were exhausted, the gloves had to come off, and our fight for survival against that totalitarian regime had to be elevated to a whole new level. In spite of the obstacles and what seemed like a hopeless situation, I somehow felt we had not reached an impasse. I was sure God could help us, as long as we stayed on the right track and did our part. I was ready to risk my shabby Soviet freedom—even my life if need be—to get us out of that place, and that meant doing something I had never done in the past.

Chapter 23

The Final Effort, Boiled Egg and Stamps

It was the end of summer, 1990, and there was not much time left before we departed from the Soviet Union—or at least we hoped so. With a great deal of secrecy, I spoke to my wife about the idea of forging our Soviet travel passports. We really had no other choice, and in order to leave the USSR we were forced to consider breaking the law. By Russian mandates, it was considered a crime to leave the country without permission, and that was exactly what we planned to do. It was, of course, also a breach of totalitarian law to run away for freedom on a floating door from Cuba, hide inside of a barge leaving China, or sneak a refugee out of the country, hidden inside the car trunk of a diplomat. In our case, as long as we entered the United States with documents legally issued to us by the U.S. Embassy for emigration, the rest of the story as to how we left our country was irrelevant. For us, forgery had become the one and only desperate option to reach American soil.

First, we agreed that in case of a catastrophic failure at the Soviet Customs border, my wife would blame the whole scheme on me. She would claim she knew nothing about the plot to forge the passports. She could easily claim she hadn't even seen her passport until I handed it to her, and even go so far as to tell the authorities that I beat her into submission to follow my orders and that I forced her to leave the Soviet Union with me. While the tale wouldn't do much for my reputation, it might salvage hers.

After thoroughly thinking through it all and evaluating everything we might have to deal with, I started looking at what could be done to enable our passports to pass the scrutiny of Customs at the Soviet airport. The danger and consequences of failure would be truly life threatening, but I considered the alternative to be just as daunting: staying in a country that was rotting away with corruption, a homeland that was killing its people with radiation. Looking back today, I am not sure whether or not that decision to do something radical and unthinkable was truly rational. Without question, it was an act of despair and determination, because we felt like hostages in the USSR, where there was no consideration of our rights or desires. Today, I might think differently about trying to move forward with such a risky, irresponsible approach to leaving; however, it was a different world back then, a world of different conditions, when everyone was in a desperate state of mind, considering what they could do to better a future that looked otherwise hopelessly grim.

The only difference between our passports and those who were getting to leave the USSR was a particular stamp on one of the pages. While we had a "Tourist Travel" stamp, everyone who was leaving the country for good had "Permanent Residence" stamped inside theirs. That one stamp was the difference that was holding us back from going where we wanted to go.

I knew the criminals in our country were not only forging single pages of passports, but also full documents and even currency. Considering there was really nothing fancy or extravagant has about the stamp, I was sure I could find some seedy character who knew how to change it from "Tourist Travel" to "Permanent Residence." I didn't know what was involved in such forgery, though, and I needed to talk to someone who did.

Considering the great deal of confidentiality required, I could only discuss my plan with people I could trust 100 percent. No one in my circle of friends was even aware we already had travel passports, other than the painter, Alexander. Considering that he not only knew about my phony invitation to American, but was also the one who called the U.S. attorney to get the wheels going, I figured he was the only man I could talk to about my idea of forging these documents.

When I went to see him, Alex was in a bad mood, so talking about my dangerous idea was very difficult for me. He was in a full-blown rant about our lame Soviet system, telling me how fed up he was about having to paint propaganda posters at work. When he told me he was at least happy to know I was going to escape the clutches of the USSR, I had to tell him it might not happen after all. I told him all about the drama with the OVIR and the U.S. Embassy bureaucracy battle that I lost, and then I finally broke the news that the only way out that I could think of was to forge our travel passports.

He looked at me as if I was proposing to blow up a school. "Do you understand what you are trying to do?" he asked.

"Absolutely."

He looked at the floor and nodded his head as he spoke with sad assurance. "I suppose you are right. I would probably do the same if I were you."

After explaining to him the details of what had to be done, I asked him about my options of changing the stamp from "Tourist Travel" to "Permanent Residence." He told me to bring my passport, and ten minutes later, I was back with my red USSR travel document in hand.

After looking at it for couple minutes, he said, "I know how to make it happen. It's actually easy. You're lucky it was not written by hand, so this stamp is a no-brainer to remove, but you have to find the way to make a new one," he said with such confidence.

I jumped up excitedly and started asking what needed to be done to achieve the task. The ink used for the stamp could be diluted and erased with a special solution, without distorting or damaging the paper. The rest would be a matter of craftsmanship and dedication. I don't know where Alex learned about that trick, and I didn't ask him. To me, it was enough that he possessed this vital information and was willing to share it.

Apparently, the key to this process was a simple hard-boiled chicken egg. The egg had to be freshly boiled and peeled, then rolled over the ink stamp. After that, the stamp could then immediately be transferred to another document by rolling the egg against the new surface. The process of making a new stamp for our passports was a more involved procedure, but we were sure it could be accomplished with the right tools and materials on hand. We needed lead printing dies, and finding them would be yet another challenging task.

"I can do the first part for you, but you have to make the stamp for me yourself," Alexander said, looking straight into my eyes.

"You want to help me? You're kidding, aren't you, Alex?" I asked in shock. "Don't you know what could happen to you if you get caught?"

"If you tell them I helped you, I could get in trouble. But you won't tell, will you?"

"Hell no!" I replied in outrage. "But I still don't want you to be involved in my mess."

"I am already involved, right? I could tell you how to do it and will give you the solutions for it, but I guarantee you will throw away your passport after you're done."

I stopped for a moment and asked him one more time, "Are you sure you want to do it yourself?"

"You can go on the street and ask, and maybe you will find other volunteers, if you're so concerned," he responded with a bit of sarcasm.

"Okay, fine," I said. "You can help me, but you need to tell me how to do it anyway. That way, if I do get busted, I can prove to the cops that I was operating solo. I don't want you to get in trouble for helping me."

It sounded like I was the one who was doing a favor for Alexander, allowing him to get involved in such extremely dangerous business. After our short deliberation, I agreed on Alex's help, realizing that he truly was trying to save my little family's future. I could not thank him enough for what he was willing to do for me, and after talking about it a little more, I headed home to deliver the news to my wife.

Finding Dies for Stamps

After I handed our passports over to Alex for the stamp removal process, I had to find material for its replacement. Once Alex was done with all his work, the proper "Permanent Residence" stamp had to be in my hands. In order to make it, all necessary letters had to be found, and the only place I knew to look for them was a newspaper printing facility. Those places were heavily guarded at all times back when I lived in the USSR. Out of fear of unauthorized anti-Soviet publications, known as "samizdat", authorities did everything in their power to prevent any printing equipment or dies from being smuggled or produced underground. It was impossible to sneak anything out of our local "Gomelskaya Pravda" printing house, where the local paper was printed. I remembered a field trip there when I was a child, and I knew there were police and guards all over the facility. The tall brick wall that surrounded the printing press was too massive for anyone to get over it. Knowing that I could not make it inside of that place, I had to search for some other alternatives. I looked at our phone book to see if there were any other small printing houses in our city, and I saw a listing for a local union newspaper office about an hour's drive away from our house.

When I arrived there, I discovered their printing shop on the production floor, which was to my surprise relatively easy to sneak into. In the several small rooms, women were selecting the proper lettering dies for printing brochures and factory newspapers. One of them was working at the big press, finishing the process. As I approached her, I noticed a bin not far away, a wooden box filled with exactly what I was looking for: all sizes of letter dies. The old lady was dressed in the typical messy attire for such a job, pressing large levers on the machine in front of her. She noticed me and asked what I was looking for.

"Well," I said, pulling a piece of paper from my pocket, "I was hoping that maybe you could help me find the letters I need for our coop business stamp." Then I showed her a list of my randomly compiled letters.

"What size are you looking for?" she replied in a loud voice, trying to be heard over the printing press.

"Seven millimeters tall, ma'am," I said, hoping no one in the vicinity would start eavesdropping on our conversation.

"Well, I can do that, but what you got for me, son?" She smiled, and there was a little twinkle in her eye.

"Will a bottle of wine do?" I asked her with the same naughty grin.

"If you go to the store for it, I will have them ready for you when you come back."

The liquor store was two blocks away, but there was a legal restriction on alcohol sales prior to two p.m., so I had to wait by the door for an hour in the long line of people who were desperate for booze. Soon, though, a bottle of cheap wine was in my hands, and I hid it inside my coat and ran to the printing house.

As promised, the old lady gave me a heavy little envelope with a lead lettering dies, all in exchange for a bottle of "Kogor" wine.

When I arrived home, I immediately started working on my new secret project. All the letters had to be glued together with epoxy so they could function as a stamp, but the process of applying them to paper was far more complicated than what I expected it would be. Once I finished that tedious step, I simply had to wait for a call from Alexander.

A couple days later, Alex called me and invited me over to his place. There, he showed me our passports, and I could not believe my eyes. The stamps were gone, and there wasn't the slightest trace of ink or tampering on the paper. "I am glad they used cheap school-grade ink. It was a piece of cake to get rid of," Alex said with a bit of pride in his voice.

"Boiled eggs and dies ... Anything else sir?..."

The next step involved the egg and lettering die trick to create the new stamps on our passports. I gave Alex the dies I had glued together. To create a uniform, legitimate-looking stamp, he had to ink and press them on the paper until the showed proper contrast and even typical minor imperfections in the stamped image. Once everything looked right, he rolled a freshly boiled and peeled egg over it and then rolled it one more time on the passport page. The synchronization and accuracy of this procedure had to be flawless, and there was no room for any mistakes. For this reason, I knew it would be better if he did it without an audience, so I wished him luck and headed home.

The next day, Alex called me again and said I needed to come down. I didn't know if the work he did had turned out great, only one passport came out good, or if both of them would have to be thrown away.

When I walked into his house, Alex was drunk. I wasn't sure how to react to that situation, and when he handed me our passports, I was afraid to open them. "How are they?" I asked, still holding the closed passports in my hands.

"Take a look," he replied as he poured another unnecessary glass of vodka.

I turned the page on my passport and was speechless. The stamp was so authentic-looking that it seemed to have been made at the OVIR office itself. Both mine and my wife's looked absolutely real, with the "Permanent Residence" stamp situated as if it had always been there. I could not thank him enough for what he had done for us. Again, he had made a priceless effort to help us with our plans to leave the USSR. After we talked about the complexity of all tricks he had to go through to make it work, we drank together, celebrating our success in that seemingly impossible project. He was as happy as I was, and finally, it looked like we were ready to go to America.

After I showed our passports to my wife, we decided to perform a little test and see if any of her relatives would notice any problems with our newly made stamps. No one spotted any signs of forgery or tampering. We pointed to the stamps without telling Natasha's relatives what we were up to, and we asked if the stamp looked like it had been made at the OVIR office. They looked at the stamp under several kinds of light and at different angles and assured us, "These cannot be faked. These must be real documents you are holding in your hands." That little test gave us even more confidence and hope that we would succeed when we tried to cross the border at the Soviet airport.

Finally, everything was in order—forged or not—for our departure to United States, and all we had to do was wait for our final documents from the Embassy so we would know our flight date.

Passing on the Root Cellar to My Brother and Preparing to Leave

It felt like the world I was trying to leave was coming to an end, and if we were lucky, we would very soon be living in the United States. I knew if I got busted at the airport with fake stamps in our passports, I would never see the outside of a Soviet jail, let alone build guitars again. Regardless, though, I had to concentrate on helping my brother Misha move forward with his growing desire to build the instruments I so loved. I knew if he was going to take over my business after I was gone, so he could also do something that interested him, I had to tell him about my material suppliers and those who did services like chroming and milling for me. He followed all of my techniques and before long, he was working on his first instrument.

I did not want to leave any unfinished work behind, so I was pushing to finish my final project before my departure. Juggling our root cellar between my brother and me made for a very busy production facility, but as I watched him, I saw that he was doing an excellent job, and it was obvious he was going to have no problem making guitars, even after I was gone. If the conditions in our country ever changed and he had the opportunity to work out in the open, I was sure he would be very successful. Unfortunately, Mikhail's future, like so many others, was still unknown; he had never received a response to his application for immigration to the USA. There was still time for him to receive a miracle answer, of course, but I decided that if I did make it to the United States, finding a way to get my brother there was going to be my highest priority.

Rumors About a Brewing Military Coup

The autumn of 1990 was cold and windy, and the typical reddish-gold leaves on the city trees soon covered the streets in a beautiful array of colors. Dusty wind chased them about in swirls as pedestrians walking in the gray, unpredictable atmosphere of the end of Perestroika times.

Rumors about a brewing military coup in the USSR were floating around on short-wave Western radio programs, and seeing the occasional military convoys rushing through the city only added the fuel to these speculations. Everyone was aware that our military was constantly undertaking war exercises, but asking them about the reasons for their more frequent gatherings only garnered bogus lies in response. Even our leaders in the Kremlin did not realize that the rumors were not too far from the truth, but the harsh reality of the totalitarian regime would prove it all in the very near future. The clock was ticking on the USSR, and people who wanted this system to go back to old hard line regime were working already on its "survival" plan.

Preparing to Leave

We could not wait to receive our travel information and flight itinerary from the Embassy or SPATE, which now was handling all our relocation process, so when the letter from that organization finally arrived, we eagerly began preparing to leave the USSR.

Our departure date was set for December 3, 1990, and we were to arrive in Chicago, Illinois. The U.S. government had chosen a volunteer organization called Catholic Charities to help us to assimilate and settle within the first couple of months after our arrival there. We are not Catholic, but that organization was the only non-Jewish one set up to help immigrants from the USSR in assimilating to American life. The refugee program was a blessing that would allow us to blend into American society, without having to fend for ourselves on the streets of a foreign land.

This made our folks at home feel better and less concerned, knowing that we would most likely not be gunned down upon our arrival by "American gangsters." The whole plan to go to Chicago did make everyone a bit nervous, though, because for years, we had been drowned in propaganda telling us that the Windy City was the world capital of crime. I did not fear any "wild jungle of crime" in America; rather, what I feared was ending up in the cold and heartless basement of the Soviet jail while trying to pass through border control with our fake stamps in the passports. Because of this terrifying concern, which was a very real one indeed, some of the excitement of our journey and our possible future was robbed. None of our relatives knew all that we had done in an effort to depart from Moscow's airport for good. We did not want them to worry, but deep inside, we both carried too much anxiety to think about a chance for a new life.

In preparation for our departure, we arranged dinners at our relatives' houses. The most common question we heard during those evening get-togethers was: "What are you going to do in America?" I told everybody I would be making guitars, to which most responded, "America already has enough unemployed guitar makers. You better learn to drive so you can work for a taxi company." People had little understanding about life in the USA, but while I was not an expert on everyday American life, I knew there were many more opportunities in the free world, and I was sure I could accomplish whatever I put my mind to. I believed—and still believe, in fact—that it would depend on me and my desire to become who I wanted to be. I had managed to build guitars for four years without any civilized sources of materials and proper conditions, so I was more than confident that even if I did have to earn a living as a taxicab driver in the USA, I could at least continue my beloved craft on the side. In the Land of Opportunity, I would be able to build my guitars without having to hide in a root cellar.

No One Had to Know

To avoid triggering the suspicions of our paranoid authorities, I had to keep our departure plans confidential from all of my friends until the very end. Even my closest friends, whom I spent years playing music, riding bikes, and sharing good and bad days of Soviet life with had to be kept in the dark for their own protection. I was desperate to share with them that we were leaving the USSR, but the great danger of not making it through Soviet Customs was reason enough to keep it to ourselves. I even had to lie to some of the more curious ones, telling them that nothing came of our attempt for refugee status at the U.S. Embassy. It was very difficult to be dishonest and keep secrets from my friends, but the less people who knew about it, the better it was for us and for them. Despite my great desire to share with them what we were up to, I had to protect us, as well our families, from any information being leaked to the KGB. If life in the USSR taught us anything, it was that we had to be secretive about extremely important aspects of our lives, often even among our closest friends and relatives. In this case, we had to follow that time-proven rule.

There was one person I needed to tell, and that was my father. When I arrived in his little village, we had a long conversation about my plans to move to America that December. It came as a great surprise to him. After all, it was the kind of news that would never come as a casual revelation, and my dad thought it almost unimaginable. He did not argue with us about it or try to talk us out of leaving the USSR, as he recognized that there were undeniable tough times ahead for the unstable nation we called home.

We didn't tell him about our trouble with travel passports or the details about how we'd managed to obtain them. He knew that whatever it took to reach that goal, it must have required much patience and an extraordinary effort. To him, America sounded so distant and unknown; it was very difficult for him to comprehend what I would do in a country where we had no relatives or friends. My desire to make guitars for a living sounded very childish and naïve to him, and his biggest fear was that I would not be able to find such a job in the USA—or anywhere. At the same time, he did not have to tell us what we could count on if we stayed in the USSR, and after a long evening supper, he gave us a little envelope with some cash in it to help with our trip. It was very kind of him to offer to help instead of ranting and lecturing us about the dangers of the unknown and fear of the foreign world. I had no way of knowing if I would ever see him again, but after saying goodbye to him and his beautiful new family, we walked together to the train station for our last trip home from his village.

Finding Dollars and an Empty Houses

We wanted to exchange all of the savings I had from guitar-making for U.S. dollars, as we knew the money would help us buy food and clothes and possibly put a roof over our heads for some time or at least keep us out of trouble. It was not very easy to find anyone in our city who could help us with the money exchange. There was still a law on the books to persecute Russian citizens for possession of foreign currency, and the black market guarded these types of exchanges with the highest level of secrecy.

To connect with someone who could help me exchange my Russian money, I went to my friends who were involved in the numismatic collectors world. Finally, through several different people, I was hooked up with the right people. Despite being introduced to them as a trusted person, I still had to prove I was not a rat (a cop or KGB informer). Not only did I have to disclose my reason for wanting the dollars, but I was openly warned with a pistol barrel shoved into my face that I would see that weapon again if I was trying to set anyone up. The deal was made, and a few hundred dollars were exchanged for our Soviet rubles.

After more than two decades of living in that cramped, small apartment, my family was actually becoming lonely. My mom now lived in her own apartment, which she shared with my brother Mikhail, and my grandma, who had lived her whole life surrounded by loved ones, would now be living alone. It seemed like an unhappy destiny for them, especially for my grandmother, who loved being around people. Leaving her behind to live on her own was a sad and difficult reality for us, but at the same time, we took some comfort in knowing that she would have some peace and quiet after coping with years of three generations crammed under one roof.

The time of our departure date was fast approaching. None of my family members were yet willing to accept the fact that we were leaving for good. Grandma insisted we would come back with our tails between our legs after America disappointed us, and while my mother hoped we could establish our lives there, she assumed we'd be able to travel back and forth whenever we wanted. For us, the biggest concern was whether or not we could make it through Customs with our forged documents. It was impossible not to worry about the risk we were taking, and we hoped for a miracle as we tried to concentrate on our preparations for departure. Since we needed a miracle, we stood in church with our travel passports and prayed that God would help us on our journey, especially after all we'd been through. There was, after all, no one else to count on at that time, and we wanted to get out of there before the stand-off between the fight for freedom and tyranny culminated in our homeland.

Relying only on God

Only a few days before our departure, we began to gather our personal items into our luggage. We packed our necessities and inexpensive items in our two small travel cases and were ready to go on our journey to an uncertain future.

Now, everything was in God's hands, and all we could do was pray, hope, and embrace one another. Whether or not we actually made it all the way to America, our lives were about to be forever changed. The last close friend I saw before our departure was Alexander, and he wished us much success and praised us for all we'd accomplished. For him, our success at the airport was a shared victory, since he had such a hand in getting us there. I told Alex to call my grandma a few days later so she could inform him of how things were going, and then, in the true Russian tradition, we shared a shot of vodka and said our friendly and grateful farewells.

Twenty-four hours later, we would be on the train to Moscow, and after our farewell to our relatives, we would quietly have to leave the city. It was the most intense day of my life as I realized that everything and everyone I had ever known was becoming part of my history, and my life—as well as my wife's—was destined to be completely different once we set foot on our journey.

On December 2, 1990, we said our tearful goodbyes to my mother, grandma, and brother, and my wife's mother and uncle escorted us to the capital. We had left Gomel for good.

Chapter 24

Another Obstacle and the Departure

After arriving in Moscow, we had a whole day before our scheduled plane departure from the Sheremetievo-2 Airport. While the time was more than adequate, the Soviet regulations about international flights required ticket registration to begun no later than four hours prior to takeoff. This scrutiny was simply another result of the extra-strict precautions taken with passports and visas control. We walked through the streets, which were blanketed in a thin coat of snow, heading toward the taxi station. On the way there, we stopped at a little coffee shop to enjoy our last lunch in the Soviet capital.

Sheremetievo-2 Airport was crowded with an army of people who were scheduled to depart for overseas destinations. Every foot of space on the floor was occupied by bags, sleeping passengers-to-be, and friends and relatives who had come to see their loved ones off. It was a chaotic atmosphere, to say the least, and after finding our Pan-Am airline departure terminal, we joined the large group of people who were also supposed to be on our flight. A couple of hours later, a representative from SPATE would be there to deliver all our immigration documents, visas, and tickets; we would be flying to Chicago, through New York City. After a jittery, sleepless night on the train, all we wanted was some rest, but the anxiety of the upcoming Customs inspection had us on high alert. Nestled against the wall, using our bags as chairs, we patiently awaited the arrival of the SPATE representatives.

All kind of things went through our minds in that stressful situation, not the least of which was the mounting fear. We were taking an ultimate risk, trying to escape the USSR with artificial stamps on our passports, and that thought assailed us with doubts and worry. The one comfort I had was knowing that after that day, I would at least have a settled future, one way or another. Regardless of how it turned out, it would be the end of my frustrations. Like a good husband, a protector, I continued to comfort my wife, telling her that everything would be fine, but deep down, I could not stop thinking that I might never see her again if we got caught.

When the people from SPATE showed up, a mob of people surrounded them. After a short briefing about the boarding process, they began to pass us our documents. It took about a half-hour, but when they were done distributing documents, there were still about twenty people left empty-handed, and among those people were my wife and me. Even with all the doubts we'd had, this was not something we expected. The lady from SPATE announced that, due to great deal of paperwork, our documents were not ready, and it would take couple days to finish them before we or the others could depart.

We didn't necessarily expect everything to go smoothly, but it was trouble none of us wanted to deal with, and several angry people in our position began screaming at the woman, condemning SPATE for his lousy work. Still, we had no interest in complaining about it because we didn't want to drum up any suspicion or ill feelings. When they told us that SPATE would put us up in a hotel until we were able to leave the USSR, everyone calmed down.

My wife's relatives cold not stay in Moscow, so the unexpected delay was very troubling for them. They had spent so much time and effort making the trip with us that they did not want to miss seeing us off on our departure from Russia, but they were forced by work obligations to return home. When we were told that the bus was waiting to take us to the hotel, we said our difficult last goodbyes to my wife's folks and made our way to the airport exit.

Scary Night

As we headed to the hotel, I became even more frustrated by the tortuous setback. After all we'd gone through to get to that point, only to be told we'd have to wait longer, it felt like the anguishing drag of our postponed travel was the work of the same invisible force that had been doing everything in its power to stop us from leaving the country. It was so difficult to deal with the circumstances after that long-awaited day had arrived. We could do nothing about it, however, and as we rode through the empty winter fields of the Moscow suburbs, I wondered if we truly would ever be able to leave.

After driving for about an hour, our bus stopped in the middle of nowhere at the large sports resort for Soviet athletes. It was a five-story building, and only a few people were staying there at the time. We were assigned to our rooms, where we would stay for a couple of days, and after a long and frustrating day, we had a short dinner and went off to bed.

The night was quiet and very cold. The heaters barely worked, so we lay beneath the blankets with our clothes on, trying to warm up. We could not fall asleep; our thoughts were too focused on our upcoming ordeal with Customs. Suddenly, a loud noise erupted on the second floor of the building. We cold hear someone trying to crawl on the balcony by the rails, and a few minutes later, we saw the shadow of climbers coming up to our level. They beamed flashlights through our window, and after a short stop on our balcony, they decided for one reason or another to go up one more story. Moments later, the noise grew louder, as police car brakes squealed outside our building. A bunch of people ran down the stairways and balconies, to the point where the noise and confusion became even more excruciating. And then, a few minutes later, everything was quiet again, and we tried again to sleep.

Back to the Airport

In the morning, we learned that local racketeers were tipped off that "reach people" departing to USA were staying in the complex. No one was injured or robbed during the skirmish, but the incident clearly reflected the situation in our country: Small gangs were forming into large, more organized groups, the ever-growing Russian mafia. The cops arrived quickly because a patrol car was nearby; otherwise, the gang raid could have taken a far worse dramatic turn. The next night, everyone stayed close to one another, and the fear of another invasion kept us on alert all night.

When the SPATE rep informed us that in one day, our documents and plane tickets would be ready for our departure, the end of our uncertainty began to close in. On December 5, we finally headed back to the airport. The group of us who had to wait gathered once again at the Pan-Am terminal, ready to fly to the USA. Our U.S. visas and sealed envelopes for INS had finally been given to us, and we were on the threshold of what would be the most monumental change in our lives. After those scary nights at the athletic resort, we were glad that all we had left to do was go to Soviet Customs and see what our destiny had in store for us.

The ticket registration and passport control on our Pan-Am flight to New York was announced few hours prior its departure. The long delay was put into effect so that the Soviet authorities who worked at Customs would have ample time to thoroughly inspect all passengers before they boarded the most "sensitive" Soviet flights: the ones leaving for the United States. The passengers took all of their luggage and got in line, and we all began to slowly move toward the militarized airport Customs checkpoint.

Crossing the Border and the Departure

At the special station, there were KGB officers sitting in a small booth, dressed in a PV (Border Army) uniform. The officers were taking documents from the passengers and slowly checking them for any discrepancy. At that moment, we consciously felt the tremendous danger of our situation, but we tried to maintain effective poker faces as we took one step after another, getting ever closer to the Customs control. As we held our passports in hand, I prayed that God to spare our souls and lives and let us peacefully cross the Soviet border.

When the officer in the window asked for our documents, I handed him everything we had. We stood casually next to the secured area, surrounded by soldiers who were watching him open our passports. For some reason, I became very relaxed. I realized that all that was happening in that moment was the culmination of all of our efforts, and whatever happened next was in God's hands.

The officer behind the glass window occasionally picked up a phone and called someone to ask questions, but we could not hear what he was saying. When he got up from his chair and walked away, I thought, "We're in trouble. It is over now".

A moment later, he returned with a bottle of water and handed my wife's documents back to her. "That way," he said, pointing to the neutral zone.

My wife stepped outside the passport control area; she was free to go to America. However, until I had my documents back in hand and his permission to move along, our mission was not truly a success. We both knew that she would be dragged back over for questioning if they realized my passport had been tampered with.

While several more minutes passed, I watched the officer carefully as he examined my passport and its "Permanent Residence" stamp. He flipped pages and looked at them under a special light, then suddenly asked, "Do you have any relatives in the USA?"

"No," I answered, swallowing the rock in my throat.

"What valuables you have with you in your luggage?"

"Not much, Officer. We are not rich people. Would you like to see?"

"No. Our X-ray machine will do that. Tell me, how much do you have on you in U.S. dollars?"

I had our converted "guitar" money in my socks, but I had no supporting documents of its OVIR currency exchange since we hadn't gone through the proper channels to exchange my rubles for it. At that point, I knew this might become a very problematic situation. While strip-searches were not common, they did happen, and I was ready to voluntarily give up all what we had; I just wanted them to accept my passport so my wife and I would be free to go. I decided to take a chance to prevent our losses and replied, "Not much, sir. Look at us," I said with an assuring gesture toward my wife and I to indicate that we had no furs or gold on our hands like some of the other immigrants in line. "As I said, we are not rich."

At that moment, a young officer looked into my yes and said, "Have a safe trip, guys," and handed my passport to me. I will never forget the sound of his voice when he uttered those words to me.

Life Long Lasting Hours

In a few seconds I walked toward my wife in total disbelief that we were only steps away from our freedom. Dragging our two small bags behind us, we could barely hold back our excitement. We wanted to cheer out loud about it, but we knew our ordeal with Soviet Customs were not quite over. In the duty-free zone, everyone who passed the border patrol was waiting the announcement of our flight departure. Through the same speakers, names of passengers were also occasionally called to report to the airport Customs office. Even after we passed this control, our documents were checked one more time in the airport's KGB office. Every time names began to be called over the loudspeakers, we cringed, touched by a shock of fear. Until we boarded the American plane, and actually departed, we knew that our joy was in danger of instantly being changed into yet another tragedy.

As we sat in front of the duty-free store, we looked at the lavish assortment of goods and luxury items. For most Russian people, those would have been considered collectible relics, absolutely out of reach. A few other would-be passengers walked around in stores, observing products we'd never seen in our lives. To us, it was almost like a museum, filled with expensive and rare treasures, but even more valuable to us were the moments ticking by as the clock crawled toward our time of departure.

More and more people from our flight began flooding into our waiting room. Most of them were refugees like us, and everyone seemed to be experiencing the same delightful, hopeful feelings about our impending flight to America. Through the large windows of the airport, we could see the huge Boeing 747 with the Pan-Am® logo painted on its fuselage. Russian KGB military soldiers, armed with AK-47s, stood around the premises of the U.S. plane, guarding it; that was standard security procedure for any American plane that landed on the Russian soil. The purpose of the tight protection had nothing to do with any terrorist or criminal threat; rather, they knew anyone who climbed on the plane would technically be standing on U.S. territory, and removing them from the plane would involved a painful diplomatic hassle. Soviet authorities realized that some Russian people were desperate to escape, and to prevent anyone, even airport personnel, from boarding the plane, they placed armed guards so no one could even get close.

When the announcement came that our plane would be boarding in five minutes, our hearts were filled with an overwhelming sense of impending freedom. Everybody got up and began forming a line, and we headed to the last airplane we would ever board during our Soviet lives. The doors to the gate opened, and our pulse quickened as we started moving into the plane. As we moved forward, we felt as if we were walking away from a battlefield, finally being rescued. The surreal feeling that we were actually leaving the USSR was very difficult to comprehend. It felt like a dream, and I couldn't help worrying that we were going to wake up any minute in some Russian jail or a KGB basement. I was sure there would be a dreadful interrogation about our failed plot to escape the USSR, that we would fail in our naïve attempt to fool the immortal totalitarian system. Fortunately, that was not happening. Instead, we were nearing the seats that we would sit in for our arrival to the United States. "Is this is it? We can't be this lucky!", I told myself, looking back at all the unbelievable steps we had to go through to land a seat on that flight.

Take Off to Freedom

About a half-hour later, the doors of the plane started closing, and the low, humming noise of the revving engines grew louder and louder. When our Boeing started to moved, it finally hit is: We were going to America! We began quietly cheering, celebrating the end of our frustrations and the success of our plot to leave the USSR. Ten minutes later, our crowded plane was picking up speed down the Russian runway toward a future we could not yet fathom. When the wheels lifted off the ground, we could see people in tears, looking out of the windows to give our homeland a final farewell.

Below us, everything became smaller and smaller, and the dim lights pierced through the cold night, eventually fading out of sight as we took to the clouds. The land I had called home for twenty-six years seemed like a fading memory already, complete with its two-millennia history, astonishing nature, unimaginable culture, and kind Russian hospitality. Below, through those small airplane windows, was a nation of great poets and writers, talented inventors, and engineers—a nation I was leaving behind.

I knew that even if I wished to, I could never return back home, and no matter how badly I had wanted to leave, that tweaked my most sensitive emotions. Those difficult feelings could only be understood by another immigrant. My friends and loved ones were being ripped away from me because of the destiny of our lives and the unpredictable turns that my motherland had taken. Everything I knew was becoming history, and I was leaving behind all my unaccomplished dreams of making guitars in Russia, as well as all the lost hopes and broken promises of Perestroika. The value of my many happy days in Russia, and some of the benefits of our Socialistic system, however, could not replace priceless freedom. The good, glorious, and terrible days of our past were coming to an end, but they would live on in my mind as in-erasable images of the Soviet life I had lived. A life like that never would have happened without the cataclysmic political event of 1917, when many of us lost our country without even leaving its soil. As we flew away, I realized I had lost my country seventy-three years earlier, even before I was born, because of the devastating consequences of the experimental Communistic utopia dogmas that were thrust upon our people.

All the fear, anxiety, and drama of our lives was now below us, going further away to the past with our plane flying higher and higher into the sky. The new life and unknown future was lying ahead of us like a clean canvas before painter. What will be painted on it was a mystery and knowing what I've lived through in the resent years, the uncertainty of life ahead for me could only be exiting.

Prays and works of God were definitely playing a role in seating at that moment at the US airplane. Knowing myself, my weaknesses and my fragile nature without a doubt would never gained such result without a Supernatural help. I was giving my life to the hands of This Power counting on mercy to my wife and family that left back home. We rested the struggle of getting free from Soviet uncertainties and flying away from our country. The mystery of tomorrow now was only flight duration time away from us. The mystery of hope, excitements and fulfillments of our dreams for which we've sacrificed the most precious possession that we ever had - our homeland.

Epilogue.

In eight hours, our plane would land in New York City, and few hours after that, we would arrive in Chicago to start our new lives. We would be swept away with culture shock from everything we would see, and the first few pages of the first chapter of our new destiny would begin in a country far different than the one we'd imagined from that cold land far away. In spite of what Soviet propaganda tried to teach us and the way Americans were painted in the USSR, the difference would be a kind, charitable people that would quickly touch our hearts.

The first months of immigration would bring excitement and thrills of a new life, as well as difficulties, limitations, and missing our loved ones. We would learn the English language from watching TV, and since there would be no other Russians around, we would have to adapt and get on our feet faster than we could have imagined.

Back home in Russia, all our friends would be in shocked when our parents shared the news with them that we had reached America. Many would beg us to help them leave the USSR, while others would jealously hope that we would fail in the new world and have to make a shameful, defeated return.

Shortly after our arrival, to everybody's surprise, my brother would get his invitation for an interview in the U.S. Embassy. However, he would ultimately be denied refugee status, so it would become our highest priority to find a way to bring him to the United States with sponsored support.

In a few months, I would find a job as a Guitar Technician at the Washburn® Musical Instruments firm. At the same time, with the American dollars I'd smuggled over in my socks, I would buy my first quality hand tools to make my first guitars at home. Absorbed in the ocean of information about instrument-building and an endless supply of resources and materials, I would become somewhat of a workaholic, making them at home after work and in all my spare time.

The fate of our motherland would turn into what we had all feared. In August of 1991, the streets of Moscow would be filled with tanks after a coup attempt by hardliners. We would watch television broadcasts in horror as cannonades of gunfire and smoke billowed from the Moscow parliament building. Only the refusal of Soviet soldiers to shoot at civilians, coupled with a disorganized plot to revert Russia to Stalinism, would prevent a catastrophic outcome for the failed coup. As a result, the Soviet Union, as we knew it, would cease to exist, breaking apart into fifteen independent states. This would spark a new and difficult time for Russia as our former nation would try to establish democracy while fighting an outbreak of crime, chaos, and economical crisis. We would be sleeping on the floor, saving our money so we could send packages of food back to our parents because the turmoil in our homeland would leave many Russian citizens poor and hungry. We would limit our own expenses to a minimum, and every extra penny would be put away to help bring my brother to the States.

In the first year, our only Friday night out would include a bicycle ride to a local Burger King. I would pedal, and my wife would sit on the frame. I would promise her that one day, we would have so much money that we would eat at Burger King every day if we wanted. That same bicycle would be our only transportation, until the freezing Chicago winter would force us to accept a donated broken car, and we would finally learn how to care for, deal with, and appreciate the automobile.

We would be living a simple, almost primitive life, but we would enjoy our humble existence with gratitude for all that America has to offer. Everything we would have, regardless of its value, would be priceless to us, and our souls would be inspired by all the potential and freedom of our new lives in the United States.

With all our effort and the help of very kind people, we would bring my brother Misha to America, and he would work for Hamer® Guitar Company and become one of the greatest guitar-makers in the business. He would marry, have children, and make a new life for himself in America.

Shortly after my employment at Washburn®, the company would recognize my potential, and I would begin building guitar prototypes, doing restorations, and making instruments for all the company's endorsees. After only a few years, the artists I had listened to on transistor radios and crummy tape recordings in the USSR would become my customers. I would be invited to rock stars' birthday parties, with private jet transportation. I would be asked to attend musical premiers, and private dinners and backstage lounges would become part of my job. Building guitars and working side by side with artists like Michael Angelo/Batio, Paul Stanley, Sammy Hagar, Dimebag Darrel, Jimmy Page, Robert Plant, and many other megastars would become part of my life—something I never would have dreamt about in my Soviet past.

On a hot August day in 1995, I would receive my official U.S. citizenship in Chicago's Soldiers Field® stadium, and my residence status in the United States of America would finally be complete. It would become our new homeland, the planting soil for our growing family, and live would forge ahead with the arrival of our daughters, Jessica and Alyssa.

I would continue making guitars at home, exercising my true passion, while staying busy at Washburn. Fascinated with inlay works and, the most difficult of all in this field, jazz guitar construction, I would spend many months creating more complicated instruments than I'd ever imagined. Some of them were conceived back in Russia, in the root cellar, but with the absence of materials and tools, they had to wait. They would be birthed upon my arrival in America.

Absorbing the Western lifestyle and blending into its culture, we would gradually begin to appreciate all the benefits of the free society. The privileges and achievements of a new world for us would help us to realize that Americans truly do not know the value of their inherited freedom, simply because they have never lived without it.

I would eventually be hired as a Senior Master Builder at Fender® Custom Shop, and in the beginning of 2000, with my family we would move to California. My new home and job would open yet another exciting chapter in the story of my life.

At the same time, the new millennium would bring heartbreaking realities. Within a couple years of my relocation to California, I would learn that some of the people closest to me had passed away, and I would not even be able to attend their funerals. At the age of ninety-three, my beloved grandma would die, and shortly after that, my father would pass away in a Russian hospital. The cause of his death would never be disclosed to his family; we would forever suspect the aftermath of Chernobyl for my father's premature passing.

In addition to my beloved relatives, two people who had placed such a crucial, life-changing role in my life would depart from this world as well. Alexander would never achieve any respect and recognition as a painter and would ultimately die as a result of his body and soul being devoured by alcohol, a fate shared by many Russians of his era. Sasha, my great friend and the true godfather of my guitar life, would be senselessly murdered near his house at the young age of thirty-nine. My family would hide this tragic news from me, knowing the scale of his loss to my soul. Only a long time after his death would the truth be revealed to me by my mother.

My seemingly picture-perfect life in America would also see its fair share of suffering and pain, for no place in this world is immune from struggles and heartbreak. From a misdiagnosed medical condition to a near-death accident to a head-on automobile collision, my life would never be short of unwanted surprises.

I would continue making guitars at Fender® Custom Shop for collectors, ordinary musicians, and music legends like Buddy Guy, Neal Schon, Keith Urban, John-5, Prince, and others. Some of my instruments would be ordinary-looking guitars, while others could only be dubbed elaborate art pieces, and some of my guitars would fetch over $100,000. Curiosity about my work and past would bring some media attention from international publications and magazines, as well as newspaper giants like The Chicago Tribune® and The Los Angeles Times®. These spoils of my labors would come, even though I'd never dreamt of them and would not want to deal with them. Many unique opportunities and happenings would occur in my American life, even though I'd never set goals to achieve them. I would only be able to credit the mighty power of God; without His great help, I know I never would have had even the tiniest bit of success in any of my endeavors.

Until all of that happened, however, the dark Atlantic ocean outside of our plane window lingered beneath us like a watery abyss, reflecting the bright stars in the sky that led us to our unknown future life in America.

Some of my work at Washburn®.

"Blue Dolphin"

18" Body Acoustic Arch top Guitar.

Hand carved Exotic woods parts

Flame maple binding.

Hand inlayed Wood,Silver, Gold, Mother of Pearl,

Abalone, and Vintage Ivory.

One of a kind instrument.

All work by author.

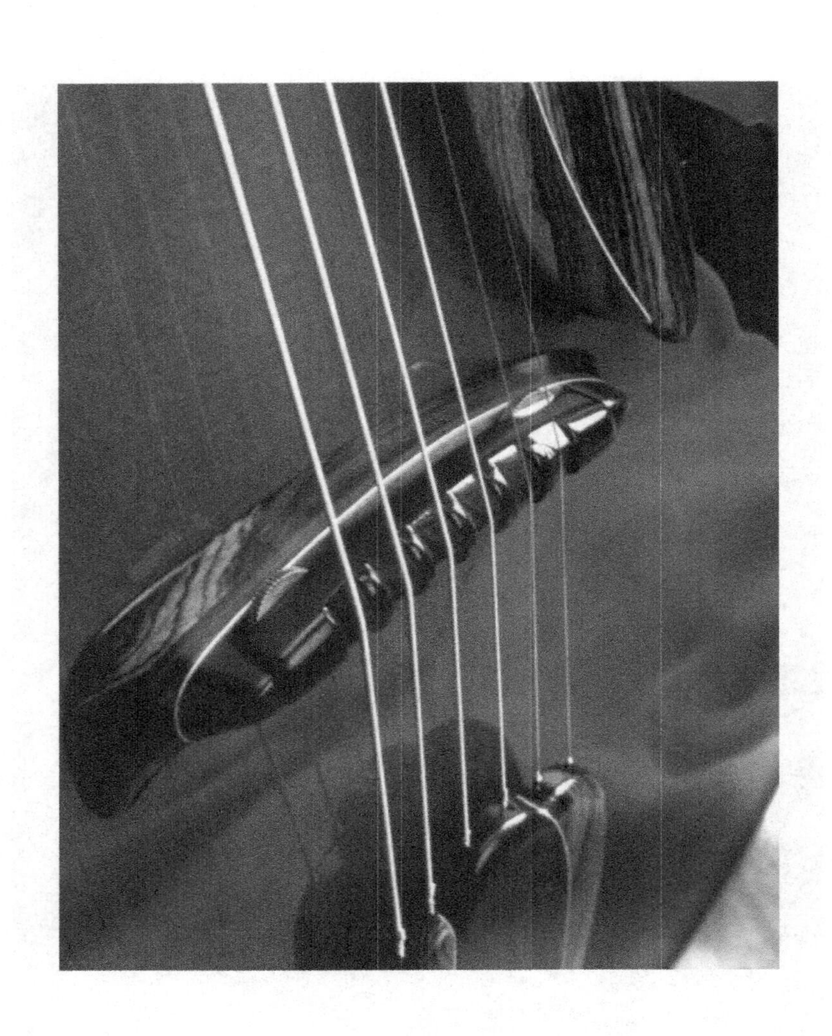

Washburn

"Galactica"

18" Arch Top Acoustic Guitar.

Hand Inlayed Mother of Pearl, Abalone, Silver and Gold.

Flame maple binding.

Hand Carved all parts .

One of a kind Instrument.

All work by author.

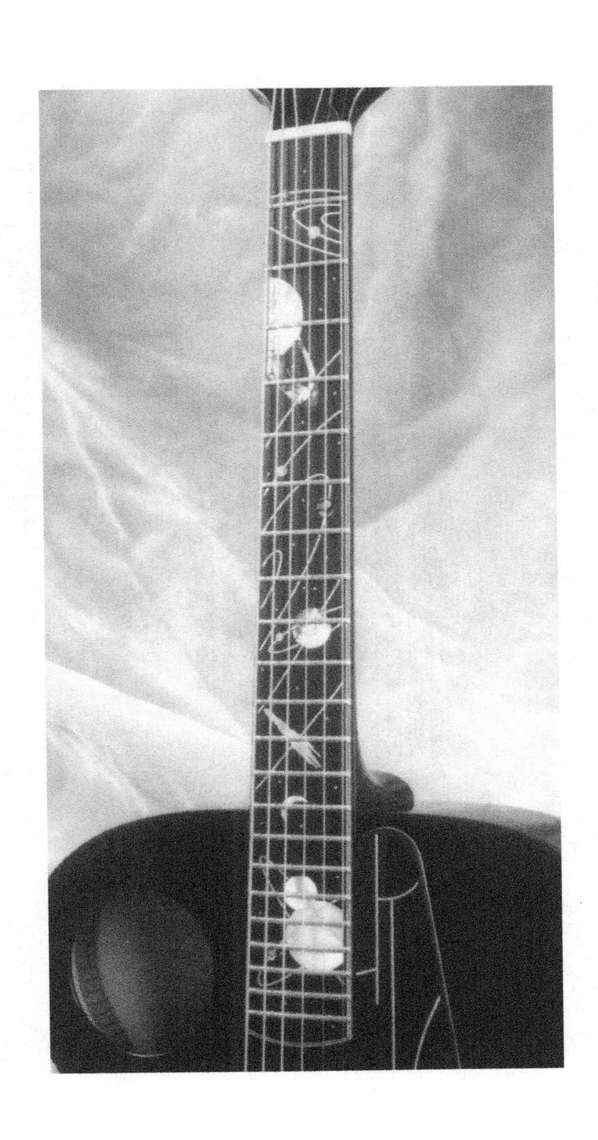

Washburn

Some of my guitars made in Chicago.

"Sunset"

17" Arch top Jazz guitar.

Cello maple and exotic woods.

Flame maple binding

Inlay Mother of Pearl accents .

All work by author.

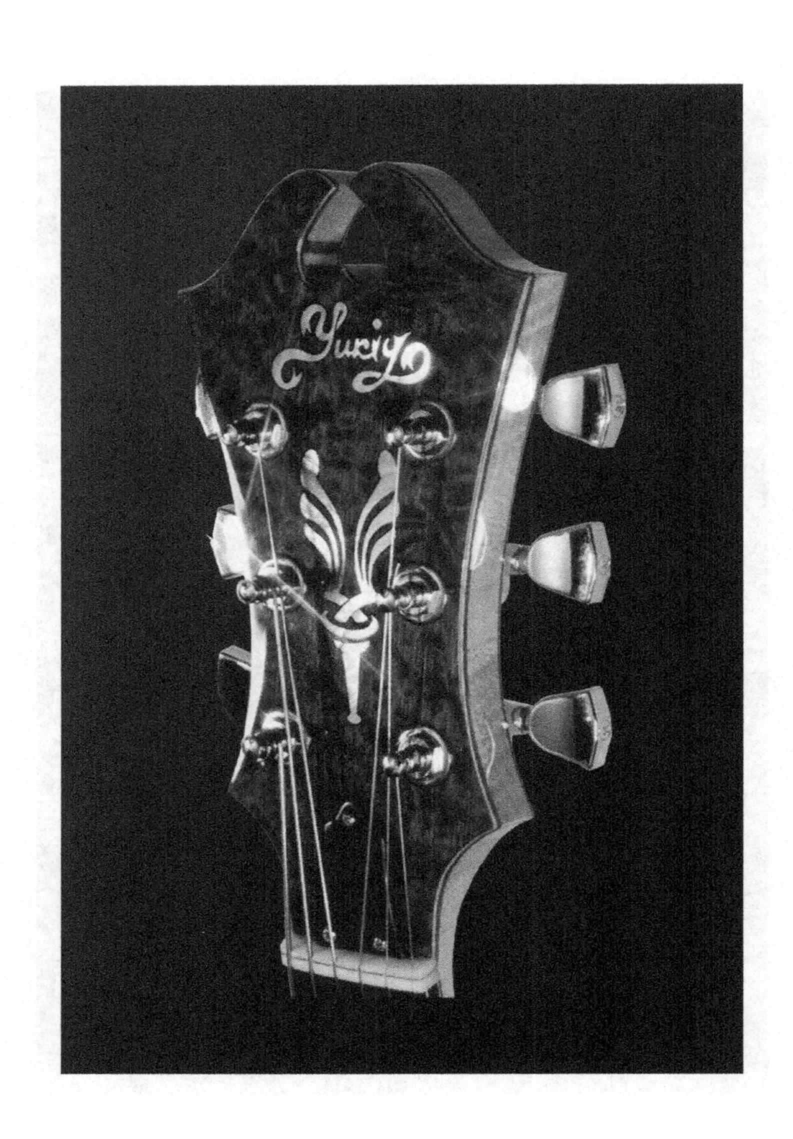
Yuriy

"Pearl Swan"

16" Arch top acoustic guitar.

Mahogany body, cedar top.

Ebony parts.

Mother of Pearl, Green, Pink and Gold Abalone Hand inlay work.

All work by author.

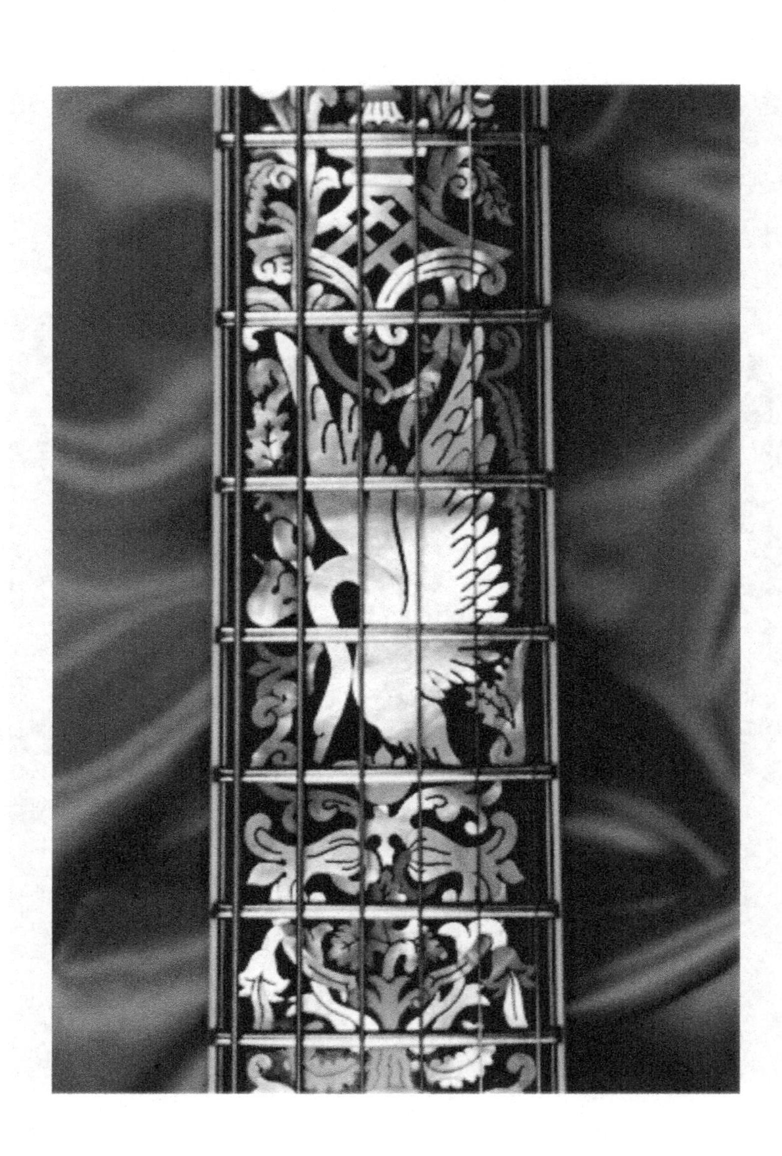

Yuriy

"Angel"

Arched Top and Back Electric Guitar.

Design conceived back in USSR.

Mahogany body.

Mother of Pearl Hand Inlay work.

All work by author.

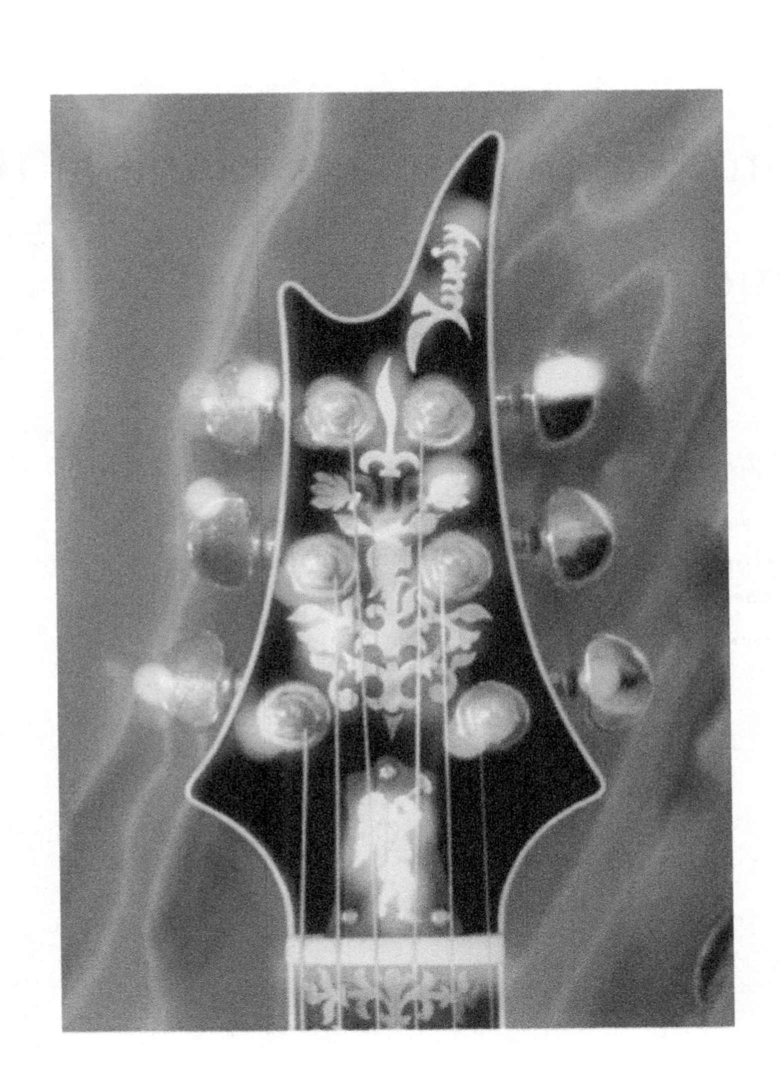

Some of my guitars made at the Fender® Custom Shop.

"Laguna Beach" Esquire®.

Oil painted artwork on canvased body.

Easel type guitar case.

Matching body panting.

All work by author.

Keith Urban "Shattered Telecaster®."

Hand cut glass mirror decorated top.

"Sphere"top surface design.

Chambered body for a light weight.

All work by author.

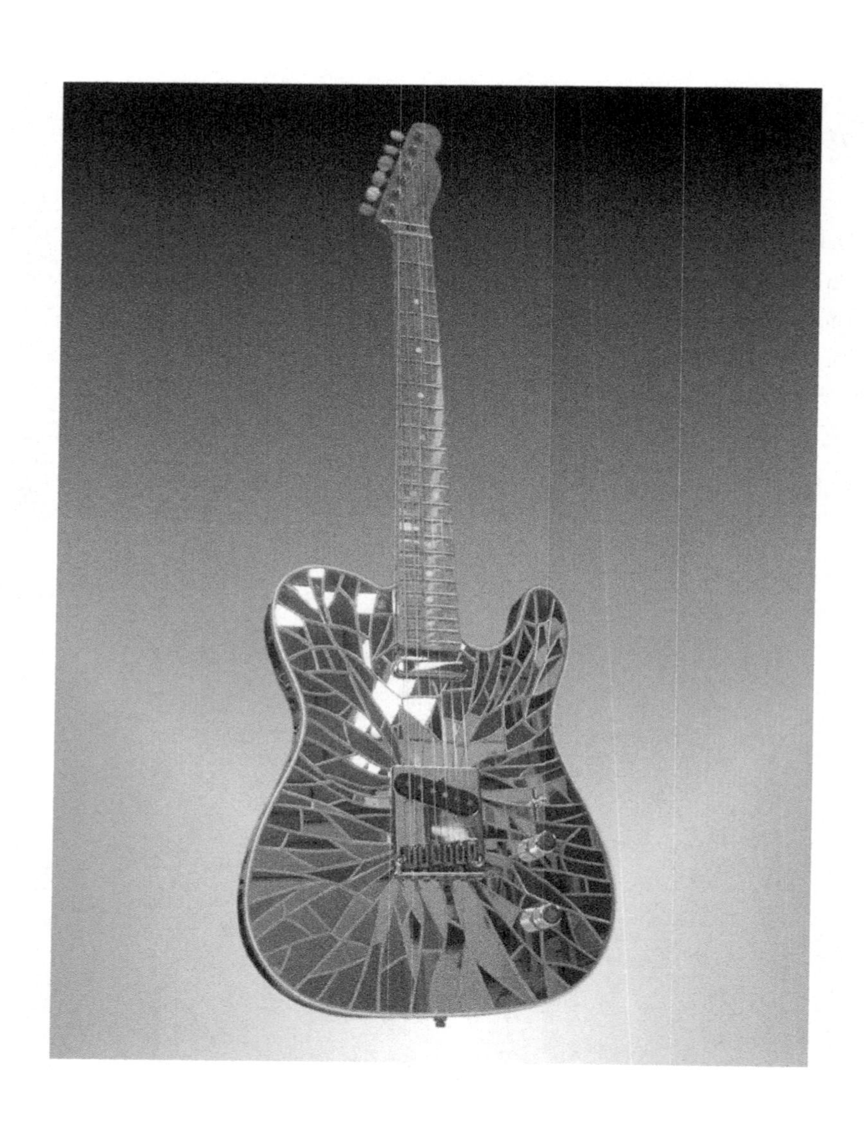

"Birdflower" Telecaster®.

Exotic wood.

Precision Hand Inlay Work using Mother of Pearl, Abalone, Silver and Copper wire.

All work by author.

Hardware engraving by Tim Adlam.

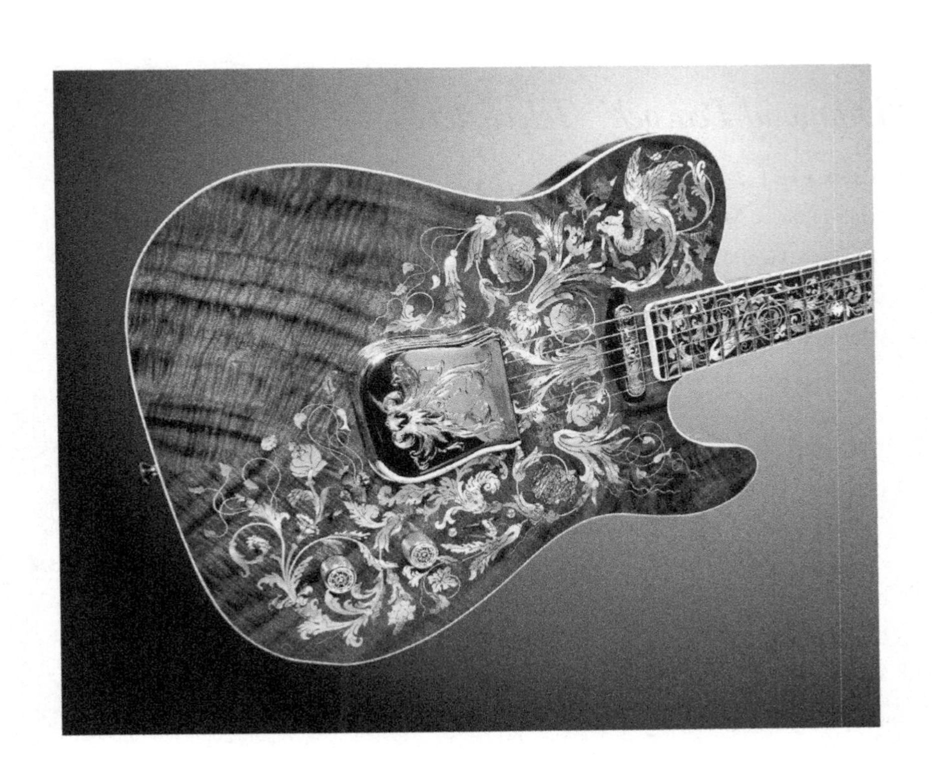

"Diamond Peacock" Telecaster®.

Exotic wood.

Hand Inlayed Mother of Pearl, Abalone, Silver and 18K Gold wire.

Decorated with Emeralds, Rubies, Sapphires, Amethyst, Gold and Diamonds.

All work by author.

Hardware engraving by Tim Adlam.

One of a kind instrument.

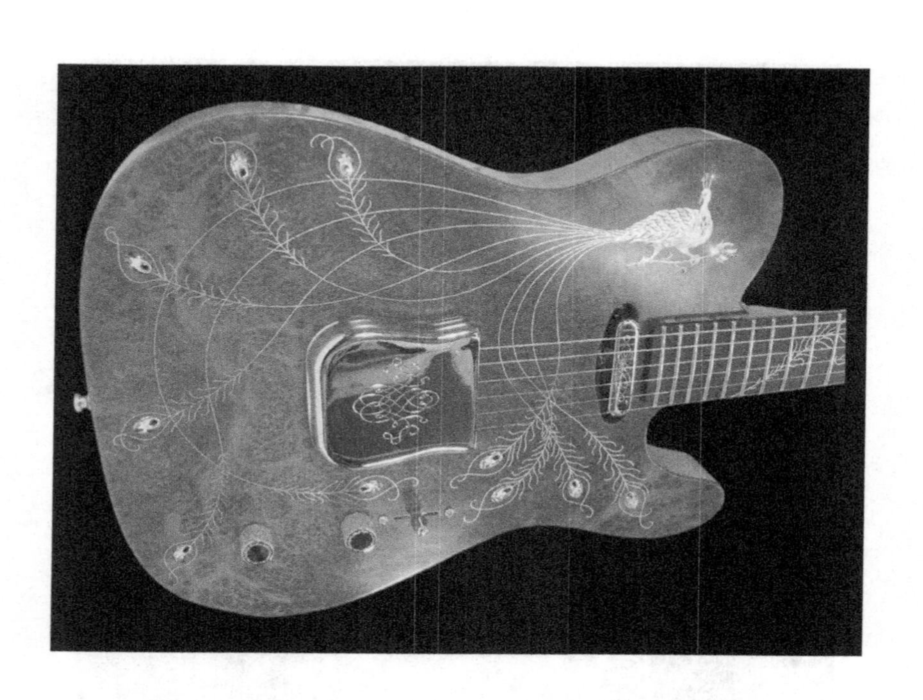

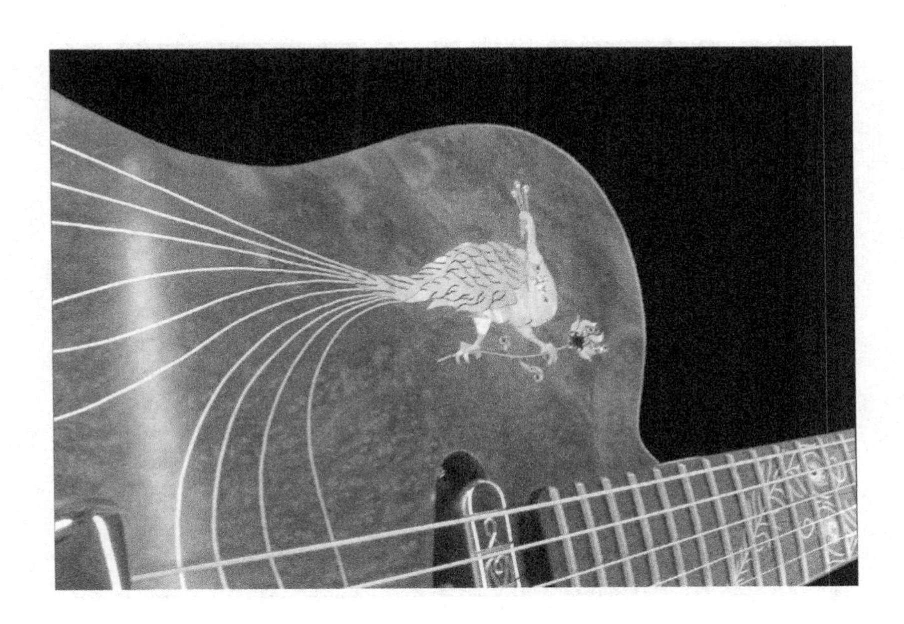

"Midnight Opulence" Stratocaster®.

One of the most extravagant guitars I've completed in 2011.

Decorated with 117 natural jewels of

Citrins, Peridots, Blue Swiss Topazes, Emeralds and 161 Diamonds.

Hand hammered into the body and neck 55 feet of Fine Silver and Rose Gold wire.

All project including design, inlay and jewelry work done by author.

Hardware engraving by Tim Adlam.

USA

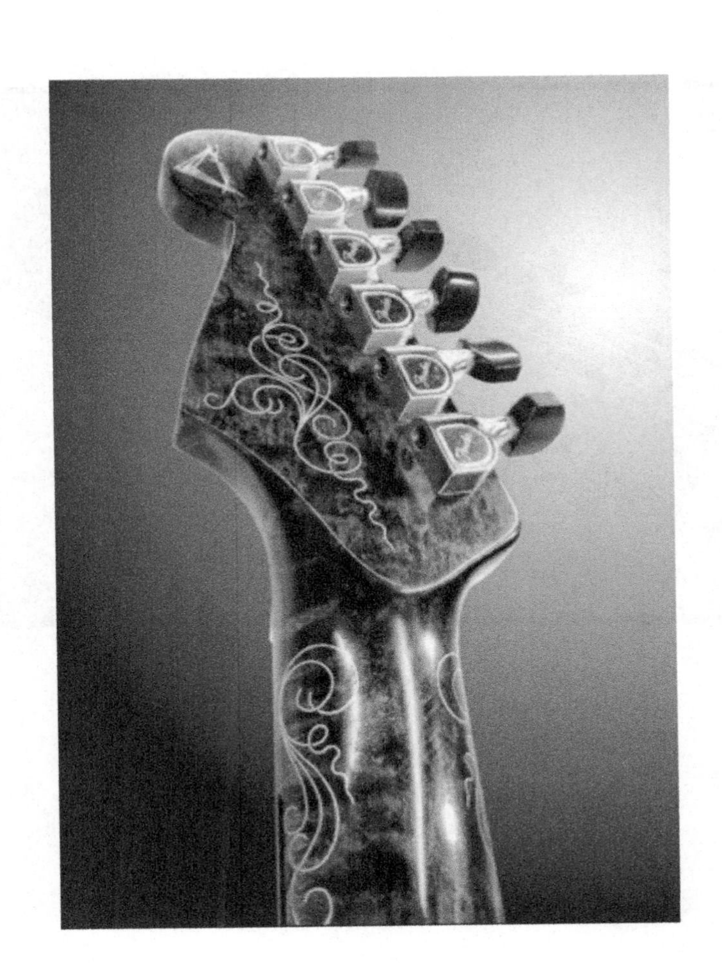

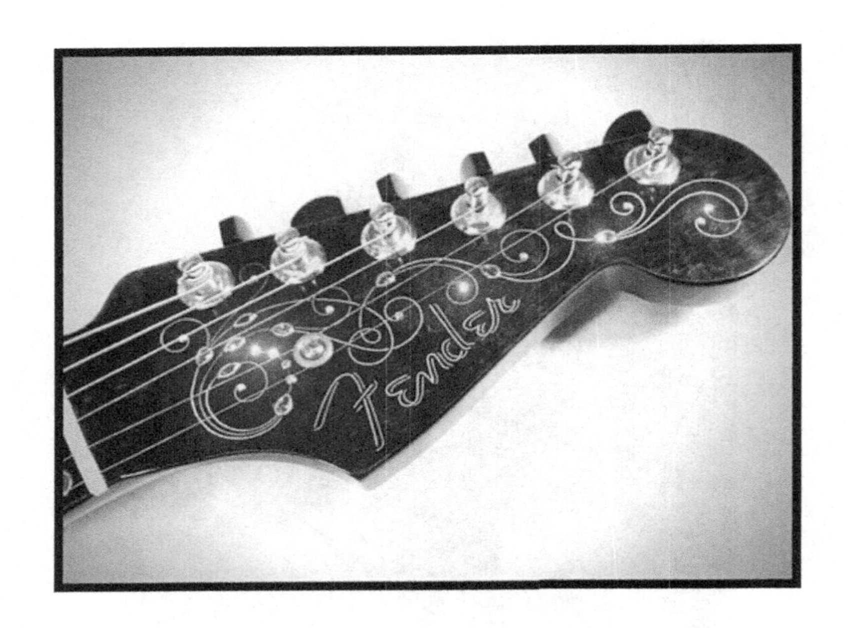
Fender

In the Shop

From My Chicago and Fender®Custom Shop Files

WARNING

Made in the USA
Las Vegas, NV
09 February 2024

85572354R10254